Natural Language Processing for Global and Local Business

Fatih Pinarbasi
Istanbul Medipol University, Turkey

M. Nurdan Taskiran
Istanbul Medipol University, Turkey

A volume in the Advances in Business Information
Systems and Analytics (ABISA) Book Series

Published in the United States of America by
IGI Global
Business Science Reference (an imprint of IGI Global)
701 E. Chocolate Avenue
Hershey PA, USA 17033
Tel: 717-533-8845
Fax: 717-533-8661
E-mail: cust@igi-global.com
Web site: http://www.igi-global.com

Library of Congress Cataloging-in-Publication Data

Names: Pinarbaşi, Fatih, 1991- editor. | Taşkıran, Nurdan Öncel, 1960-
   editor.
Title: Natural language processing for global and local business / Fatih
   Pinarbaşi and M. Nurdan Oncel Taskiran, editors.
Description: Hershey, PA : Business Science Reference, [2020] | Includes
   bibliographical references and index. | Summary: "This book explores the
   theoretical and practical phenomenon of natural language processing
   through different languages and platforms in terms of today's
   conditions"-- Provided by publisher.
Identifiers: LCCN 2019059926 (print) | LCCN 2019059927 (ebook) | ISBN
   9781799842408 (hardcover) | ISBN 9781799851349 (paperback) | ISBN
   9781799842415 (ebook)
Subjects: LCSH: Natural language processing (Computer science) |
   Computational linguistics. | Discourse analysis--Data processing. |
   Emotive (Linguistics)
Classification: LCC QA76.9.N38 N388 2020 (print) | LCC QA76.9.N38 (ebook)
   | DDC 006.3/5--dc23
LC record available at https://lccn.loc.gov/2019059926
LC ebook record available at https://lccn.loc.gov/2019059927

This book is published in the IGI Global book series Advances in Business Information Systems and Analytics (ABISA) (ISSN: 2327-3275; eISSN: 2327-3283)

British Cataloguing in Publication Data
A Cataloguing in Publication record for this book is available from the British Library.

For electronic access to this publication, please contact: eresources@igi-global.com.

Advances in Business Information Systems and Analytics (ABISA) Book Series

Madjid Tavana
La Salle University, USA

ISSN:2327-3275
EISSN:2327-3283

MISSION

The successful development and management of information systems and business analytics is crucial to the success of an organization. New technological developments and methods for data analysis have allowed organizations to not only improve their processes and allow for greater productivity, but have also provided businesses with a venue through which to cut costs, plan for the future, and maintain competitive advantage in the information age.

The **Advances in Business Information Systems and Analytics (ABISA) Book Series** aims to present diverse and timely research in the development, deployment, and management of business information systems and business analytics for continued organizational development and improved business value.

COVERAGE

- Performance Metrics
- Algorithms
- Business Models
- Data Strategy
- Forecasting
- Legal information systems
- Business Information Security
- Statistics
- Strategic Information Systems
- Geo-BIS

IGI Global is currently accepting manuscripts for publication within this series. To submit a proposal for a volume in this series, please contact our Acquisition Editors at Acquisitions@igi-global.com or visit: http://www.igi-global.com/publish/.

Titles in this Series

For a list of additional titles in this series, please visit:
https://www.igi-global.com/book-series/advances-business-information-systems-analytics/37155

Applications of Big Data and Business Analytics in Management
Sneha Kumari (Vaikunth Mehta National Institute of Cooperative Management, India) K. K. Tripathy (Vaikunth Mehta National Institute of Cooperative Management, India) and Vidya Kumbhar (Symbiosis International University (Deemed, India)
Business Science Reference • © 2020 • 300pp • H/C (ISBN: 9781799832614) • US $225.00

Handbook of Research on Integrating Industry 4.0 in Business and Manufacturing
Isak Karabegović (Academy of Sciences and Arts of Bosnia and Herzegovina, Bosnia and Herzegovina) Ahmed Kovačević (City, University London, UK) Lejla Banjanović-Mehmedović (University of Tuzla, Bosnia and Herzegovina) and Predrag Dašić (High Technical Mechanical School of Professional Studies in Trstenik, Serbia)
Business Science Reference • © 2020 • 661pp • H/C (ISBN: 9781799827252) • US $265.00

Internet of Things (IoT) Applications for Enterprise Productivity
Erdinç Koç (Bingol University, Turkey)
Business Science Reference • © 2020 • 357pp • H/C (ISBN: 9781799831754) • US $215.00

Trends and Issues in International Planning for Businesses
Babayemi Adekunle (Arden University, UK) Husam Helmi Alharahsheh (University of Wales Trinity Saint David, UK) and Abraham Pius (Arden University, UK)
Business Science Reference • © 2020 • 225pp • H/C (ISBN: 9781799825470) • US $225.00

Institutional Assistance Support for Small and Medium Enterprise Development in Africa
Isaac Oluwajoba Abereijo (Obafemi Awolowo University, Nigeria)
Business Science Reference • © 2020 • 280pp • H/C (ISBN: 9781522594819) • US $205.00

Role of Regional Development Agencies in Entrepreneurial and Rural Development Emerging Research and Opportunities
Milan B. Vemić (Union – Nikola Tesla University, Serbia)
Business Science Reference • © 2020 • 246pp • H/C (ISBN: 9781799826415) • US $175.00

Using Applied Mathematical Models for Business Transformation
Antoine Trad (IBISTM, France) and Damir Kalpić (University of Zagreb, Croatia)
Business Science Reference • © 2020 • 543pp • H/C (ISBN: 9781799810094) • US $265.00

701 East Chocolate Avenue, Hershey, PA 17033, USA
Tel: 717-533-8845 x100 • Fax: 717-533-8661
E-Mail: cust@igi-global.com • www.igi-global.com

Table of Contents

Section 2
Natural Language Processing in Business

Section 3
Diversity Among Languages Over Natural Language Processing

Detailed Table of Contents

Section 1
A General Outlook on Natural Language Processing

This chapter presents a view of how the use of NLP knowledge might change the relation between universities and companies. Products from NLP analysis are expected in both ends of this at times not so reciprocal exchange. But history has shown the products developed by universities and companies are complementary for the development of NLP. The great volume of data the world is producing is requiring newer perspectives to provide understanding. These newer aspects found on big data may provide the comprehension of human language categorization and therefore possibly human language acquisition. But to process data more data need to be produced and not all companies have the time to dedicate for this task. This chapter aims to present through sharing literature review and experience in the field that partnerships are the most reliable resource for the cycle of knowledge production in NLP. Companies need to be receptive of the theoretical knowledge the university may provide, and universities must turn their theoretical knowledge for a more applied envionment.

The wealth of information produced over the internet empowers businesses to become data-driven organizations, increasing their ability to predict consumer behavior, take more informed strategic decisions, and remain competitive on the market. However, past research did not identify which online data sources companies should choose to achieve such an objective. This chapter aims to analyse how online news articles, social media messages, and user reviews can be exploited by businesses using natural language processing (NLP) techniques to build business intelligence. NLP techniques assist computers to understand

and derive a valuable meaning from human (natural) languages. Following a brief introduction to NLP and a description of how these three text streams differ from each other, the chapter discusses six main factors that can assist businesses in choosing one data source from another. The chapter concludes with future directions towards improving business applications involving NLP techniques.

Chapter 3

Gunjan Ansari, JSS Academy of Technical Education, Noida, India
Shilpi Gupta, JSS Academy of Technical Education, Noida, India
Niraj Singhal, Shobhit Institute of Engineering and Technology (Deemed), Meerut, India

The analysis of the online data posted on various e-commerce sites is required to improve consumer experience and thus enhance global business. The increase in the volume of social media content in the recent years led to the problem of overfitting in review classification. Thus, there arises a need to select relevant features to reduce computational cost and improve classifier performance. This chapter investigates various statistical feature selection methods that are time efficient but result in selection of few redundant features. To overcome this issue, wrapper methods such as sequential feature selection (SFS) and recursive feature elimination (RFE) are employed for selection of optimal feature set. The empirical analysis was conducted on movie review dataset using three different classifiers and the results depict that SVM could achieve f-measure of 96% with only 8% selected features using RFE method.

Chapter 4

Akshi Kumar, Delhi Technological University, India
Divya Gupta, Galgotias University, India

With the accelerated evolution of social networks, there is a tremendous increase in opinions by the people about products or services. While this user-generated content in natural language is intended to be valuable, its large amounts require use of content mining methods and NLP to uncover the knowledge for various tasks. In this study, sentiment analysis is used to analyze and understand the opinions of users using statistical approaches, knowledge-based approaches, hybrid approaches, and concept-based ontologies. Unfortunately, sentiment analysis also experiences a range of difficulties like colloquial words, negation handling, ambiguity in word sense, coreference resolution, which highlight another perspective emphasizing that sentiment analysis is certainly a restricted NLP problem. The purpose of this chapter is to discover how sentiment analysis is a restricted NLP problem. Thus, this chapter discussed the concept of sentiment analysis in the field of NLP and explored that sentiment analysis is a restricted NLP problem due to the sophisticated nature of natural language.

Chapter 5

Vincent Karas, University of Augsburg, Germany
Björn W. Schuller, University of Augsburg, Germany

Sentiment analysis is an important area of natural language processing that can help inform business decisions by extracting sentiment information from documents. The purpose of this chapter is to introduce the reader to selected concepts and methods of deep learning and show how deep models can be used to increase performance in sentiment analysis. It discusses the latest advances in the field and covers topics including traditional sentiment analysis approaches, the fundamentals of sentence modelling, popular neural network architectures, autoencoders, attention modelling, transformers, data augmentation methods, the benefits of transfer learning, the potential of adversarial networks, and perspectives on explainable AI. The authors' intent is that through this chapter, the reader can gain an understanding of recent developments in this area as well as current trends and potentials for future research.

Section 2
Natural Language Processing in Business

Chapter 6
Sunny Rai, Mahindra Ecole Centrale, Hyderabad, India
Shampa Chakraverty, Netaji Subhas University of Technology, India
Devendra Kumar Tayal, Indira Gandhi Delhi Technical University for Women, India

Commercial advertisements, social campaigns, and ubiquitous online reviews are a few non-literary domains where creative text is profusely embedded to capture a viewer's imagination. Recent AI business applications such as chatbots and interactive digital campaigns emphasise the need to process creative text for a seamless and fulfilling user experience. Figurative text in human communication conveys implicit perceptions and unspoken emotions. Metaphor is one such figure of speech that maps a latent idea in a target domain to an evocative concept from a source domain. This chapter explores the problem of computational metaphor interpretation through the glass of subjectivity. The world wide web is mined to learn about the source domain concept. Ekman emotion categories and pretrained word embeddings are used to model the subjectivity. The performance evaluation is performed to determine the reader's preference for emotive vs non emotive meanings. This chapter establishes the role of subjectivity and user inclination towards the meaning that fits in their existing cognitive schema.

Chapter 7
Roney Lira de Sales Santos, University of Sao Paulo, Brazil
Carlos Augusto de Sa, Federal University of Piaui, Brazil
Rogerio Figueredo de Sousa, University of Sao Paulo, Brazil
Rafael Torres Anchiêta, University of Sao Paulo, Brazil
Ricardo de Andrade Lira Rabelo, Federal University of Piaui, Brazil
Raimundo Santos Moura, Federal University of Piaui, Brazil

The evolution of e-commerce has contributed to the increase of the information available, making the task of analyzing the reviews manually almost impossible. Due to the amount of information, the creation of automatic methods of knowledge extraction and data mining has become necessary. Currently, to facilitate the analysis of reviews, some websites use filters such as votes by the utility or by stars. However, the use of these filters is not a good practice because they may exclude reviews that have recently been submitted to the voting process. One possible solution is to filter the reviews based on their textual descriptions, author information, and other measures. This chapter has a propose of approaches to estimate the importance of reviews about products and services using fuzzy systems and artificial neural networks. The results were encouraging, obtaining better results when detecting the most important reviews, achieving approximately 82% when f-measure is analyzed.

Chapter 8

Ainhoa Serna, University of the Basque Country, Spain
Jon Kepa Gerrikagoitia, BRTA Basque Research and Technology Alliance, Spain

In recent years, digital technology and research methods have developed natural language processing for better understanding consumers and what they share in social media. There are hardly any studies in transportation analysis with TripAdvisor, and moreover, there is not a complete analysis from the point of view of sentiment analysis. The aim of study is to investigate and discover the presence of sustainable transport modes underlying in non-categorized TripAdvisor texts, such as walking mobility in order to impact positively in public services and businesses. The methodology follows a quantitative and qualitative approach based on knowledge discovery techniques. Thus, data gathering, normalization, classification, polarity analysis, and labelling tasks have been carried out to obtain sentiment labelled training data set in the transport domain as a valuable contribution for predictive analytics. This research has allowed the authors to discover sustainable transport modes underlying the texts, focused on walking mobility but extensible to other means of transport and social media sources.

Chapter 9

Sayani Ghosal, Ambedkar Institute of Advanced Communication Technologies and Research, India
Amita Jain, Ambedkar Institute of Advanced Communication Technologies and Research, India

Hate content detection is the most prospective and challenging research area under the natural language processing domain. Hate speech abuse individuals or groups of people based on religion, caste, language, or sex. Enormous growth of digital media and cyberspace has encouraged researchers to work on hatred speech detection. A commonly acceptable automatic hate detection system is required to stop flowing hate-motivated data. Anonymous hate content is affecting the young generation and adults on social networking sites. Through numerous studies and review papers, the chapter identifies the need for artificial intelligence (AI) in hate speech research. The chapter explores the current state-of-the-art and prospects of AI in natural language processing (NLP) and machine learning algorithms. The chapter aims to identify the most successful methods or techniques for hate speech detection to date. Revolution in this research helps social media to provide a healthy environment for everyone.

Chapter 10

Matthias Hölscher, Institute for IT Management and Digitization, FOM University, Germany
Rudiger Buchkremer, Institute for IT Management and Digitization, FOM University, Germany

Rare diseases in their entirety have a substantial impact on the healthcare market, as they affect a large number of patients worldwide. Governments provide financial support for diagnosis and treatment. Market orientation is crucial for any market participant to achieve business profitability. However, the market for rare diseases is opaque. The authors compare results from search engines and healthcare databases utilizing natural language processing. The approach starts with an information retrieval process, applying the MeSH thesaurus. The results are prioritized and visualized, using word clouds. In total, the chapter is about the examination of 30 rare diseases and about 500,000 search results in the databases Pubmed, FindZebra, and the search engine Google. The authors compare their results to the search for common diseases. The authors conclude that FindZebra and Google provide relatively good results for the evaluation of therapies and diagnoses. However, the quantity of the findings from professional databases such as Pubmed remains unsurpassed.

Chapter 11

Increased use of computer-assisted translation (CAT) technology in business settings with augmented amounts of tasks, collaborative work, and short deadlines give rise to errors and the need for quality assurance (QA). The research has three operational aims: 1) methodological framework for QA analysis, 2) comparative evaluation of four QA tools, 3) to justify introduction of QA into CAT process. The research includes building of translation memory, terminology extraction, and creation of terminology base. Error categorization is conducted by multidimensional quality (MQM) framework. The level of mistake is calculated considering detected, false, and not detected errors. Weights are assigned to errors (minor, major, or critical), penalties are calculated, and quality estimation for translation memory is given. Results show that process is prone to errors due to differences in error detection, harmonization, and error counting. Data analysis of detected errors leads to further data-driven decisions related to the quality of output results and improved efficacy of translation business process.

Section 3
Diversity Among Languages Over Natural Language Processing

In this study, the authors give both theoretical and experimental information about text mining, which is one of the natural language processing topics. Three different text mining problems such as news classification, sentiment analysis, and author recognition are discussed for Turkish. They aim to reduce the running time and increase the performance of machine learning algorithms. Four different machine learning algorithms and two different feature selection metrics are used to solve these text classification problems. Classification algorithms are random forest (RF), logistic regression (LR), naive bayes (NB), and sequential minimal optimization (SMO). Chi-square and information gain metrics are used as the feature selection method. The highest classification performance achieved in this study is 0.895 according to the F-measure metric. This result is obtained by using the SMO classifier and information gain metric for news classification. This study is important in terms of comparing the performances of classification algorithms and feature selection methods.

Chapter 13

Hichem Rahab, ICISI Laboratory, University of Khenchela, Algeria
Mahieddine Djoudi, TechNE Laboratory, University of Poitiers, France
Abdelhafid Zitouni, LIRE Laboratory, University of Constantine 2, Algeria

Today, it is usual that a consumer seeks for others' feelings about their purchasing experience on the web before a simple decision of buying a product or a service. Sentiment analysis intends to help people in taking profit from the available opinionated texts on the web for their decision making, and business is one of its challenging areas. Considerable work of sentiment analysis has been achieved in English and other Indo-European languages. Despite the important number of Arabic speakers and internet users, studies in Arabic sentiment analysis are still insufficient. The current chapter vocation is to give the main challenges of Arabic sentiment together with their recent proposed solutions in the literature. The chapter flowchart is presented in a novel manner that obtains the main challenges from presented literature works. Then it gives the proposed solutions for each challenge. The chapter reaches the finding that the future tendency will be toward rule-based techniques and deep learning, allowing for more dealings with Arabic language inherent characteristics.

Chapter 14

Sumaya Sulaiman Al Ameri, Khalifa University of Science and Technology, UAE
Abdulhadi Shoufan, Center for Cyber-Physical Systems, Khalifa University of Science and Technology, UAE

The natural language processing of Arabic dialects faces a major difficulty, which is the lack of lexical resources. This problem complicates the penetration and the business of related technologies such as machine translation, speech recognition, and sentiment analysis. Current solutions frequently use lexica, which are specific to the task at hand and limited to some language variety. Modern communication platforms including social media gather people from different nations and regions. This has increased the demand for general-purpose lexica towards effective natural language processing solutions. This chapter presents a collaborative web-based platform for building a cross-dialectical, general-purpose lexicon for Arabic dialects. This solution was tested by a team of two annotators, a reviewer, and a lexicographer. The lexicon expansion rate was measured and analyzed to estimate the overhead required to reach the desired size of the lexicon. The inter-annotator reliability was analyzed using Cohen's Kappa.

Chapter 15

César Aguilar, Pontificia Universidad Católica de Chile, Chile
Olga Acosta, Singularyta SpA, Chile

This chapter presents a critical review of the current state of natural language processing in Chile and Mexico. Specifically, a general review is made regarding the technological evolution of these countries in this area of research and development, as well as the progress they have made so far. Subsequently, the remaining problems and challenges are addressed. Specifically, two are analyzed in detail here: (1)

the lack of a strategic policy that helps to establish stronger links between academia and industry and (2) the lack of a technological inclusion of the indigenous languages, which causes a deep digital divide between Spanish (considered in Chile and Mexico as their official language) with them.

Foreword

Natural Language Processing has attracted the attention of scholars since last century. Thanks to the developments in computer technology and digitalisation of text materials, linguists have found ample resources to study on. Programming languages have recently been enriched by special NLP libraries and third-party tools have been available for the use of NLP analyses. These developments may suggest that things are much easier than they were before. On the contrary, these developments have increased the research appetite and enthused scholars to study more challenging subjects. Today, works of James Joyce and Edgar Alan Poe are compared in terms of their lexical, colocation, colligation or adjective usage. Holy Books are compared with one another to extract similarities. Even sentiment analyses are done for each verse. As the user generated data (UGD) increase, NLP have started to do great jobs and become a part of artificial intelligence already. Machines are trained to understand or perceive what people really say taking similes, metaphors, ironies into account. Today, some machines are aware of the difference between lexical and grammatical ambiguities and they are still learning. Suffice it to say, these developments are the ones leading us to web 4.0 which is expected to be a semantic web era. Any small or big contribution to NLP takes us to semantic web times inches by inches.

This book is truly one of them. It gives practical implementations of NLP through text mining. That is done using real data corpus rather than toy data sets. Most importantly, user generated data have been used. By analysing UGD with proper text mining models, naïve users' opinions have been extracted, and this is presented very well in the book. This shows that questionnaires and surveys have already become obsolete when it comes to get user reflections. Using text not only in English but also in other languages like Arabic and Turkish enriches the content of the book.

I congratulate editors and authors for producing such a great book. I am sure the book will be very helpful for those who want to see real life examples of NLP implementations. This is a work which will broaden NPL horizons of readers.

Gökhan Silahtaroğlu
Istanbul Medipol Universitesi, Turkey

Preface

The attempt of humankind to interpret signs and imaginations is almost the same age as the adventure of life on earth. Interpreting complex signals/visions to specific meanings, survival instinct and the humankind dominance on the world depend on recognition, understanding and interpretation of the world outside. The communication effort that started with strange sounds, and the process of self-expression of people who continue with the cave drawings, has undergone many changes in the thousands of years of human life adventure, with different tools and media in different forms.

The cultural and sociological changes experienced by human beings have affected self-expression, language tools and language structure. While all of these are important in the world paradigm where people are at the centre, there has been a transition from this paradigm to a technology-based communication paradigm over the past 50 years. Based on the new paradigm, this book is prepared as a work fed by the common point where technology meets language.

LANGUAGE AND HUMANITY

Among the most curious topics in language studies were questions such as how the first human beings could communicate with each other, how they reconcile in a universal language, and how they derive words. The question of whether the paintings on the walls of the Lascaux cave, which remain alive today, to leave a trace of themselves or as an expression of their dreams, still retains its mystery. However, as one of the two features that distinguish human from animal, language is a unique feature, and it is the only tool that provides communication with the environment, conveys emotions and thoughts, and imposes various meanings. The language acquisition that starts in the family develops and improves its use throughout education life. Language changes with the development and progress of the human being by adapting to the environment; Being dynamic is one of its distinguishing features. Man's interpretation of language has changed since the Stone Age. Today, human beings can interpret the language in the digital world better with the help of technology.

DIGITAL WORLD

In today's world, technology and digital tools play an essential role in human life. Today, human beings spend some of their days in the digital world with the help of technological tools, establish their communication with other people from here and can socialize in a digital "social" world. Understanding and interpreting the prints of people and businesses in this digital world has become one of the significant issues in today's business. The whole set of methods specified as "natural language processing" refers to processing the languages in which people express themselves with the help of technology and making inferences. In this method, it is aimed to make the messages that human beings tell in various ways, understandable with the help of machines and make interpretations on them.

OBJECTIVE OF THE BOOK

This book aims to address the current state of natural language processing, one of the most critical issues in recent years, to interpret it in terms of businesses and to present examples of different languages. The chapters of the book are grouped into three main sections accordingly—the book targets both the academic community and practitioners as a target audience.

CONTENT OF THE STUDY

The organization of study consists of three main sections; a general outlook, business applications and diversity for NLP.

Section 1: A General Outlook on Natural Language Processing

The first section of the project refers to a general outlook of NLP for the beginning part of the book. This section has five chapters for evaluating NLP in general.

Chapter 1: Academy and Companies' Needs: The Past and the Future of NLP

In the first study, the author evaluated the past and future of NLP with the focus of the academy and business world. A brief history of NLP through the years is included in the study, and the author highlighted the importance of collaboration between universities and companies. Some theoretical corners are also discussed in the study, while a view of the future of NLP is included.

Chapter 2: Exploiting Online Data Sources for the Use of NLP

The second chapter focuses on the data source side of NLP and evaluates the data sources by three groups; online news articles, social media messages and user reviews. The author also included six main factors for assisting businesses about the selection of data sources.

Chapter 3: Natural Language Processing in Online Reviews

Following the starting of the NLP concept with data sources concept, this study continues the subject of online reviews in terms of NLP. The authors emphasize the increase of social media content data volume and investigate various statistical feature selection methods in the study. In an empirical analysis on movie review dataset, three different classifiers are compared.

Chapter 4: Sentiment Analysis as a Restricted NLP Problem

Following the data concept of NLP, this chapter focuses on the methodology of Sentiment analysis and evaluates it as a restricted problem. Sentiment analysis is evaluated in this study in terms of types, levels, techniques and applications. Consistent with "restricted" highlight in the title of the study, the authors also included challenges for sentiment analysis.

Chapter 5: Deep Learning for Sentiment Analysis – An Overview and Perspectives

The final study of the first section examines sentiment analysis with deep learning concept. Selected methods and concepts of deep learning are included in the study. At the same time, authors presented how deep models could be used for increasing performance in sentiment analysis. The authors also examine recent developments in the area.

Section 2: Natural Language Processing in Business

Following an overview of the NLP concept, Section 2 focuses on the business side of NLP and includes various implementation of NLP. There are six chapters in this section.

Chapter 6: Metaphors in Business Applications – Modelling Subjectivity Through Emotions for Metaphor Comprehension

Understanding the meanings hidden in the text is crucial for businesses, and some problems may block understanding. This study evaluates one of these blocks -metaphors- in NLP topic and explores the metaphor interpretation in terms of subjectivity. Modelling of subjectivity in the study includes Ekman emotion categories and pre-trained word embeddings. The performance evaluation is implemented for reader's preference for emotive vs non-emotive meanings.

Chapter 7: Estimating Importance From Web Reviews Through Textual Description and Metrics Extraction

Since the web reviews concept contains different sub-concepts inside, different approaches can be used for evaluating web reviews in NLP methodology. This study focuses on web reviews in terms of importance and uses Fuzzy Systems and Artificial Neural Networks as methodologies. The authors conclude approximately 85% performance for detecting most essential reviews.

Chapter 8: Discovery of Sustainable Transport Modes Underlying in TripAdvisor Reviews With Sentiment Analysis – Transport Domain Adaptation of Sentiment Labeled Data Set

Online reviews are rich forms with different meanings underlying them, and different approaches with different focuses can be used for NLP based studies. This study evaluates the concept of the review in TripAdvisor context. It evaluates the reviews for the discovery of sustainable transport modes. The methodology of the study included both quantitative and qualitative approach based on knowledge discovery techniques.

Chapter 9: Research Journey of Hate Content Detection From Cyberspace

As people produce content online and share the ideas online, some topics emerge by time, like hate content. This study focuses on one of the different sides of NLP. It evaluates hate content detection as the subject of study. Identifying the most successful techniques and methodologies for hate speech detection is aimed in the study.

Chapter 10: The Use of Natural Language Processing for Market Orientation on Rare Diseases

This study evaluates rare diseases as the subject and 30 rare diseases, and about 500.000 search results are examined. It is concluded that FindZebra and Google provide good results regarding the evaluation of therapies and diagnoses, while the quantity of findings from professional databases is still unexcelled.

Chapter 11: Quality Assurance in Computer-Assisted Translation in Business Environment

Computer-assisted translation is the subject of this study, and the study includes three aims; presenting a methodological framework for quality assurance analysis, comparative evaluation for four quality assurance tools and justifying the introduction of quality assurance in the computer-assisted translation process. It is concluded that process is prone to errors because of the differences in error detection, harmonization and error counting.

Section 3: Diversity Among Language Over Natural Language Processing

After the business implementations of NLP in several aspects, the final section of the book includes four chapters. It evaluates different languages/areas for NLP.

Chapter 12: An Extensive Text Mining Study for the Turkish Language – Author Recognition, Sentiment Analysis, and Text Classification

Employing different languages as a focus of NLP studies is essential, and Turkish is one of the most spoken languages in the world. This study focuses on Turkish language and combines three different problems for methodology section; author recognition, sentiment analysis and text classification. The study uses four machine learning algorithms and two feature selection metrics for the methodology.

Chapter 13: Sentiment Analysis of Arabic Documents – Main Challenges and Recent Advances

The study focuses on the Arabic language, which is one of the other most spoken languages in the world and highlights the insufficiency of Arabic NLP studies. Main challenges and recent advances regarding

Arabic NLP are discussed in the chapter. At the same time, the future tendency with rule-based techniques and deep learning is concluded.

Chapter 14: Building Lexical Resources for Dialectical Arabic

This study also evaluates the Arabic language, but it differs from the previous study by including a methodological approach. The study evaluates the main steps of building lexical resources for dialectical Arabic. A collaborative web-based platform to build a cross-dialectical and general-purpose lexicon for Arabic dialects is discussed in the chapter.

Chapter 15: A Landscape About the Advances in Natural Language Processing in Chile and México

Natural language processing is affected by technological advances and country-based advancements. Final study of the book includes examining the advances in NLP for Chile and México. Lack of strategic policy which helps establishing stronger links between academia and industry and lack of inclusion of indigenous languages are concluded in the study.

CONTRIBUTION AND CONCLUSION

The three issues related to NLP addressed in this book project are; i) General outlook of NLP, ii) NLP and business, iii) diversity of languages for NLP. As the content and audience of each issue (addressed as sections in this project) differ by their characteristics, the impact of the sections is different, too.

The first section aiming general outlook of NLP would be useful for starters of NLP research areas. In contrast, the section presents an overview with different topics like academy and company needs, online reviews, sentiment analysis. The readers can use this section to have a piece of brief information about what NLP means for general perspective. The second section (as it is consistent to the title of the book "NLP in Global and Local Business") is related to the business side of NLP since one of the main areas of this project refers to the business implementation of NLP. Various studies in the section include different business practises related to NLP, and the readers can use each section for the purpose they focus on. Finally, the last section of our book project refers to the diversity side of NLP as the technique includes various languages in its scope. Evaluating the different languages and regions is crucial for improving the usage of NLP for other languages.

This book project includes studies for both the academic community and private sector practitioners. Readers can use this book to both have general information about NLP and to examine sectoral practices.

Acknowledgment

First of all, we would like to acknowledge to our families who support us in every minute of our lives; to whom form the basis for our projects including this study, our precious teachers and professors; to Istanbul Medipol University and its employees for the technical equipment and infrastructure support; additionally to Mehmet Hulusi Ekren and Enver Sait Kurtaran for their support who helped with the promotion of the book; lastly we also thank to Zeynep Türkyılmaz and Gökhan Silahtaroğlu for their precious contributions.

Our special thanks to our dear writers from different regions of the world (Algeria, Brazil, Chile, Croatia, France, Germany, India, Malta, Slovenia, Spain, Turkey, UAE) 12 countries / 38 authors, who are the real architects of this wonderful book project, by patiently fulfilling our revisions many times, justifying our meticulous work.

Section 1
A General Outlook on Natural Language Processing

Chapter 1
Academy and Company Needs:
The Past and Future of NLP

Tiago Martins da Cunha
UNILAB, Brazil

ABSTRACT

This chapter presents a view of how the use of NLP knowledge might change the relation between universities and companies. Products from NLP analysis are expected in both ends of this at times not so reciprocal exchange. But history has shown the products developed by universities and companies are complementary for the development of NLP. The great volume of data the world is producing is requiring newer perspectives to provide understanding. These newer aspects found on big data may provide the comprehension of human language categorization and therefore possibly human language acquisition. But to process data more data need to be produced and not all companies have the time to dedicate for this task. This chapter aims to present through sharing literature review and experience in the field that partnerships are the most reliable resource for the cycle of knowledge production in NLP. Companies need to be receptive of the theoretical knowledge the university may provide, and universities must turn their theoretical knowledge for a more applied envionment.

INTRODUCTION

As a researcher in Computational Linguistics focusing on Machine Translation (MT) I had the opportunity to work for a project from the partnership between a mobile company and a University on the creation of a mobile personal assistant. This great interdisciplinary team had the opportunity to put some of the theoretical architecture of my doctoral thesis on hybrid MT in practical work. The architecture was naive, but the outcome was greater than expected.

With the compound use of statistical algorithm and the creation of rules based on the learning from the use of the prototype application the results were almost scary. The same architecture in two different mobile phones with two different team training the data with different context made the same system produce two different outcomes, almost as personality. But would this be the reach of singularity in Artificial Intelligence (AI)? Probably a lot more work would need to be done to be even talking about

DOI: 10.4018/978-1-7998-4240-8.ch001

it. But this research reached something great in a very short period of time due to its interdisciplinary approach and the high quality of its team.

This project opportunity along with the experience of a linguistic professor made me wonder what the future promises for NLP might. In the University, very differently from the experience with that mobile company project, the rhythm in each resources and data is produced is very different. Although it is those academic resources that lay the groundwork for companies' projects like the one mentioned. So, this got me thinking on how these different rhythms are related to the future of NLP.

Much has been said about the future of NLP. On applications, the popular interest in Bots and personal assistants bring science fiction closer to our everyday life. Personal assistants and conversational agents designed to tutor or auxiliar tasks are provided for many everyday activities. However, the range of understanding of popular conversationa agents and personal assistants is very limited. It is limited to a controlled language expectation. And the specific language frame within the expect context in not a controlled language.

The real-world discourse is very broad in meaning and context. Humans are designed or trained, depending on your theoratical belief, to understand language. Four years of our life is spent to master a mother language. Machines do not have this natural design. The levels of language understanding a unliterate human have is absurdly bigger than most of the complexes AI systems. The struggle to manage unstructured data is the real challenge in NLP researches. The less you struggle is the key to success in such researches. You may even find satisfaction on the implementation of computer readable resources that may provide the desired range of reachable language analysis for some NLP tools.

The volume of data is increasing everyday. Kapil, Agrawal & Khan (2016) affirm that the volume of data increased 45% to 50% in the last two years and will grow from 0,8 ZB to 35 ZB until 2020. And the biggest portion of them is text. So, many researchers aim their focus on techniques for analyzing this great volume of data. Big Data, it is called. Although this focus may be more than necessary, the effort may be given at the wrong end of the spectrum of information. Improving analysis must have reliable computational linguistic resources to get our control data from. Although a narrowed view may be given through analysis using probabilistic models to a variety of text, these resources may require a more subjective point of view. But how can these subjective analyses be implemented into such a technical field?

Well, that's what AI is all about. But not just a machine to machine analysis. By machine to machine, it is related to the use of evolutionary or genetic algorithms that produce stages of analysis not readable by humans. Understand, I'm not saying not to use statistical methods to analyze language data, but to produce readable stages so humans can shrive through. The key may lie on building hybrid methods. The use of statistical approaches to build rule-based engines that could be groomed by language experts.

However, the rules that have been mention here are not just syntactical or semantical, but cognitive as well. And not separated from each other either. Syntactical and semantical theories have been broadly used in NLP due to it extensive testing of their structured formats. The more these theories interact the more they may showed satisfying results. The limitations of syntactic and semantic systems have already showed themselves problematic. The accuracy of such approaches has reached a limit that many researchers have struggle to break through in broad context.

Many big corporation systems in spite their great success have reached a dead end on data analysis. The construction of specific context framework might not always be worth the work even though it may be the only solution for some of these big corporation problems. In the case of mobile applications, the problem now is not the specific context but the opposite.

The possible context of a short sentence said to a personal assistant on the phone could or should be analyzed in a wide variety of contexts. For machines a short sentence leaves too little information on a few data to analyze on. But how do we, humans, do it? Humans are capable of evaluating the context trhough our life experience. I'm not saying life should be given to machines, but experience. Humans sort a new experience and compare with previous similar ones and then these are choosen. Not always the choice correctly made, thus, making mistakes is human. But mistakes are learned from this. My humble opinion is that much of this analysis that rely on linguistic theory must be renewed. Recent works on Neurosciences, Psycholinguistics and Cognitive Linguistics must be incorporated in the implementation of Corpus, Ontology and Grammar Building for instance.

The rise of these field of studies in NLP and its wide variety of implementation contexts might change the perspective of resources created today. The investment on computing human behavior, social interactions and structure possibilities need to encounter our primitive psychological/biological needs that are represented as language. Conceptual Metaphors, one of the main issues on Cognitive Linguistics may be one the options to drag some of syntactical/semantical analysis from stagnation. The enhancement of Corpus data with linguistic information adopting a cognitive perspective may be a solution for many systems, but that's not the near future of NLP.

The future of NLP might be seen in undergraduate stages. Computing theoratical knowledge should be basic during a university major. The universities enabling the creation of this enhanced resources will be the next step. The so desired interdisciplinary behavior must be stimulated. The blended knowledge from different university majors must be reinforced to navigate without the restrictions of departments. Also, the adaptation of the linguistic curriculum is needed. To provide a more integrated view of the diverse disciplines within linguistic knowledge, such as Phonetics, Morphology, Syntax, Semantics and Pragmatics to interface more freely with one another. Computational Linguistics need to enter these curricular components not just to provide theory or to test it but to produce data, computational linguistic data.

New approaches to part-of-speech tagging, new criteria for tagset implementation, efficient syntactic-semantics grammar formalism engineering, specific context word framing, new declarative forms of accessing these frames, a new theoretical approaches for corpus building (not just based on human production but on human reasoning), conceptual ontologies creation, context specific sentiment analysis data training are some of the few new type of resources the world of NLP stills require. Investing in partnerships with academic group early on and creating the productive mind field in these youngsters might be solution come up with creative solutions to our stagnated results.

The aim of this chapter is to present how NLP has been developing over the years and how it might unfold the structure within related areas. First, the brief development of NLP through history and in the last decade is presented. A reflection on the ups and downs of researches on NLP have had over the years and their social and theoratical issues is shared. Then a discussion on some theoratical corners this field of study must turn to keep on improving is made. And, finally, a view of what the future of NLP may bring into the context of theoratical and practical interface is presented.

NLP RESEARCH CONTEXT

Brief History: Beginning With Translation

The development of NLP is not a linear frame to present. It can be represented by different branches of studies and investigation paths. A brief illustration is presented in figure 1 in which is clarified along this section. This figure does not illustrate intersections with linguistic, mathematical and computational developments.

Figure 1. NLP brief history timeline

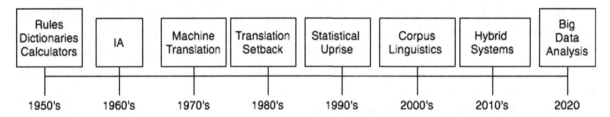

The birth of NLP in the early 50's was within the Translation Studies. Its quest of providing MT results "perfectly" provided the NLP's greatest achievments and also its greatest desappointments. The perfect quality of translation is something arguable even between human professional translators. Deternining the levels of quality a translation depended on the amount of reference translation to be compared on. Managing and pairing the amount of translation products to serve as reference has been the great challenges in MT systems. Since the beginning the development of NLP depended on massive human struggle, mainly to produce machine-readle material or evaluating systems.

World War II and the Cold War were largely responsible for the initial development of research in this area (GARRÃO, 1998). Americans and English, in spying on Soviet intelligence agencies, to get inside information as quickly as possible, developed a scientific calculator with enough data to perform literal word-for-word translations of texts, without considering syntactic or semantic aspects (LOFFLER- LAURIAN, 1996). Hutchins (2003) states that machine translation projects consisted of huge dictionaries that performed direct translation with statistical analysis. There were no linguistic theories, at the time, to support the design of translation systems (LOFFLER-LAURIAN, 1996). Many theorists have questioned the efficiency of information manipulation by these automatic systems.

From the beginning NLP was developed through "brute force", as Wilks (2008) would say. The manual labor of dicionary construction was the base of the first statistical methodologies for language processing (HUTCHINS, 2003). At this time the theoratical issues of dictionary making were too young and Lexicography and Terminology had not yet determined themselves as fields of studies. With the advent of Artificial Intelligence, scholars designed small programs that illustrated translational possibilities. Soon later grammar and syntax information was introduced to speed up and improve the automatic query (GARRÃO, 1998). According to Wilks (2009), AI's role in MT was mainly theoretical in nature. The logic system of calculators was not sufficient to solve the logical elements in language.

Setbacks in Development

In 1966, a report by the Advisory Committee on Automatic Language Processing (ALPAC) made statements discrediting the potential of MT to produce good quality translations (HUTCHINS, 2003). These statements sowed skepticism about this field of study, leading to a general cut in government funding for such research (SANTOS, 2012). Even without financial support, systems such as SYSTRAN and TAUM, from the Montreal University, continued to manually perform the translations and catalog them in their system. This example-based machine translation approach reuses existing translations as the basis for new translations (SOMERS, 2003). This example-based approach is the backbone of one of the most professionaly translation systems used used, Translation Memories (TM) system.

TM systems are not MT systems, but Computer Assisted Tools. All the translations are suggestions for the user to choose from as the translation is manually edited. Even though TMs are not MTs, they share similar architectures for the user suggestions. Groves (2005a) discusses several hybrid approaches on data-focused MT systems such as statistical example-based. These authors investigate the different ways of linking syntactic knowledge with statistical data. Using TM system require the user to feed, initially, the system with translations. This pairs the translation more reliably. Other MT system do the pairing without supervision. But MT products must go through a evaluation process to rank their efficiency. And that requires human professionals to evaluate the quality of the translations automatically generated by the MT system. MT as any NLP system evaluation require human attention.

New devolepment in NLP still require great amount of human collaboration, and this can be aquired through academic involvement or entreprise financing. Back in the 70's, the lack of good translation ratings from MT systems resulted in the skepticism and, subsequentially, in the Entreprise fleeing academic partnerships. Without external financing most researches were carried in the academic limits, as TAUM from Montreal University is cited. Later, due to linguistic and mathematical theory development the good results started to come and soon after the entreprise interest.

Lexicography is a good example of theoratical development that made a practical real-world difference. Lexicography is the discipline of describing, analyzing and responsible for craft of compiling, writin and editing dictionaries according to semantic, sintactic and pragmatic relationships (BÉJOINT, 2000). Due to technological issues, lexicographers rarely shared their views with other colegues in the 60's (ZGUSTA, 2010).

New Theories to Approach Data

However, with the globalization scenario this discipline was one to manage to organize its principles and views. Lexicography was one of the first disciplines to provide data and to manage to organize them according a theoratical criteria. Following the organization provided by Lexicography but with a longer historic gap between the arise Corpus Linguistics was one to boost NLP theories and analysis. Corpus Linguistics is so powerfull IBM announced, back in the 50's at the very beginning of Corpus Linguistics advances, that a supercomputer running the Brown Corpus would soon master the English language. This was shortly corrected as an academic prank (MASTERMAN & KAY, 1959). Since then, much of the process has evolved. First from paper punch card to hard drive memories. But the philosophy behind Corpus Linguistics has not changed much.

According to Sardinha (2004), corpus linguistics is the science that deals with the collection and exploration of corpora, or carefully collected textual linguistic data sets, for the purpose of serving to searching for a language or linguistic variety. According to Oliveira (2009), this area represents a new philosophical approach to language studies and can be considered as the "modern face" of empirical linguistics. In corpus linguistics the process of text selection to compose the corpus and its arrangement in the database is very important. There are several ways to compose a corpus. The corpus can be composed of texts of one language or several languages, in this case called the multilingual corpus. The multilingual corpus can be aligned in parallel. According to Simões (2004), the parallel corpus can be aligned at different levels, e.g. in paragraphs, sentences, segments, words and even characters. The parallel corpus can be used for different purposes, such as foreign language teaching, terminology studies, information retrieval systems and MT.

Brown Corpus is one of the most popular corpora in the world. Its format has served as a template for new corpora since its construction. It is a million-word collection from 500 hundred written texts from different genres (JURAFSKY and MARTIN, 2009). The Brown Corpus had initially only the words themselves. After several years Part-of-Speech (POS) was applied (GREENE and RUBIN, 1971). The POS tagging process had been extensively revised. Now the Brown Corpus has been serving as a model for the design of new corpora not just on its format but on it linguistic resources. Much linguistic enrichment work has been extensively done. POS tagging has added to each word a morphossintactial label in which the tagset has been replicated in many different corpora in many different languages.

The annotation of POS is popularly done by the use of probabilistic models. Today the state of art in accuracy of probabilistic POS tagging is over 96%. Thus, the linguistic enrichment through POS tagging require a carefull revision to turn the annotated corpus into a gold-standard model. Once in a gold-standard stage, the corpus can be used as model for automatically assigning POS tags to new texts or corpora. Although POS tagging can be done in a variety of ways, statistical models are the most commonly used. Statistical implementation of algorithms has followed NLP since its beginning with MT calculators. Probabilistic models are crucial for capturing every kind of linguistic Knowledge (JURAFSKY and MARTIN, 2009). Hidden Markov Models are one of the most used in the field and and the advantage of probabilistic approaches is the robustness for solving any kind of ambiguity and providing a possible answer. Remember that a possible answer not necessarily means a reliable one.

As statistical POS tagging, once again, attention must be called that this is not the only way to achieve a linguistic enrichment of a corpus. There are State Machines and Rule-based system are also capable of annotating new texts or different corpora, but their implementations are not as popular as the statistical ones and the construction and rule implementation is a extensive and expert tiring work, but with products up to 100% reliable.

POS tagging is one of the processes in the pipeline of NLP to enrich linguistically a corpus. Other stages can be the syntactical annotation, thematic roles and lexical semantic annotation. The syntactical information is commonly stored as treebanks. The Penn Treebank is a highly enriched corpus and it gathers not only syntactical information but sense annotation as well (PRASAD et al., 2008).

The interface of Syntax and Semantics in a corpus helps all sort of parallel studies. A syntactically annotated corpus can serve as a sample for grammar extraction, which may serve as grammar corrector or speech identifier. Linguistic information in different levels of depth can be used as resource of a number of intelligent systems. Other systems that rely on decision making and through the use of different models imply intelligent machines are Conversational Agents or Dialogue systems, such as chatterbots. Chatterbots are systems that seek to interact and maintain human communication. Alan Turing in his famous paper "Can a machine think" proposes a philosophical task of daring a human to maintan a conversation with an unknown subject and then guess if the interaction happened with a human or a machine, passing as human (TURING, 1956). As the use of State Machines or Rule systems can be augmented by probalistic models, the resemblance of intelligence from a machine is more and more human-like. The proposition from Turing (1956), later called the Turing test, turned a philosophical query into a sciency fictional symbol and later a near reality.

In the 80's the design of chatterbots was at its peak. Projects like ELIZA (WEIZENBAUM, 1966) was one of the first chatterbots to maintain a limited conversation with the user. ELIZA (WEIZENBAUM, 1966) and ALICE (WALLACE, 1995), as open source softwares, are commonly used as the backgroung architecture for the design of new chatterbot for specific domains (RAHMAN, 2012). The architecture of their AIML (Artifitial Intelligence Markup Language) was replicated in many other projects but their indicated poor results. The poor results were based on the human effort to maintan the conversation or the cyclical loop of interaction from the chatterbots. These results more than a decade ago made many enthusiasts lose their attention to such systems.

Today with the hybridization of the systems, conversational agents are popular again. This time chatterbots are been used to represent institutions and to facilitate interactions with clients. This scenario is very controlled domain for a chatterbot chose its replies. Governamental and educational institutions are interested in chatterbots to provide tutorial instructions or even question and answering for educational purposes. And a little time must be dedicated to clarify the difference between a chatterbot and a personal assistant. Differently from a chatterbot the personal assistant is not compeled to maintain a conversation, but to quickly converge the user request into an excutable action to be performed. Personal assitants can help you to find an address via GPS embarked on the phone, execute a transaction or solve a problem as a call-center attendant.

For better illustrating the difference between Personal assistants and Conversationa Agents, many intelligent systems, nowadays, are applied in the healthcare domain. And let's imagine you have a system that monitor your heart rate in the case of a cardiac patient. If you heart rate is going flat, you would want a personal assistant to notice the issue and react calling for help. A conversational agent would try to maintain a conversation with you while you are having a stroke and keep you interacted as your life fades away. Jokes aside, a high-performance personal assistant will only maintain a converstation while it gathers information, not primarily clear, on what excutable action the user is instructing the personal assistant to perform.

Now there are even probabilistic models that mimic human-like personality (GALVAO et al., 2004). Or even projects like Pelling and Gardner (2019) that reflect on Alan Turing's philosophical question and search of the Artifitial Intelligence singularity. But those are the ones pushing NLP possibilities forward without seeking guaranteed rewards. In the last decade NLP research does not differ from what happened in the early 70's with MT or in the late 80's with conversational agents. The potential of great results is anxiously waited, and many times the ansiety of great unrealistic results in a short period of time withdraw finantial support for projects. Much in NLP has been done and great results have been reached, but the curve of development in many fields of studies are coming to a seemly plateau. If that was not worrisome enough, in 2008 a great world economic crisis stroke (BUCHANAN, 2008). This economic crisis held back new investment and made partnerships collapse. And once again, the trail of NLP was back to the academic track and to its slower pace of development.

The Last Decade

The crisis, which initially started in Europe years later reached South America. In Some developing countries, like Brazil, the crisis made major NLP researches pause or even quit their work during this period. As some stand by the crisis, others had to seek deeper in the interdisciplinary nature of language processing to keep on developing the field. The 7th Empirical Methods on Cognitive Linguistics Workshops (EMCL) at the height of the Brazilian crisis, in 2015, for instance, had the goal to look for different experiemental hypothesis and methods for data collection. These new views on cognitive systems and neurosciense proposals gained the opportunity of computational application (CHEN, ARGENTINIS, & WEBER 2016).

Partnerships between the academy and enterprises that were maintanined during the crisis were the biggest responsibles for the development of NLP during the period of crisis. And the most experimental hypotheses were developed and tested during this period. The use of Social Media as corpus for Sentiment Analysis had great development and positive results at around this time. The trend on social media usage provided the data, on opinion and behavior, that this field of information retrieval required to manage its texts classification and processing tasks (LIU, 2010). The uprise of Sentiments Analysis made the already newly important Big Data even more interesting. Major volume of data was gaining focus at the beginning of this decade, and the development of Data Science and new methods of analysis were the elements it needed for providing the effective filter and categorization of results (PRIYADARSHINI et. al., 2020). These results were soon seen on the market for pattern behavior recognition and resulted popularly on adversting suggestions and security protocols.

Some methods relied on Ontology building, but its contruction could be very time consuming (TORRES, 2012). Combined approaches of different techniques, as constraint grammar analysis, terms extraction and statistic algorithms are used to try to support the Ontology learning methods. These are some of the researchs that tried to auxiliar on the analysis of great volumes of data. Chen, Argentinis & Weber (2016) say although more data are available than ever, only a fraction is being integrated, understood, and analyzed. The 7th EMCLworkshops focused on different ways on applying cognitive solutions to different types of data in media. And IBM's Watson has been using cognitive computing technology on its latest version.

SOLUTIONS AND RECOMMENDATIONS

Many years ago, the foundations of NLP would rely on rule structuring and recognition. Important projects as the TreeBank (TAYLOR et al., 2003), PropBank (KINGSBURY & PALMER, 2002) as Snow et al. (2008) say they played an important role to NLP encourageing novel ideas, tasks and algorithms. And that made the development of Grammar Engineering possible. Although Rule-based systems showed themselves uneffective to dealing with large amount of data hybrid systems gained more and more focus on NLP (GROVES & WAY, 2005b).

However, the mix of statistical algorithms with language structured models soon reached a peak of improvement but no further, reliably. Although this peak represents the best results in the last decade, the rate of accuracy, purely statistical without supervision, is still not reliable enough on its own. Researchers as Gildea & Jurafsky (2002) and Pease (2011) seeked for other linguistic areas to keep on improving this field of studies. Semantics was for many years the source of theoratical material to enrich data.

Projects as FrameNet (BAKER ET AL, 2008) and WordNet (MILLER, 1998) are great achievements in the interface between Syntax and Semantics.

Projects like FrameNet and WordNet brought the semantic enrichment many people thought was the thing that was missing to improve machine learning. However, the network of word and terms relations operate with a sintactical interface and therefore would only improve syntactic ratings, not the implied idea of meaning within semantics, as wrongly expected. Many researchers went on the search for new source of language material on Pragmatics and discourse knowledge. And even though many progresses had been made with theses investments, computational pragmatics is still too related to language semantics withing Syntax. Many of the protocols used on IBM's Watson relied on Semantics and even thought it is one of the most efficient and precise Artifitial Intelligence tools nowadays, IBM knew it could go further.

Chen et al. (2019) believed that cognitive computing, based on aspects of human thinking, may unveil a variety of insights of how to digest and understand data. Relating to language theory, Cognitive Linguistics (CL) has brought many aspects of human language acquisition into the circle of studies and many patterns of categorization have been studied. The application of such studies is still in development. The kind of source material that CL might provide handles language within its most fundamental aspects. Lakoff and Johnson (2008) propose that conceptual metaphors are presented in everyday language and they are universaly used, therefore a systematic part o human language organization. Concepts presented by Lakoff and Jonhson (2008) are still in development to be structured in a patterned language set.

Think like image recognition. Many shapes and distortion of ideal shapes have to be classified so an algorithm may sugest probabilistically righter what a candidate image might be. The Conceptual Metaphor presented by Lakoff and Jonhson (2008) still need to be extensively tested to indentify which concepts are performed universily (LAKOFF & JONHSON, 2020). And work with universal concepts is the jewel seeked in every multi-language project.

In MT, there is illustrative image, the triangle of Vauquois. This image presents a triangle in which in the bottom there are the most structural elements of the language, as words and phonemes. As you climb the pyramid the depth of analysis becomes greater. The space that represents the distance between two languagues becames narrower and narrower, makig the need for a transfer system from the source to the target language smaller and smaller. When you reach the top of the triangle, there is no need for the transfer system and the distance between two languages has vanished. The top of the triangle is what it is called an interlingua system. Interlingua is deeply connected to the astract representation of meaning and the practical implementation in MT systems has not been done massively. In large scale the work of Arnold et al. (1994) presents as a utopic idea.

But the CL is working on formalizing the theory and it would be a great step towards an efficient implementation of this symbolic approach. If words, sentences and utterances could be managed to be clustered according to its primitive intentions, most of the products related to NLP would gain new or enhanced application. Information Retrieval would not encounter problematic labeling of issues, machine translation's engine would work on a, what Jurafsky and Martin (2009) say, interlingua level, and conversational agents would engage in dialogue according to the user's behavior.Understanding concepts of, for instance, hunger and desire are connected to human survival instincts, may guide to converge meanings. If how humans classify and categorize all things is understood, and then how they aquire language concepts related to those categoties, soon, machines could probably do as well.

FUTURE RESEARCH DIRECTIONS

CL still struggling with the methodology to test such primitive aspects of human language, but many progres has been done with big data analysis. This reciprocal exchange promises a theoratical revolution on NLP and the areas related to it. At first, this new linguistic data would have to be accessible in large volume of machine-readable text. As said by Sales et al. (2018), human linguistic annotation is crucial for NLP, but it can be expensive and time-consuming. And not always such an experimental idea has the chance to be tested due to these finacial hurdles.

In 2013, a project requested by the mobile branch of the South- Korean conglomerate LG started a partnership with the Research Group, GReat from the Federal University of Ceara in Brazil. The project was designed to develop a personal assistant for that mobile company. The research group started to hire researchers from all NLP related areas already working or studying at the University. The assemble created a high-quality team that was responsible for structuring a prototype to present as proof of concept back to LG. In only three months, this team was capable of structuring a not just a proof of concept but a system prototype. This prototype was presented to the LG headquarters in South Korea and, amazingly, it outperformed a previous personal assistant project LG had been working on for two years.

Although the Brazilian prototype seemed to work better on a much simpler system architecture, the South Korean company chose to maintain their previous native project. This, along with the Brazilian economic crisis of 2015, made a potential efiecient system architecture not to be public used or shared. The system architecture that surprassed was built over Cunha (2013). This work created a CAT system, a TM system, that was designed to create machine translation engines based on the linguistics enrichment of the occurances processed through the TM. A TM system stores and recalls previous text translated by the user. The architecture used by Cunha (2013) uses not only the occurance of the sentence to verify already existant memory, but the grammar within the sentence and its constranint grammar.

The verification of already existant constraint rules was performed by a sequence of modules within the Computational Linguistc pipeline. A chunker, followed by a Part-of-Speech (POS) tagger collected the string of POS tags to a Grammar Memory (GM). If the phrase chunk occurance is not found within the TM, the input is directed for GM. If the GM identifies the the rule within the grammar engine and dictionary, it proceeds to translate the input via a rule-based approach. Otherwise, if the rule is not existant in the GM the input is directed to a statistical engine that performs the translation of the input chunk missing from the engines and suggest an output for the user.

The outuput that goes to the user if confirmed or edited goes back to the system pipeline and updates all the engines that flanked the first submission from the user. This interface with TM and a machine learnig process was able to outcome popularly used machine translations system freely available on the internet (CUNHA, 2013). Although this system rotine seems to be quite naïve, it enabled a greater view of machine learning possibilities. This system from Cunha (2013) was based on constraint structures and dictionaries entries. However, if the modules, engines and dictionaries were to learn how to communicate or classify interaction with a user. This system would pair not source and target language, but user input and system output. And it would learn throughout its examlpes of interaction with the user (FRANCO et al. 2014).

This system architecture was one of the great successes of the project. And even thought the Brazilian project of the personal assistant was not maintained by LG, its original models help to auxiliar lacking data from the South Korean one. Cunha & Soares (2015) e Cunha & Silva (2015) reflected on the aspects of this collaboration and the theoratical issues the demands from the South-korean project brought to light. One of the main issues was the lack of data on interaction human-machine and the need of a broader view of the concept of corpus (CUNHA & SOARES, 2015). Other aspect was the quality of the interaction between human and machine and the lack of criteria for evaluating this quality of communication (CUNHA & SILVA, 2015). When those ideas were presented by Cunha & Soares (2015) e Cunha & Silva (2015) intellectuals the Corpus Linguistics field expressed their outrage for the idea of a machine-generated corpus via human engineered grammar and to be validated by native humans. But the idea was well received by companies with ongoing NLP projects that need this sort of data.

The University does not aim on profit but on improvement of the field of sudies. This might take more time than companies may expect to access such knowledge and that is where the NLP future may rely. The University produces knowledge and analysis on data the market need processing. Why not bond these two universes? Some of the most productive experiments come from the partnership between Universities and companies. Even theoratical fields of study that are not directly interested in computational sciences produce a great amount of data that are unexcusably not machine readable. Logic philosophy and grammatical formalism are some examples of studies that are computationaly interesting but not necessarily are implemented.

Most of the applied sciences may be related to NLP. And many solutions to different fields of application might come from NLP. Many majors could dedicate some curriculum time for the NLP basics and data analysis. Surely, many undergraduate students would carry on to more advanced levels of analisys and even they might provide the market with knowledge products that might make more and more partnerships possible.

CONCLUSION

NLP research has survived over moments of crisis and for the near future many crises are to come. Popular interests in NLP has been appearing in a cycle. And the turn of the cycle depend on the pontential results a theory might bring. Ther greater the expectation, the greater is the frustration, when good results do not come.

Historically, the implementation of some theories that were frustrated by bad results returns with greater potential as theories and technology evolve. It has happened with MT, Conversational Agents and many probabilistic areas of NLP. Hybrid systems provide new results and different balance of this hybridization promotes different results. The University is the space for creating and testing theories. Experimentation is the fundamental key of research.

My experience as a NLP researcher led me to believe the more interdisciplinary the team is the greater the possibilities of success are. I worked with Computatinal Linguistics research in companies and in the University. The pace of both researchs are completely different but the products, they both produce, are complementary. The theories that rise to analyze new behavior will never cease to appear as behavior will never cease to change or evolve. Acknowledge change is one of the main goals of the University, but its attachment to older theories can not keep the University from updating itself. University must be open for applied theory and for showing the potential o implementation of all theories in the real world. In case, a theory is not applied for the real world, what is the point, if not only informational, to acknowledge this theory.

Today the world turns around data. The volume of data the society produces is greater than ever and it just grows and grows everyday. Every new application, every new behavior and appliance provides more and more data. Nowadays the knowledge on how to analyze data is one of the most valuable products the University has to offer. The analysis of great amounts of even chunks of them is valid. And the possibility of applying this knowledge to real world appliences is one of the most desired ascpects companies may offer. The approximation of theoratical scholars and implementation researchers to market needs and companies support should be encouraged at the University. The University is not the place where profit should be the focus, but the improvement of society, through different fields of studies.

However, the future of NLP may not rely on the enriched appliances it may occasinaly provide, but the data they produce. And this will be for long theoraticaly and practically useful. As long as society produces data, NLP will have ground to work on. New appliances that enable new behavior are released every now and then. And the creative human mind will keep on reliesing new appliances as long the human deseire for consumption exists. This pattern will be for as long as our societal dynamic is maintaned. But the data and knowledge produced, while using those new appliances, highlight new patterns and theories to be tested.

The understanding of data increases everyday. More and more data analisysy research unveil characteristics of the human behavior that brings us closer to Pragmatic levels. Although, the Pragmatic ratings of implementation are not yet so reliable. Maybe in the near future, as CL succeed on converging the human behavior. CL is advancing using analysis from Big Data. And many aspects of our primitive beings are becoming clear as this field of studies verify their theories. The theories need great amounts of data to prove reliable results and the world is producing lots of data and it is not going to decrease any time soon. But to analyze data, more data is needed, and the University is the perfect place for such extensive task. And companies and the market are the ones to compel the University to do so.

Comprehending the deeper structure, the primitives, of human language behavior and the mecanics of language acquisition may help improving aspects of data analysis. As the analisys of structure faces a more abstract concept the more universal this analisys turns out to be. Managing to go deeper into the structure of one language breaks the barrier that separates all languages and unites all in a conceptual system, an interlingua.

Moments of crisis will always come and go but the human curiosity will never stop wondering. History has shown the cicle of co-dependency between theory and practice, therefore university and companies in the field of NLP. Computaional researches are not the most expensive if compared to other fields, but it can be very time consuming from experts or plain human colaborators. Time dedicated for a reaserch can be relative to its needs, but unquestionably the knowledge it aquires, no matter the nature of the level of theoratical depth, piles up, seemly, indefinitely.

Partnership between companies and Universities must be encouraged. As the academic views of their theoratical aknowledge should be seen as a market product. A product to be advertised and shown. Knowledge must imply applied usage of it. Therefore, theoratical majors must open the door and grant space for practical implementation. The application of theory can benefit the class learning, student engagement, improvement of the field of studies and society.

REFERENCES

Arnold, D., Lorna, B., Siety, M., Humphreys, R. L., & Sadler, L. (1994). *Machine translation: An introductory guide*. Blackwells-NCC.

Baker, C. F., Fillmore, C. J., & Lowe, J. B. (1998, August). The berkeley framenet project. In *Proceedings of the 17th international conference on Computational linguistics-Volume 1* (pp. 86-90). Association for Computational Linguistics.

Béjoint, H. (2000). *Modern lexicography: An introduction.* Oxford: Oxford University Press.

Buchanan, M. (2008). This economy does not compute. *New York Times, 1.*

Chen, M., Li, W., Fortino, G., Hao, Y., Hu, L., & Humar, I. (2019). A dynamic service migration mechanism in edge cognitive computing. *ACM Transactions on Internet Technology, 19*(2), 1–15. doi:10.1145/3239565

Chen, Y., Argentinis, J. E., & Weber, G. (2016). IBM Watson: How cognitive computing can be applied to big data challenges in life sciences research. *Clinical Therapeutics, 38*(4), 688–701. doi:10.1016/j.clinthera.2015.12.001 PMID:27130797

Cunha, T. M. D. (2013). *A criação de um sistema híbrido de tradução automática para a conversão de expressões nominais da língua inglesa.* Academic Press.

Cunha, T. M. D., & Silva, P. B. L. D. (2015a, November). A Criação de um Corpus de Sentenças Através de Gramáticas Livres de Contexto. In *Anais do X Simpósio Brasileiro de Tecnologia da Informação e da Linguagem Humana* (pp. 241–248). SBC.

Cunha, T. M. D., & Soares, D. D. F. B. (2015b, November). A Utilização de Atos de Diálogo em Sistemas de Diálogo para Dispositivos Móveis. In *Anais do X Simpósio Brasileiro de Tecnologia da Informação e da Linguagem Humana* (pp. 225–232). SBC.

Franco, W., Gomes, T. C. J. P. P., Castro, R., Andrade, R. M., & Castro, M. F. (2014). *Example-based dialog modeling for a mobile system.* Academic Press.

Galvao, A. M., Barros, F. A., Neves, A. M., & Ramalho, G. L. (2004, July). Persona-AIML: an architecture for developing chatterbots with personality. In *Proceedings of the Third International Joint Conference on Autonomous Agents and Multiagent Systems, 2004. AAMAS 2004.* (pp. 1266-1267). IEEE.

Garrão, M. D. U. (2001). Tradução automática: ainda um enigma multidisciplinar. In Congresso nacional de linguística e filologia (Vol. 5, pp. 8-12). Academic Press.

Gildea, D., & Jurafsky, D. (2002). Automatic labeling of semantic roles. *Computational Linguistics, 28*(3), 245–288. doi:10.1162/089120102760275983

Greene, B. B., & Rubin, G. M. (1971). *Automatic grammatical tagging of English.* Department of Linguistics, Brown University.

Groves, D., & Way, A. (2005a). Hybrid data-driven models of machine translation. *Machine Translation, 19*(3-4), 301–323. doi:10.100710590-006-9015-5

Groves, D., & Way, A. (2005b). Hybrid example-based SMT: the best of both worlds? In *Proceedings of the ACL Workshop on Building and Using Parallel Texts* (pp. 183-190). Association for Computational Linguistics. 10.3115/1654449.1654490

Jurafsky, D., & Martin, J. H. (2008). *Speech and Language Processing: An introduction to speech recognition, computational linguistics and natural language processing*. Prentice Hall.

Kapil, G., Agrawal, A., & Khan, R. A. (2016, October). A study of big data characteristics. In *2016 International Conference on Communication and Electronics Systems (ICCES)* (pp. 1-4). IEEE.

Kingsbury, P., & Palmer, M. (2002, May). From TreeBank to PropBank. In LREC (pp. 1989-1993). Academic Press.

Lakoff, G., & Johnson, M. (2008). *Metaphors we live by*. University of Chicago press.

Lakoff, G., & Johnson, M. (2020). The embodied mind. *Shaping Entrepreneurship Research: Made, as Well as Found*, 80.

Liu, B. (2010). Sentiment analysis and subjectivity. Handbook of Natural Language Processing, 2(2010), 627-666.

Loffler-Laurian, A. M. (1996). La traduction automatique. Presses Univ. Septentrion.

Masterman, M., & Kay, M. (1959). *Operational system (IBM-USAF Translator Mark I)*. Foreign Technology Division, USAF.

Miller, G. A. (1998). *WordNet: An electronic lexical database*. MIT Press.

Oliveira, L. P. (2009). Linguística de Corpus: teoria, interfaces e aplicações. *Matraga-Revista do Programa de Pós-Graduação em Letras da UERJ, 16*(24).

Pease, A. (2011). *Ontology: A practical guide*. Articulate Software Press.

Pelling, C., & Gardner, H. (2019, August). Two Human-Like Imitation-Learning Bots with Probabilistic Behaviors. In *2019 IEEE Conference on Games (CoG)* (pp. 1-7). IEEE. 10.1109/CIG.2019.8847995

Prasad, R., Dinesh, N., Lee, A., Miltsakaki, E., Robaldo, L., Joshi, A. K., & Webber, B. L. (2008, May). The Penn Discourse TreeBank 2.0. LREC.

Priyadarshini, R., Barik, R. K., Panigrahi, C., Dubey, H., & Mishra, B. K. (2020). An investigation into the efficacy of deep learning tools for big data analysis in health care. In Deep Learning and Neural Networks: Concepts, Methodologies, Tools, and Applications (pp. 654-666). IGI Global.

Rahman, J. (2012). *Implementation of ALICE chatbot as domain specific knowledge bot for BRAC U (FAQ bot)* (Doctoral dissertation). BRAC University.

Sales, J. E., Barzegar, S., Franco, W., Bermeitinger, B., Cunha, T., Davis, B., . . . Handschuh, S. (2018, May). A Multilingual Test Collection for the Semantic Search of Entity Categories. In *Proceedings of the Eleventh International Conference on Language Resources and Evaluation (LREC 2018)*. Academic Press.

Santos, C. C. (2012). Os corpora eletrônicos nos estudos da tradução automática. *Revista Letras Raras, 1*(1), 48–64. doi:10.35572/rlr.v1i1.81

Sardinha, T. B. (2004). *Lingüística de corpus*. Editora Manole Ltda.

Simões, A. (2004). *Parallel corpora word alignment and applications* (Doctoral dissertation).

Snow, R., O'Connor, B., Jurafsky, D., & Ng, A. Y. (2008, October). Cheap and fast---but is it good?: evaluating non-expert annotations for natural language tasks. In *Proceedings of the conference on empirical methods in natural language processing* (pp. 254-263). Association for Computational Linguistics. 10.3115/1613715.1613751

Taylor, A., Marcus, M., & Santorini, B. (2003). The Penn treebank: an overview. In *Treebanks* (pp. 5–22). Springer. doi:10.1007/978-94-010-0201-1_1

Torres, C. E. A. (2012). *Uso de informação linguística e análise de conceitos formais no aprendizado de ontologies* (Doctoral dissertation). Universidade de São Paulo.

Turing, A. M. (1956). Can a machine think. *The World of Mathematics, 4*, 2099-2123.

Wallace, R. (1995). *Artificial linguistic internet computer entity (alice)*. Academic Press.

Weizenbaum, J. (1966). ELIZA---a computer program for the study of natural language communication between man and machine. *Communications of the ACM, 9*(1), 36–45. doi:10.1145/365153.365168

Wilks, Y. (2008). *Machine translation: its scope and limits*. Springer Science & Business Media.

Zgusta, L. (2010). *Manual of lexicography* (Vol. 39). Walter de Gruyter.

ADDITIONAL READING

Goldsmith, J. (2007). Probability for linguists. *Mathématiques et sciences humaines. Mathematical Social Sciences*, (180), 73–98.

Katz, J. J. (1997). Analyticity, necessity, and the epistemology of semantics. *Philosophy and Phenomenological Research: A Quarterly Journal*, 1-28.

Koehn, P. (2009). *Statistical machine translation*. Cambridge University Press. doi:10.1017/CBO9780511815829

Lakoff, G. (2008). *Women, fire, and dangerous things*. University of Chicago press.

Manning, C. D., Manning, C. D., & Schütze, H. (1999). *Foundations of statistical natural language processing*. MIT press.

Mitkov, R. (Ed.). (2004). *The Oxford handbook of computational linguistics*. Oxford University Press.

Papageorgiou, H., Cranias, L., & Piperidis, S. (1994, June). Automatic alignment in parallel corpora. In *Proceedings of the 32nd annual meeting on Association for Computational Linguistics* (pp. 334-336). Association for Computational Linguistics. 10.3115/981732.981784

Ratnaparkhi, A. (1996). A Maximum En tropy Part of Speech Tagger. In *Proc. ACLSIGDAT Conference on Empirical Methods in Natural Language Processing*.

Tendahl, M., & Gibbs, R. W. Jr. (2008). Complementary perspectives on metaphor: Cognitive linguistics and relevance theory. *Journal of Pragmatics, 40*(11), 1823–1864. doi:10.1016/j.pragma.2008.02.001

KEY TERMS AND DEFINITIONS

Big Data: It is a term used in the field of Information Technology that difines a large volume of data. It can be related to the analisys and interpretation of a variety of data. It is related as the instrument used in Data science.

Categorization: It is the human cognitive process of organizing concepts and the classifying things according to their aspects of similarities or differences. It is involuntary human behavior related to the aquicsition on language and cultural patterns.

Cognitive Linguistics: It is a discipline within applied linguistics that combines knowledge from both psychology and linguistics. It aims to describe how language is processed cognitively and studies of patterns of behavior within human language.

Conceptual Methafors: They are everyday language discourse words and terms that represent a higher conceptual domain of meaning and believed to be universaly used. They are generated throughout the relations of humans with their own embodied experiences.

Conversational Agents: They are dialogue system built to create or maintain a conversation with a human user. They can be used as tutorial system for educational or governamental institutions.

Machine Translation: The field of NLP that handles the task of automatically converting one source language text into another target language though pairing similar word, terms or sentence according parallel data or language transfer engines.

Partnership: It is the process of a collaborative dynamic. This sort of assossiation must be reciprocal for all parts related. The bond of the relationship could be finantial, emotional for people, a business or organization.

Personal Assistant: It is a system designed to assist or perform task for the user. It mayrepresent a call-center attendant of organization or institution. It may execute everyday mobile assessible tasks.

Pragmatics: It is a linguistic discipline that handles language discourse, the contexts in which is used and the pattern or cultural protocols of language behavior usage.

Chapter 2
Deriving Business Value From Online Data Sources Using Natural Language Processing Techniques

Stephen Camilleri
University of Malta, Malta

ABSTRACT

The wealth of information produced over the internet empowers businesses to become data-driven organizations, increasing their ability to predict consumer behavior, take more informed strategic decisions, and remain competitive on the market. However, past research did not identify which online data sources companies should choose to achieve such an objective. This chapter aims to analyse how online news articles, social media messages, and user reviews can be exploited by businesses using natural language processing (NLP) techniques to build business intelligence. NLP techniques assist computers to understand and derive a valuable meaning from human (natural) languages. Following a brief introduction to NLP and a description of how these three text streams differ from each other, the chapter discusses six main factors that can assist businesses in choosing one data source from another. The chapter concludes with future directions towards improving business applications involving NLP techniques.

INTRODUCTION

The Internet has revolutionized the way information is communicated and how social interaction takes place. Its extraordinary growth has led people to become more connected together, giving businesses the possibility to achieve competitive advantage from data submitted online. 2018 was characterized with 3 billion active social media users (Egan, 2020), while the Global Datasphere is forecasted to grow from 33 trillion GB in 2018 to 175 trillion GB by 2025 (Reinsel, Gantz, & Rydning, 2018). However, the business value lies not in the wealth of data that is harvested but what businesses do with that data.

DOI: 10.4018/978-1-7998-4240-8.ch002

Dedicating human resources to process and analyze large volumes of data can become challenging, expensive and time-consuming.

Businesses can already avail themselves from transactional data, that is gathered from day-to-day operations. This data source, which may consist of orders, invoices, payments, deliveries etc. provides visibility of what consumers want and what they tend to look for. However, businesses also need to automatically predict market trends and changes; understand and react more quickly to the rapid shifts in consumers' demands and expectations; increase automation to improve performance and; identify new niche markets to remain sustainable. Such intelligence could be harvested from online data sources.

Past research has so far not identified the basis for which a business should opt to exploit one data source over another. This chapter aims to provide a better understanding of how news articles, social media messages and user reviews can be exploited by businesses using natural language processing techniques to provide value to the business. News agency sites, whose content is maintained by editors, have been traditionally used for distributing information about events and activities. This approach has been challenged following the introduction and rapid increase of social media platforms, where active social media users have become valuable real-time info and news contributors. Users have also been given the opportunity to voice their feedback on purchased products and services via company platforms, focused on logging user reviews. This chapter introduces these three data streams and provides the basis for which businesses should choose one data source from another. The chapter also lists potential areas of growth within the context of business intelligence and text analytics.

The chapter is structured in the following manner. Section 2 introduces natural language processing and the three data sources discussed in this chapter – news articles, social media messages and user reviews. The main focus of this chapter is defined in section 3, where the recommendations are given on the basis for which businesses should opt to harvest one data source from another. Section 4 discusses future directions in relation to commercial text mining and analysis, followed by concluding remarks in section 5. The list of references cited in this chapter are then provided, along with supplemental readings and key terms mentioned in this chapter.

BACKGROUND

Technology has changed the way life is lived; the way interactions take place; the way games are played; the way business is conducted; the way information is handled. What seemed to be impossible up to some decades ago, has become ubiquitous in today's world and man is constantly automating tasks that are closer to what human beings do.

Natural Language Processing

The emergence of **natural language processing** (NLP) as a branch of Artificial Intelligence, is increasingly focused on improving such impersonification, by programming computers to understand spoken and written human (natural) languages (Pinto, Oliveira & Oliveira Alves, 2016; Al Omran & Treude, 2017). As humans normally interact through text and speech, NLP tools have been developed to accept text and voice streams as inputs; decode such inputs in a machine-readable way; understand the message by identifying the underlying structures governing the syntax and semantics of the language and; derive a valuable meaning from the human language. The knowledge that the machine 'acquires' can then be stored in a repository or used to produce another written text (through a process called **natural-language generation**). The generated text can ultimately be read by a text-to-speech tool.

Originally, systems which processed natural language made use of human-programmable rules to understand the language structure. Later in time, research embarked on instructing machines to learn new rules by making probabilistic decisions, so that it could maximize the number of systems, which could use NLP techniques to interact similarly to humans. In fact, NLP is nowadays used to gather important information on events (Avvenuti, Del Vigna, Cresci, Marchetti & Tesconi, 2015; Imran, Castillo, Diaz & Vieweg, 2015; Panagiotou, Katakis, & Gunopulos, 2016); to detect topics and carry out sentiment analysis (Anta, Chiroque, Morere & Santo, 2013); to analyze software documentation (Al Omran & Treude, 2017); to build user and product profiles from user reviews (Chen, Chen & Wang, 2015); to improve answers to user questions (Fang, Wu, Zhao, Duan, Zhuang & Ester, 2016); to improve advertising techniques (Lee, Hosanagar, & Nair, 2018) and; to detect fake user reviews (Levinson, 2019).

This chapter focuses on applying NLP techniques on digital content submitted by users, communities and organizations on the Web, which has become a popular network of interactivity and a massive data repository. The following section introduces three examples of online text streams that could be mined for information – news articles that are published on news agency sites; messages that are posted on social media platforms and; reviews posted by users on company platforms. These text streams are considered to be **unstructured sources**, given that they do not follow a particular format or model (He, Zha & Li, 2013; Kaushik & Naithani, 2016). This increases the complexity involved for NLP techniques to process and analyze the content and to turn raw data into valuable information that can be stored in a more structured format.

News Articles

News articles deal with current affairs, usually discussing a particular event, opinion or topic. Events are reported differently by different news agencies, with some highlighting some aspects more than others (Alfonseca, Pighin & Garrido, 2013). As a result, harvesting different news agency sites simultaneously can help businesses acquire a more accurate picture of the actual event (Camilleri, Agius & Azzopardi, 2020). The content is generally reviewed by editors, or by columnists, who are requested to share their viewpoints and knowledge on specific subjects. News reports are sometimes supported with first-hand information (including photos and videos). The content is then placed in (unstructured) HTML-formatted pages using templates specific to the news agency and published on the news agency sites, as illustrated in Figure 1. The templates of the HTML page differ from one news agency to another.

Some news agencies also broadcast their news through dedicated API and/or RSS endpoints (Camilleri, Azzopardi & Agius, 2019), which are considered to be semi-structured sources. **Semi-structured sources** are not bound with the structure of a repository (He et al., 2013; Kaushik & Naithani, 2016). Every API and RSS endpoint contains a selection of news items, chosen specifically by the news agency and ordered by date of publication. Each news item is wrapped around metadata, usually containing the headline of the news article; a timestamp when the news article was published; the hyperlink to the content on the news agency site and; an excerpt (or complete) news content.

Figure 1. Sketch illustrating the homepage of a news portal

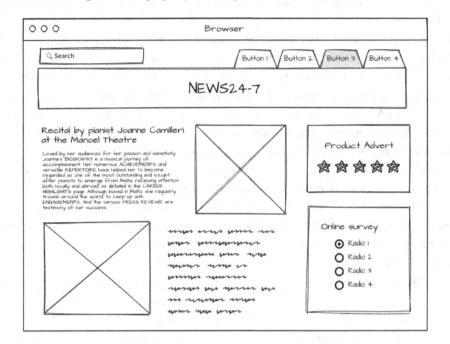

Difference Between API and RSS Endpoints

An **API** (Application Programming Interface) endpoint enables data to be transmitted between parties or services using programmed functions. Three news agencies which expose their data through APIs are Google News[1], The Guardian[2] and Die Zeit[3]. The advantage of API endpoints is that users can narrow down the search results or the amount of data that is retrieved through designated parameters. Responses received from APIs are structured in JSON format, as illustrated in Figure 2. **JSON** (JavaScript Object Notation) is a lightweight structure for exchanging data.

An **RSS** (Really Simple Syndication) endpoint is a web feed, which gives users the possibility to receive updates in a semi-structured format. Examples of news agencies, which broadcast news using this channel include News24[4], El Pais[5] and Shanghai Daily[6]. Data in RSS is outputted in an XML-structure format and does not support filtering of search results (Figure 3).

Social Media Messages

Social media platforms, which include blogs, microblogs, discussion forums, networking sites and multimedia sharing sites, have become increasingly popular throughout the years as means for the general public to share their outspoken opinions, reactions, news and emotions (Panagiotou, Katakis & Gunopulos, 2016). Businesses also use such channels for marketing purposes (Lin, Swarna & Bruning, 2017; Lee, Hosanagar & Nair, 2018). Interaction on this widespread medium is strengthened when comments are added to social media messages; when such messages are backed with user likes (a feature used to show support on a comment) and; when messages are reposted on the individual's personal news feed or shared with others as private messages.

Figure 2. A sample response from an API endpoint

```json
{
    "response": {
        "status": 200,
        "totalpages": 13,
        "currentpage": 4,
        "orderBy": "newest",
        "articles": [
            {
                "id": "22321433214",
                "tags": "music",
                "published": "2020-06-02T12:05:47Z",
                "title": "Recital by pianist Joanne Camilleri at the Manoel Theatre",
                "webURL": "www.joannecamilleri.com/english/engagements.htm"
            }
        ]
    }
}
```

Figure 3. A sample response from an RSS endpoint

```xml
<?xml version="1.0" encoding="utf-8"?>
<feed
    xmlns="http://www.w3.org/2005/Atom">
    <id>www.joannecamilleri.com/rss</id>
    <title>Joanne Camilleri - Professional Pianist</title>
    <logo>www.joannecamilleri.com/img/logo.gif</logo>
    <link rel="self" type="application/atom+xml" href="www.joannecamilleri.com/english/engagements.htm?category_id=" />
    <updated>2020-06-02T12:05:47-01:00</updated>
    <rights>Copyright (c) 2020, JOANNE CAMILLERI</rights>
    <icon>http://www.joannecamilleri.com/favicon.ico</icon>
    <entry>
        <id>www.joannecamilleri.com/english/engagements.htm</id>
        <title>Recital by pianist Joanne Camilleri at the Manoel Theatre</title>
        <link href="www.joannecamilleri.com/english/engagements.htm" />
        <updated>2020-06-21T13:25:00-03:00</updated>
        <summary></summary>
        <content type="xhtml">
            <div
                xmlns="http://www.w3.org/1999/xhtml">Regarded as one of the most outstanding and sought-after
                pianists to emerge from Malta, described by international pianist William Fong as "a musician of
                high intelligence and artistic vision", loved by her audiences for her passion and sensitivity,
                Joanne Camilleri is a rising star in the world of music.
            </div>
        </content>
        <author>
            <name>joannecamilleri.com</name>
            <uri>www.joannecamilleri.com</uri>
            <email>noreply@joannecamilleri.com</email>
        </author>
        <category term="Music" />
    </entry>
</feed>
```

Social media messages are usually shorter than news articles, as illustrated in Figure 4. They give users the possibility to submit immediate accounts of events and activities and voice their reactions and feelings on different subjects. As reporting is more personal and subjective and messages are published without being reviewed by a moderator, the content is considered to be less accurate, reliable and authentic when compared to news articles (Bruno, 2011; Imran et al., 2015; Rauchfleisch, Artho, Metag, Post &

Schäfer, 2017). Bursty behavior (a substantial amount of messages posted in a very short timeframe) has also been detected following an event or activity that has affected or experienced by a wide audience for example when a major earthquake takes place somewhere around the world (Liang, Caverlee & Mander, 2013; Avvenuti et al., 2015; Panagiotou, Katakis & Gunopulos, 2016). Usually, a single event burst lasts between one or two days; however, it may be the case that a series of bursts are recorded, representing multiple sub-events within a single event.

Figure 4. Screenshot of a tweet posted by a Maltese professional pianist

Rich in Content

Social media messages allow users to embed **hashtags** (a phrase that has no spaces and is preceded by a # symbol, containing important keywords or topics) and **user mentions** (a tag which contains the user's account name preceded by @ symbol, linking other users to a post). Hashtags are useful for businesses to associate messages with specific subjects or events and so, beneficial for tracking topics across space and time. On the other hand, user mentions are valuable to grab the user's attention and can be used to build connections with users.

Usage

Social media platforms have seen a growth in popularity. As shown in Figure 5, according to Statista and TNW sources, Facebook is recording the highest reported number of active users, supporting 2.5 billion users, followed by YouTube and Whatsapp (Ortiz-Ospina, 2019). It has been reported that 510,000 comments are posted, 293,000 statuses are updated, and 136,000 photos are uploaded on Facebook every minute, while in 2017, Twitter dispatched over 455,000 tweets per minute (Egan, 2020). Businesses could avail of this rich data to understand better the user's areas of interest, capture and track topics that captivate the user's attention and identify the activities engaged by the user.

Social media messages have also been used to capture the attitude of users towards specific businesses on a daily basis (Yu, Duan & Caoa, 2013); to identify events (Benson, Haghighi, & Barzilay, 2011); to understand how customer responds to marketing on social media platforms (Lee, Hosanagar & Nair, 2018) and the ways to increase brand marketing (Lin, Swarna & Bruning, 2017); to efficiently identify the geographical region where earthquakes took place (Liang et al., 2013; Avvenuti et al., 2015; Panagiotou et al., 2016); to detect rumours during emergency situations (Zeng, Starbird, & Spiro, 2016); to personalize social tag recommendations (Feng & Wang, 2012; Nam & Kannan, 2014); to identify spam tweets and spam in emerging topics (without any prior knowledge of the tweet author) (Martinez-Romo & Araujo, 2013); as well as to facilitate collaborative question answering (Kayes, Kourtellis, Quercia, Iamnitchi & Bonchi, 2015; Fang et al., 2016).

Harvesting Social Media Messages

Historical and real-time social media messages can be harvested from APIs designated specifically by the social media platforms (e.g. Twitter Public API) or; purchased directly from the social media platforms or by an alternative service provider. Real-time data is more expensive to procure and more difficult to manage due to the substantial amount of data that needs to be instantly processed and handled. However, unlike historical data, harvesting data in real-time give businesses the possibility to instantly analyze the information that is being conveyed by users. Throughout these past years, social media platforms have been minimizing the amount of data that is made available by the social media organization. For example, the amount of Twitter data that is made freely available is only 1% (Khumoyun, Cui & Lee, 2016; Goswami, Chakraborty, Ghosh, Chakrabarti & Chakraborty, 2018).

Some data providers also give users the possibility to download datasets containing historical social media messages. These datasets are beneficial as they provide businesses with a preliminary analysis of what kind of data they will be dealing it. However, harvesting messages in real-time from APIs give businesses more additional value than isolated datasets as data can be instantly processed and analyzed and the number of social messages that is harvested may be narrowed down using filters based on keywords; specific user account/s; geographical areas or within a specific timeframe. In addition, the size of the dataset (i.e. the number of rows) may not be sufficient for the organization and some of the fields which are made available by the social media platform and which are required by the organization, may not have been harvested by the owner of the dataset.

The fields that are available for downloading vary from one social platform to another. For example in the case of Twitter, each downloaded message is encapsulated with the message reference ID; the user account ID; the message content; in which language the content was written; the geographical coordinates from where the message was submitted (if enabled); date/time when the message was submitted; the number of times a message has been reposted; hashtags, symbols, user mentions and links used; the number of followers etc. On the other hand, Facebook messages are encapsulated with the message media type (i.e. status, link, video or photo), the number of likes, number of comments and the number of times the message had been shared.

Figure 5. The number of active users using social media platforms
Source: (Ortiz-Ospina, 2019).

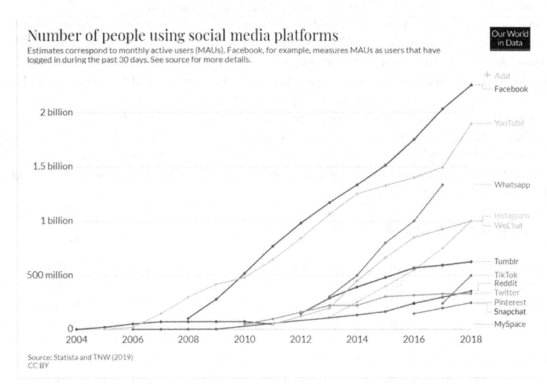

User Reviews

User reviews are invaluable information for businesses to understand their customers' perceptions, demands and expectations; to get insight on clients' behavior toward their purchases (Wang, Wezel & Forgues, 2015; Zhao, Stylianou & Zheng, 2018); to improve trust and build relationships; to gain new customers and increase sales (Levinson, 2019) and; to gain competitive advantage. Reviews also tend to encourage other users to voice their opinions, hence increasing the chance of generating a chain of reactions (Zhao, Stylianou & Zheng, 2018). They usually allow the user to submit feedback through a message box and a rating. Other platforms such as Amazon also summarize the ratings. Some of the popular platforms, which allow customers to comment on their products or services are Amazon (Singh, Irani, Rana, Dwivedi, Saumya & Roy, 2017; Levinson, 2019), Trip Advisor (Park, 2018), Yelp and Foursquare.

User reviews are different from professional non-profit reviews, whereby external experts are sought by the company to evaluate their products and services. However, user reviews also have their downsides. As these are voluntarily inputted by the customers (Park, 2018), platforms allowing user reviews may suffer from lack of feedback as clients may be reluctant to spend time to give feedback. In addition, customers may also intentionally submit malicious comments to try to harm businesses (Park, 2018; Levinson, 2019).

As businesses expand over time, it would become more challenging for businesses to handle the number of user reviews that are posted, given the amount of time needed to review and react on the user comments. However, businesses can leverage the use of text analytics to transform customer experience to customer loyalty, by retrieving online user reviews and carry out NLP techniques on them to gauge the customer's sentiment (through **sentiment analysis**); to identify common criticism; to respond and react more efficiently to consumer's feedback; to automatically order real-time user reviews by placing highly positive user reviews at the top (Park, 2018) and; to recommend products and services, which have been highly commendable by past customers (Chen, Chen & Wang, 2015).

Data is an invaluable source, that can be exploited by businesses to build intelligence. This section introduced the distinctive features of three different text streams that could be mined for information – online news articles, whose content is produced by news agencies; social media messages, whereby each active social user becomes a valuable real-time info contributor and; user reviews, which logs feedback on specific products or services. The following section provides the basis for which businesses should opt to harvest any of these three data sources.

SOLUTIONS AND RECOMMENDATIONS

The rapid surge of online content presents an opportunity for businesses that once harnessed, can lead to sustained growth. This growth can be achieved by initially identifying which online data sources could be used to strengthen business intelligence and add value to the business.

This section discusses six main factors that can assist businesses in choosing online news articles, social media messages and/or through user reviews, namely whether data needs to be harvested as soon as the event is unfolding (**time-bound**); the level of importance given to the reliability of data and whether content needs to be reviewed by moderators prior to being published (**authenticity**); the type of content that needs to be analyzed (**content-type**); the level of detail discussed in the content (**length of content**); how robust NLP algorithms are to interpret this raw data (**tools**) and; the amount of capital that the organization is willing to invest to acquire data (**data availability**).

Time-Bound

Businesses have different levels of sensitivity when it comes to understanding and reacting to online consumer behavior. French personal care company L'Oréal invested heavily to identify trending topics containing customer questions on social media and rapidly provided replies with embedded how-to-do video solutions (Lambrecht, Tucker & Wiertz, 2018). Similarly, analysis of TripAdvisor user reviews has shown a higher business activity whenever London hotels listened and rapidly reacted to consumers' negative feedback in a professional manner (Wang, Wezel & Forgues, 2015). In these cases, exploiting social media messages and user reviews gave such businesses a better chance to build a better rapport with their customers. Other organizations such as Faculty (2020) are more interested in capturing views of businesses from news articles on a daily basis and so are less time-bound with analyzing the online harvested content. Understanding the level of swiftness in reacting to online external sources is, for this reason, one of the determining factors for deciding which type of data, businesses need to harvest.

Authenticity

Reportage

The level of importance given to the reliability of data may also be another motive for choosing against different data streams. Information reported in online news articles is usually reviewed by news editors before being published and so, can be considered as more factual, reliable and accurate than social media messages (Wilson, 2012; McClure & Velluppillai, 2013; Popoola, Krasnoshtan, Toth, Naroditskiy, Castillo, Meier & Rahwan, 2013; Imran et al., 2015; Camilleri, Azzopardi & Agius, 2019). While social media users can be considered as important news reporters, the user-generated content posted on social media is highly dependent on the attitude and views of the user (Bruno, 2011; Vij & Sharma, 2013). For example, stock market returns are influenced by people's positive or negative outlook expressed on tweets (Sul, Dennis & Yuan, 2014) and a consumer's feedback posted on TripAdvisor may significantly differ (Wang, Wezel & Forgues, 2015) given some users being more cautious than others when posting.

At the same time, an earthquake victim posting messages can provide a more accurate detailed account of the events that are unfolding, than an editor, who is reporting the event behind the desk (Abdelhaq, Sengstock & Gertz, 2013). Research has also shown that low-income social media users tend to be more optimists and emit higher anxiety messages than social media users with higher income (Preoţiuc-Pietro, Volkovam, Lampos, Bachrach & Aletras, 2015). High-income earners tend to convey emotions related to fear and anger, as social media is used for a more 'professional' reason than low-income earners, who use it just for interaction and for expressing emotions and opinions (Preoţiuc-Pietro et al., 2015).

Data profiling is as important as harvesting online data. Companies, whose business require more accurate data but which are not bound with time, should rely more on news articles. Others, whose decision-making is more dependent on real-time data, should opt for user-generated content such as social media messages and user reviews. However, listening and reacting professionally to online consumer feedback is crucial to maintain a solid customer relationship.

Accuracy

The accuracy of geo-referenced messages (i.e. that contains the latitude and longitude coordinates, from where the message has been sent) has also been questioned, given that a social media user may set static coordinates on his/her device, which results in the inaccurate posting of coordinates (Abdelhaq, Sengstock & Gertz, 2013; Koswatte, Mcdougall & Liu, 2015). However, algorithms have been programmed to validate the location where tweets were posted (Popoola et al., 2013; Koswatte et al., 2015), e.g. by setting a threshold number of tweets or by noticing a relationship between the time Twitter users tweeted and the time the event took place (Panagiotou et al., 2016).

Type of Content

Different businesses require different kinds of data to be analyzed. Companies requiring information about events and activities taking place around the world should rely more on news articles. Opinions of 'experts' may also be harvested from this data stream and serve to provide businesses with a better insight on specific subjects. On the other hand, social media messages cover a wider array of subjects and current affairs, which give businesses a better approach to generate customer analytics, to directly engage with customers and to define and target a smaller market for a niche business. Both news articles and social media messages can embed media such as images, videos and links to other pages. On the other hand, user reviews discuss the specific product or service solely, and for this reason, this kind of data is crucial for businesses to appease unsatisfied customers and provide superior customer service, to maintain customer loyalty and good public relations and to mitigate the possibility of negative reviews by other customers in the near future.

Length of Content

Another determining factor in deciding which type of data is to be harvested is the length of content. News articles tend to provide more information about the events and activities, as they are not restricted with the number of characters, imposed by social media platforms. Twitter imposes a 140-character limit on the posted tweet (Bontcheva, Derczynski, Funk, Greenwood, Maynard & Aswani, 2013; Derczynski, Ritter, Clark & Bontcheva, 2013; Madani, Boussaid & Zegour, 2014), while Facebook messages cannot be longer than 420 characters. For this reason, Facebook can be considered more reliable than Twitter (Lee et al., 2018). Picasa's comments are restricted to 512 characters, while personal status messages on Windows Live Messenger are limited to 128 characters (Salina & Ilavarasan, 2014). In the case of user reviews, the limit on the number of characters is usually higher. Businesses should harvest a substantial amount of social media messages and user reviews, to build intelligence, if they wish to rely on such data streams. In this way, the information that is harvested could be cross-referenced.

Words are usually also abbreviated by the social media user to include as much content as possible (Bontcheva et al., 2013). Examples of abbreviations used in social media messages include AFAIK (as far as I know), BR (best regards), BTW (by the way), ICYMI (in case you missed it) etc. Such restriction leads to increased challenges when it comes to analyzing, processing, clustering and extracting information from social media messages and a higher likelihood that messages are taken out-of-context and misinterpreted by information systems (McClure & Velluppillai, 2013). More rigorous NLP tools also need to be used to interpret the context of social media messages and to understand what part-of-speech the word is. Specialized tools have been developed to identify and translate some of these abbreviations, as detailed in the following section.

Tools

The decision to choose one online data source from another must also be complemented with the adoption of NLP tools to analyze the content. TweetNLP (Owoputi, O'Connor, Dyer, Gimpel, Schneider & Smith, 2013) and TwitIE (Bontcheva et al., 2013) are more specialized in parsing tweets, while Python NLTK, Stanford CoreNLP, GATE, OpenNLP, OpenCalais are more accurate in parsing corpora with longer content (Derczynski et al., 2013; Pinto, Oliveira & Oliveira Alves, 2016; Al Omran & Treude, 2017). The choice of the NLP tool is also highly dependent on what kind of NLP operations the business needs to execute, including part-of-speech (POS) tagging, dependency parsing and the level of pre-processing that has to be carried out on the content.

Part-of-Speech Tagging

Part-of-speech tagging refers to the process whereby each word is analyzed to determine whether it is a cardinal or a derivation of a noun, verb, pronoun, preposition, adverb, conjunction, participle or article (Jurafsky & Martin, 2014). This process takes place after carrying out sentence segmentation and tokenization. **Sentence segmentation** involves identifying the boundaries of sentences using punctuation and splitting the content into sentences. **Tokenization** refers to the process whereby each sentence is split further into words using the spaces, with each word represented as a token. Figure 6 presents an example of part-of-speech tagging being affected on the following phrase: "Teaching your dog not to chase your cat takes time and consistency, but the reward of not having to constantly worry about Fido chasing Fluffy is more than worth it!".

Table 1 contains the list of tag abbreviations, coined by Penn Treebank Project and used by NLP Python-programmable parsers, for marking words to a corresponding parts-of-speech. Individual words (**uni-grams**) may also be grouped into **bi-grams** (two-word phrases), **tri-grams** (three-word phrases) or **n-grams** (phrases containing multiple words) (Anta et al., 2013).

Figure 6. Example showing part-of-speech tagging being carried out on a sentence

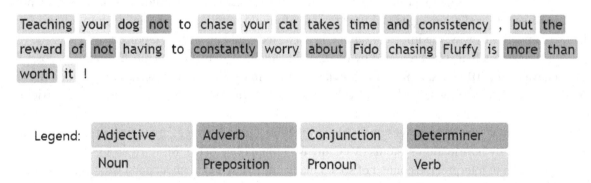

POS tagging is more difficult to be carried out on tweets because tweets are often bursty (Abdelhaq et al., 2013; Avvenuti et al., 2015) and tend to contain noisy, fragmented and unstructured content (Derczynski et al., 2013; Avvenuti et al., 2015), as well as colloquial or slang language (Derczynski et al., 2013). However, specialized POS taggers have been developed to understand better the semantic context of these kinds of texts. In fact, as more abbreviations are used in social media messages due to the limited number of characters, the error rate involved when processing tweets is higher (Wilson, 2012; Derczynski et al., 2013; Imran et al., 2015) than the mining of news data (Derczynski et al., 2013). In addition, certain NLP tools have a higher likelihood of running into the ambiguity problem, due to social media messages being shorter than news articles. The **ambiguity problem** takes place when a single word has more than one meaning (e.g. the word 'bear' can refer to an animal or a verb) or different words convey the same meaning. As a result, businesses, which choose social media messages for building business intelligence, need to choose the right tools to sufficiently make sense from the content.

Table 1. The Penn Treebank tagset, used by NLP Python-programmable parsers to mark words to a corresponding part-of-speech

CC	Coordinating conjunction	PRP$	Possessive pronoun
CD	Cardinal number	RB	Adverb
DT	Determiner	RBR	Adverb, comparative
EX	Existential there	RBS	Adverb, superlative
FW	Foreign word	RP	Particle
IN	Preposition or subordinating conjunction	SYM	Symbol
JJ	Adjective	TO	To
JJR	Adjective, comparative	UH	Interjection
JJS	Adjective, superlative	VB	Verb, base form
LS	List item marker	VBD	Verb, past tense
MD	Modal	VBG	Verb, gerund or present participle
NN	Noun, singular or mass	VBN	Verb, past participle
NNS	Noun, plural	VBP	Verb, non-3rd person singular present
NNP	Proper noun, singular	VBZ	Verb, 3rd person singular present
NNPS	Proper noun, plural	WDT	Wh-determiner
PDT	Predeterminer	WP	Wh-pronoun
POS	Possessive ending	WP$	Possessive wh-pronoun
PRP	Personal pronoun	WRB	Wh-adverb

Source: (Santorini, 1990)

Dependency Parsing

Dependency parsing and entity linking have also been utilized as a preparatory process for producing headings for content and to identify crisis from tweets (Alfonseca et al., 2013; Imran et al., 2015). **Dependency parsing** describes a sentence as a set of words connected together to form the sentence structure (Jurafsky & Martin, 2014), as illustrated in Figure 7. It can be referred to as a directed graph, with words correspond vertices representing the word. **Entity linking** refers to the automatic association of different expressions representing the same entity, e.g. 'Dr. Robert Abela' and 'Prime Minister of Malta'.

Figure 7. Dependency parsing being carried out on a sentence using Stanford CoreNLP 4.0

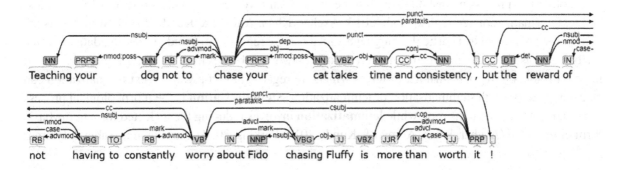

Pre-Processing Content

Different NLP tools deal with raw harvested content in different ways. Businesses, who have opted to build their intelligence from news articles are required to capture the tags where the news content is found. HTML tags vary from one website to another. Figure 8 shows a snippet of one of the HTML pages with the content (displayed in black) being enclosed in a 'p' tag with 'class' tag named 'wow fadeInUp'. The rest of the unstructured HTML page may be discarded including HTML tags and elements that are used for displaying site adverts, menus, headers and footers, as well as embedded JavaScript and CSS (Cascading Style Sheets).

Figure 8. A snippet of the HTML code

```
<!-- MAIN BODY -->
<section id="about" data-stellar-background-ratio="0.5">
    <div class="container">
        <div class="row">
            <div class="about-info">
                <div class="section-title wow fadeInUp" data-wow-delay="0.2s">
                    <div class="col-md-12 col-sm-12">
                        <h4><!-- InstanceBeginEditable name="subtitle" -->Who am I<!-- InstanceEndEditable --></h4>
                        <h2><!-- InstanceBeginEditable name="title" -->Biography<!-- InstanceEndEditable --></h2>
                        <p> </p>
                        <!-- InstanceBeginEditable name="content" -->
                    <div class="col-md-8 col-sm-4">
                        <div class="wow fadeInUp" data-wow-delay="0.2s">
                            <article>
                                <p>Regarded as <font color=#133C55><strong>one of the most outstanding and sought-after pianists</strong></font> to emerge from
Malta, described by international pianist William Fong as "<font color=#133C55><strong>a musician of high intelligence and artistic vision</strong></font>", loved by her
audiences for her passion and sensitivity, Joanne Camilleri is a rising star in the world of music.</p>

                            <p> </p>

                                <p>Joanne regularly performs a wide-ranging repertoire both in her native Malta and around Europe. Her performances have taken her
to Tunisia, Sweden, Switzerland, Wales, Ireland, the Isle of Man, around the UK, as well as to America and Asia. She has been <font color=#133C55><strong>invited to
perform at prestigious functions</strong></font> including those at the President's Palace in Malta, at the German Ambassador's Residency and the American Ambassador's
Residency, as well as other concerts organised under the auspices of the Ambassadors for Ireland, UK, Tunisia and China. Commemorative events have seen her<font
color=#133C55><strong> perform alongside other prominent international musicians</strong></font> such as British pianist Ann Rachlin at the age of 13 at the National
Manoel Theatre in a Mozart Night, alongside Russian pianist Vladimir Ovchinnikov in a millennium year concert of Twentieth Century Music and alongside London Symphony
Orchestra leader Carmine Lauri in a concert to celebrate Malta's Independence Day in London. As concerto soloist and orchestral pianist, she has performed with the Malta
Philharmonic Orchestra, the Armenian State Symphony Orchestra and British Orchestras, collaborating with distinguished conductors such as Wayne Marshall, Lancelot Fuhry,
Clark Rundell, Eric Hull, Philip Walsh, Karl Jenkins and Michael Laus.</p>
```

Some NLP parsers and processing tools may suffer when handling text containing language-specific characters (e.g. à, á, â, ä, ç, è, é, ê, ë, í, î, ï, ñ, ó, ô, ù, ú, û, ü) and for this reason, these characters need to be replaced with the English character set. Businesses may also avail themselves from the rich content found in messages such as **emoticons** and **emojis** (used by users to express their feelings through characters), **hashtags** (to invite users to view messages on the same theme or content) (Anta et al., 2013) and **user mentions** (to tag users to the submitted post). However, if businesses wish to process the text further, they need to remove these tags, together with special characters such as large dashes (—), guillemets (‹ › « »), lozenges (◊), hashes (#) and question marks (¿), so as prevent NLP tools from running into any errors during processing.

Another pre-processing task that needs to be carried out involves removing stopwords from the text and text normalization (Abdelhaq et al., 2013; Asghar, Khan, Ahmad & Kundi, 2014). **Stop words** are common words found in a particular language, and these are removed to avoid processing data unnecessarily. There is no single universal compiled list of stop words which is used by all NLP tools. However, most NLP tools have their own list of terms which are regarded as stopwords. Text normalization can be carried out through stemmatisation or lemmatization. **Stemmatisation** is the morphological process of reducing each word to its root, while **lemmatization** involves reducing the inflected form to the basic form of the word (Asghar, Khan, Ahmad & Kundi, 2014; Perkins, 2014). As shown in Table 2, lemmatizing texts reduces the noise involved when inflecting words but requires deeper linguistics knowledge to inflect the words. Text normalization is required for businesses to map documents to common topics, to expand a query search by including other documents, for sentiment analysis, as well as for document clustering.

Table 2. Example of stemmatisation and lemmatization employed on a phrase

Phrase	The U.S. Supreme Court on Monday left in place a Kentucky restriction requiring doctors to show and describe ultrasound images to women seeking an abortion, turning away a challenge arguing that the measure violates the free speech rights of physicians.
Stemmed phrase (using Porter's technique)	The U . S . Suprem Court on Monday left in place a Kentucki restrict requir doctor to show and describ ultrasound imag to women seek an abort, turn away a challeng argu that the measur violat the free speech right of physician
Lemmatized phrase (using WordNet's Lemmatizer)	The U . S . Supreme Court on Monday left in place a Kentucky restriction requiring doctor to show and describe ultrasound image to woman seeking an abortion, turning away a challenge arguing that the measure violates the free speech right of physician .

Source: (Hurley, 2019)

Data Availability

Businesses also need to determine how much capital they are willing to invest to retrieve data. News articles can be harvested for free. User reviews can be easily extracted from the business' platform, although it can be labor intensive to review and react to user comments. However, harvesting social media messages can come at a huge cost if data is procured from social media platforms or alternative data sources (Goswami et al., 2018). At the same time, the amount of data that is made publicly available can also be limited – in the case of Twitter, it is restricted to 1% (Khumoyun, Cui & Lee, 2016; Goswami et al., 2018). Despite this limitation, this small percentage of data translates into millions of tweets, which is still beneficial if one is trying to run analytics on a substantial amount of data.

Businesses need to evaluate what external data sources they should use to maximize the information needed to strengthen business intelligence. This section has discussed the foundations for choosing to harvest news articles, social media or user reviews. Researchers have also tried making use of more than one data source, although this was found to be a challenging task, as they do not have any variables in common. In fact, mapping social media messages with content published on news agency websites has been carried out using dates in conjunction with hashtags from social messages and named entities from news articles (Guo, Li, Ji & Diab, 2013) and by using the URLs found in social media messages, linking to a news article (Štajner, Thomee, Popescu, Pennacchiotti & Jaimes, 2013).

FUTURE RESEARCH DIRECTIONS

Although NLP technology has been in development for some time, commercial research is still finding new ways to serve businesses; to improve the precision of existing NLP tools and; to automate tasks which could help build business intelligence. Chatboxes need to be improved to perform more complex tasks and to provide answers for queries containing concepts, which have not been understood or which have not been programmed by the application. More complex algorithms need to be developed to process and understand unstructured texts, including the automatic tagging of telephone numbers, product names and part numbers. Automatic analysis becomes more complex if the unstructured data is inspected as soon as it is streamed.

In addition, NLP parsers need to be improved to automatically handle texts containing language-specific characters, without the possibility of running into exceptions. Part-of-speech tagging also needs to be improved by better taking into consideration the context in which the content has been written, similar to how human beings understand text (Bontcheva et al., 2013; Guo et al., 2013). Such automatic tools can reduce the effort involved in the processing, provide more accurate real-time information discovery and retrieval and improve the results outputted by question and answering systems and search engines.

Commercial research also needs to find ways to automatically predict future business scenarios based on current macro and microeconomic events, using NLP and machine learning techniques. Similarly, the detection and neutralization of fake news and misinformation need to be improved. Fake news and misinformation have a negative impact on businesses. Identifying deceivers spreading false news can be a huge headache for businesses as they could deter potential customers from making use of products or services (Zeng, Starbird, Spiro, 2016). Such a solution could potentially help businesses to build counter-campaigns to minimize the impact involved.

CONCLUSION

Mimicking how humans think and process language is a challenging task to accomplish. The exponential growth in text data that is being submitted over the Web and the fast-paced research that is being carried out within the NLP domain, has led businesses to automate tasks that up to some decades ago, was inconceivable to accomplish. Some of the NLP tasks that were adopted by businesses include search autocomplete, financial trading, creditworthiness assessment, advertising and audience analysis, chatboxes and sentiment analysis.

This chapter has laid the foundations for businesses, that wish to embrace this technology to gain more insights, build business intelligence and transform customer experience to customer loyalty. It introduced three online unstructured data sources that could be used to transform meaningless data into valuable information that can help achieve a competitive advantage over their competitors. The three text sources discussed in this chapter are news articles, social media messages and user reviews. Following this, the chapter provides the main reasons for choosing amongst different online external sources. These are grouped under six factors, specifically the level of importance given to extract intelligence in real-time; how authentic the data is; what type of data that will be exploited; the length of content; the NLP tools that are needed to execute the data and any pre-processing steps that need to be exerted and; the amount of data that is made available. The chapter concludes with potential areas of interest within the text mining domain that can stimulate businesses to exploit ways to mimic human actions in the future.

NLP is a promising technology for businesses, which can help unlock a world of opportunities. If mastered correctly, businesses can transform computer interaction to become more human-like help; can automate in real-time the process of understanding and reacting to consumer feedback submitted on different data streams; can create the perfect venue for marketing and; facilitate sustained business growth. However, there are still several challenges that need to be overcome within the context of text analytics, especially in relation to unstructured data. These include the difficulties involved to correctly map entities identified in unstructured data with entities stored in business' database; achieve full language understanding and perform inferences on top of textual data and; improve the semantical analysis of text.

The application of NLP technology has come a long way since its inception. Despite such challenges, the integration of NLP into the daily business operations, coupled with the harvesting of online data, should help businesses achieve their objectives in a more efficient manner. Such accessibility is precisely what makes NLP so valuable.

REFERENCES

Abdelhaq, H., Sengstock, C., & Gertz, M. (2013). EvenTweet: Online localized event detection from Twitter. *Proceedings of the VLDB Endowment International Conference on Very Large Data Bases*, *6*(12), 1326–1329. doi:10.14778/2536274.2536307

Al Omran, F. N. A., & Treude, C. (2017). Choosing an NLP library for analyzing software documentation: A systematic literature review and a series of experiments. In *Proceedings of the 14th International Conference on Mining Software Repositories*, (pp. 187-197). IEEE Press. 10.1109/MSR.2017.42

Alfonseca, E., Pighin, D., & Garrido, G. (2013). HEADY: News headline abstraction through event pattern clustering. In *Proceedings of the 51st Annual Meeting of the Association for Computational Linguistics* (*Vol. 1*, pp. 1243-1253). Association for Computational Linguistics.

Anta, A. F., Chiroque, L. N., Morere, P., & Santo, A. (2013). Sentiment analysis and topic detection of Spanish Tweets: A comparative study of NLP techniques. *Procesamiento de Lenguaje Natural*, *50*, 45–52.

Arendse, B. (2016). *A thorough comparison of NLP tools for requirements quality improvement* (Master's thesis). Utrecht University.

Asghar, M. Z., Khan, A., Ahmad, S., & Kundi, F. M. (2014). A review of feature extraction in sentiment analysis. *Journal of Basic and Applied Scientific Research*, *4*(3), 181–186.

Avvenuti, M., Del Vigna, F., Cresci, S., Marchetti, A., & Tesconi, M. (2015). Pulling information from social media in the aftermath of unpredictable disasters. In *2015 2nd International Conference on Information and Communication Technologies for Disaster Management (ICT-DM)*, (pp. 258-264). IEEE. 10.1109/ICT-DM.2015.7402058

Benson, E., Haghighi, A., & Barzilay, R. (2011). Event Discovery in Social Media Feeds. In *Proceedings of the 49th Annual Meeting of the Association for Computational Linguistics: Human Language Technologies*, (pp. 389-398). Association for Computational Linguistics.

Bontcheva, K., Derczynski, L., Funk, A., Greenwood, M. A., Maynard, D., & Aswani, N. (2013). TwitIE: An open-source information extraction pipeline for microblog text. *International Conference Recent Advances in Natural Language Processing (RANLP)*, 83-90.

Bruno, N. (2011). *Tweet first, verify later? How real-time information is changing the coverage of worldwide crisis events*. Retrieved June 1, 2020, from https://reutersinstitute.politics.ox.ac.uk/our-research/tweet-first-verify-later-how-real-time-information-changing-coverage-worldwide-crisis

Camilleri, S., Agius, M. R., & Azzopardi, J. (2020). Analysis of online news coverage on earthquakes through text mining. *Frontiers of Earth Science, 8*(141).

Camilleri, S., Azzopardi, J., & Agius, M. R. (2019). Investigating the relationship between earthquakes and online news. *2019 IEEE Second International Conference on Artificial Intelligence and Knowledge Engineering*, 203-210. 10.1109/AIKE.2019.00043

Chen, L., Chen, G., & Wang, F. (2015). Recommender systems based on user reviews: The state of the art. *User Modeling and User-Adapted Interaction, 25*(2), 99–154. doi:10.100711257-015-9155-5

Derczynski, L., Ritter, A., Clark, S., & Bontcheva, K. (2013). Twitter part-of-speech tagging for all: Overcoming sparse and noisy data. In *Proceedings of Recent Advances in Natural Language Processing* (pp. 198–206). Association for Computational Linguistics.

Egan, J. (2020). Marketing communications. SAGE Publications Ltd.

Faculty. (2020). *Applying NLP to news articles to trace business sentiment.* Retrieved June 1, 2020 from https://faculty.ai/ourwork/applying-nlp-to-news-articles-to-trace-business-sentiment/

Fang, H., Wu, F., Zhao, Z., Duan, X., Zhuang, Y., & Ester, M. (2016). Community-based question answering via heterogeneous social network learning. In *Proceedings of the Thirtieth AAAI Conference on Artificial Intelligence*, (pp. 122-128). AAAI Press.

Feng, W., & Wang, J. (2012). Incorporating Heterogeneous Information for Personalized Tag Recommendation in Social Tagging Systems. In *Proceedings of the 18th ACM SIGKDD international conference on Knowledge discovery and data mining*, (pp. 1276-1284). Association for Computing Machinery. 10.1145/2339530.2339729

Goswami, S., Chakraborty, S., Ghosh, S., Chakrabarti, A., & Chakraborty, B. (2018). A review on application of data mining techniques to combat natural disasters. *Ain Shams Engineering Journal, 9*(3), 365–378. doi:10.1016/j.asej.2016.01.012

Guo, W., Li, H., Ji, H., & Diab, M. (2013). *Linking Tweets to News: A Framework to Enrich Short Text Data in Social Media. Proceedings of the 51st Annual Meeting of the Association for Computational Linguistics*, 1, 239-249.

He, W., Zha, S., & Li, L. (2013). Social media competitive analysis and text mining: A case study in the pizza industry. *International Journal of Information Management, 33*(3), 464–472. doi:10.1016/j.ijinfomgt.2013.01.001

Hurley, L. (2019, December 9). *U.S. Supreme Court leaves in place Kentucky abortion restriction.* Retrieved June 1, 2020 from https://www.reuters.com/article/us-usa-court-abortion/u-s-supreme-court-leaves-in-place-kentucky-abortion-restriction-idUSKBN1YD1JX

Imran, M., Castillo, C., Diaz, F., & Vieweg, S. (2015). Processing social media messages in mass emergency: A survey. *ACM Computing Surveys, 47*(4), 67. doi:10.1145/2771588

Jurafsky, D., & Martin, J. H. (2014). *Speech and language processing.* Pearson London.

Kaushik, A., & Naithani, S. (2016). A comprehensive study of text mining approach. *International Journal of Computer Science and Network Security (IJC-SNS), 16*(2), 69-76.

Kayes, I., Kourtellis, N., Quercia, D., Iamnitchi, A., & Bonchi, F. (2015). The social world of content abusers in community question answers. *Proceedings of the 24th International Conference on World Wide Web*, 570-580. 10.1145/2736277.2741674

Khumoyun, A., Cui, Y., & Lee, H. (2016). Real-time information classification in Twitter using Storm. *Bangkok 6th International Conference, 49*, 1-4.

Koswatte, S., McDougall, K., & Liu, X. (2015). SDI and crowdsourced spatial information management automation for disaster management. *Survey Review, 47*(344), 307–315. doi:10.1179/1752270615Y.0000000008

Lambrecht, A., Tucker, C., & Wiertz, C. (2018). Advertising to Early Trend Propagators: Evidence from Twitter. *Marketing Science, 37*(2), 177–199. doi:10.1287/mksc.2017.1062

Lee, D., Hosanagar, K., & Nair, H. (2018). Advertising Content and Consumer Engagement on Social Media: Evidence from Facebook. *Management Science, 64*(11), 4967–5460. doi:10.1287/mnsc.2017.2902

Levinson, B. (2019, June 10). *Don't Lie To Me: Integrating Client-Side Web Scraping And Review Behavioral Analysis To Detect Fake Reviews*. Undergraduate Research Scholars Program. Retrieved June 1, 2020 from http://hdl.handle.net/1969.1/175409

Liang, Y., Caverlee, J., & Mander, J. (2013). Text vs. images: On the viability of social media to assess earthquake damage. In *Proceedings of the 22nd International Conference on World Wide Web*, (pp. 1003-1006). ACM. 10.1145/2487788.2488102

Lin, H. C., Swarna, H., & Bruning, P. F. (2017). Taking a global view on brand post popularity: Six social media brand post practices for global markets. *Business Horizons, 60*(5), 621–633. doi:10.1016/j.bushor.2017.05.006

Madani, A., Boussaid, O., & Zegour, D. E. (2014). What's happening: A survey of tweets event detection. *Proceedings of the 3rd International Conference on Communications, Computation, Networks and Technologies*, 16-22.

Martinez-Romo, J., & Araujo, L. (2013). Detecting malicious tweets in trending topics using a statistical analysis of language. *Expert Systems with Applications, 40*(8), 2992–3000. doi:10.1016/j.eswa.2012.12.015

McClure, J., & Velluppillai, J. (2013). The effects of news media reports on earthquake attributions and preventability judgments: Mixed messages about the Canterbury earthquake. *Australasian Journal of Disaster and Trauma Studies, 2013*(1), 27–36.

Nam, H., & Kannan, P. K. (2014). The Informational Value of Social Tagging Networks. *Journal of Marketing, 78*(4), 21–40. doi:10.1509/jm.12.0151

Ortiz-Ospina, E. (2019, September 18). *The rise of social media*. Retrieved June 1, 2020 from https://ourworldindata.org/rise-of-social-media

Owoputi, O., O'Connor, B., Dyer, C., Gimpel, K., Schneider, N. A., & Smith, N. A. (2013). Improved part-of-speech tagging for online conversational text with word clusters. *Proceedings of NAACL-HLT*, 380-390.

Panagiotou, N., Katakis, I., & Gunopulos, D. (2016). Detecting events in online social networks: Definitions, trends and challenges. In *Solving Large Scale Learning Tasks. Challenges and Algorithms* (pp. 42–84). Springer. doi:10.1007/978-3-319-41706-6_2

Park, Y. J. (2018). Predicting the Helpfulness of Online Customer Reviews across Different Product Types. *Sustainability, MDPI, 10*(6), 1–20. doi:10.3390u10061735

Perkins, J. (2014). *Python 3 text processing with NLTK 3 cookbook*. Packt Publishing Ltd.

Pinto, A., Oliveira, H. G., & Oliveira Alves, A. (2016). Comparing the performance of different NLP toolkits in formal and social media text. In *OpenAccess Series in Informatics, 51, 1-16*. Dagstuhl Publishing.

Popoola, A., Krasnoshtan, D., Toth, A. P., Naroditskiy, V., Castillo, C., Meier, P., & Rahwan, I. (2013). Information verification during natural disasters. In *Proceedings of the 22nd International Conference on World Wide Web, WWW '13 Companion*, (pp. 1029-1032). New York. ACM. 10.1145/2487788.2488111

Preoţiuc-Pietro, D., Volkova, S., Lampos, V., Bachrach, Y., & Aletras, N. (2015, September 22). Studying User Income through Language, Behaviour and Affect in Social Media. *PLoS One, 10*(9), e0138717. Advance online publication. Retrieved June 1, 2020, from. doi:10.1371/journal.pone.0138717 PMID:26394145

Rauchfleisch, A., Artho, X., Metag, J., Post, S., & Schäfer, M. S. (2017). How journalists verify user-generated content during terrorist crises. Analyzing Twitter communication during the Brussels attacks. *Social Media and Society, 3*(3), 1–13. doi:10.1177/2056305117717888

Reinsel, D., Gantz, J., & Rydning, J. (2018, November). *The Digitization of the World From Edge to Core*. Retrieved June 1, 2020 from https://www.seagate.com/gb/en/our-story/data-age-2025/

Salina, A., & Ilavarasan, E. (2014). Mining Usable Customer feedback from Social networking data for Business Intelligence. *GJMS Special Issue for Recent Advances in Mathematical Sciences and Applications, 13*(2), 1–9.

Santorini, B. (1990). *Part-of-speech tagging guidelines for the Penn Treebank Project*. Technical report MS-CIS-90-47, Department of Computer and Information Science, University of Pennsylvania.

Singh, J. P., Irani, S., Rana, N. P., Dwivedi, Y. K., Saumya, S., & Roy, P. K. (2017). Predicting the "helpfulness" of online consumer reviews. *Journal of Business Research, 70*, 346–355. doi:10.1016/j.jbusres.2016.08.008

Štajner, T., Thomee, B., Popescu, A. M., Pennacchiotti, M., & Jaimes, A. (2013). Automatic Selection of Social Media Responses to News. In *Proceedings of the 19th ACM SIGKDD International Conference on Knowledge Discovery and Data Mining, KDD '13*. ACM. 10.1145/2487575.2487659

Sul, H., Dennis, A. R., & Yuan, L. I. (2014). Trading on Twitter: The Financial Information Content of Emotion in Social Media. *Proceedings of the Annual Hawaii International Conference on System Sciences*, 806-815.

Vij, S., & Sharma, J. (2013). An Empirical Study on Social Media Behaviour of Consumers and Social Media Marketing Practices of Marketers. In *Proceedings of the 5th IIMA Conference on Marketing in Emerging Economies*. Indian Institute of Management, Ahmedabad.

Wang, T., Wezel, F. C., & Forgues, B. (2015). Protecting Market Identity: When and How Do Organizations Respond to Consumers' Devaluations? *Academy of Management Journal, 59*(1), 135–162. doi:10.5465/amj.2014.0205

Wilson, J. K. (2012). *Responding to natural disasters with social media: A case study of the 2011 earthquake and tsunami in Japan* (Master's thesis). Simon Fraser University.

Yu, Y., Duan, W., & Cao, Q. (2013). The impact of social and conventional media on firm equity value: A sentiment analysis approach. *Decision Support Systems, 55*(4), 919–926. doi:10.1016/j.dss.2012.12.028

Zeng, L., Starbird, K., & Spiro, E. S. (2016). #Unconfirmed: Classifying Rumor Stance in Crisis-Related Social Media Messages. In *Proceedings of the 10th International AAAI Conference on Web and Social Media (ICWSM 2016)*, (pp. 747-750). AAAI Publications.

Zhao, K., Stylianou, A. C., & Zheng, Y. (2018). Sources and impacts of social influence from online anonymous user reviews. *Information & Management, 55*(1), 16–30. doi:10.1016/j.im.2017.03.006

ADDITIONAL READING

Anand, A., Sharma, R., & Coltman, T. (2016). Four Steps to Realizing Business Value from Digital Data Streams. *MIS Quarterly Executive, 15*, 259–278.

Fisher, I. E., Garnsey, M. R., & Hughes, M. E. (2016). Natural Language Processing in Accounting, Auditing and Finance: A Synthesis of the Literature with a Roadmap for Future Research. *Intelligent Systems in Accounting, Finance & Management, 23*(3), 157–214. doi:10.1002/isaf.1386

Haddia, E., Liua, X., & Shib, Y. (2013). *The Role of Text Pre-processing in Sentiment Analysis*. Information Technology and Quantitative Management. *Procedia Computer Science, 17*, 26–32. doi:10.1016/j.procs.2013.05.005

Ioanid, A., & Scarlat, C. (2017). Factors Influencing Social Networks Use for Business: Twitter and YouTube Analysis. *Procedia Engineering, 181*, 977–983. doi:10.1016/j.proeng.2017.02.496

Noce, L., Zamberletti, A., Gallo, I., Piccoli, G., & Rodriguez, J. A. (2014). Automatic Prediction of Future Business Conditions. *Advances in Natural Language Processing, 8686*, 371–383. doi:10.1007/978-3-319-10888-9_37

Virmani, D., & Taneja, S. (2018). A Text Preprocessing Approach for Efficacious Information Retrieval. In *Proceedings in Smart Innovations in Communication and Computational Sciences, 669, 13-22*. Springer.

Xu, S., Lu, B., Baldea, M., Edgar, T. F., Wojsznis, W., Blevins, T., & Nixon, M. (2015). Data cleaning in the process industries. *Reviews in Chemical Engineering, 31*(5), 453–490. doi:10.1515/revce-2015-0022

KEY TERMS AND DEFINITIONS

API (Application Programming Interface): Enables data to be transmitted between parties or services using programmed functions.

Dependency Parsing: Describes a sentence as a set of words connected together to form the sentence structure (Jurafsky & Martin, 2014).

Entity Linking: Refers to the automatic association of different expressions representing the same entity.

Hashtags: A phrase that has no spaces and is preceded by a # symbol, containing important keywords or topics.

JSON (JavaScript Object Notation): A lightweight structure for exchanging data.

Lemmatization: Reducing the inflected form to the basic form of the word.

NLP Parser: An application, which identifies the grammatical and morphological structure of sentences, which includes the rules that govern the arrangement of words; identify part-of-speech of words (nouns, verbs); grouping of words into phrases and the word order typology.

Part-of-Speech Tagging: Refers to the process whereby each word is analyzed to determine whether it is a cardinal or a derivation of a noun, verb, pronoun, preposition, adverb, conjunction, participle or article (Jurafsky & Martin, 2014).

RSS (Really Simple Syndication): A web feed, which gives users the possibility to receive updates in a structured format.

Semantics: Concerned with the meaning of the words used within that structure.

Semi-Structured Sources: Are not bound with the structure of a repository (He et al., 2013; Kaushik & Naithani, 2016).

Sentence Segmentation: Involves identifying the boundaries of sentences using punctuation and splitting the content into sentences.

Sentiment Analysis: Automatically analyses and classifies user's emotions.

Stemmatisation: The morphological process of reducing each word to its root.

Stop Words: Common words found in a particular language and these are removed to avoid processing data unnecessarily.

Structured Sources: A digital location, which stores data in a structured format.

Syntax: Denotes the grammatical structure.

Tokenization: Refers to the process whereby each sentence is split further into words using the spaces, with each word represented as a token.

Unstructured Sources: A digital location, whose content does not follow a particular format or mode.

User Mentions: A tag which contains the user's account name preceded by @ symbol, linking other users to a post.

ENDNOTES

[1] **Google News API Documentation**. Retrieved June 1, 2020 from https://newsapi.org/s/google-news-api.

[2] **The Guardian API Documentation**. Retrieved June 1, 2020 from https://open-platform.theguardian.com/documentation/.

[3] **Die Zeit API Documentation**. Retrieved June 1, 2020 from http://developer.zeit.de/index/.

[4] **News24 RSS Feeds**. Retrieved June 1, 2020 from https://www.news24.com/SiteElements/Services/News24-RSS-Feeds-20070614-2.

[5] **El Pais RSS Feeds**. Retrieved June 1, 2020 from https://servicios.elpais.com/rss/.

[6] **Shanghai Daily RSS Feeds**. Retrieved June 1, 2020 from https://archive.shine.cn/siteinfo/rss.aspx.

Chapter 3
Natural Language Processing in Online Reviews

Gunjan Ansari
 https://orcid.org/0000-0001-6935-2897
JSS Academy of Technical Education, Noida, India

Shilpi Gupta
JSS Academy of Technical Education, Noida, India

Niraj Singhal
 https://orcid.org/0000-0002-2614-4788
Shobhit Institute of Engineering and Technology (Deemed), Meerut, India

ABSTRACT

The analysis of the online data posted on various e-commerce sites is required to improve consumer experience and thus enhance global business. The increase in the volume of social media content in the recent years led to the problem of overfitting in review classification. Thus, there arises a need to select relevant features to reduce computational cost and improve classifier performance. This chapter investigates various statistical feature selection methods that are time efficient but result in selection of few redundant features. To overcome this issue, wrapper methods such as sequential feature selection (SFS) and recursive feature elimination (RFE) are employed for selection of optimal feature set. The empirical analysis was conducted on movie review dataset using three different classifiers and the results depict that SVM could achieve f-measure of 96% with only 8% selected features using RFE method.

INTRODUCTION

With the rise of various e-commerce sites, 72% buyers rely on online reviews before purchasing any product or service. Online review statistics show that 85% of consumers prefer to buy products from sites with reviews and users trust 12 times more on customer reviews than description given by product manufacturers. Reviews are the third most significant factor used for the ranking of e-commerce sites by

DOI: 10.4018/978-1-7998-4240-8.ch003

Google. Facebook reviews statistics reveal that every four out of five users rely on local business having positive reviews. However, one negative review may adversely impact 35% of customers. Twitter statistics showed that the reviews shared through tweets in 2019 increased the sale by 6.46% on e-commerce sites (Galov et al.,2020).

With the remarkable rise in the social media content in the past few years, there arises a need to analyze this online data to enhance user's experience which will further lead to an improvement in the local and global business of the e-commerce sites. Due to the availability of annotated datasets of product, movie, restaurant, reviews, etc. the researchers are developing various supervised learning approaches in recent years for extracting useful patterns from the online content. Although the supervised learning approaches are found to be quite useful, they suffer from the curse of dimensionality due to the generation of ample feature space from the vast amount of online content. The selection of relevant and non-redundant features from the extracted features have shown to achieve promising results in terms of accuracy and time.

The chapter will provide a theoretical and empirical study of different filter (Yang & Pederson,1997; Chandrashekhar & Sahin, 2014) and wrapper (Zheng et al.,2003) based feature selection methods for improving classification. The filter-based feature selection methods rank each feature based on the correlation between the feature and the class using various statistical tests. The top-ranked features are then selected for training the classification model. However, the filter-based methods are computationally fast; they result in the selection of redundant features. To overcome this drawback, wrapper-based feature selection methods such as Recursive Feature Elimination and Sequential Feature Selection are employed in this study. They evaluate each feature subset based on its performance on the classifier. The selected features in wrapper methods are more relevant and non-redundant as compared to filter methods, thus leading to better performance of the classifier.

The first section of the chapter will introduce elementary Natural Language Processing (NLP) tasks related to online review classification. An insight into a few tools used for scraping data (Mitchell, 2015) from online review sites will be covered in this section. The reviews posted on these sites are generally noisy and contain misspelt words, abbreviations etc. To handle these issues, pre-processing of reviews (Kowsari et al.,2019) is required which convert raw data into an appropriate format for the implementation of the machine learning model. Few parsing techniques such as Parts-of-Speech (PoS) tagging and dependency parsing are the primary tasks required for extracting opinion from the review in applications such as Sentiment Analysis (Liu, 2012), Named entity recognition (Hanafiah & Quix, 2014) etc.

After pre-processing of reviews, there is a need to represent each review document into a learning vector for designing any machine learning model. The section will also provide a review of elementary feature representation models used in various applications of text classification (Ahuja et al., 2019) such as Term-Frequency (TF) or Bag-of-Words (BoW) and Term Frequency- Inverse Document Frequency (TF-IDF) (Qaiser & Ali, 2018). However, these schemes are easy to implement; their negative aspect is that they ignore the position of feature and its semantic relationship with other features in the given review document. This issue can be resolved by using the model (Uchida et al.,2018) that converts document of the given corpus into low dimensional embedding vector using deep learning and neural networks-based techniques. The Doc2vec model for representing feature vectors will also be covered in the section.

The extracted features are significant in number resulting in high dimensionality of feature space when BoW and TF-IDF are used as feature representation schemes. To reduce feature space and improve accuracy of classifier, there is a need to select relevant and non-redundant features. The next section will introduce classification and need for feature selection in classification algorithms. It will also cover the statistical background of three widely-used classifiers such as Naive Bayes (NB), Support Vector Machine (SVM) and Logistic Regression (LR) employed in the proposed methodology. The filter and wrapper-based feature selection methods will also be discussed in this section. The filter-based feature selection methods employed in this study are Chi-square, Mutual information, Gini Index, Document Frequency, Standard deviation and Distinguishing feature selection and the wrapper based methods discussed in this section are Sequential Feature Selection, Backward Feature Elimination and Recursive Feature Elimination.

The Solutions and Recommendations section in this chapter will provide the methodology of the proposed solution for feature selection. The section will also cover result analysis of an empirical study conducted on Movie Review dataset using both filter and wrapper methods for selecting relevant features with varying size of feature set. The results depict that that best performance of around 96% is achieved by SVM using RFE feature selection method with small feature set size of around 8%. The next section on future research directions discusses future scope in the area of review classification. Finally, the conclusion of the proposed work is presented in the last section.

ELEMENTARY NLP TASKS FOR ONLINE REVIEW CLASSIFICATION

Brief Overview of Web Scraping

The data analysis starts with the extraction of the reviews posted by customers on various e-commerce sites. There are different methods employed in past years for extracting informative data from these websites for the application of data analytics. The information from these sites can be extracted by accessing the HTML of the webpage and this process is known as Web Scraping. The process of scraping is performed in two steps. In the first step, HTTP request is sent to the URL of the webpage and HTML content of the webpage is received by the server, and in the second step, information is parsed and extracted from the retrieved HTML content. There are number of tools available in Python, Java and other programming languages for performing task of Crawling and Scraping. Python is most preferable for Web Scraping because it is easy to use, has large number of libraries and easily understandable. The name and description of few libraries used for Web Scraping in Python are discussed in Table 1:

Table 1. Short Description of Scraping Tools in Python

Scraping Tools	Description
urllib (Severance, 2013)	urllib is the package used to fetch Uniform Resource Locators (URLs). It handles all of the HTTP protocol and header details. It uses urlopen function to fetch URLs from web pages using various protocols. This package includes many other modules like urllib.request, urllib.parse, urllib.error, and urllib.robotparser.
Scrapy (Mitchell, 2015)	Scrapy is web crawling framework which download web pages, browse them, and saves them in files. It is a unified system engine which controls the flow of data between all components and consist of a scheduler, downloader and spider. The role of scheduler is to receive request, downloader help to fetch web pages and spider is used to parse response and extract information.
Selenium (Gojare et al., 2015)	Selenium is an open-source, highly portable, web-based automation testing tool. However, it is a testing tool; it can be used to extract any information from the web page. The tool is preferred if a website relies on Javascript. It has an advantage as it is compatible with multiple web browsers like Firefox, Chrome etc.
LXML (Mitchell, 2015)	LXML library allows easy handling of XML and HTML files. It is secure to use and consumes very less time to process large XML files. etree, one of the modules of LXML, is responsible for creating and structuring the elements.

From the survey of the above-mentioned tools, it can be concluded that Scrapy is the most widely used libraries in Python for scrapping and crawling tasks. Due to its high speed and low power consumption, Scrapy is preferred for complex scrapping operation.

The result after scrapping review of product "iphone6s" from amazon using Scrapy is shown in Table 2 as follows:

Table 2. Scrapped Review in CSV format

Input Review	Output (Scrapped Review)		
Okay ; if you are reading this, you must be buying this 6s in 2018 onwards. So honestly, this is what I thought when I ordered it 6 months back. I have been through all the reviews and then I was so sure that yes i really should order this and, i am so happy with my choice now. (Above review is posted by Aayushi J and review rating is 5.0 out of 5 stars)	Name	Review	Rating
	Aayushi J	Okay ; if you are reading this, you must be buying this 6s in 2018 onwards. So honestly, this is what I thought when I ordered it 6 months back. I have been through all the reviews and then I was so sure that yes i really should order this and, i am so happy with my choice now.	5.0 out of 5 stars

Pre-Processing of Reviews

The reviews extracted from online sites needs to be pre-processed before passing the review to the next phase of feature extraction as review text is unstructured and poorly written. Some of the pre-processing steps are discussed as follows:

Tokenization

After conversion of crawled review into lowercase and dealing with other types of noises in review text such as misspelt words, abbreviations etc., and review document is split into smaller parts (words or sentences) by a process known as tokenization. This is implemented by importing Natural Language Toolkit (NLTK) in Python (Bird et al., 2009). Many tools such as tokenization, stemming, word count etc. for text analysis are available in this library.

Table 3 showed the results after applying sentence and word tokenization on sample review extracted from flipkart site.

Table 3. Review after sentence and word tokenization

Input Review	Review after sentence tokenization	Review after word tokenization
Guys the iphone 6s is amazing nothing beats it I order it from flipkart the delivery is fast, moreover the phone was in good condition the features of the phone is to what I expected l love it .Everything is fine.	['Guys the iphone 6s is amazing nothing beats it I order it from flipkart the delivery is fast, moreover the phone was in good condition the features of the phone is to what I expected l love it.', 'Everything is fine.']	['Guys', 'the','iphone', '6s', 'is', 'amazing', 'nothing', 'beats', 'it', 'I', 'order', 'it', 'from', 'flipkart', 'the', 'delivery', 'is', 'fast', ',', 'moreover', 'the', 'phone', 'was', 'in', 'good', 'condition', 'the', 'features', 'of', 'the', 'phone', 'is', 'to', 'what', 'I', 'expected', 'I', 'love', 'it', '..Everything', 'is', 'fine', '.']

Removal of Stop Words

Frequent words such as "an", "about", "across", "the", "at", "is" etc. does not contribute in deciding the polarity of the review. These words are known as stop words or empty words. The removal of such words reduces the number of tokens in the review, thereby reducing the dimension of feature space.

The tokens generated after removal of stop words are shown above in Table 4.

Table 4. Review after stop word removal

Input Review	Review after stop word removal
Guys the iphone 6s is amazing nothing beats it I order it from flipkart the delivery is fast, moreover the phone was in good condition the features of the phone is to what I expected l love it ..Everything is fine.	['Guys', 'iphone', '6s', 'amazing', 'nothing', 'beats', 'I', 'order', 'flipkart', 'delivery', 'fast', ',', 'moreover', 'phone', 'good', 'condition', 'features', 'phone', 'I', 'expected', 'l', 'love', '..Everything', 'fine', '.']

Normalization of Words Using Lemmatization

The process of removing irrelevant words from the collection of extracted review is known as normalization. In the review, the noise can also be obtained by representing a single word in many ways. Lemmatization is the process of obtaining the root form of the word by establishing the part of speech and utilizing detailed database of the language. The review is lemmatized and the output obtained is shown in Table 5 as follows:

Table 5. Lemmatized Review

Input Review	Lemmatized Review
Guys the iphone 6s is amazing nothing beats it I order it from flipkart the delivery is fast, moreover the phone was in good condition the features of the phone is to what I expected l love it ..Everything is fine.	Guys the iphone 6 is amazing nothing beat it I order it from flipkart the delivery is fast, moreover the phone was in good condition the feature of the phone is to what I expected l love it ..Everything is fine

From the review, the words 'beats' and 'features' are lemmatized to beat and feature. This is implemented by importing WordNetLemmatizer from NLTK.

Parts-of-Speech (PoS) Tagging

PoS tagging or dependency parsing are the primary tasks of natural language processing which are required in applications such as Sentiment Analysis, Named Entity Recognition, Word Sense Disambiguation etc. PoS tagging assign tags to the extracted tokens of the review which are categorized as noun, pronoun, verb, adverb, adjective, preposition, conjunctions and interjections. The output of PoS tagger of NLTK is shown below:

Table 6 represents the output of PoS tagger of NLTK.

Table 6. PoS tagging of tokens in review

Input Review	Review after PoS tagging
Guys the iphone 6s is amazing nothing beats it I order it from flipkart the delivery is fast, moreover the phone was in good condition the features of the phone is to what I expected l love it ..Everything is fine.	[('Guys', 'NNP'), ('the', 'DT'), ('iphone', 'NN'), ('6s', 'CD'), ('is', 'VBZ'), ('amazing', 'VBG'), ('nothing', 'NN'), ('beats', 'VBZ'), ('it', 'PRP'), ('I', 'PRP'), ('order', 'NN'), ('it', 'PRP'), ('from', 'IN'), ('flipkart', 'VBG'), ('the', 'DT'), ('delivery', 'NN'), ('is', 'VBZ'), ('fast', 'RB'), (',', ','), ('moreover', 'RB'), ('the', 'DT'), ('phone', 'NN'), ('was', 'VBD'), ('in', 'IN'), ('good', 'JJ'), ('condition', 'NN'), ('the', 'DT'), ('features', 'NNS'), ('of', 'IN'), ('the', 'DT'), ('phone', 'NN'), ('is', 'VBZ'), ('to', 'TO'), ('what', 'WP'), ('I', 'PRP'), ('expected', 'VBD'), ('l', 'RB'), ('love', 'VB'), ('it', 'PRP'), ('..Everything', 'VBG'), ('is', 'VBZ'), ('fine', 'JJ')]

Features Representation Schemes for Classification

Each review needs to be represented in a vector form for applying any machine learning model. In this phase, a feature vector of size r x f where r is number of reviews and f is the number of features is constructed from the available corpus. Some of the feature representation schemes (Mitchell, 2015) and their implementation results using Python sklearn library are discussed as follows:

Bag-of-Words (BoW)

In BoW model, the list of tokens are termed as features and value in feature vector is computed using the occurrence of features within a given review. However, the model is easy to implement; it assigns more weightage to frequently occurring features which may not achieve accurate results in few text classification applications.

Table 7. BoW model on review samples

Input Reviews	BoW	Feature Vector of size 3 x 28 where the size of vocabulary =28
corpus = ['Nice product value for money As usual Flipkart Rocks...', 'nice product thanks for the flipkart offer sale.... loved it...', 'good product looking very nice.. battery donot compare with others feel like not good but manageable']	{'nice': 15, 'product': 19, 'value': 25, 'for': 7, 'money': 14, 'as': 0, 'usual': 24, 'flipkart': 6, 'rocks': 20, 'thanks': 22, 'the': 23, 'offer': 17, 'sale': 21, 'loved': 12, 'it': 9, 'good': 8, 'looking': 11, 'very': 26, 'battery': 1, 'donot': 4, 'compare': 3, 'with': 27, 'others': 18, 'feel': 5, 'like': 10, 'not': 16, 'but': 2, 'manageable': 13}	[[1 0 0 0 0 0 1 1 0 0 0 0 0 0 1 1 0 0 0 1 1 0 0 0 1 1 0 0] [0 0 0 0 0 0 1 1 0 1 0 0 1 0 0 1 0 1 0 1 0 1 1 1 0 0 0 0] [0 1 1 1 1 1 0 0 2 0 1 1 0 1 0 1 1 0 1 1 0 0 0 0 0 0 1 1]]

The result of BoW model on review samples is shown in Table 7.

Term Frequency- Inverse Document Frequency (TF-IDF)

The other method to represent feature vector is TF-IDF, a statistical model which computes the weightage of given feature using trade-off between its occurrence in a review (TF) and its importance (IDF) in the corpus. The results of TF-IDF model on review samples is shown below:

Table 8 shows the results of TF-IDF on review samples.

Table 8. TF-IDF model on review samples

Reviews: docA = "Nice product value for money As usual Flipkart Rocks" docB = "Nice product thanks for the Flipkart offer sale, loved it"	
Term Frequency for document 1 {'loved': 0.0, 'for': 0.1111111111111111, 'thanks': 0.0, 'Rocks': 0.1111111111111111, 'sale,': 0.0, 'value': 0.1111111111111111, 'As': 0.1111111111111111, 'it': 0.0, 'Flipkart': 0.1111111111111111, 'usual': 0.1111111111111111, 'offer': 0.0, 'Nice': 0.1111111111111111, 'money': 0.1111111111111111, 'product': 0.1111111111111111, 'the': 0.0}	**Term Frequency for document 2** {'loved': 0.1, 'for': 0.1, 'thanks': 0.1, 'Rocks': 0.0, 'sale,': 0.1, 'value': 0.0, 'As': 0.0, 'it': 0.1, 'Flipkart': 0.1, 'usual': 0.0, 'offer': 0.1, 'Nice': 0.1, 'money': 0.0, 'product': 0.1, 'the': 0.1}
IDF computation {'loved': 0.3010299956639812, 'for': 0.0, 'thanks': 0.3010299956639812, 'Rocks': 0.3010299956639812, 'sale,': 0.3010299956639812, 'value': 0.3010299956639812, 'As': 0.3010299956639812, 'it': 0.3010299956639812, 'Flipkart': 0.0, 'usual': 0.3010299956639812, 'offer': 0.3010299956639812, 'Nice': 0.0, 'money': 0.3010299956639812, 'product': 0.0, 'the': 0.3010299956639812}	
Feature vector of size 2 x 15 loved for thanks Rocks ... Nice money product the 0 0.000000 0.0 0.000000 0.033448 ... 0.0 0.033448 0.0 0.000000 1 0.030103 0.0 0.030103 0.000000 ... 0.0 0.000000 0.0 0.030103	

Document to Vector (doc2vec)

The limitation of above-mentioned models is that they ignore the position of features and its semantic relationship with other features in the given review document. This issue can be resolved by using doc2vec model (Quoc & Tomas, 2014) that convert document or review of the given corpus into low dimensional embedding vector using the concept of deep learning and neural networks-based techniques as used in word2vec model (Jang et al., 2019). Word2vec is a two-layer neural network model used for word embedding, which vectorises the word in a given review. This model finds the syntactic and semantic relationship between the words. It helps to categorize similar words together in vector space, thus overcoming the problem of sparse vector generation that occurs in TF-IDF and BoW techniques. Though word2vec vectorises the word in a given review, doc2vec computes feature vector for every document and find similarity between documents in the corpus. Table 9 shows the implementation of doc2vec model using gensim library of Python (Rehurek & Sojka, 2010).

The above result is implemented by importing doc2vec from gensim. Gensim is an open-source library for natural language processing in Python used for topic modelling and similarity measure. After data preprocessing, the model is trained by setting vector size as 20, min_count=1, maximum no. of epochs=100, alpha=0.025, distributed memory=1 and vector representation of the document is obtained by using training vector.

Table 9. doc2vec model on review samples

Input Reviews	Feature Vector of size 1 x 20
corpus = ['Nice product value for money As usual Flipkart Rocks...', 'nice product thanks for the flipkart offer sale.... loved it...', 'good product looking very nice.. battery donot compare with others feel like not good but manageable']	[-0.00181341 -0.0109626 0.01808534 -0.01223498 -0.01348515 0.01312689 0.00939472 0.00387317 -0.00697212 0.01512301 0.00848521 0.00407578 -0.00071359 0.0116848 0.00962164 -0.01037175 -0.00630024 -0.01729558 0.01891079 0.00790605]

SUPERVISED LEARNING TECHNIQUES USED FOR KNOWLEDGE DISCOVERY FROM ONLINE REVIEWS

After feature representation of online data, there is a need for automatic extraction of useful patterns and knowledge discovery for various applications such as Sentiment Analysis, Recommendation system etc. The researchers are developing various machine learning approaches for analyzing this vast amount of data to save time and expense of manufacturers and customers on data analysis. These techniques can be classified into three different approaches: Supervised, Unsupervised and Semi-Supervised Learning. Supervised Learning approaches predict the class of new instance using the massive amount of training data. This training data is a collection of review instances with their predetermined class. The classifier is trained using this data in supervised learning to determine the class of testing data. Unsupervised learning approaches are utilized for data analysis where the class of the instances is not known. In these approaches, patterns are discovered using similarity between various instances. Semi-supervised learning approaches predict the class of unlabeled instances from few labelled instances. The advantage of semi-supervised learning approaches is that they save time and expense required for annotating large data as in the case of supervised learning approaches. In this section, problem of review classification, few popular classification algorithms and need for feature selection methods for classification and their techniques are discussed.

Review Classification

Given a training data D of n-reviews {R_1, R_2..... R_n} where each review R_i is represented by a set of m-features {f_1, f_2....f_m} and labeled to a class C_i ε {1, 2...c} where c is the number of classes. In the training phase, the classification algorithm will utilize the class label and training data to learn a map function F (or a classifier) from review features to class label as shown below:

$$F(f) \rightarrow C_i \tag{1}$$

In the prediction phase, the unknown review instance is represented by the feature set and the map function learned from the training phase is used to predict the class of this instance.

Few popular classification algorithms such as Naïve Bayes classifier, Support Vector Machine and Logistic Regression have been employed in the past for text classification. The brief overview of these classifiers is presented below.

Naïve Bayes Classifier (NB): Naïve Bayes classifier is probabilistic learning algorithm popularly used for text classification problems (Frank & Bouckaert, 2006; Kim et al., 2006). It uses Bayes theorem to predict the probability of a given set of features to the particular class using Equation 2:

$$P\left(C_i | features\right) = \frac{P\left(C_i\right) * P\left(features | C_i\right)}{P\left(features\right)} \qquad (2)$$

where $P(C_i)$ is the ith class prior probability. *P(features|C_i)* is the prior probability of feature set belonging to class i. P (features) is the prior probability of feature set which is a constant for all classes, so it is ignored. The class of feature set is determined from the maximum value for which P (C_i | features) is maximized.

Support Vector Machine (SVM): In mid-90s, SVM was introduced as a novel supervised learning method (Cortes & Vapnik, 1995). The algorithm has been popularized in text classification (Tong & Koller, 2001) due to its low computational cost and high accuracy value. The classifier is most suitable for significant data size problems as it is less prone to overfitting problem. SVM searches for the maximal marginal hyperplane using support vectors that are tuples carrying maximum information required for classifying the data.

Logistic Regression (LR): Logistic Regression is a variant of linear regression technique and is an effective method used for classification (Bishop, 2006). Logistic regression uses a linear combination of feature variables to generate an output variable as shown in Equation 3. Here, the corresponding output lies between 0 and 1 which is mapped to binary value using threshold or cut off value. The computation of logistic function on input vector is shown in Equation 3.

$$\sigma\left(X\right) = \frac{1}{(1 + \exp(-(b_0 + \sum_{i=1}^{n} b_i X_i)))} \qquad (3)$$

Where n is the number of features, b_i is the regression coefficient for input vector $\{X_1, X_2 \ldots \ldots X_n\}$. The regression coefficient can be estimated based on the data.

Feature Selection for Classification

In past few years, there has been huge growth in the number of online reviews posted by buyers on various e-commerce sites. Due to the generation of large feature space from online data, the classification algorithms suffer from curse of dimensionality when BoW and TF-IDF are used as feature representation schemes. The accuracy and computational speed of classification algorithms can be improved by employing feature selection before classification.

Feature selection methods for data classification was introduced in Dash & Liu (1997)'s study. They aimed to select a subset of relevant and non-redundant features from the original feature set. The selected feature subset can easily discriminate between two different classes of reviews. For example in the review *"Guys the iphone 6s is **amazing** nothing beats it I order it from flipkart the delivery is **fast** ,moreover the phone was in **good** condition the features of the phone is to what I expected l love it ..Everything is fine"*, it can be seen that the features "amazing", "fast" and "good" are relevant unigram features that can easily discriminate between a "positive" or "negative" review while classification. These relevant features are highly correlated with one class while having low correlation with other classes, thus having high discrimination power.

Feature selection is one of the significant step in classification problem as it results in better classification performance, low computation cost, better representation of training data with less memory storage. Feature selection methods consist of four elementary steps (Liu, 2012) as shown in Figure 1:

Figure 1. Flow diagram of Feature Selection

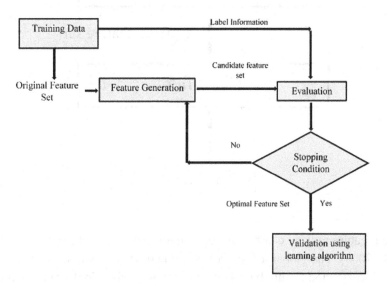

In the first step, the feature subset is generated according to the search strategy from the original feature set of training data. The next step evaluates each feature subset based on evaluation criteria. After the stopping condition is met, optimal feature set is selected that best fits the criterion function. This optimal feature set is utilized by different learning algorithms for validation in the last phase.

The problem of optimal feature selection from the extracted features for improving classifier performance can be solved using two different methods (Chandrashekhar & Sahin, 2014): Filter-based feature selection and wrapper-based feature selection. The feature selection is independent of classifier in filter methods and involve classifier in wrapper based methods. The study of both these methods is discussed below.

Filter-Based Feature Selection Methods

Filter-based approaches are two-step process as shown in Figure 2. In the first step, all n-features extracted from training data are ranked using statistical correlation between individual feature and class and in the next step the classifier's performance is evaluated using k optimal features.

The filter methods are computationally fast as each feature is ranked independent of other features in feature space and thus are useful in classification of high dimensional datasets.

Figure 2. General framework of Filter-based Feature Selection method

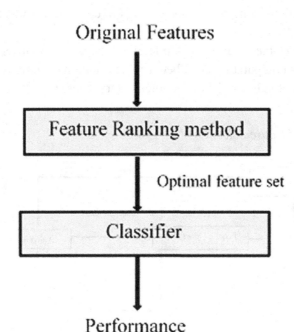

The filter-based feature rankers can be further categorized as global (Yang & Pederson, 1997) and local (Zheng et al., 2003). The global feature selection methods are two-sided metric and compute the positive score of each extracted feature based on its utility in predicting the class of a review document. The local feature rankers assign both positive and negative score to each extracted features based on membership and non-membership to a given class respectively. For example, the feature " good" has high positive score for positive class and high negative score for negative class as this feature is absent in most of the negative reviews of training set. If negative score of feature is higher than its positive score, it is termed as a negative feature. Past studies (Uysal, 2016; Ansari et al.,2018) found that integration of few negative features into the set of positive features while selection of optimal feature set improves the discriminating power of the classifiers thus increasing their performance. Past works have proposed different evaluation criteria for local and global filter-based feature selection methods as discussed below.

Chi-square Test: Chi-square test (Yang & Pederson, 1997) is statistical feature selection method which computes a positive score as shown in Equation (4) to find the degree of correlation between feature and class. A higher value of feature-class score implies feature relevancy and thus helps to filter irrelevant features before classification. The formula used to calculate the Chi-square score of a feature is as follows:

$$CHI(f, C_k) = \frac{N(AB - CD)^2}{(A+C)(A+D)(B+C)(B+D)} \tag{4}$$

Where f is a feature, C_k is k^{th} class, and k=1, 2...c, c is the number of classes, n is the number of documents in the dataset, A is the number of documents in which f and C_k co-occur, B is the number of documents that neither contain f nor C_k, C is the number of documents in which f occurs without C_k and D is the number of documents in which C_k occur without f.

Information Gain: Information Gain (Yang & Pederson,1997) computes score of each feature using its presence or absence in a document for predicting its correct class. The features having higher information gain are selected for classification as they have more discriminating power.

The formula to calculate IG score is as follows:

$$IG\left(feature\right) = -\sum_{k=1}^{c} P\left(C_k\right) \log P\left(C_k\right)$$

$$+ P\left(feature\right) \sum_{k=1}^{c} P\left(C_k | feature\right) \log P\left(C_k | feature\right) \tag{5}$$

$$+ P\left(\overline{feature}\right) \sum_{k=1}^{c} P\left(C_k | \overline{feature}\right) \log P\left(C_k | \overline{feature}\right)$$

Where 1<=k<=c and c is the number of classes

$P(C_k)$: Probability of a class C_k P (feature): Probability of feature
$P(C_k | feature)$: Conditional probability of class C_k given presence of feature
$P(\overline{feature})$: Probability of absence of feature
$P\left(C_k | \overline{feature}\right)$: Conditional Probability of class C_k given absence of feature

Document Frequency: Document Frequency of a feature is computed by counting the number of documents that contain that feature. It is the simplest method and based on the concept that more useful features occur more frequently in the dataset.

Standard Deviation: Standard deviation (SD) is used to measure deviation of value from its mean. The concept is used in feature selection (Yousefpour et al., 2014) to calculate the amount of dispersion of a feature from its average in the feature space. The features that show higher deviation are termed as relevant as they have more discrimination power. Standard deviation (SD) of a feature f_i for binary classification problem is shown in Equation 6 and Standard deviation of feature f_i for C_k class where k ε {0, 1} termed as Sdev is computed as shown in Equation 7.

$$SD\left(f_i\right) = \left|Sdev\left(f_i, C_1\right) - Sdev\left(f_i, C_2\right)\right| \tag{6}$$

$$Sdev\left(f_i, C_k\right) = \sqrt{\frac{1}{N} \sum_{j=1}^{N} \left(x_{ji} - mean_k\left(f_i\right)\right)^2} \tag{7}$$

Where x_{ji} is the weight of jth feature in the ith sample and $mean_k$ is the mean of the ith feature in the kth class.

Gini Index: Gini Index (GI) is a statistical feature selector that uses probability theory to assign global positive score to each extracted feature from the dataset. The method is employed (Forman, 2003; Shang et al., 2007) for ranking features in text categorization problems. The GI score of each feature is computed as follows:

$$GI\left(feature\right) = \sum_{k=1}^{c} P\left(feature \mid C_k\right)^2 P\left(C_k \mid feature\right)^2 \tag{8}$$

Where $1 <= k <= c$ and c is the number of classes

$P\left(C_k \mid feature\right)$: Conditional probability of class C_k given presence of feature
$P\left(feature \mid C_k\right)$: Conditional probability of feature given presence of class C_k

Distinguishing Feature Selection (DFS): DFS is used to filter irrelevant or non-informative features from the extracted large number of features using the global rank of the features (Uysal & Gunal, 2012). The method assigns a positive score to each feature for m different classes using probability theory as shown in Equation 9.

$$DFS\left(feature\right) = \sum_{k=1}^{c} \frac{P\left(C_k \mid feature\right)}{\left[P\left(\overline{feature} \mid C_k\right) + P\left(feature \mid \overline{C_k}\right) + 1\right]} \tag{9}$$

where $1 <= k <= c$ and c is the number of classes

$P\left(C_k \mid feature\right)$: Conditional Probability of class C_k given the presence of feature
$P\left(\overline{feature} \mid C_k\right)$: Conditional Probability of absence of feature given the presence of class C_k
$P\left(feature \mid C_k\right)$: Conditional Probability of feature given the presence of class C_k

Odds Ratio (OR): It is local feature selection method and assigns a negative and positive score to a feature with reference to the kth class (Forman, 2003) as shown in Equation 10. This score is assigned based on its membership and non-membership to the class. For example, if a feature f is present in all reviews belonging to classes C_1, C_2 and C_3 and not present in any reviews of class C_4, then OR (f $|C_4$) assigns f a negative score. If absolute value of OR (f $|C_4$) is higher than the absolute values of OR (f $|C_1$), OR (f $|C_2$) and OR (f $|C_3$), then this feature f is termed as a negative feature. The selection of few negative features can be useful in distinguishing between different classes.

$$OR\left(feature \mid C_k\right) = log \frac{P\left(feature \mid C_k\right)\left[1 - P\left(feature \mid \overline{C_k}\right)\right]}{\left[1 - P\left(feature \mid C_k\right)\right] P\left(feature \mid \overline{C_k}\right)} \tag{10}$$

Where $1 <= k <= c$ and c is the number of classes

$P(feature|C_k)$: Probability of a feature in the presence of class C_k

$P\left(feature \mid \overline{C_k}\right)$: Probability of a feature in the absence of class C_k

Correlation coefficient (CC): Correlation coefficient (Zheng et al., 2003) is one-sided or local feature selection method. CC is a variant of the CHI metric where $CC^2=CHI (f, C_k)^2$. The positive values correspond to membership of feature to a class while negative values correspond to its non-membership to a class. The features having maximum CC values are selected to filter irrelevant terms.

Wrapper-Based Feature Selection Methods

The filter methods do not involve feature interaction leading to selection of redundant features. For selection of more relevant and non-redundant features, wrapper approaches are quite useful. They evaluate each feature subset based on its performance on classifier which makes the approach computationally slow. Wrapper methods for feature selection were first introduced in Kohavi & John (1997)'s study. The three essential components of wrapper approaches (see Figure 3) are: Feature subset generation, Feature subset evaluation that involves a classifier for estimating the performance and final evaluation on test data using the optimal feature subset selected in the second step.

Figure 3. General framework of Wrapper-based Feature Selection method

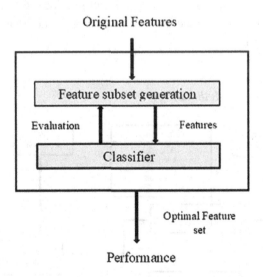

Wrapper based methods are employed in this study for selection of better feature set. Though the wrapper methods are quite slow as compared to filter methods as they involve classifier for selecting appropriate feature set, they obtain better classification performance.

The three Wrapper-based Feature Selection approaches such as Sequential Feature Selection, Backward Feature Elimination and Recursive Feature Elimination are utilized in our study for selection of relevant and non-redundant feature set. The process used in these methods for feature selection is presented below.

Sequential Feature Selection (SFS): SFS is an iterative method (Maldonado & Weber, 2009) which starts with a null model and then start fitting the classifier with each feature one at a time and select the feature f1 that maximises its performance. In the next iteration, the model is again fitted with f1 with all remaining features and the feature that maximizes the classifier's performance is selected. The process continues till a specified number of features say k is selected by the model.

Backward Feature Elimination (BFE): In Backward Feature Elimination (Maldonado & Weber, 2009), the procedure starts by including all the features in the feature set and then at every iteration remove the feature that minimizes the classifier performance. The process stops when there is no improvement on removal of features or when specified number of features are selected by the model.

Recursive Feature Elimination (RFE): RFE is another Wrapper-based Feature Selection method and is a variant of Backward Feature Elimination. RFE fits the classifier with all features at the beginning of the process. Then, it ranks these features based on the value of the model's coefficient. At each step, the method recursively removes few features that have least weights (Guyon et al., 2002). The procedure continues until optimal features are found. This optimal number of features need to be specified in advance.

SOLUTIONS AND RECOMMENDATIONS

Proposed Methodology

This section presents the architecture of the proposed methodology for selecting optimal features to improve review classification. The architecture of the proposed methodology (see Figure 4) and its components are explained in this section.

Figure 4. Architecture of Proposed Methodology

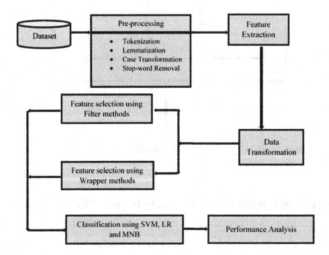

Dataset Used

The accessible Movie review dataset is utilized in our work for the task of sentiment analysis. The dataset was retrieved and employed in early 2000 (Pang et al., 2002), and its cleaned version was released and employed in Pang & Lee (2004)'s study. The dataset is balanced, comprising of 1000 positive and 1000 negative movie reviews.

Preprocessing Data and Feature Extraction

The pre-processing steps such as lowercase conversion, dealing with noisy content, removal of all stop words, tokenization and lemmatization are applied on the content of the review using NLTK library (Bird et al., 2009). After pre-processing, 39389 unigrams were extracted as features from the dataset.

Data Transformation

In this study, the TF-IDF is employed to convert extracted unigrams into a review feature vector.

Feature Selection Methods

The global filter-based feature selection methods employed in the proposed work for comparison in terms of real performance of classifiers are Chi-Square (CHI), Information Gain (IG), Gini Index (GI), Distinguishing Feature Selection (DFS), Standard Deviation (SD) and Document Frequency (DF) and wrapper methods utilized in our work for experimental analysis are Sequential Feature Selector (SFS) and Recursive Feature Elimination (RFE).

Classification Methods

The results are evaluated using three classifiers - NB, SVM and LR. Scikit-learn (sklearn), a machine learning toolkit in Python (Pedregosa et al., 2011) is used for sentiment classification to conduct experimental study. The classifiers employed in this work for training are SVM with linear kernel, Multinomial version of NB and Logistic Regression. The model is tested using cross-validation technique to yield better and less biased results of classifiers.

It was found that the use of cross validation technique for evaluating the performance of the classifier yields in less biased result (Bolon-Canedo et al., 2014). The evaluation in cross-validation techniques divides data into m-folds where m-1 folds are used for model training and one fold for model testing. In each iteration, test fold is varied to evaluate classifier performance on the remaining training data and its average is computed for generating the overall evaluation score. In the experimental study, 5-fold cross validation is employed to achieve more effective classification results.

Performance Evaluation

To evaluate classifier performance, F-measure is the best measure that uses the combination of both Precision and Recall value. In Han & Kamber (2006)'s study, the performance metrics and their computation are presented for evaluating the classification algorithms. The number of accurately classified instances out of the total number of classified instances is termed as Precision (P). The number of accurately classified instances out of the total number of instances belonging to a particular class is called Recall(R). The formula for computing P and R are shown in Equation 11 and 12 respectively. The harmonic mean between Precision and Recall is termed as F-measure and its computation is shown in Equation 13.

$$Precision\,(P) = \frac{TP}{TP+FP} \tag{11}$$

$$Recall\,(R) = \frac{TP}{TP+FN} \tag{12}$$

$$F-measure = \frac{2*P*R}{(P+R)} \tag{13}$$

Here TP (True Positive) are the positive objects that are accurately classified as positive, TN (True Negative) are the negative objects that are accurately classified as negative, FP (False Positive) are the negative objects inaccurately classified as positive, and FN (False Negative) are the positive objects inaccurately classified as negative.

Result Analysis

In this section, a comparative study of various filter and wrapper based methods is presented. However, few of the widely used filter and wrapper methods for feature selection have been presented theoretically in the previous section, empirical analysis for comparing these approaches using f-measure as performance evaluation metrics is covered in this section. The results of SVM, MNB and LR without feature selection on Movie dataset is achieved as 0.84, 0.82 and 0.821 respectively on Movie Review dataset. Table 10-15 shows the performance of all three classifiers on the same dataset using different filter-based feature selection methods. The number of selected features for testing the classifier performance is varied from 5-20% in case of all feature selection methods.

Table 10. Comparative Analysis between SVM, MNB and LR on Movie dataset using DFS feature selection method

Size of Selected feature set	SVM	MNB	LR
2000	0.731	0.776	0.761
4000	0.791	0.822	0.82
6000	0.831	0.829	0.847
8000	0.846	0.829	0.847

As observed from Table 10, LR shows improvement up to 3% in terms of f-measure when DFS is used as a filter method and the selected features are 20% of total feature set of size 40000.

It has been observed in Table 11 that all classifiers get benefitted by using CHI as feature selection method and best f-measure of 91.5% is obtained when SVM is chosen as classifier and 20% features are selected.

Table 11. Comparative Analysis between SVM, MNB and LR on Movie dataset using CHI feature selection method

Size of Selected feature set	SVM	MNB	LR
2000	0.907	0.902	0.862
4000	0.914	0.905	0.873
6000	0.915	0.905	0.884
8000	0.915	0.908	0.88

As observed from Table 12, IG shows f-measure of around 2% when 20% features are selected and SVM is employed as classifier.

Table 12. Comparative Analysis between SVM, MNB and LR on Movie dataset using IG feature selection method

Size of Selected feature set	SVM	MNB	LR
2000	0.842	0.819	0.8
4000	0.86	0.831	0.817
6000	0.858	0.829	0.82
8000	0.861	0.829	0.823

The results shown in Table 13 depicts that GI improves by around 2% on all classifiers on selected 20% features.

Table 13. Comparative Analysis between SVM, MNB and LR on Movie dataset using GI feature selection method

Size of Selected feature set	SVM	MNB	LR
2000	0.85	0.841	0.845
4000	0.866	0.834	0.867
6000	0.871	0.843	0.843
8000	0.869	0.84	0.843

The results observed from Table 14 depicts that on utilizing standard deviation as feature selection method, the performance of NB classifier outperforms SVM and LR and shows an improvement of 6% on selected 20% features.

Table 14. Comparative Analysis between SVM, MNB and LR on Movie dataset using SD feature selection method

Size of Selected feature set	SVM	MNB	LR
2000	0.826	0.833	0.823
4000	0.855	0.865	0.852
6000	0.869	0.877	0.857
8000	0.88	0.883	0.868

As observed from Table 15, DF shows an improvement of only 1% when SVM and LR are employed as classifier and shows no improvement on MNB classifier. The result analysis on all classifiers shows that the best performance is achieved on selecting 20% features from the extracted unigrams and it can be concluded that CHI method for selecting features outperforms all other feature selection methods.

Table 15. Comparative Analysis between SVM, MNB and LR on Movie dataset using DF feature selection method

Size of Selected feature set	SVM	MNB	LR
2000	0.833	0.811	0.829
4000	0.854	0.823	0.836
6000	0.852	0.825	0.829
8000	0.854	0.823	0.831

However, the statistical feature rankers are computationally fast and show improved performance on all classifiers; they result in selection of few redundant and irrelevant features that increase selected feature set size and degrade classifiers' performance. Thus, in the proposed work the classifiers' performance is improved with a reduced feature set size by utilizing two wrapper-based feature selection approaches- SFS and RFE. To prove efficacy of wrapper methods over filter methods, the performance of all three classifiers is evaluated using SFS and RFE methods on Movie dataset.

Table 16-17 shows the performance of all three classifiers- MNB, SVM and LR when RFE and SFS are used as feature selection methods on Movie Review dataset. Before applying RFE and SFE for feature selection, unigrams that occur in less than five documents are also filtered in addition to other pre-processing steps. In RFE and SFE, vector is constructed from filtered 13057 unigrams or features. This filtering is applied to improve the execution time of wrapper-based approaches. Table 16 shows the performance of RFE feature selection method that recursively eliminates the feature based on its performance on the chosen model.

Table 16. Comparative Analysis between SVM, MNB and LR on Movie dataset using RFE feature selection method

Size of Selected feature set	SVM	MNB	LR
600	0.952	0.352	0.866
800	0.953	0.371	0.881
1000	0.962	0.389	0.882
1200	0.961	0.411	0.887

As depicted in Table 16, the SVM and LR show good performance when RFE is used as feature selection method whereas MNB is unable to perform well with the same. As observed from the same, SVM achieves 96% f-measure value with a small feature set size of around 8%. Also, LR classifier achieves around 89% f-measure value with around 9% features when RFE is used as a feature selection method. It can be remarked from the observed results that the stability of this wrapper-based approach depends heavily on the chosen model or classifier that is used for feature ranking at each iteration.

As depicted in Table 17, all three classifiers show better performance when SFS is used as the feature selection method. As observed from the same, SVM, MNB and LR achieve f-measure value as 95%, 93% and 92% respectively with selection of small feature size of around 10%.

Table 17. Comparative Analysis between SVM, MNB and LR on Movie dataset using SFS feature selection method

Size of Selected feature set	SVM	MNB	LR
600	0.923	0.907	0.890
800	0.935	0.912	0.897
1000	0.945	0.922	0.912
1200	0.948	0.935	0.918

It can be concluded from the observed results that the RFE improves the classifiers' performance over CHI-square feature selection method by around 5% on SVM and 2% on LR. On the other hand, SFS improves the classifiers' performance over CHI-square feature selection method by 3% on SVM, 3% on MNB and 4% on LR. Both these wrapper methods show a reduction in terms of feature subset size as compared to filter methods.

FUTURE RESEARCH DIRECTIONS

The advantages of both filter and wrapper methods for online review classification can be utilized by designing a hybrid approach for feature selection that first filters the irrelevant features using computationally fast feature ranking method and then apply wrapper method to remove all redundant features. The hybrid approach utilized in few works of movie and product review domains (Ansari et al., 2019;

Agarwal & Mittal, 2013; Yousefpour et al., 2017) generates more accurate classification results with less number of selected features. With the increase in the online content over the last few years, the online review analysis is a problem of big data analytics. To overcome this issue, parallel approach for online review classification (Liu et al., 2013) can be designed in future. Semi-supervised learning model can be designed to annotate a large set of crawled reviews with the small set of annotated reviews for aspect term extraction from online reviews (Ansari G. et al., 2020). In Zhu (2005)'s study, Graph-based semi-supervised learning, co-training, self-training, Transductive SVM and other methods are discussed which can be employed to design semi-supervised learning models. In future, there is a need to design better deep learning models for various natural language processing tasks as presented in the study (Young et al., 2018) that can work on unlabeled data as well. Thatha et al. (2020) proposed a modification in the TF-IDF scheme for selecting better features for improving results of clustering. This enhanced feature selection can be employed in other learning tasks for improving their performance.

CONCLUSION

The chapter presented a thorough study of various natural language processing tasks involved in the process of online review classification. The different tools and techniques used for extraction and cleaning of online review data and their implementation results are also covered in this chapter. This chapter also investigates three different feature representation schemes employed in the past by machine learning models for representation of review document into a feature vector. The focus of the work is to improve the task of feature selection that is needed to reduce feature space and thus solve the problem of curse of dimensionality that occurs while review classification. The chapter has presented application of different Filter and Wrapper methods for selection of optimal feature set. The comparison in terms of f-measure between three classifiers - SVM, MNB and LR using six different statistical feature selection methods on Movie review datasets is presented in this chapter. Finally, Wrapper-based methods such as SFS and RFE are employed for feature selection on the same dataset to improve classifiers' performance and reduce feature space. The observed results indicates the efficacy of Wrapper-based approaches over filter-based approaches for optimal feature selection in online review classification.

REFERENCES

Agarwal, B., & Mittal, N. (2013). Sentiment classification using rough set based hybrid feature selection. In *Proceedings of 4th Workshop on Computational Approaches to Subjectivity, Sentiment and Social Media Analysis* (pp.115-119). Academic Press.

Ahuja, R., Chug, A., Kohli, S., Gupta, S., & Ahuja, P. (2019). The impact of features extraction on the sentiment analysis. In *Proceedings of International Conference on Pervasive Computing Advances and Applications* (vol. 152, pp. 341-348). 10.1016/j.procs.2019.05.008

Ansari, G., Ahmad, T., & Doja, M. N. (2018). Spam review classification using ensemble of global and local feature selectors. *Cybernetics and Information Technologies*, 8(4), 29–42. doi:10.2478/cait-2018-0046

Ansari, G., Ahmad, T., & Doja, M. N. (2019). Hybrid filter–wrapper feature selection method for sentiment classification. *Arabian Journal for Science and Engineering*, *44*(11), 9191–9208. doi:10.100713369-019-04064-6

Ansari, G., Saxena, C., Ahmad, T., & Doja, M. N. (2020). *Aspect Term Extraction using Graph-based Semi-Supervised Learning*. arXiv preprint arXiv:2003.04968

Bird, S., Klein, E., & Loper, E. (2009). *Natural Language Processing with Python – Analyzing Text with the Natural Language Toolkit*. O'Reilly Media.

Bishop, C. M. (2006). *Pattern recognition and machine learning*. Springer-Verlag New York.

Bolon-Canedo, V., Sanchez-Marono, N., Alonso-Betanzos, A., Benitez, J. M., & Herrera, F. (2014). A review of microarray datasets and applied feature selection methods. *Information Sciences*, *282*, 111–135. doi:10.1016/j.ins.2014.05.042

Chandrashekar, G., & Sahin, F. (2014). A survey on feature selection methods. *Computers & Electrical Engineering*, *40*(1), 16–28. doi:10.1016/j.compeleceng.2013.11.024

Cortes, C., & Vapnik, V. (1995). Support Vector Machine. *Machine Learning*, *20*(3), 273–297. doi:10.1007/BF00994018

Dash, M., & Liu, H. (1997). Feature selection for classification. *Intelligent Data Analysis*, *1*(1-4), 131–156. doi:10.1016/S1088-467X(97)00008-5

Forman, G. (2003). An extensive empirical study of feature selection metrics for text classification. *Journal of Machine Learning Research*, *3*, 1289–1305.

Frank, E., & Bouckaert, R. R. (2006). Naive bayes for text classification with unbalanced classes. In *Proceedings of 10th European Conference on Principles & Practice of Knowledge Discovery in Databases* (vol. 4213). 10.1007/11871637_49

Galov, N., Krstic, B., & Chakarov, R. (2020). *67+ Staggering Online Review Statistics That Will Help You Improve Your Business in 2020*. Retrieved from https://hostingtribunal.com/blog/online-review-statistics/

Gojare, S., Joshi, R., & Gaigaware, D. (2015). Analysis and design of selenium webdriver automation testing framework. *Procedia Computer Science*, *50*, 341–346. doi:10.1016/j.procs.2015.04.038

Guyon, I., Weston, J., Barnhill, S., & Vapnik, V. (2002). Gene selection for cancer classification using support vector machines. *Machine Learning*, *46*(1–3), 389–422. doi:10.1023/A:1012487302797

Han, J., & Kamber, M. (2006). *Data mining: Concepts and Techniques*. Morgan Kaufmann Publishers, Elsevier.

Hanafiah, N., & Quix, C. (2014) Entity recognition in information extraction. In *6th Asian Conference on Intelligent Information and Database Systems*. (vol. 8397, pp. 113–122). 10.1007/978-3-319-05476-6_12

Jang, B., Kim, I., & Kim, J. W. (2019). Word2vec convolutional neural networks for classification of news articles and tweets. *PLOS ONE, 14*(8), 1-20.

Kim, S. B., Han, K. S., Rim, H. C. R., & Myaeng, S. H. (2006). Some effective techniques for naive bayes text classification. *IEEE Transactions on Knowledge and Data Engineering*, *18*(11), 1457–1466. doi:10.1109/TKDE.2006.180

Kohavi, R., & John, G. (1997). Wrappers for feature subset selection. *Artificial Intelligence*, *97*(1-2), 273–324. doi:10.1016/S0004-3702(97)00043-X

Kowsari, K., Meimandi, K. J., Heidarysafa, M., Mendu, S., Barnes, L. E., & Brown, D. E. (2019). Text classification algorithms: A survey. *Informations*, *10*(4), 150. doi:10.3390/info10040150

Liu, B. (2012). *Sentiment Analysis and Opinion Mining*. University of Illinois at Chicago, Morgan & Claypool Publishers. doi:10.2200/S00416ED1V01Y201204HLT016

Liu, B., Blasch, E., Chen, Y. L., Shen, D., & Chen, G. (2013). Scalable sentiment classification for big data analysis using naïve bayes classifier. In *2013 IEEE International Conference on Big Data*, (pp. 99-104). Santa Clara, CA: IEEE. 10.1109/BigData.2013.6691740

Maldonado, S., & Weber, R. (2009). A wrapper method for feature selection using support vector machines. *Information Sciences*, *179*(13), 2208–2217. doi:10.1016/j.ins.2009.02.014

Mitchell, R. (2015). *Web Scraping with Python*. O'Reilly Publishers.

Pang, B., & Lee, L. (2004). A sentimental education: Sentiment Analysis using subjectivity summarization based on minimum cuts. In *Proceedings of the 42nd Annual Meeting on Association for Computational Linguistics*, (pp. 271-278). 10.3115/1218955.1218990

Pang, B., Lee, L., & Vaithyanathan, S. (2002). Thumbs up? Sentiment classification using machine learning techniques. In *Proceedings of the Conference on Empirical Methods in Natural Language Processing (EMNLP)*, (pp.79-86). 10.3115/1118693.1118704

Pedregosa, F., Varoquaux, G., & Gramfort, A. (2011). Scikit-learn: Machine Learning in Python. *Journal of Machine Learning Research*, *12*(85), 2825–2830.

Qaiser, S., & Ali, R. (2018). Text Mining: Use of TF-IDF to examine the relevance of words to documents. *International Journal of Computers and Applications*, *181*(1), 25–29. doi:10.5120/ijca2018917395

Quoc, L., & Tomas, M. (2014). Distributed representations of sentences and documents. *Proceedings of the 31 st International Conference on Machine Learning*, *32*.

Rehurek, R., & Sojka, P. (2010). Software framework for topic modelling with large corpora. *Proceedings of the LREC 2010 Workshop on New Challenges for NLP Frameworks*, 45-50.

Severance, C. (2013). *Python for informatics: Exploring information* (1st ed.). CreateSpace Independent Publishing Platform.

Shang, W., Huang, H., Zhu, H., Lin, Y., Qu, Y., & Wang, Z. (2007). A novel feature selection algorithm for text categorization. *Expert Systems with Applications*, *33*(1), 1–5. doi:10.1016/j.eswa.2006.04.001

Thatha, V. N., Babu, A. S., & Haritha, D. (2019). An Enhanced Feature Selection for Text Documents. In *Smart Intelligent Computing and Applications* (pp. 21–29). Springer.

Tong, S., & Koller, D. (2001). Support vector machine active learning with applications to text classification. *Journal of Machine Learning Research, 2*(11), 45–66.

Uchida, S., Yoshikawa, T., & Furuhashi, T. (2018). Application of output embedding on Word2Vec. *Proceedings of Joint Tenth International Conference on Soft Computing and Intelligent Systems and 19th International Symposium on Advanced Intelligent System, 1433-1436.*

Uysal, A. K. (2016). An improved global feature selection scheme for text classification. *Expert Systems with Applications, 43*(1), 82–92. doi:10.1016/j.eswa.2015.08.050

Uysal, A. K., & Gunal, S. (2012). A novel probabilistic feature selection method for text classification. *Knowledge-Based Systems, 36*, 226–235. doi:10.1016/j.knosys.2012.06.005

Yang, Y., & Pederson, J. O. (1997). A comparative study of feature selection in text categorization. *Proceedings of the Fourteenth International Conference on Machine Learning, 412-420.*

Young, T., Hazarika, D., Poria, S., & Cambria, E. (2018). Recent trends in deep learning based natural language processing. *IEEE Computational Intelligence Magazine, 13*(3), 55–75. doi:10.1109/MCI.2018.2840738

Yousefpour, A., Ibrahim, R., Abdull Hamed, H. N., & Hajmohammadi, M. S. (2014). Feature reduction using standard deviation with different subsets selection in sentiment analysis. *Asian Conference on Intelligent Information and Database Systems*, 33-41. 10.1007/978-3-319-05458-2_4

Yousefpour, A., Ibrahim, R., & Hamed, H. N. A. (2017). Ordinal-based and frequency-based integration of feature selection methods for sentiment analysis. *Expert Systems with Applications, 75*, 80–93. doi:10.1016/j.eswa.2017.01.009

Zheng, Z., Srihari, R., & Srihari, S. (2003). A feature selection framework for text filtering. *Proceedings of Third IEEE International Conference on Data Mining*, 705-708. 10.1109/ICDM.2003.1251013

Zhu, X. (2005). *Semi-supervised learning literature survey*. University of Wisconsin-Madison Department of Computer Sciences.

ADDITIONAL READING

Das, B., & Chakraborty, S. (2018). An improved text sentiment classification model using TF-IDF and next word negation. arXiv preprint arXiv:1806.06407.

Haddi, E., Liu, X., & Shi, Y. (2013). The role of text pre-processing in sentiment analysis. *Procedia Computer Science, 17*, 26–32. doi:10.1016/j.procs.2013.05.005

Lau, J. H., & Baldwin, T. (2016). An empirical evaluation of doc2vec with practical insights into document embedding generation. In *Proceedings of the 1st Workshop on Representation Learning for NLP*. Berlin, Germany. 10.18653/v1/W16-1609

Liu, B., & Yu, L. (2005). Toward integrating feature selection algorithms for classification and clustering. *IEEE Transactions on Knowledge and Data Engineering, 17*(4), 491–502. doi:10.1109/TKDE.2005.66

Mishra, V. K., & Tiruwa, H. (2020). Aspect-Based sentiment analysis of online product reviews. In *Natural Language Processing: Concepts, Methodologies, Tools, and Applications* (pp. 31–47). International Publisher of Information Science and Technology Research. doi:10.4018/978-1-7998-0951-7.ch003

Shelke, N. M., & Deshpande, S. P. (2020). Exploiting chi square method for sentiment analysis of product reviews. In *Natural Language Processing: Concepts, Methodologies, Tools, and Applications* (pp. 422–439). International Publisher of Information Science and Technology Research. doi:10.4018/978-1-7998-0951-7.ch022

Tang, J., Alelyani, S., & Liu, H. (2014). Feature selection for classification: a review. In *Data Classification: Algorithms and Applications* (p. 37). CRC Press.

Wang, J., Yu, L., Lai, K. R., & Zhang, X. (2020). Tree-Structured Regional CNN-LSTM Model for Dimensional Sentiment Analysis. *IEEE/ACM Transactions on Audio, Speech, and Language Processing*, *28*, 581–591. doi:10.1109/TASLP.2019.2959251

Zhong, G., Wang, L. N., Ling, X., & Dong, J. (2016). An overview on data representation learning: From traditional feature learning to recent deep learning. *The Journal of Finance and Data Science*, *2*(4), 265–278. doi:10.1016/j.jfds.2017.05.001

Zhu, P., Chen, Z., Zheng, H., & Qian, T. (2019). Aspect Aware Learning for Aspect Category Sentiment Analysis. *ACM Transactions on Knowledge Discovery from Data*, *13*(6), 1–21. doi:10.1145/3350487

KEY TERMS AND DEFINITIONS

Deep Learning: It is a subarea of machine learning, where the models are built using multiple layers of artificial neural networks for learning useful patterns from raw data.

Feature Selection: It is used to select appropriate features from the available data for improving efficiency of machine learning algorithms.

Filter-Based Feature Selection: It filters irrelevant features from the extracted features on the basis of their association with the output class.

Semi-Supervised Learning: It is a machine learning algorithm in which the machine learns from both labeled and unlabeled instances to build a model for predicting the class of unlabeled instances.

Supervised Learning: It is machine learning algorithm in which the model learns from ample amount of available labeled data to predict the class of unseen instances.

Unsupervised Learning: In unsupervised machine learning algorithms, the model learns from unlabeled data instances by finding the similarity or association between them.

Wrapper-Based Feature Selection: This method selects the most useful and non-redundant features from the extracted features on the basis of their performance on the classifier.

Chapter 4
Sentiment Analysis as a Restricted NLP Problem

Akshi Kumar
Delhi Technological University, India

Divya Gupta
Galgotias University, India

ABSTRACT

With the accelerated evolution of social networks, there is a tremendous increase in opinions by the people about products or services. While this user-generated content in natural language is intended to be valuable, its large amounts require use of content mining methods and NLP to uncover the knowledge for various tasks. In this study, sentiment analysis is used to analyze and understand the opinions of users using statistical approaches, knowledge-based approaches, hybrid approaches, and concept-based ontologies. Unfortunately, sentiment analysis also experiences a range of difficulties like colloquial words, negation handling, ambiguity in word sense, coreference resolution, which highlight another perspective emphasizing that sentiment analysis is certainly a restricted NLP problem. The purpose of this chapter is to discover how sentiment analysis is a restricted NLP problem. Thus, this chapter discussed the concept of sentiment analysis in the field of NLP and explored that sentiment analysis is a restricted NLP problem due to the sophisticated nature of natural language.

INTRODUCTION

With the emergence of WWW and the Internet, the interest of social media has increased tremendously over the past few years. This new wave of social media has generated a boundless amount of data which contains the emotions, feelings, sentiments or opinions of the users. This abundant data on the web is in the form of micro-blogs, web journals, posts, comments, audits and reviews in the Natural Language. The scientific communities and business world are utilizing this user opinionated data accessible on various social media sites to gather, process and extract the learning through natural language processing. In this way, there is a need to detect and distinguish the sentiments, attitudes, emotions and opinions of

DOI: 10.4018/978-1-7998-4240-8.ch004

the users from the user's generated content. Sentiment Analysis is the process which aids to recognize and classify the emotions and opinions of users in the communicated information, in order to determine whether the opinion of the user towards a specific service or product is positive, negative or neutral through NLP, computational linguistics and text analysis. While this user opinionated data is intended to be useful, the bulk of this data requires preprocessing and text mining techniques for the evaluation of sentiments from the text written in natural language. Sentiment Analysis permits organizations to trace their brand reception and popularity, enquire about new product perception and anticipation by the consumers, improve customer relation models, enquire company reputation in the eyes of customers and to track the stock market. According to the Local consumer review survey (Bloem, 2017), 84 percent of the total people trust online reviews as much as a personal recommendation given to them. Thus, it is important to mine online reviews to determine the hidden sentiments behind them.

According to Techopedia (2014), Sentiment Analysis is defined as "*a type of data mining that measures the inclination of people's opinions through NLP, computational linguistics and text analysis, which are used to extract and analyze subjective information from the Web- mostly social media and similar sources*". The analyzed data measures the consumer's experiences and opinions towards the products, services or proposed schemes and discloses the contextual orientation of the content. Sentiment analysis encounters many challenges due to its analysis process. These challenges become hindrances in examining the precise significance of sentiments and identifying the sentiment polarity. Some of the common challenges faced by sentiment analysis include difficulties in feature extraction, increased complexity in analyzing label opinionated data, the complication in analysis of other regional languages, requirements of world knowledge, increased domain dependency etc. Unfortunately, sentiment analysis also experiences various difficulties due to the sophisticated nature of the natural language that is being used in the user opinionated data. Some of these issues are generated by NLP overheads like colloquial words, coreference resolution, word sense disambiguation and so on. These issues add more difficulty to the process of sentiment analysis and emphasize that sentiment analysis is a restricted NLP problem. Different algorithms have been applied to analyze the sentiments of the user-generated data. The techniques applied to the user-generated data ranges from statistical to knowledge-based techniques. Even hybrid techniques have been used for the sentiment analysis. Various algorithms, as discussed above, have been employed by sentiment analysis to provide good results, but they have their own limitations in providing high accuracy. It is found from the literature that deep learning methodologies are being used for extracting knowledge from huge amounts of content to reveal useful information and hidden sentiments. Many researchers have explored sentiment analysis from various perspectives but none of the work has focused on explaining sentiment analysis as a restricted NLP problem.

Thus, this chapter presents an overview of Sentiment analysis, which is followed by the related work in section 2, then the detailed description of generally employed methodologies and techniques in Sentiment analysis are discussed in Section 3. Section 4 explains the applications of Sentiment Analysis. Section 5 describes the challenges faced by the Sentiment Analysis and then the challenges relevant to NLP are discussed in Section 6. Section 7 explores the solutions and recommendations to resolve the challenges and in the next section, some future research directions have been explored.

RELATED WORK

As sentiment analysis is a progressing field of research, thus a lot of research has been done and still going on in this field. Cambria (2016) have discussed the sentiment analysis and its basic process as sentiment detection and its polarity classification. Zhang et al. (2018) examined the sentiment analysis from three perspectives, i.e. sentence level, document level and feature-based level. Ainur et al. (2006), Noura et al. (2010), Nikos et al. (2011), Thomas (2013), Haochen & Fei (2015) have examined sentiment analysis at various levels such as document, sentence and feature-based level. Patel et al. (2015) have also studied sentiment analysis on various levels. The researchers have also discussed various methods of sentiment analysis, like SVM and Naive Bayes. Tsytsarau et al. (2012) reviewed the various sentiment analysis techniques such as machine learning, corpus-based, semantic-based and statistical-based techniques. The researchers have also examined the document-level sentiment analysis. Pang & Lee (2008) have also provided a wide overview of the various methodologies and techniques used in the process of sentiment analysis. The researchers were encouraged to resolve the difficulties in the sentiment analysis. Kharde et al. (2016) have reviewed the process of sentiment analysis on the twitter dataset. The researchers have also compared the sentiment analysis techniques that incorporate machine learning as well as lexicon-based techniques. The issues and challenges associated with the process of sentiment analysis, as well as the various applications where sentiment analysis can be employed were also investigated by the researchers. Kalchbrenner et al. (2014) have also employed machine learning techniques like dynamic CNN for sentiment analysis and achieved great outcomes. Similarly, the machine learning techniques were discussed by Tang et al. (2009) for customer survey for analyzing the sentiments at the document level.

Yanyan et al. (2017) presented a strategy to develop an enormous sentiment word reference for microblog data to elevate the performance of sentiment analysis. Li et al. (2015) have explored different highlights of an SVM classifier for analyzing the sentiments. Turney et al. (2003) and Yang et al. (2013) have discussed vocabulary-based techniques. Researchers, Turney et al. (2003) have also proffered an algorithm to investigate the inclination of the text towards sentiments extremity. Hu and Liu (2004) produced a lexicon consisting of both positive and negative sentiment keywords through seed words in WordNet. Bravo-Marquez et al. (2016) presented a strategy of enlarging the dictionary in a supervised way for better sentiment analysis. Yang et al. (2013) introduced an improved method for emotional dictionary modelling.

Pang & Lee (2008) have reviewed the different methods and applications of sentiment analysis. The researchers have discussed sentiment analysis of document level by focusing primarily on the machine learning techniques of sentiment analysis. Zhang et al. (2018) have employed deep learning techniques for sentiment analysis whereas Kim (2014) proposed an improved strategy which is based on CNN to identify the sentiments from English language text at the sentence level by utilizing dynamic and static keywords embeddings. Liu et al. (2016) proposed a hybrid technique for bilingual context incorporating deep learning attributes. Many researchers have studied sentiment analysis on languages other than English. Al-Azani & El-Alfy (2018) have classified sentiments of non-verbal features, i.e. emojis in Arabic language microblogs by employing the deep recurrent neural networks techniques. In the research article, the researchers have also compared the performance of baseline traditional learning methods and deep neural networks to reveal that the best results are attained when using bidirectional GRU. Dahou et al. (2016) have also worked on Arabic language tweets and audits for sentiment classification. Alayba et al. (2017) discussed the analysis of sentiments of Arabic health issues. Sallab et al. (2015) discussed

Arabic sentiment analysis by employing deep learning. Similarly, Abbes et al. (2017) employed deep neural networks to discover sentiments from reviews written in the Arabic language. Aziz & Tao (2016) have utilized machine learning techniques such as SVMs, Naive Bayesian, random forests and decision trees to identify the sentiments from multiple datasets of Arabic languages.

Many researchers like Ling et al. (2014), Chalothom et al. (2015), Matthew et al. (2015) have presented and discussed various applications of sentiment analysis. Kharde et al. (2016) have investigated the different approaches, including machine learning as well as vocabulary-based approaches that are used for sentiment analysis. The researchers have additionally examined the issues in extracting sentiments from unstructured and heterogeneous context. Issues like sarcasm detection, thwarted expression, entity recognition are studied by the researchers. Kharde et al. (2016) also suggested that the sentiments are classified precisely if the data in consideration is clean and less noisy. Varghese et al. (2013) have investigated the challenges involved with the sentiment analysis.

METHODOLOGY OF SENTIMENT ANALYSIS

Types of Sentiment Analysis

Analyzing the sentiments of the user from the user-generated content is generally classified into two types, as described in Figure 1:

1. **Polarity based Sentiment Analysis:** In polarity-based sentiment analysis, the expressed sentiments of the user in a document, sentence or an entity feature are grouped into three polarities, i.e. positive, negative and neutral. It implies that the consumer's opinion about the product or service in consideration could be at any one of the extremities, i.e. it could be either positive, negative or neutral. If the review by a user is, "The customer service provided by your organization is so poor, that it is killing me!", then the polarity-based sentiment classification can predict that the polarity of review is negative.

Figure 1. Types of Sentiment Analysis

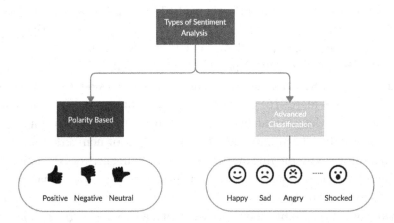

2. **Advanced classification-based sentiment analysis:** In the advanced classification-based sentiment analysis, the sentiments of the user are beyond the above-mentioned extremities. The sentiments are classified into further classification states. For instance, the user expressed sentiment can be considered on the basis of emotional states such as anger, happiness, sadness and excitement. If the review by a user is, "The customer service provided by your organization is so poor, that it is killing me!", then the advanced sentiment classification can predict that the review expresses anger of the user.

An alternative technique for evaluating the sentiments of the user in the user-generated data is the use of scaling framework. In this technique, the user's sentiments are grouped in the ranks on the scale of -10 to +10.

Levels of Sentiment Analysis

The primary aim of Sentiment Mining is to process the sentence and analyze the sentiments of a given expression and to determine the polarity of the sentiments. Sentiment analysis has been explored from various perspectives. The most prominent perspective is to classify the sentiment analysis at three levels, described as follows in Figure 2:

1. Document-level: At document-level, the overall sentiment of the whole document is determined. For the small data set, the document level sentiment analysis shows great accuracy. This stage treats the document as an individual entity. For example: If a document is written about a particular element, the aim is to evaluate the sentiment polarity for that element i.e. whether the document conveys positive, negative or neutral sentiment about the entity in consideration (Khaled et al., 2015) (Aggarwal, 2018). For instance, the reviews of a particular laptop is that it has amazing resolution and the size is sleek. The processor seems good but one can get better configurations in the said price. Thus, at document level, the overall sentiment of the customer review is evaluated to be negative.
2. Sentence-level: At the Sentence-level, the degree of examination is nearly a subjective arrangement, and the analysis at this level is restricted to the sentences and their communicated sentiments. In particular, this stage decides if each sentence communicates a positive, negative or neutral sentiment (Safrin, 2017) (Aggarwal, 2018). For the same example of the review of a particular laptop. The review will be broken down into multiple sentences and the polarity of each sentence will be determined separately.

Figure 2. Levels of Sentiment Analysis

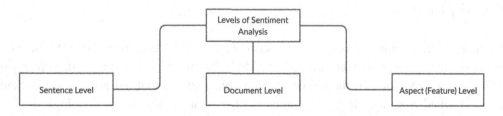

3.   Aspect (feature) level: Aspect-level sentiment analysis is more complex than the other two levels. At aspect level, instead of inspecting language constructs (like sentences, passages or documents), a finer-grained inspection of different aspects of each product is performed. Aspect level sentiment analysis first extracts the different features for a product in consideration and then discerns the polarity for the various features of that particular product. For example, different characters like size, memory, price, camera etc. of mobile will be distinguished at the first stage, and then the polarity of each of these characteristics will be determined at the second stage (Beigi et al., 2016).

Process of Sentiment Analysis

The process of perceiving and classifying the sentiments in the opinionated text, so as to find out whether the frame of mind of the user about a particular item is positive, negative or neutral, principally contains five phases: Collection of Data, Preprocessing and Text Preparation, Subjectivity Detection, Sentiment Classification and Presentation of Output.

The graphical representation of the methodology of the sentiment analysis is described in Figure 3:

A. Collection of Data

The first phase of the sentiment analysis process is Collecting data, which is the most significant phase of sentiment analysis. If the amount of the information is inadequate or the quality of the gathered information is poor, then the general performance of the model is impeded. Administration clients or product users post their emotions, opinions and experience about the products online via web-based networking media like web journals, blogs, reviews etc. Collection of data from a wide range of data sources such as blogs, micro-blogging sites, review sites and social media platforms is the primary job.

B. Preprocessing Data and Text Preparation

The second phase of the sentiment analysis process is preprocessing data and text preparation. As the opinions and emotions are communicated in various ways, with various settings of composing, technical words, utilization of short structures and slang due to which the information becomes tremendous and complicated. Manual examination of this user-generated data is basically incomprehensible. Thus, unique programming languages and strategies are utilized to process and investigate the user-generated content (Seerat & Azam, 2012). Preprocessing is the process of removal of stopwords, punctuation, numbers, emoticons, hashtags; stemming and lemmatization. In the task of text preparation, the user-generated opinionated context is filtered. It incorporates recognizing and eliminating non-literary and non-relevant data (i.e. the data which is not important to the field or subject of concentrate) from the user-generated content (Chandni et al., 2015).

C. Subjectivity Detection

The third phase of the sentiment analysis process is the subjectivity detection phase. In this phase, all the sentences of the user-generated data are reviewed for subjectivity. The sentences that convey subjective expressions are kept, whereas the sentences with objective articulations are discarded. Sentiment analysis is performed at various levels of language such as at the lexical, morphological, discourse,

Figure 3. Process of sentiment analysis

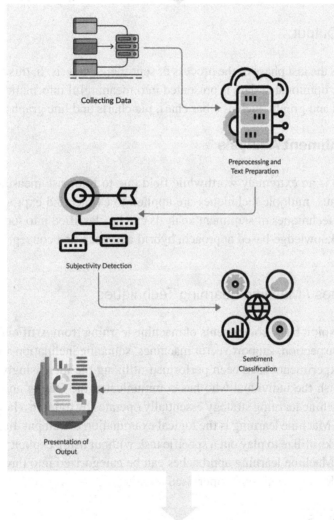

semantic and pragmatic levels, using prevalent computational procedures like Unigrams, Frequency count, lemmas and negation.

D. Sentiment Classification

The next stage of the sentiment analysis process is classifying the sentiments from the opinionated data into various categories. Sentiments are commonly categorized into three classes, i.e. positive, negative and neutral. In this stage of the sentiment analysis process, all subjective sentences are classified into the sentiment classes such as positive, negative, neutral, bad, good, like, dislike.

E. Presentation of Output

Presentation of output is the last phase of the process of sentiment analysis. In this phase, the orientation of the unstructured user opinionated data is presented into meaningful information, which is displayed in the form of diagrams and graphs such as a bar chart, pie charts and line graphs.

Techniques of Sentiment Analysis

Sentiment investigation is an extremely worthwhile field due to immense measure of information accessible on the web. Thus, multiple techniques are applied to extract and express the sentiments of a product or service. The techniques of sentiment analysis can be classified into four key categories such as statistical approach, knowledge-based approach, hybrid approach and concept-based approaches, as shown in Figure 4.

Statistical Approaches / Machine Learning Techniques

Statistical approaches exploit basic components of machine learning from Artificial Intelligent systems, for example, semantic inspection, support vector machines, semantic inclination and bag of words (Aggarwal, 2018). Many experiments have been performed utilizing the increasingly advanced strategies that attempt to distinguish the individual who has communicated the feeling and the objective of the user-generated data. Machine learning strategy essentially operates by training a large data set and learning from its experience. Machine learning is the logical examination of computation and factual models that computer frameworks utilize to play out a specific task without using explicit guidelines, relying on patterns and inference. Machine learning approaches can be categorized into three classes: supervised learning, unsupervised learning and semi-supervised learning.

Supervised Techniques

Supervised learning relies on the presence of marked data. The two datasets are utilized in this methodology. The first set of input data is also known as training data and has a known label value or result, for example, valid/invalid or value of any commodity at a time. This data is utilized for training on the selected classifier. A model is set up through a preparation procedure wherein it is required to make predictions and is adjusted when those predictions are not right. The process continues until the desired level of accuracy is not achieved on the training data. The prime reason is that the algorithm can learn

Figure 4. Techniques of Sentiment Analysis

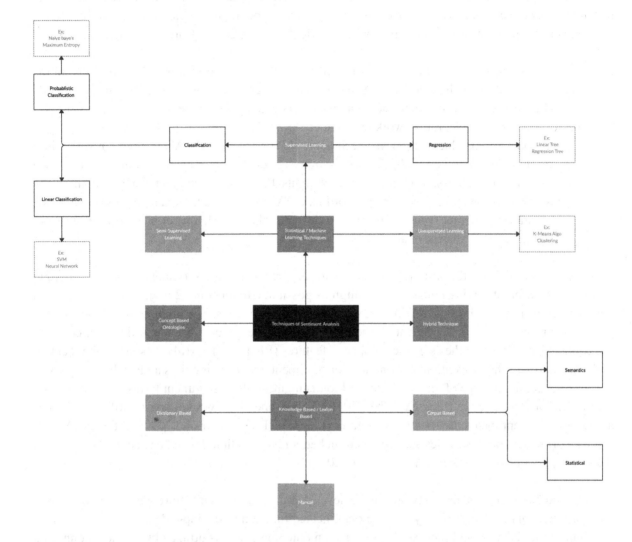

by analyzing and comparing the actual values with the instructed values to discover the extremity of the sentiments. The second set of data is the unlabeled test data on which this learnt ability is applied to predict the label values known as classes (Kamble & Itkikar, 2018) (Yadlapalli et al., 2019).

Thus, it can be implied that in supervised learning, all data is marked and the machine is trained for every input with a particular target. The input variable (X) and the output variable (Y) is known. Y =f(X) The machine has to predict the function f that maps X to Y. The common problems of supervised learning are further categorized into two methodologies: classification and regression (Ahmad et al., 2017). If the output variable is a category, like 'costly' or 'cheap', then the problem is called a classification problem. If the output variable is a real value, like 'price', then the problem is a regression problem (Medhat et al., 2014) (Samal et al., 2017) (Sharma et al., 2019).

1.   **Classification problem:**

The classification problem is generally about identifying or predicting a label. It filters the data in different classes, e.g. when given some comment; the data can be filtered out as 'positive' or 'negative'. Classification can be linear as well as probabilistic (Medhat et al., 2014) (Kamble & Itkikar, 2018).

a. Linear classification: A linear classifier identifies the class of an object based on the value of the linear combination of characteristics. A linear classifier can represent any mapping that is linearly separable. There are various types of linear classifiers, among which the most popular are Support Vector Machine and Neural Network (Medhat et al., 2014) (Kamble & Itkikar, 2018).

    i. Support Vector Machine (SVM): A Support Vector Machine (SVM) is a type of supervised machine learning, that is also known as high edge classifiers. This technique is mainly used to segregate (or classify) multiple types of inputs. Each individual input can be hypothetically represented on a plane as a single coordinate. SVMs are used to create a hypothetical plane separating different types of inputs into different classes (Medhat et al., 2014) (Kamble & Itkikar, 2018) (Sharma et al., 2019).

In sentiment analysis, the text is divided by a hyperplane as per the sentiments where the margin between the different sentiment classes is as high as possible (Bhuta et al., 2014). This technique can deal with enormous feature spaces with a large number of dimensions. The learning capability of support vector machines is not dependent on the dimensions of the feature space as it does not compute the complexity of the hypothesis by the number of features (Bhuta et al., 2014). In spite of the fact that SVM outflanks all the conventional techniques for sentiment classification, it is a black box strategy. It is hard to examine the type of classification and to distinguish which sentiment terms are increasingly significant for classification (Sharma & Dey, 2012). This is one of the weaknesses of utilizing SVM as a technique for sentiment classification (Bhuta et al., 2014). There are various possibilities in SVM. It can take off some outlier samples and still result in better classification. It can be used to classify more than two types of inputs as well (Chandni et al., 2015).

    ii. Neural Network: A neural network can be defined as a complex architecture with numerous layers of interconnected units. Every unit is a complicated function of the input data. From the previous unit, input is taken and processed to provide an outcome which is utilized by the next connected unit. All these connected units are individually known as the neuron, and the whole combined architecture is known as a Neural Network. The values processed to the functions of each unit are acquired as the training of the neural network. The neural system replicates the above behaviour to learn about gathered information and to predict the outcomes (Ouyang et al., 2015).

All the neural networks consist of one input and one output layer whose design is application-specific. For instance, in the process of sentiment analysis, the sentences that need to be analyzed can be considered as the input, and the classifier which would yield the sentiment to be positive, negative or neutral can be the output.

The inner layers of the neural network are known as hidden layers. A neural network can have a number of hidden layers, and each hidden layer can have several units. Every unit (which is also known as a neuron) influences the overall outcome. As every unit can only influence the overall result just marginally, the impact is magnified when that result goes through a few layers of neurons and provides extremely precise outcomes (Aggarwal et al., 2019).

b.   Probabilistic classification: Probabilistic classifier is a classifier which works on probability and is able to estimate a probabilistic distribution over a set of classes rather than giving a class to which an object belongs to. Probability classification can be done using Naïve Bayes or Maximum Entropy Techniques.

i.   Naïve Bayes: Naive Bayes algorithm is a supervised machine learning technique in the family of sample probabilistic classifiers which is based on the probabilistic methodology. This algorithm is primarily utilized for training the classifiers, which are then employed to classify the sentiments in a text. The main principle behind this methodology is the assumption that the features are independent of each other as it is based on BOWs and does not take the position of features in the text into consideration (Sharma et al., 2019). This technique is one of the least complex and common techniques for the training of the classifier. It is based on the likelihood of occurrence of feature words in the document. It utilizes Bayes Theorem to foresee the likelihood that a given list of features has a place with a specific label (Kamble & Itkikar, 2018). The probability that a sentiment (ST) occurs in a given sentence (SN) is determined by the rule: "P(ST/SN) =P(ST)P(SN/ST)/P(SN)" (Ahmad et al., 2017) (Kamble & Itkikar, 2018).

The prime advantage of this methodology is that this technique is easy to interpret, and the outcomes are determined proficiently (Ahmad et al., 2017). One of the major disadvantages is the presumption that the features are independent of each other in the feature space (Desai & Mehta, 2016) (Ahmad et al., 2017).

ii.   Maximum entropy classifier: The maximum entropy classifier is also a probabilistic classifier like Naïve Bayes except that it doesn't assume that features act independently. It is associated with the category of exponential models. It is employed mainly when very little information is available about the prior distributions. The distribution of the feature should be as uniform as possible, which implies that it should have the highest possible entropy. The distribution is constrained to be the least non-uniform (Bhuta et al., 2014).

It is normally used in sentiment analysis for text classification where the words are not independent. The time required for training is more in Maximum entropy as compared to Naïve Bayes (Sharef et al.,2016). The major advantage of this methodology is that it does not experience the ill effects of the independence assumption (Bhuta et al., 2014). Whereas, due to the evaluation of constraints from the labelled data, the data could be inadequate and dispersed, which may cause the technique to experience the issues of overfitting. To enhance the performance remarkably a prior for all the features can be introduced.

2.   Regression Problem

Unlike classification problems, where output is a discrete value, regression problems have continuous values. The different regression algorithms are linear regression, regression trees etc. Predicting the temperature in a city is a regression problem because it is a real value whereas predicting the trend in the stock market is not a regression problem because it is a discrete value(rise/fall).

Unsupervised Techniques

Supervised learning techniques employ labelled information which is difficult to produce and gather the labelled data for training. Whereas collecting the unlabeled user-generated data is simpler and is possible in great quantity from web-based sources. It can be gathered either by utilizing a few of the prevailing tools or by building custom tools to capture the user-generated data. As the unsupervised techniques do not employ the usage of the labelled data, thus, the limitation of labelled training data can be controlled by utilizing unsupervised methods for sentiment analysis. Unsupervised techniques need enormous amounts of training data. This is the primary issue of employing unsupervised techniques. Regardless of the issues, this methodology tenders an approach to get information from the unannotated user-generated data (Pang & Lee, 2008).

Unsupervised techniques include K- means technique. K-means clustering is one of the fundamental and popular approaches for data clustering. It is an iterative algorithm and is based on partition of data into clusters. The input to this algorithm is the count of vital clusters and it yields the centroids of the clusters as the outputs. In the initial step of this algorithm, "n" arbitrary data entries are selected as the centroids and in every successive step, all other data entries are allotted to their nearest centroid on the basis of the euclidean distance. In the next progression, the centroid is recalibrated as the average of all the data entries that are assigned to the particular cluster. These steps are repeated until the desired distance value is achieved or they have no modification. The sentiment score is awarded on the basis of the cluster they belong to. The k-means approach is a simple and fast technique. The small and noisy data can induce high sparseness in the dataset, which inturn reduces the efficiency of the approach (Zul et al., 2018) (Orkphol et al., 2019) (Wu et al., 2019).

Semi-Supervised Techniques

This model uses both supervised and unsupervised approaches. It uses both unlabeled as well as labelled data to gain knowledge, which is not there in Supervised or Unsupervised learning.

This approach was proposed because of the absence of volume of labelled data. In the semi-supervised techniques, unlabeled data is used to gain information about the knowledge about joint distribution over classification attributes as this data does not include information about the different categories of sentiments in the user-generated data. Due to the absence of volume of labelled data, employing the semi-supervised approaches would yield better outcomes as compared to the supervised approaches. Semi-supervised approaches also have an advantage over the non-supervised approaches as the semi-supervised approaches include some prior knowledge into the unsupervised models. Most commonly used semi-supervised learning algorithms are generative models, multi-view learning, graph-based methods, and self-training (Gieseke et al., 2012) (Shahnawaj & Astya, 2017).

Knowledge-Based (Rule/lexicon) Approach

Knowledge-based Approaches for sentiment analysis utilizes the sentiment dictionaries with sentiment reflecting words and compare it with data under consideration to determine the polarity of the sentiments (Andrea et al., 2017). This technique classifies the opinionated data on the occurrence of unequivocal influence expressions, for example, tragic, cheerful, exhausted, and terrified. Few knowledge bases additionally allot abstract words a presumably liking to certain feelings along with the record of evident influence terms. The task of creating a sentiment lexicon can be accomplished in three ways as follows (Vohra & Teraiya, 2013):

1. **Manual Construction Approach:** It is a very monotonous, wearying and time-consuming process and thus is rarely used nowadays.
2. **Dictionary Based Approach:** In the dictionary-based approach, the words that reflect the sentiments of the users are gathered manually. The orientation of these words is known apriori. Then the collection of words are developed gradually via looking through words in Corpora or thesaurus for their opposites and equivalent words. This cycle is terminated when there are no more words left to explore. The limitation of the dictionary-based approach is that it is not reliable to discover the sentiments of the user corresponding to the domain specification (Kumar & Sebastian, 2012).
3. **Corpus-Based Approach:** Corpus-based methodology eliminates the issues of dictionary-based approach. It acquires the sentiment labels as well as the context which is generally utilized in machine learning techniques. The accuracy of this method is also relatively high. But this methodology is not as proficient as a dictionary-based methodology as it requires an enormous corpus to enclose the terms of English language, which is a very tedious process. Regardless of this drawback, this approach is commonly employed as a result of its huge preferred function of furnishing the sentiment terms with domain-specific polarities. This approach uses two different techniques, namely, Statistical and Semantic.

The main advantage of knowledge-based approaches general knowledge sentiment lexicons has more extensive term inclusion. One of the major limitations of this technique is the finite count of phrases and terms in the lexicons, which might cause difficulty in determining sentiments from dynamic environments. Another challenge with this technique is that dictionaries allocate a fixed sentiment polarity and score to the opinion terms without considering the utilization of these opinion terms in the data under consideration (Andrea et al., 2017).

Hybrid Approaches

This methodology utilizes statistical as well as the lexicon-based techniques. It incorporates the advantages of both the approaches – stability and readability of knowledge-based approach and high performance and accuracy from a supervised machine learning approach. Implementing the statistical and knowledge-based techniques combined helps in enhancing the performance and accuracy of the process of sentiment analysis. The advantages of hybrid techniques include lexicon-learning symbiosis, detection and analysis of sentiments at the concept level and lesser sensitivity to modifications in the subject domain. The disadvantage of this technique is that the data with noise (i.e. data that contains superfluous and unrelated terms for the topic of the review) are generally associated with unbiased tags as this approach is unsuccessful in identifying any sentiment (Andrea et al., 2017).

Concept-Based Ontologies

Ontologies can be described as "explicit, machine-readable specification of a shared conceptualization" (Studer et al., 1998). Ontologies are utilized for exhibiting the expressions in a domain of interest as well as to represent the association between these expressions. Ontologies can be implemented in and are now applied in different fields such as Sentimental analysis. Ontologies are employed as the principal mode of knowledge presented in the Semantic Web. This approach uses a huge knowledge-base, and with this, we can analyze the conceptual information of natural language opinion behind multiword expressions. Sentimental analysis often uses web ontologies for semantic networks. In Concept-based Ontologies techniques, the primary task is to create an ontology that comprises features, their attributes and components, that were discussed by individuals who are vigorously offering their opinions on the social web. The ontology can be generated in Web Ontology Language (OWL). After developing an ontology, the created ontology is then utilized for extraction of the object-features and attributes from the specified domain. The data collected is preprocessed, and then the input vector for classification is created. The output is the data categorized into three categories of sentiments, i.e. positive, negative or neutral. In the event of determining the sentiments via concept-based ontologies techniques, the feature extraction is a simple and time-efficient process (Kumar & Joshi, 2017).

APPLICATIONS OF SENTIMENT ANALYSIS

With the evolution of the Internet, an individual's lifestyle has been changed to being highly revealing of their perspectives and expressions. This inclination assisted the researchers in receiving consumer-produced data. The user-generated content can be utilized by sentiment analysis for various tasks. The major application tasks of sentiment analysis are shown in Figure 5:

1. **Purchasing Product or Service:** Buying an item or service is no longer a troublesome errand. Using sentiment analysis, one can assess another's conclusion and experience about any item or administration without much difficulty. Thus, making the comparison of the items with the contending brands easier. At present, individuals would not prefer to depend on an external expert. Sentiment Analysis is employed to obtain consumer's opinions and sentiments from the web content and analyze it to present them in a highly structured and understandable manner.

Figure 5. Application tasks of Sentiment Analysis

2. **Quality Improvement in Product or service:** The producers can gather the public's sentiments and opinions of products and services through sentiment analysis and thus one can improve the quality of the products with respect to the criticism and favourable opinions received. The online product reviews can be collected from websites like Amazon, Rotten Tomatoes and IMDb.

3. **Marketing research:** Sentiment Analysis techniques can be used for marketing research. The recent trends of the buyers about some products and services or the ongoing frame of mind of the overall population towards some new government strategy can be investigated by the process of sentiment analysis. In this way, sentiment analysis can contribute to the collective intelligent research.

4. **Recommendation Systems:** Sentiment analysis can be employed in recommendation systems. The sentiments and opinions of the individuals can be assessed as positive, negative and neutral. The framework can suggest individuals, the products with positive sentiments and avoid those with negative responses of the user.

5. **Detection of "flame":** Analyzing the user-generated content of social media can be done effectively by the process of sentiment analysis. Arrogant expressions, over warmed words or contempt language utilized in messages, discussion passages or tweets on different web sources, can be detected automatically in sentiment analysis.

6. **Spam Review Detection:** Since the web can be accessed by everyone, anyone can post anything on the web; this enhanced the probability of spam data on the web. In the world of online reviews, where there are genuine reviews, there exists a lot of spam reviews also which can be given by some individuals or maybe the organizations themselves for their advertisement. Detection of spam reviews is a big application in sentiment analysis, e.g. an e-mail may be considered as 'spam' or 'not spam'. This task has a great impact on industrial communities also.

7. **Policy-Making:** Sentiment analysis techniques are used by the policymakers to take people's perspective towards policies into consideration and to utilize this data to make new policies.

8. **Decision Making:** User's sentiments and opinions are extremely valuable components in the decision-making process. Sentiment analysis provides analyzed sentiments of the users, which can be viably utilized in the process of decision making.

As discussed above, it is contemplated that sentiment analysis is a fast-growing tool used in the world of Natural Language Processing in order to detect and evaluate the user's emotions, feelings, views and different perspectives about a certain product or service, and can be utilized to perform various tasks. Sentiment analysis is an advanced stage of data mining which utilizes different processes to extract the information from a certain unstructured text, and it has gained a lot of popularity because of the implementation of these tasks in versatile applications in the various fields. Some of the applications are as displayed by Figure 6:

1. **Social Media:** People use social networking sites nowadays to express their views in many contexts. The media may be Facebook, Twitter, etc. The current issues are discussed on social networking websites through blogs or different forums, which gives researchers an opportunity to analyze the text in various forms and come up with even better algorithms.

2. **Industries or business organization:** Sentiment analysis plays a significant role in the business world. Industries can take the survey of their products or services from their consumers and hence improve the same. Different customers will have different views about some product and service.

Figure 6. Application areas of Sentiment Analysis

And the data set is quite large to manually deal with. Hence a sentiment analysis or opinion mining tool will prove to be very helpful in understanding the average customer reviews.

3. **Education:** In the education field also, sentiment analysis plays a significant role. Since the feedback is taken by the students or parents at the end of the session, the analysis of this feedback will give way out to improve the teaching-learning process. The faculty will come to know the expectations of the students and the limitations of self. This analysis may help the faculty to improve his teaching methods. Not only this, it can be quite helpful for the management also like if they get the summarized feedback of faculty through an automated analysis tool, thus the appraisal process can be done in an efficient manner.

4. **E-Commerce:** Purchasing and selling of products and services online are known as e-commerce. Sentiment analysis is very helpful in this context. If a person wants to buy something online, he can take a survey of the reviews given by other persons who bought the same product, before buying one. If all the reviews are analyzed and summarized, it will save a great deal of time and effort of the buyer. Sentiment analysis can assist in summarizing the different reviews. Similarly, if a user wants to sell something, he can take a survey of the market before actually quoting the price of his product.

5. **Finance Sector:** Sentiment analysis plays a significant role in the finance sector. A user can look at the market trends before investing in the stock market. Monitoring of financial news on the web can be done with the help of automatic sentiment detection tools.

6. **Hospitality industry:** People share their experiences about their travels like hotels or travel providers. Many sites which are very popular for this are TripAdvisor, Trivago etc. Before getting the bookings done, people look for reviews of other users and analyze them manually to reach any conclusion. If some automated analysis tool is available for analyzing the reviews, the task becomes much easier. Not only the customers are benefited from this, but also the hotel management authorities and travel providers can improve their services by looking at the analysis of feedback given by customers.

7. **Politics:** The views of voters about various issues can be analyzed by politicians in order to work in a better way. During elections, various surveys take place, which, when analyzed, can help a common man in deciding the right candidate.

8. **Entertainment:** In the field of entertainment, sentiment analysis plays an essential role. People look at the reviews of a movie or play or any other event before watching them. From the several

reviews, if the feature-based extraction is done like the story of a movie is good, the direction is bad, casting is good, the music is very good, and so on, then a user can easily decide whether to go for that movie or not based on his preferences about different features of a movie.

9. **Medical sector:** The views of doctors and patients about a particular treatment or medicine can help the authorities to work in a particular direction, e.g. if a particular procedure is reviewed as costly by many patients, then the price factor may be reconsidered for future perspectives.

CHALLENGES OF SENTIMENT ANALYSIS

The principal purpose of the sentiment analysis is to acquire the expressed sentiments from the unstructured user opinionated data and to categorize the sentiment into three classes of sentiment orientation, i.e. positive, negative or neutral. But recognizing the polarity words is a strenuous and complex procedure, and it faces many difficulties as users rarely express their sentiments in the same way. Thus, there are numerous aspects due to which sentiment analysis is considered complicated and difficult. Some of these challenges are exhibited in Figure 7, are:

Figure 7. Challenges of Sentiment Analysis

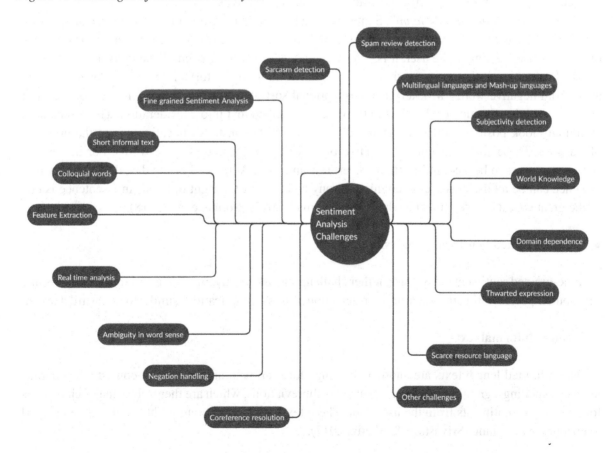

- **Spam review detection:**

Social web networks are represented by obscurity and anonymity of their clients, which might be utilized to misguide different clients on web networks. On the one hand, the surveys and reviews on a specific service or product are exceptionally useful, but on the other hand, there are many fake and phoney reviews too. These fake reviews mislead the users by presenting undeserving positive assessments and untruthful negative assessments. An individual or some association to promote or ruin the overall rating of a specific product or service in political aspects as well as in other areas where the posted reviews can influence user's evaluation of the product or service in consideration might publish the spam reviews and surveys. These spams and fake reviews make sentiment analysis worthless in many application areas. Identifying these phoney (spam) reviews from non-spam sentiments is a major test in the field of sentiment analysis. The issue for sentiment analysis is to build up the appropriate systems and advanced techniques for recognizing and filtering non-spam reviews from the spams in the user opinionated data. Despite the fact that numerous researches have been done in this area in order to overcome this challenge, yet it still is a major concern in the process of sentiment analysis (Seerat & Azam, 2012).

- **Sarcasm detection:**

According to Wikipedia (2020), Sarcasm can be characterized as "*a sharp, bitter, or cutting expression or remark; a bitter gibe or taunt*". Sentences in a text might be straight forward as well as sarcastic sentences. Sarcastic sentences are an extraordinary kind of sentences which characterize the converse of the expressed feeling of the user. It is constantly indicated utilizing strengthened positive or positive words. Posting sarcastic messages via web-based networking media turns into another fashion to stay away from negative words. Mockery is an exceptional sort of sentiment expression that, for the most part, reverses the direction of the view in the user opinionated text into consideration. These sentences commonly look positive; however, the overall orientation demonstrates negative due to the presence of sarcasm. These sentences convey negative opinions by employing positive words. For instance: a sentence appears to be a compliment; however, it is an insult. At the end of the day, the extremity of a sentence can be a false positive. Recognizing irony and finding the right opinions in a sentence is one of the greatest tests for sentiment analysis (Mohammad, 2017) (Soman et al., 2018).

- **Fine-grained Sentiment Analysis**

Fine-grained sentiment analysis is another challenging task. Analyzing the fine grains sentiments like a rumour, aspect identification, and emotion detection possess complications similar to sarcasm detection.

- **Short informal text**

These limited length texts are another challenge for sentiment analysis. They consist of numerous incorrect spellings, grammatical errors, slang and abbreviations, which are themselves major challenges for analysis of sentiments from the user data. These texts also incorporate hashtags that are employed to encourage searching (Srivastava & Bhatia, 2017).

- **Colloquial words / Abbreviations and slangs**

Using slang and abbreviations is a fashion statement nowadays. There are a large number of slangs and abbreviations that are utilized in communication. To analyze the text while considering these slangs and abbreviations is a major challenge that is to be handled while working with sentiment analysis.

- **Feature Extraction**

To distinguish the attributes of a product or service in consideration is an immensely exhausting and difficult process. If the attributes of the object are not distinguished accurately, then the polarity of the sentiments expressed cannot be determined appropriately (Seerat & Azam, 2012).

- **Real-time analysis**

Static information can be analyzed effectively with contrast to the real-time dynamic data (Ebrahimi et al., 2017). With the expansion in the utilization of social media websites, enormous information is accessible for sentiment mining that increases the requirement for an automated system.

- **Sentiment analysis on audio and video**

Numerous explorers are continuing for content examination in the field of sentiment mining. Along with the text documents, user opinions about a particular product and service can be as audio and video data. Thus the information obtained in the form of audio and video data should be analyzed additionally. But analyzing and determining sentiments from the audio and video content is a very strenuous task.

- **Ambiguity in word sense**

This problem arises when the same term can have diverse interpretations in various contexts. It increases the efforts to develop language-oriented vocabularies and lexicons. In some situations, it also reduces the precision of interpretation of different dialects into the English language. For example, Smaller size would be considered as a positive opinion for laptop chargers, but the same phrase would be regarded as negative if the object in consideration is the cinema multiplex. Thus, to investigate the significance and accurate context of a word is a challenging task.

- **Negation handling**

Negations in a sentence are used to inverse the extremity of that sentence. Negation words like no, not, never etc. are used to reverse the polarity of the sentiments. For instance: "The novel is boring", is a negative polarity sentence whereas "the novel is not boring", is a positive polarity sentence due to the utilization of the negation keyword "not". Negation handling is thus one of the largest challenges, and if not handled properly, the results would be disastrous (Soman et al., 2018).

- **Coreference resolution**

Coreference resolution is the process of discovering all expressions that are concerned with the same object in the given text. In sentences that contain two or more expressions that indicate the same entity then one expression is usually an antecedent and the other expressions are an anaphor (i.e. a truncated structure) (Sonagi & Gore, 2013). For instance: We went to the picnic and had lunch; it was terrible. In this sentence, one needs to determine the reference of "it" in relation to the picnic and dinner. Coreference resolution improves the precision of sentiment analysis as it provides detailed information (Vohra & Teraiya, 2013). If the expressions and phrases referring to the same entity are not identified accurately, then it makes it difficult to understand the sentiments, and it also impacts the accuracy of the sentiment analysis (Vohra & Teraiya, 2013).

- **Multilingual languages and Mashup languages**

Most of the research has been performed in the English language. Thus, most of the tools, libraries and resources have been generated and are available only for the English language. As a large percentage of people around the world are non-native English speakers, thus there is a need to analyze the sentiments from other languages. But due to the different characteristics of the languages (like Arabic, Chinese, German) and limited available resources (El-beltagy & Ali 2013), it is difficult to process the sentiments of the text of these languages. Employing the resources of English to analyze the sentiments from other languages is very cumbersome, and the results are mainly unreliable. Along with other languages, analyzing the mashup languages like Hinglish, which is a combination of Hindi and English, is critical for the analyzers (Soman et al., 2018).

- **Scarce resource language (Sentiment Analysis of data in mother tongue)**

Analysis of sentiments for scarce resource language is a challenge. Those languages and dialects whose annotated corpus, resources and tools are limited or unavailable; their reviews need to be translated into other languages like English for sentiment analysis (Soman et al., 2018).

- **Thwarted expression**

Sometimes, there are sentences where a small number of contents determines the overall polarity (Nasukawa & Yi, 2003) (Vohra & Teraiya, 2013) (Collomb et al., 2014) (Soman et al., 2018). For instance, the cinematography was admirable, the acting was decent, and songs were nice, but the movie is crappy. In such cases, an easy bag of words approach is not suitable as the majority of terms used are positive, but the principal sentiment is negative due to the critical final sentence. In traditional sentiment analysis, the sentence would have been classified as positive due to the greater importance to the word frequency than the word presence.

- **Domain dependence**

Sentiment analysis profoundly relies on the domain. If the domain from where the training data is obtained and classifier are prepared differently from the domain of the test data, then it performs ineffectively. In general, the words that are utilized for communicating the sentiments have different orientations in different domains, which makes it a very challenging task (Vohra & Teraiya, 2013) (Soman et al., 2018).

- **World Knowledge**

To analyze the sentiments of the user from the user opinionated data, sometimes it is important to have the information about the new trends, facts and history of the world. For instance: to analyze the sentence and predict its polarity, "There is no difference between the character of him and Hitler", the system must have the knowledge about the character of Hitler, else the sentence will not be classified into the appropriate sentiment polarity category (Vohra & Teraiya 2013).

- **Subjectivity detection**

Subjectivity detection is also one of the major challenges that are encountered by sentiment analysis (Pang & Lee, 2008) (Soman et al., 2018). Subjectivity detection is the process of differentiating between opinionated and non-opinionated phrases. In sentiment analysis, the strategy of determining subjectivity is one of the crucial activities and is utilized to predict objective phrases. Subjectivity detection is an extremely challenging task for humans as well as for machines with limited emotional potential as the exhibited sentiment can be associated with the same entity as well as with the overall objective of the sentiment analysis (Soman et al., 2018). In real-life applications, the user needs to comprehend the sentiments accurately, thus demands exhaustive and elaborate sentiment analysis of text, which necessitates the characterization of subjective and objective phrases (Liu, 2010). If the subjectivity is determined accurately, it can enhance the system performance (Soman et al., 2018).

- **Other challenges**

Some of the other challenges that are faced by the sentiment analysis are due to the Bipolar words (Ghaleb & Vijendran, 2017) and Grammatical Errors. When a huge amount of data is considered for sentiment analysis, some of the data might be grammatically wrong. To discover the sentiment polarity of a sentence, the grammatical mistakes are to be managed. Sometimes, the data to be analyzed contains noise along with the relevant required data. This noise needs to be filtered before analyzing the data that makes the sentiment analysis task complicated. Thus, noise removal is another challenge that sentiment analysis deals with.

ISSUES RELATED TO SENTIMENT ANALYSIS AND NLP

Natural language processing deals with the manipulation of natural language (i.e. language used by humans) by utilizing computers and artificial intelligence to process and analyze vast amounts of natural language data for various applications like automatic summarization to disease prediction.

It is evident that despite the wide range of applications of Natural language processing, it faces various challenges which are briefly described below:

- **Ambiguity:** One of the major challenges of NLP is the ambiguity of expressions in a text that has variable context. In natural language, many phrases have various interpretations depending on the context in which they are being assessed. The same expression in the sentence can have various implications depending on the manner of interpretation. The ambiguity in a text can be Lexical ambiguity, Syntactic ambiguity or Semantic ambiguity.

- **Personality, intention and style:** An idea can be communicated in various styles depending on the goal or intention in a particular situation. Some of the opinions have contrary polarities than the actual one. These expressions could be ironic or sarcastic and thus would have different inclination from the original sentence. Sarcasm and irony detection in natural language is a major challenge.
- **Grammatical and spelling errors:** The detection and recovery of grammatical and spelling mistakes is a highly demanding and challenging task. Sometimes, accurate words are mapped as mistakes and erroneously used phrases such as homophones are distinguished as correct ones causing a lot of trouble in natural language processing.
- **Named Entity Recognition:** Named Entity recognition is one of the tasks of Natural language processing. In this task, explicit words and expressions are distinguished and classified for different entities like people, area or qualities (Aronson, 2011). This task is made difficult by word order variation, derivation by the usage of suffixes and prefixes, synonymy and polysemy (Nadkarni et al., 2011).
- **Negations:** Some words in natural language are used to inverse the polarity of the intended meaning.
- **Colloquial words:** Abbreviations and slangs used in natural language made the processing difficult and a challenging task. Most of these words are not present in the dictionary of the original language.

As sentiment analysis is considered as a branch of Natural Language Processing intended to mine various sources of data for opinions and sentiment extraction and classification. But there are several issues which pose a barrier in carrying out the fair evaluation of sentiments and makes it unrealistic and difficult to detect and analyze the sentiments. As shown, some of those issues are Colloquial words, negation handling, ambiguity in word sense, coreference resolution, sarcasm detection and bipolar words. Most of these challenges are due to NLP constructs which restrict in-depth investigation of sentiments in a given text, thus impacting the process of sentiment analysis and making this a formidable task. Therefore, it is concluded that Sentiment analysis is a restricted Natural Language Processing (NLP) problem.

SOLUTIONS AND RECOMMENDATIONS

- RNN for ambiguity: The advanced deep learning methodology for analyzing sentiments is employed for morphology, language syntax and semantics. Recursive neural networks (RNN) is considered the best one for this purpose. The advancements of Recursive neural networks are valuable for eliminating ambiguity and for tasks that employ grammatical tree structure. It is also supportive of tasks that refer to certain specified phrases. For situations that involve nested hierarchy and an intrinsic recursive structure, Recursive neural networks are considered ideal for them. The syntactic principles of language are exceptionally recursive. Thus, the recursive structure is exploited through a model that regards it. An additional advantage of designing sentences with RNN is that the phrases and sentences with variable length can be taken as an input. Moreover, the RNN works more efficiently than the other methodologies for semantic segmentation.

- Deep learning for sarcasm detection: Sarcasm detection is one of the crucial challenges of Natural Language Processing (NLP) as well as sentiment analysis. Deep learning methodologies prove to be very effective and accurate in analyzing the polarity of the sentiments from the sarcastic text. Kumar et al. (2017) proposed a specified deep learning-based model which is based on CNN-LSTM-FF architecture. This technique which is known as deep neural networks (DNNs) performed better than all the previous techniques, and it exhibits the most significant level of accuracy for numerical sarcasm identification. DNN was not just the best for numerical sarcasm; it was better than all other sarcasm detection approaches as well. Ghosh & Veale (2016) proposed another model which is a fusion of a convolutional neural network, a long short-term memory (LSTM) network, and a DNN. This integrated model was an improvement over the previous models like recursive support vector machines (SVMs).
- Another researcher, Al-kabi et al. (2014), has applied lexicon-based methods that depend on POS tagging. The technique is applied to the dataset that deals with the emoticons, chat data and Arabizi. This technique overcame the issues related to domain dependence and multilingual challenges and determined the polarity of the sentiments from the dataset with an accuracy of 93.9% (Hussein, 2018).
- Languages other than English, for instance: Japanese, Arabic and Chinese generally do not possess definite word boundary markers, and thus tokenization is not a necessity. Instead, it requires word segmentation, which is a critical issue for languages other than English. Conditional Random Fields (CRFs) (Lafferty et al., 2001) have been applied that proved to be a success to resolve this complication. CRFs have exhibited better results than hidden Markov models and maximum- entropy Markov models (Kudo et al., 2004) (Peng et al., 2004) (Tseng et al., 2005). In another attempt, word embeddings and deep learning-based methodologies have been applied to the Chinese word segmentation (Chen et al., 2015) (Ma et al., 2015) (Sun et al., 2017).

FUTURE RESEARCH DIRECTIONS

In the past few years, deep learning and soft computing techniques have progressed due to its practical and promising application in the field of sentiment analysis. Deep learning is an advancement over the traditional methods due to the machine's capacity to learn on its own and develop. Deep learning algorithms employing neural networks are immensely powerful and understand sentiments better than the traditional approaches. Recursive and Recurrent Neural Networks specifically LSTMs and GRUs can be further explored to overcome the challenges faced by sentiment analysis.

Hybrid techniques have performed satisfactorily but their utilization for implicit sentiment analysis can be investigated further. As shown that deep learning techniques can resolve and limit the challenges faced by the sentiment analysis due to NLP constructs. An interesting progression to pursue in this regard is to move towards deep learning and soft computing techniques along with their integrated techniques in the field of natural language to resolve restricted issues of sentiment analysis. This endeavour will be very rewarding and will attempt in uncovering the useful hidden information from the user generated data. Deep learning and soft computing will be key for stepping forward in the process of improving the accuracy of the tasks of sentiment analysis as well as it can be employed to solve the open problems discussed in the chapter. The solutions to many such problems have been provided in the chapter. However, many challenges in this field of study remain unsolved. More future research could be dedicated to these challenges. The chapter has uncovered many interesting open challenges that can be promising directions for future research.

CONCLUSION

With the tremendous increase in the online reviews, opinions, recommendations, ratings, and feedback by the people, in the past decade, the focus on the content generated by the user has also proliferated. This wealth of information is thus rewarding for organizations and individuals for various purposes. In this chapter, an overview of sentiment analysis has been presented. The sentiment analysis can be applied on various levels and thus different levels of sentiment analysis as well as the process of sentiment analysis has been explained in detail. The various methodology and techniques, i.e. statistical approach, knowledge-based approach, hybrid approach and concept-based approaches, employed for analyzing the sentiments have been explored and described. This newly produced knowledge from analyzing the sentiments can be successfully employed in the various application domains, as explained in the chapter.

The focus of the chapter has been on the challenges faced by the Sentiment analysis. The major challenges of sentiment analysis like spam review detection, sarcasm detection, colloquial words, multimodal data analysis, negation handling, real-time analysis, multilingual and mashup languages; that still needs to be overcome have been discussed. Despite the numerous researches being done in the field of sentiment analysis, there are some Natural Language Processing (NLP) related issues being faced by sentiment analysis. Most of the issues that are faced by the sentiment analysis are due to the natural language constructs. Some of these issues are colloquial words, negation keywords, ambiguity, coreference resolution. It is evident that these challenges impact the process of Sentiment Analysis and makes it difficult to understand the sentiments. Few of the issues have been resolved using deep learning and advanced integration techniques that have been discussed in the chapter. The basic constructs of the natural language impose restrictions on the analyzing of the sentiments from the user-generated data and making this a formidable task. It acts as a barrier to the advancements in this area. Thus, it can be inferred that the sentiment analysis is a restricted Natural Language Processing (NLP) problem.

ACKNOWLEDGMENT

We would like to thank the scholars of Web Research Group, Department of Computer Science and Engineering, Delhi Technological University for their constant support during the preparation of this manuscript. We would also like to thank "www.flaticon.com" to provide the icons for our figures.

REFERENCES

Abbes, M., Kechaou, Z., & Alimi, A. M. (2017). Enhanced deep learning models for sentiment analysis in Arab social media. *International Conference on Neural Information Processing*. 667-676. 10.1007/978-3-319-70139-4_68

Aggarwal, D., Bali, V., & Mittal, S. (2019). An insight into machine learning techniques for Predictive Analysis and Feature Selection. *International Journal of Innovative Technology and Exploring Engineering*, *8*(9S), 342–349. doi:10.35940/ijitee.I1055.0789S19

Aggarwal, D. G. (2018). *Review Paper Sentiment Analysis: An Insight into Techniques, Application and Challenges*. Academic Press.

Ahmad, M., Aftab, S., Muhammad, S. S., & Ahmad, S. (2017). Machine Learning Techniques for Sentiment Analysis: A Review. *International Journal of Multidisciplinary Sciences and Engineering.*, *8*(3), 27–32.

Ainur, Y., Yisong, Y., & Claire, C. (2010). Multi-level structured models for document-level sentiment classification. *Proceedings of the 2010 Conference on Empirical Methods in Natural Language Processing*, 1046–1056.

Al-Azani, S., & El-Alfy, E. (2018). Emojis-Based Sentiment Classification of Arabic Microblogs Using Deep Recurrent Neural Networks. *2018 International Conference on Computing Sciences and Engineering (ICCSE)*, 1-6. 10.1109/ICCSE1.2018.8374211

Al-kabi, Gigieh, Alsmadi, & Wahsheh. (2014). *Opinion Mining and Analysis for Arabic Language*. Academic Press.

Alayba, A. M., Palade, V., England, M., & Iqbal, R. (2017). Arabic language sentiment analysis on health services. *2017 1st International Workshop on Arabic Script Analysis and Recognition (ASAR)*, 114-118.

Andrea, A. D., Ferri, F., Grifoni, P., Guzzo, T. (2015). Approaches, Tools and Applications for Sentiment Analysis Implementation. *International Journal of Computer Applications, 125*(3), 26-33.

Aronson, A. R. (2001). Effective mapping of biomedical text to the UMLS Metathesaurus: the MetaMap program. *Proceedings. AMIA Symposium*, 17–21.

Aziz, A. A., & Tao, L. (2016). Word embeddings for Arabic sentiment analysis. *IEEE International Conference on Big Data*, 7, 3820-3825.

Beigi, G., Hu, X., Maciejewski, R., & Liu, H. (2016). An overview of sentiment analysis in social media and its applications in disaster relief. Sentiment analysis and ontology engineering, 313-340.

Bhuta, S., Doshi, A., Doshi, U., & Narvekar, M. (2014). A Review of Techniques for Sentiment Analysis Of Twitter Data. *2014 International Conference on Issues and Challenges in Intelligent Computing Techniques (ICICT)*, 583-591. 10.1109/ICICICT.2014.6781346

Bloem, C. (2017, July 31). *84 Percent of People Trust Online Reviews As Much As Friends. Here's How to Manage What They See*. Retrieved from https://www.inc.com/craig-bloem/84-percent-of-people-trust-online-reviews-as-much-.html

Bravo-Marquez, F., Frank, E., & Pfahringer, B. (2016). Building a Twitter opinion lexicon from automatically-annotated tweets. *Knowledge-Based Systems*, *108*, 65–78. doi:10.1016/j.knosys.2016.05.018

Cambria, E. (2016). Affective computing and sentiment analysis. *IEEE Intelligent Systems*, *31*(2), 102–107. doi:10.1109/MIS.2016.31

Chalothom, T., & Ellman, J. (2015). Simple approaches of sentiment analysis via ensemble learning. Information Science and Applications, 631-639.

Chandni, Chandra, N., Gupta, S., & Pahade, R. (2015). Sentiment analysis and its challenges. *International Journal of Engineering Research & Technology (Ahmedabad)*, *4*(3), 968–970.

Chen, X., Qiu, X., Zhu, C., & Huang, X. J. (2015). Gated recursive neural network for Chinese word segmentation. *Proceedings of the 53rd Annual Meeting of the Association for Computational Linguistics and the 7th International Joint Conference on Natural Language Processing*, 1, 1744-1753. 10.3115/v1/P15-1168

Collomb, A., Costea, C., Joyeux, D., Hasan, O., & Brunie, L. (2014). A study and comparison of sentiment analysis methods for reputation evaluation. *Rapport de recherche RR-LIRIS-2014-002*.

Dahou, A., Xiong, S., Zhou, J., Haddoud, M. H., & Duan, P. (2016). Word embeddings and convolutional neural network for Arabic sentiment classification. *The 26th International Conference on Computational Linguistics (COLING 2016)*, 2418-2427.

Desai, M., & Mehta, M. A. (2016). Techniques for Sentiment Analysis of Twitter Data: A Comprehensive Survey. *International Conference on Computing, Communication and Automation (ICCCA2016)*, 149-154. 10.1109/CCAA.2016.7813707

Ebrahimi, M., Yazdavar, A. H., & Sheth, A. (2017). Challenges of sentiment analysis for dynamic events. *IEEE Intelligent Systems*, *32*(5), 70–75. doi:10.1109/MIS.2017.3711649

El-Beltagy, S. R., & Ali, A. (2013). Open issues in the sentiment analysis of Arabic social media: A case study. *2013 9th International Conference on Innovations in Information Technology (IIT)*, 215-220. 10.1109/Innovations.2013.6544421

Ghaleb, O. A. M., & Vijendran, A. S. (2017). The Challenges of Sentiment Analysis on Social Web Communities. *International Journal of Advance Research in Science and Engineering.*, *6*(12), 117–125.

Ghosh, A., & Veale, T. (2016). Fracking sarcasm using neural network. *Proceedings of the 7th workshop on computational approaches to subjectivity, sentiment and social media analysis*, 161-169. 10.18653/v1/W16-0425

Gieseke, F., Kramer, O. I., Airola, A., & Pahikkala, T. (2012). Efficient recurrent local search strategies for semi- and unsupervised regularized least-squares classification. *Evolutionary Intelligence*, *2012*(5), 189–205. doi:10.100712065-012-0068-5

Haochen, Z., & Fei, S. (2015). Aspect-level sentiment analysis based on a generalized probabilistic topic and syntax model. In *Proceedings of the Twenty-Eighth International Florida Artificial Intelligence Research Society Conference*. Association for the Advancement of Artificial Intelligence.

Hu, M., & Liu, B. (2004). Mining and summarizing customer reviews. *Proceedings of the tenth ACM SIGKDD international conference on Knowledge discovery and data mining*, 168-177.

Hussein, D. M. E. D. M. (2018). A survey on sentiment analysis challenges. *Journal of King Saud University-Engineering Sciences.*, *30*(4), 330–338. doi:10.1016/j.jksues.2016.04.002

Kalchbrenner, N., Grefenstette, E., & Blunsom, P. (2014). A Convolutional Neural Network for Modelling Sentences. *Computation and Language.*, 655–665. doi:10.3115/v1/P14-1062

Kamble, S. S., & Itkikar, A. R. (2018). Study of supervised machine learning approaches for sentiment analysis. *International Research Journal of Engineering and Technology*, 5(4), 3045–3047.

Khaled, A., Tazi, N. E., & Hossny, A. H. (2015). Sentiment Analysis over Social Networks: An Overview. *2015 IEEE International Conference on Systems, Man, and Cybernetics*, 2174-2179.

Kharde, V., & Sonawane, P. (2016). *Sentiment analysis of twitter data: A survey of techniques.* arXiv preprint arXiv:1601.06971

Kim, Y. (2014). *Convolutional neural networks for sentence classification.* Academic Press.

Kudo, T., Yamamoto, K., & Matsumoto, Y. (2004). Applying conditional random fields to Japanese morphological analysis. *Proceedings of the 2004 Conference on Empirical Methods in Natural Language Processing*, 230–237.

Kumar, A., & Joshi, A. (2017). Ontology-Driven Sentiment Analysis on Social Web for Government Intelligence. *ICEGOV '17: Proceedings of the Special Collection on eGovernment Innovations in India*, 134–139. 10.1145/3055219.3055229

Kumar, A., & Sebastian, T. M. (2012). Sentiment Analysis: A Perspective on Its Past, Present and Future. *International Journal of Intelligent Systems and Applications,* 1–14.

Kumar, L., Somani, A., Bhattacharyya, P. (2017). *"Having 2 Hours to Write a Paper Is Fun!": Detecting Sarcasm in Numerical Portions of Text.* ArXiv, abs/1709.01950

Lafferty, J., McCallum, A., & Pereira, F. C. (2001). Conditional random fields: Probabilistic models for segmenting and labeling sequence data. *Proceedings of the 8th International Conference on Machine Learning*, 282–289.

Li, P., Xu, W., Ma, C., Sun, J., & Yan, Y. (2015). IOA: Improving SVM based sentiment classification through post processing. *Proc. 9th Int. Workshop Semantic Evaluation*, 545–550. 10.18653/v1/S15-2091

Lincy, W., & Kumar, N. M. (2016). A survey on challenges in sentiment analysis. *International Journal of Emerging Technology in Computer Science & Electronics*, 21(3), 409–412.

Ling, P., Geng, C., Menghou, Z., & Chunya, L. (2014). *What Do Seller Manipulations of Online Product Reviews Mean to Consumers?* (HKIBS Working Paper Series 070-1314) Hong Kong Institute of Business Studies, Lingnan University, Hong Kong.

Liu, B. (2010). Sentiment Analysis: A Multi-Faceted Problem. *IEEE Intelligent Systems.*

Liu, G., Xu, X., Deng, B., Chen, S., & Li, L. (n.d.). A hybrid method for bilingual text sentiment classification based on deep learning. *17th IEEE/ACIS International Conference on Software Engineering Artificial Intelligence Networking and Parallel/Distributed Computing (SNPD)*, 93-98. 10.1109/SNPD.2016.7515884

Ma, J., & Hinrichs, E. (2015). Accurate linear-time Chinese word segmentation via embedding matching. *Proceedings of the 53rd Annual Meeting of the Association for Computational Linguistics and the 7th International Joint Conference on Natural Language Processing*, 1, 1733–1743. 10.3115/v1/P15-1167

Matthew, J. K., Spencer, G., & Andrea, Z. (2015). Potential applications of sentiment analysis in educational research and practice – Is SITE the friendliest conference? In *Proceedings of Society for Information Technology & Teacher Education International Conference 2015*. Association for the Advancement of Computing in Education (AACE).

Medhat, W., Hassan, A., & Korashy, H. (2014). Sentiment analysis algorithms and applications: A survey. *Ain Shams Engineering Journal. Elsevier.*, 5(4), 1093–1113. doi:10.1016/j.asej.2014.04.011

Mohammad, S. M. (2017). Challenges in sentiment analysis. In A practical guide to sentiment analysis. Springer.

Nadkarni, P. M., Ohno-Machado, L., & Chapman, W. W. (2011). Natural language processing: An introduction. *Journal of the American Medical Informatics Association*, 18(5), 544–551. doi:10.1136/amiajnl-2011-000464 PMID:21846786

Nasukawa, T., & Yi, J. (2003). Sentiment analysis: Capturing favorability using natural language processing. *Proceedings of the 2nd international conference on Knowledge capture*, 70-77. 10.1145/945645.945658

Nikos, E., Angeliki, L., Georgios, P., & Konstantinos, C. 2011. ELS: a word-level method for entity-level sentiment analysis. *WIMS '11 Proceedings of the International Conference on Web Intelligence, Mining and Semantics.*

Noura, F., Elie, C., Rawad, A. A., & Hazem, H. 2010. Sentence-level and document-level sentiment mining for Arabic texts. *Proceeding IEEE International Conference on Data Mining Workshops.*

Orkphol, K., Yang, W. (2019). Sentiment Analysis on Microblogging with K-Means Clustering and Artificial Bee Colony. *International Journal of Computational Intelligence and Applications, 18*(3).

Osimo & Mureddu. (2011). *Research Challenge on Opinion Mining and Sentiment Analysis*. Academic Press.

Ouyang, X., Zhou, P., Li, C. H., & Liu, L. (2015). Sentiment Analysis using Convolutional Neural Network. *2015 IEEE International Conference on Computer and Information Technology; Ubiquitous Computing and Communications; Dependable, Autonomic and Secure Computing; Pervasive Intelligence and Computing*, 2359-2364.

Pang, B., & Lee, L. (2008). Opinion Mining and Sentiment Analysis. *Foundations and Trends in Information Retrieval.*, 2(1), 1–135. doi:10.1561/1500000011

Patel, V., Prabhu, G., & Bhowmick, K. (2015). A Survey of Opinion Mining and Sentiment Analysis. *International Journal of Computers and Applications, 131*(1), 24–27. doi:10.5120/ijca2015907218

Peng, F., Feng, F., & McCallum, A. (2004). Chinese segmentation and new word detection using conditional random fields. *Proceedings of the 20th International Conference on Computational Linguistics*, 562–568. 10.3115/1220355.1220436

Safrin, R. (2017). *Sentiment Analysis on Online Product Review*. Academic Press.

Sallab, A. A. A., Baly, R., Badaro, G., Hajj, H., Hajj, W. E., & Shaban, K. B. (2015). Deep learning models for sentiment analysis in Arabic. *Proceedings of the Second Workshop on Arabic Natural Language Processing*, 9–17. 10.18653/v1/W15-3202

Samal, B. R., Behera, A. K., & Panda, M. (2017). Performance Analysis of Supervised Machine Learning Techniques for Sentiment Analysis. *2017 IEEE 3rd International Conference on Sensing, Signal Processing and Security (ICSSS)*, 128-133.

Seerat, B., & Azam, F. (2012). Opinion mining: Issues and challenges (A Survey). *International Journal of Computers and Applications*, *49*(9), 42–51. doi:10.5120/7658-0762

Shahnawaz, A. P. (2017). Sentiment Analysis: Approaches and Open Issues. *International Conference on Computing, Communication and Automation (ICCCA2017)*, 154-158.

Sharef, N. M., Zin, H. M., & Nadali, S. (2016). Overview and Future Opportunities of Sentiment Analysis Approaches for Big Data. *Journal of Computational Science*, *12*(3), 153–168. doi:10.3844/jcssp.2016.153.168

Sharma, A., & Dey, S. (2012). A comparative study of feature selection and machine learning techniques for sentiment analysis. *Proceedings of the 2012 ACM Research in Applied Computation Symposium*, 1-7. 10.1145/2401603.2401605

Sharma, D., Sabharwal, M., Goyal, V., & Vij, M. (2019). Sentiment Analysis Techniques for Social Media Data: A Review. *First International Conference on Sustainable Technologies for Computational Intelligence. Proceedings of ICTSCI 2019*, 75-90.

Soman, S. J., Swaminathan, P., Anandan, R., Kalaivani, K. (2018). A comparative review of the challenges encountered in sentiment analysis of Indian regional language tweets vs English language tweets. *International Journal of Engineering & Technology*, *7*(2), 319-322.

Sonagi, A., & Gore, D. (2013). Sentiment Analysis and Challenges Involved: A Survey. *International Journal of Scientific Research (Ahmedabad, India)*, *4*(1), 1928–1932.

Srivastava, R., & Bhatia, M. P. S. (2017). Challenges with sentiment analysis of on-line micro-texts. *International Journal of Intelligent Systems and Applications*, *9*(7), 31–40. doi:10.5815/ijisa.2017.07.04

Studer, R., Benjamins, R., & Fensel, D. (1998). Knowledge engineering: Principles and methods. *Data & Knowledge Engineering*, *25*(1–2), 161–198. doi:10.1016/S0169-023X(97)00056-6

Sun, S., Luo, C., & Chen, J. (2017). A Review of Natural Language Processing Techniques for Opinion Mining Systems. *Information Fusion*, *36*, 10–25. doi:10.1016/j.inffus.2016.10.004

Tang, H., Tan, S., & Cheng, X. (2009). A survey on sentiment detection of reviews. *Expert Systems with Applications*, *36*(7), 10760–10773. doi:10.1016/j.eswa.2009.02.063

Tawunrat, C., Jeremy, E., 2015. Chapter Information Science and Applications, Simple Approaches of Sentiment Analysis via Ensemble Learning. *Lecture Notes in Electrical Engineering, 339*.

Techopedia. (2014, January 21). *Sentiment Analysis*. Retrieved from https://www.techopedia.com/definition/29695/sentiment-analysis

Thomas, B. (2013). *What Consumers Think About Brands on Social Media, and What Businesses Need to do About it Report*. Keep Social Honest.

Tseng, H., Chang, P. C., Andrew, G., Jurafsky, D., & Manning, C. D. (2005). A conditional random field word segmenter for sighan bakeoff 2005. *Proceedings of the fourth SIGHAN workshop on Chinese language Processing*, 168–171.

Tsytsarau, M., & Palpanas, T. (2012). Survey on mining subjective data on the web. *Data Mining and Knowledge Discovery*, *24*(3), 478–514. doi:10.100710618-011-0238-6

Turney, P. D., & Littman, M. L. (2003). Measuring praise and criticism: Inference of semantic orientation from association. *ACM Transactions on Information Systems*, *21*(4), 315–346. doi:10.1145/944012.944013

Varghese, R., & Jayasree, M. (2013). A Survey on Sentiment Analysis and Opinion Mining. *IJRET: International Journal of Research in Engineering and Technology.*, *2*(11), 312–317. doi:10.15623/ijret.2013.0211048

Vohra, S., & Teraiya, J. (2013). Applications and Challenges for Sentiment Analysis: A Survey. *International Journal of Engineering Research & Technology (Ahmedabad)*, *2*(2), 1–5.

Wikipedia. (2020, May 29). *Sarcasm*. Retrieved from https://en.wikipedia.org/wiki/Sarcasm#:~:text=From%20Wikipedia%2C%20the%20free%20encyclopedia,sarcasm%20is%20not%20necessarily%20ironic

Wu, S., Liu, Y., Wang, J., & Li, Q. (2019). Sentiment Analysis Method Based on K-means and Online Transfer Learning. *CMC-Computers Materials & Continua*, *60*(3), 1207–1222. doi:10.32604/cmc.2019.05835

Yadlapalli, S. S., Reddy, R. R., & Sasikala, T. (2019). Advanced Twitter sentiment analysis using supervised techniques and minimalistic features. Ambient Communications and Computer Systems, RACCCS 2019, 91-104.

Yang, A. M., Lin, J. H., Zhou, Y. M., & Chen, J. (2013). Research on building a Chinese sentiment lexicon based on SO-PMI. Applied Mechanics and Materials, 263, 1688-1693.

Yanyan, Z., Bing, Q., & Qiuhui, S., & Ting, L. (2017). Large-scale sentiment lexicon collection and its application in sentiment classification. *Journal of Chinese Information Processing.*, *31*(2), 187–193.

Zhang, L., Wang, S., & Liu, B. (2018). Deep learning for sentiment analysis: A survey. *Wiley Interdisciplinary Reviews. Data Mining and Knowledge Discovery*, *8*(4), e1253. doi:10.1002/widm.1253

Zul, M. I., Yulia, F., & Nurmalasari, D. (2018). Social Media Sentiment Analysis Using K-Means and Naïve Bayes Algorithm. *2nd International Conference on Electrical Engineering and Informatics (ICon EEI)*, 24-29. 10.1109/ICon-EEI.2018.8784326

ADDITIONAL READING

Cambria, E., Das, D., Bandyopadhyay, S., & Feraco, A. (2017). *A Practical Guide to Sentiment Analysis.* Springer. doi:10.1007/978-3-319-55394-8

Cambria, E., Poria, S., Gelbukh, A., & Thelwall, M. (2017). Sentiment Analysis is a Big Suitcase. *IEEE Intelligent Systems, 32*(6), 74–80. doi:10.1109/MIS.2017.4531228

Chaturvedi, I., Poria, S., & Cambria, E. (2017). Basic tasks of sentiment analysis. Encyclopedia of Social Network Analysis and Mining. 1-28.

Khaled, A., Tazi, N. E., & Hossny, A. H. (2015). Sentiment Analysis over Social Networks: An Overview. *2015 IEEE International Conference on Systems, Man, and Cybernetics.* 2174-2179.

Kumar, A., & Sebastian, T. M. (2012). Sentiment Analysis on Twitter. *IJCSI International Journal of Computer Science Issues.* 9(4,3). 372-378.

Kumar, A., & Sebastian, T. M. (2012). Sentiment Analysis: A Perspective on Its Past, Present and Future. *International Journal of Intelligent Systems and Applications.* 1–14.

Montoyo, A., Martínez-Barco, P., & Balahur, A. (2012). Subjectivity and sentiment analysis: An overview of the current state of the area and envisaged developments. *Decision Support Systems. Elsevier., 53*(4), 675–679. doi:10.1016/j.dss.2012.05.022

Taboada, M. (2016). Sentiment Analysis: An Overview from Linguistics. *Annual Review of Linguistics, 2*(1), 325–347. doi:10.1146/annurev-linguistics-011415-040518

KEY TERMS AND DEFINITIONS

Natural Language Processing: Natural language processing is a process that deals with the manipulation of natural language (i.e., language used by humans) by utilizing computers and artificial intelligence to process and analyze huge amounts of natural language data for various applications ranging from automatic summarization to disease prediction.

Opinionated Text: Opinionated text can be defined as the text acquired from blogs, social networking sites or any other online portal in which the users have expressed their disposition and point of view towards any particular product or service.

Scarce Resource language: Scarce resource languages are those languages that lack text processing resources and only have basic dictionaries. The sentiment analysis of these languages is difficult due to the absence of developed processing tools and resources for these languages.

Sentiment Analysis: Sentiment Analysis is the technique that aids to recognize and classify the emotions and opinions of users in the communicated information, so that the opinion of the user for a certain utility or commodity can be determined as being positive, negative or neutral through NLP and content analysis.

Sentiment Polarity: Sentiment polarity for an element defines the orientation of the expressed sentiment, i.e., it determines if the text expresses the positive, negative or neutral sentiment of the user about the entity in consideration.

Subjectivity Detection: Subjectivity detection is the process of differentiating between opinionated and non-opinionated phrases.

Word Sense Disambiguation: Word sense disambiguation is described as a process of recognizing the implication of a term with respect to the context of the sentence. This problem arises when the same word can have diverse meanings in various contexts.

Chapter 5
Deep Learning for Sentiment Analysis:
An Overview and Perspectives

Vincent Karas
University of Augsburg, Germany

Björn W. Schuller
University of Augsburg, Germany

ABSTRACT

Sentiment analysis is an important area of natural language processing that can help inform business decisions by extracting sentiment information from documents. The purpose of this chapter is to introduce the reader to selected concepts and methods of deep learning and show how deep models can be used to increase performance in sentiment analysis. It discusses the latest advances in the field and covers topics including traditional sentiment analysis approaches, the fundamentals of sentence modelling, popular neural network architectures, autoencoders, attention modelling, transformers, data augmentation methods, the benefits of transfer learning, the potential of adversarial networks, and perspectives on explainable AI. The authors' intent is that through this chapter, the reader can gain an understanding of recent developments in this area as well as current trends and potentials for future research.

INTRODUCTION

In recent years, the amount of information available on the Internet has grown rapidly. At the beginning of 2019, Twitter had 326 million monthly active users, and 500 million tweets were sent per day Cooper (2019). Facebook, the largest social media platform, reported 2.41 billion monthly active users for the second quarter of 2019 Facebook (2019). Every minute, 4.5 million YouTube videos and 1 million Twitch videos are viewed, and the Google search engine processes 3.8 million queries (Desjardins, 2019). This trove of online content constitutes a valuable resource for business applications, e.g. for providing the users with personalised search recommendations and tailored advertisements. If the data is harnessed

DOI: 10.4018/978-1-7998-4240-8.ch005

properly, it may deliver new insights that can help improve existing products and services and inspire future business models. Among the available content, text, in particular, is rich in information, as it can contain nuanced emotions, multiple layers of meaning and ambiguities. However, this complexity also results in it being challenging to analyse. Natural Language Processing (NLP), which addresses this challenge, has become a popular field of research.

Sentiment Analysis (SA), which is often also referred to as opinion mining or comment mining in the literature, is a discipline of NLP-based text analysis whose goal is to determine the writer's feelings about a particular topic. Emotions have been shown to play an essential role in human decision making (Bechara, Damasio, & Damasio, 2000) and behaviour in general. Consequentially, SA has many conceivable applications in business and academia. Examples include companies looking to improve their services by automatically assessing customer reviews (Hu & Liu, 2004), (Zvarevashe & Olugbara, 2018), comparing products online, or analysing newspaper headlines (Rameshbhai & Paulose, 2019).

Sentiment also plays an important role in the financial market. Ranjit, Shrestha, Subedi, and Shakya (2018) used SA to predict the exchange rates of foreign currencies. Shah, Isah, and Zulkernine (2018) predicted stock prices in the pharmaceutical industry based on the sentiment in news coverage. C. Du, Tsai, and Wang (2019) classified financial reports in terms of expected financial risk using SA.

In addition, there are medical applications for SA. Müller and Salathé (2019) introduced an open platform for tracking health trends on social media. Luo, Zimet, and Shah (2019) created an NLP framework to investigate sentiment fluctuation on the subject of HPV vaccination, expressed by Twitter users between 2008 and 2017.

Furthermore, political analysts and campaigns can benefit from mining the opinions and emotions expressed towards candidates, issues and parties on social media. Jose and Chooralil (2016) used an ensemble classifier approach to predict results of the 2015 election in Delhi. Joyce and Deng (2017) applied SA to tweets collected in the run-up to the 2016 US presidential election and compared them to polling data. They found that automatic labelling of tweets outperformed manual labelling.

Many tools used in sentiment analysis are designed for a specific application, which negatively impacts their diffusion. Joshi and Simon (2018) introduced a cloud-based open-source tool which provides various APIs in order to perform SA on data from arbitrary sources.

While SA has attracted considerable attention, the field still faces challenges. These include domain dependence, negations, handling fake reviews (Hussein, Doaa Mohey El-Din Mohamed, 2018), as well as incorporating context, dealing with data imbalance and ensuring high-quality annotations (Boaz Shmueli & Lun-Wei Ku, 2019).

This chapter introduces the reader to selected methods used for sentiment analysis, with a focus on techniques based on deep learning. Its contribution consists of a discussion of the latest advances in the state of the art, as well as an outlook concerning ongoing trends in the field and recommendations on future research directions.

The rest of the chapter is structured as follows. In the next section, the fundamentals of SA and select machine learning concepts are presented. Topics covered include a categorisation of analysis approaches by level of granularity, how to measure sentiment, traditional sentiment analysis methods employing lexica and machine learning, as well as tools for word embedding and sentence modelling such as autoencoders, GloVe, fastText and Word2vec. The chapter will then continue with its main section, focusing on current developments in deep learning-based SA. Topics include popular neural network architectures and their combination into hybrid models, capturing contextual information by adding attention, Transformer networks and the challenges and benefits of transfer learning. In the following section, solutions and recommendations for readers seeking to apply state-of-the-art models to SA are presented. The subsequent section involves an overview of promising research opportunities in the field. Recent data augmentation techniques, zero-shot learning and the potential of generative adversarial networks are covered. In addition, the need for developing explainable AI systems is discussed as well as improving generalisation across topics and languages and defending against adversarial attacks. Finally, a conclusion sums up this chapter.

BACKGROUND

This section presents a taxonomy of sentiment analysis and key methods and frameworks used for sentence modelling and generating word embeddings.

Levels of Sentiment Analysis

A text can be analysed for its sentiment content at different levels. These are document, sentence and phrase levels (P. Balaji, O. Nagaraju, & D. Haritha, 2017). Sentiment analysis at phrase level is also commonly referred to as aspect level analysis, a name that will be adopted for this chapter. The level of analysis informs the choice of deep learning models.

As a motivational example, consider an automotive company wanting to classify product reviews of their cars. A review might read as follows:

"This is a great car. It handles well in corners and has superb acceleration. Like its predecessor, it has a V6 engine. However, I do not like what they did with the new voice-controlled infotainment system. It gets confused too easily to be useful."

The following subsections illustrate the application of SA at different levels based on the example review:

Document Level SA

The task at this level is to classify the entire document as having a positive or negative sentiment (Pang, Lee, & Vaithyanathan, 2002). Such an analysis can serve to determine a general verdict, e.g. to find out whether a reviewer likes or dislikes a product. Therefore, this approach can work only if the document describes a single issue.

For the example review, it appears that the customer has an overall positive opinion. However, there is also criticism. In order to understand the positive and negative feelings expressed by the customer, the document needs to be examined in greater detail.

Sentence Level SA

At this level, individual sentences are examined for their sentiment content. This approach requires splitting the document into objective sentences, which contain factual information, and subjective sentences that reflect opinions and feelings. The classification of subjectivity was investigated by Wiebe, Bruce, and O'Hara (1999). Subjective sentences are then subjected to SA and rated accordingly. Performing

SA at sentence level makes a similar assumption to document level SA in that individual sentences are referring to only one entity, which will often not be true (Christy Daniel & Shyamala, 2019).

Considering our sample review at the sentence level, a more detailed picture emerges: The customer expresses positive sentiment in the first two sentences. The third sentence is a factual statement. The last two sentences show negative sentiment.

Aspect Level SA

Aspect-level analysis examines individual entities within sentences, making it more fine-grained than the previous approaches. It can discover in detail which elements of a topic are liked or disliked, which is useful since the author's opinion on a subject will rarely be entirely positive or negative. Thus, the objective of an aspect-level analysis is to discover the slant of the text (P. Balaji et al., 2017). Multiple sub-tasks can be defined at this level:

1. **Target extraction:** This identifies the entities that sentiments refer to.
2. **Sentiment classification:** The rating of the sentiment.
3. **Temporal opinion mining:** This task is concerned with discovering the temporal relationships in the text and how those affect the evolution of sentiment.
4. **Opinion holder identification:** A text may reference different persons, each having individual opinions.

For the example review, a targeted aspect-level analysis can reveal that the customer approves of the car's driving characteristics, as they commend the acceleration and handling in corners. At the same time, the customer disapproves of a new feature in the infotainment system. For the manufacturer, this is valuable information for identifying the strengths and weaknesses of the product. Opinion holder identification is also quite useful for this task. The example review features a single customer who emphasises a good driving experience, but there could also be references to, e.g. family members having different priorities.

Now that the basic approaches for extracting sentiment from documents have been identified, the next subsection will address the question of how sentiment can be quantified.

Measuring Sentiment

Just as the analysis of a document may be performed at different levels, the discovered sentiment may also be measured at different levels of granularity. One possibility is a binary approach based on polarity, i.e. the text is positive or negative. A neutral state may be added as a third class. Alternatively, categorical emotions may be used. Ekman (1999) identified six basic emotions, namely, happiness, anger, sadness, disgust, surprise and fear. A more fine-grained description is provided by continuous affect dimensions such as valence, arousal, dominance, or novelty. Plutchik (1980) introduced a model which combines elements of the categorical and continuous approaches. It encompasses eight types of emotions, namely joy, anticipation, trust, surprise, fear, anger, disgust and sadness. The emotions are arranged as opposing pairs in a wheel. In addition, each emotion can appear at different levels of intensity, e.g. trust ranges from acceptance to admiration.

Consider the sentences "This car is all right." and "This car is great." Both express a positive sentiment, but it is much stronger in the second sentence, which should result in a higher level of valence being detected.

Having introduced levels of granularity and ways to measure sentiment, the next section will explore algorithms traditionally used in SA:

Traditional Approaches for Sentiment Analysis

The methods used for SA can be placed into two broad categories: lexica-based approaches and machine learning approaches. This chapter considers deep learning-based algorithms separately in the following section; therefore, they are not discussed among the machine learning algorithms in this section.

Lexicon-Based Approach

The lexicon-based approach aggregates the polarity and strength of individual words in the document to calculate the overall sentiment. (Turney, 2002). It requires a dictionary of words with associated semantic orientation. The research into lexica-based SA has largely focused on adjectives, cf. Hatzivassiloglou and McKeown (1997), Hu and Liu (2004), Wiebe (2000) and Taboada, Anthony, and Voll (2006).

The dictionary or lexicon can be compiled manually (Taboada, Brooke, Tofiloski, Voll, & Stede, 2011) or automatically starting from a seed list of opinion words. Automatic lexicon compilation is accomplished with thesaurus-based and corpus-based methods. Thesaurus-based methods expand the seed list by parsing existing dictionaries for synonyms or antonyms, while corpus-based methods exploit statistical co-occurrence of words with similar polarity in a corpus, or calculate similarity measures between words (Kaur, Mangat, & Nidhi, 2017).

Machine Learning-Based Approach

Machine learning algorithms perform sentiment classification or regression according to features contained in the text. They can – among many possible discriminations – be divided into linear classifiers and probabilistic classifiers.

Support Vector Machine (SVM) is an example of an (in principle) linear classifier, i.e. it attempts to predict a label y (+1 or -1) from features x based on the function:

$$y = f(x) = w^T x + b \tag{1}$$

It was developed within the statistical learning theory (Vapnik, 2000). The algorithm searches a hypothesis space of functions in order to find a hyperplane that separates classes. In the simple case, considered up to now, of a linear SVM, the hyperplane lies in the input space. In the generalised form of SVM, a dot product called a kernel is used to define a Reproducing Kernel Hilbert Space as the feature space (Evgeniou & Pontil, 2001). SVM attempts to maximise the distance between the named hyperplane and the instances of each of the two classes (extensions for more than two classes exist, such as one vs one, or one vs all).

Naïve Bayes (NB) is an example of a probabilistic classifier, which predicts a conditional probability $p(y|x)$. Naïve Bayes uses Bayes' rule to determine the probability of a class c belonging to a vector of BoW features x:

$$p(c \mid x) = \frac{p(c)p(x \mid c)}{p(x)} \tag{2}$$

This simple algorithm assumes that the features are conditionally independent, which allows it to decompose the numerator (Pang et al., 2002). The classifier then takes the form:

$$p_{NB}(c \mid x_1, \cdots, x_n) = \frac{p(c)\prod_{i=1}^{n}p(x_i \mid c)}{p(x)} \tag{3}$$

Maximum Entropy (ME) is another probabilistic algorithm. It has been used for SA of tweets (Neethu & Rajasree, 2013), (Gautam & Yadav, 2014). The intuitive assumption of this classifier is that the underlying probability distribution should have maximum entropy, i.e. be as uniform as possible within the constraints imposed by the training data (Nigam, Lafferty, & Mccallum, 1999). Those constraints apply to the feature functions $f_i(d, c)$, whose expected value within the model and the training data are demanded to be equal. The probability distribution takes an exponential form (Della Pietra, Della Pietra, & Lafferty, 1997):

$$p_{ME}(c \mid d) = \frac{1}{Z_d}e^{\sum_{i=1}^{n}\lambda_i f_i(d,c)} \tag{4}$$

Here Z_d is a normalisation factor, and λ_i is a parameter to be estimated. Unlike NB, ME does not assume independence of features, and therefore, it can outperform NB on tasks where that assumption does not hold (Pang et al., 2002).

Sentence Modelling and Word Embeddings

In order to perform SA on a document, the text first has to be converted into a form that the SA algorithm can process. This is done by assigning a vector to each word in the document. A simple solution would be to use an approach known as Bag-of-Words (BoW). The number of occurrences of each unique word within the corpus is determined and used to sort the words in descending order. Then, a one-hot encoding can be applied to that list of words. The same approach can be used with n-grams (word sequences of length n).

A naïve BoW, as described above, is easy to implement but has several disadvantages. First, it can result in very high-dimensional representations, up to the number of entries in the vocabulary. Second, such an encoding does not capture the linguistic relationships between words. However, the goal of sentence modelling should be to obtain feature representations which guarantee that the similarity between two vectors reflects the semantic and syntactic relationship between the corresponding words.

The following subsections introduce a selection of established methods and tools that can be used to discover useful representations for NLP tasks, including but not limited to SA.

Autoencoders

A useful representation should capture the relevant information contained in the raw data, allow for clustering into categories, and reduce the number of features sufficiently to avoid the curse of dimensionality. An example of a deep architecture designed to learn such representations in an unsupervised manner is the autoencoder.

An autoencoder (AE) consists of two networks connected in sequence: The encoder processes the input data and generates a feature vector at its output layer. That vector is usually of lower dimensionality than the input; however, a variant called sparse autoencoder may increase the dimensionality of the encoder output but regularise it to produce sparse activations. The features generated by the encoder are used as the input to the decoder, which produces an output of the same shape as the input data. The autoencoder is trained by setting the target of the decoder to be the same as the input data. Since the layer in the middle of the network has fewer parameters, it acts as a bottleneck, forcing the network to learn how to compress the input into a compact representation. This process can be called self-supervised, as the autoencoder learns by optimising the reconstructing error of the data without a need for labels. Figure 1 illustrates the basic structure of an autoencoder.

Figure 1. Autoencoder architecture. Input is compressed by the encoder, then reconstructed by the decoder. This forces the network to learn an efficient representation of the data.

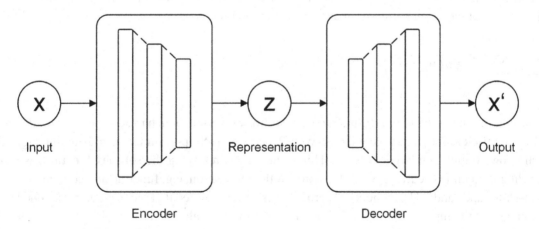

AEs and their variants are popular tools for sentiment analysis. They are frequently employed in semi-supervised strategies when only part of the data is labelled. The variational autoencoder (VAE) learns latent representations in a probabilistic manner (Kingma & Welling, 2013). Examples from the literature that utilise VAEs for SA include aspect-level classification of user reviews (Fu et al., 2019), multi-task learning for improved generalisation (Lu, Zhao, Yin, Yang, & Li, 2018) and a semi-supervised variant that makes use of the labels in the decoder to boost accuracy (W. Xu, Sun, Deng, & Tan, 2017). Winner-take-all autoencoders (Makhzani & Frey, 2015) enforce sparsity by having the neurons in the embedding layer compete for contributing to the output. Maitra and Sarkhel (2018) used a shallow winner-take-all autoencoder to classify social media texts in multiple languages as overtly, covertly or non-aggressive.

Denoising autoencoders (DA) make the representation more robust by corrupting the input with noise and learning to reconstruct a clean version. A stacked denoising autoencoder (SDA) combines multiple denoising autoencoders, with the latent representation of one AE acting as input to the next one (Vincent, Larochelle, Bengio, & Manzagol, 2008). This allows for learning potent representations while keeping the number of parameters small, saving computational resources and reducing the amount of training data needed to prevent overfitting. During training, the layers are tuned one by one. (Sagha, Cummins, & Schuller, 2017).

Conventional autoencoders have recently become less relevant for generating word embeddings, as NLP researchers increasingly favour the new Transformer networks, which are discussed separately in this chapter's main section on deep learning. The following subsections present several popular open-source frameworks that provide pre-trained word embeddings. For tasks that involve small datasets, pre-trained embeddings learned on large corpora can help mitigate the problem of encountering unseen words at test time (Hsu & Ku, 2018).

Word2vec

Word2vec[1] was introduced by Mikolov, Chen, Corrado, and Dean (2013). It is an extension of the continuous Skip-gram model developed by Mikolov, Sutskever, Chen, Corrado, and Dean (2013). Skip-gram is a log-linear model; the choice of linearity is motivated by training efficiency being valued over additional complexity in the representations. It analyses a sequence of training words T and for each word w, attempts to predict both previous and subsequent words within a context c. The objective that Skip-Gram attempts to maximise is an average log probability given by:

$$\frac{1}{T}\sum_{t=1}^{T}\sum_{-c\leq j\leq c, j\neq 0}\log p\left(w_{t+j} \mid w_t\right) \tag{5}$$

The conditional probability is formulated as a softmax function, which makes the computation of the gradient inefficient for large vocabularies. Word2vec extends Skip-gram by optimising the algorithm, which allows training on larger corpora. This is done by simplifying the softmax function, as well as discarding frequently occurring words that carry little information, e.g. function and conjunction words such as "the" and "and". The authors of Word2vec also demonstrated that phrases can be encoded by the model and that the linear properties of the learned word vectors allow reasoning based on simple arithmetic. For example, the representation of the word "queen" could be found by the following expression:

$$v_{queen} = v_{king} - v_{man} + v_{woman} \tag{6}$$

GloVe

GloVe[2] (Global Vectors) was derived by Pennington, Socher, and Manning (2014). The name reflects that global statistics of a corpus are captured. It is a log-bilinear model with a weighted least-squares objective function for unsupervised learning of word representations. The objective function that GloVe attempts to minimise is given by:

$$J = \sum_{i,j=1}^{V} f\left(X_{ij}\right)\left(w_i^T \tilde{w}_j + b_i + b_j - \log X_{ij}\right) \tag{7}$$

GloVe operates on word co-occurrence counts, i.e. on a matrix X whose entries show how many times a word appears in the context of other words. The set of all words together forms the vocabulary V. The word learning of GloVe is based on the ratios of word co-occurrence probabilities, which compared to the raw probabilities are better at distinguishing relevant words (Pennington et al., 2014).

fastText

fastText[3] is an open-source library for text representation learning and text classifier learning provided by Facebook AI Research. It is based on the works of Bojanowski, Grave, Joulin, and Mikolov (2017) and Joulin, Grave, Bojanowski, and Mikolov (2017). In fastText, instead of assigning a fixed vector to each word, words are modelled as bags of character n-grams. For text classification, simple linear models are used, whose performance on SA tasks has been shown to be comparable with deep architectures while being lightweight and faster to train.

THE CURRENT STATE OF DEEP LEARNING-BASED SA

In this section, a number of key concepts and methods for deep learning are presented.

Advantages and Applications of Deep Learning

Deep learning is a popular form of machine learning that has allowed researchers to achieve breakthroughs in many fields, including computer vision (Krizhevsky, Sutskever, & Hinton, 2012) and speech recognition (Hinton et al., 2012). This part of the chapter will introduce key concepts of deep learning.

Deep learning is based on deep neural networks, i.e. models which contain hidden layers. This multi-layered architecture allows deep models to overcome a shortcoming of conventional machine learning algorithms such as SVM, which is the requirement of feature engineering. Those algorithms needed a suitable feature extractor to turn raw data into representations they could learn from, which required considerable expertise and effort from the researcher (LeCun, Bengio, & Hinton, 2015).

On the other hand, deep models can adjust their internal states to find appropriate representations without the need for extensive preprocessing of the data. They are capable of learning advanced concepts through a stack of modules connected by nonlinear functions. Each module processes the features extracted by the previous ones, which leads to the development of increasingly complex representations. Bengio,

Courville, and Vincent (2013) provide an in-depth discussion of desirable properties of representations and how various deep learning methods can be leveraged for representation learning.

Common Network Architectures

Models based on deep learning have the capability of detecting intricate patterns in data and continue to produce state of the art results in many fields. The following subsections introduce important architectures and techniques and examples of their application to sentiment analysis.

Recurrent Neural Network (RNN)

Recurrent Neural Networks are capable of processing sequential inputs, which makes them attractive for handling data of varying length, e.g. speech or text. An RNN makes use of its hidden units to maintain a state vector, which stores information on the previous elements in the input sequence (LeCun et al., 2015). Thus, the RNN can remember the inputs it has seen. The network can be unfolded along the temporal dimension, effectively making it a deep feedforward architecture, with each unit processing one element in the input sequence and generating an output and a state, which feeds into the next unit. The equations for an RNN are as follows:

$$h_t = \sigma\left(U^h x_t + W^h h_{t-1} + b^h\right), \tag{8}$$

$$o_t = softmax(W^o h_t + b^o) \tag{9}$$

With h, x, o being the hidden state, input and output respectively and subscripts denoting the time step. U and W are parameter matrices, and b are bias vectors. An illustration of an unfolded RNN can be seen in Figure 2.

Figure 2. Unfolded RNN architecture. Data is processed sequentially, with the hidden state being propagated through time.

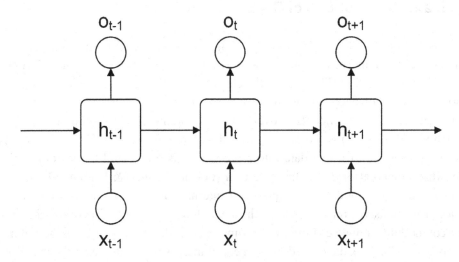

In some cases, it can be desirable to use both past and future information contained in a sequence. Bidirectional RNNs achieve this by combining two RNNs, with each net reading the sequence in a different direction. They have been extensively used in NLP, including in sentiment analysis (Tian, Rong, Shi, Liu, & Xiong, 2018).

Plain RNNs suffer from a common problem in training deep architectures with backpropagation, which is that gradients either tend to zero or become very large across many layers. These effects are known as the vanishing gradient problem and exploding gradient problem, respectively. They make it difficult to learn relationships across large time intervals.

To address this problem, Hochreiter and Schmidhuber (1997) proposed an RNN variant called Long Short-Term Memory (LSTM). In this architecture, the standard recurrent cells in the hidden layers are replaced with memory blocks designed to maintain information (Graves, 2012). The original LSTM is built around a self-recurrent internal structure called a constant error carousel (CEC), which prevents the error from vanishing. Furthermore, it uses two multiplicative gates to regulate its connections: the input gate restricts information entering the cell, and the output gate controls information leaving the cell. Gers, Schmidhuber, and Cummins (2000) improved the LSTM by adding a third gate, named forget gate, in place of the fixed CEC connection. This allows the network to reset its previously learned state, which solves the problem of internal states growing too large over long sequences. The LSTM cell can now be described by the following equations:

$$i_t = \sigma\left(W^i x_t + U^i h_{t-1} + b^i\right), \tag{10}$$

$$f_t = \sigma\left(W^f x_t + U^f h_{t-1} + b^f\right), \tag{11}$$

$$o_t = \sigma\left(W^o x_t + U^o h_{t-1} + b^o\right), \tag{12}$$

$$g_t = \tanh\left(W^g x_t + U^g h_{t-1} + b^g\right), \tag{13}$$

$$c_t = f_t \cdot c_{t-1} + i_t \cdot g_t, \tag{14}$$

$$h_t = o_t \cdot \tanh(c_t) \tag{15}$$

Here c_t is the cell state at time t.

Cho, van Merriënboer, Bahdanau, and Bengio (2014) introduced the Gated Recurrent Network (GRU), which simplifies the LSTM cells. The hidden cells contain two gates: a reset gate which makes the cell forget its hidden state and replace it with the current input, and an update gate which controls the contribution of the previous hidden state to the next time step.

An example of the application of RNNs to sentiment analysis is the work of D. Tang, Qin, and Liu (2015). They performed document-level SA on four large datasets containing IMDB and Yelp reviews, using two gated RNN models with adaptive sentence modelling.

Convolutional Neural Network (CNN)

Convolutional Neural Networks process data in the form of arrays (e.g. videos, images, audio spectrograms and word embeddings) through multiple layers that extract hierarchical features. This is achieved by a combination of convolutional layers and pooling layers.

A convolutional layer makes use of arrays of weights called filter banks. A filter slides across the input data, computing a weighted sum at each position. This results in a new array called a feature map, whose size can be adjusted by zero-padding the input data or changing the filter dimensions and stride. A convolutional layer can construct multiple feature maps by applying different filters. The results are passed through a nonlinear activation, e.g. a (potentially "leaky") rectified linear unit (ReLU). The idea behind the use of these filters is to detect certain features in the input data by matching it to the pattern specified by the filter. For a visual recognition system, those features could be simple lines or edges in the first layers, which are then combined to form objects of increasing complexity. The name convolutional layer is due to the fact that the sliding filter effectively performs a discrete convolution of the input.

Pooling layers merge the information contained in neighbouring cells of a feature map. Implementations of CNNs commonly use max-pooling layers, which will retain only the maximum value of the features in a patch, resulting in a smaller map. Pooling has the advantage of reducing the dimension of the internal representations, as well as introducing an invariance to small shifts and distortions (LeCun et al., 2015).

In addition to sequences of convolutional layers, nonlinearities and pooling for feature extraction, CNNs also incorporate fully connected layers to combine the features for classification. The complete network can be trained through backpropagation. Figure 3 illustrates an example of a CNN architecture.

Figure 3. CNN architecture. A stack of convolutional and pooling layers is used to extract features, which are combined by fully connected layers for classification.

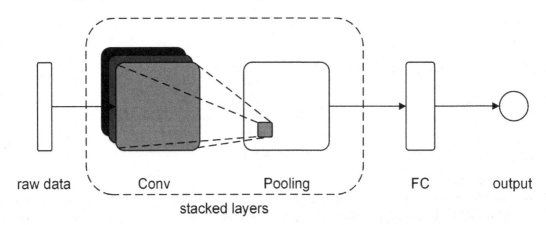

The breakthrough of CNNs came in the field of computer vision in 2012, when a model by Krizhevsky et al. (2012) won the ImageNet Large Scale Visual Recognition Challenge (ILSVRC) with a top-5 test error rate of 15.3%, which was more than 10% ahead of the second-best entry. CNNs can also be applied to sentiment analysis of text. Kim (2014) showed that a simple CNN which processed embeddings generated by word2vec could perform very well in sentence classification, even improving upon the state of the art at the time.

Hybrid Network

A hybrid network includes components from multiple basic neural network architectures. An example of this is combinations of convolutional and recurrent nets (C-RNNs). As shown previously, CNNs are useful for feature extraction in a hierarchical manner, while RNNs are well suited for processing sequential data and capturing important aspects in memory. A C-RNN allows for the combination of these advantages by processing word embeddings through convolutions and feeding the resulting features to a recurrent network.

Hybrid models are a widely used technique in SA. X. Wang, Jiang, and Luo (2016) performed SA on short texts using combinations of word2vec and randomly initialised word vectors and CNN-GRU/CNN-LSTM models, finding that the joint architecture outperformed CNN and RNN alone. More recently, Hassan and Mahmood (2018) proposed a C-RNN architecture that uses recurrent layers instead of pooling layers in order to overcome the problem of CNNs extracting features locally at each stage and thus needing to be very deep to capture long-term dependencies.

The previously discussed methods can be enhanced through a concept called attention, which will be introduced next.

Capturing Context Through Attention

When sentiment analysis is performed on a text, some words will matter more than others. To determine the sentiment towards a certain target requires knowing the context, i.e., relevant words in the rest of the sequence. When an encoder attempts to model those relationships implicitly, as, e.g., RNNs do when compressing the entire input sequence into a fixed-length representation vector, this can lead to problems with long-term dependencies in very long texts. What is needed is a way for the network to learn how to focus on specific elements of the input, as a human reader would do. This is achieved through the attention mechanism.

Attention was first proposed by Bahdanau, Cho, and Bengio (2014), who used it for the purpose of neural machine translation. A common approach to that task is to use an encoder-decoder structure, with the encoder creating a high-level representation of the input sentence and the decoder turning it into an output sentence in a different language. This model was expanded by an attention component which taught it how to align certain words in the input and output sequences, leading to improved performance in English-French translation.

A general way of describing attention is as a function that takes a query Q and a set of key-value pairs (K_i, V_i) and computes a weighted sum of the values based on a comparison between the query and the keys (Vaswani et al., 2017). Thus, assuming an input sequence of hidden states $(h_1,...,h_T)$ as the keys, a context vector c_i is computed by:

$$\alpha_{ij} = \frac{\exp\left(e_{ij}\right)}{\sum_{k=1}^{T}\exp\left(e_{ik}\right)}, \tag{16}$$

$$c_i = \sum_{j=1}^{T} \alpha_{ij} h_i \qquad (17)$$

Here, e_{ij} is an alignment model that functions as a measure of similarity between the query and a key. It is used to compute the weight α_{ij} of each value through a softmax function, and the context vector is the sum of those contributions (Bahdanau et al., 2014). Figure 4 illustrates the concept of attention.

Figure 4. Dot product attention. The dot product is used as a similarity measure between query and keys. A softmax function computes the attention weights of the values, which are then summed into the output.

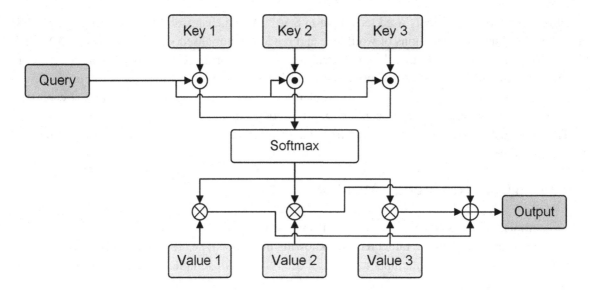

Attention has become a popular method in sentiment analysis. Works that use attention for aspect-level SA include Q. Liu, Zhang, Zeng, Huang, and Wu (2018), Chen, Sun, Bing, and Yang (2017), and D. Tang, Qin, and Liu (2016). It has been combined with RNNs (Ran, 2019), (G. Liu & Guo, 2019), CNNs (J. Du, Gui, Xu, & He, 2018), (Wu, Cai, Li, Xu, & Leung, 2018) and employed in hybrid networks (Zhu, Gao, Zhang, Liu, & Zhang, 2018). Deng, Jing, Yu, and Sun (2019) used an LSTM with sparse self-attention to construct a sentiment lexicon.

Zichao Yang et al. (2016) proposed a hierarchical attention network (HAN) for document classification that applied attention at word and sentence level. Z. Liu et al. (2019) used HAN for sentence representation learning. N. Xu (2017) combined a text HAN with an image HAN for public sentiment classification. Another work by Niu and Hou (2017) used hierarchical attention with bidirectional LSTM for text modelling. Stappen et al. (2019) employed HAN for detecting sentiment change in transcripts of interviews.

A significant development in the fields of SA and NLP in general that has been enabled by attention was the invention and subsequent popularisation of Transformer networks.

Transformer Networks

Vaswani et al. (2017) introduced a novel type of networks known as Transformers, which do not require recurrent or convolutional layers. Instead, those networks rely on self-attention, i.e. computing attention between all the elements in the input sequence, and make use of multiple structures called attention heads for fine-grained analysis (G. Tang, Müller, Rios, & Sennrich, 2018). The architecture of a Transformer is illustrated in Figure 5, based on Vaswani et al. (2017). The Transformer consists of an encoder and a decoder block, followed by a linear layer and a softmax layer. The encoder and decoder are composed of N blocks, with each block containing multi-head attention and a feedforward network, as well as residual connections and layer normalisation. Positional encoding is added to the input and output embeddings to allow the model to understand word order.

Figure 5. Transformer architecture

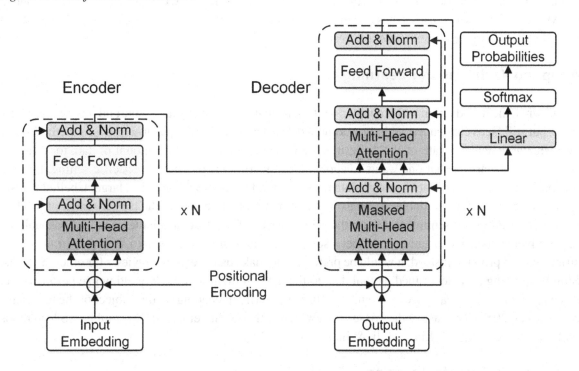

Recently, the work by Devlin, Chang, Lee, and Toutanova (2018) on transformers has led to a major breakthrough in NLP. They introduced a framework named Bidirectional Encoder Representations from Transformers (BERT). BERT involves two steps:

1. **Pre-training:** BERT is pre-trained on a document-level corpus using unsupervised learning on two tasks: A Masked Language Model (MLM) randomly masks input tokens in order to teach BERT to predict words based on their context. In addition, Next Sentence Prediction (NSP) is used to learn the relationships between sentences.

2. **Fine-tuning**: The pre-training is used to initialise models for the downstream tasks that BERT should solve. Each model is then fine-tuned separately through end-to-end learning with task-specific data.

The main contribution of BERT is its improvement upon previous unsupervised representation learning methods by using a bidirectional architecture to generate more powerful representations. Models created with BERT showed excellent performance, surpassing the state of the art in eleven NLP tasks by wide margins, including a 7.7% improvement on the GLUE, a benchmark task for natural language understanding (A. Wang et al., 2018). This has led to great popularity of this type of models in the NLP research community.

Among many other applications, Transformers have also been used for sentiment analysis. Q. Zhang, Lu, Wang, Zhu, and Liu (2019) introduced interactive multi-head attention (IMAN) pre-trained on BERT to achieve new state of the art results in aspect-level SA. Jiang, Wu, Shi, and Zhang (2019) proposed a Transformer-based memory network (TF-MN) for sentiment-based Q&A. Cheng et al. (2019) introduced a VAE framework which uses Transformers as encoder and decoder. Gao, Feng, Song, and Wu (2019) used BERT for targeted sentiment classification.

Adapting With Transfer Learning

As shown in the introduction to this chapter, sentiment analysis has many academic and business applications, but still faces challenges, including domain dependence. While deep learning-based methods have been shown to achieve state-of-the-art results, they require a considerable amount of data for training. A common scenario is that one wants to apply a deep learning approach to a specific setting, but it is not feasible to collect and label enough data to train a model. However, there is a large, labelled dataset from a different setting available. As an example of this problem consider the classification of product reviews depending on sentiment. Given the wide variety of products available, it would probably be prohibitively expensive to gather and label a sufficiently large amount of data to separately train a classifier for each product. Instead, it would be preferable to make use of existing reviews for other products. Simply applying a model trained on that data to the new problem will likely yield worse performance, since the same words may have different meaning or polarity depending on the subject of the text (Save & Shekokar, 2017). Because of these issues, a new research field has emerged that combines SA methods with transfer learning (R. Liu, Shi, Ji, & Jia, 2019).

Definitions of Transfer Learning

In their survey paper, Pan and Yang (2010) present a useful categorisation of transfer learning and its relation to other fields. They define machine learning problems in terms of domains D and tasks T. A domain D consists of a feature space spanning all possible features X and a marginal probability distribution $P(X)$. A task T encompasses a label space Y and a function $f(\bullet)$:

$$D = \{X, P(X)\} \tag{18}$$

$$T = \{Y, f(\bullet)\} \tag{19}$$

In transfer learning, as opposed to traditional machine learning, the domains and/or tasks of the source and target settings are different. The survey paper distinguishes the following variants: Inductive transfer learning (the domains are identical, and the tasks are different), Transductive transfer learning (the domains are different, and the tasks are identical) and Unsupervised transfer learning (domains and tasks may be different and labels are not available in each case). In addition, four categories are presented based on what is being transferred: instances, feature representations, model parameters and relational knowledge. Weiss, Khoshgoftaar, and Wang (2016) follow this categorisation in their survey on recent transfer learning methods, while also distinguishing between homogeneous (same feature space in source and target) and heterogeneous (different feature spaces) transfer learning approaches.

For the purpose of this chapter, the focus is placed on transductive transfer learning. This problem is closely related to domain adaptation, and the terms transfer learning and domain adaptation are used somewhat interchangeably in NLP (Pan & Yang, 2010). Within the context of sentiment analysis, the term cross-domain sentiment classification is also commonly used in the literature. Its definition is equivalent to that of transductive transfer learning. A recent survey on the topic of cross-domain transfer learning can be found in R. Liu et al. (2019). Next, several transfer methods are presented along with examples of their applications to SA.

Methods of Transfer

Structural Correspondence Learning (SCL) was introduced by Blitzer, McDonald, and Pereira (2006). It is a feature transfer algorithm that relies on domain-independent features called pivots to learn correspondences between features in the source and target domains. Those pivots are then used to map source and target features into a common latent space, making SCL an example of a symmetric feature transfer algorithm (Weiss et al., 2016). SCL only considers one-to-one mappings between features. N. Li, Zhai, Zhang, and Liu (2017) extended SCL to include one-to-many mappings and used it for cross-lingual SA, with English as the source and Chinese as the target. Spectral Feature Alignment (SFA) was proposed by Pan, Ni, Sun, Yang, and Chen (2010). This algorithm creates clusters of source and target features in a common latent space. It constructs a bipartite graph, using domain-independent features as a bridge to bring corresponding domain-specific features closer together. The pivots are selected by computing the mutual information between features and domains. SFA does not require labelled data in the target domain. Recently, Hao et al. (2019) introduced CrossWord, which makes use of stochastic word embedding to learn an alignment between domains.

Autoencoders have been successfully applied to transfer learning as well. Glorot, Bordes, and Bengio (2011) extracted a high-level shared representation across multiple domains (Amazon product reviews) in an unsupervised manner with SDAs. The benefit of this approach is that is scales well with larger amounts of data. Zhou, Zhu, He, and Hu (2016) used SDAs to learn language-independent features and perform cross-lingual SA from English to Chinese. Long, Wang, Cao, Sun, and Yu (2016) proposed a framework combining unsupervised pre-training with denoising autoencoders and supervised fine-tuning with deep neural nets to improve transferability.

Ganin et al. (2016) introduced Domain-Adversarial Neural Network (DANN) to improve upon existing autoencoder-based methods. DANN is an augmentation technique for feedforward networks, allowing them to learn features that are both discriminative and invariant to domain shift while being trainable with backpropagation.

Yu and Jiang (2016) apply the pivot prediction concept of SCL to neural networks. They introduce two auxiliary binary tasks to detect the presence of positive and negative domain-independent words in a sentence. The network is then jointly trained to learn both the feature embedding and the classifier at the same time, outperforming several state-of-the-art methods.

Attention models can also be applied to cross-domain SA. Z. Li, Zhang, Wei, Wu, and Yang (2017) introduced the Adversarial Memory Network (AMN) as an improvement over previous deep learning-based methods in terms of interpretability of the pivots. Z. Li, Wei, Zhang, and Yang (2018) developed the Hierarchical Attention Transfer Network (HATN). HATN consists of two subsets named P-Net and NP-Net. The P-Net discovers pivots, and the NP-Net performs feature alignment using the pivots as a bridge. The advantage of this method over algorithms like SCL and SFA is that the pivots are selected automatically. CCHAN (Manshu & Xuemin, 2019) is another combined attention model, consisting of a cloze task network (CTN) performing the word embedding task and a convolutional HAN (CHAN) for sentiment classification. The two networks are jointly trained in an end-to-end fashion. The Hierarchical Attention Network with Prior knowledge information (HANP) was further recently proposed by Manshu and Bing (2019). It adds prior knowledge of the contextual meaning of sentiment words via a sentiment dictionary match (SDM) layer to identify domain-dependent and domain-independent features simultaneously.

Yin, Liu, Zhu, Li, and Wang (2019) introduced Capsule Net with Identifying Transferable Knowledge (CITK). This method includes domain-invariant knowledge extracted with a lexicon-based method in the network to help with pivot identification and generalisation.

Transformers have also shown promising results for cross-domain applications due to their capability of learning high-level feature representations. A recent example is the work by Myagmar, Li, and Kimura (2019), applying transformers to Amazon product reviews.

SOLUTIONS AND RECOMMENDATIONS

This section presents solutions and makes recommendations for readers interesting in applying state-of-the-art models to SA problems. First, a number of popular datasets and challenges are described.

Datasets and Tasks

IMDB Dataset

The IMDB dataset[4] (Maas et al., 2011) contains 50000 movie reviews that are annotated as positive or negative. The reviews are highly polarised, and the data is split evenly between positive and negative reviews.

Yelp Dataset

The Yelp review dataset[5] (X. Zhang, Zhao, & LeCun, 2015) was created from the ongoing Yelp Dataset Challenge. It encompasses two tasks: predicting the review polarity and predicting the number of stars given by the user. The dataset is evenly split between classes, with 280000 training and 19000 test samples for each polarity and 130000 training and 10000 test samples for each star rating.

Stanford Sentiment Treebank

The Stanford Sentiment Treebank (SST) dataset[6] (Socher et al., 2013) contains 215154 phrases parsed from 11855 sentences that were extracted from movie reviews. It provides both coarse-grained (binary) and fine-grained (five points) annotations.

SemEval-2017 Task 4

Task 4 of the International Workshop on Semantic Evaluation (Rosenthal, Farra, & Nakov, 2017) is concerned with SA on Twitter. The task was held yearly since 2013 and continuously expanded. The 2017 task added Arabic as a second language to English. There were five subtasks: polarity classification of single tweets, targeted polarity classification of single tweets in two and five classes, estimating the distribution of a set of tweets across two and five classes.

Applying State of the Art Models

The current state of the art in SA, as well as NLP in general, is based on Transformer networks. This means that pre-trained word embeddings generated by GloVe, Word2vec and fastText are no longer recommended. In 2018, all competitors in the SocialNLP EmotionX Challenge (Hsu & Ku, 2018) used one of those toolkits. By 2019, all the best contributions were utilizing pre-trained embeddings generated with BERT.

As discussed in the previous section, BERT provides powerful text representations through pre-training on a large document corpus. Versions of BERT trained for various languages and of different sizes (named BERT-Base and BERT-Large) have been made publicly available[7]. Thus, the recommended workflow for readers interested in using BERT for SA is to obtain a suitable pre-trained model, e.g. BERT-Large in English, and then further adapt it to their specific task.

An instructive example of how this tuning can be achieved is given in the work of C. Sun, Qiu, Xu, and Huang (2019). They outline three steps for improving the performance of BERT-Base and BERT-Large:

1. **Further Pre-training:** BERT is pre-trained on a large collection of documents. In a subsequent step, additional pre-training on within-task or in-domain data is performed.
2. **Multi-Task Learning:** The model is trained on multiple tasks simultaneously, with the tasks sharing layers except for the final classification layer. This allows knowledge from different tasks to be shared.
3. **Fine-Tuning on the target task:** The model is further trained to adapt it to a specific task.

Following this approach and testing a number of fine-tuning strategies, including the layer-wise optimisation approach from Howard and Ruder (2018), (C. Sun et al.) developed BERT_large+ITPT, which achieved new state-of-the-art results on a number of text processing tasks, including SA. Specifically, the model obtained test error rates of 4,21% on the IMDB dataset and 1.81% and 28.62% on the coarse-grained and fine-grained tasks of the Yelp dataset, respectively.

Transformer-based methods are continuing to evolve. Many researchers develop variants of BERT, such as RoBERTa (Y. Liu et al., 2019), which further optimises the training process. Recently, Zhilin Yang et al. (2019) introduced XLNet, which replaces the autoencoding paradigm of BERT with generalised autoregression. XLNet incorporates ideas from the Transformer-XL (Dai et al., 2019), an autoregressive model which improves upon the standard Transformer by better handling long-term dependencies. The advantages of XLNet over BERT are that it predicts permutations of a sequence, allowing it to learn bidirectional context more effectively and that it does not rely on masking, which solves several inherent problems of BERT, such as the assumption that masked tokens are independent.

XLNet further improved upon the state of the art in a number of language understanding tasks including SA, yielding test error rates of 3.20% on IMDB, 1.37% on coarse-grained Yelp and 27.05% on fine-grained Yelp, as well as 3.2% on SST.

To conclude this section, readers are recommended to use the latest developments in Transformer models for SA. While XLNet has outperformed BERT in a number of popular SA tasks and may become the new standard due to its powerful permutation-based language modelling, BERT variants like RoBERTa could still be useful depending on the problem to be solved. Thus, the readers are encouraged to experiment with these models while observing further developments in the field.

FUTURE RESEARCH DIRECTIONS

NLP in general and sentiment analysis in particular are already being used in many business applications, as discussed in the introduction to this chapter. The amount and diversity of available data continue to grow, which motivates the use of deep learning techniques due to their potent feature extraction capabilities. This section outlines a number of trends and promising research opportunities.

Data Augmentation

One open issue is the need for compensating class imbalance, i.e. the number of instances of each class not being evenly distributed in a labelled dataset. Class imbalance affects many datasets collected in realistic settings, and often a minority class will be of great interest. This is problematic since many classifiers, including deep learning methods, will exhibit a bias towards the majority class (Johnson & Khoshgoftaar, 2019).

Data augmentation is a data-based solution to this problem. It enriches the dataset with additional examples of minority instances. While such augmentation can be easily applied to image data, e.g. by adding noise, rotating or mirroring, it is less straightforward for NLP, as the resulting text sample still needs to make sense. Consequentially, this technique has received comparatively little attention in textual SA. Recently, however, a promising approach for applying data augmentation to SA has been presented by Rizos, Hemker, and Schuller (2019), who use it for improving online hate speech classification. The strategies employed in the paper include: replacing words with synonyms which are discovered through similarities of their embeddings, shifting the positions of words within the sentence, and generating new text through sequential prediction with RNNs or transformers.

Zero-Shot Learning

Aside from improving training through data augmentation, an interesting strategy for dealing with missing data is to apply zero-shot learning techniques. The goal of zero-shot learning, also referred to as zero-data learning, is to recognise classes at test time that were not seen during training (Larochelle,

Erhan, & Bengio, 2008), i.e. there were no instances of those classes for the model to learn from. In the related case where only a few instances are present in the training data, methods are commonly referred to as one-shot or few-shot learning.

Zero-shot learning is increasingly used for large-scale classification problems where annotating all classes extensively is not possible. For the field of visual object detection, there already exist numerous benchmark datasets such as Animals with Attributes (AWA) (Lampert, Nickisch, & Harmeling, 2014). Recently, Xian, Lampert, Schiele, and Akata (2019) published an overview of the state of the art in zero-shot learning, finding a proliferation of approaches but a lack of comparability and flaws of methodology, and introduced a novel dataset called Animals with Attributes 2 (AWA2), along with proposing a standardised evaluation procedure.

Zero-shot learning techniques frequently rely on knowledge in a semantic embedding space (Norouzi et al., 2014), (Z. Zhang & Saligrama, 2015). Applying such techniques to NLP and SA tasks in particular is a promising research direction.

Adversarial Learning

The concept of adversarial networks was introduced by Goodfellow et al. (2014). In a generative adversarial network (GAN), two networks, named generator and discriminator, compete with each other, with the generator attempting to produce samples resembling that of a target distribution and the discriminator attempting to differentiate between real and artificial samples. A basic GAN architecture is depicted in Figure 6.

Figure 6. GAN architecture. The generator creates a fake sample mimicking the training data. The discriminator attempts to tell real from fake samples. Both networks are trained against each other until an equilibrium is reached.

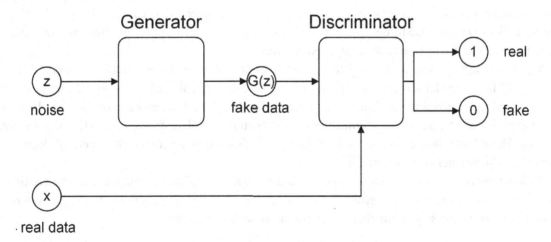

The concept of adversarial training has been applied to many disciplines, including sentiment analysis. Numerous works make use of adversarial networks for cross-domain sentiment classification (Y. Zhang, Barzilay, & Jaakkola, 2017), (Duan, Zhou, Jing, Zhang, & Chen, 2018), (W. Liu & Fu, 2018). In addition, adversarial networks can be used in a generative way to change the style of sentences, outperforming previous approaches based on encoder-decoder architectures (Choi, Choi, Park, & Lee, 2019), (John, Mou, Bahuleyan, & Vechtomova, 2019). While these results are promising, adversarial networks applied to text and speech have yet to reach the same levels of performance as in image generation (Han, Zhang, Cummins, & Schuller, 2019).

Transfer Learning

An emerging trend that is certain to play a major role in the future is the proliferation and improvement of transfer learning methods. This will allow businesses to leverage existing knowledge in the form of models and datasets for new applications, which could significantly speed up time to market and reduce development costs. In terms of research opportunities, cross-lingual transfer is attractive, since most studies on sentiment analysis focus on English documents.

Explainable AI

While deep learning-based models have achieved impressive results, they are frequently applied in a black-box manner, i.e., no information is given about how those systems reach a conclusion. This is a consequence of the massive datasets processed and the highly complex features derived from them by the deep learning algorithms, which may be difficult or impossible for humans to understand. This lack of transparency limits the effectiveness of such systems and is the motivation for the development of explainable AI (XAI). XAI aims to create models that can maintain high levels of performance while allowing humans to understand and trust their decisions (Mathews, 2019).

XAI strategies can be classified into two broad categories: model-based (intrinsic) and post-hoc explainability (Murdoch, Singh, Kumbier, Abbasi-Asl, & Yu, 2019). Intrinsic approaches aim to make the model itself more explainable, e.g. by reducing its complexity. Post-hoc methods are designed to analyse an existing model. An example of a popular post-hoc framework is LIME (Marco Tulio Ribeiro, Singh, & Guestrin, 2016). Murdoch et al. (2019) formulate three criteria for grading an interpretation: predictive accuracy, descriptive accuracy, and relevancy.

A possible solution for interpretability is the use of attention. (Letarte, Paradis, Giguère, & Laviolette, 2018) introduced a self-attention network based on the Transformer. They found that visualising the relationships between words found by attention helped explain differences in the model's behaviour between topic classification and sentiment analysis. (Peters, Niculae, & Martins, 2018) demonstrated how regularised attention can be used to create sparse, ordered structures in the layers of deep neural networks, which benefits interpretability.

As automated solutions spread and become increasingly complex, explainable AI will continue to become more relevant, both as a means for building trust with the customers employing a system and as a way for the business offering that system to improve performance.

Defending Against Adversarial Attacks

On a related note, an important area of research that is starting to be explored is the robustness of NLP algorithms. Complex classifiers, while being powerful pattern detectors, are also prone to changing their predictions based on small perturbations in the input data. This weakness has been shown to be exploitable through so-called adversarial attacks. The attacker designs manipulated instances of input data (adversarial samples), which are misclassified by the targeted model. Recently, M. T. Ribeiro, Singh, and Guestrin (2018) demonstrated how to apply this concept to NLP, using semantically equivalent adversarial rules (SEARs) to construct adversarial examples from text while maintaining the semantic content. Given these vulnerabilities, further investigation into adversarial attacks in order to improve models and make them safer to use is a promising line of research.

Multimodal Sentiment Analysis

Another interesting research direction is to perform SA based on multiple modalities, e.g. text, audio and visual data from videos. This will allow for a more robust sentiment detection, as the model can combine information across modalities for decision making. A recent work on cross-domain sentiment analysis that makes use of Bag-of-Words features derived from text, speech and facial expressions is (Cummins et al., 2018).

CONCLUSION

This chapter has introduced sentiment analysis as an important topic in natural language processing. It has highlighted numerous business and academic applications, including customer analytics, financial market predictions and estimating public sentiment from social media posts, and provided a categorisation of sentiment analysis approaches. Deep learning was presented as a useful collection of methods to extract information from increasingly large amounts of unstructured data. The basic architectures of CNNs and RNNs were introduced, as well as their combination into hybrid networks. Current trends and state-of-the-art methods were explored, covering attention, transfer learning and Transformer networks. The challenges of explainable AI, data augmentation, zero-shot learning, adversarial learning. the threat of adversarial attacks and the potential of multimodal analysis were explained and highlighted as opportunities for future research.

ACKNOWLEDGMENT

This research was supported by the BMW Group.

REFERENCES

Bahdanau, D., Cho, K., & Bengio, Y. (2014, September 1). *Neural Machine Translation by Jointly Learning to Align and Translate*. Retrieved from https://arxiv.org/pdf/1409.0473v7

Balaji, P., Nagaraju, O., & Haritha, D. (2017). Levels of sentiment analysis and its challenges: A literature review. In *Proceedings of the 2017 International Conference on Big Data Analytics and Computational Intelligence (ICBDAC)* (pp. 436–439). IEEE. 10.1109/ICBDACI.2017.8070879

Bechara, A., Damasio, H., & Damasio, A. R. (2000). Emotion, decision making and the orbitofrontal cortex. *Cerebral Cortex (New York, N.Y.)*, *10*(3), 295–307. doi:10.1093/cercor/10.3.295 PMID:10731224

Bengio, Y., Courville, A., & Vincent, P. (2013). Representation Learning: A Review and New Perspectives. *IEEE Transactions on Pattern Analysis and Machine Intelligence*, *35*(8), 1798–1828. doi:10.1109/TPAMI.2013.50 PMID:23787338

Blitzer, J., McDonald, R., & Pereira, F. (2006). Domain Adaptation with Structural Correspondence Learning. In *EMNLP '06, Proceedings of the 2006 Conference on Empirical Methods in Natural Language Processing* (pp. 120–128). Association for Computational Linguistics. doi:10.3115/1610075.1610094

Bojanowski, P., Grave, E., Joulin, A., & Mikolov, T. (2017). Enriching Word Vectors with Subword Information. *Transactions of the Association for Computational Linguistics*, *5*, 135–146. doi:10.1162/tacl_a_00051

Chen, P., Sun, Z., Bing, L., & Yang, W. (2017). Recurrent Attention Network on Memory for Aspect Sentiment Analysis. In *Proceedings of the 2017 Conference on Empirical Methods in Natural Language Processing* (pp. 452–461). Copenhagen, Denmark: Association for Computational Linguistics. 10.18653/v1/D17-1047

Cheng, X., Xu, W., & Wang, T., Chu, W., Huang, W., Chen, K., & Hu, J. (2019). Variational Semi-Supervised Aspect-Term Sentiment Analysis via Transformer. In *Proceedings of the 23rd Conference on Computational Natural Language Learning (CoNLL)* (pp. 961–969). Hong Kong, China: Association for Computational Linguistics. 10.18653/v1/K19-1090

Cho, K., van Merriënboer, B., Bahdanau, D., & Bengio, Y. (2014). On the Properties of Neural Machine Translation: Encoder-Decoder Approaches. In *Proceedings of SSST-8, Eighth Workshop on Syntax, Semantics and Structure in Statistical Translation* (pp. 103–111). Doha, Qatar: Association for Computational Linguistics. 10.3115/v1/W14-4012

Choi, W., Choi, S. J., Park, S., & Lee, S. (2019). Adversarial Style Transfer for Long Sentences. *2019 International Conference on Electronics, Information, and Communication (ICEIC)*. 10.23919/ELIN-FOCOM.2019.8706482

Christy Daniel, D., & Shyamala, L. (2019). An insight on sentiment analysis research from text using deep learning methods. *International Journal of Innovative Technology and Exploring Engineering*, *8*(10), 2033–2048. doi:10.35940/ijitee.J9316.0881019

Cooper, P. (2019). *28 Twitter Statistics All Marketers Need to Know in 2019*. Retrieved from https://blog.hootsuite.com/twitter-statistics/

Cummins, N., Amiriparian, S., Ottl, S., Gerczuk, M., Schmitt, M., & Schuller, B. (2018). Multimodal Bag-of-Words for Cross Domains Sentiment Analysis. In *ICASSP-2018, Proceedings of the 2018 IEEE International Conference on Acoustics, Speech and Signal Processing (ICASSP)* (pp. 4954–4958). IEEE. 10.1109/ICASSP.2018.8462660

Dai, Z., & Yang, Z., Yang, Y., Carbonell, J., Le, Q., & Salakhutdinov, R. (2019). Transformer-XL: Attentive Language Models beyond a Fixed-Length Context. In *Proceedings of the 57th Annual Meeting of the Association for Computational Linguistics* (pp. 2978–2988). Florence, Italy: Association for Computational Linguistics. 10.18653/v1/P19-1285

Della Pietra, S., Della Pietra, V., & Lafferty, J. (1997). Inducing features of random fields. *IEEE Transactions on Pattern Analysis and Machine Intelligence*, *19*(4), 380–393. doi:10.1109/34.588021

Deng, D., Jing, L., Yu, J., & Sun, S. (2019). Sparse Self-Attention LSTM for Sentiment Lexicon Construction. *IEEE/ACM Transactions on Audio, Speech, and Language Processing*, *27*(11), 1777–1790. doi:10.1109/TASLP.2019.2933326

Desjardins, J. (2019). *What Happens in an Internet Minute in 2019?* Retrieved from https://www.visualcapitalist.com/what-happens-in-an-internet-minute-in-2019/

Devlin, J., Chang, M.-W., Lee, K., & Toutanova, K. (2018). *BERT: Pre-training of Deep Bidirectional Transformers for Language Understanding.* CoRR, abs/1810.04805

Du, C., Tsai, M., & Wang, C. (2019). Beyond Word-level to Sentence-level Sentiment Analysis for Financial Reports. *Proceedings of the 2019 IEEE International Conference on Acoustics, Speech and Signal Processing (ICASSP)*. 10.1109/ICASSP.2019.8683085

Du, J., Gui, L., Xu, R., & He, Y. (2018). A Convolutional Attention Model for Text Classification. In X. Huang, J. Jiang, D. Zhao, Y. Feng, & Y. Hong (Eds.), Lecture Notes in Computer Science: Vol. 10619. *Natural Language Processing and Chinese Computing* (pp. 183–195). Springer International Publishing. doi:10.1007/978-3-319-73618-1_16

Duan, X., Zhou, Y., Jing, C., Zhang, L., & Chen, R. (2018). Cross-domain Sentiment Classification Based on Transfer Learning and Adversarial Network. In *Proceedings of the 2018 IEEE 4th International Conference on Computer and Communications (ICCC)* (pp. 2302–2306). IEEE. 10.1109/CompComm.2018.8780771

Ekman, P. (1999). Basic emotions. Handbook of Cognition and Emotion, 98(45-60), 16.

Evgeniou, T., & Pontil, M. (2001). *Support Vector Machines: Theory and Applications* (Vol. 2049). Springer. doi:10.1007/3-540-44673-7_12

Facebook. (2019). *Facebook Reports Second Quarter 2019 Results.* Retrieved from https://investor.fb.com/investor-news/press-release-details/2019/Facebook-Reports-Second-Quarter-2019-Results/default.aspx

Fu, X., Wei, Y., Xu, F., Wang, T., Lu, Y., Li, J., & Huang, J. Z. (2019). Semi-supervised Aspect-level Sentiment Classification Model based on Variational Autoencoder. *Knowledge-Based Systems*, *171*, 81–92. doi:10.1016/j.knosys.2019.02.008

Ganin, Y., Ustinova, E., Ajakan, H., Germain, P., Larochelle, H., Laviolette, F., . . . Lempitsky, V. S. (2016). Domain-Adversarial Training of Neural Networks. *J. Mach. Learn. Res., 17*, 59:1-59:35. Retrieved from http://jmlr.org/papers/v17/15-239.html

Gao, Z., Feng, A., Song, X., & Wu, X. (2019). Target-Dependent Sentiment Classification With BERT. *IEEE Access: Practical Innovations, Open Solutions, 7*, 154290–154299. doi:10.1109/ACCESS.2019.2946594

Gautam, G., & Yadav, D. (2014). Sentiment analysis of twitter data using machine learning approaches and semantic analysis. In M. Parashar (Ed.), *Proceedings of the 2014 Seventh International Conference on Contemporary Computing (IC3): 7 - 9 Aug. 2014, Noida, India* (pp. 437–442). Piscataway, NJ: IEEE. 10.1109/IC3.2014.6897213

Gers, F. A., Schmidhuber, J., & Cummins, F. (2000). Learning to forget: Continual prediction with LSTM. *Neural Computation, 12*(10), 2451–2471. doi:10.1162/089976600300015015 PMID:11032042

Glorot, X., Bordes, A., & Bengio, Y. (2011). Domain Adaptation for Large-scale Sentiment Classification: A Deep Learning Approach. In *ICML'11, Proceedings of the 28th International Conference on International Conference on Machine Learning* (pp. 513–520). Omnipress. Retrieved from https://dl.acm.org/citation.cfm?id=3104482.3104547

Goodfellow, I. J., Pouget-Abadie, J., Mirza, M., Xu, B., Warde-Farley, D., Ozair, S., & Bengio, Y. (2014). Generative Adversarial Nets. In *NIPS'14, Proceedings of the 27th International Conference on Neural Information Processing Systems* (Vol. 2, pp. 2672–2680). MIT Press. Retrieved from https://dl.acm.org/citation.cfm?id=2969033.2969125

Graves, A. (2012). Supervised Sequence Labelling with Recurrent Neural Networks (2nd ed.). In Studies in Computational Intelligence: Vol. 385. Berlin: Springer Berlin Heidelberg. doi:10.1007/978-3-642-24797-2

Han, J., Zhang, Z., Cummins, N., & Schuller, B. (2019). Adversarial Training in Affective Computing and Sentiment Analysis: Recent Advances and Perspectives [Review Article]. *IEEE Computational Intelligence Magazine, 14*(2), 68–81. doi:10.1109/MCI.2019.2901088

Hao, Y., Mu, T., Hong, R., Wang, M., Liu, X., & Goulermas, J. Y. (2019). Cross-domain Sentiment Encoding through Stochastic Word Embedding. *IEEE Transactions on Knowledge and Data Engineering, 1*, 1. Advance online publication. doi:10.1109/TKDE.2019.2913379

Hassan, A., & Mahmood, A. (2018). Convolutional Recurrent Deep Learning Model for Sentence Classification. *IEEE Access: Practical Innovations, Open Solutions, 6*, 13949–13957. doi:10.1109/ACCESS.2018.2814818

Hatzivassiloglou, V., & McKeown, K. (1997). Predicting the Semantic Orientation of Adjectives. In *Proceedings of the 35th Annual Meeting of the Association for Computational Linguistics and 8th Conference of the European Chapter of the Association for Computational Linguistics* (pp. 174–181). Madrid, Spain: Association for Computational Linguistics. 10.3115/976909.979640

Hinton, G., Deng, L., Yu, D., Dahl, G., Mohamed, A., Jaitly, N., Senior, A., Vanhoucke, V., Nguyen, P., Sainath, T., & Kingsbury, B. (2012). Deep Neural Networks for Acoustic Modeling in Speech Recognition: The Shared Views of Four Research Groups. *IEEE Signal Processing Magazine, 29*(6), 82–97. doi:10.1109/MSP.2012.2205597

Hochreiter, S., & Schmidhuber, J. (1997). Long short-term memory. *Neural Computation, 9*(8), 1735–1780. doi:10.1162/neco.1997.9.8.1735 PMID:9377276

Howard, J., & Ruder, S. (2018). Universal language model fine-tuning for text classification. In *Proceedings of the 56th Annual Meeting of the Association for Computational Linguistics (*Volume 1*: Long Papers)*. Melbourne, Australia: Association for Computational Linguistics. 10.18653/v1/P18-1031

Hsu, C.-C., & Ku, L.-W. (2018). SocialNLP 2018 EmotionX Challenge Overview: Recognizing Emotions in Dialogues. In *Proceedings of the Sixth International Workshop on Natural Language Processing for Social Media* (pp. 27–31). Melbourne, Australia: Association for Computational Linguistics. 10.18653/v1/W18-3505

Hu, M., & Liu, B. (2004). Mining and Summarizing Customer Reviews. In *KDD '04, Proceedings of the Tenth ACM SIGKDD International Conference on Knowledge Discovery and Data Mining* (pp. 168–177). New York, NY: ACM. 10.1145/1014052.1014073

Hussein, D. M. E.-D. M. (2018). A survey on sentiment analysis challenges. *Journal of King Saud University -. Engineering and Science, 30*(4), 330–338. doi:10.1016/j.jksues.2016.04.002

Jiang, M., Wu, J., Shi, X., & Zhang, M. (2019). Transformer Based Memory Network for Sentiment Analysis of Web Comments. *IEEE Access: Practical Innovations, Open Solutions, 1*, 179942–179953. Advance online publication. doi:10.1109/ACCESS.2019.2957192

John, V., Mou, L., Bahuleyan, H., & Vechtomova, O. (2019). Disentangled Representation Learning for Non-Parallel Text Style Transfer. In *Proceedings of the 57th Annual Meeting of the Association for Computational Linguistics* (pp. 424–434). Florence, Italy: Association for Computational Linguistics. 10.18653/v1/P19-1041

Johnson, J. M., & Khoshgoftaar, T. M. (2019). Survey on deep learning with class imbalance. *Journal of Big Data, 6*(1), 27. doi:10.118640537-019-0192-5

Jose, R., & Chooralil, V. S. (2016). Prediction of election result by enhanced sentiment analysis on twitter data using classifier ensemble Approach. In *Proceedings of the 2016 International Conference on Data Mining and Advanced Computing (SAPIENCE)* (pp. 64–67). IEEE. 10.1109/SAPIENCE.2016.7684133

Joshi, O. S., & Simon, G. (2018). Sentiment Analysis Tool on Cloud: Software as a Service Model. In *Proceedings of the 2018 International Conference On Advances in Communication and Computing Technology (ICACCT)* (pp. 459–462). Sangamner, India: Springer. 10.1109/ICACCT.2018.8529649

Joulin, A., Grave, E., Bojanowski, P., & Mikolov, T. (2017). Bag of Tricks for Efficient Text Classification. In *Proceedings of the 15th Conference of the European Chapter of the Association for Computational Linguistics: Volume 2, Short Papers* (pp. 427–431). Valencia, Spain: Association for Computational Linguistics. Retrieved from https://www.aclweb.org/anthology/E17-2068

Joyce, B., & Deng, J. (2017). Sentiment analysis of tweets for the 2016 US presidential election. In *Proceedings of the 2017 IEEE MIT Undergraduate Research Technology Conference (URTC)* (pp. 1–4). IEEE. 10.1109/URTC.2017.8284176

Kaur, H., & Mangat, V., & Nidhi (2017). A survey of sentiment analysis techniques. *2017 International Conference on I-SMAC (IoT in Social, Mobile, Analytics and Cloud) (I-SMAC)*. 10.1109/I-SMAC.2017.8058315

Kim, Y. (2014). Convolutional Neural Networks for Sentence Classification. In *Proceedings of the 2014 Conference on Empirical Methods in Natural Language Processing (EMNLP)* (pp. 1746–1751). Doha, Qatar: Association for Computational Linguistics. 10.3115/v1/D14-1181

Kingma, D. P., & Welling, M. (2013, December 20). *Auto-Encoding Variational Bayes*. Retrieved from https://arxiv.org/pdf/1312.6114v10

Krizhevsky, A., Sutskever, I., & Hinton, G. E. (2012). ImageNet Classification with Deep Convolutional Neural Networks. In *NIPS'12, Proceedings of the 25th International Conference on Neural Information Processing Systems* - Volume 1 (pp. 1097–1105). Curran Associates Inc.

Lampert, C. H., Nickisch, H., & Harmeling, S. (2014). Attribute-Based Classification for Zero-Shot Visual Object Categorization. *IEEE Transactions on Pattern Analysis and Machine Intelligence*, *36*(3), 453–465. doi:10.1109/TPAMI.2013.140 PMID:24457503

Larochelle, H., Erhan, D., & Bengio, Y. (2008). Zero-data Learning of New Tasks. In *AAAI'08, Proceedings of the 23rd National Conference on Artificial Intelligence* (Vol. 2, pp. 646–651). AAAI Press. Retrieved from https://dl.acm.org/citation.cfm?id=1620163.1620172

LeCun, Y., Bengio, Y., & Hinton, G. (2015). Deep learning. *Nature*, *521*(7553), 436–444. doi:10.1038/nature14539 PMID:26017442

Letarte, G., Paradis, F., Giguère, P., & Laviolette, F. (2018). Importance of Self-Attention for Sentiment Analysis. In *Proceedings of the 2018 EMNLP Workshop BlackboxNLP: Analyzing and Interpreting Neural Networks for NLP* (pp. 267–275). Brussels, Belgium: Association for Computational Linguistics. 10.18653/v1/W18-5429

Li, N., Zhai, S., & Zhang, Z., & Liu, B. (2017). Structural Correspondence Learning for Cross-lingual Sentiment Classification with One-to-many Mappings. In *AAAI'17, Proceedings of the Thirty-First AAAI Conference on Artificial Intelligence* (pp. 3490–3496). AAAI Press. Retrieved from https://dl.acm.org/citation.cfm?id=3298023.3298075

Li, Z., & Wei, Y., Zhang, Y., & Yang, Q. (2018). Hierarchical Attention Transfer Network for Cross-Domain Sentiment Classification. *AAAI Conference on Artificial Intelligence; Thirty-Second AAAI Conference on Artificial Intelligence*. Retrieved from https://aaai.org/ocs/index.php/AAAI/AAAI18/paper/view/16873

Li, Z., & Zhang, Y., Wei, Y., Wu, Y., & Yang, Q. (2017). End-to-end Adversarial Memory Network for Cross-domain Sentiment Classification. In C. Sierra (Ed.), *IJCAI'17, Proceedings of the 26th International Joint Conference on Artificial Intelligence* (pp. 2237–2243). AAAI Press. Retrieved from https://dl.acm.org/citation.cfm?id=3172077.3172199

Liu, G., & Guo, J. (2019). Bidirectional LSTM with attention mechanism and convolutional layer for text classification. *Neurocomputing*, *337*, 325–338. doi:10.1016/j.neucom.2019.01.078

Liu, Q., Zhang, H., Zeng, Y., Huang, Z., & Wu, Z. (2018). Content Attention Model for Aspect Based Sentiment Analysis. In *WWW '18, Proceedings of the 2018 World Wide Web Conference* (pp. 1023–1032). Geneva, Switzerland: International World Wide Web Conferences Steering Committee. 10.1145/3178876.3186001

Liu, R., Shi, Y., Ji, C., & Jia, M. (2019). A Survey of Sentiment Analysis Based on Transfer Learning. *IEEE Access: Practical Innovations, Open Solutions*, 7, 85401–85412. doi:10.1109/ACCESS.2019.2925059

Liu, W., & Fu, X. (2018). Introduce More Characteristics of Samples into Cross-domain Sentiment Classification. In *ICPR 2018, Proceedings of the 2018 24th International Conference on Pattern Recognition (ICPR)* (pp. 25–30). IEEE. 10.1109/ICPR.2018.8545331

Liu, Y., Ott, M., Goyal, N., Du Jingfei, Joshi, M., Chen, D., . . . Stoyanov, V. (2019, July 26). *RoBERTa: A Robustly Optimized BERT Pretraining Approach*. Retrieved from https://arxiv.org/pdf/1907.11692v1

Liu, Z., Bai, X., Cai, T., Chen, C., Zhang, W., & Jiang, L. (2019). Improving Sentence Representations with Local and Global Attention for Classification. In *IJCNN 2019, Proceedings of the 2019 International Joint Conference on Neural Networks (IJCNN)* (pp. 1–7). Curran Associates, Inc. 10.1109/IJCNN.2019.8852436

Long, M., Wang, J., Cao, Y., Sun, J., & Yu, P. S. (2016). Deep Learning of Transferable Representation for Scalable Domain Adaptation. *IEEE Transactions on Knowledge and Data Engineering*, 28(8), 2027–2040. doi:10.1109/TKDE.2016.2554549

Lu, G., Zhao, X., Yin, J., & Yang, W., & Li, B. (2018). Multi-task learning using variational auto-encoder for sentiment classification. *Pattern Recognition Letters*. Advance online publication. doi:10.1016/j.patrec.2018.06.027

Luo, X., Zimet, G., & Shah, S. (2019). A natural language processing framework to analyse the opinions on HPV vaccination reflected in twitter over 10 years (2008 - 2017). *Human Vaccines & Immunotherapeutics*, 15(7-8), 1496–1504. doi:10.1080/21645515.2019.1627821 PMID:31194609

Maas, A. L., Daly, R. E., Pham, P. T., Huang, D., Ng, A. Y., & Potts, C. (2011). Learning Word Vectors for Sentiment Analysis. In *Proceedings of the 49th Annual Meeting of the Association for Computational Linguistics: Human Language Technologies* (pp. 142–150). Association for Computational Linguistics. Retrieved from https://www.aclweb.org/anthology/P11-1015

Maitra, P., & Sarkhel, R. (2018). A K-Competitive Autoencoder for Aggression Detection in Social Media Text. In *Proceedings of the First Workshop on Trolling, Aggression and Cyberbullying (TRAC-2018)* (pp. 80–89). Association for Computational Linguistics. Retrieved from https://www.aclweb.org/anthology/W18-4410

Makhzani, A., & Frey, B. (2015). *Winner-take-all autoencoders*. MIT Press.

Manshu, T., & Bing, W. (2019). Adding Prior Knowledge in Hierarchical Attention Neural Network for Cross Domain Sentiment Classification. *IEEE Access: Practical Innovations, Open Solutions*, 7, 32578–32588. doi:10.1109/ACCESS.2019.2901929

Manshu, T., & Xuemin, Z. (2019). CCHAN: An End to End Model for Cross Domain Sentiment Classification. *IEEE Access: Practical Innovations, Open Solutions*, 7, 50232–50239. doi:10.1109/ACCESS.2019.2910300

Mathews, S. M. (2019). Explainable Artificial Intelligence Applications in NLP, Biomedical, and Malware Classification: A Literature Review. *Advances in Intelligent Systems and Computing*, *998*, 1269–1292. doi:10.1007/978-3-030-22868-2_90

Mikolov, T., Chen, K., Corrado, G. S., & Dean, J. (2013). *Efficient Estimation of Word Representations in Vector Space*. Retrieved from https://arxiv.org/pdf/1301.3781.pdf

Mikolov, T., Sutskever, I., & Chen, K., Corrado, G., & Dean, J. (2013). Distributed Representations of Words and Phrases and Their Compositionality. In *NIPS'13, Proceedings of the 26th International Conference on Neural Information Processing Systems - Volume 2* (pp. 3111–3119). Curran Associates Inc. Retrieved from https://dl.acm.org/citation.cfm?id=2999792.2999959

Müller, M. M., & Salathé, M. (2019). Crowdbreaks: Tracking health trends using public social media data and crowdsourcing. *Frontiers in Public Health*, *7*(APR), 81. Advance online publication. doi:10.3389/fpubh.2019.00081 PMID:31037238

Murdoch, W. J., Singh, C., Kumbier, K., Abbasi-Asl, R., & Yu, B. (2019). Definitions, methods, and applications in interpretable machine learning. *Proceedings of the National Academy of Sciences of the United States of America*, *116*(44), 22071–22080. doi:10.1073/pnas.1900654116 PMID:31619572

Myagmar, B., Li, J., & Kimura, S. (2019). Cross-Domain Sentiment Classification With Bidirectional Contextualized Transformer Language Models. *IEEE Access: Practical Innovations, Open Solutions*, *7*, 163219–163230. doi:10.1109/ACCESS.2019.2952360

Neethu, M. S., & Rajasree, R. (2013). Sentiment analysis in twitter using machine learning techniques. In *2013 Fourth International Conference on Computing, Communications and Networking Technologies (ICCCNT)* (pp. 1–5). IEEE. 10.1109/ICCCNT.2013.6726818

Nigam, K., & Lafferty, J., & Mccallum, A. (1999). Using maximum entropy for text classification. In *IJCAI-99, Proceedings of the IJCAI-99 Workshop on Machine Learning for Information Filtering* (pp. 61–67). AAAI Press.

Niu, X., & Hou, Y. (2017). Hierarchical Attention BLSTM for Modeling Sentences and Documents. Lecture Notes in Computer Science, 10635, 167–177. doi:10.1007/978-3-319-70096-0_18

Norouzi, M., Mikolov, T., Bengio, S., Singer, Y., Shlens, J., Frome, A., . . . Dean, J. (2014). Zero-Shot Learning by Convex Combination of Semantic Embeddings. In *2nd International Conference on Learning Representations, ICLR 2014*. Conference Track Proceedings.

Pan, S. J., Ni, X., Sun, J.-T., Yang, Q., & Chen, Z. (2010). Cross-domain Sentiment Classification via Spectral Feature Alignment. In *WWW '10, Proceedings of the 19th International Conference on World Wide Web* (pp. 751–760). New York, NY: ACM. 10.1145/1772690.1772767

Pan, S. J., & Yang, Q. (2010). A Survey on Transfer Learning. *IEEE Transactions on Knowledge and Data Engineering*, *22*(10), 1345–1359. doi:10.1109/TKDE.2009.191

Pang, B., Lee, L., & Vaithyanathan, S. (2002). *Thumbs up? Sentiment classification using machine learning techniques*. Association for Computational Linguistics. Retrieved from https://dl.acm.org/ft_gateway.cfm?id=1118704&type=pdf

Pennington, J., Socher, R., & Manning, C. D. (2014). Glove: Global Vectors for Word Representation. *Proceedings of the 2014 Conference on Empirical Methods in Natural Language Processing (EMNLP)*. Retrieved from https://www.aclweb.org/anthology/D14-1162.pdf

Peters, B., Niculae, V., & Martins, A. F. T. (2018). Interpretable Structure Induction via Sparse Attention. In *Proceedings of the 2018 EMNLP Workshop BlackboxNLP: Analyzing and Interpreting Neural Networks for NLP* (pp. 365–367). Brussels, Belgium: Association for Computational Linguistics. 10.18653/v1/W18-5450

Plutchik, R. (1980). A general psychoevolutionary theory of emotion. In R. Plutchik & H. Kellerman (Eds.), *Theories of Emotion* (pp. 3–33). Academic Press. doi:10.1016/B978-0-12-558701-3.50007-7

Rameshbhai, C. J., & Paulose, J. (2019). Opinion mining on newspaper headlines using SVM and NLP. *Iranian Journal of Electrical and Computer Engineering*, 9(3), 2152–2163. doi:10.11591/ijece.v9i3.pp2152-2163

Ran, J. (2019). A Self-attention Based LSTM Network for Text Classification. *Journal of Physics: Conference Series*, 1207, 12008. doi:10.1088/1742-6596/1207/1/012008

Ranjit, S., Shrestha, S., Subedi, S., & Shakya, S. (2018). Foreign Rate Exchange Prediction Using Neural Network and Sentiment Analysis. *2018 International Conference on Advances in Computing, Communication Control and Networking (ICACCCN)*. 10.1109/ICACCCN.2018.8748819

Ribeiro, M. T., Singh, S., & Guestrin, C. (2016). Why Should I Trust You?": Explaining the Predictions of Any Classifier. In *KDD '16, Proceedings of the 22Nd ACM SIGKDD International Conference on Knowledge Discovery and Data Mining* (pp. 1135–1144). New York, NY: ACM. 10.1145/2939672.2939778

Ribeiro, M. T., Singh, S., & Guestrin, C. (Eds.). (2018). *Semantically equivalent adversarial rules for debugging NLP models*. Retrieved from https://www2.scopus.com/inward/record.uri?eid=2-s2.0-85061785761&partnerID=40&md5=be8d9d4a9111c0f0f6ba388f3dcc16bb

Rizos, G., Hemker, K., & Schuller, B. (2019). Augment to Prevent: Short-Text Data Augmentation in Deep Learning for Hate-Speech Classification. In *CIKM '19, Proceedings of the 28th ACM International Conference on Information and Knowledge Management* (pp. 991–1000). New York, NY: ACM. 10.1145/3357384.3358040

Rosenthal, S., Farra, N., & Nakov, P. (2017). SemEval-2017 Task 4: Sentiment Analysis in Twitter. In *Proceedings of the 11th International Workshop on Semantic Evaluation (SemEval-2017)* (pp. 502–518). Vancouver, Canada: Association for Computational Linguistics. 10.18653/v1/S17-2088

Sagha, H., Cummins, N., & Schuller, B. (2017). Stacked denoising autoencoders for sentiment analysis: A review. *Wiley Interdisciplinary Reviews. Data Mining and Knowledge Discovery*, 7(5), e1212. doi:10.1002/widm.1212

Save, A., & Shekokar, N. (2017). Analysis of cross domain sentiment techniques. *2017 International Conference on Electrical, Electronics, Communication, Computer, and Optimization Techniques (ICEEC-COT)*. 10.1109/ICEECCOT.2017.8284637

Shah, D., Isah, H., & Zulkernine, F. (2018). Predicting the Effects of News Sentiments on the Stock Market. *2018 IEEE International Conference on Big Data (Big Data)*. 10.1109/BigData.2018.8621884

Shmueli, B., & Ku, L.-W. (2019). *SocialNLP EmotionX 2019 Challenge Overview: Predicting Emotions in Spoken Dialogues and Chats*. Retrieved from https://arxiv.org/abs/1909.07734

Socher, R., Perelygin, A., Wu, J., Chuang, J., Manning, C. D., Ng, A., & Potts, C. (2013). Recursive Deep Models for Semantic Compositionality Over a Sentiment Treebank. In *Proceedings of the 2013 Conference on Empirical Methods in Natural Language Processing* (pp. 1631–1642). Seattle, WA: Association for Computational Linguistics. Retrieved from https://www.aclweb.org/anthology/D13-1170

Stappen, L., Cummins, N., Meßner, E.-M., Baumeister, H., Dineley, J., & Schuller, B. W. (2019). Context Modelling Using Hierarchical Attention Networks for Sentiment and Self-assessed Emotion Detection in Spoken Narratives. In *Proceedings of the 2019 IEEE International Conference on Acoustics, Speech and Signal Processing (ICASSP)* (pp. 6680–6684). Brighton: IEEE. 10.1109/ICASSP.2019.8683801

Sun, C., Qiu, X., Xu, Y., & Huang, X. (2019). How to Fine-Tune BERT for Text Classification? In M. Sun, X. Huang, H. Ji, Z. Liu, & Y. Liu (Eds.), *LNCS sublibrary. SL 7, Artificial intelligence: v. 11856. Chinese Computational Linguistics: 18th China National Conference, CCL 2019, Kunming, China, October 18-20, 2019, Proceedings* (pp. 194–206). Cham: Springer. 10.1007/978-3-030-32381-3_16

Taboada, M., Anthony, C., & Voll, K. (2006). Methods for Creating Semantic Orientation Databases. *Proceeding of LREC-06, the 5th International Conference on Language Resources and Evaluation.* Retrieved from https://www.microsoft.com/en-us/research/publication/methods-for-creating-semantic-orientation-databases/

Taboada, M., Brooke, J., Tofiloski, M., Voll, K., & Stede, M. (2011). Lexicon-based methods for sentiment analysis. *Computational Linguistics*, *37*(2), 267–307. doi:10.1162/COLI_a_00049

Tang, D., Qin, B., & Liu, T. (2015). Document Modeling with Gated Recurrent Neural Network for Sentiment Classification. In *Proceedings of the 2015 Conference on Empirical Methods in Natural Language Processing* (pp. 1422–1432). Lisbon, Portugal: Association for Computational Linguistics. 10.18653/v1/D15-1167

Tang, D., Qin, B., & Liu, T. (2016). Aspect Level Sentiment Classification with Deep Memory Network. In *Proceedings of the 2016 Conference on Empirical Methods in Natural Language Processing* (pp. 214–224). Austin, TX: Association for Computational Linguistics. 10.18653/v1/D16-1021

Tang, G., Müller, M., Rios, A., & Sennrich, R. (2018). Why Self-Attention? A Targeted Evaluation of Neural Machine Translation Architectures. In *Proceedings of the 2018 Conference on Empirical Methods in Natural Language Processing* (pp. 4263–4272). Brussels, Belgium: Association for Computational Linguistics. 10.18653/v1/D18-1458

Tian, Z., Rong, W., Shi, L., Liu, J., & Xiong, Z. (2018). Attention Aware Bidirectional Gated Recurrent Unit Based Framework for Sentiment Analysis. In W. Liu, F. Giunchiglia, & B. Yang (Eds.), *Knowledge Science, Engineering and Management* (pp. 67–78). Springer International Publishing. doi:10.1007/978-3-319-99365-2_6

Turney, P. D. (2002). *Thumbs up or thumbs down?: semantic orientation applied to unsupervised classification of reviews*: Association for Computational Linguistics. Retrieved from https://dl.acm.org/ft_gateway.cfm?id=1073153&type=pdf

Vapnik, V. N. (2000). *The Nature of Statistical Learning Theory*. Springer New York., doi:10.1007/978-1-4757-3264-1

Vaswani, A., Shazeer, N., Parmar, N., Uszkoreit, J., Jones, L., Gomez, A. N., & Polosukhin, I. (2017). Attention is All you Need. In I. Guyon, U. V. Luxburg, S. Bengio, H. Wallach, R. Fergus, S. Vishwanathan, & R. Garnett (Eds.), Advances in Neural Information Processing Systems (Vol. 30, pp. 5998–6008). Curran Associates, Inc. Retrieved from http://papers.nips.cc/paper/7181-attention-is-all-you-need.pdf

Vincent, P., Larochelle, H., Bengio, Y., & Manzagol, P.-A. (2008). Extracting and Composing Robust Features with Denoising Autoencoders. In *ICML '08, Proceedings of the 25th International Conference on Machine Learning* (pp. 1096–1103). New York, NY: ACM. 10.1145/1390156.1390294

Wang, A., Singh, A., Michael, J., Hill, F., Levy, O., & Bowman, S. (2018). GLUE: A Multi-Task Benchmark and Analysis Platform for Natural Language Understanding. In *Proceedings of the 2018 EMNLP Workshop BlackboxNLP: Analyzing and Interpreting Neural Networks for NLP* (pp. 353–355). Brussels, Belgium: Association for Computational Linguistics. 10.18653/v1/W18-5446

Wang, X., Jiang, W., & Luo, Z. (2016). Combination of Convolutional and Recurrent Neural Network for Sentiment Analysis of Short Texts. *Proceedings of COLING 2016, the 26th International Conference on Computational Linguistics: Technical Papers*. Retrieved from https://www.aclweb.org/anthology/C16-1229.pdf

Weiss, K., Khoshgoftaar, T. M., & Wang, D. (2016). A survey of transfer learning. *Journal of Big Data*, *3*(1), 1817. doi:10.118640537-016-0043-6

Wiebe, J. (2000). Learning Subjective Adjectives from Corpora. In *Proceedings of the Seventeenth National Conference on Artificial Intelligence and Twelfth Conference on Innovative Applications of Artificial Intelligence* (pp. 735–740). AAAI Press. Retrieved from https://dl.acm.org/citation.cfm?id=647288.721121

Wiebe, J., Bruce, R., & O'Hara, T. P. (1999). Development and Use of a Gold-Standard Data Set for Subjectivity Classifications. *Proceedings of the 37th Annual Meeting of the Association for Computational Linguistics*. Retrieved from https://www.aclweb.org/anthology/P99-1032.pdf

Wu, X., Cai, Y., Li, Q., Xu, J., & Leung, H.-F. (2018). Combining Contextual Information by Self-attention Mechanism in Convolutional Neural Networks for Text Classification. Lecture Notes in Computer Science, 11233, 453–467. doi:10.1007/978-3-030-02922-7_31

Xian, Y., Lampert, C. H., Schiele, B., & Akata, Z. (2019). Zero-Shot Learning—A Comprehensive Evaluation of the Good, the Bad and the Ugly. *IEEE Transactions on Pattern Analysis and Machine Intelligence*, *41*(9), 2251–2265. doi:10.1109/TPAMI.2018.2857768 PMID:30028691

Xu, N. (2017). Analyzing multimodal public sentiment based on hierarchical semantic attentional network. In *Proceedings of the 2017 IEEE International Conference on Intelligence and Security Informatics (ISI)* (pp. 152–154). IEEE. 10.1109/ISI.2017.8004895

Xu, W., Sun, H., Deng, C., & Tan, Y. (2017). Variational Autoencoder for Semi-Supervised Text Classification. In *AAAI'17: Proceedings of the Thirty-First AAAI Conference on Artificial Intelligence* (Vol. 4, pp. 3358–3364). San Francisco, CA: AAAI Press.

Yang, Z., Yang, D., Dyer, C., He, X., Smola, A., & Hovy, E. (2016). Hierarchical Attention Networks for Document Classification. In *Proceedings of the 2016 Conference of the North American Chapter of the Association for Computational Linguistics: Human Language Technologies* (pp. 1480–1489). San Diego, CA: Association for Computational Linguistics. 10.18653/v1/N16-1174

Yang, Z., Dai, Z., Yang, Y., Carbonell, J., Salakhutdinov, R. R., & Le, Q. V. (2019). XLNet: Generalized Autoregressive Pretraining for Language Understanding. In *Advances in Neural Information Processing Systems 32* (pp. 5754–5764). Curran Associates, Inc. Retrieved from http://papers.nips.cc/paper/8812-xlnet-generalized-autoregressive-pretraining-for-language-understanding.pdf

Yin, H., Liu, P., Zhu, Z., Li, W., & Wang, Q. (2019). Capsule Network With Identifying Transferable Knowledge for Cross-Domain Sentiment Classification. *IEEE Access: Practical Innovations, Open Solutions, 7*, 153171–153182. doi:10.1109/ACCESS.2019.2948628

Yu, J., & Jiang, J. (2016). Learning Sentence Embeddings with Auxiliary Tasks for Cross-Domain Sentiment Classification. In *Proceedings of the 2016 Conference on Empirical Methods in Natural Language Processing* (pp. 236–246). Austin, TX: Association for Computational Linguistics. 10.18653/v1/D16-1023

Zhang, Q., Lu, R., Wang, Q., Zhu, Z., & Liu, P. (2019). Interactive Multi-Head Attention Networks for Aspect-Level Sentiment Classification. *IEEE Access: Practical Innovations, Open Solutions, 7*, 160017–160028. doi:10.1109/ACCESS.2019.2951283

Zhang, X., Zhao, J., & LeCun, Y. (2015). Character-Level Convolutional Networks for Text Classification. In *NIPS'15, Proceedings of the 28th International Conference on Neural Information Processing Systems* - Volume 1 (pp. 649–657). Cambridge, MA: MIT Press.

Zhang, Y., Barzilay, R., & Jaakkola, T. (2017). Aspect-augmented Adversarial Networks for Domain Adaptation. *Transactions of the Association for Computational Linguistics, 5*(1), 515–528. doi:10.1162/tacl_a_00077

Zhang, Z., & Saligrama, V. (2015). Zero-Shot Learning via Semantic Similarity Embedding. In *ICCV'15, Proceedings of the 2015 IEEE International Conference on Computer Vision (ICCV)* (pp. 4166–4174). ACM. 10.1109/ICCV.2015.474

Zhou, G., Zhu, Z., He, T., & Hu, X. T. (2016). Cross-lingual sentiment classification with stacked autoencoders. *Knowledge and Information Systems, 47*(1), 27–44. doi:10.100710115-015-0849-0

Zhu, Y., Gao, X., Zhang, W., Liu, S., & Zhang, Y. (2018). A bi-directional LSTM-CNN model with attention for Aspect-level text classification. *Future Internet.* Advance online publication. doi:10.3390/fi10120116

Zvarevashe, K., & Olugbara, O. O. (2018). A framework for sentiment analysis with opinion mining of hotel reviews. *Proceedings of the 2018 Conference on Information Communications Technology and Society (ICTAS).* 10.1109/ICTAS.2018.8368746

ADDITIONAL READING

Manning, C., Surdeanu, M., Bauer, J., Finkel, J., Bethard, S., & McClosky, D. (2014). The Stanford CoreNLP Natural Language Processing Toolkit. In *Proceedings of 52nd Annual Meeting of the Association for Computational Linguistics: System Demonstrations* (pp. 55–60). Baltimore, Maryland: Association for Computational Linguistics. 10.3115/v1/P14-5010

Peters, M., Neumann, M., Iyyer, M., Gardner, M., Clark, C., Lee, K., & Zettlemoyer, L. (2018). Deep Contextualized Word Representations. *In Proceedings of the 2018 Conference of the North American Chapter of the Association for Computational Linguistics: Human Language Technologies*, Volume 1 *(Long Papers)* (pp. 2227–2237). New Orleans, Louisiana: Association for Computational Linguistics. 10.18653/v1/N18-1202

Poria, S., Cambria, E., Bajpai, R., & Hussain, A. (2017). A review of affective computing: From unimodal analysis to multimodal fusion. *Information Fusion*, *37*, 98–125. doi:10.1016/j.inffus.2017.02.003

Thongtan, T., & Phienthrakul, T. (2019). Sentiment Classification Using Document Embeddings Trained with Cosine Similarity. In *Proceedings of the 57th Annual Meeting of the Association for Computational Linguistics: Student Research Workshop* (pp. 407–414). Florence, Italy: Association for Computational Linguistics. 10.18653/v1/P19-2057

Zimbra, D., Abbasi, A., Zeng, D., & Chen, H. (2018). The State-of-the-Art in Twitter Sentiment Analysis: A Review and Benchmark Evaluation. *ACM Trans. Manage. Inf. Syst.*, *9*(2), 5:1-5:29. doi:10.1145/3185045

KEY TERMS AND DEFINITIONS

Adversarial Learning: A learning paradigm based on two models attempting to achieve opposing goals.

Attention: A mechanism which allows a model to place additional emphasis on specific features.

Autoencoder: A network composed of an encoder and a decoder that can learn compact representations of its input data in a self-supervised manner.

Data Augmentation: A technique for improving the performance of a model by enriching the training data, e.g. by generating additional instances of minority classes.

Deep Learning: A form of machine learning which uses multi-layered architectures to automatically learn complex representations of the input data. Deep models deliver state-of-the-art results across many fields, e.g. computer vision and NLP.

Explainable AI: An emerging area of research whose goal is to make the decision-making processes of deep models understandable for humans.

Sentence Modelling: The task of converting a text into a representation that can be processed by a machine learning algorithm.

Sentiment Analysis: The task of discovering the underlying feelings expressed in a text. Methods are commonly classified by their scope, i.e. whether they consider aspects, sentences, or the entire document.

Transfer Learning: A collective term for machine learning techniques concerned with adapting a model across different domains and/or tasks.

Transformer: A type of deep model with an encoder-decoder structure that combines self-attention with feedforward networks.

ENDNOTES

[1]   The code for Word2vec has been made publicly available at https://code.google.com/archive/p/word2vec/.

[2]   The code for GloVe, along with pre-trained word vectors, is publicly available at https://github.com/stanfordnlp/GloVe.

[3]   The code for fastText is publicly available at https://github.com/facebookresearch/fastText.

[4]   The IMDB dataset is available at http://ai.stanford.edu/~amaas/data/sentiment/. It is also included in Tensorflow https://www.tensorflow.org/datasets/catalog/imdb_reviews.

[5]   The Yelp dataset is available at https://github.com/zzhang83/Yelp_Sentiment_Analysis or in Tensorflow https://www.tensorflow.org/datasets/catalog/yelp_polarity_reviews.

[6]   The SST dataset is publicly available at http://nlp.stanford.edu/~socherr/stanfordSentimentTreebank.zip.

[7]   Implementations of both BERT-Base and BERT-Large are publicly available at https://github.com/google-research/bert.

Section 2
Natural Language Processing in Business

Chapter 6
Metaphors in Business Applications:
Modelling Subjectivity Through Emotions for Metaphor Comprehension

Sunny Rai
Mahindra Ecole Centrale, Hyderabad, India

Shampa Chakraverty
Netaji Subhas University of Technology, India

Devendra Kumar Tayal
Indira Gandhi Delhi Technical University for Women, India

ABSTRACT

Commercial advertisements, social campaigns, and ubiquitous online reviews are a few non-literary domains where creative text is profusely embedded to capture a viewer's imagination. Recent AI business applications such as chatbots and interactive digital campaigns emphasise the need to process creative text for a seamless and fulfilling user experience. Figurative text in human communication conveys implicit perceptions and unspoken emotions. Metaphor is one such figure of speech that maps a latent idea in a target domain to an evocative concept from a source domain. This chapter explores the problem of computational metaphor interpretation through the glass of subjectivity. The world wide web is mined to learn about the source domain concept. Ekman emotion categories and pretrained word embeddings are used to model the subjectivity. The performance evaluation is performed to determine the reader's preference for emotive vs non emotive meanings. This chapter establishes the role of subjectivity and user inclination towards the meaning that fits in their existing cognitive schema.

DOI: 10.4018/978-1-7998-4240-8.ch006

INTRODUCTION

The growing significance of creative text in today's digital world is indisputable. From interactive digital advertisements to ubiquitous product reviews, it has become imperative for business organizations to automatically process as well as generate novel creative constructs to engage users actively. A text is said to be *creative or figurative* if its intended meaning is different from its literal meaning. Metaphor, sarcasm, and irony are few such figurative speeches, used frequently in one's daily communications on social media.

Today's digital market, including Zomato, AirBnB and Amazon, has *user's ratings and product reviews* at its core for product promotion. In fact, the popularity of a business model is often gauged by its mentions on social media platforms. A significant chunk of research work strives to accurately mine user's opinion and brand perception in the market (Asur and Huberman, 2010; Zadeh and Sharda, 2014; Jurafsky et al., 2014). One of the major hurdles in processing online reviews is creative texts. Consider the following product reviews on Amazon to understand this point:

(1) "At first she was just there with no support. She sat in that hole with no protection. Shifting, jiggling not knowing what can happen. There has to be something I can do. I looked and search and what I found is the "Fabric Case" for Alexa. This is it! *A support she will be happy to wear*. No more accidental popping out, no more shifting and readjusting, *she is finally safe*."

(2) "I must add that this *jacket's repellent powers are infinitely multiplied when coupled with the included Medal of Yavin*. Without it, the untrained female eye may confuse this ceremonial jacket with a Justin Timberlake style biker coat."

As in utterance (1), metaphorical references such as '*A support she will be happy to wear*' and '*she is finally safe*' convey strong opinion in reviews or feedback. Similarly, in utterance (2), the buyer is not pleased about his purchase, *a visually-unappealing jacket* and thus sarcastically expresses his displeasure towards the product. Traditional opinion mining techniques struggle to accurately capture the intended intent or sentiment for figurative texts. Nevertheless, these creative constructs convey strong reactions whether positive or negative in comparison with a literal feedback and thus, act as a significant factor in determining the true feelings of the user.

Figure 1. Metaphors in Advertisements: (a) Nokia (Source: Nokia Connecting People Campaign[1]) (b) Audi Wake up Campaign (Source: Audi Wake up Campaign[2])

Once widely popular digital campaign *Connecting People* of NOKIA, with its vivid imagery forges mental associations leaving an unforgettable imprint on the viewer's mind. In Fig. 1-(a), the phrase *connecting people* has an emotional connotation which subtly associates the human's basic instinct to reach out and build bonds with NOKIA. Various studies demonstrate that the human mind enjoys a bit of an enigma and often, metaphorical advertisements enforce viewer's attention along with providing a sense of pleasure (Danesi, 2002). Another such campaign 'Wake up!' by Audi is provided in Fig. 1-(b). At first glance, one merely sees white lane markings on a tar road. However, the quest to make sense of it, takes us to the fine print on this ad. This provides the context of *Audi automobiles* and *fatigue*. Here, this campaign makes a clever yet intriguing use of lane markings to convey shut eyes. Through this visual metaphor, Audi automobiles promote the feature *fatigue detector* in their cars while simultaneously, providing an 'Aha!' moment for its audience on deciphering this puzzling ad.

Figure 2. Google Translate: Translating creative text literally

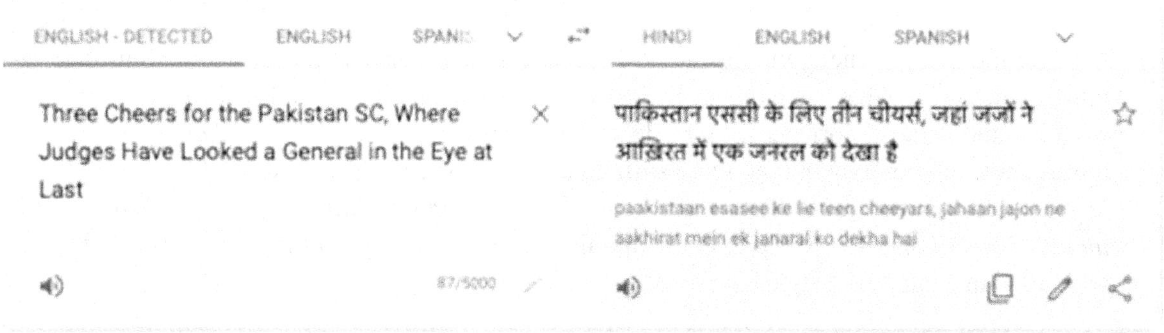

Language becomes a hurdle for global marketeers looking to reach a multilingual user base (Jain et al., 2019). A well curated app localization immensely improves the brand's visibility in the marketplace and thereby its revenues (Henry, 2017). Many websites and mobile apps rely heavily on machine translation to achieve localization. In Fig. 2, *Google translate* literally translates an English figurative phrase "*have looked a General in the eye*" to Hindi language and thus, fails to convey the intended metaphorical sense "*fearlessness or unwavering will of Pakistan SC*". While translating a language, the inherent concepts and ideas from the source language need to be transformed aptly to retain the intended figurative senses in the target language. The current machine translation technologies need to incorporate a module for creative text translation which may include (a) identifying creative text, (b) understanding the intended meaning and thus, (c) mapping it to the right concepts in the target language for appropriate translation.

Upcoming artificial intelligence applications including *Google Duplex* and *Alexa* are continuously fine-tuned to mimic realistic human conversation. The ongoing struggle to interpret latent meaning in spoken commands encompasses understanding creative speeches. To achieve a seamless human-system interaction, a system needs to detect and comprehend figurative commands. Noting the significance of figurative text in business applications, this chapter introduces the problem of metaphor processing. The role of subjectivity and individual's perception are explored in context of metaphor comprehension. Emotion driven Metaphor Understanding model proposed by Rai et al. (2019) is discussed to illustrate the role of emotions in modelling subjectivity.

BACKGROUND

What is a Metaphor?

A metaphor is a latent cognitive construct forged by mapping two dissimilar conceptual domains namely Target Domain and Source Domain (Fainsilber and Ortony, 1987; Lakoff and Johnson, 2008). The target domain concept is often abstract and thus, reconceptualized into a relatively concrete concept from the source domain for improved understandability. Consider the following metaphorical utterances:

(3) My watchman is a *lion*.
     [HUMAN IS **ANIMAL**] - Type- I Metaphor (Noun)
(4) My car *drinks* gasoline.
     [CAR IS **ANIMATE**] - Type-II Metaphor (Verb)
(5) Teenagers have a *bitter* mood.
     [MOOD IS **TASTE**] - Type-III Metaphor (Adjective)
(6) He spoke *fluidly*.
     [COMMUNICATION IS **LIQUID**] - Type-IV Metaphor (Adverb)

In utterances (3)-(6), the italicized text is the metaphor. In square brackets, the intended conceptual mapping in the format, [TARGET IS **SOURCE**] is provided. The underlined text indicates the type of metaphor. Here, content metaphors such as nouns, verbs, adjectives and adverbs are shown. However, other parts of speeches such as prepositions and conjunctions can also be used metaphorically.

In utterance (3), a group of properties such as *fearsome* or *hairy* from the domain ANIMAL (*lion*) is transferred to the target domain HUMAN (watchman). Here, the metaphorical concept is a noun and thus, these types of metaphors are also known as Nominal metaphors. Likewise, in utterance (4), a verb *drink* is used metaphorically to convey the property 'ability to drink'. Here, a car (NON-ANIMATE entity) has been portrayed similar to an ANIMATE entity which can *drink*. It may be noted that *drink* also exemplifies a high rate of consumption by the automobile. In utterance (5), an adjective *bitter* is used figuratively to indicate a person's MOOD and it is compared with TASTE where *bitter* would indicate unpleasant and *sweet* would refer to a pleasant experience (Rai et al, 2018b). In utterance (6), an adverb *fluidly* is employed to emphasize the smooth communication skills of an individual, thus forming the mapping between COMMUNICATION and the domain of LIQUID. Similar to a liquid substance such as water, the flow of words from one's mouth is smooth and clear.

A freshly forged metaphorical mapping is considered a *novel metaphor*. With time and their repeated use, these mappings may eventually acquire standard meanings and lose their novelty, thus turning them into *dead metaphors*. For instance, in the metaphorical phrase '*goldmine* of knowledge', the metaphor *goldmine* has an acquired meaning that is, a significant source. In literature, the dead metaphors are considered equivalent to the literal text. The standard word sense disambiguation techniques are applied on dead metaphors to identify the intended meaning.

Computational Metaphor Processing

Computational metaphor processing involves two sub problems, (a) to **detect metaphors** in text and (b) to **interpret** them by identifying its intended figurative meaning. The problem of metaphor detection is posed either as (i) a *classification problem* that is, label an utterance as either metaphorical or literal (Shutova et al., 2010; Birke and Sarkar, 2006; Veale and Hao, 2008; Rai et al., 2018a, 2017a, 2017b) or (ii) a *sequence labelling task* where every word in a given utterance is assigned a label (Klebanov et al., 2014; Rai et al., 2016; Wu et al., 2018; Gao et al., 2018). While performing detection, one does not need to understand the underlying mapping. Using the notion of *semantic incongruity*, it is possible to detect the majority of the metaphors. Various statistical approaches employing *lexico-syntactic relations, abstractness-concreteness,* and even pre-trained *word embeddings* have been proposed to identify metaphorical usage in English language. More recently, the development is spilling over to other languages such as Russian (Tsvetkov, 2014) and Polish.

The problem of computational metaphor comprehension can be formulated as (i) *identifying the transferred property set* (Su et al., 2016, 2017), or (ii) *identifying the underlying conceptual mapping* (Rosen, 2018), or (iii) *generation of literal substitute paraphrase* (for verb metaphors) (Shutova, 2010; Bollegala and Shutova, 2013). Metaphor interpretation is a relatively tough nut to crack as it involves acquiring the knowledge base for the mapped domains and then, identifying the most likely property transfer. A detailed explanation on different aspects of computational metaphor processing is provided in (Rai and Chakraverty, 2020). In this chapter, the emphasis is on *extraction of transferred properties* to comprehend metaphorical connections.

Computational Metaphor Comprehension

In *Poetics,* Aristotle introduced the principle of analogy that is, if A: B:: C: D, then B can be used in place of D and vice versa. That is, relational structure applicable in one domain is transferable to another domain. Let us consider a simple analogy, *kitten: cat:: puppy: dog*, the relation between *kitten* and *cat* is also applicable between *puppy* and *dog*. Here, the relation is clearly depicted which eases the process of understanding for users. However, a metaphor compares two domains without explicitly stating the type of correspondence. For instance, consider the mapping of *shark-lawyer*. It is difficult to precisely state the relation between the mapped concepts *shark* and *lawyer* unless more contextual information is provided. A crude way would be to analyze all possible relations to identify the most appropriate relation between the mapped concepts. Approaches based on Aristotelian theory essentially treats a metaphor as a *condensed simile* and thus, compares the mapped domains based on a set of common perceptual attributes shared by both domains. For instance, consider the phrase,

(7) My **lawyer** is a *shark.*
      => My **lawyer** is like a *shark.*
      => <u>behaves/appears like a shark</u>

In utterance (7), a lawyer is compared to a *shark*. This utterance can be syntactically rephrased into a simile: 'A lawyer is like a shark'. The idea is to identify a set of perceptual properties of *shark* which are simultaneously applicable to *lawyers* in order to interpret this comparison. In Fig. 3, a set of perceptual as well as behavioral properties of *shark* and *lawyer* are listed. On careful analysis, it is possible to identify overlapping properties which are applicable on both domains. Few such perceptual properties are *fearsome, huge, aggressive, violent, etc.* However, it is not possible to precisely interpret the given mapping. Often, researchers provide a set of meanings or the most accepted meaning while comprehending a metaphorical utterance.

Figure 3. Properties for 'My lawyer is shark.'

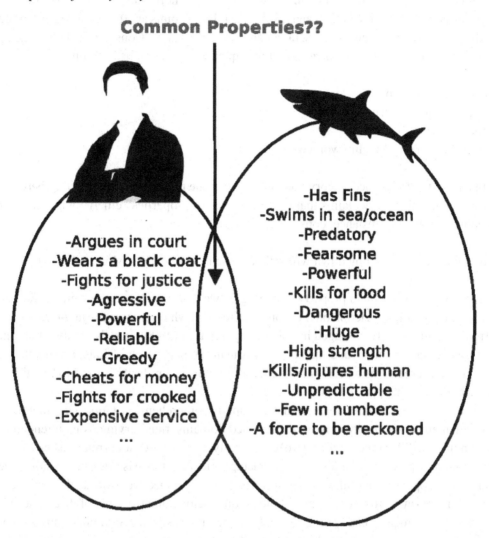

Su et al. (2016) provide a computational approach to comprehend metaphor using the notion of *latent similarity*. For instance, the property *soft* is a synonym of *delicate* which in turn is a synonym of *tender* in WordNet. So, the word pair <*soft, tender*> will be said to have latent similarity between them. Similarly, a property *p* from source domain which has latent similarity with at least one of the attributes of mapped target domain, is said to be the interpretation of a given metaphorical mapping. Su et al. (2017) later proposed an approach using pre-trained word embeddings and the most likely property was computed using cosine similarity with the target domain. Xiao et al., (2016) puts forward a statistical model to learn concept relations using a large corpus. They enhance their model, *meta4meaning* through a set of metrics to choose the most relevant properties.

A more sophisticated way to compare the source and target domains is achieved through relational *analogy* which further encapsulates functional attributes of the domains. For instance, a shark *lays a trap to lure its prey.* In a similar way, a lawyer is likely to lay the trap with right arguments for desirable judgement. Veale and Hao (2008) introduce a 'fluid knowledge representation' model using conceptual 'talking points'. To acquire source domain knowledge, the authors mine the web by crafting lexico-syntactic patterns such as *IS-A*, *LIKE-A*, and *AS-A*. The talking points are then inserted and/or deleted in *Slipnet* to discover an analogy between the target and source domains. Consider the below metaphorical expression, "*Make-up* is a *Western burqa*" and the sequence of operations in Slipnet.

"Make-up => typically worn by women
    => expected to be worn by women
    => must be worn by women
    => must be worn by Muslim women => Burqa"

Moving ahead, the Relevance Theory contends against the plain property matching between source and target domain. This theory claims that the "meanings or properties" emerge when the source and target domains interact. For instance, consider the phrase

(8)   Getting married and settling down will kill her. She is a *butterfly*. - Moreno (2014)

In utterance (8), it is not plain property matching between *butterfly* and the woman. Rather, it possibly conveys the possible restriction on the woman's free will which emerged from *butterfly's* behavior to move freely for survival. Encouraged by this theory, Kintsch (2000) models the dynamic interaction between the meanings of source and target domains using the approach of Latent Semantic Analysis. Each concept is represented as a vector and the notion of cosine similarity is used to identify common concepts for both of the mapped domains.

To conclude, prior techniques for nominal metaphor comprehension emphasize identification of properties which are semantically close to the mapped domains, thus serving as its intended meaning. However, Samur et al. (2015) and Davitz (2016) empirically demonstrate the correlation between emotions and the resultant metaphorical manifestations. A metaphorical utterance is often not an utterance devoid of opinion. The mapping is carefully chosen to reflect one's perspective towards the target domain. It further derives its meaning from one's immediate cultural setting and the topic of discourse. Moreover, the approaches which require hand crafted knowledge resources such as Sardonicus struggle with data sparsity and depend on timely manual upgrading. This limits the system performance in identifying recently acquired senses and thus, in understanding the intended meaning of the metaphorical mapping.

ROLE OF SUBJECTIVITY IN METAPHOR COMPREHENSION

Subjectivity refers to thoughts, feelings, beliefs, and desires that comprise a person's self-identity. While interpreting metaphors, the natural tendency is to recall one's prior experiences about the source domain and then try to see if the extracted understanding fits their acquired cognitive schema for the target domain. Let us reconsider utterance (7). The metaphor *shark* emphasizes a set of attributes of the *lawyer*. A distressing prior experience which may be due to watching *violent movies on sharks,* or *news on shark attacks, or even a simple warning about fatal shark attacks* will evoke senses indicating *aggression,* or *fear*. Whereas, someone who has seen sharks mostly in a controlled environment such as a zoo or Discovery channel would perceive it positively, evoking senses of *strength* and *dominance*. Here, the underlying emotion would act as a context of interpretation. The former interpretation conveys degrading trust and impending termination of the lawyer. In contrast, the other interpretation hints towards the lawyer's notable skills and the client's confidence. Depending on the context of usage or underlying emotion, the mapping expresses different metaphorical senses including *powerful, aggressive, vicious, trustworthy, and fearsome*.

Researchers have so far attempted to understand metaphors by identifying a set of similar properties between the mapped domains such as in the works of Kintsch (2000) and Su et al. (2017). However, Gibbs Jr (2010) and Rai et al. (2019) contend that a metaphor is open to multiple senses depending on the reader's perception. For instance, a person may have a terrifying experience with *sharks* or s/he may have felt *amazement* on seeing its tremendous size. That is, perceptions are fundamentally derived from one's prior experiences and can thus be categorized on the basis of their inherent emotions.

Emotion Driven Metaphor Understanding

Type-I metaphors (also known as Nominal metaphors) are constructed by directly mapping the source and target domains. The lexical manifestation is generated by gluing together the mapped domains using a copular verb such as *to be, was, is,* and *am*. In utterance (7), the copular verb *is,* is used to propose a relation between the target domain *lawyer* and the source domain *shark*. To extract the subject and the direct object from a given utterance, a dependency parse is employed.

Emotion-driven Metaphor Understanding (EMU) system incorporates a module to assign emotion strength to each property. A block diagram for EMU is provided in Fig. 4. A nominal metaphorical utterance is parsed to identify the target and source domain concepts. Consequently, a tuple $<T$ (target domain), S (source domain)$>$ is created which serves as the input to the EMU system.

Figure 4. Block Diagram for Emotion-driven Metaphor Understanding System

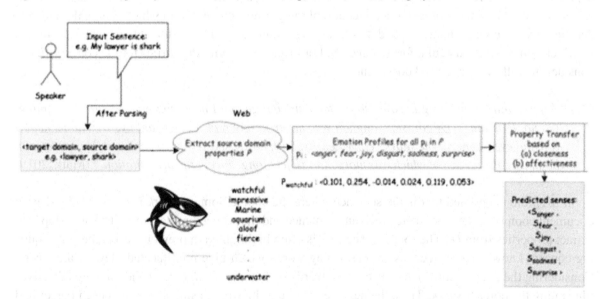

The EMU consists of the following sub-modules:

(A) *Property Extraction*: This module characterizes the source domain by extracting its properties from the web.

(B) *Emotion Extraction*: The extracted properties are given emotion profiles on the basis of their affinity towards Ekman emotion categories (Ekman, 1984).

(C) *Property Transfer:* This module carefully selects a property set on the basis of emotion and the given target domain.

The sub-modules are explained in detail below.

Property Extraction: Profiling Source Domain Concept

Before comprehending a metaphorical expression, there is a need to first understand the meaning of the source domain concept. Only then, its meaning can be tuned to align with the target domain concept. For instance, consider the concept of *fish*. The Cambridge Dictionary defines *fish*[3] as "an animal that lives in water, is covered with scales, and breathes by taking water in through its mouth, or the flesh of these animals eaten as food". That is, a concept is understood by its properties such as *living in water, eating flesh, scales on its body* and so on. The World Wide Web acts as a big collection of documents which can be tapped to learn existing human understanding and knowledge of this world. Thus, one of the unsupervised ways to extract concept knowledge is through probing the web.

The procedure includes (a) *retrieval of documents* containing the term source domain S from the web using a search engine such Google, Bing or even Yandex. Then, the aim is to (b) capture the relevant context of *S* from the collected documents. The concept of context can be defined in multifarious ways depending on one's requirement. It could be of one sentence, a paragraph or even a complete document. Rai et al. (2019) consider context as a collection of the present sentence s_0 in which source domain *S* is detected, its preceding sentence s_{-1} and its succeeding sentence s_{+1}. This results into a textual document D_s which comprises all useful information on S. For instance, to build the corpus for the concept *shark,* consider the following retrieved document:

(d1) " *"If you think something is going to try to come and get me I need you guys to start screaming, 'Oh no, look out.'"* <u>*Of course, Gaughan was never in any real danger and two assistants kept a watchful eye whenever the* **sharks** *came nearby.*</u> *Still, he ducked several times to avoid contact with the sharks, the largest of which was more than 10 feet long, during the presentation."* (Mark, 2019)

In (d1), the underlined text is the sentence where the source domain *shark* is present. The overall document comprises the immediate preceding sentence and the succeeding sentence. The next step is to extract properties from D_s. The role of adjectives is often highlighted in previous researches on acquiring concept knowledge. Adjectives are describing words which give multifaceted view of a concept. Considering the document (d1), the descriptive words such as *watchful, largest* and *long* are adjectives illustrating the domain *shark*. Thus, the next step is to tag the words using a part of speech tagger and retain only adjectives which act as attributes of the concept. One such tool is Stanford CoreNLP parser (Manning et al., 2014).

However, as with any data scraping procedure, it becomes important to filter out noisy and unrelated adjectives. To determine the relevance of an adjective with respect to the source domain, the notion of semantic relatedness is widely employed. One of the popular ways to compute semantic relatedness is by computing cosine similarity between the vector representations of the property and the source domain. Only those adjectives whose relatedness that is, $\cos(p,S)$ exceed a predefined limit γ_L (source), are retained for further examination. For instance, adjectives such as *disqualified, crystal or hazardous* can be removed in the context of *shark*. Similarly, the highly specific adjectives such as *mammal, aquarium, underwater* become irrelevant in the study of metaphorical meaning and shall be removed using a preset upper threshold γ_U (source). In the similar way, the properties which do not make sense in respect to the target domain can be removed using the rule of $\cos(p,T) \geq \gamma_L$(target).

Emotion Extraction: Unsupervised Emotion Extraction Using word2vec

To build emotion profiles for the extracted properties, the traditional approach is to use knowledge resources such as WordNet-Affect (Strapparava et al., 2004) and NRC Emotion Lexicon (Mohammad and Turney, 2010, 2013). The existing knowledge resources are often marked with binary scale, that is, 0 or 1 indicating the presence or absence of a certain emotion in a given word. Binary scale is useful when the objective is to just identify the inherent emotion in a concept however, it does not provide the intensity of the marked emotion. Another issue is the limited coverage of hand-crafted knowledge resources.

More recently, the trend has shifted to word embeddings trained on huge corpus to learn semantic orientation and other word properties. The embeddings are fundamentally based on the concept of distributional hypothesis, that is, *"words that occur in the same contexts tend to have similar meanings"* (Pantel, 2005). More recent applications include sentiment analysis (Zhang et al., 2015) and metaphor detection (Rai and Chakraverty, 2017; Rai et al., 2016). In (Rai et al., 2019), the authors make the use of pre trained *word2vec* embeddings to generate emotion profiles.

Dalgleish and Power (2000) note that humans commonly express their feelings using six basic emotions namely *anger, fear, happiness, disgust, sadness,* and *surprise* irrespective of their culture and geographical location. Let a set $\mathbf{E} = \{$ *'anger', 'fear', 'happiness', 'disgust', 'sadness', 'surprise'*$\}$. Thus, an emotion profile of a concept can be defined by quantifying its closeness towards each emotion $e\ \hat{I}\ \mathbf{E}$. That is, emotion profile $\overrightarrow{EP}$ for a property is defined as follows:

$$\overrightarrow{EP} = \langle cos(p,'anger'), cos(p,'fear'),$$
$$cos(p,'happiness'), cos(p,'disgust'), cos(p,'sad'), cos(p,'surprise') \rangle$$

For instance, document (d1) provides one of many affective profiles of the concept *shark*. The given context projects the animal *shark* as a fatal and terrifying creature. The underlined descriptive word *watchful* guides us towards the notion of fear. Thus, the resultant emotion profile $\overrightarrow{EP}$ is calculated as: < 0.1011, 0.2548, -0.0144, 0.0249, 0.119, 0.0531 >.

The obtained vector for the concept *watchful* majorly elicits *fear*. The notion of fear is often associated with the state of being *watchful*. On further observing the vector, it can be gathered that the next predominant emotion is *sadness* whereas *happiness* scored a value of -0.0144, highlighting its negative correlation with the state of watchfulness.

Figure 5. Clusters of Words with similar affective Profile

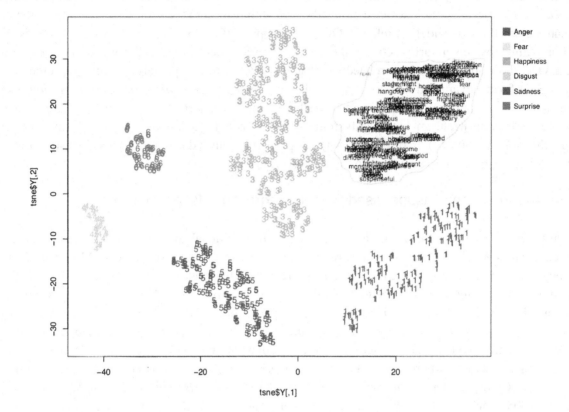

T-SNE (Maaten and Hinton, 2008) visualization technique is used to verify the hypothesis that "words of similar affective categories will have similar emotion profiles". That is, similar affective words cluster together. A set of 934 unique affective words with its predominant emotion is extracted from WordNet-Affect (Strapparava et al., 2004).

Using *Rtsne* library (Krijthe (2015), these words are plotted in the vector space of their emotion profiles. From Fig. 5, it is clear that the words with similar affective categories (marked with the same color) are clustered together. A snippet for class- *'fear'* circled in yellow is provided where words such as *suspenseful, frightening and monstrous* are clustered together indicating the similitude in their obtained vector profiles. It is an interesting yet unsupervised way to derive emotion profiles for words which can be further applied for other problems. This technique removes the obstruction of relying on hand crafted knowledge resources.

Property Transfer

The next step is to select the most relevant property while taking into account (a) its suitability with respect to the target domain and (b) its ability to evoke a certain emotion *e*. The underlying intuition is to identify the property which optimizes emotional relatedness of a property along with the semantic relatedness. Rai et al. (2019) use the product operation and define criterion for choosing $\hat{p}_e$ as in eq. 1.

$$\hat{p}_e = argmax_{\forall p \in P}\left(cos\left(p,e\right) * cos\left(p,T\right)\right) \tag{1}$$

Using this method, a set of six emotion-oriented senses of a metaphor are computed. The property $\hat{p}_{fear}$ for the sentence (7) was deduced to be *unscrupulous,* that is, 'My lawyer is *<fear*: unscrupulous>'. Likewise, $\hat{p}_{happiness}$ is *stoic,* $\hat{p}_{anger/disgust}$ is *uncaring,* $\hat{p}_{sadness}$ is *difficult and* $\hat{p}_{surprise}$ is *ridiculous*. There could be better ways to optimize the weights to be assigned for semantic relatedness and emotional relatedness. There are many optimization algorithms including Genetic algorithms which might further improve the process of property selection.

EXPERIMENT AND RESULTS

The EMU was implemented in Python V2.7. From the NLTK package ((Loper and Bird, 2002)), Stanford CoreNLP parser (Manning et al., 2014) is deployed to parse the input text. A nominal metaphor dataset (Rai and Chakraverty, 2017) is used for performance evaluation. This dataset comprises 75 instances. One could also choose to work on nominal metaphor dataset provided in (Krishnakumaran and Zhu, 2007) and (Roncero and Almeida, 2015).

Baseline

For every new model, it is necessary to evaluate the performance gain with respect to either an existing model or a random baseline if no prior model exists. EMU strongly favors the inclusion of emotion with semantic relatedness while selecting the most relevant property. Thus, the most appropriate baseline would be a model which does not factor in the component of emotions. Consequently, Rai et al (2019) implements a baseline approach B_T inspired from the approach proposed by Su et al. (2017). The baseline, B_T generates a set **P** of top six properties on the basis of its semantic relatedness with the target domain.

Performance Evaluation and Human Evaluators

Language is an ever-evolving entity. The meaning of concepts often starts to vary even if there is a slight transition in space (geophysical location) or time. For the majority of subjective applications in NLP, the idea of evaluation is essentially based on recruiting a set of human evaluators and asking for their opinion. The assumption is the collective shared meaning of each concept through which a communication can be carried on. The notion of inter annotator agreement is used to quantify the extent of agreement among annotators or evaluators. Thus, if the majority of the evaluators agree for a specific meaning, then it is considered as the correct or acceptable meaning.

Metaphor comprehension is a complex cognitive procedure. Thus, a group of English speakers were asked to mark the appropriateness of the meanings suggested through the approaches, B_T and EMU. The granularity of the scale for *appropriateness* can be selected in accordance with the application. For instance, it could simply be *appropriate meaning* vs *inappropriate meaning*. Or, it could also be *appropriate, slightly appropriate or inappropriate*. The increasing granularity often leads to lower inter annotator agreement. That is, one evaluator may mark the suggested meaning of a given utterance as *somewhat appropriate* whereas another evaluator may consider the same meaning as *highly appropriate*. However, if there are only two possibilities namely *appropriate* vs *inappropriate* then, it is more likely that both would have marked it as *appropriate,* thus increasing the agreement amongst annotators.

Rai et al. (2019) asked the evaluators independently to rate the appropriateness of each of the predicted senses on a Likert scale (Likert, 1932) of '1' to '5' where '1': *Highly inappropriate*; '2': *Somewhat inappropriate*; '3': *Average*; '4': *Somewhat appropriate* and, '5': *Highly appropriate*. Only when the average score for a predicted sense is below 3, it is marked as an *inappropriate* meaning otherwise it is regarded as a correct suggestion.

Results

The B_T approach provided an accuracy of 83.82% whereas the EMU system performed the best with an improvement of 13.19% in sense correctness that is, an overall accuracy of 97.01%. The improved accuracy hints towards the preference to subjective meanings by the evaluators. On providing a varied set of senses, evaluators were able to find the one which matched with their prior mental patterns. For instance, consider the following metaphorical phrase,

(9)   New moon is a *banana.*

For utterance (9), the B_T approach generates the property set as {*silvery, dark, bluish, daylight, volcanic, dwarf}*. The meanings mostly refer to the lighting effects of the moon such as *dark, bluish* or *silvery*. In contrast, the EMU generates varied senses as: {<*anger:* volcanic>, <*fear*: dark>, <*happiness*: beautiful>, <*disgust*: yellowish>, <*sadness:* beautiful>, and <*surprise*: odd>} under different emotional parameters. It is visible that EMU has imported source domain knowledge such as *yellowish tint, beauty* as well as the *crazy* or *odd* sense associated with the concept of *banana.*

Subjective Metaphor Interpretation Using Emotions

To verify if a metaphor can have multiple senses according to the perception of a reader towards the target domain T, a study was conducted to analyze the number of correct senses for each metaphorical utterance. Let us consider the following utterance.

(10) My marriage is *war.*

For sentence (10), the property set generated using B_T approach is {sexual, *eldest, societal, religious, civil, unrequited*} whereas the EMU property set comprises: {<*anger:* bitter>, <*fear*: unspoken>, <*happiness*: passionate>, <*disgust*: vindictive>, <*sadness*: terrible> and <*surprise*: inevitable>}. It is amusing to see varied experiences one may have towards marriage when it is equated to a war. The senses ranging from *bitterness* a war may ensue between its participants to unspoken (*its consequences not being discussed anymore)*, are quite interesting. These senses illustrate that the EMU brings forth varied yet apt senses of a metaphor.

The results show that more than 90% of the instances have at least two correct EMU senses, giving weight to the hypothesis of subjective interpretation. Through B_T approach, almost 59% of instances were identified with at least 2 correct senses. The percentage gradually declines on considering the higher number of correct senses. That is, 76.47% of the instances had more than two correctly predicted senses for EMU whereas it is merely 32.4% for B_T. The percentage eventually goes down to 67.65% when the number of correct senses is greater than 3 whereas for B_T, it went down to 20.6%. The numbers favor the EMU system in identifying multiple yet valid senses over B_T approach.

Interpretation Sans Emotion vs EMU

In order to validate that a metaphor can indeed be better analyzed when different emotion undertones are incorporated, the evaluators were asked to state their preference for the senses generated by EMU vs the baseline approach B_T. For instance, consider the following statement:

(11) My rat's fur is *silk*.

In sentence (11), the concept of *silk* emphasizes the abstract properties of fur. The B_T senses are < silk, garment, dyed, fabric, viscose, silkworm>. Whereas its possible EMU senses are: { <*anger*: coarse>, <*fear*: artificial>, <*happiness*: comfortable>, <*disgust*: coarse>, <*sadness*: lustrous> and <*surprise*: warm>}. The senses such as *coarse* or *artificial* carry a subtle affective connotation. Interestingly, both senses can be deemed to be appropriate if given appropriate context. This variety in set of senses often facilitates the selection of the sense which fits well with the reader's mental pattern. This process also brings out the latent concepts associated with fur such as such as *warmth* or even *lustrousness* which could not be captured through B_T approach.

From the experiments, it was found that evaluators preferred EMU interpretations over interpretations sans emotion for almost half of the instances. For 39.7% of instances, evaluators did not show any clear preference between EMU and B_T interpretations. However, B_T senses were chosen over the EMU senses for 13.24% instances. This indicates that novel metaphors often tend to have varied interpretation initially as there is no clearly established meaning. However, as time passes by, these novel metaphors eventually become dead metaphors leading to standard emotionless interpretation.

SOLUTION AND RECOMMENDATIONS

The results clearly favor the idea of emotive interpretations over senses devoid of emotions. Emotion categories are a way to model different contexts of usage. For real data including reviews and feedback, the appropriate approach would be to extract the right emotion from the surrounding context of a metaphorical phrase. Consider the review of Amazon Alexa case provided in (1) reproduced below.

<FEAR, SADNESS, SURPRISE {At first, she was just there with no support. She sat in that hole with no protection. Shifting, jiggling not knowing what can happen. There has to be something I can do}>. <HAPPINESS {I looked and search and what I found is the "Fabric Case" for Alexa. This is it! *A support she will be happy to wear.* No more accidental popping out, no more shifting and readjusting, *she is finally safe*}>.

On observing the above review, a transition from the initial gamut of emotions <FEAR, SADNESS, SURPRISE> to <HAPPINESS> is observed. The metaphorical content is present in the context of emotion <HAPPINESS>. Thus, we only need to provide the meaning corresponding to the emotion HAPPINESS and analyze the overall sentiment accordingly.

Let us consider a possible comment on an online post on the newly proposed economic policies.

(12) The new policies have *strangulated* the market.

In the above utterance, the concept of *strangulation* is used metaphorically. Here, there are no other concepts which evoke any emotion or sentiment other than the metaphor itself. The word *strangulation* has a negative connotation in itself and thus, the senses inclined towards <ANGER, DISGUST, FEAR> would be retrieved. However, let us consider a slight variation of utterance (12).

(13) The new policies have *strangulated* the black market.

In utterance (13), the word *strangulation* evokes a positive or joyous sense due to negative connotation of entity 'black market' that is, illegal trading of goods. Thus, a metaphor comprehension model needs to identify the transition in emotions from the given input as well as gather the inherent sentiments of entities.

CONCLUSION

This chapter discussed the role of subjectivity in identifying the property transferred between the mapped domains. The reader's inclination towards meanings which reflect their own beliefs and experiences were analyzed. Treading the path of unsupervised learning, the world wide web was mined to learn about the source domain. An interesting application of word embeddings was discussed which helped in profiling emotion spread for concepts denoted by a word. Overall, this chapter established the need to take user's background knowledge into account while comprehending a metaphor. Applications such as marketing & advertising which are dependent on demographics, may use such systems to analyze the impact and sentiment their content may leave on the viewer's mind. Likewise, reviews and feedback processing systems need to consider the writer's viewpoint while interpreting creative constructs.

FUTURE RESEARCH DIRECTIONS

Understanding metaphorical text is an interesting computational research problem with intricate dimensions. The inspiration is often taken from one's daily lives while forging new metaphors. As metaphor comprehension is clearly guided by one's surroundings, it becomes pertinent to account for cultural and societal settings. Personalized metaphor processing could be an interesting avenue to explore in the future. In today's multilingual society, a generic model applicable on multilingual or code-mixed text would solve many business issues. One of the future directions would be towards a cross-lingual metaphor processing such as Hindi-English or Turkish-English.

From this chapter, it is evident that there are quite a few approaches for nominal metaphors where the source domain is explicit. However, verb or adjective metaphors have an implicit mapping between the mapped domains and thus, a property matching model is not directly applicable. Another interesting direction would be to extract the inherent source domain concept from Type-II/III metaphorical text.

REFERENCES

Asur, S., & Huberman, B. A. (2010). Predicting the future with social media. In *Proceedings of the 2010 IEEE/WIC/ACM International Conference on Web Intelligence and Intelligent Agent Technology-Volume 01*, (pp. 492–499). IEEE Computer Society. 10.1109/WI-IAT.2010.63

Birke, J., & Sarkar, A. (2006). A clustering approach for nearly unsupervised recognition of nonliteral language. 11th Conference of the European Chapter of the Association for Computational Linguistics, 329–336.

Bollegala, D., & Shutova, E. (2013). Metaphor interpretation using paraphrases extracted from the web. *PLoS One*, *8*(9), e74304. doi:10.1371/journal.pone.0074304 PMID:24073207

Dalgleish, T., & Power, M. (2000). *Handbook of cognition and emotion*. John Wiley & Sons.

Danesi, M. (2002). *The puzzle instinct: The meaning of puzzles in human life*. Indiana University Press.

Davitz, J. R. (2016). *The language of emotion*. Academic Press.

Ekman, P. (1984). Expression and the nature of emotion. *Approaches to Emotion, 3*(19), 344.

Fainsilber, L., & Ortony, A. (1987). Metaphorical uses of language in the expression of emotions. *Metaphor and Symbol*, *2*(4), 239–250. doi:10.120715327868ms0204_2

Gao, G., Choi, E., Choi, Y., & Zettlemoyer, L. (2018). *Neural metaphor detection in context*. arXiv preprint arXiv:1808.09653

Gibbs, R. W., Jr. (2010). The dynamic complexities of metaphor interpretation. *DELTA: Documentac,a ̃o de Estudos em Linguʹ́istica Teoʹrica e Aplicada*, *26*(SPE), 657–677.

Henry, N. (2017). Why app localization matters. *Localize Blog*. Available at https://localizeblog.com/app-localization-matters/

Jain, A., Tayal, D. K., & Rai, S. (2015). Shrinking digital gap through automatic generation of WordNet for Indian languages. *AI & Society*, *30*(2), 215–222. doi:10.100700146-014-0548-5

Jurafsky, D., Chahuneau, V., Routledge, B. R., & Smith, N. A. (2014). Narrative framing of consumer sentiment in online restaurant reviews. *First Monday*, *19*(4). Advance online publication. doi:10.5210/fm.v19i4.4944

Kintsch, W. (2000). Metaphor comprehension: A computational theory. *Psychonomic Bulletin & Review*, *7*(2), 257–266. doi:10.3758/BF03212981 PMID:10909133

Klebanov, B. B., Leong, B., Heilman, M., & Flor, M. (2014). Different texts, same metaphors: Unigrams and beyond. *Proceedings of the Second Workshop on Metaphor in NLP*, 11–17. 10.3115/v1/W14-2302

Krijthe, J. (2015). Rtsne: T-distributed stochastic neighbor embedding using barnes-hut implementation. *R package version 0.10*. https://cran. r-project. org/package= Rtsne.

Krishnakumaran, S., & Zhu, X. (2007, April). Hunting Elusive Metaphors Using Lexical Resources. *Proceedings of the Workshop on Computational approaches to Figurative Language*, 13-20. 10.3115/1611528.1611531

Lakoff, G., & Johnson, M. (2008). *Metaphors we live by*. University of Chicago press.

Likert, R. (1932). A technique for the measurement of attitudes. *Archives de Psychologie*.

Loper, E., & Bird, S. (2002). Nltk: The natural language toolkit. In *Proceedings of the ACL-02 Workshop on Effective tools and methodologies for teaching natural language processing and computational linguistics-Volume 1*, (pp. 63–70). Philadelphia, PA: Association for Computational Linguistics.

Maaten, L. d., & Hinton, G. (2008). Visualizing data using t-sne. *Journal of Machine Learning Research*, 9(Nov), 2579–2605.

Manning, C. D., Surdeanu, M., Bauer, J., Finkel, J. R., Bethard, S., & McClosky, D. (2014). The stanford corenlp natural language processing toolkit. ACL (System Demonstrations), 55–60. doi:10.3115/v1/P14-5010

Mark, H. (2019). *Nascar driver gaughan swims with the sharks at newport aquarium to teach kids about teamwork* [blog post]. retrieved from https://www.nkytribune.com/2016/09/nascar-driver-gaughan-swims-with-the-sharks-at-newport-aquarium-to-teach-kids-about-teamwork/. *Northern Kentucky Tribune*.

Martin, J. H. (2006). A corpus-based analysis of context effects on metaphor comprehension. *Trends in Linguistics Studies and Monographs, 171*, 214.

Mikolov, T., Sutskever, I., Chen, K., Corrado, G. S., & Dean, J. (2013). Distributed representations of words and phrases and their compositionality. Advances in neural information processing systems, 3111–3119.

Mohammad, S. M., & Turney, P. D. (2010). Emotions evoked by common words and phrases: Using mechanical turk to create an emotion lexicon. In *Proceedings of the NAACL HLT 2010 workshop on computational approaches to analysis and generation of emotion in text*, (pp. 26–34). Los Angeles, CA: Association for Computational Linguistics.

Mohammad, S. M., & Turney, P. D. (2013). Crowdsourcing a word–emotion association lexicon. *Computational Intelligence, 29*(3), 436–465. doi:10.1111/j.1467-8640.2012.00460.x

Moreno, R. E. V. (2004). Metaphor interpretation and emergence. *UCL Working Papers in Linguistics, 16*, 297-322.

Pantel, P. (2005). Inducing ontological co-occurrence vectors. In *Proceedings of the 43rd Annual Meeting on Association for Computational Linguistics*, (pp. 125–132). Ann Arbor, MI: Association for Computational Linguistics.

Rai, S., & Chakraverty, S. (2017). Metaphor detection using fuzzy rough sets. In *International Joint Conference on Rough Sets*, (pp. 271–279). Olsztyn, Poland: Springer. 10.1007/978-3-319-60837-2_23

Rai, S., & Chakraverty, S. (2020). A Survey on Computational Metaphor Processing. *ACM Computing Surveys, 53*(2), 1–37. doi:10.1145/3373265

Rai, S., Chakraverty, S., & Garg, A. (2018b). Effect of Classifiers on Type-III Metaphor Detection. In *Towards Extensible and Adaptable Methods in Computing* (pp. 241–249). Springer. doi:10.1007/978-981-13-2348-5_18

Rai, S., Chakraverty, S., & Tayal, D. K. (2016). Supervised metaphor detection using conditional random fields. In *Proceedings of the Fourth Workshop on Metaphor in NLP*, (pp. 18–27). San Diego, CA: Association of Computational Linguistics. 10.18653/v1/W16-1103

Rai, S., Chakraverty, S., & Tayal, D. K. (2017a, May). Identifying metaphors using fuzzy conceptual features. In *International Conference on Information, Communication and Computing Technology* (pp. 379-386). Springer. 10.1007/978-981-10-6544-6_34

Rai, S., Chakraverty, S., Tayal, D. K., & Kukreti, Y. (2017b). Soft metaphor detection using fuzzy c-means. In *International Conference on Mining Intelligence and Knowledge Exploration*, (pp. 402–411). Springer. 10.1007/978-3-319-71928-3_38

Rai, S., Chakraverty, S., Tayal, D. K., & Kukreti, Y. (2018a). A study on impact of context on metaphor detection. *The Computer Journal*, *61*(11), 1667–1682. doi:10.1093/comjnl/bxy032

Rai, S., Chakraverty, S., Tayal, D. K., Sharma, D., & Garg, A. (2019). Understanding metaphors using emotions. *New Generation Computing*, *37*(1), 5–27. doi:10.100700354-018-0045-3

Roncero, C., & de Almeida, R. G. (2015). Semantic properties, aptness, familiarity, conventionality, and interpretive diversity scores for 84 metaphors and similes. *Behavior Research Methods*, *47*(3), 800–812. doi:10.375813428-014-0502-y PMID:25007859

Rosen, Z. (2018). Computationally constructed concepts: A machine learning approach to metaphor interpretation using usage-based construction grammatical cues. *Proceedings of the Workshop on Figurative Language Processing*, 102–109. 10.18653/v1/W18-0912

Samur, D., Lai, V. T., Hagoort, P., & Willems, R. M. (2015). Emotional context modulates embodied metaphor comprehension. *Neuropsychologia*, *78*, 108–114. doi:10.1016/j.neuropsychologia.2015.10.003 PMID:26449989

Shutova, E. (2010). Automatic metaphor interpretation as a paraphrasing task. In *Human Language Technologies: The 2010 Annual Conference of the North American Chapter of the Association for Computational Linguistics*, (pp. 1029–1037). Association for Computational Linguistics.

Shutova, E., Sun, L., & Korhonen, A. (2010). Metaphor identification using verb and noun clustering. In *Proceedings of the 23rd International Conference on Computational Linguistics*, (pp. 1002–1010), Beijing, China. Association for Computational Linguistics.

Strapparava, C., & Valitutti, A. (2004). Wordnet affect: an affective extension of wordnet. LREC, 4, 1083–1086.

Su, C., Huang, S., & Chen, Y. (2017). Automatic detection and interpretation of nominal metaphor based on the theory of meaning. *Neurocomputing*, *219*, 300–311. doi:10.1016/j.neucom.2016.09.030

Su, C., Tian, J., & Chen, Y. (2016). Latent semantic similarity based interpretation of chinese metaphors. *Engineering Applications of Artificial Intelligence*, *48*, 188–203. doi:10.1016/j.engappai.2015.10.014

Tsvetkov, Y., Boytsov, L., Gershman, A., Nyberg, E., & Dyer, C. (2014, June). Metaphor detection with cross-lingual model transfer. In *Proceedings of the 52nd Annual Meeting of the Association for Computational Linguistics (Volume 1: Long Papers)* (pp. 248-258). 10.3115/v1/P14-1024

Veale, T., & Hao, Y. (2007). Comprehending and generating apt metaphors: a web-driven, case-based approach to figurative language. AAAI, 1471–1476.

Veale, T., & Hao, Y. (2008). A fluid knowledge representation for understanding and generating creative metaphors. In *Proceedings of the 22nd International Conference on Computational Linguistics-Volume 1*, (pp. 945–952). Manchester, UK: Association for Computational Linguistics. 10.3115/1599081.1599200

Wilks, Y. (1978). Making preferences more active. *Artificial Intelligence*, *11*(3), 197–223. doi:10.1016/0004-3702(78)90001-2

Wu, C., Wu, F., Chen, Y., Wu, S., Yuan, Z., & Huang, Y. (2018). Neural metaphor detecting with cnn-lstm model. *Proceedings of the Workshop on Figurative Language Processing*, 110–114. 10.18653/v1/W18-0913

Xiao, P., Alnajjar, K., Granroth-Wilding, M., Agres, K., & Toivonen, H. (2016). Meta4meaning: Automatic metaphor interpretation using corpus-derived word associations. *Proceedings of the 7th International Conference on Computational Creativity (ICCC)*.

Zadeh, A. H., & Sharda, R. (2014). Modeling brand post popularity dynamics in online social networks. *Decision Support Systems*, *65*, 59–68. doi:10.1016/j.dss.2014.05.003

Zhang, D., Xu, H., Su, Z., & Xu, Y. (2015). Chinese comments sentiment classification based on word2vec and svm perf. *Expert Systems with Applications*, *42*(4), 1857–1863. doi:10.1016/j.eswa.2014.09.011

ADDITIONAL READING

Berkman, R. I. (2008). *The art of strategic listening: finding market intelligence through blogs and other social media*. Paramount Market Publishing.

Bremer, K., & Lee, M. (1997). *Metaphors in marketing: Review and implications for marketers*. ACR North American Advances.

Camp, E. (2006). Metaphor in the Mind: The Cognition of Metaphor 1. *Philosophy Compass*, *1*(2), 154–170. doi:10.1111/j.1747-9991.2006.00013.x

Kelly, A., Lawlor, K., & O'Donohoe, S. (2005). Encoding advertisements: The creative perspective. *Journal of Marketing Management*, *21*(5-6), 505–528. doi:10.1362/0267257054307390

McQuarrie, E. F., & Phillips, B. J. (2005). Indirect persuasion in advertising: How consumers process metaphors presented in pictures and words. *Journal of Advertising*, *34*(2), 7–20. doi:10.1080/00913367.2005.10639188

Rai, S., & Chakraverty, S. (2020). A Survey on Computational Metaphor Processing. [CSUR]. *ACM Computing Surveys*, *53*(2), 1–37. doi:10.1145/3373265

Reyes, A., Rosso, P., & Buscaldi, D. (2012). From humor recognition to irony detection: The figurative language of social media. *Data & Knowledge Engineering, 74,* 1–12. doi:10.1016/j.datak.2012.02.005

Zaltman, G., & Zaltman, L. H. (2008). *Marketing metaphoria: What deep metaphors reveal about the minds of consumers.* Harvard Business Press.

KEY TERMS AND DEFINITIONS

Cosine Similarity: It is defined as cosine of the angle between two non-zero word vectors, used to measure word or text similarity.

Emotion: An immediate yet brief reaction or perception of a feeling towards an event such as meeting your long-lost friend or delicious meal.

Figurative Text: A text is said to be figurative text if the phrase is not intended to be understood literally.

Localization: The transformation of a product such as a mobile app or website to incorporate the linguistic and cultural aspects of a local market.

Nominal Metaphor: An explicit mapping between a concept from Target Domain and a concept from Source Domain where a copular verb is used as an adhesive.

Perception: A psychological process to interpret sensory stimuli such as visual, auditory, or gustatory on the basis of one's past experiences.

Word Embedding: A learned numerical representation for a word where words having similar meaning have a similar representation.

ENDNOTES

[1]   *Nokia Connecting People Campaign.* [Accessed on June 11 2020]. Available at: <https://www.pinclipart.com/pindetail/iixJJwi_nokia-with-hands-connecting-people-png-nokia-connecting/>

[2]   Audi Wake up Campaign. [Accessed on June 11, 2020]. Available at: https://www.adsoftheworld.com/media/print/audi_wake_up

[3]   Fish: https://dictionary.cambridge.org/dictionary/english/fish

Chapter 7
Estimating Importance From Web Reviews Through Textual Description and Metrics Extraction

Roney Lira de Sales Santos
https://orcid.org/0000-0001-9562-0605
University of Sao Paulo, Brazil

Rafael Torres Anchiêta
https://orcid.org/0000-0003-4209-9013
University of Sao Paulo, Brazil

Carlos Augusto de Sa
Federal University of Piaui, Brazil

Ricardo de Andrade Lira Rabelo
Federal University of Piaui, Brazil

Rogerio Figueredo de Sousa
https://orcid.org/0000-0003-4589-6157
University of Sao Paulo, Brazil

Raimundo Santos Moura
Federal University of Piaui, Brazil

ABSTRACT

The evolution of e-commerce has contributed to the increase of the information available, making the task of analyzing the reviews manually almost impossible. Due to the amount of information, the creation of automatic methods of knowledge extraction and data mining has become necessary. Currently, to facilitate the analysis of reviews, some websites use filters such as votes by the utility or by stars. However, the use of these filters is not a good practice because they may exclude reviews that have recently been submitted to the voting process. One possible solution is to filter the reviews based on their textual descriptions, author information, and other measures. This chapter has a propose of approaches to estimate the importance of reviews about products and services using fuzzy systems and artificial neural networks. The results were encouraging, obtaining better results when detecting the most important reviews, achieving approximately 82% when f-measure is analyzed.

DOI: 10.4018/978-1-7998-4240-8.ch007

INTRODUCTION

Nowadays, a web user has a common practice to search for reviews when there is an interest in purchasing a product or service. Also, the companies that manufacture products or provide services are interested in customers opinions or feedback, mainly to guide marketing actions and decision-making process.

One of the main places of this kind of data is e-commerce, which includes sites for buying and selling products and providing services. E-commerce is one of the main activities present on the internet, in which exceeding the mark of 12 million stores around the planet (Digital Commerce 360, 2014). NLP researches area have tried to extract useful data from unstructured data, as around 95% of relevant information originates in an unstructured way, mainly texts such as emails, surveys, posts on social networks and forums, among others, and every day 2.5 quintillion of bytes of data are created, so much so that 90% of the data in the world today was created only in the last two years (Santos et al., 2015). This large amount of data makes manual analysis an impossible task, requiring the creation of automatic methods to analyze the data (Liu, 2010).

According to Liu (2010), this interest has always existed. However, considering the growing of data on the web, there is another way of sending opinions and making information available. Due to web popularization, people and companies have had new ways to deliver and collect opinions. Recently, social networks showed an increase in supply available places to store the content generated by customers about some products or service. Thus, consumer reviews are important to the success or failure of a product or service, because a satisfied customer will probably make a positive comment about some product that was purchased to close people, while a not satisfied customer will do a negative review.

Since there are a large number of reviews published by users, the reviews are usually classified by stars, most recent or most relevant, but are not always the most important or useful opinions for a particular user. On some buying and selling websites, users can vote on reviews that they consider useful or useless when they are searching for a product or service. However, not always only polarity information from the review is sufficient, as other problems may happen, as highlighted by Li et al., (2013): newer reviews that have not been voted yet will be hard to read and voted on. Thus, providing the most important reviews, based on the textual description, the richness of the vocabulary, and the quality of the author are factors that must be considered. In this way, new users can analyze a small set of reviews for decision-making.

Sousa et al. (2015) approach presented one possible solution to such problems, by filtering the reviews based on some features such as author reputation and textual description measures. In the end, their approach estimates the importance degree of reviews about products or services that were written by web users, allowing the knowledge of which reviews were most relevant to the user's final evaluation. Their work also used some Natural Language Processing (NLP) techniques and Fuzzy Systems (FS). Thus, the main aim of this paper is to present a study with an approach to estimate the importance degree of reviews, using some NLP techniques but made some changes in the computational model to Artificial Neural Network (ANN). Moreover, this work proposes adaptations in two input variables proposed by Sousa et al. (2015): author reputation and vocabulary richness.

This work has as contributions:

- Creation of a corpus manually annotated, to be used in the experiments of this work and others with the same approach or intention;
- Measures to define author reputation and vocabulary richness;

- Ease for user and companies in filtering reviews based not only on utility and more recent but from textual description;

It is important to emphasize that, in addition to the theoretical contributions mentioned in the first two items above, the main practical implication of this work is to reduce the difficulty of users when reading the various comments about the products and services. The automation of this task becomes something relevant and possible because by returning the most important comments, the users can analyze a small but rich set of comments for their decision-making.

The rest of this paper is organized as follows: Section *Related Works* the works related to the research are presented; Section *Proposed Approach* presents the approaches proposed in this paper, as well as the adaptations made in relation to previous work (base approach); Section *Experiments and Discussions* reports all performed experiments on the proposed approaches and finally, Section *Conclusions* concludes the paper and presents future work.

RELATED WORKS

In this section are shown the related studies that are the base of this work. They are split into two sub-sections: works about opinion extraction and works about the machine learning approaches used in this paper in the scope of opinion mining.

Opinion Extraction

A methodology to identify opinions in reviews that address more than one product was proposed by Liu et al. (2006), in what they included two steps: opinion indexing and opinion retrieving. The first one consists in the identification of opinion fragments and, after this, to make the opinion tuples like <product, feature, sentiment>. The last one is referred to look up the opinion tuples which represents the users' retrieving interests. Using the C4.5 approach on a dataset with 376 documents, the authors achieved 70% accuracy when all opinions were processed and 80% accuracy when they used the *Non-Disagreement* criteria, i. e., when the reviews were not with different annotates on the feature.

In the Jeong et al. (2011) study, they proposed a system for extraction and refinement of features based on nominal phrases and semantic information of the words, which they denominate of FEROM. Due to problems leading to unsatisfactory results in the extraction of aspects at the time, the authors proposed a preprocessing step, where all the words of the reviews are tagged with their grammatical classes and then identify the noun phrases. In addition, in the same preprocessing step there is a sentence separator, which keeps each aspect and its opinion words in the same sentence.

The main goal of Silva et al. (2012) was to present the *SAPair*, a more refined process of sentiment analysis, entering the level of features. The proposal aimed to classify the polarity of opinions on each feature of the object being monitored, by means of the pairs <feature, opinion word>, since some adjectives change their polarity when they follow a certain noun, for example, "hot pizza" and "hot beer", respectively, positive and negative. Experiments have shown that the proposed process has high efficacy, in which it overcomes other existing methods, such as the proposal of Turney (2002).

In the approach presented in this work, the opinion extraction step is similar to the proposal by Jeong et al. (2011). However, it was additionally used the phrasal structure of the sentence to identify the features and its respective quality words. So, from a review, all tuples <feature, opinion word> are identified.

Fuzzy Systems and Artificial Neural Networks in Opinion Mining

The propose of Kar and Mandal (2011) was an approach with Fuzzy techniques for analyzing the opinion contained in a review, focusing on the sentiment evaluation in the review by a score for decision-making. Three steps were used: i) mining products features commonly addressed by users; ii) identifying the sentences that contain opinions in each review and extract the opinion expressions in each opinion sentence; and iii) from these opinion expressions, to measure their score in order to summarize by their strength.

A Fuzzy logic system was proposed by Nadali et al. (2010) with the aim to analyze the sentiment of users' reviews. First, the reviews were classified (by experts) in various levels (e.g., strongly positive or negative, moderately positive or negative, weakly positive or negative, and very weakly positive or negative). Then, they used three membership functions for the Fuzzy System: low, moderate and high, which the boundaries also being defined by experts. In this work, the authors did not report their results.

The aim of Srivastava and Bhatia (2013) was to quantify the strength of subjective expressions when used modifiers (usually adverbs) and if they make changes in the opinion word strength. From the examples like "screen is beautiful", "screen is very beautiful" and "screen is slightly very beautiful", the authors compared the results with a manual annotation, and they found an average error less than 0.0118, considered by authors acceptable.

The approach presented in this work is different from all the above related works in the proposal of the use of models to infer the review importance and not only the strength of opinion word. Thus, the main contribution of our approach is to propose a model with fuzzy system and ANNs to estimate the importance of review and set the TOP(X) most relevant reviews. Also, it is important to highlight that our approach reduces the task of processing the uncountable user reviews of product or service.

Approaches using artificial neural networks in the scientific literature can be divided into some subjects, such as classify opinions about products and services, market predictions and social networks. Sharma and Dey (2012) proposed a sentiment classification model using backpropagation, using the Information Gain method and popular sentiment lexicons to extract sentiment representing features that are used to train and test the network. The results showed that the proposed approach had better performance in order to reduce the network dimensionality while producing an accurate sentiment-based classification of text.

The possibility to improve the accuracy of stock market indicators predictions by using data about psychological states of Twitter users was discussed by Porshnev et al. (2013) in their study. For their analysis, they used a lexicon-based approach to allow evaluating the presence of eight basic emotions in more than 755 million tweets to apply to neural networks algorithms.

In none of the related works, there is a reason for the use of other machine learning technique, which is discussed in this work. In the authors' previous work (Santos, Sousa, Rabelo & Moura, 2016), it was made an initial comparative study between Sousa et al. (2015) approach with Fuzzy System (which is explained in the following section) and the implementation of an approach with the same characteristics, but changing the algorithm of machine learning for the Artificial Neural Network, obtaining good results, however, it was still below than expected.

Table 1 summarizes the main related works presented in this section, highlighting the approach used, most important features and results.

Table 1. Summarized table with related works in this section

Related Work	Approach	Features	Result
Liu et al. (2006)	C4.5	Triple <product, feature, opinion word>	0.791 (accuracy)
Jeong et al. (2011)	Feature-based	Semantic information of words	0.847 (f-measure)
Silva et al. (2012)	NGD	Pair <feature, opinion word>	0.658 (f-measure)
Kar and Mandal (2011)	Fuzzy	Opinion words (adjectives and adverbs)	0.701 (their own measure)
Nadali et al. (2010)	Fuzzy	Adjectives, adverbs, verbs and nouns (as opinion words)	no result
Srivastava and Bhatia (2013)	Fuzzy	Adverbial modifiers, unigram, bigram and trigram patterns	0.0118 (avg error)
Sharma and Dey (2012)	Neural Network	Sentiment words	0.95 (f-measure)
Porshnev et al. (2013)	Neural Network and SVM	Frequency of words and semantic information of words	0.641 (accuracy)

PROPOSED APPROACH

In this work, adaptations were proposed in three input variables of the system previously proposed by Sousa et al. (2015). The base approach and the adaptations are described in the next subsections.

In addition, in this section, the proposed models in this work are detailed: an approach with Fuzzy Systems and Artificial Neural Networks. Fuzzy Systems have the advantage of being able to implement control techniques based on expert experience and intuitive aspects, using linguistic propositions (rules) and imprecise entries. The approach of Sousa et al. (2015) allows the user to define the rule base in a personalized way. Thus, when choosing a Fuzzy Inference System to determine which set of comments the user should read to make a decision, i. e., to calculate the importance of a comment, an action/control strategy is obtained that can be monitored and interpreted, including from a linguistic point of view. Then, with the exploration of each dimension of the base approach, new metrics (variables) at the input of the model were introduced, making it impractical to use a Fuzzy System. With this, new models with the use of Artificial Neural Networks were proposed. Finally, to make the authors' choices more flexible, two types of Artificial Neural Networks were analyzed: Multi-Layer Perceptron and Radial Basis Function.

Artificial Neural Networks are computational models inspired by the nervous system of living beings, being an attempt to model the information processing capacities of nervous systems (Rojas, 2013). The computational elements, called artificial neurons, are simplified models of biological neurons, inspired by the work of Hodgkin and Huxley (1952). The artificial neurons used in nonlinear ANN models provide typically continuous outputs and perform simple functions, such as collecting the existing signals at their inputs, aggregating them according to their operational function and producing a response, taking into account their inherent activation function.

The Base Approach

Sousa et al. (2015) proposed an approach that infers the importance degree of reviews in relation to products and services using a Fuzzy System containing three main inputs: author reputation, number of tuples (feature, opinion word) and correctness. Then, these inputs are applied to a Fuzzy System, which returns the importance degree of the review. Some parts about the Fuzzy System configuration proposed by them were not detailed in this work, being available in Sousa et al. (2015). In what follows, the proposed adaptations in this work are detailed.

Adaptations

Author Reputation

In this work, six metrics were defined, taking into account the maximum of information that could be used to evaluate the author reputation, as follows (extracted of Sa et al. (2017)):

- **Review Date**: the date in which the review was posted, converted to days compared to the initial date of corpus data collection. The more recent a review is, the more updated the review will be and, consequently, should be better evaluated. However, the most recent reviews may be disadvantaged by this metric there was not enough time for users to read it;
- **Website Register Date**: the date the author registered at the website, converted to days in comparison to the corpus collection date. This metric evaluates veteran authors with a better reputation than newcomer authors;
- **Positive Votes**: a number of positive votes received from other users. The more positive votes a user receives, the better their reputation;
- **Negative Votes**: a number of negative votes received from other users. Inversely proportional to positive votes, the more negative votes a user's reviews receive, the worse their reputation will be;
- **Total of Votes**: the general sum of all votes received in a review. In a general, hypothetical sense, the more votes a user's review has, either positive or negative, the better the author reputation since this means the author is more largely observed;
- **Total of reviews by the review's author**: number of reviews the user has posted on the website. It is relevant because this information shows the active participation of the user on the website.

Thus, the proposed solution was the implementation of an MLP ANN that receives as input the six variables described in this section. The hidden layer, consist of eight neurons and the output layer uses one neuron, classifying all possible author grades (0 to 10). Next, the author grades were grouped into three categories (low, medium and high) to define how good the author reputation of the review is. The ANN obtained the test precision of 91.01% (it was used 2,000 comments were used for training, and 356 for testing) and the resulting reputation served as a single input in the Fuzzy Inference System to be explained in Section *Experiments and Discussion*. The ANN is shown in Figure 1.

The tool used to perform the neural network was the statistical analysis software SPSS (Spss, 2011). In the input layer, there are six variables, each one representing a measure to evaluate the author's reputation. These metrics were considered important to evaluate the author reputation in the context of the collected corpus. It is important to note that in Online Social Networks (OSN) other metrics may be ap-

Figure 1: ANN topology for author reputation

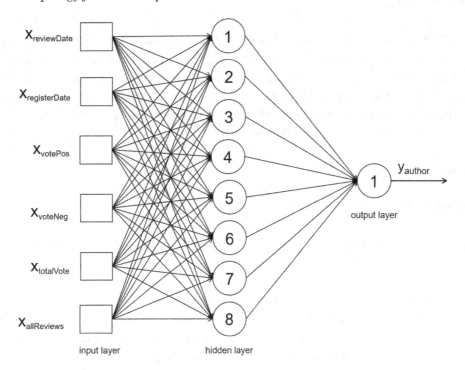

plied to calculate author reputation, for example, the number of followers on Twitter (Kwak et al., 2010; Weng et al., 2010; Aggarwal and Kumaraguru, 2014). However, these metrics are still not available on e-commerce websites, which makes it a big challenge to integrate user profiles from e-commerce websites and OSNs. Further information about the author reputation approach can be found in Sa et al. (2017).

Vocabulary Richness

In this work, in addition to considering the correctness of the review, it is proposed to use three more variables that measure the lexical richness of the text: the TTR index (Type-Token Ratio) (Templin, 1957), the Maas index (Mass, 1972) and the MTLD index (Measure of Textual Lexical Diversity) (McCarthy, 2005).

Torruella and Capsada (2013) affirm that the lexical richness of a text gives an idea of the number of different terms used and vocabulary diversity. In addition, it defines three classes of indexes that calculate vocabulary richness.

The first class of indexes is based on the direct relationship between the number of terms and words. The TTR index is defined by $TTR = t/n$ where t is the number of unique terms, and n is the number of words of the review.

The second class of indexes has been developed based on logarithms. The justification is that the function grows in such a way to adapt itself better to the behaviour of the relationship between the different terms and the number of words in the text. The Maas index, defined by $Maas = (\log n - \log t)/(\log n)^2$ where, again, t is the number of unique terms and n is the quantity of words.

There is also a third class of indexes, obtained from more complex calculations, where the MTLD index is found. The calculation of the MTLD index is performed by dividing the text into segments and the TTR index is calculated for each segment. The size of each segment is variable, and depends precisely on the value of the TTR index (here, the default size is 0.72). A segment is considered complete when the TTR index of the last word is less than 0.72. So, if the TTR index of the last word is upper to 0.72, it is considered to calculate the partial segment of the text as $PS = (1 - TTR_{last\ word})/(1 - 0.72)$ where $TTR_{last\ word}$ is the value of the TTR index in the last word of the text. At the end of the text, the number of segments in which the text was divided is counted, and the MTLD index value is calculated by $MTLD = n/(s+PS)$ where n is the size of the text in number of words, s is the number of complete segments, and PS is the quantity of partial segments. New execution of the MTLD index is done with the text being processed in reverse. The average of the two values is the final value of the MTLD index (McCarthy and Jarvis, 2010).

In relation to the text size, Torruella and Capsada (2013) proved that the indices belonging to the first class are sensitive to the text size, while the indices belonging to the second and third classes are not. In addition, the Maas index proved to be the most stable with respect to the text size.

The use of indexes is justified by their ability to detect and quantify the differences in lexical richness among different reviews. The more correct and rich vocabulary is the review, the more important it becomes. Thus, to map the vocabulary richness, it was considered the four variables described: i) the correctness; ii) the lexical richness measured by the TTR index; iii) the lexical richness measured by the Maas index; and iv) the lexical richness measured by the MTLD index.

For the calculation of the word's review correctness variable, a dictionary of words was taken from *WordNet.BR* (Dias-da-Silva, 2010) containing 250,196 words. The calculation of the variables related to the TTR, Maas, and MTLD indexes was done by obtaining the values of the number of different terms that are expressed in the review and the number of words in the review through tokenization and word count method in the NLTK library.

As justified in the adaptation of author reputation variable, the vocabulary richness variable must also have only one output. Thus, the proposed solution was the implementation of an MLP-type ANN that receives as input the four variables described in this section and returns as output a real value between 0 and 3 that defines how good the vocabulary richness of the review is. The ANN is illustrated in Figure 2.

The ANN topology was also defined by the SPSS software. The ANN contains four inputs, five neurons in the hidden layer and one neuron in the output layer. The error function used was cross-entropy.

For training and testing, the reviews were manually classified as Low (LW), Medium (MD), Good (GD), and Excellent (EX) with reference to the values of correctness, TTR, Maas, and MTLD. These reviews were used in the training of the ANN, considering the values 0, 1, 2, and 3 for the classes Low, Medium, Good and Excellent, respectively. The use of such classes was based on the Likert scale (Likert, 1932), which usually resorts to five levels of response. In our case, the lowest level was automatically removed as it was considered useless comments. The percentage of correctness in the classes performed in the testing step of the ANN proposed for the vocabulary richness variable was 82.5%.

Finally, it is noted that the author reputation and vocabulary richness are relevant metrics to infer the importance degree of reviews and they serve as inputs to the approach using the FS to be explained in next subsection and as a basis for the approach using ANN to be discussed in subsection after.

Figure 2: ANN topology for vocabulary richness

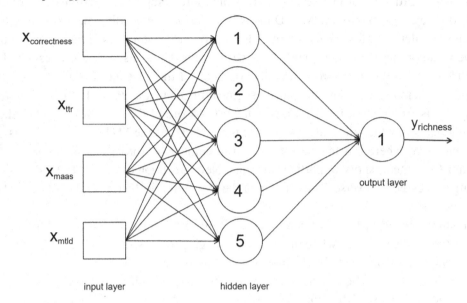

Approach With Fuzzy System

Taking into account the three input variables proposed in Sousa et al. (2015) and the adaptations here proposed, the general scheme of the FS approach is presented in Figure 3.

The approach uses the Mamdani inference model (Mamdani and Assilian, 1975), due to the use of linguistic variables in the input and output of the inference system, which makes the system modelling process more intuitive.

Fuzzy Inference Systems contains three steps: fuzzification, fuzzy inference process and defuzzification. The first performed task was to define the linguistic values for each system variables, both the input variables and the output variable. The linguistic values of each variable are shown in Table 2.

Table 2. Linguistic values of Fuzzy Inference System variables

Variable	Linguistic Variables
Author Reputation	Low, Medium and High
Quantity of Tuples	Low, Medium and High
Vocabulary Richness	Low, Medium, Good and Excellent
Importance	Insufficient, Sufficient, Good and Excellent

The linguistic values of all variables were based on Sousa et al. (2015). It was necessary to adapt the vocabulary richness variable because, as explained in Subsection *Vocabulary Richness*, the resulting value comes from an ANN that includes four inputs and returns an output which value is between 0 and 3, mapping each of the numerical outputs to a linguistic variable.

In the fuzzification step is obtained the membership degree of which each input is related to each Fuzzy set. The degree is obtained through the analysis of the membership functions involved in the system. The membership functions of the proposed approach are shown in Figure 4: author reputation (5a), the quantity of tuples (5b), vocabulary richness (5c) and the importance of the review (5d).

Figure 3. Fuzzy Inference System approach

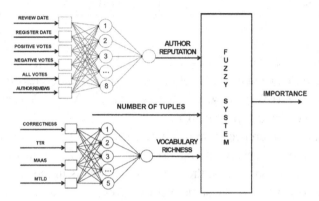

The inference process step receives the fuzzified entries and applies them according to each rule contained in the rule base. The rule base contains the Fuzzy rules that represent the knowledge of the process. The structure of a rule is:

IF $(v_{e1}=a)$ **AND** $(v_{e2}=b)$ **AND** $(v_{e3}=c)$ **THEN** $(v_s=d)$,

where v_{e1}, v_{e2}, and v_{e3} are the input variables and v_s is the output variable. The proposed rule base for the FS approach is shown in Table 3.

Figure 4. Membership Functions

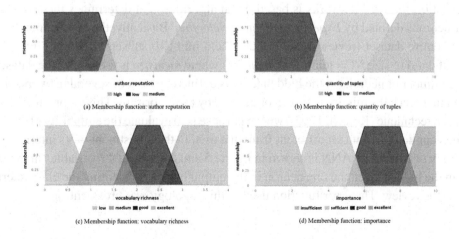

Table 3. Fuzzy inference system rule base

Author	Quantity of Tuples/Vocabulary Richness											
	LW/ LW	LW/ MD	LW/ GD	LW/ EX	MD/ LW	MD/ MD	MD/ EX	MD/ EX	HG/ LW	HG/ MD	HG/ GD	HG/ EX
LW	IF	IF	IF	SF	IF	SF	SF	GD	SF	SF	GD	GD
MD	IF	IF	IF	SF	SF	SF	GD	GD	SF	SF	GD	EX
HG	SF	SF	SF	GD	SF	GD	GD	EX	GD	GD	EX	EX

As an example of reading the rules of Table 3, it is used the values referring to the intersection of the first line (referring to the author) and the first column (referring to the tuples and vocabulary richness). The inputs are: Author = *Low* (LW), Number of tuples = *Low* (LW) and Vocabulary Richness = *Low* (LW), resulting in Importance = *Insufficient* (IF).

The final step of the Fuzzy inference system is defuzzification. To obtain a numerical value for the output variable importance of the review, it was used the centre of area method, which could be the centre of gravity or centroid. In most cases, the centre of the area is in the same position as the centre of gravity, so these names often denote the same method (Weber and Klein, 2003).

Approach With Fuzzy System

The choice of an ANN was due to its power in solving problems involving the classification of patterns. The definition of the approach was made by three steps: i) definition of ANN architecture; ii) definition of ANN topology; and iii) ANN training and testing.

In the ANN architecture definition phase, two types of networks were studied: a Multi-Layer Perceptron (MLP) using the backpropagation training algorithm and Radial Basis Function (RBF).

It was considered 323 reviews, manually classified in Insufficient, Sufficient, Good and Excellent. This was the analogy of the Fuzzy System, since the Fuzzy System approach linguistic variables proposed in this work result in this classification, and for this reason, the ANN output must follow the same pattern.

The next step was to define the topologies to be used. It should be noted that the entire task of defining the architecture, topology (number of neurons in the hidden layer, error and activation functions), and ANN execution was performed in the SPSS software. According to its documentation (Spss, 2011), the topology definition for MLP networks is based on an algorithm that determines the "best" number of hidden layer neurons defined by *Expert Architecture Selection*. Basically, the algorithm takes a random sample of the entire dataset (reviews) and divides them into two subsets: training (70% of data) and testing (30% of data) of size $NC= \min(1000, memsize)$ where *memsize* is the size of the dataset stored in memory. The number of neurons in the hidden layer is defined by tests of several networks trained with the set of data that reach the minimum test error defined by the algorithm. This algorithm is based on the cross-validation technique (Kohavi, 1995), whose purpose is to evaluate the suitability of each candidate topology when applied to a data set different from that used in the adjustment of its internal parameters.

The topology of MLP-type ANN is shown in Figure 5 and consists of 11 variables in the input layer, six neurons in the hidden layer and one neuron in the output layer, representing the class referring to the importance of the review. The error function used in this topology was cross-entropy.

The definition of the topology for the RBF networks followed practically the same procedures used in the definition of MLP network topology. SPSS uses an algorithm that determines the "best" number of neurons in the hidden layer of the RBF network, defined by *Automatic Selection of Number of Basic Functions* (Spss, 2011), and automatically calculates the minimum and maximum values of a user-defined range and finds the best number of neurons within that range.

Figure 5. Topology: MLP-type ANN

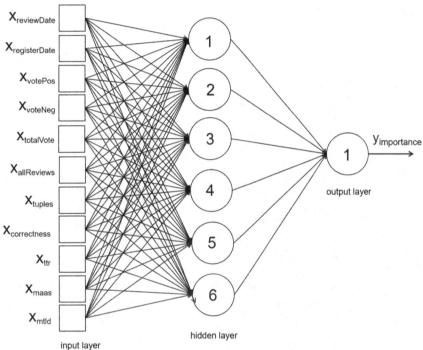

The topology of RBF-type ANN is illustrated in Figure 6 and consists of 11 variables in the input layer, seven neurons in the hidden layer and one neuron in the output layer. The Softmax activation function was used in the hidden layer, and the function applied to the output layer was the identity. The reason for using the softmax function in the hidden layer is because the training in the first stage uses only radial-based functions, called in this case the Normalized Radial Basis Function (NRBF) (Bugmann, 1998; Heimes et al., 1998), which uses the softmax function (Duch and Jankowski, 1999). The error function used in this topology was the sum of the square errors.

Unlike the one proposed in the Fuzzy System explained in Subsection *Approach with Fuzzy System*, the ANN approach supports very well all the variables being considered together, facilitating the final analysis and avoiding that one of the ANN inputs is another ANN, just as it is one of the entries of the proposed Fuzzy Inference System.

SOLUTIONS AND RECOMMENDATIONS

In this section, the solutions regarding the approaches proposed in this paper and recommendations that are important are discussed. In addition, here is explain the collection and preparation of the corpus that serves as the basis for the experiments. The computational model based on MLP and RBF ANN are analyzed, taking into account the importance of the input variables in relation to the output of the model. In the end, a comparison of the computational models is performed, along with the base approach.

Figure 6. Topology: RBF-type ANN

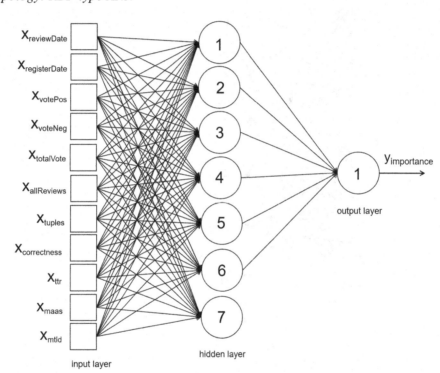

Collect and Preparation of Corpus

For the evaluation of the approach, it was necessary to build a corpus of reviews. The data collection process was performed on September 28 and 29, 2016, at the Buscapé website (Buscapé, 2016). Some smartphones models were selected and the users' reviews were collected. Initially, a total of 2,433 reviews were collected, but an adjustment was made in the reviews by eliminating the duplicates and empty to avoid inconsistencies. In the end, there were 2,000 reviews, of which 1,000 were positive and 1,000 negative polarities. The semantic orientation of the reviews was defined by the review author and are presented to the readers separately, through guides with positive and negative reviews. It is noteworthy that the works in the area have usually used only 2,000 reviews in the experiments and evaluations, due to the difficulty of the corpus annotation process.

However, when analyzed more closely, the semantic review orientation did not always present the reality of the review. Thus, some reviews marked as positive could actually have a negative orientation or vice versa. In addition, it was noticed that many reviews were neither positive nor negative, being neutral with respect to the product for which they were intended. To solve this problem, it was decided to create a corpus annotated with the intention of evaluating the approaches. In this process, four experts from the opinion mining area were selected to evaluate the reviews, with 1,000 reviews for each pair. They evaluated the reviews according to the following orientations: positive, negative, neutral or trash (reviews without useful content). At the end of this stage, a fifth expert was responsible for resolving the discrepancies. All the experts are students graduated in Computer Science and act as researchers in the NLP area. Figure 7 shows the corpus annotation workflow.

The annotated corpus after the analysis of the specialists has 923 positive, 602 negative, 141 neutral, and 334 trash reviews. Note that a large number of reviews were marked as trash. This is due to the fact that several users post their collaborations on the sites without owning the product or even posting something without the least sense.

Figure 7. Corpus Annotation Workflow

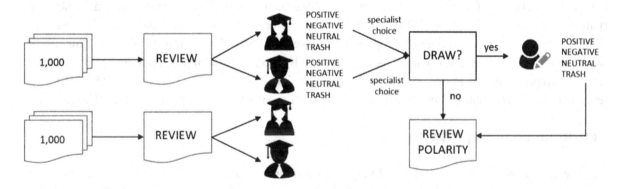

A total of 356 reviews were randomly selected, being 138 positives and 218 negatives, to be evaluated according to their importance. This procedure was necessary in order to evaluate the accuracy of the base approach and also the new approaches being presented in this paper. The number of reviews was chosen by means of a statistical analysis that takes into account the level of confidence and the margin of error of the sample. Being q is the minimum quantity of reviews belonging to the sample, the calculation is done by the equations (Hamburg, 1974)

$$x = Z\left(\frac{c}{100}\right)^2 r(100 - r) \quad q = \left[\frac{T_x}{\left((T-1)E^2 + x\right)}\right]^2$$

where $Z\left(\dfrac{c}{100}\right)$ is the critical value of the confidence level c chosen, r is the distribution of responses, i. e., what answers are expected for each review (usually 0.5), since if the sample is highly distorted, the

Table 4. Base approach: matrix

Real Value	Predict Value				Total
	EXCELLENT	**GOOD**	**SUFFICIENT**	**INSUFFICIENT**	
EXCELLENT	6	4	23	0	33
GOOD	4	19	42	1	66
SUFFICIENT	8	16	121	9	154
INSUFFICIENT	1	8	70	24	103
Total	19	47	256	34	356

population will probably be, T is the size of the corpus and E is the margin of error. For this work, the confidence level chosen was 95%, and the margin of error chosen was 5%.

The manual analysis procedure was performed by five experts, all masters students of the course of Portuguese Literature, using the same method of evaluation of the revised corpus. The experts manually evaluated each of the reviews by assigning an importance degree: Insufficient (IF), Sufficient (SF), Good (GD) or Excellent (EX), according to the verification of features about the smartphones, vocabulary richness and observation of the author reputation. Variables related to the author reputation and vocabulary richness were assigned a score of 0 to 10 by the expert in each review encompassing all the variables proposed in this work, according to the reputation inferred by ANNs. For definition purposes, this subset with 356 reviews analyzed was named as **Importance Reference Subcorpus**, containing 33 Excellent reviews (16 positives and 17 negatives), 66 Good reviews (19 positives and 47 negatives), 154 Sufficient reviews (51 positives and 103 negatives), and 103 Insufficient reviews (52 positives and 51 negatives).

Performance of Approaches

Experiments were performed with the Importance Reference Subcorpus. For each review, the same methods were used to extract the information from the input variables of each approach. The results are presented by a confusion matrix, containing the number of correct classifications as opposed to the classifications predicted for each class. For the evaluation of the models, the precision measures (P), recall (R) and F-measure (F) were calculated for each class, as well as the error rate. The overall accuracy of the approach, which represents the accuracy of the model, was also calculated. It is important to note that these measures are usually used in the evaluation of machine learning approaches (Powers, 2011).

Table 4 shows the confusion matrix for the TOP(X) base approach, used as the basis for the comparison process. The measures of precision, recall, F-measure and error rate per class are given in Table 5.

Table 5. Base approach: measures

Class	PRECISION	RECALL	F-MEASURE	Error
EXCELLENT	0.315	0.182	0.23	0.818
GOOD	0.404	0.288	0.336	0.712
SUFFICIENT	0.472	0.786	0.59	0.214
INSUFFICIENT	0.705	0.233	0.35	0.767

It should be noted that precision is calculated as the percentage of examples correctly classified as positive in each class, by means of the equation:

$$P = \frac{TP}{(TP + FP)}.$$

where *TP* represents the reviews classified correctly (*true positive*) and *FP* represents the reviews classified incorrectly (*false positive*). For example, for the EX class, six reviews were correctly classified, but 13 reviews were incorrectly classified, with the precision being 6/(6+13) = 31.57%. For the GD class, 19 reviews were correctly classified (TP), but 28 reviews were classified incorrectly (FP), reaching precision equal to 19/(19+28) = 40.42%.

The recall is obtained by means of the percentage of examples correctly classified as positive in relation to the total of instances of the Importance Reference Subcorpus, by means of the formula

$$R = \frac{TP}{(TP + FN)}.$$

where *TP* represents the reviews correctly classified, and *FN* represents the reviews that are incorrectly classified in relation to the Importance Reference Subcorpus (*false negative*). For example, for the EX class, the recall is equal to 6/(6+27) = 18.18%, since 6 reviews were correctly classified (TP), but 27 reviews were incorrectly classified (FN).

The F-measure is a harmonic mean between precision and recall derived from Rijsbergen (1979). The calculation of the F-measure is performed according to the equation

$$F = \frac{2 * P * R}{(P + R)}.$$

where *P* represents the value of the precision, and *R* represents the value of the recall. There are ways to weight precision and recall values according to the calculation goal (Piskorski and Yangarber, 2013), but in this work, it was not necessary to ponder since the purpose of using the F-measure was to evaluate the complete approach in its precision and recall in each class. In the case of class EX, the F-measure is equal to 23.07%, and for the GD class, the F-measure reached 33.62%.

The error rate is calculated as the number of reviews classified incorrectly divided by the total of reviews belonging to the class. For example, for the EX class, the error rate is equal to 27/33 = 81.82%.

Finally, the overall accuracy of the approach is calculated as the number of correctly classified samples in each class by the total sample overall. In the case, one has 6+19+121+24 = 170 reviews correctly classified. Therefore, the overall accuracy of the base approach is equal to 170/356 = 47.7%.

Table 6 presents the confusion matrix for the Fuzzy System approach with adaptations, and Table 7 shows the measures of precision, recall, F-measure and error rate per class. The overall accuracy of the approach was 61.23% (29+55+47+87 = 218; 218/356 = 0.6123).

Table 6. Fuzzy System approach: matrix

Real Value	Predict Value				Total
	EXCELLENT	GOOD	SUFFICIENT	INSUFFICIENT	
EXCELLENT	29	1	1	2	33
GOOD	2	55	7	2	66
SUFFICIENT	6	1	47	100	154
INSUFFICIENT	1	0	15	87	103
Total	38	57	70	191	356

Table 7. Fuzzy System approach: measures

Class	PRECISION	RECALL	F-MEASURE	Error
EXCELLENT	0.763	0.877	0.816	0.123
GOOD	0.964	0.834	0.894	0.166
SUFFICIENT	0.671	0.306	0.419	0.694
INSUFFICIENT	0.455	0.846	0.591	0.154

The confusion matrix for the approach with MLP-type ANN is shown in Table 8 and in Table 9 the accuracy, recall, F-measure and error rate for each class. The overall accuracy of this approach was 62.35% (22+54+88+58 = 222; 222/356 = 0.6235).

Table 8. MLP approach: matrix

Real Value	Predict Value				Total
	EXCELLENT	GOOD	SUFFICIENT	INSUFFICIENT	
EXCELLENT	22	7	4	0	33
GOOD	1	54	10	1	66
SUFFICIENT	2	25	88	39	154
INSUFFICIENT	1	5	39	58	103
Total	26	91	141	98	356

Table 9. MLP approach: measures

Class	PRECISION	RECALL	F-MEASURE	Error
EXCELLENT	0.846	0.667	0.745	0.333
GOOD	0.593	0.818	0.687	0.182
SUFFICIENT	0.671	0.306	0.419	0.694
INSUFFICIENT	0.455	0.845	0.591	0.155

The confusion matrix for the RBF-type ANN approach is shown in Table 10, while values of accuracy, coverage, F-measure and error rate per class are shown in Table 11. Its overall accuracy was 59.26% (23+51+72+65 = 211; 211/356 = 0.5926).

Table 10. RBF approach: matrix

Real Value	Predict Value				Total
	EXCELLENT	GOOD	SUFFICIENT	INSUFFICIENT	
EXCELLENT	23	6	4	0	33
GOOD	4	51	9	2	66
SUFFICIENT	10	29	72	43	154
INSUFFICIENT	0	5	33	65	103
Total	37	91	118	110	356

Table 11. RBF approach: measures

Class	PRECISION	RECALL	F-MEASURE	Error
EXCELLENT	0.621	0.697	0.657	0.303
GOOD	0.56	0.773	0.649	0.227
SUFFICIENT	0.61	0.468	0.529	0.532
INSUFFICIENT	0.59	0.631	0.61	0.369

DISCUSSION

After the results of the execution of the approaches were presented through their confusion matrices, it was possible to compare the proposed approaches in this work. As the approaches using the Fuzzy System and Artificial Neural Network are parametric, a carefully planned comparison was made.

It is verified that the approach using MLP-type ANN obtained better overall accuracy, achieving 62.35% when compared to the others. The Base TOP(X) obtained 47.7%, FS with Adaptations obtained 61.23%, and the RBF-type ANN achieved 59.26%. However, evaluating the performance of the classification model only with the measure of accuracy is not fully accepted by the community, as it is considered a weak measure (Provost, 1997), and that a model whose objective is to maximize accuracy may apparently have a good rating because it may consider the information irrelevant (Schütze et al., 2008). For this reason, it was decided to analyze the approaches through their classes, that is, their degrees of importance with other measures of evaluation. The first measure analyzed is the F-measure, as shown in Table 12.

One can be observed that with regard to the reviews of the EX and GD classes (excellent and good), the approach with FS with adaptations obtained a better value of F-measure with 81.69% and 89.43%, while the approach with MLP-type ANN obtained better F-measure value (59.6%) in the SF (sufficient) class. The RBF-type ANN approach had a better F-measure value (61%) to ISF (insufficient) samples.

Another measure used was the Matthews Correlation Coefficient (Matthews, 1975), which takes into account the true and false positives and is considered a balanced measure that can be used even if the classes are unbalanced (different sizes). The coefficient calculation returns a value in the interval [-1, 1], where the coefficient of +1 represents a perfect prediction, 0 represents a mean random prediction, and -1 a reverse prediction. The equation that returns the coefficient is

$$\varphi = \frac{(TP \times TN) - (FP \times FN)}{\sqrt{(TP + FP)(TP + FN)(TN + FP)(TN + FN)}}$$

where *TN* represents the reviews correctly classified as not being of the analyzed class (*true negative*). It is the measure that is most accurate for the comparison of the approaches proposed in this work, and it is generally considered to be one of the best metrics to measure the performance of a system (Powers, 2011). Besides, the value of this metric has an interpretation which indicates how close to perfection the algorithm is. The values for each class are given in Table 13.

Table 12. F-measure per class of each approach

Class	Base TOP(X)	FS with adaptations	MLP-type ANN	RBF-type ANN
EXCELLENT	0.23	**0.816**	0.745	0.657
GOOD	0.336	**0.894**	0.687	0.649
SUFFICIENT	0.59	0.419	**0.596**	0.529
INSUFFICIENT	0.35	0.591	0.577	**0.61**

Table 13. Matthews Correlation Coefficient per class of each approach

Class	Base TOP(X)	FS with adaptations	MLP-type ANN	RBF-type ANN
EXCELLENT	0.18	**0.80**	0.73	0.62
GOOD	0.22	**0.88**	0.62	0.57
SUFFICIENT	0.13	0.24	0.31	**0.57**
INSUFFICIENT	0.30	0.39	0.41	**0.44**

As verified in the results concerning the F-measure, the correlation coefficients for each class of each approach show that the Fuzzy System with adaptations obtained the best value in relation to the other approaches with reference to the reviews of the class EX and GD. The RBF-type ANN approach achieved better coefficients in the remaining classes. Again, the base approach got worse coefficients in all classes.

Finally, an analysis of the approaches from the semantic orientation of the reviews was performed. Table 14 shows the F-measure of each class, divided by the polarity of the review: positive or negative. It should be noted that in this analysis the reviews considered excellent and good were joined in a single class by the fact that these classes had a small number of reviews for individual analysis, being called Excellent and Good (EX+GD).

Table 14. F-measure by the polarity of each class of each approach

Class		Base TOP(X)	FS with adaptations	MLP-type ANN	RBF-type ANN
POSITIVES	EXCELLENT+GOOD	0.176	**0.325**	0.204	0.235
	SUFFICIENT	**0.533**	0.376	0.339	0.361
	INSUFFICIENT	0.405	0.608	0.598	**0.625**
NEGATIVES	EXCELLENT+GOOD	0.174	0.148	**0.317**	0.311
	SUFFICIENT	0.593	0.38	**0.604**	0.522
	INSUFFICIENT	0.166	0.449	0.476	**0.489**

There is a blend in which approach best detects the most important reviews, represented here in this work by the excellent and good reviews. In the positive reviews, the Fuzzy System with adaptations was the approach that obtained better results. When analyzed the negative reviews, the approaches with ANN (MLP-type and RBF-type) stood out in relation to the approaches with the Fuzzy System and the defined baseline, the Base TOP(X), being MLP-type ANN a little better than RBF-type ANN.

From the analysis of the three measures calculated in this experiment, the comparison of the approaches allows to take the following interpretations:

- For analysis of the most important reviews, that is, the reviews considered excellent, the approach with the **Fuzzy System with adaptations** obtained better results;
- In order to analyze the most important **positive** reviews, the approach with the **Fuzzy System with adaptations** obtained better results, and for the analysis of the most important **negative** reviews the approach with the **MLP-type ANN** obtained better results;

Therefore, in comparison of statistical measures between the approaches proposed in this work, with all the adaptations and justifications made in previous sections, one can be observed that the approach that best identifies the most important reviews of a corpus of reviews on smartphones is using the Fuzzy System, while the approach that best identifies the most important reviews of a corpus of reviews on smartphones annotated with its semantic orientation is using the Fuzzy Systems for positive reviews and the MLP-type Artificial Neural Network for negative reviews.

CONCLUSION

In order to automate the task of analyzing textual descriptions due to a large number of reviews on the web, this work aimed to estimate the importance degree using computational models based on Fuzzy System and Artificial Neural Networks. As a practical implication, the reduction of the difficulty of users when reading the various comments about the products and services becomes something relevant and possible, in order to return a small set of comments which are rich of information for the user's decision-making.

Such computational models are parametric, which made a comparison between them carefully planned and performed. Specific objectives of this work were to adapt the input variables of the base approach:

author reputation, the number of tuples <feature, opinion word> and vocabulary richness. Since the focus of this work is about the proposed models, one used simple linguistic features to show up how our models can perform the task of estimate the importance of reviews.

The approaches were compared using the computational models inspired by Fuzzy Systems and Artificial Neural Networks after the experiment. The confusion matrices generated by the execution of the approaches were used to perform a statistical comparison of accuracy, precision, recall, F-measure, and correlation. It was interpreted that in the analysis of the most important reviews (excellent and good reviews), the approach using Fuzzy System with adaptations obtained better performance. In case of to detect the most important reviews when defined the semantic orientation of each review, when positive approach using the Fuzzy System was better, and the approach using MLP-type ANN had better results when applied to negative reviews.

Some limitations can be mentioned, namely: i) the difficulty of building an annotated corpus is due to the lack of standard in the choice of the classes of reviews (excellent and good, for example) by experts. As alternatives, the use of classification examples such as a set of rules to classify the review in such class and the use of the Likert Scale (Likert, 1932); and ii) the performance of tools used at work, such as the tagger and language patterns. The first one can be seen in relation to the features that were not correctly tagged due to writing errors and words outside the formal context, such as the Internet language or spelling errors. The Internet Language is known as a grafolinguistics form that spread in texts like chats, blogs, and other OSNs as a writing practice characterized by the divergent record of the standard cultured, taken as "simplification of writing" (Komesu and Tenani, 2010). The second can be explained by the fact of the manual detection of such linguistic patterns, in which not all possible ones are listed, which could be done automatically by methods existing in the literature.

FUTURE RESEARCH DIRECTIONS

As future works, it is intended to use word embeddings as input to a number of tuples entry, which may produce better results when performed new experiments. Besides, other metrics can be defined to calculate the importance degree of the review, such as the time the review was done and the size of the text; to propose a new approach using Neuro-Fuzzy Systems, which integrates the two computational models explored in this work, as well as other architectures of machine learning, such as Convolutional Neural Networks (LeCun and Bengio, 1995; Vieira and Moura, 2017); and to study errors of detection in the reviews, which can be solved through the construction of bases of slang, ironies and sarcasm, based on normalization of texts.

Finally, it is important to emphasize that the focus of this work is on the proposed models, not on its current inputs, which are simple to the present moment. The future work proposition above deals with what still needs to be done for the model to achieve even better performance. Besides, this work is part of a larger project that aims to analyze information about products and/or services based on three sources: sites of product and/or service manufacturers, sales and complaints websites. In this way, it aims to generate a broader knowledge when evaluating the product offered by a company, by comparing common opinions and notably negative opinions.

REFERENCES

Aggarwal, A., & Kumaraguru, P. (2014). *Followers or phantoms? An anatomy of purchased Twitter followers.* arXiv preprint arXiv:1408.1534

Braga, A. P., Ferreira, A. C. P. L., & Ludermir, T. B. (2007). *Redes neurais artificiais: teoria e aplicações.* LTC Editora.

Bugmann, G. (1998). Normalized Gaussian radial basis function networks. *Neurocomputing, 20*(1-3), 97–110. doi:10.1016/S0925-2312(98)00027-7

Buscapé. (2016). Retrieved September 28, 2016, from https://www.buscape.com.br/

Dias-da-Silva, B. C. (2010). Brazilian Portuguese WordNet: A computational-linguistic exercise of encoding bilingual relational lexicons. *International Journal of Computational Linguistics and Applications, 1*(1-2), 137–150.

Digital Commerce 360. (2014). Retrieved August 18, 2016, from https://www.internetretailer.com/commentary/2014/12/04/how-many-online-stores-are-there-world?p=1

Duch, W., & Jankowski, N. (1999). Survey of neural transfer functions. *Neural Computing Surveys, 2*(1), 163-212.

Hamburg, M. (1974). *Basic statistics: A modern approach.* Houghton Mifflin Harcourt P.

He, X., & Lapedes, A. (1994). Nonlinear modelling and prediction by successive approximation using radial basis functions. *Physica D. Nonlinear Phenomena, 70*(3), 289–301. doi:10.1016/0167-2789(94)90018-3

Heimes, F., & van Heuveln, B. (1998). The normalized radial basis function neural network. In *SMC'98 Conference Proceedings. 1998 IEEE International Conference on Systems, Man, and Cybernetics (Cat. No. 98CH36218)* (Vol. 2, pp. 1609-1614). IEEE. 10.1109/ICSMC.1998.728118

Hodgkin, A. L., & Huxley, A. F. (1952). A quantitative description of membrane current and its application to conduction and excitation in nerve. *The Journal of Physiology, 117*(4), 500–544. doi:10.1113/jphysiol.1952.sp004764 PMID:12991237

Jeong, H., Shin, D., & Choi, J. (2011). Ferom: Feature extraction and refinement for opinion mining. *ETRI Journal, 33*(5), 720–730. doi:10.4218/etrij.11.0110.0627

Kar, A., & Mandal, D. P. (2011). Finding opinion strength using fuzzy logic on web reviews. *International Journal of Engineering and Industries, 2*(1), 37–43. doi:10.4156/ijei.vol2.issue1.5

Kohavi, R. (1995). A study of cross-validation and bootstrap for accuracy estimation and model selection. *IJCAI (United States), 14*(2), 1137–1145.

Komesu, F., & Tenani, L. (2010). Considerações sobre o conceito de "internetês" nos estudos da linguagem. *Linguagem em (Dis) curso, 9*(3), 621-643.

Kwak, H., Lee, C., Park, H., & Moon, S. (2010). What is Twitter, a social network or a news media? In *Proceedings of the 19th international conference on World wide web* (pp. 591-600). ACM. 10.1145/1772690.1772751

LeCun, Y., & Bengio, Y. (1995). Convolutional networks for images, speech, and time series. The handbook of brain theory and neural networks, 3361(10), 1995.

Li, M., Huang, L., Tan, C. H., & Wei, K. K. (2013). Helpfulness of online product reviews as seen by consumers: Source and content features. *International Journal of Electronic Commerce, 17*(4), 101–136. doi:10.2753/JEC1086-4415170404

Likert, R. (1932). A technique for the measurement of attitudes. *Archives de Psychologie, 22*(140), 1–55.

Liu, B. (2012). Sentiment analysis and opinion mining. *Synthesis lectures on human language technologies, 5*(1), 1-167.

Liu, J., Wu, G., & Yao, J. (2006). Opinion searching in multi-product reviews. In *The Sixth IEEE International Conference on Computer and Information Technology* (pp. 25-25). IEEE. 10.1109/CIT.2006.132

Mamdani, E. H., & Assilian, S. (1975). An experiment in linguistic synthesis with a fuzzy logic controller. *International Journal of Man-Machine Studies, 7*(1), 1–13. doi:10.1016/S0020-7373(75)80002-2

Mass, H. D. (1972). Über den Zusammenhang zwischen wortschatzumfang und länge eines textes. *Lili. Zeitschrift für Literaturwissenschaft und Linguistik, 2*(8), 73.

Matthews, B. W. (1975). Comparison of the predicted and observed secondary structure of T4 phage lysozyme. *Biochimica et Biophysica Acta (BBA)-. Protein Structure, 405*(2), 442–451. doi:10.1016/0005-2795(75)90109-9 PMID:1180967

McCarthy, P. M. (2005). *An assessment of the range and usefulness of lexical diversity measures and the potential of the measure of textual, lexical diversity (MTLD)* (Doctoral dissertation). The University of Memphis.

McCarthy, P. M., & Jarvis, S. (2010). MTLD, vocd-D, and HD-D: A validation study of sophisticated approaches to lexical diversity assessment. *Behavior Research Methods, 42*(2), 381–392. doi:10.3758/BRM.42.2.381 PMID:20479170

Nadali, S., Murad, M. A. A., & Kadir, R. A. (2010). Sentiment classification of customer reviews based on fuzzy logic. In *2010 International Symposium on Information Technology* (Vol. 2, pp. 1037-1044). IEEE. 10.1109/ITSIM.2010.5561583

Piskorski, J., & Yangarber, R. (2013). Information extraction: Past, present and future. In *Multi-source, multilingual information extraction and summarization* (pp. 23–49). Springer. doi:10.1007/978-3-642-28569-1_2

Porshnev, A., Redkin, I., & Shevchenko, A. (2013). Machine learning in prediction of stock market indicators based on historical data and data from twitter sentiment analysis. In *2013 IEEE 13th International Conference on Data Mining Workshops* (pp. 440-444). IEEE. 10.1109/ICDMW.2013.111

Powers, D. M. (2011). Evaluation: From precision, recall and F-measure to ROC, informedness, markedness and correlation. *Journal of Machine Learning Technologies, 2*(1), 37–63.

Provost, F. J., & Fawcett, T. (1997, August). Analysis and visualization of classifier performance: Comparison under imprecise class and cost distributions. *KDD: Proceedings / International Conference on Knowledge Discovery & Data Mining. International Conference on Knowledge Discovery & Data Mining*, *97*, 43–48.

Rojas, R. (2013). *Neural networks: a systematic introduction*. Springer Science & Business Media.

Sa, C. A., Santos, R. L. D. S., & Moura, R. S. (2017). An approach for defining the author reputation of comments on products. In *International Conference on Applications of Natural Language to Information Systems* (pp. 326-331). Springer.

Santos, R. L. D. S., de Sousa, R. F., Rabelo, R. A., & Moura, R. S. (2016). An experimental study based on fuzzy systems and artificial neural networks to estimate the importance of reviews about product and services. In *2016 International Joint Conference on Neural Networks* (pp. 647-653). IEEE. 10.1109/IJCNN.2016.7727261

Schütze, H., Manning, C. D., & Raghavan, P. (2008). Introduction to information retrieval. In *Proceedings of the international communication of association for computing machinery conference* (p. 260). Academic Press.

Sharma, A., & Dey, S. (2012). An artificial neural network based approach for sentiment analysis of opinionated text. In *Proceedings of the 2012 ACM Research in Applied Computation Symposium* (pp. 37-42). ACM. 10.1145/2401603.2401611

Silva, N. R., Lima, D., & Barros, F. (2012). Sapair: Um processo de análise de sentimento no nível de característica. *IV International Workshop on Web and Text Intelligence*.

Sousa, R. F., Rabêlo, R. A., & Moura, R. S. (2015). A fuzzy system-based approach to estimate the importance of online customer reviews. In *2015 IEEE International Conference on Fuzzy Systems* (pp. 1-8). IEEE. 10.1109/FUZZ-IEEE.2015.7337914

Spss, I. I. B. M. (2011). IBM SPSS statistics for Windows, version 20.0. New York: IBM Corp.

Srivastava, R., & Bhatia, M. P. S. (2013). Quantifying modified opinion strength: A fuzzy inference system for sentiment analysis. In *2013 International Conference on Advances in Computing, Communications and Informatics* (pp. 1512-1519). IEEE. 10.1109/ICACCI.2013.6637404

Templin, M. C. (1957). *Certain language skills in children; their development and interrelationships*. University of Minnesota Press. doi:10.5749/j.ctttv2st

Torruella, J., & Capsada, R. (2013). Lexical statistics and tipological structures: A measure of lexical richness. *Procedia: Social and Behavioral Sciences*, *95*, 447–454. doi:10.1016/j.sbspro.2013.10.668

Turney, P. D. (2002). Thumbs up or thumbs down?: semantic orientation applied to unsupervised classification of reviews. In *Proceedings of the 40th annual meeting on association for computational linguistics* (pp. 417-424). Association for Computational Linguistics.

van Rijsbergen, C. J. (1979). *Information Retrieval*. Butterworth-Heinemann.

Vieira, J. P. A., & Moura, R. S. (2017). An analysis of convolutional neural networks for sentence classification. In *2017 XLIII Latin American Computer Conference (CLEI)* (pp. 1-5). IEEE. 10.1109/CLEI.2017.8226381

Weber, L., & Klein, P. A. T. (2003). *Aplicação da lógica fuzzy em software e hardware.* Editora da ULBRA.

Weng, J., Lim, E. P., Jiang, J., & He, Q. (2010). Twitterrank: finding topic-sensitive influential twitterers. In *Proceedings of the third ACM international conference on Web search and data mining* (pp. 261-270). ACM. 10.1145/1718487.1718520

ADDITIONAL READING

Baowaly, M. K., Tu, Y. P., & Chen, K. T. (2019). Predicting the helpfulness of game reviews: A case study on the Steam store. *Journal of Intelligent & Fuzzy Systems, 36*(5), 1–12. doi:10.3233/JIFS-179022

Chen, C., Yang, Y., Zhou, J., Li, X., & Bao, F. (2018, June). Cross-domain review helpfulness prediction based on convolutional neural networks with auxiliary domain discriminators. In *Proceedings of the 2018 Conference of the North American Chapter of the Association for Computational Linguistics: Human Language Technologies*, Volume 2 *(Short Papers)* (pp. 602-607). 10.18653/v1/N18-2095

Diaz, G. O., & Ng, V. (2018). Modeling and prediction of online product review helpfulness: a survey. In *Proceedings of the 56th Annual Meeting of the Association for Computational Linguistics (*Volume 1*: Long Papers)* (pp. 698-708). 10.18653/v1/P18-1065

Huang, A. H., Chen, K., Yen, D. C., & Tran, T. P. (2015). A study of factors that contribute to online review helpfulness. *Computers in Human Behavior, 48*, 17–27. doi:10.1016/j.chb.2015.01.010

Krishnamoorthy, S. (2015). Linguistic features for review helpfulness prediction. *Expert Systems with Applications, 42*(7), 3751–3759. doi:10.1016/j.eswa.2014.12.044

Malik, M. S. I., & Hussain, A. (2017). Helpfulness of product reviews as a function of discrete positive and negative emotions. *Computers in Human Behavior, 73*, 290–302. doi:10.1016/j.chb.2017.03.053

Qazi, A., Syed, K. B. S., Raj, R. G., Cambria, E., Tahir, M., & Alghazzawi, D. (2016). A concept-level approach to the analysis of online review helpfulness. *Computers in Human Behavior, 58*, 75–81. doi:10.1016/j.chb.2015.12.028

Tang, J., Gao, H., Hu, X., & Liu, H. (2013, October). Context-aware review helpfulness rating prediction. In *Proceedings of the 7th ACM conference on Recommender systems* (pp. 1-8). ACM.

Wang, Y., Wang, J., & Yao, T. (2019). What makes a helpful online review? A meta-analysis of review characteristics. *Electronic Commerce Research, 19*(2), 257–284. doi:10.100710660-018-9310-2

Zeng, Y. C., Ku, T., Wu, S. H., Chen, L. P., & Chen, G. D. (2014). Modeling the helpful opinion mining of online consumer reviews as a classification problem. *International Journal of Computational Linguistics & Chinese Language Processing, 19*(2).

KEY TERMS AND DEFINITIONS

Corpus: A dataset about some specific subject. Widely used in comptational linguistic area.

Helpfulness: A quality of being helpful in some subject.

Importance Degree: A measure to define which object of study is more important than other one.

Neural Network: A set of algorithms based on human brain usually used to recognize patterns.

Opinion Mining: The task of identify and extract subjective information in texts.

Review: A description of user's opinion about some product or service and it should be positive, negative, or neutral.

Vocabulary Richness: The measure of correctness and lexical variety of the sentence or document.

Chapter 8

Discovery of Sustainable Transport Modes Underlying TripAdvisor Reviews With Sentiment Analysis:
Transport Domain Adaptation of Sentiment Labelled Data Set

Ainhoa Serna

https://orcid.org/0000-0003-4750-3222

University of the Basque Country, Spain

Jon Kepa Gerrikagoitia

BRTA Basque Research and Technology Alliance, Spain

ABSTRACT

In recent years, digital technology and research methods have developed natural language processing for better understanding consumers and what they share in social media. There are hardly any studies in transportation analysis with TripAdvisor, and moreover, there is not a complete analysis from the point of view of sentiment analysis. The aim of study is to investigate and discover the presence of sustainable transport modes underlying in non-categorized TripAdvisor texts, such as walking mobility in order to impact positively in public services and businesses. The methodology follows a quantitative and qualitative approach based on knowledge discovery techniques. Thus, data gathering, normalization, classification, polarity analysis, and labelling tasks have been carried out to obtain sentiment labelled training data set in the transport domain as a valuable contribution for predictive analytics. This research has allowed the authors to discover sustainable transport modes underlying the texts, focused on walking mobility but extensible to other means of transport and social media sources.

DOI: 10.4018/978-1-7998-4240-8.ch008

INTRODUCTION

Mobility with motor vehicles has a negative environmental impact. Over time, means of transportation have emerged as an alternative to the use of motor vehicles. Examples of sustainable transport are bicycle, public transport (subway, tram, bus), electric car, and so on. Conforming to the EU Transport Council in 2001, "*a sustainable transport system is one that allows individuals and societies to meet their needs for access to areas of activity with total safely, in a manner consistent with human and ecosystem health, and that is also balanced equally between different generations*" (European Commission - Mobility and Transport, 2018).

Additionally, tourist activity generates wealth in the receiving place and is an excellent great source of employment. However, as a counterpart, it can also be a destructive activity. It is estimated that tourism activity produces up to 8% of global greenhouse gas emissions from 2009 to 2013 (Lenzen, Sun, Faturay et al., 2018). Even if we take into account the energy used in hotels, transport or hygiene products, it represents up to 12.5% (Sánchez, 2018). Moreover, cities across Europe have adopted or strengthened Low Emission Zones (LEZ) in response to the growing air pollution crisis. These measures have been taken by more than 250 EU cities. A study shows that 67% of interviewees favour the adoption of LEZ either strongly or slightly. LEZ should move forward to zero-emission mobility zones (ZEZ), that will eventually be turned into policies to promote transitioning to healthier alternatives like walking, cycling jointly with the electrification of all forms of transport like taxis, public transport and private vehicles (Müller and Le Petit, 2019).

Furthermore, tourism produces large quantities of the content generated by users (User Generated Content) that is rapidly growing. There is a wide variety of subjects in this type of content, and one of them is mobility. On the other hand, the different languages and contexts are relevant to react when consumers around the world are speaking various languages and as digital platforms increase the range of users on these platforms, such as Social Media data of TripAdvisor platform. Being platforms worldwide that include users from different countries, the variety and richness of the data that can be extracted and the knowledge that can be created with them can be very relevant for different companies, both public and private.

In recent years, in particular, digital technology and research methods have developed the concept of Natural Language Processing that has become a preferred means for better understanding consumers and what they share in. Regarding the economic and business relevance of NLP, forecasts that Global NLP Market is projected to rise to $26.4 billion by 2024 and the CAGR (Compound Annual Growth Rate) of 21% from 2019 (MarketsandMarkets, 2019) will continue to increase. Given the current importance of this area and future forecasts, this research will focus on the application of NLP in the field of transport, since the contribution of this research can be relevant both at the level of global and local business. For this reason, this investigation analyses the different transport modes, focus on sustainable transports. In this research, natural language processing techniques are applied to Social Media data (UGC), to evaluate the impressions of visitors regarding success factors that can be used as planning aid tools. The study has been developed according to transport mode used and languages.

Regarding the novelty of this research, it should be noted that there are numerous TripAdvisor articles but mainly focused on tourism, such as monuments, hotels, restaurants, attractions...etc. There are hardly any studies in transportation analysis with TripAdvisor, and moreover, there is no a complete analysis of sentiment analysis. This article proposes TripAdvisor as a data source for the study of modes of transport, user ratings and automated sentiment-detection algorithms.

Study aims to investigate and discover the presence of sustainable transport modes underlying in non-categorized TripAdvisor texts, such as walking mobility in order to impact positively in public services and businesses. The research is based on a qualitative and quantitative method following (KDD) Knowledge discovery in databases techniques. Thus, data gathering, normalization, classification, polarity analysis and labelling tasks have been carried out to obtain sentiment labelled training data set, in the transport domain as a valuable contribution for predictive analytics.

For this purpose, the use case is focused in Croatia. It includes essential information about activities and travels of UGC from TripAdvisor in Spanish and English languages, aiming to demonstrate the value of Social Media-related data as a valuable data source to get a better understanding of tourism mobility (easy mobility across all transport) and transport modes to enhance the tourism destination management.

The chapter is structured according to the following: section 2 lays out the background, analysis of the Social Media research in the transport area and the progress of one of the most sustainable means of transport, the bicycle, also, the contributions of the authors. The key focus of this chapter is defined in section 3, describing the research methodology and phases. Afterwards, section 4 details the solutions and recommendations with the main results of the phases. Finally, the paper presents future lines and the conclusions of the research. Additionally, after the references section, the suggestions on additional readings and key terms defined by the authors are added.

BACKGROUND

The literature review is divided into two parts. The first part reviews the literature on the study of Social Media in the transport sector in general. The second part shows the progress of one of the most sustainable means of transport, the bicycle.

Social Media Analysis in the Urban Transport Area

TripAdvisor is a database for travel analysis for recent work in the field of sentiment analysis. Gal-Tzur (2018) focuses on TripAdvisor's Q&A forums section and offers a framework for automatically categorizing transportation-related issues addressed in those forums and collecting travel-related questions. Ali et al. (2019) propose a latent Dirichlet allocation (LDA) model based on topics and an ontology, with embedding words approach for the classification of sentiment. The proposed framework collects transport content from social networks, eliminates irrelevant content to extract meaningful information, and uses LDA to create topics and features from the data collected.

Recent researches regarding Social Media in urban transport (Kuflik, Minkov, Nocera et al., 2017; Serna, Gerrikagoitia, Bernabe and Ruiz, 2017a) are worthy of note in order to explore urban mobility from another viewpoint. Newly, there has been a substantial increase in research in this field. A system for collecting, processing and mining Geo-located tweets has been designed and developed by Pereira (2017). More specifically, the program provides functionality for the parallel selection of geo-located tweets, preprocessing of English or Portuguese tweets, thematic modelling, transport-specific text classifications, and aggregation and data visualizers, from several predefined areas or cities. Furthermore, there are numerous possible sources of transport data, which are differentiated by the vast quantity of available material, the speed at which it is accessed and the diversity of formats to be delivered (Ruiz, Mars, Arroyo and Serna, 2016). The application of this knowledge on Transport Planning is a task involving advanced techniques of data mining. The authors identified plausible applicable Social Media data sources that could be utilized in planning of transport and discussed their benefits and disadvantages. A summary of incipient developments for planning of transport is then addressed. Besides, several opportunities to use Big Data related to social networks, in particular, are emphasized.

Others researches discuss probable Social Media activities for providers of transport services and makers of transport policy suggesting that substantial transport policy knowledge can be obtained from UGC (Gal-Tzur et al., 2014). Information on technology challenges linked to social network data mining in transport are presented in Grant-Muller (2014). A text mining method is provided, which provides the foundation for novel investigation in this field, to obtain significant transportation sector data, including taxonomy, polarity analysis, and measuring accuracy. In 2015, Grant-Muller (2015) confirmed the alternative of adding data from content produced by users can complement, improve and even replace conventional data gathering and highlight the need to develop automated methods to gathering and analyzing transport-related Social Media data.

Conforming to Serna, Gerrikagoitia, Bernabe & Ruiz (2017b) empirically evidence the viability of the automated identification of the difficulties in in the field of sustainable urban mobility using the user generated-content reviews. The methodology improves knowledge in conventional surveys and expands quantitative research by using big data approaches. Gu, Qian & Chen (2016) propose that Twitter posts provide an accurate and cost-effective option to classify incident data on both arterials and highways. Moreover, they present a method for crawling, processing and filtering tweets which are accessible openly.

Social Media Analysis Focus on the Bicycle Transport Mode

The public bicycle shared (PBS) systems research area has drawn the attention of researchers who in recent years have published their findings from a variety of viewpoints. Several studies have investigated the area of study on PBS transport modes (Serna & Gasparovic, 2018; Nickkar et al., 2019; Serna, Ruiz, Gerrikagoitia & Arroyo, 2019). For example, according to Serna et al., (2019), so far, the literature has overlooked the effect of Social Media on public bicycle shared systems alongside official statistics data that include following data: populations, the quantity of docking stations and weather information such as temperature, raininess, humidity, pressure, etc. Their research filled this gap and led to a novel investigation source to supplement current information with knowledge derived from Social Media in order to understand the conduct of travel and establish predictive models for the use of the mode of travel.

In 2019, Serna et al. (2019) also provide a comprehensive literature review on PBS systems, showing, for example, that some researchers, such as Shaheen, Guzman, and Zhang (2010) researched PBS systems as a feasible choice for mobility, demonstrating the progress of 3 generations of public bicycle shared systems in three continents (Asia, America and Europe) from 1965 until 2010. Other research works have concentrated on the facilities of the network, and the operational features that are strongly associated to the utilization of PBS systems, such as convenient sign-up procedures, 24/7 opening hours or sign-up opportunities (Buck & Buehler, 2013; El-Assi, Mahmoud & Habib, 2017). Also, researchers considered the socio-demographic features, including population, employment, mixed-use and retail density as well as riders' educational rates were related to increased public use of bicycles (Hampshire & Marla, 2012; Buck and Buehler, 2012; Rixey 2013; El-Assi et al.,2017). Moreover, the environment was also analyzed to show that storm, strong wind, rain and low temperatures negatively affect the use of bike shares (Gebhart, and Noland, 2014). Furthermore, users' digital footprint was an essential source of data to fill the demand-supply gap for bike-sharing (Zhao, Wang and Deng, 2015; Bordagaray, dell'Olio, Fonzone, Ibeas, 2016).

RESEARCH METHODOLOGY

The methodology follows a qualitative and quantitative approach that consists of two main phases (see Figure 1). The first phase consists of identifying, obtaining, capturing, normalizing, analyzing, classifying and discovering the different modes of transport in the TripAdvisor reviews, also applying the sentiment analysis to assign polarity (positivity, negativity, neutrality). Besides, a dashboard is developed to understand and manage the results easily. The second phase developed involves the process of collecting a set of data automatically labelled with sentiment based on the reviews rated with 5 and 1 stars and measuring their accuracy.

Figure 1. Research methodology and general process

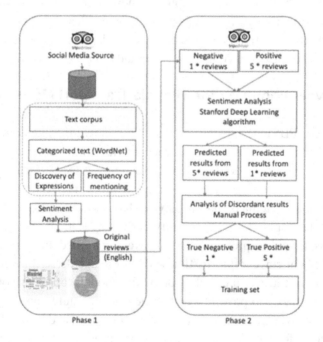

Case Study

The case study is focused in Croatia and includes UGC from TripAdvisor in Spanish and English languages, demonstrating the value of Social Media data as a valuable data source to get a better understanding of tourism, mobility and transport modes. English and Spanish are the top two languages. One fact to emphasize is that about 91 per cent of reviews were posted in English.

Regarding the methodology, the first phase comprises the following steps: source identification, Social Media source acquisition, data preparation for the analysis, sentiment analysis, storage and data visualization (Serna & Gasparovic, 2018).

Phase 1

Step 1: Source Identification

TripAdvisor includes impressions of travellers for different purposes: business, leisure, and so on. The information-gathering was implemented with reviews that include data about mobility in different sections of transportation (taxis & shuttles, ferries, bus transportation, tramways, funicular railway…etc.) within TripAdvisor.

Step 2: Social Media Source Acquisition

This technique involves the processing of raw and unstructured data, consists of data acquisition, normalization and cleaning. Web scraper software has been implemented to acquire information from TripAdvisor.

Step 3: Data Preparation for the Analysis

The discovery of expressions relating to walking mobility and the morph-syntactic analysis is realized in two distinct processes. The starting step is to load the reviews one by one to identify the language with the Shuyo language detector (Shuyo, 2010). Next, Freeling that is an Open Source library which offers a broad range of linguistic analysis services for several languages for automatic multilingual processing (Padró and Stanilovsky, 2012) with the corresponding WordNet lexicons version 3.1 (2012) (Miller, 1995; Fellbaum, 1998), and GNU Aspell spell checker version 0.60.8 (2019) (Atkinson, 2003) for specific languages are established. For example, in the spell checker, some improvements to be able to detect localism and abbreviation are added. In order to correct the texts, the spell checker is applied. The normalization of the reviews is a crucial procedure which involves the management and adaptation of the emoticons and abbreviations. The normalization of the reviews is a crucial procedure which covers both abbreviations and emoticons

After this process, the next task is the discovery of expressions and synonyms related to walking mobility. This process has been carried out for reviews written in Spanish. Words and expressions that are synonymous with walking mobility on foot are identified. Then they are added in the category of mobility on foot to avoid their loss. In this way, the developed software tool can identify and add them automatically, improving these shortcomings.

Next, Freeling Analyzer including WordNet database integration and an ad-hoc software is used, each word being labelled morph-syntactically within a transport classification as a result of this method. Furthermore, numerous nouns are described by transport modes with their adjectives, and common nouns have been categorized by the number of occurrences in order to obtain exhaustive details.

Step 4: Sentiment Analysis

In this step, the polarity is calculated with the SentiWordNet polarity lexicon (Baccianella, Esuli & Sebastiani, 2010; Esuli & Sebastiani, 2006). In order to select the correct meaning depending on the context, the UKB Word Sense Disambiguation program (Agirre & Soroa, 2009), has been used.

Step 5: Storage

For the scalable data storage and management, it is necessary this process. The downloaded reviews are homogenized and stored in the Apache Solr search Engine in JSON, a standard format (Smiley & Pugh, 2011).

Step 6: Data Visualization

The previous steps are implemented in a software workflow that provides data to be shown in a visual (dashboard) interface to monitor and interpret information quickly. The dashboard has been developed with a robust and versatile UI (user interface), customizable pie charts and histogram and so on, based on the Solr Apache Foundation (open source). The data provided by the workflow has been indexed to provide efficient response time to queries.

Phase 2: Sentiment Labelled Data Set

This phase consists of the creation of a "*Sentiment Labelled Data Set*" as a training dataset for supervised learning algorithms.

Step 1: Filtered

First, the reviews written in English have been filtered (rated on 1 to 5 stars scale). The process consisted of selecting only the reviews rated with 1 and 5 stars in order to get the extremes in both positivities (5 *) and negativity (1 *).

Step 2: Stanford Deep Learning Algorithm

In this step, sentiment analysis is applied using Stanford Deep learning algorithm (Socher et al., 2013). Many sentiment prediction systems (polarity orientation) only work with terms/concepts isolating that offer positive and negative scores for positive and negative terms respectively and summarize these scores. Therefore, the order of terms is overlooked, and essential knowledge is lost. In comparison, this deep learning model constructs a illustration of whole phrases based on the form of the sentence. It calculates the sentiment based on how the terms constitute the meaning of longer sentences.

To order to achieve a better precision in the transport domain, a random manual review will then be carried out of the 10 per cent of the overall evaluations listed as positive or negative. Later, during the selection process, two files were created, one containing the positive reviews and the other with the negative ones, respectively.

Step 3: Analysis of Discordant Results

Therefore, these two files (positive and negative) have to be cleaned manually, which ensures that the reviews are positive or negative with total certainty. This step is crucial, otherwise, the results of both, the training set and the created model would be inconsistent and invalid in order to predict reliably.

SOLUTIONS AND RECOMMENDATIONS

Phase 1

A dashboard with dynamic graphics was created to analyze TripAdvisor's Social Media reviews data which recognizes positive and negative factors and their potential impacts on sustainable tourism and transportation. Also, different means of transport are classified and selected according to day/month/year, term/word, mode of transport, place, ranking, language, city, adjective, adverb, transport company...etc. Besides, the original review and its corresponding title are obtained.

This dashboard allows different visual representations with dymanic graphics (tabular, historical data evolution, word cloud, and pie chart) to interpret the results. Beginning from Figure 2 (upper part) on the top left, the first block helps to choose by date. The next block enables to search and filter by a concept or term. Afterward, there is a cloud tag showing the diverse means of transport that were discovered. Following, a dymanic pie chart containing the top languages. Lastly, a description of the dates information is given in the last block of the upper part of the section.

In the central division of Figure 2, the first findings are defined in a timeline diagram with the number of TripAdvisor's observations (reviews), and it is showed as an example filtering from 12/12/2007 to 03/07/2018. The years on the x-axis are shown and the number of the reviews y-axis. Additionally, Figure 2 illustrates that the topic of research is becoming more and more important in Social Media year after year. This histogram is also a dynamic graph, which allows you to choose different time frames and update the graph automatically.

The bottom section allows filtering by word (nouns), adverb and adjective, city and review rating.

Figure 2. Visual Analytics Dashboard

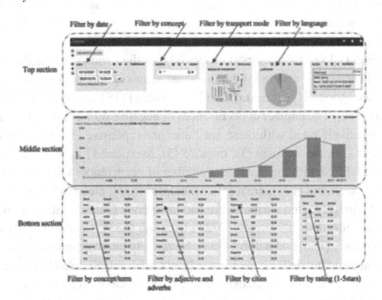

In TripAdvisor, the different transport modes are grouped and represented as follows: *cable car* 36% (called Tramway), *taxis and shuttles* with 22.4% of reviews; *funicular railway* 2.9% (called Mass Transportation Systems), *ferries* with 2.5%, and *bus* transportation with 0.4%.

Sustainable transport such as a bicycle or walking mobility are not included in the Transportation section of TripAdvisor, but it is possible to find these modes of transportation in "Walking & Biking Tours" section that encompasses two subsections, "Walking Tours" and "Bike & Mountain Bike Tours" (walking 32.6%, bike 3.1%).

It should be noted that 74.7% of transport is sustainable transport such as bicycle, walking, public transport (cable car, funicular railway), and that walking is the 2nd most reviewed mode of transport after the cable car.

Table 1. Top 7 Transport modes in the reviews.

Transport Mode	Sustainable Transport ranking	# Reviews
Cable car	2	10,352
Walking	1	9,354
Taxi and shuttles	4	6,437
Bicycle	1	882
Funicular Railway	2	845
Ferry	3	717
Bus	3	112

Furthermore, 86% of the reviews rate the *cable car* and 73% the *funicular railway* with the two highest scores (excellent and very good) and only 4% and 3% respectively, with the worst scores (poor and terrible). 96% and 89% of the reviews about *walking* and *bicycles* respectively are rated with the maximum rate (excellent). In *ferries* transport modes 69% of the reviews are rated with the two highest scores (excellent and very good) and 18% with the worst scores (poor and terrible).

The *cable car* is rated good (2494 times), great (2240), nice (1118), spectacular (860), beautiful (859), short (769), stunning (757). The number of occurrences of negative ratings is much smaller than positive ones, specifically, negatively rated with these attributes are expensive (1015), Long queues (16), bad information/ service (5), disappointment (3), mistake (5), overpriced (3), dangerous (2), regretful (1). *Taxis & shuttles* are qualified with the maximum number of occurrences with these adjectives friendly (1592), good (1771), excellent (1123), great (1624), helpful (835), clean (827), professional (790) and comfortable (757). Negatively rated attributes are bad taxi driver (4), official complaint (1), a thief (2). *Private Buses* are rated with good (2897), great (2727), friendly (1635), excellent (1337), nice (1187), clean (899), beautiful (880), easy (856) and helpful (838). Negatively rated attributes are waste of money and waste of day (4), rushed and hurried (2), mediocre (2), not pleasant (8), late (16), rude (7), stressful (5).

Ferries are positively rated with special experience, friendly, kind, excellent, well organized, the best way, fantastic, clean, brilliant, gorgeous. Negatively rated are disappointed (10), guide rude (4), rushed (4), racist (1), abusive (1). *Walking* is positively rated with great, best, fantastic, terrific, vibrant, guide passionate, amazing guide, knowledgeable, caring. Negatively rated attributes are almost inexistent, one example would be the expression "too long to walk". *Bicycle* is positively rated with amazing, excellent customer service, great bikes, strongly recommend, great quality, very good condition and perfectly maintained, stunning, Friendly helpful service. There are very few negative reviews, with these adjectives: unsuccessfully (10), disappointed (12).

Discovery of Expression Related to "Walking Mobility" Results

In this task, reviews written in Spanish on walking mobility that was not identified are discovered in the reviews. This manages to discover 59% of occurrences concerning to the number of reviews with the automatic categorization of the walking mobility as a mode of transport.

The results of the task about the discovery of expressions and disambiguation in the walking mobility are shown in the following tables (tables 2 and 3). For this, expressions or words that refer to walking mobility are added and those in different context does not mean the same are disambiguated. As an example, part of these expressions is shown in table 2:

Table 2. Discovery of synonymous expressions related to walking mobility (in Spanish)

Synonymous expressions of walking mobility		
"andar"	"ir a pie"	"desplazarse a pie"
"pasear"	"rondar"	"corretear"
"deambular"	"atravesar"	"correr"
"transitar"	"caminar"	"trotar"
"vagar"	"circular"	"marchar a pie"
"zanquear"	"avanzar"	"visitar a pie"
"recorrer"	"venir a pie"	"trasladarse a pie"
"patear"	"callejear"	"moverse a pie"
"acceder a pie"		

Besides, the Spanish expression "a pie" (on foot) depending on the context has different meanings. In one case, it means that the mode of mobility is walking, but in another case, it means close, that it is close to a place.

In Table 3, as an example, original sentences of the reviews are shown, with synonymous expressions that indicate walking mobility. Also, examples of the different meaning of the expression "a pie" (on foot) are shown depending on the context.

Phase 2: Sentiment Labelled Data Set Results

This process uses reviews written in English, it is described in phase 2 of the "Research methodology" section (graphically represented in Figure 3), and this section shows the obtained results.

The results corroborated the hypothesis that users rate reviews with five stars, that is, the maximum score, but each sentence that makes up that review can have different polarity orientation, we can find

Table 3. Original sentences with the discovered expressions related to walking mobility (in Spanish)

Original sentence	Meaning
"Muy bien ubicado para **acceder a pie** a varias de las atracciones."	walking transport mode
"También dispones de un tranvía **a pie de** la plaza Ban Jelačić."	near
"… nos permitió **recorrer a pie** las mejores zonas de Zagreb."	walking transport mode
"… para conocer la ciudad **a pie** y disfrutarla."	walking transport mode
",….. a 5 minutos **a pie** de la plaza Ban Jelačić"	walking transport mode
"Muy bien situado cerca de la plaza Ban Jelačić **a pie del** hotel."	near
"…., ofrece un **paseo a pie** inmejorable."	walking transport mode
"Nos ha encantado, la ubicación perfecta para **ir a pie** a un montón de sitios. "	walking transport mode
"Se puede ir **pateando** a los sitios más representativos de la ciudad."	walking transport mode
"… ideal para **visitar a pie** ….."	walking transport mode
"… la verdad es q en 15-20 min **andando** se llega perfectamente."	walking transport mode
"..unos cinco o diez minutos **andando** y bien comunicado con el centro de la ciudad"	walking transport mode
"..con una parada de tranvía al lado y **andando** a 20 minutos"	walking transport mode
"que te permite llegar al centro **paseando** un cuarto de hora o coger directamente el tranvía."	walking transport mode
"…. **caminando** 10 minutos llegas a la calle ….."	walking transport mode

* discovered expressions are highlighted in bold in the sentence (first column).

Figure 3. Phase 2: Sentiment Labelled Data Set process

positive, negative and neutral sentences. In the same way, it happens with the very negative reviews, those scored with one star.

Furthermore, the results of analyzing the 5 * reviews sentence by sentence with the Stanford Sentiment algorithm, were that 25% of the sentences in the positive reviews file are classified as neutral and, or negative. As for the negative reviews, 23% of the reviews scored with 1 * are considered neutral and, or positive. The accuracy, according to the following formula is 76%.

$$Accuracy = \frac{TP + TN}{TP + FP + FN + TN}$$

Where True Positive, True Negative, False Positive and False Negative are represented by TP, TN, FP and FN, respectively.

Analyzing the results manually, it is observed that some of the sentences are valued as negative due to the word "war" although they are really neutral sentences, as can be seen in the following table, in the sentences of the reviews made to the means of transport "cable car" (in English).

Table 4. Prediction and True sentiment related to cable car mobility (rated with five stars)

Original sentence	Sentiment Prediction	True Sentiment
"Loved the War museum, spent ages there."	positive	positive
"There is evidence of the war and a museum explains what happened to Dubrovnik and the role of the fort during the war in 80s/90s."	negative	neutral
"There is an old fort there that now has a display showing pictures of the recent war in Croatia."	negative	neutral
"The fort has interesting history going back to Napoleon and was used extensively by Croatians during the 1991-1995 war."	negative	positive
"Be sure while you are on the top of the mountain to visit the fortress, where you will see the shell holes from the Serb bombardment during the siege of Dubrovnik."	negative	neutral
"Have lunch at the top and be sure to visit the fortress to learn about the 90s Balkan war (from a decidedly Croatian perspective)."	negative	positive
"If you go to the war museum at Fort Imperial and go up the steps to the roof then you get even better views than the cable car observation deck."	negative	neutral

Next, in Figure 4, a tree-shaped sentiment of the sentence *"There is evidence of the war and a museum explains what happened to Dubrovnik and the role of the fort during the war in 80s/90s."* is shown. The calculus of the orientation is wrong predicted (negative) since it is a neutral sentence. Negative nodes are marked with x in the figure.

Figure 4. Example of negative prediction for neutral sentiment

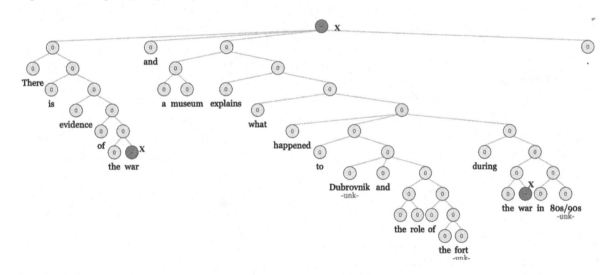

Analyzing the predictions of the negative reviews manually, it is observed that one of the sentences is valued as positive due to the word "*cheaper*", although it is a negative sentence. Also, it is observed that some sentences with the expression "*would not recommend*", despite being identified as negative, the adverbial particle "*not*", when evaluated separately from the verb "*recommend*" to which it is linked, the algorithm is wrong and assigns a positive value to the sentence. Besides, some very negative sentences (such as the first three sentences and the fifth in Table 5) are predicted as neutral.

Table 5. Prediction and true sentiment related to cable car mobility (rated 1 star)

Original sentence	Sentiment Prediction	True Sentiment
"False information ! ! !"	neutral	negative
"It was scary."	neutral	negative
"Tourist trap."	neutral	negative
"Consider booking a return trip in a taxi it would be alot cheaper ! !"	positive	negative
"Please look at alternatives before you book with these thieves."	neutral	negative
"I definitely would not recommend this taxi service to anyone."	positive	negative
"Would NOT recommend this Company."	positive	negative

Next, in Figure 5, a tree-shaped sentiment of the "*I definitely would not recommend this taxi service to anyone*" sentence is shown. The calculus of the orientation is wrong predicted (positive) since it is a negative sentence.

Figure 5. Example of positive prediction for negative sentiment

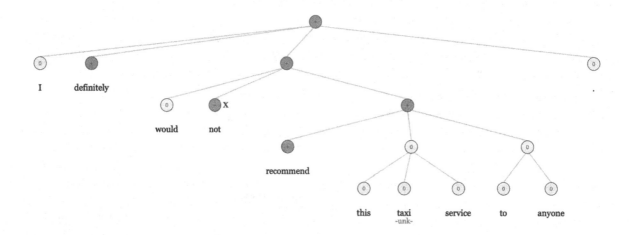

FUTURE RESEARCH DIRECTIONS

First of all, as future research, it is proposed to develop a new phase that consists of the development of models using machine learning (ML) techniques, taking advantage of the labelled data set (positive and negative reviews). Thus, for the purpose of predictive analysis, this investigation provides sentiment labelled data collection. With these two classifications (positive and negative reviews), algorithms can be trained with a supervised learning approach using the previously analyzed data model. In order to improve labelling precision, an ensemble agreement (consensus) approach can be used. Ensemble agreement means that many algorithms predicted the same class of an occurrence (Jurka et al., 2013).

Another future line can focus on testing the data valued with 5 and 1 star related to the transport domain with different algorithms to see the accuracy achieved in the automatic labelling of the data set, making a detailed analysis of the wrong predictions.

Moreover, it would be convenient to feed the training set with a more extensive data set, adding transport data from other data sources such as Twitter, Facebook, transport forums, etc. and analyze how it affects the models and their accuracy.

Besides, considering the energy model transition that is taking place nowadays, it would be relevant to analyze the presence of electric mobility electric bicycles, electric scooters, electric cars, electric buses, electric Tuk Tuk, etc. On the other hand, it would be beneficial to extend the search for synonymous expressions of mobility "on foot" to other languages besides Spanish.

CONCLUSION

Regarding the main findings of the research, first, the reference social network in trips/travels (TripAdvisor) has been characterized by modes of transport, analyzing reviews within categorized transport sections and reviews that are published in any other section such as Hotels, Things to do, Restaurants, Shopping, etc. Second, the sentiment of the characteristics of the different modes of transport has been identified, beyond the rating of the reviews, since it has been shown that there is not always a correspondence between the user's ratings and the sentiment orientation (positive, negative, neutral).

Our research has allowed us to discover sustainable transport modes underlying in the texts, such as walking mobility. Although the research has been focused on walking transport mode, our approach makes it possible to find occurrences of different non-categorized modes of transport that were initially hidden. This finding can be used to discriminate the positive and negative aspects of the diverse transport modes.

Moreover, we have developed a dashboard to evaluate and assess positive and negative features and their influence on sustainable transport using TripAdvisor's reviews. Besides, the distinct forms of transport are gathered and extracted by day/month/year, term/word, mode of transport, place, ranking, language, city, adjective, adverb, transport company, and so on. The platform and its ability to analyze the results obtained from Social Media by dynamic graphics and sentimental analysis techniques makes it easy and user-friendly to interpret the results to end-users. This platform provides, therefore, a powerful tool to classify the potential impact on sustainable transport considering positive and negative factors.

Furthermore, another contribution is the creation of a "Sentiment Labelled Data Set" as a training dataset for SML (Supervised Machine Learning) algorithms. The data set has been achieved developing models for ML taking advantage of the available labelled data set (positive and negative reviews) of the research. Thus, this sentiment labelled data set can be used for predictive analytics.

There may be inconsistencies between user ratings and Sentiment Analysis methods because users sometimes write negative sentences with positive opinions and vice versa as has been demonstrated. Therefore, new approaches must be used to assess positivity, negativity and neutrality employing consensus among Sentiment Analysis methods. Users in TripAdvisor can describe their experiences openly and influence impacting the viability of a business. To identify the weaknesses and strengths of public and private transport, it is therefore essential to apply Sentiment Analysis techniques to reviews, such as TripAdvisor. Furthermore, because of a large number of applications in the tourism sector, the quality enhancement of mobility aspects in the various transport modes through Sentiment Analysis techniques has great potential and impact.

Regarding the results, the exceptionally high presence of the means of sustainable transport should be noted very positively. In fact, 74.7% of transport is sustainable transport such as a bicycle, walking, public transport (cable car, funicular railway). Walking is the second most reviewed mode of transport after the cable car. 68% of reviews are rated with the highest score, and only 1.4% are rated with the worst score. As we can conclude, that there is a positive assessment about overall results.

Besides, knowing the users' opinions about the different modes of transport, as well as the characteristics that they value positively and negatively, is crucial to improve the service.

About the data we can extract from TripAdvisor, UGC presents the lack of socio-demographic data in the Social Media in most cases, and it is not generalizable to the entire population. Nowadays, TripAdvisor 's data quality is good as there are abundant and wide-ranging data, several languages, etc. Moreover, visitors that write reviews in TripAdvisor also explain the positive and poor characteristics of the different modes of transportation. Depending on the language to be analyzed, the difficulties are not the same. On the one hand, languages such as English are the first to benefit from advances in PLN, and yet, for other languages with few speakers such as Maltese, there is little progress and development. On the other hand, Spanish language is a vibrant language in synonymous. That characteristic that makes it such a rich language, with a wide range of expressive possibilities, is also a problem for PLN techniques, since it hinders the accuracy of automatic analysis, even having PLN resources.

Social Media provides basic features of data (variables) that can be acquired such as the language, mode of transport, date, country, town, city, state of transportation, punctuality, pricing, route, service, polarity analysis (neutral-positive), etc. Comparing to conventional surveys, the gaps and, or supplementary data you need and can be obtained from daily surveys mainly include demographic data, area (location), age, gender; occupation, personal data on education level, living arrangements, for example on your own, with children, with parents; the main motivations for visiting, the flight scheduling, when they plan to make a journey, what is the first airport of departure, the airline used, etc. Moreover, the Croatian Tourism Authority was conscious that travelers from other countries are hesitant to respond to surveys, but interestingly they write reviews in TripAdvisor and, thanks to the system and method developed, their feedback can be taken into account.

Regarding limitations, the automatic data gathering process has important shortcomings. TripAdvisor, frequently changes the structure of its content, making it difficult to search and download content automatically. Thus, it is necessary to verify the data manually and update the URL's (uniform resource locator). Also, the information on the different means of transport even having a category for it, does not combine all the means of transport that are scattered in different sections. Therefore, for proper data capture, the platform needs to be updated and tested with relative frequency. Another problem is that TripAdvisor uses automatic translations of different languages, so in this investigation the data analysis has been carried out discarding such translations, capturing only the original reviews to avoid mistakes related to wrong translations.

REFERENCES

Agirre, E., & Soroa, A. (2009). Personalizing pagerank for word sense disambiguation. *Proceedings of the 12th Conference of the European Chapter of the Association for Computational Linguistics (EACL 2009)*, 33–41. 10.3115/1609067.1609070

Ali, F., Kwak, D., Khan, P., El-Sappagh, S., Ali, A., Ullah, S., Kim, K. H., & Kwak, K. S. (2019). Transportation sentiment analysis using word embedding and ontology-based topic modeling. *Knowledge-Based Systems*, *174*, 27–42. doi:10.1016/j.knosys.2019.02.033

Atkinson, K. (2003). *GNU Aspell*. Retrieved from http://aspell.sourceforge.net/

Baccianella, S., Esuli, A., & Sebastiani, F. (2010). SentiWordNet 3.0: An enhanced lexical resource for sentiment analysis and opinion mining. *LREC*, *10*, 2200–2204.

Bordagaray, M., dell'Olio, L., Fonzone, A., & Ibeas, Á. (2016). Capturing the conditions that introduce systematic variation in bike-sharing travel behavior using data mining techniques. *Transportation Research Part C, Emerging Technologies*, *71*, 231–248. doi:10.1016/j.trc.2016.07.009

Buck, D., & Buehler, R. (2012). Bike lanes and other determinants of capital bikeshare trips. *Proceedings of the 91st Transportation Research Board Annual Meeting*.

Buck, D., Buehler, R., Happ, P., Rawls, B., Chung, P., & Borecki, N. (2013). Are bikeshare users different from regular cyclists? A first look at short-term users, annual members, and area cyclists in the Washington, DC, region. *Transportation Research Record: Journal of the Transportation Research Board*, *2387*(1), 112–119. doi:10.3141/2387-13

El-Assi, W., Mahmoud, M. S., & Habib, K. N. (2017). Effects of built environment and weather on bike sharing demand: A station level analysis of commercial bike sharing in Toronto. *Transportation*, *44*(3), 589–613. doi:10.100711116-015-9669-z

Esuli, A., & Sebastiani, F. (2006). Sentiwordnet: A publicly available lexical resource for opinion mining. *LREC*, *6*, 417–422.

European Commission. (2018). *Mobility and Transport*. Retrieved from https://ec.europa.eu/transport/themes/sustainable_en

Fellbaum, C. (Ed.). (1998). WordNet: An Electronic Lexical Database. Cambridge, MA: MIT Press.

Gal-Tzur, A., Grant-Muller, S. M., Kuflik, T., Minkov, E., Nocera, S., & Shoor, I. (2014). The potential of Social Media in delivering transport policy goals. *Transport Policy*, *32*, 115–123. doi:10.1016/j.tranpol.2014.01.007

Gal-Tzur, A., Rechavi, A., Beimel, D., & Freund, S. (2018). An improved methodology for extracting information required for transport-related decisions from Q&A forums: A case study of TripAdvisor. *Travel Behaviour & Society*, *10*, 1–9. doi:10.1016/j.tbs.2017.08.001

Gebhart, K., & Noland, R. B. (2014). The impact of weather conditions on capital bikeshare trips. *Transportation, 41*, 1205–1225. doi:10.100711116-014-9540-7

Grant-Muller, S. M., Gal-Tzur, A., Minkov, E., Nocera, S., Kuflik, T., & Shoor, I. (2014). Enhancing transport data collection through Social Media sources: Methods, challenges and opportunities for textual data. *IET Intelligent Transport Systems, 9*(4), 407–417. doi:10.1049/iet-its.2013.0214

Gu, Y., Qian, Z. S., & Chen, F. (2016). From Twitter to detector: Real-time traffic incident detection using Social Media data. *Transportation Research Part C, Emerging Technologies, 67*, 321–342. doi:10.1016/j.trc.2016.02.011

Hampshire, R. C., & Marla, L. (2012). An analysis of bike sharing usage: Explaining trip generation and attraction from observed demand. *Proceedings of the 91st Annual Meeting of the Transportation Research Board*, 22–26.

Jurka, T. P., Collingwood, L., Boydstun, A. E., Grossman, E., & van Atteveldt, W. (2013). RTextTools: A Supervised Learning Package for Text Classification. *The R Journal, 5*(1), 6. doi:10.32614/RJ-2013-001

Kuflik, T., Minkov, E., Nocera, S., Grant-Muller, S., Gal-Tzur, A., & Shoor, I. (2017). Automating a framework to extract and analyse transport related Social Media content: The potential and the challenges. *Transportation Research Part C: Emerging Technologies, 77*, 275-291.

Lenzen, M., Sun, Y., Faturay, F., Ting, Y.-P., Geschke, A., & Malik, A. (2018). The carbon footprint of global tourism. *Nature Climate Change, 8*(6), 522–528. doi:10.103841558-018-0141-x

MarketsandMarkets. (2019). *Natural Language Processing Market by Component, Deployment Mode, Organization Size, Type, Application, Vertical And Region - Global Forecast to 2024*. Retrieved from https://www.reportlinker.com/p05834031/Natural-Language-Processing-Market-by-Component-Deployment-Mode-Organization-Size-Type-Application-Vertical-And-Region-Global-Forecast-to.html

Miller, G. A. (1995). WordNet: A Lexical Database for English. *Communications of the ACM, 38*(11), 39–41. doi:10.1145/219717.219748

Müller, J., & Le Petit, Y. (2019). *Transport & Environment*. Retrieved from https://www.transportenvironment.org/sites/te/files/publications/2019_09_Briefing_LEZ-ZEZ_final.pdf

Nickkar, A., Banerjee, S., Chavis, C., Bhuyan, I. A., & Barnes, P. (2019). A spatial-temporal gender and land use analysis of bikeshare ridership: The case study of Baltimore City. *City Cult. Soc, 18*, 100291. doi:10.1016/j.ccs.2019.100291

Padró, L., & Stanilovsky, E. (2012). Freeling 3.0: Towards Wider Multilinguality. *Proceedings of the Eight International Conference on Language Resources and Evaluation (LREC'12)*.

Pereira, J. F. F. (2017). *Social Media Text Processing and Semantic Analysis for Smart Cities*. arXiv preprint arXiv:1709.03406

Rixey, R. A. (2013). Station-level forecasting of bikesharing ridership: Station network effects in three US systems. *Transportation Research Record: Journal of the Transportation Research Board, 2387*(1), 46–55. doi:10.3141/2387-06

Ruiz, T., Mars, L., Arroyo, R., & Serna, A. (2016). Social Networks, Big Data and Transport Planning. *Transportation Research Procedia, 18*, 446-452.

Sánchez, J. (2018). *Cómo hacer turismo sostenible.* Retrieved from: https://www.ecologiaverde.com/como-hacer-turismo-sostenible-1216.html

Serna, A., & Gasparovic, S. (2018). Transport analysis approach based on big data and text mining analysis from social media. *Transportation Research Procedia, 33*, 291–298. doi:10.1016/j.trpro.2018.10.105

Serna, A., Gerrikagoitia, J. K., Bernabé, U., & Ruiz, T. (2017a). Sustainability analysis on Urban Mobility based on Social Media content. *Transportation Research Procedia, 24*, 1–8. doi:10.1016/j.trpro.2017.05.059

Serna, A., Gerrikagoitia, J. K., Bernabe, U., & Ruiz, T. (2017b). A method to assess sustainable mobility for sustainable tourism: The case of the public bike systems. In *Information and Communication Technologies in Tourism 2017* (pp. 727–739). Springer. doi:10.1007/978-3-319-51168-9_52

Serna, A., Ruiz, T., Gerrikagoitia, J. K., & Arroyo, R. (2019). Identification of Enablers and Barriers for Public Bike Share System Adoption using Social Media and Statistical Models. *Sustainability, 11*(22), 6259. doi:10.3390u11226259

Shaheen, S. A., Guzman, S., & Zhang, H. (2010). Bikesharing in Europe, the Americas, and Asia: Past, present, and future. *Transportation Research Record: Journal of the Transportation Research Board, 2143*(1), 159–167. doi:10.3141/2143-20

Shuyo, N. (2010). *Language Detection Library for Java.* Retrieved from https://github.com/shuyo/language-detection/

Smiley, D., & Pugh, D. E. (2011). *Apache Solr 3 Enterprise Search Server.* Packt Publishing Ltd.

Socher, R., Perelygin, A., Wu, J., Chuang, J., Manning, C. D., Ng, A. Y., & Potts, C. (2013, October). Recursive deep models for semantic compositionality over a sentiment treebank. In *Proceedings of the 2013 conference on empirical methods in natural language processing* (pp. 1631-1642). Academic Press.

Zhao, J., Wang, J., & Deng, W. (2015). Exploring bikesharing travel time and trip chain by gender and day of the week. *Transportation Research Part C, Emerging Technologies, 58*, 251–264. doi:10.1016/j.trc.2015.01.030

ADDITIONAL READING

Gräbner, D., Zanker, M., Fliedl, G., & Fuchs, M. (2012, January). Classification of customer reviews based on sentiment analysis. In *Information and Comm. Technologies in Tourism* (pp. 460–470). Springer. doi:10.1007/978-3-7091-1142-0_40

Guzman, E., & Maalej, W. (2014, August). How do users like this feature? a fine grained sentiment analysis of app reviews. In *2014 IEEE 22nd international requirements engineering conference (RE)* (pp. 153-162). IEEE.

Ivo Cré, P. (2019). *European Platform on sustainable urban mobility plans*. Retrieved from https://www.eltis.org/sites/default/files/urban_vehicle_access_regulations_and_sustainable_urban_mo bil-ity_planning.pdf

Kadriu, A., Abazi, L., & Abazi, H. (2019). Albanian Text Classification: Bag of Words Model and Word Analogies. *Business Systems Research Journal*, *10*(1), 74–87. doi:10.2478/bsrj-2019-0006

Klopotan, I., Zoroja, J., & Meško, M. (2018). Early warning system in business, finance, and economics: Bibliometric and topic analysis. *International Journal of Engineering Business Management*, *10*, 1847979018797013. doi:10.1177/1847979018797013

Palakvangsa-Na-Ayudhya, S., Sriarunrungreung, V., Thongprasan, P., & Porcharoen, S. (2011, May). Nebular: A sentiment classification system for the tourism business. In *2011 eighth international joint conference on computer science and software engineering (JCSSE)* (pp. 293-298). IEEE. 10.1109/JCSSE.2011.5930137

Pejic-Bach, M., Bertoncel, T., Meško, M., & Krstic, Ž. (2020). Text mining of industry 4.0 job advertisements. *International Journal of Information Management*, *50*, 416–431. doi:10.1016/j.ijinfomgt.2019.07.014

Pejic Bach, M., Krstic, Ž., Seljan, S., & Turulja, L. (2019). Text mining for big data analysis in financial sector: A literature review. *Sustainability*, *11*(5), 1277. doi:10.3390u11051277

Pejic Bach, M., Pivar, J., & Dumicic, K. (2017). Data anonymization patent landscape. *Croatian Operational Research Review*, *8*(1), 265–281. doi:10.17535/crorr.2017.0017

Rashidi, T. H., Abbasi, A., Maghrebi, M., Hasan, S., & Waller, T. S. (2017). Exploring the capacity of social media data for modelling travel behaviour: Opportunities and challenges. *Transportation Research Part C, Emerging Technologies*, *75*, 197–211. doi:10.1016/j.trc.2016.12.008

KEY TERMS AND DEFINITIONS

Natural Language: Language created as a mode of communication between people.

Natural Language Processing or NLP: It is a subset of Artificial Intelligence that makes possible through different computer algorithms to process digital content generated by people (natural language). NLP aims to simulate the interpretation of humans.

Sentiment Analysis: It is a natural language processing technique (NLP), which describes the sentiment orientation (positive, negative, neutral) underlying into the information.

Sentiment Labelled Data Set: They are sets of data, composed of sentences taken from real reviews of people, to which polarity (sentiment orientation) is added, so these sentences are labelled with a positive or negative or neutral sentiment.

Supervised Learning: It is an algorithm that uses labelled data and analyses the training data and accordingly produces an inferred model, which can be used to classify new data.

Sustainable Transport: Are those modes of transport that reduce environmental pollution impacting collective well-being and besides, some of them even reduce traffic congestion and promote health.

Unsupervised Learning: It is an algorithm that uses unlabelled data, where the model works on its own to discover information.

Chapter 9
Research Journey of Hate Content Detection From Cyberspace

Sayani Ghosal

iD https://orcid.org/0000-0002-0979-0788

Ambedkar Institute of Advanced Communication Technologies and Research, India

Amita Jain

Ambedkar Institute of Advanced Communication Technologies and Research, India

ABSTRACT

Hate content detection is the most prospective and challenging research area under the natural language processing domain. Hate speech abuse individuals or groups of people based on religion, caste, language, or sex. Enormous growth of digital media and cyberspace has encouraged researchers to work on hatred speech detection. A commonly acceptable automatic hate detection system is required to stop flowing hate-motivated data. Anonymous hate content is affecting the young generation and adults on social networking sites. Through numerous studies and review papers, the chapter identifies the need for artificial intelligence (AI) in hate speech research. The chapter explores the current state-of-the-art and prospects of AI in natural language processing (NLP) and machine learning algorithms. The chapter aims to identify the most successful methods or techniques for hate speech detection to date. Revolution in this research helps social media to provide a healthy environment for everyone.

INTRODUCTION

In the 21st century, digital media provides scope for everyone to share information. People from all age groups are using the cyberspace every day. As per the survey from Statista (Clement, 2019), 100% of users of 18-29 age groups and more than 90% of the adult populations are using the internet in the United States in 2019. UK government presents national statistics (Prescott, 2019) where 99% of users of 16-44 age groups are using cyberspace. World Atlas survey shows (Dillinger, 2019) most internet

DOI: 10.4018/978-1-7998-4240-8.ch009

users countries are China and India. Surveys indicate the effects of hate speech, cyberbullying, online extremism on social networking sites are very high. To protect the world from such negative situations, all tech giants are rigorously trying to improve automatic detection systems.

Hate speech is the action that abuse individual or groups based on various features like gender, colour, race, religion, nationality, and disability, etc. Every day numerous hate contents are posted by various users that are difficult to trace. Manual detection of hate content is laborious, time-consuming, and not scalable. Usually, manual approaches block websites or remove paragraphs that contain slur words. Social webs usually have a mechanism to report hate posts by user reviews, but automatic recognition of hate content is one of the priorities. During recent years, the importance of the automatic system of hate speech detection has grown. Various shortcomings still exist for automatic systems. Numerous posts circulating on the web are laborious for researchers to identify as a hate post.

Figure 1. Hate texts from internet

"all Mexicans are rapists"

"thugs" when talking about young Black men

referring to ALL Muslims as "terrorists"

The chapter significantly emphasizes automatic hate speech detection techniques and challenges. It also critically analyses the theoretical framework for hate speech as well as techniques to develop automatic hate speech detections systems. Different existing algorithms and feature representations performance in automatic systems are also part of this study. The majority of the study in hate-motivated speech classification relies on Natural Langue Processing (NLP) with various Machine Learning models. These have applied for binary classification and multi-class classification or both. Different supervised techniques (like SVM, Logistic regression, Decision Trees), unsupervised algorithms (k-means, bootstrapping) and deep learning methods (like CNN, LSTM, RNN) has employed to predict the hate posts. Evaluation measures section with various existing models helps to identify the progress of research.

The chapter aims to identify the most successful methods or techniques for hate speech detection to date. The chapter is structured with two fundamental parts related to the hate posts detection methods which help readers to gain knowledge for current Natural Language Processing Research. The theoretical framework and technical framework are the main part of this chapter that comes under the solution and recommendation section. The theoretical framework described with several related concepts and rules for hatred speech classification, whereas technical framework illustrated with various approaches implemented in the latest research. The next section will describe the research analysis of hate speech detection using the scientometric method. In the last section, the chapter ends with the future direction of hate content detection research.

BACKGROUND

In today's world, cyberspace plays a very crucial role in our life. However, one negative side of the social web is cyberhate. Negative sentiments flowing in social media can potentially ruin social balance in society. Leading social webs describe hate speech as a violent speech that can be harmful to people. Online hate speech affects the youth of many countries, where they experienced severe depression. Automatic hate content detection research helps to balance social harmony. The automatic system is highly essential to protect cyberspace from hate speech effects. To shield society from hate speech, many countries are considered this as an illegal address.

The automatic cyberhate detection research is a novel and challenging area. The numbers of research in this field are limited. The necessity of this research arises in the last ten years. Researchers from the computer science domain have applied various algorithms to detect hate text from cyberspace. Most of the research evolved with Artificial Intelligence. AI-based research is continuously struggling for the perfect detection of hate content. Recognition of negative sentiment from natural language, NLP is the key solution. Artificial Intelligence is the root of NLP that processed human languages. Automatic or semi-automatic systems are the only solution to prevent extreme harm in the social environment. Numeral machine learning approaches have been implemented by NLP researchers for toxic post detection. NLP researchers are rigorously trying to increase accuracy.

Figure 2. Basic flow of automatic hate texts detection system

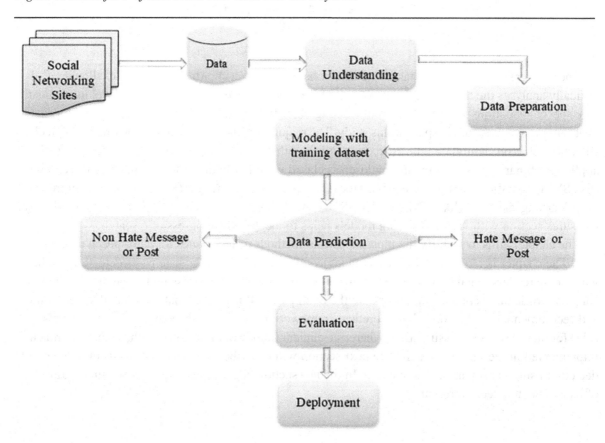

The major success in the background of hate speech research will motivate readers. That will also help to find more useful feature extractions and classification approaches. As per our findings, the leading approach for hate speech detection research in recent years specified below. The majority of the study depends on the Dictionary (Liu & Forss, 2015) and Bag of Word (Burnap, & Williams, 2016) features. Lexical features also showed significant achievement in the message level (Chen, Zhou, Zhu, & Xu, 2012). Another notable research has achieved 95.6% accuracy with N-grams and TF-IDF (Gaydhani, Doma, Kendre, & Bhagwat, 2018). Offensive language detection has also shown 0.932 F-measure by applied Recurrent Neural Network with LSTM classifiers (Pitsilis, Ramampiaro & Langseth, 2018). In 2019, the Paragraph2Vec feature and MLP classifier achieved 0.99 AUC (Alorainy, Burnap, Liu & Williams, 2019). Another recent study considered multiple platform dataset where they have used one ensemble approach XGBoost classifier has achieved 0.92 F1-score (Salminen, Hopf, Chowdhury, Jung, Almerekhi, & Jansen, 2020). The above significant studies inspire researchers for more future research.

With the above successful stories of hate content research, there is also a prerequisite to know the basic flow of the automatic detection system. Figure 2 shows the flow of hate posts detection system. Large data from social network initially work for data understanding and data preparation part in cyberhate mining. Annotation or labelling of toxic words is also a part of the system. Labelling hate words with subject matter experts directly employed in classification tasks. Model selection for data prediction is the next significant part that directly affects the accuracy of the model. Detection of hate post or non-hate post is the goal of any algorithm.

SOLUTIONS AND RECOMMENDATIONS

The main focus of this chapter evolved with the theoretical framework section and technical framework section that comes under solution and recommendation. Readers of the automatic hate speech detection chapter will gain knowledge and direction from both sections.

Theoretical Framework: Hate Speech

The theoretical section describes the various related concepts of hate speech that can help NLP communities for their research. Description of many notations like Abusive, Hostile, Profanity, Misogyny, and Offensive has considered in this part. Classification rules for hate speech will help readers for their research. Researchers can easily understand the theory behind hatred speech detection.

Concepts of Hate Speech

Speech is a way of communication where people share their thought, belief, and sentiments. Hate speech is part of speech that abuses an individual or mass based on various features, like racism, sexism, gender, skin colour, nationality, caste, religion, etc. Hate texts in social networks provoke different destructive activities. Hate crime articulated as hate influenced attack. Cyberhate is dangerous in real life. As per the recent research, author has shown the main four destructive activities that evolved around the cyberspace like hate speech, crime from hate posts, extremism and terrorism (Chetty & Alathur, 2018). With these four major violent activities, cyberbullying/cyberstalking and cyber exploitation have also grown every day. Hate crime and cyber terrorism are similar activities that occur from hate speech. Extremists and terrorists can consider cyberspace to plot the attack because they can easily contact and spread hate within people.

The research shows that hate speech generates an event in four phases. It starts with the influence phase. The influence phase occurred after an event triggered. In the next phase, hate speech are reduced named as mediation phase. Then hate speech reduced to zero named as response phase. Lastly, the rebirth may appear in rebirth phase (Chetty & Alathur, 2018). The event generation life cycle for hate speech in cyberspace has followed the above phases.

Categories of Hate Posts

- **Sexism:** Sexism is a term related to gender discrimination and aggression for a particular gender. Posts that abuse a specific gender has considered hate speech. Hostile posts generally hurt a specific gender, whereas Benevolent denotes more insults compare to hostile. (Al-Hassan & Al-Dossari, 2019). Some research reports that cyberspace is mostly targeting women. Most users have threatened women for rape, and they have used opprobrious words against women. Recent research in sexism classification has achieved significant accuracy using 16000 twitter data (Pitsilis, Ramampiaro & Langseth, 2018).

- **Racism:** This category for prejudice includes negative expression against tribal, immigrant, minority and refugees. Racism occurred when hate expression evolved with various reasons like geographic regions, tribal communities, and countries. (Al-Hassan & Al-Dossari, 2019). When people show their pride for skin colour is also considered racist comments. Cyberspace is the primary media to harass common people based on racism.

- **Religious:** This hate expression occurred based on a particular religion like Hindu, Muslim, and Christian, etc. Social networking sites are the media for expressing hate against a specific religion. People spread hate toward spiritual people by post various messages and images to abuse them. Islamophobia notation has used to show anti-Muslim expression. Many researchers have considered religious hate content analysis for their research. Cyberspace provides the platform to spread hate against a particular religion and use scurrilous words to provoke extremism.

- **Disability:** Hate expression about the psychic state or physical disability of people considered for this category. Physical disability based on the medical ground is an excuse to insults people. Many patients have to choose disability to survive in the long run. Some people consider this situation to express their disgust against disabled people.

- **Hybrid:** Hate expressions of any combination categories (protected, unprotected and Quasi- protected category) circulating in cyberspace called hybrid category (Ting, Wang, Chi & Wu, 2013). Online hate speech triggers terrorist activity. Insecure people with behavioural problems also show their hate expressions. Sensitive and insecure personalities come under the behavioural category. Drunk and shallow people another target for this category. Clash between rich and poor class people also a reason for hate posts.

Related Notions

- **Cyberbullying:** Cyberbullying and cyberstalking both are significant research areas in the text mining domain. Aggressive behaviour for abuse a person is defined as cyberbullying. Hate speech occur based on the common topic but cyberbullying targeting one person repeatedly.

- **Abusive Language:** The abusive language concept includes hate speech and vulgarity. This notation denotes destructive message that troubles people strongly.
- **Profanity:** Profanity words originate from the medieval era that is offensive or swear words. It mainly used to show disrespect for religious relationships. It can be present in a sarcastic way. Many popular countries punished citizens for the practice of profanity words.
- **Discrimination:** This concept is social behaviour to target a group. Discrimination occurred based on multiple factors like caste, religion, family status, disability, nationality, ethnicity and many more.
- **Flaming:** The flaming notion defines the profane, aggressive, antagonistic post to hurt the sentiment of a particular community. Flaming is a subset of hate content.
- **Toxic comment:** Toxic posts use to disrespect group of people. A vulgar comment against any person provokes to leave the conversation or make the person violent. Every toxic sentence is not categorized as hate speech.
- **Misogyny:** The concept refers to the hate emotions against women or girls. It essentially used to show the superiority of the male sex against femininity.
- **Extremism:** Extremist behaviour comes from some group of people who spread hate, violence, and target for segmented people based on their hate opinion. Extremist repeatedly used hate speech to target a group of people or an organization.
- **Radicalization:** The concept focused on the terrorist group, patriotism, and racism. The radical words have used for strong hate content. It also influenced by extremism that shows strong negative emotion.

Guidelines for Classification

Classification of abusive content is not commonly accepted by common people as well as experts. Some researchers report categorization of hate content depends on various guidelines. Some of the rules to classify as hate are listed below.

- Bad speech about any country is acceptable, but insulting any people based on nationality is classified as hate speech (Krause & Grassegger, 2016).
- Abusive statement about any religious people is hate-motivated speech, but speaking about any religion is allowed (Krause & Grassegger, 2016).
- Hate statement related to the religious association is also considered (Krause & Grassegger, 2016).
- Hate message linking of two protected categories are considered as hate content (Krause & Grassegger, 2016).
- Merging unprotected and protected categories is an unprotected category. So, the sentence related to this is allowed (Krause & Grassegger, 2016).
- Under some particular situation, another category is considered named Quasi-Protected, where some sentences are not allowed (Krause & Grassegger, 2016).
- Use of any offensive word that comes under the hate category (Warner & Hirschberg, 2012).
- Any association related to a terrorist group or hate crime also expressed hate (Warner & Hirschberg, 2012).
- Discrimination related to any religion or country is not permitted (Fortuna & Nunes, 2018).

- Any term related to racial which harm individual or group of people is also displayed hate (Fortuna & Nunes, 2018).
- Negative message for any minority group is not acceptable (Ross, Rist, Carbonell, Cabrera, Kurowsky & Wojatzki, 2017)
- A statement that mocks the disabled person has represented hate speech.
- The sentence shows racial disgraces as well as sexist insults.

Hate Posts Influenced Violence

Hate content represents various dimensions. As per the existing research, one of the important dimensions is violence or attack influenced by hate-motivated speech (Chetty & Alathur, 2018). Hate speech and hate crimes both influenced for extremism. After that extremism concludes with violence. The present study shows that discrimination is also a reason for the crime. Subcategories of hate speech (racism, sexism, nationalism and religious, etc.) caused the extremism and violation activities between people.

Violence related activity in the social network is a major concern for everyone. The online social network is an e-relational network for all global users. Social webs represent an essential role that builds and maintain connections with people. A new relation developed based on some common concerns where they share positive and negative information. But a minor subset of e-user used hate speech, hate crime, and terrorism. (Chetty & Alathur, 2018).

Hate Content in Business

Popular social network companies are Facebook, Twitter, LinkedIn, and YouTube. Fake users, fake news, hate, and abusive language flows extremely in these social networks. Every day global tech giants face challenges to remove such contains that harm the society. These situations not only destroyed healthy social life as well as various local and global businesses. Social media provide platforms to spread hate posts that affect people. Controlling hate speech helps to balance social harmony. Tech giants' investors invest billion dollars for enhancing safety measures.

Online users are not only spread hate speech on personal levels that also threat to business levels. One of the famous feminine care company Honey Pot has recently flooded with lots of hate and negative reviews for their products. After the owner was featured in an advertisement, the company has faced 1-star and 2-star ratings for their products. CEO Beatrice Dixon, Lady with black skin colour who is the owner of the Honey Pot. The racist attack has impacted directly in their product rating and reviews. This is not only one recent story. Many companies also impacted due to racist, sexist and extremist statements (Williams, 2020).

In 2018, another situation happened when popular social network site Gab has temporarily barred their service after GoDaddy has pulled the support. The key reason behind this decision was hate speech. GoDaddy identified that various hate speech, discrimination, and numerous contents that provoke hate crime on the website. Due to cyberhate in social sites, many businesses have impacted (Wolfe, 2018). In the same year, another business relation has terminated due to the provocation of hate speech. Payment service provider PayPal bans another American company Infowars for promoting hate speech on its websites (Brandom, 2018). In 2017, another incident happened based on hate speech commercial from British retailer Marks and Spencer. Google has expressed regret after advert this radical commercial on

YouTube (Cellan-Jones, 2017). So promoting hate speech has terminated many business relations as well as that also affects brand reputation.

With above all global business incidents, local small scale businesses also faced threats through hate speech. Usually, any company that provides service to local people named as a local business. So cyber hate speech that emerged by the local population has mainly damaged local businesses. Local businesses can be affected by various political issues. Political issues can be a stance for hate speech that affects sales. Majority of the hate text circulated through social media or any chat system in community labels. The identification of hate text circulation chain is significant to stop the destruction. Many new firms have started their business with hate speech detection tool. They provide service at the local levels as well as global levels to stop hate content.

Technical Framework: Hate Content Detection

Technical framework section is responsible for the reader to gain basic knowledge regarding hate speech detection techniques. Comparative analysis of different feature extraction and classification algorithm will help researchers to think about the future direction of hate speech detection research. Analysis of NLP techniques based on the latest significant research will help readers to comprehend the advantages and drawbacks.

Automatic Hate Speech Detection Method

Explosive data in social webs motivate researchers to apply NLP techniques. Manual detection of hate speech is very challenging. It takes a lot of manual effort and time. The automatic classification of hate, non-hate, racism, sexism post is the main research point. Many machine learning algorithms are used by the researchers to perform automatic detection. Research of the automatic detection method is in the initial phase. Lots more research work is required to overcome existing challenges. Below advantages can help to interpret the need for automatic hate speech detection system.

Advantage of automatic hate posts detection systems

- Automatic hate posts identification.
- Maintain a healthy social environment.
- Economical and efficient techniques.
- Identification of hate speech spreaders.
- Beneficial for social web business.

An automatic classification system is highly required. Protect the social environment from negatively motivate people is a responsibility for every human being. Hate speech categorization is not a commonly accepted topic. The semi-automatic approach has considered domain experts that required costly effort. NLP researchers have rigorously worked to fix the challenges.

Automatic hate content detection methods include four steps to classify hate speech. Initially, data extraction from different websites like Whisper, Yahoo!, Twitter, Facebook, and YouTube is the initial step for any Natural Language Processing research. After the extraction of data, pre-processing of data is the second part. Pre-processing of data will directly affect the efficiency of hate speech classification. Labelling corpora or data annotation is an important part that includes in the detection process. Both manual and crowdsourcing process has used for data annotation. In the third step, pre-processed data has used for feature extraction. Feature extraction is the method that converts raw pre-processed data to fewer variables based on categorize information. NLP researchers have used n-gram, unigram, semantic-based, sentiment-based, pattern-based features. Finally, the classification approach has employed to feature extracted data. Random Forest (RF), Logistic Regression (LR), Support Vector Machine (SVM), and Decision Tree (DT) these entire traditional algorithms, as well as many other algorithms, are already shown significant performance for classification tasks. The below sections describe all the steps in detail for automatic detection systems.

Figure 3. Automatic hate speech detection with Natural Language Processing

Data Extraction and Annotation

Manual hate posts detection can be possible for a small amount of data. Automatic detection has required for large quantities. The extraction of data from social networking sites is an essential step. A huge source of social networking data provides more challenges for NLP research communities. Researchers are continually working on analysing the enormous amount of unstructured multilingual data. The objective is to convert any unstructured data to the system understandable format.

Data extraction from social webs has performed through various APIs. Social websites data have used for research like Twitter, Instagram, Facebook, YouTube, Whisper, ask.fm and yahoo. Data extraction for hate post-classification is mainly required specific topic or any topic related to racism, sexism, nationalism or religion, etc. NLP researchers also provide executed labelled datasets for future use. That will easy for comparison of various models.

Pre-processing of data directly affects the model performance. Researchers extracted unstructured data from social webs. Analysis of unstructured and ambiguous data is difficult for researchers. Pre-processing is the part where the user-generated unstructured text has converted into the system understandable format. In various ways, text data has pre-processed. Cleaning these data is a very initial task in the pre-processing part. Each sentence usually consists of Html link, alphanumeric, stop word, capitalization. If any sentence with a capital word or mixed case that provides an unusual output or no proper output at all (Example of mixed cases- India, Italy). Mixed case words mapped into the lower case for data cleaning. Remove stop words in any sentence means it extract only high information words (Example of stop words- a, an, the, is). Html link from a sentence is also not useful for machines. Union of words like numeric and alphabets named as alphanumeric (Example- agxy004, mk664). Researchers first clean text and convert each sentence into tokens. Data pre-processing also includes stemming and lemmatization. Each word used by the user can write in various forms, which may not be understandable by the systems. Convert inflected words to their root word is called stemming. The concept of stemming is necessary for pre-processing, like fishery, fishing, fished from root word fish. The Group of all inflected forms of words that identify the root word is called lemmatization helps in pre-processing (geese, goose from root word goose). Both the concepts of stemming and lemmatization are very similar. The difference between lemmatization and stemming is that lemmatization converts words to their actual root. Lemmatization returns the morphological root of a word, whereas stemming returns the nearest word or word map of a stem. Data annotation for analysis is also part of the pre-processing tasks. Data annotation means each sentence labeled with some unique identification. All this linguistic process of NLP has employed for pre-processing tasks. Convert unstructured data to algorithm usable format is challenging as well as valuable tasks.

Data annotation is an essential phase in this research. The huge dataset is annotated manually or by domain experts. Crowdsourcing is also another option for data annotation. Manual annotation for data is a time-taking and costly procedure. Researchers usually adopt a crowdsourcing method compare to a manual one. But crowdsourcing annotation is also suffered from the quality annotation. Classification of a post in the hate category and classification rules is a challenging task. The data set size is also a critical factor in any research that will affect learning algorithms and feature detection. Data sparsity issues generally occurred based on data size. The randomly generated dataset for data annotation creates challenges. Randomly generated training data may contain less hate category text compare to the total dataset that directly impacts on accuracy. Training and testing datasets distribution is another important factor where it desired balance of hate text (Schmidt & Wiegand, 2017).

Feature Extraction Approaches

All unstructured raw pre-processed data is classified based on some characteristics of data. In the text mining, classification tasks required feature extraction of data. Categorized all unstructured information to a fewer variable based on different features is feature extraction. Hate speech detection also follows the same approach to classifying data. The chapter considers recent studies that categorize and compares all the features (Fortuna & Nunes 2018).

Figure 4. Various Feature Extraction Approaches

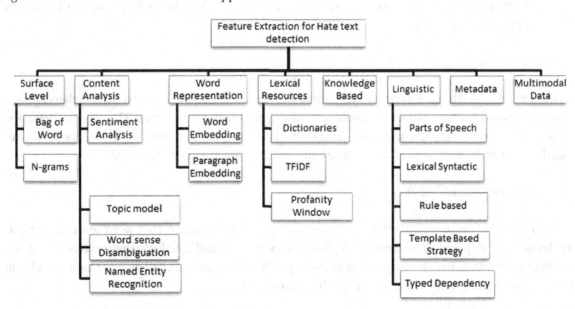

- **Surface Level Feature:** The surface-level feature is played a very important role in NLP research. Specially N-gram features extraction is included by many researchers in hate speech detection tasks. Below surface-level features are helpful for a variety of NLP research as well as in abusive language detection tasks.

- Bag of Words:

This model is extensively used in information retrieval, computer vision, as well as NLP research. It creates a corpus based on training data where texts are represented as a set of words with considering the frequency of every word. The BOW method mostly used for classification tasks, but it has some limitations. BOW is not able to consider syntactic and semantic features for any text. The sequence of words in a text is also ignored by the method (Fortuna & Nunes 2018). Bag of word feature implemented in hate speech detection study where data set collected from Twitter used for binary classification (Burnap, & Williams, 2016).

- N-grams:

N-grams feature is commonly employed in various hate text detection and related research. N-grams consider N sequential words. N defines the size of the word in the list. It considers all occurrence and sequence which improve the classification performance compared to BOW model. Character N-grams model comes into play where it considered N character. It mostly used when spelling discrepancy is observed in NLP research. A combination of N-grams features with other features makes remarkable classifier performance (Schmidt & Wiegand, 2017). Recently N-grams feature with TF-IDF has successfully implemented in toxic content detection where Twitter data has extracted for classification of hate post into three categories – offensive, hateful and clean (Gaydhani, Doma, Kendre, & Bhagwat, 2018).

- **Content Analysis Feature:** Content Analysis feature is used to analyse the content of the text for hate category classification. Content analysis features include sentiment analysis, topic model, word sense disambiguation and named entity recognition which helps to predict post category (Fortuna & Nunes 2018).

- Sentiment Analysis:

The method is used to identify negative, positive and neutral sentiment from text. Researchers applied sentiment analysis features extraction combined with various feature extraction. Hate speech detection is improved by using sentiment analysis where single and multistep sentiment analysis approaches are applied. Based on high degrees of negative sentiment, hate speech can be identified.

- Word Sense Disambiguation:

When one word denotes a different sense based on a particular sentence, then word sense disambiguation features are required. Hate speech detection is very much complicated. Various sentences may not contain abusive words but are categorized as hate speech. This complex challenge for hate speech can be overcome by using word sense disambiguation techniques.

- Name Entity Recognition:

Natural language processing techniques mostly use for unstructured text. Identifying names and entities from the same text is another essential work for language processing. Various posts contain terrorist organization names or any famous extremist. This feature can help to identify that extremist or terrorist group in a text.

- Topic Model:

The topic model is a text mining approach that extracts similar pattern words from large datasets. It helps to improve the classification tasks to organize a large quantity of data. LDA is a popular topic model. The goal of this topic model is to segregate text based on each topic. Topic extraction, classification, and topic similarity all features have applied as feature extraction of hate speech.

- **Word Representation Feature:** The majority of deep learning research has employed word representation features for better prediction results in NLP research. Word2Vec, Paragraph2Vec, Content2Vec, and BERT all these models come under word representation feature in hate speech research.

- Word Embedding:

Word embedding represents as a vector for each word to find similarity between different words. It measures the semantic similarity of a text. A computed vector for each word is used to classify the features.

- Paragraph Embedding:

Paragraph embedding concepts is an unsupervised method which influenced by word embedding feature. The concepts of paragraph vector representation perform better compare to other embedding model, and it increases the embedding performance. This feature with Multilayer Perceptron (MLP) classifier has effectively classified the hateful and neutral comments based on racism, sexism, religion, and disability (Alorainy, Burnap, Liu & Williams, 2019)

- **Lexical Feature:** Lexical feature concepts denote the language vocabulary. It includes word and phrase which differentiates based on grammatical concepts. Lexical features widely used by NLP researchers that also play a significant role in hate-motivated post detection.

- Dictionaries:

This feature has widely used in NLP research. It makes a word list that contains the occurrence of each word in a passage. This feature helps to identify similar offensive words or a list of abusive words. The various website contains such negative word lists.

- TF-IDF:

This is a statistical method to recognize word significance in a file. TF-IDF also considers word appearance count in a text. TF-IDF normalization method plays very significant success using Naïve Bayes (NB), SVM and Logistic regression machine learning algorithms (Gaydhani, Doma, Kendre, & Bhagwat, 2018).

- Lexical Syntactic:

This lexical method is known as LSF or Lexical Syntactic Feature. It detects the grammatical relationship in a sentence. It works a word pair in a sentence to find the relationship. To obtain hate motivation in sentence, researchers also applied these features.

- Profanity Window:

Dictionary and N-grams feature influenced the concepts; the profane word shows disrespectful comments towards religious people or religious beliefs. This concept aims to identify the second person related to a profane word. The window size limit is fixed for the same (Fortuna & Nunes 2018).

- **Knowledge-Based Feature:** Hate speech detection does not only depend on particular word occurrences, but the knowledge-based feature is also required to identify the motivation of a sentence. Contextual information for a text is considered to classify hate category.
- **Linguistic Feature:** Linguistic features include POS tagging, rule and template-based approach and typed dependency for grammatical corrections. Majority of NLP research employed POS tagging to find the importance of words. Toxic content detection in any post highly relies on linguistic features.

- Parts of Speech:

The POS method identifies the role and significance of a particular word within a sentence. It detects the word category like adjective, verb form, pronoun, etc. Hate speech detection in a sentence is largely required POS tagging (Fortuna & Nunes 2018).

- Rule-Based:

In NLP domain, researchers have used rule-based techniques to classify based on a particular condition. The rule-based technique used dictionary features for particular subjective activity. This method has enhanced by linguistic features. This approach detects the sense of group activities (Gitari, Zuping, Damien & Long, 2015).

- Template Based Strategy:

This linguistic feature used to create a corpus of words where it gathers more related words that happened around each word from the corpus. The template-based feature helps to detect the particular context of a sentence.

- Typed Dependency:

Grammatical connections are required to identify the sense of a sentence. The typed dependency feature is used to provide the subject-based grammatical relationship. Expertise for a particular language is not required to detect grammatical structure for pair words.

- **Metadata:** Information about data is denoted as metadata. Metadata feature extraction is also a significant technique for abusive sentence detection. When any user-posted hate content repeatedly, then user identification can help to predict hate post. Not only is the user identification, but the gender factor also considered for prediction. One study considered that hate post from male gender is more compare to female gender (Waseem & Hovy, 2016). Metadata concepts in hate context detection also considered many other factors like the number of followers who frequently post hate messages, geographic region, the number of posts replied to hate message and many more. But a recent survey shows that metadata should be considered based on the information type and instigated source (Schmidt & Wiegand, 2017).
- **Multimodal Data:** Now a day, social networking sites also use multimodal data such as image, video and audio posts. Classifying hate posts from all multimodal data is very much challenging. Visual data attract people most. Most of the abusive post-detection research comes from the text but audio, video, image, memes, and all gif format used for hate spreading in cyberspace. Combinations of text and image also communication medium for scattering hate. Image recognition, OCR, and audio-video translation techniques have implemented to overcome these challenges (Vidgen, Harris, Nguyen, Tromble, Hale & Margetts, 2019). To analyse the vulnerable attack in cyberspace multimodal research using pixel feature extraction has considered for 3000 pictures (Zhong, Li, Squicciarini, Rajtmajer, Griffin, Miller, & Caragea, 2016). In recent multimodal abusive content detection research 160M images has considered from 2.6B posts to categorize the racist meme (Zannettou, Caulfield, Blackburn, De Cristofaro, Stringhini, Sirivianos & Suarez-Tangil, 2018).

Knowledge of all feature extraction approaches concerning hate speech research is not sufficient for future research scope. Below table 1 shows the advantages and limitations for all features to compare them and help to get the right path for new research.

Machine Learning Classification Algorithm

After completion of feature extraction from abusive posts, machine learning classification algorithms take place to detect hate speech. Machine learning algorithms are mainly used for classification. Machine learning algorithms categorized as below (Al-Hassan & Al-Dossari, 2019).

- **Supervised Classification Algorithm:** Supervised learning comes under the machine learning approach where it required supervision. This approach depends on labelling the huge volume of data. Data annotation for large data is a time-dependent solution. The supervised method is the most usable in hate speech detection research. Machine learning algorithms for the supervised approach is fully depends on particular domain knowledge. To detect hateful people and symbol, researchers implemented the logistic regression algorithm (Waseem & Hovy, 2016). Majority of

*Table 1. **Advantages and Disadvantages** of hate speech detection feature extraction techniques*

Features	Advantages	Limitations
Surface Level	• N-gram, character level features, help to detect various spelling of slur words. • Highly predictive features for classification.	• Data sparsity problem arises for large datasets. • Bag of Word not able to consider the co-occurrence of words
Content Analysis	• Multi-step approach includes sentiment polarity features. • Complex challenges can be addressed by this feature.	• Humour or sarcasm hate post-detection face challenges.
Word Representation	• Word clustering concepts address the data sparsity issue. • Word embedding and paragraph embedding features enhanced classification tasks.	• Morphologically rich language face challenges for word embedding feature.
Lexical	• Lists of slur words improve the prediction of hate posts. • Assigning weight based on hate degrees is also a valuable feature.	• Insufficient feature as a stand-alone mode.
Knowledge-Based	• Aspect information and world knowledge highly useful. • Semantic concepts of expression behind user posts are also valuable.	• This model cannot perform well in inter-domain concepts. • More manual effort is required for coding.
Linguistic	• POS tagging helps to find the importance of words. • Grammatical connections extraction is a significant feature.	• Detection is difficult by modelling large datasets.
Metadata	• Different Meta information extracted by social webs API is valuable. • Social users' background data is also important.	• Dependency based on information type or data origin is a significant limitation.
Multimodal	• Image Posts based on pixel-level analysis is valuable. • Feature of visual posts and captions analysis are important criteria.	• Analysis cost is high for multimodal data.

the hate context detection research has implemented support vector machine to classify the hateful posts where the supervised approach has followed (Warner & Hirschberg, 2012; Wiegand, Ruppenhofer, Schmidt, & Greenberg, 2018; Liu, Burnap, Alorainy & Williams, 2019).

- **Semi-supervised Classification Algorithm**: This approach deals with a large volume of unlabeled and labeled data. The combination of both types of data helps to improve model performance. Many semi-supervised algorithms successfully implemented in NLP research. The semi-supervised approach has applied in hate speech detection research where the logistic regression algorithm used for classification (Xiang, Fan, Wang, Hong & Rose, 2012). In another research, the AdaBoost algorithm has implemented to identify the supporters of Jihadism (Kaati, Omer, Prucha & Shrestha, 2015). Some of the researchers also employed a semi-supervised bootstrapping algorithm in abusive language detection (Gitari, Zuping, Damien & Long, 2015; Davidson, Bhattacharya & Weber, 2019).

- **Unsupervised Classification Algorithm:** Unsupervised approach is very much useful when huge data are unlabeled. This approach can able to extract key terms dynamically from the training dataset. The unsupervised approach deals with various types of content, and it can be dependent for a particular domain. Model scalability is the advantage of the semi-supervised approach. Detection of extremism and online hate research applied unsupervised approach (Wadhwa & Bhatia, 2013).

- **Deep Learning:** This technique is a subsection of machine learning that influenced by the concept of human brain neurons. These models are significantly performed well in various NLP research. Hate speech is not the exception domain. An artificial Neural Network concept in deep learning is one of the old concepts which commendably used in many research domains. NLP researchers are widely used multiple deep learning techniques in hate content classification where one study has implemented FastText, CNN model (Convolutional Neural Network) & LSTMs Neural Network approach (Badjatiya, Gupta, Gupta, & Varma, 2017). A comparison with baseline models has required for any research. One existing research follows the various existing model comparison approaches and employed incorporation of CNN approach & GRU Neural Network techniques to distinguish sexism, racism (Zhang, Robinson & Tepper, 2018). Multilayer (MLP) Neural Network architecture also achieved 0.99 AUC (Alorainy, Burnap, Liu & Williams, 2019). A latest study has applied CNN architecture with a transfer learning approach to detect hate context in multilingual sentences (Rajput, Kapoor, Mathur, Kumaraguru & Shah, 2020).

Performance Measured

Evaluation of any algorithm is a significant step to infer the future scope for research. Hate speech detection performance has measured by various metrics like AUC, Precision, F- score, Recall, and Accuracy. State-of-art and future models compare based on evaluation metrics. NLP community executes distinct metrics based on the hate speech classification.

Figure 5. Evaluation metrics for hate speech detection

$$P(Precision) = \frac{TP(TruePositive)}{TP(TruePositive) + FP(FalsePositive)}$$

$$R(Recall) = \frac{TP(TruePositive)}{TP(TruePositive) + FN(FalseNegative)}$$

$$F\ score = 2 * \frac{P(Precision) * R(Recall)}{P(Precision) + R(Recall)}$$

$$A(Accuracy) = \frac{TP(TruePositive) + TN(TrueNegative)}{TotalMeasure(TP + TN + FP + FN)}$$

Hate speech classification research evaluates with **Recall** (percentage of measure classified by proposed method), **Precision** (percentage of measure which is relevant), F score (performance measure considering Precision and Recall both), **AUC** (Measures the performance of true positive with false positive for all probable values), **Accuracy** (measure the performance of classification for positive and negative both), **ROC** (predict finest threshold value). Precision, Recall, and F- score values range between 0 to 1, where 0 represents the poorest and 1 represents the best performance. False positive rate minimization is the objective of any hate content classification system (Burnap, & Williams, 2016). All performance evaluation formulas have displayed in figure 5. Below table 2 shows the analysis of the evaluation metric from recent significant hate speech detection research.

Shortcomings of Hate Speech Detection Methods

Research in hate posts classification is in the initial stage where researchers face many challenges for classifications of offensive words. NLP researchers have reported many limitations (Nobata, Tetreaul, Thomas, Mehdad, & Chang, 2016; Raisi & Huang, 2016; Schmidt & Wiegand, 2017).

- Data sparsity issues occurred due to dataset volume. Offensive content increase on a regular basis that creates challenges for researchers to overcome the issue of data sparsity.
- People also depend on multimodal posts. The multi-mode of communications creates complexities to detect toxic comments from posts.
- Hate speech exists in a single language, multiple languages and the combination of different languages in a single sentence. Multilingual hate content detection is also a challenge for researchers.
- Languages used in social media are changing every day. Morphological evaluation creates difficulties for hate content detection.
- Reliable annotation faces challenges with datasets. Crowdsourcing annotation is also unsuccessful in developed quality labelling.
- In hate posts also contain various permutations of word or phrase which create difficulties for simple keyword identifying processes.
- Every day the slur words are changing, which creates problems for detection. The specific list of words for racism is toxic for one group but may be suitable for another group.
- The majority of the posts are grammatically accurate and fluent that makes difficulties for researchers.
- In a post, majority sentences have categorized as non-hateful, but for particularly one sentence refer to the total post as hate post. Detection of inter-relation between sentences generates challenges for this cyber hate research.
- Irony recognition is a very perplexing task where humour posts may contain abusive meaning.

RESEARCH GROWTH ANALYSIS IN HATE CONTENT CLASSIFICATION

It is essential to visualize the statistical analysis of the research trends of hate speech detection with NLP. **Web of Science** database gives the appropriate idea for the growth of hate speech research. The statistical analysis of the web of science data shows the growth of hate posts research in current ages. The significant fact is the recent development of research in hate speech detection is fairly high. Analysis

*Table 2. **Analysis of Precision, Recall and F-score value from recent hate speech detection research***

Year	Features	Classification Algorithm	Hate Classes	P	R	F	Research Paper
2012	Parts of speech, Template-Based	SVM	Anti-Semitic, Non-anti-Semitic	59.00	68.00	63.00	(Warner & Hirschberg, 2012)
2013	TFIDF	Naïve Bayes	Hate, Like	78.6	73.3	75.9	(Ting, Wang, Chi & Wu, 2013)
2014	n-gram reduced type dependency, Hateful Terms	Bayesian Logistic Regression	Yes and No	89.00	69.00	77.00	(Burnap & Williams, 2014)
2015	subjectivity detection, Lexicon, semantic, theme-based	Rule-Based approach	Not Hateful, Weakly Hateful, Strongly Hateful	73.42	68.42	70.83	(Gitari, Zuping, Damien & Long, 2015)
2016	char n-grams	Logistic Regression	Racism, Sexism, None	72.87	77.75	73.89	(Waseem & Hovy, 2016)
2017	Random embedding	GBDT, LSTM	Racism, Sexism, None	93.00	93.00	93.00	(Badjatiya, Gupta, Gupta, & Varma, 2017)
2017	Random Vector	CNN	Racism, Sexism, both, non-hate	86.68	67.26	75.63	(Gambäck & Sikdar, 2017)
2018	Word - frequency vectorization	RNN, LSTM	Sexism, Racism, Neutral	93.05	93.34	93.20	(Pitsilis, Ramampiaro & Langseth, 2018)
2018	n-grams, TFIDF	Logistic Regression	Hateful, Offensive, Clean	96.00	96.00	96.00	(Gaydhani, Doma, Kendre, & Bhagwat, 2018)
2019	Paragraph Embedding	MLP	Hateful, Neutral	99.00	99.00	99.00	(Alorainy, Burnap, Liu & Williams, 2019)
2019	Semantic, sentiment, pattern, unigram	Logistic Regression, DNN	Hate, Offensive and Neither	98.72	98.03	98.37	(Al-Makhadmeh & Tolba, 2020)
2020	Word Ngrams, char Ngrams, syntactic feature, sentiment (negative)	SVM, RF, GB	Hate, Offensive & Free posts	50.00	80.00	50.00	Oriola & Kotzi 2020)
2020	Bag of word, TF-IDF, BERT and Word2Vec	XGBoost	Hateful and Non-hateful	-----	-----	92.40	(Salminen, Hopf, Chowdhury, Jung, Almerekhi, & Jansen, 2020)

Figure 6. Growth of hatred speech research with NLP

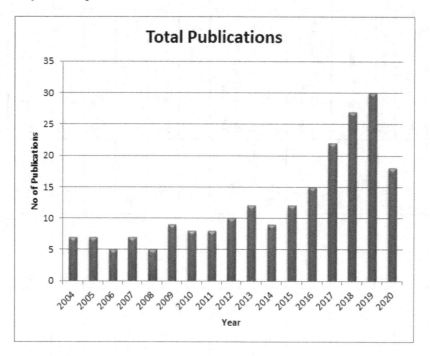

of total publication has considered for the year 2004 to 2020. To plot the growth of hate speech research diagram (figure 6) below query has applied in the web of science database.

TOPIC: (hate speech detection) OR TOPIC: (racism detection) OR TOPIC: (sexism detection) OR TOPIC: (offensive language detection) OR TOPIC: (toxic word detection) OR TOPIC: (cyberhate)

In every research area, there exist various control terms that evolved around this research. These control terms are very much important for the researchers. Readers will be benefitted if they want to know the research area in detail. In figure 7, control terms are modelled into the visualization of density cluster. Extracted web of science data has considered for the cluster density diagram. Control terms interrelated to each other belong to the same clusters. Required keywords for cluster density analysis has extracted from the **WoS (Web of Science)** database. In figure 7, VOSviewer tool is used to show the cluster density of keywords related to hate content detection research (Van Eck & Waltman, 2010). The same above query has also applied in the web of science database to plot the cluster density diagram with the help of the VOSviewer tool.

In order to extract the cluster density plot from the VOSviewer tool, the minimum occurrence of control terms to be set by 10. After analysing the number of occurrence of control terms by VOSviewer software, the total 113 control terms has picked. In the next step, the relevance score for each control term has calculated. Based on that score, the most relevant control terms are elected. Finally, 60% of default criteria have selected for final control terms. The final cluster density plot has displayed by 60 control terms for hate speech detection research.

The cluster density diagram for hate speech research has mainly consisted of four clusters. Selected 60 control terms are correlated based on various aspects of hate speech. The first cluster exhibits control terms evolved with categories of hate speech like racism, sexism, and woman. Another cluster mainly focused on languages, words, speakers of hate speech research. The third cluster focused on the terms

Figure 7. Cluster density diagram of control terms

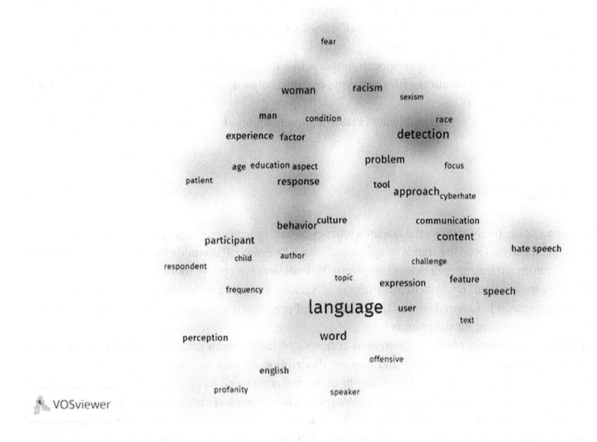

that related to the communication of hate speech like cyberhate, hate speech, content, and text. The final and fourth clusters show the various persons that surrounded by hate speech like an author, child, patient, age, etc. The importance of these clusters shows that studies of every interrelated term are necessary for research.

FUTURE RESEARCH DIRECTIONS

This section presents various future advancements possible for automatic hate content detection systems. Information gathers related to the research is not enough for readers. Existing open issues will provide the right track for future research directions. The research of hate text detection is a recent field. So the number of open issues and challenges is more. Through a systematic analysis, the chapter has allowed pointing out the various possibilities in this field. Future research can follow the succeeding details for automatic hate speech detection system.

- Semi-automatic systems using NLP will be highly acceptable in the existing tech world. These systems required human involvement and expertise.
- NLP researchers should evaluate algorithms considering the large dataset.

- The multimodal dataset is also a critical challenge for researchers to classify the hate speech.
- Various combinations of posts will be valuable data for research.
- Hate speech detection using a hybrid of various toxic words from multilingual datasets is also another future research direction.
- A combination of various hate speech subparts like racism with ethnicity, disability with skin colour, gender discrimination with misogyny, etc. posts classification will be another responsibility for NLP researchers.
- Algorithm accuracy with multi-label classification is highly desirable to implement in social networking sites.

CONCLUSION

The chapter collectively exhibits the research journey of hate speech detection systems from the computer science perspective. Growing trends of cyberspace have forced NLP communities to conceive about the accurate automatic hate speech detection system. Researchers are getting more challenges and great opportunities in this field. By systematic analysis of various features and techniques, the chapter reveals that more research is required in this field. Successful presentation of hate speech research journey is very much informative for the readers.

Initially, the chapter presents theoretical concepts of hate speech and the critical terms evolving around hate speech theory. A brief and concise description of various characteristics of hate speech has also included in this chapter. The majority of the research work has considered racism and sexism categories. The review finds that the hybrid category of hate speech is also required more research work with respect to the computer science domain. The chapter also frames the rules behind the classification theory of hate speech that motivates researchers for future work. The theoretical core of hate speech, relevant terms, and distinctions among them are also significant for readers. This chapter also includes the effects of online hate speech in the business domain. The various social media giants, online commercials, e-products have faced threats from cyberhate. With the critical analysis of hate speech affects in the business domain, the recent examples also included. The analysis pointed out that cyberhate made a negative impact on the industry.

After a systematic and concise explanation of theoretical concepts of hate speech, the chapter focused on the technical concepts of automatic detection systems. Section initiate with the basic flow of a cyberhate text recognition system. The research is in early-stage, so the collection and annotation of new text datasets is part of the process. Many datasets of the past research paper are not accessible to the public. Detection in a multimodal dataset is also another challenge in hate content research. Additionally, the section also presents diverse feature extractions approaches that employed in automatic hate speech detection systems. Feature extractions of online hate text detection research are classified based on various NLP techniques. Most existing research has employed supervised learning methods. Generally, studies have applied generic features for hate speech. The section further compares diverse feature extractions that have used in different algorithms in the last few years. Future models can incorporate more specific features of hate speech than generic features. Identification of successful features and classification algorithms for hate text research is the objective of this chapter. Performance measures for past research are an essential phase. Brief concepts of standard evaluation criteria for this area have also included in this section. The outline of significant research by various machine learning algorithms has also shown in the evaluation section. It comforts readers to get appropriate knowledge and opportunities in this field. Lastly, the technical section includes various limitations of this research to date.

Apart from the theoretical and technical section, the chapter uniquely showed the research growth plot from Web of Science data. Clear clarity of existing hate speech research in the computer science domain demands more research in automatic detection systems. Researchers will able to identify the right path by future research direction section. With this work, it expressed the establishment of the current state-of-art. In conclusion, the chapter actively identifies the significant approaches for hate speech detection to date.

REFERENCES

Al-Hassan, A., & Al-Dossari, H. (2019). Detection of hate speech in social networks: a survey on multilingual corpus. *6th International Conference on Computer Science and Information Technology*. 10.5121/csit.2019.90208

Al-Makhadmeh, Z., & Tolba, A. (2020). Automatic hate speech detection using killer natural language processing optimizing ensemble deep learning approach. *Computing, 102*(2), 501–522. doi:10.100700607-019-00745-0

Alorainy, W., Burnap, P., Liu, H., & Williams, M. L. (2019). "The Enemy Among Us" Detecting Cyber Hate Speech with Threats-based Othering Language Embeddings. *ACM Transactions on the Web, 13*(3), 1–26. doi:10.1145/3324997

Badjatiya, P., Gupta, S., Gupta, M., & Varma, V. (2017, April). Deep learning for hate speech detection in tweets. In *Proceedings of the 26th International Conference on World Wide Web Companion* (pp. 759-760). 10.1145/3041021.3054223

Brandom, R. (2018, Sep 21). *PayPal bans Infowars for promoting hate.* Retrieved from https://www.theverge.com/2018/9/21/17887138/paypal-infowars-ban-alex-jones-hate-speech-deplatform

Burnap, P., & Williams, M. L. (2014). *Hate speech, machine classification and statistical modelling of information flows on Twitter: Interpretation and communication for policy decision making.* Academic Press.

Burnap, P., & Williams, M. L. (2016). Us and them: Identifying cyber hate on Twitter across multiple protected characteristics. *EPJ Data Science, 5*(1), 11. doi:10.1140/epjds13688-016-0072-6 PMID:32355598

Cellan-Jones, R. (2017, 20 March). *Google's crisis of confidence.* Retrieved from https://www.bbc.com/news/technology-39331204

Chen, Y., Zhou, Y., Zhu, S., & Xu, H. (2012, September). Detecting offensive language in social media to protect adolescent online safety. In *2012 International Conference on Privacy, Security, Risk and Trust and 2012 International Conference on Social Computing* (pp. 71-80). IEEE. 10.1109/SocialCom-PASSAT.2012.55

Chetty, N., & Alathur, S. (2018). Hate speech review in the context of online social networks. *Aggression and Violent Behavior, 40*, 108–118. doi:10.1016/j.avb.2018.05.003

Clement, J. (2019). *Share of adults in the United States who use the internet in 2019, by age group.* Retrieved from https://www.statista.com/statistics/266587/percentage-of-internet-users-by-age-groups-in-the-us/

Davidson, T., Bhattacharya, D., & Weber, I. (2019). *Racial bias in hate speech and abusive language detection datasets.* arXiv preprint arXiv:1905.12516

Dillinger, J. (2019, September 6). *List Of Countries By Internet Users.* Retrieved from https://www.worldatlas.com/articles/the-20-countries-with-the-most-internet-users.html

Fortuna, P., & Nunes, S. (2018). A survey on automatic detection of hate speech in text. *ACM Computing Surveys*, *51*(4), 1–30. doi:10.1145/3232676

Gambäck, B., & Sikdar, U. K. (2017, August). Using convolutional neural networks to classify hate-speech. In *Proceedings of the first workshop on abusive language online* (pp. 85-90). 10.18653/v1/W17-3013

Gaydhani, A., Doma, V., Kendre, S., & Bhagwat, L. (2018). *Detecting hate speech and offensive language on twitter using machine learning: An n-gram and tfidf based approach.* arXiv preprint arXiv:1809.08651

Gitari, N. D., Zuping, Z., Damien, H., & Long, J. (2015). A lexicon-based approach for hate speech detection. *International Journal of Multimedia and Ubiquitous Engineering*, *10*(4), 215–230. doi:10.14257/ijmue.2015.10.4.21

Kaati, L., Omer, E., Prucha, N., & Shrestha, A. (2015, November). Detecting multipliers of jihadism on twitter. In *2015 IEEE International Conference on Data Mining Workshop (ICDMW)* (pp. 954-960). IEEE. 10.1109/ICDMW.2015.9

Krause, T., & Grassegger, H. (2016). *Facebook's secret rules of deletion.* Retrieved from https://international.sueddeutsche.de/post/154543271930/facebooks-secret-rules-of-deletion

Liu, H., Burnap, P., Alorainy, W., & Williams, M. L. (2019). A fuzzy approach to text classification with two-stage training for ambiguous instances. *IEEE Transactions on Computational Social Systems*, *6*(2), 227–240. doi:10.1109/TCSS.2019.2892037

Liu, S., & Forss, T. (2015, November). New classification models for detecting Hate and Violence web content. In *2015 7th international joint conference on knowledge discovery, knowledge engineering and knowledge management (IC3K)* (Vol. 1, pp. 487-495). IEEE. 10.5220/0005636704870495

Nobata, C., Tetreault, J., Thomas, A., Mehdad, Y., & Chang, Y. (2016, April). Abusive language detection in online user content. In *Proceedings of the 25th international conference on world wide web* (pp. 145-153). 10.1145/2872427.2883062

Oriola, O., & Kotzi, E. (2020). Evaluating Machine Learning Techniques for Detecting Offensive and Hate Speech in South African Tweets. *IEEE Access: Practical Innovations, Open Solutions*, *8*, 21496–21509. doi:10.1109/ACCESS.2020.2968173

Pitsilis, G. K., Ramampiaro, H., & Langseth, H. (2018). *Detecting offensive language in tweets using deep learning.* arXiv preprint arXiv:1801.04433

Prescott, C. (2019, May 24). *Internet users, UK: 2019*. Retrieved from https://www.ons.gov.uk/businessindustryandtrade/itandinternetindustry/bulletins/internetusers/2019

Qian, J., ElSherief, M., Belding, E. M., & Wang, W. Y. (2018). *Leveraging intra-user and inter-user representation learning for automated hate speech detection.* arXiv preprint arXiv:1804.03124

Raisi, E., & Huang, B. (2016). *Cyberbullying identification using participant-vocabulary consistency.* arXiv preprint arXiv:1606.08084

Rajput, K., Kapoor, R., Mathur, P., Kumaraguru, P., & Shah, R. R. (2020). Transfer Learning for Detecting Hateful Sentiments in Code Switched Language. In *Deep Learning-Based Approaches for Sentiment Analysis* (pp. 159–192). Springer. doi:10.1007/978-981-15-1216-2_7

Ross, B., Rist, M., Carbonell, G., Cabrera, B., Kurowsky, N., & Wojatzki, M. (2017). *Measuring the reliability of hate speech annotations: The case of the European refugee crisis.* arXiv preprint arXiv:1701.08118

Salminen, J., Hopf, M., Chowdhury, S. A., Jung, S. G., Almerekhi, H., & Jansen, B. J. (2020). Developing an online hate classifier for multiple social media platforms. *Human-centric Computing and Information Sciences, 10*(1), 1. doi:10.118613673-019-0205-6

Schmidt, A., & Wiegand, M. (2017, April). A survey on hate speech detection using natural language processing. In *Proceedings of the Fifth International Workshop on Natural Language Processing for Social Media* (pp. 1-10). 10.18653/v1/W17-1101

Ting, I. H., Wang, S. L., Chi, H. M., & Wu, J. S. (2013, August). Content matters: A study of hate groups detection based on social networks analysis and web mining. In *Proceedings of the 2013 IEEE/ACM International Conference on Advances in Social Networks Analysis and Mining* (pp. 1196-1201). 10.1145/2492517.2500254

Van Eck, N., & Waltman, L. (2010). Software survey: VOSviewer, a computer program for bibliometric mapping. *Scientometrics, 84*(2), 523-538.

Vidgen, B., Harris, A., Nguyen, D., Tromble, R., Hale, S., & Margetts, H. (2019, August). *Challenges and frontiers in abusive content detection.* Association for Computational Linguistics.

Wadhwa, P., & Bhatia, M. P. S. (2013, February). Tracking on-line radicalization using investigative data mining. In *2013 National Conference on Communications (NCC)* (pp. 1-5). IEEE. 10.1109/NCC.2013.6488046

Warner, W., & Hirschberg, J. (2012, June). Detecting hate speech on the world wide web. In *Proceedings of the second workshop on language in social media* (pp. 19-26). Association for Computational Linguistics.

Waseem, Z., & Hovy, D. (2016, June). Hateful symbols or hateful people? predictive features for hate speech detection on twitter. In *Proceedings of the NAACL student research workshop* (pp. 88-93). 10.18653/v1/N16-2013

Wiegand, M., Ruppenhofer, J., Schmidt, A., & Greenberg, C. (2018). *Inducing a lexicon of abusive words–a feature-based approach.* Academic Press.

WilliamsD. (2020, March 5). *CNN Business.* Retrieved from https://edition.cnn.com/2020/03/04/business/target-commercial-race-reviews-trnd/index.html

Wolfe, S. (2018, October 29). *Gab, the social network popular with the far right, has temporarily shut down after GoDaddy pulled its support.* Retrieved from https://finance.yahoo.com/news/gab-social-network-popular-far-162103840.html

Xiang, G., Fan, B., Wang, L., Hong, J., & Rose, C. (2012, October). Detecting offensive tweets via topical feature discovery over a large scale twitter corpus. In *Proceedings of the 21st ACM international conference on Information and knowledge management* (pp. 1980-1984). 10.1145/2396761.2398556

Zannettou, S., Caulfield, T., Blackburn, J., De Cristofaro, E., Sirivianos, M., Stringhini, G., & Suarez-Tangil, G. (2018, October). On the origins of memes by means of fringe web communities. In *Proceedings of the Internet Measurement Conference 2018* (pp. 188-202). 10.1145/3278532.3278550

Zhang, Z., Robinson, D., & Tepper, J. (2018, June). Detecting hate speech on twitter using a convolution-gru based deep neural network. In *European semantic web conference* (pp. 745-760). Springer. 10.1007/978-3-319-93417-4_48

Zhong, H., Li, H., Squicciarini, A. C., Rajtmajer, S. M., Griffin, C., Miller, D. J., & Caragea, C. (2016, July). Content-Driven Detection of Cyberbullying on the Instagram Social Network. IJCAI, 3952-3958.

ADDITIONAL READING

Blaya, C. (2019). Cyberhate: A review and content analysis of intervention strategies. *Aggression and Violent Behavior, 45,* 163–172. doi:10.1016/j.avb.2018.05.006

Kaakinen, M., Räsänen, P., Näsi, M., Minkkinen, J., Keipi, T., & Oksanen, A. (2018). Social capital and online hate production: A four country survey. *Crime, Law, and Social Change, 69*(1), 25–39. doi:10.100710611-017-9764-5

Khieu, B. T., & Moh, M. (2020). Neural Network Applications in Hate Speech Detection. In Neural Networks for Natural Language Processing (pp. 188-204). IGI Global. doi:10.4018/978-1-7998-1159-6.ch012

Malmasi, S., & Zampieri, M. (2018). Challenges in discriminating profanity from hate speech. *Journal of Experimental & Theoretical Artificial Intelligence, 30*(2), 187–202. doi:10.1080/0952813X.2017.1409284

Mishra, P., Yannakoudakis, H., & Shutova, E. (2019). *Tackling Online Abuse: A Survey of Automated Abuse Detection Methods.* arXiv preprint arXiv:1908.06024.

Noriega, C. A., & Iribarren, F. J. (2012). *Social Networks for Hate Speech.* Working Paper, UCLA, Chicano Studies Research Center.

Pacheco, E., & Melhuish, N. (2018). *Online hate speech: A survey on personal experiences and exposure among adult New Zealanders.* Available at SSRN 3272148.

van Aken, B., Risch, J., Krestel, R., & Löser, A. (2018). *Challenges for toxic comment classification: An in-depth error analysis.* arXiv preprint arXiv:1809.07572.

Weinstein, J. (2018). *Hate speech, pornography, and radical attacks on free speech doctrine*. Routledge. doi:10.4324/9780429500046

KEY TERMS AND DEFINITIONS

Context: Situation happens behind particular posts or messages.

Data Annotation: Preparing data with data labelling for machine learning techniques is called data annotation.

Data Sparsity: Data sparsity problem occurs when the numbers of non-zero values are very less compare to zero values in datasets. In NLP, the data sparsity problem occurs when a document converted to vector form.

Deep Learning: Deep learning approach is a subfield of the machine learning technique. The concepts of deep learning influenced by neuron and brain structure based on ANN (Artificial Neural Network).

Machine Learning: Machine Learning is a statistical or mathematical model that performs data analysis, prediction, and clustering. This science is a subfield of Artificial Intelligence.

Natural Language Processing: NLP is a Linguistic approach to interact with human language and computer. This field comes under Artificial Intelligence and Computer Science.

Text Mining: Text mining extracting unstructured data from any web source and processed to semi-structured or structured form for analysis.

Chapter 10
The Use of Natural Language Processing for Market Orientation on Rare Diseases

Matthias Hölscher

Institute for IT Management and Digitization, FOM University, Germany

Rudiger Buchkremer

iD https://orcid.org/0000-0002-4130-9253

Institute for IT Management and Digitization, FOM University, Germany

ABSTRACT

Rare diseases in their entirety have a substantial impact on the healthcare market, as they affect a large number of patients worldwide. Governments provide financial support for diagnosis and treatment. Market orientation is crucial for any market participant to achieve business profitability. However, the market for rare diseases is opaque. The authors compare results from search engines and healthcare databases utilizing natural language processing. The approach starts with an information retrieval process, applying the MeSH thesaurus. The results are prioritized and visualized, using word clouds. In total, the chapter is about the examination of 30 rare diseases and about 500,000 search results in the databases Pubmed, FindZebra, and the search engine Google. The authors compare their results to the search for common diseases. The authors conclude that FindZebra and Google provide relatively good results for the evaluation of therapies and diagnoses. However, the quantity of the findings from professional databases such as Pubmed remains unsurpassed.

INTRODUCTION

In this article, we describe different ways for a market player to get information about the rare disease healthcare market. As rare diseases are concerned, there is little information available, and it is challenging to integrate the topic into a comprehensive market strategy with information flows. Stakeholders are dependent on search engines and databases, and it is essential to know which is the most appropriate.

DOI: 10.4018/978-1-7998-4240-8.ch010

A relatively small number of articles on rare diseases exists; however, the quantity is still a challenge, especially if several rare diseases are searched simultaneously. Natural Language Processing can provide support through finding relevant articles quickly, and by helping to find the "needle in the haystack" through mathematical operations and subsequent visualizations. These methods also represent an essential accomplishment for physicians, as they can usually only control a small part of known diseases. Furthermore, NLP is crucial for patients, relatives, and other stakeholders who are not familiar with the subject matter.

A low prevalence characterizes rare diseases, and the global number of incidences for each disease is low. The impression may arise that they do not impact the health care market. However, the situation is different: Collectively, about 10% of the US population is affected by a rare (also called orphan) disease as many countries are undertaking efforts to provide patients with orphan diseases with highly qualified medicines. In the USA, the Orphan Drug Act has been in place since 1983, and in China, efforts are being made to improve patient care (Kang et al., 2019). Rare diseases affect the medical market in at least two ways.

On the one hand, these drugs are commonly quite expensive because they become visible in the market. On the other hand, it generally takes several years until a rare disease is discovered at all so that unnecessary examinations and treatments cost enormous amounts of money (Svenstrup et al., 2015). Therefore, healthcare professionals need to quickly discover the right information on rare diseases, and Natural Language Processing (NLP) can provide useful help.

The problem with transparency in the rare diseases market is that there is little information about specific rare diseases, and it can be very laborious to find orientation in the market. Thus, how do we orientate ourselves in a market about which hardly any information is available? Moreover, how do we find our way through it?

The proclamation for a business that improves its market orientation also expands its market performance has been issued for more than 60 years. Narver and Slater (1990) introduce an efficient instrument the degree of market orientation in 1990 and show that customer and competitor orientation includes all activities to obtain information about buyers and competitors. It is essential to cover the target market and to disseminate the resulting reports internally. In 2005, Kirca et al. provide a quantitative summary of the bivariate findings regarding forerunners and the effects of performing market-orientation research and confirm that market intelligence is a compulsory prerequisite to participate in a market successfully. Intelligence seems feasible for a transparent and information-rich market, but information on rare diseases is scarce. For a large corporation or an organization in a transparent market, it is not challenging to establish a sophisticated marketing strategy. However, if management attention is scarce to investigate an opaque market such as the marketing of rare diseases, the trade-off for a strategy is the in-situ information search in the Web and literature databases (see also Christen et al., 2009). Thus, we need to look for ways to utilize search engines to get a quick overview of the market. Besides, it is crucial that we also evaluate the results. It is, therefore, advisable to compare the results with professional databases. FindZebra is a database that focuses on rare diseases, and MEDLINE or PubMed is a database of medical articles.

Thus, in this article, we examine whether Internet search engines like Google and professional healthcare databases, such as PubMed and FindZebra, are comprehensive tools for diagnosing and searching for therapeutic approaches to rare diseases. Although there is relatively little information available about rare diseases, the number of hits is so large that the search results can be examined and compared much more transparently with a new approach, national language processing, as the authors show with this article.

Furthermore, the approach described in this paper offers an opportunity and, thus, a solution to one of the profound research drawbacks, mainly to study a highly fragmented market where information on fragments (here: rare diseases) is scarce and difficult to comprehend. Natural language processing can assist if the transparency about the market fragments is not given.

In this chapter, we will begin with an outline concerning the scientific background of rare diseases and medical search portals. After comparatively examining similar studies, we methodically classify our approach. The implementation starts with a selection of rare and common diseases and a description of our approach. After presenting our results, we discuss the findings, prioritize the selected search portals, and finally present an outlook.

BACKGROUND

Search Engines and Healthcare Literature Databases

The Pew Research Center's Internet & American Life Project reveals that 35% of all adult U. S. Americans apply Internet search engines to diagnose diseases (Fox & Duggan, 2013). Of these, only 13% start their search on health information websites such as WebMD[1]. 1. 77% of people use search engines such as Google, Bing, or Yahoo. 35% do not visit a doctor to confirm the results of their research (Cooper et al., 1997). Of the respondents who subsequently presented their results to a doctor, 41% were correct with their researched diagnosis, but 18% were wrong with their results. The results of the study indicate that the search for healthcare information about diseases is anything but trivial.

In recent years, there has been an exponential increase in peer-reviewed literature, including the medical field. In 2006, the MEDLINE[2] database contained 16 million scientific articles, of which around 700,000 were added in the previous year alone (Hunter & Cohen, 2006). By 2017, this figure had risen to 24 million (U.S. National Library of Medicine, 2018). It is becoming increasingly common for patients to reveal correct diagnoses that doctors have not taken into account (Bouwman et al., 2010).

The exact definition of rare diseases varies worldwide, but the disease is generally considered rare when less than one in two thousand people are affected (Dragusin et al., 2013). The authors of this study obtain the list of rare diseases from the National Organization for Rare Disorders (NORD) to select the diseases to be examined. NORD is a charitable health organization in the USA that aims to help people with rare diseases and supporting organizations. Its database includes medical reports on more than 1,200 rare diseases. (Rare Disorders NZ, 2019)

To gain more insight into the search for rare diseases, the authors compare the outcome with those for common diseases. The list of the most frequent causes of death of the Burden of Disease (BOD) Study 2000-2016 of the World Health Organization (WHO)[3] has been applied, which has already been examined by Buchkremer et al. (2019). The top 10 diseases with the highest YLL values (years of life lost) are selected.

Related Work

Jhaveri et al. (2013) see the advent of the Internet as a dramatic development in the way medical decision making is conducted. The Internet has become a valuable information resource for patients, doctors, and other healthcare market stakeholders. They use search engines such as Google to help diagnose diseases. For this reason, Jhaveri et al. (2013) investigate how Google can be applied to diagnose diseases. Krause et al. (2011) conduct a study where 33 physicians in emergency medicine initially answer 71 clinical questions. A second run takes place a week later. The doctors are allowed to use Google as a source of information. In the first test, the participants answered an average of 32% correctly, and 28% incorrectly. In 40% of the questions, the test participants gave "uncertain" answers. The second attempt, which included Google search, yielded 59% correct, 33% incorrect, and only 8% uncertain answers.

The results of this study suggest that an internet search engine can provide clinically useful information to doctors. Falagas et al. (2009) analyze 26 case studies from the New England Journal of Medicine of the year 2005. In the course of solving medical challenges from the journal, the participants mention only a little help using a search engine. The accuracy increased slightly with the three study participants by 15,4%, 2,9%, and 11,5%. Tang and Ng (2006) extracted 3-5major keywords from each case and searched Google on this basis. The search revealed the correct diagnosis in 15 out of 26 cases. Jhaveri et al. (2013) conclude that while Internet search engines such as Google are helpful for doctors to diagnose rare diseases, however, it cannot be a replacement for the heuristic opinion of an expert. Lombardi et al. (2009) assess the accuracy of diagnoses for complex immune and allergic diseases. They select 45 articles with clinical cases from peer-reviewed journals. The authors extract clinical data from the articles with abstracts, journal titles, and diagnoses removed. They subsequently hand the data over to the study participants. In most cases, the study participants reveal the correct diagnosis by looking at the first three search results.

Dragusin et al. (2011) investigate the hypothesis that search engines like Google have not been designed and optimized to search for severe medical cases such as rare diseases. Clinicians' requests are long lists of symptoms, while web searches typically expect short requests. Recommender algorithms show mainly popular websites among the first results, while information on rare diseases is generally rare. The researchers conclude that the search for diagnosis and treatment for rare diseases has characteristics that differ from traditional information retrieval on the web and that its application may not be optimal. They conclude that the search for rare diseases remains to be a challenge. Thus, they further investigate 56 cases of rare diseases in a subsequent study. The search for the diagnoses is performed in the search engine Google. However, this time, the authors consult PubMed and the specially developed search engine FindZebra. With the help of the FindZebra search engine, the investigators correctly diagnose 38 from 56 selected cases (62.5%) by selecting the top 20 hits in the FindZebra search engine. Ferrucci et al. study to make clinical diagnoses using Watson technology.

Watson was developed by IBM and is a program that can find and formulate answers to questions in naturally formulated language. Without any adjustments, Watson achieved a hit rate of 49% among the top 10 search results in the first run of 188 questions. After the run on 1322 questions as training data and after some subsequent adjustments, Watson achieved a hit rate of 77% on 5000 questions in the top 10 search results. (Ferrucci et al., 2013). In a study by Svenstrup et al. (2015), FindZebra is confronted with medical questions from the ACP's "Doctor's Dilemma" competition. The hit rate was 53% by taking only the first ten search results into account.

Thus, by looking at these results, one can conclude that Google and FindZebra are useful tools to gather information related to rare diseases. However, the error rate is still very high. Thus, in this study, Google and FindZebra are selected, but PubMed, a database not explicitly designed for rare diseases, is included. Walewski et al. (2019) state that Pubmed provides a useful source for research on rare diseases and conclude that there are two shortcomings: about 7% of the global population suffers from rare diseases, only 0.2% of the scientific literature (i.e., PubMed) refers to these. Furthermore, the authors discuss another dilemma. Many of the essential journal articles are behind paywalls, which are a particular problem for third world countries. It is where our study can contribute, because, through visual enhancements and natural language processing, some of the abstracts and keywords can be extracted, as we will show. Brasil et al. (2019) provide an overview of the use of artificial intelligence methods to study rare diseases. They explain that most approaches include machine learning and mention only a limited number of semantic approaches, mainly for phenotype analysis.

In summary, we conclude that all three sources need to be included in the analysis of rare diseases.

Natural Language Processing and Information Retrieval

NLP is considered one of the founding technologies of artificial intelligence (Minsky, 1961). It is understood to be the methodical examination of a naturally spoken or written text so that the content is perceived as if a human were reading it (McKeown et al., 2016). The primary methods can be sorted into syntactic, semantic, and statistical categories, with some overlapping. Additional insights can be acquired from texts employing machine learning (Sebastiani & Fabrizio, 2002), and in recent years, the investigation of text patterns and text mining has attracted attention (Citron & Ginsparg, 2015; Srinivasan, 2004). A fundamental methodology has been summarized as information retrieval (Sanderson & Croft, 2012), which has existed for many decades and combines these three primary methods. The procedure is particularly useful if the information to be examined is additionally labeled. It is significant for diseases and especially for rare diseases, as there are usually many names for one (Abel, 2018). If these keywords are structured, the compendium is designated as taxonomy or ontology (Spasic, 2005). The essential advantage of the PubMed database is that the content is tagged with a systematic taxonomy, and dependencies can be mapped. Many names for a disease are searched simultaneously, and the results can be reduced to diagnoses or therapies. This advantage has been exploited in this study, and the results have been further examined and graphically displayed using other NLP procedures. Here, we have mainly exploited proximities (Schenkel et al., 2007), i.e., we have investigated which terms frequently occur in the vicinity of others, thus quickly obtaining an overview of the essential terms in a diagnostic market, for example. In the further course of the study, we have generated word clouds (Heimerl et al., 2014) from our results, which can quickly provide a market overview of the diagnosis and treatment of rare diseases.

METHODOLOGY

Overview

This paper examines search results for 30 rare diseases from the list of the National Organization for Rare Disorders (NORD). The authors analyze the ten most frequent causes of death of a Burden of Disease (BoD) study of the World Health Organization (WHO) to compare rare to common diseases (Murray and Lopez, 2013). In addition to the comparison between rare and frequently occurring diseases, the authors differentiate results according to their suitability for diagnostic and therapeutic questions utilizing natural language processing. The authors deal with the differences in the results, but also with the similarities.

Research Design and Procedure

The investigators of this work apply parts of the artificial intelligence double funnel for natural language processing (NLP). This model illustrates the steps required to analyze a considerable amount of text. The procedure starts with a large opening for many documents, concentrates on the cleansed corpus, and potentially produces a large number of results (Buchkremer et al., 2019). The MeSH browser can be applied to create search queries since the authors select articles from the PubMed database. Such a lexicon-based approach enhances the performance of NLP (Almatarneh & Gamallo, 2018).

In the search for diseases, a particular problem occurs, which is even more massive in rare diseases. There are many names for the same disease. To mitigate the errors from multiple disease names, the authors of this article select all known names for diseases from the MeSH database. The selection makes steps like bootstrapping or taxonomy enhancement from the STIRL procedure obsolete. The historic analysis is also not part of this work, nor is the predictive analysis. The medical search engine PubMed from the U.S. National Library of Medicine (NLM) is applied to generate a corpus of metadata from scientific articles. However, the following two elements, in particular, are decisive factors for the market: diagnosis and therapy (Verzulli et al., 2017).

For this reason, the authors extend the search for the disease to cover additional market-relevant factors such as diagnoses and therapies. Thus, the first study section includes the selection of diseases as well as the derivation of search strings. The queries can be generated in PubMed to obtain results for specific categories. For example, "Alkaptonuria/diagnosis" [Mesh] reveals all tagged search results for diagnosing the disease "Alkaptonuria" and "Alkaptonuria/therapy" [Mesh] reveals search results for the therapy. Not for all rare diseases, mesh codes already exist, but for most, as shown in Table 1. The search for the few cases where no code is available, the diseases are entered by name in the search field.

The "National Center for Biotechnology Information" (NCBI) provides the "Entrez Programming Utilities" (E-Utilities) to automate and simplify the retrieval of information from the PubMed database, for example, with data mining tools. The search for common diseases is being done accordingly (see Table 2):

The tool RapidMiner[4] is applied to analyze the data. It has been developed at the department of artificial intelligence at the Technical University of Dortmund, Germany. For research purposes, an education license is available, which is chosen for this study.

Thus, the next study section involves applying a web crawler, which is used for selecting the current 1,231 (status February 2, 2019) list elements from the NORD list and for subsequent search results. Selected diseases are numbered in ascending order, and 30 rare diseases are selected using a pseudo-random number generator from Wolfram|Alpha®. The resulting random number serves as the identification (ID) of a disease. It is supplemented with the suffix "_d" for diagnosis and "_t" for therapy. For example, "54_d" indicates data that is related to diagnosing the disease. "Alpers Disease" and "54_t" stand for results concerning therapeutic aspects.

To compare database results to Google, we download the search engine hits via the Google custom API (application programming interface). It is advantageous since metadata of search results are returned as well. The API in its free version is limited to 100 search queries per day. The results are returned in the JASON data format. The crawler can also be linked to the FindZebra API to select search results.

All preceding process steps serve to generate the final document corpus. It serves as a central repository for all subsequent investigations, such as NLP and visualizations. The main aim of the preparatory

Table 1. PubMed MeSH search queries for diagnoses and therapies of rare diseases

ID	Suffix	Rare Disease (NORD-List)	Search Query (PubMed)
54	_d	Alpers Disease	"Diffuse Cerebral Sclerosis of Schilder/diagnosis" [Mesh]
54	_t		"Diffuse Cerebral Sclerosis of Schilder/therapy" [Mesh]
61	_d	Alternating Hemiplegia of Childhood	"Hemiplegia/diagnosis"[Mesh]
61	_t		"Hemiplegia/therapy"[Mesh]
241	_d	Chromosome 11, Partial Monosomy 11q	"Jacobsen Distal 11q Deletion Syndrome/diagnosis"[Mesh]
241	_t		"Jacobsen Distal 11q Deletion Syndrome/therapy"[Mesh]
263	_d	Chromosome 6, Partial Trisomy 6q	-
263	_t		-
278	_d	Citrullinemia Type 1	"Citrullinemia/diagnosis"[Mesh]
278	_t		"Citrullinemia/therapy" [Mesh]
284	_d	Coats Disease	"Retinal Telangiectasis/diagnosis"[Mesh]
284	_t		"Retinal Telangiectasis/therapy"[Mesh]
306	_d	Congenital Lactic Acidosis	"Acidosis, Lactic/diagnosis"[Mesh]
306	_t		"Acidosis, Lactic/therapy" [Mesh]
393	_d	Encephalocele	"Encephalocele/diagnosis"[Mesh]
393	_t		"Encephalocele/therapy"[Mesh]
402	_d	Epidermal Nevus Syndromes	-
402	_t		-
451	_d	Fibrosing Mediastinitis	-
451	_t		-
464	_d	Fragile X Syndrome	"Fragile X Syndrome/diagnosis"[Mesh]
464	_t		"Fragile X Syndrome/therapy"[Mesh]
505	_d	Glycogen Storage Disease Type I	"Glycogen Storage Disease Type I/diagnosis" [Mesh]
505	_t		"Glycogen Storage Disease Type I/therapy" [Mesh]
539	_d	Hemophilia A	"Hemophilia A/diagnosis" [Mesh]
539	_t		"Hemophilia A/therapy" [Mesh]
587	_d	Hyperostosis Frontalis Interna	"Hyperostosis Frontalis Interna/diagnosis"[Mesh]
587	_t		"Hyperostosis Frontalis Interna/therapy"[Mesh]
619	_d	Incontinentia Pigmenti	"Incontinentia Pigmenti/diagnosis"[Mesh]
619	_t		"Incontinentia Pigmenti/therapy"[Mesh]
642	_d	Kearns Sayre Syndrome	"Kearns-Sayre Syndrome/diagnosis"[Mesh]
642	_t		"Kearns-Sayre Syndrome/therapy"[Mesh]
715	_d	Machado-Joseph Disease	"Machado-Joseph Disease/diagnosis" [Mesh]
715	_t		"Machado-Joseph Disease/therapy" [Mesh]
736	_d	May Hegglin Anomaly	-
736	_t		-
787	_d	Mucopolysaccharidosis Type I	"Mucopolysaccharidosis I/diagnosis" [Mesh]
787	_t		"Mucopolysaccharidosis I/therapy" [Mesh]

continues on following page

Table 1. Continued

ID	Suffix	Rare Disease (NORD-List)	Search Query (PubMed)
833	_d	Neuroacanthocytosis	"Neuroacanthocytosis/diagnosis"[Mesh]
833	_t		"Neuroacanthocytosis/therapy"[Mesh]
844	_d	Non-24-Hour Sleep-Wake Disorder	"Sleep Disorders, Circadian Rhythm/diagnosis" [Mesh]
844	_t		"Sleep Disorders, Circadian Rhythm/therapy" [Mesh]
859	_d	Oculocutaneous Albinism	"Albinism, Oculocutaneous/diagnosis" [Mesh]
859	_t		"Albinism, Oculocutaneous/therapy" [Mesh]
868	_d	Orocraniodigital Syndrome	"Orofaciodigital Syndromes/diagnosis"[Mesh]
868	_t		"Orofaciodigital Syndromes/therapy" [Mesh]
877	_d	PEPCK Deficiency	-
877	_t		-
894	_d	Papillon Lefèvre Syndrome	"Papillon-Lefèvre Disease/diagnosis"[Mesh]
894	_t		"Papillon-Lefèvre Disease/therapy" [Mesh]
919	_d	Pitt-Hopkins Syndrome	-
919	_t		-
934	_d	Porphyria	"Porphyrias/diagnosis"[Mesh]
934	_t		"Porphyrias/therapy"[Mesh]
1078	_d	Spinocerebellar Ataxia with Axonal Neuropathy	-
1078	_t		-
1110	_d	TORCH Syndrome	-
1110	_t		-
1166	_d	Ulcerative Colitis	"Colitis, Ulcerative/diagnosis"[Mesh]
1166	_t		"Colitis, Ulcerative/therapy"[Mesh]

work is to generate a uniform data format to eliminate duplicates and to mitigate data and retrieval errors (Buchkremer et al., 2019).

Intersecting Diagnosis and Therapy

The next study section comprises the generation of a text corpus from search results for further processing. To calculate the intersections for diagnosis and therapy of a disease, the list of results is transferred to a RapidMiner process called "inner join." For PubMed, we utilize the PMID. Google's and FindZebra's results are characterized by the link to the source of the results. The list created by this step contains intersecting hits only. The equation for subsequently calculating the correlation coefficient is the following:

$$Correl\left(X,Y\right) = \frac{\sum\left(x-\overline{x}\right)\left(y-\overline{y}\right)}{\sqrt{\sum\left(x-\overline{x}\right)^2 \sum\left(y-\overline{y}\right)^2}}.$$

The following applies: $\overline{x}$ and $\overline{y}$ are the mean values for all result sets, and all intersections of the search results on diagnoses and therapies of a disease.

Table 2. PubMed MeSH search queries for diagnoses and therapies of common diseases

ID	Suffix	Common Disease	Search Query (Pubmed)
CD0	_d	Ischaemic heart disease	"Myocardial Ischemia/diagnosis" [Mesh]
CD0	_t		"Myocardial Ischemia/therapy" [Mesh]
CD1	_d	Lower respiratory infections	"Respiratory Tract Infections/diagnosis"[Mesh]
CD1	_t		"Respiratory Tract Infections/therapy"[Mesh]
CD2	_d	Stroke	"Stroke/diagnosis"[Mesh]
CD2	_t		"Stroke/therapy"[Mesh]
CD3	_d	Preterm birth complications	-
CD3	_t		-
CD4	_d	Diarrhoeal diseases	"Diarrhea/diagnosis"[Mesh]
CD4	_t		"Diarrhea/therapy" [Mesh]
CD5	_d	Road injury	-
CD5	_t		-
CD6	_d	Birth asphyxia and birth trauma	"Infant, Newborn, Diseases/diagnosis" [Mesh]
CD6	_t		"Infant, Newborn, Diseases/therapy" [Mesh]
CD7	_d	Chronic obstructive pulmonary disease	"Pulmonary Disease, Chronic Obstructive/diagnosis" [Mesh]
CD7	_t		"Pulmonary Disease, Chronic Obstructive/therapy"[Mesh]
CD8	_d	HIV/AIDS	"HIV Infections/diagnosis"[Mesh]
CD8	_t		"HIV Infections/therapy"[Mesh]
CD9	_d	Congenital anomalies	"Congenital Abnormalities/diagnosis"[Mesh]
CD9	_t		"Congenital Abnormalities/therapy"[Mesh]

Word Frequencies

With the next study section, word lists are created for diagnosis and therapy, respectively, and they are transferred to word clouds. The first 100 search results are evaluated in this section. Finally, word clouds are generated to provide images related to word frequencies (Salloum et al., 2018). Since RapidMiner allows the execution of R scripts, word clouds are generated via the "wordcloud" library (Fellows, 2018; R Core Team, 2018).

Cluster Analysis

To further specify results from the quantitative analysis, the next study section classifies search results with the K-Means algorithm to generate topic clusters (Salloum et al., 2018). The cosine similarity is used to evaluate the similarity of words (Huang, 2008; Karaa et al., 2016). It is followed by the vectorizing of the texts. This step allows us to convert the text via the Tf-IDF measure (Wu et al., 2008) into a vectorized format. A measure of 3 clusters appears to be suitable for our search results. We assign individual search engine results as one class. As a result of this, it is possible to evaluate both the number of hits as well as the percentage. This step clarifies whether documents from a particular search engine dominate a cluster. In order to assess the homogeneity of the distribution of the entire data set, the mean value of the standard deviations is calculated. The calculation of the standard deviation uses the following formula:

$$\sqrt{\frac{\sum(x - \bar{x})^2}{n}}$$

Here "x" is the sample mean value of the individual percentage of search results from one search engine where "n" equals the sample size, in this case, "3".

Metadata Analysis and Preprocessing

The scientific basis of the search engines PubMed and FindZebra are well known. It is a known fact that Google search results are not exclusively derived from scientific sources. However, in contrast to the Google search in the browser, the custom API provides useful metadata, and thus, it can be applied to determine which of the results come from scientific journals. After the hits have been identified and downloaded, it is necessary to revise the data, remove unnecessary information, and correct errors, according to Buchkremer et al. (2019).

The Selection of the Databases

The MEDLINE database, which is offered via PubMed, has been one of the most important sources of medical information for many years. Lorenzetti et al. (2014) discuss, that there are many other medical databases available, such as EMBASE or the Cochrane Library, to name two of the most important. We want to focus on free databases, and in this context, PubMed appears to be the best and most relevant medical database because it is easily accessible via the web and offers many additional search tools.

Research Drawbacks and Downsides

To achieve market transparency in a highly fragmented market, it is crucial to obtain information about the fragments. Rare diseases represent a large market in their entirety, but the information about the fragments is spread over many different places. Three sources are particularly well suited to find this market information. One is FindZebra, a meta platform with contents that are focused on rare diseases. There is a well accessible medical portal, PubMed, which mainly contains scientific articles. Last but not least, there is the web itself, which can be searched using Google, for example. All three provide much information about rare diseases. Therefore, it is essential to find a way to present essential contents from each platform quickly and to compare the outputs. Natural language processing offers ways to find relevant information quickly, applying algorithms and ontologies. Furthermore, some simple visualization tools, such as word clouds, provide ways to compare results from various sources quickly. Word clouds are more suitable than tables because they provide a visual overview of a topic more quickly. They can also be created rapidly. A downside of word clouds is that some aspects can be overlooked in word clouds; however, it is not particularly relevant in this study, since the essential aspects of a disease are to be covered.

RESULTS AND DISCUSSION

The total numbers of search results, abstracts, and documents are listed in Tables 3 and 4. The quantities for some results appear to be low because limitations for the maximum search results need to be accepted. These are 10,000 hits for PubMed, only 100 for Google and 10,000 for FindZebra. A total of 44 search strings for rare diseases and 16 search strings for common diseases were examined. Thus, on average, about 6,400 documents are retrieved per search result for rare diseases. For common diseases, an average set of 14,069 documents per search is collected. Table 3 illustrates that FindZebra returns most results for rare diseases, and all hits contain documents. Only 2/3 of PubMed results have no abstracts and thus are not eligible for word clouds. Table 4 reveals that PubMed delivers more abstracts for common diseases; however, it is interesting to note that the rare-disease database FindZebra presents many results for common diseases. It may indicate that rare and common diseases are not so far apart when all perspectives (multi-omics) are considered.

Table 3. Quantitative analysis: rare diseases

Results PubMed	Abstracts PubMed	Results Google	Documents Google	Results FindZebra	Documents FindZebra
49,916	31,907	4,247	4,038	209,800	209,796
Total number of hits: 263,963					
Documents: 245,741					

Table 4. Quantitative analysis: common diseases

Results PubMed	Abstracts PubMed	Results Google	Documents Google	Results FindZebra	Documents FindZebra
153,353	129,913	1,600	1,521	93,669	93,669
Total number of hits: 248,622					
Documents: 225,103					

Word Frequencies

All word frequencies are initially listed in tables. These tables contain the numbers of documents, word occurrences, and the total number concerning the overall result. To gain immediate context transparency, word clouds for the most common 30 words are created. Frequently occurring words are displayed larger. Figure 1 visualizes ID 278_d – the diagnosis of the disease "Citrullinemia Type 1".

With this, a rough overview can be obtained without the need to read the whole text. In the case of Citrullinemia Type 1 (CTLN1) that results from a gene mutation ("gene," "mutat"), liver damages may provide a diagnostic indication. Furthermore, the ("liver") damage results from a deficit ("defici") of enzymes ("enzyme"), hitherto resulting from a disturbed urea cycle ("urea", "cycle"). Citrullinemia type I is induced by a deficiency of argininosuccinate synthetase. It can transform citrulline and aspartate into argininosuccinate (Faghfoury et al., 2011). The information provided in the clouds provides a first impres-

Figure 1. Word Clouds 278_d - from left to right: PubMed, Google und FindZebra

sion of the diagnosis market of the disease. It appears to be a genetic disease, and thus, genetic testing, as well as the investigation of the liver, will play a major role in diagnosing the disease. Liver damage appears to be the initial presentation of the disease. A molecular (genetic) analysis will be carried out in the further course of the diagnosis. The most informative diagnostic description in Figure 1 appears to be given by the PubMed cloud since argininosuccinate ("argininosuccin") is prominently presented, and a mutation is strongly displayed. It is also the only cloud that provides evidence of "neonatal" aspects. CTLN1 is typically occurring in the neonatal phase or during infancy.

Overlaps Between Different Search Engines

The following are the results of the analysis of intersections of search results from individual search engines. By looking at all search results for rare diseases (Figure 3), on average, 1,134 hits are returned per disease from PubMed, 97 from Google, and 4,768 from FindZebra. On average, only five Google hits referred to documents that are present in PubMed results. 1.5 hits from Google results are present in FindZebra results concerning rare diseases. We do not see an overlap of hits between PubMed and FindZebra. The hit lists for common diseases yielded an average of 9,585 PubMed searches, 100 (API limit) Google hits, and 5,854 FindZebra results. For us, it was a bit astounding to get that many hits with common diseases on FindZebra, because this database is mainly intended for rare diseases. Among the 100 Google results, we found, on average, only three documents from PubMed, and only 0.6 Google hits are present in FindZebra search results. Once again, there was no overlap between PubMed and FindZebra hits.

In conclusion, the following results are obtained for both rare and common diseases (see Figure 2).

Occasionally, it is required to get a result as quickly as possible. Therefore, the following Figure 3 shows the overlaps for the first 100 hits.

One conclusion of this investigation so far is that the three search portals examine almost entirely different sources. To achieve better comparability, we compare the most frequent 100 words from the hit lists (RD100 and CD100). It is performed for every search string (see Tables 1 and 2). The value for the degree of overlapping is calculated from the respective intersections of the words. To match various data sets, the overall mean value is calculated. Thus, the word frequencies present an overlap of about 61% between PubMed and Google. Here we find a 43% overlap between PubMed and FindZebra and 48%

Figure 2. Query hits for rare and common diseases

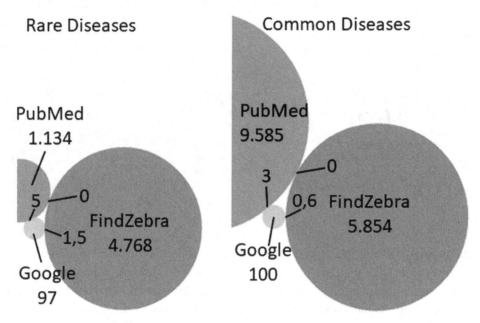

Figure 3. Query hits for rare and common diseases

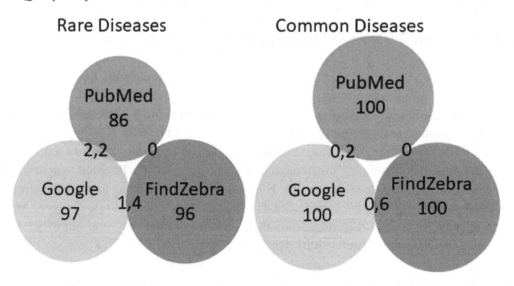

between Google and FindZebra (see Figure 4). As the chart also reveals, we observe an average overlap of about 50%. It is not significantly different if we compare the first 100 hits only. It is also interesting that the degree of overlap does not change significantly once we switch to common diseases. Hence, for a quick overview, we recommend looking at all three portals

Figure 5. Intersections Diagnosis/Therapy

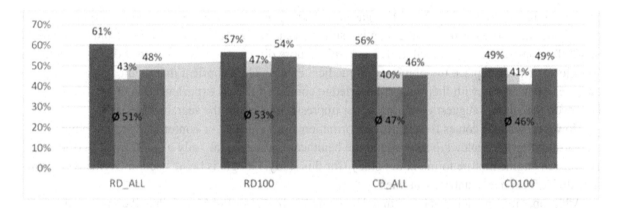

Figure 4. The average similarity of word frequencies

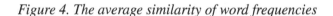

Metadata Analyses

Using the metadata returned via the Google Custom API, the amounts of ISSNs for scientific articles indicate that 9% - 47% of Google results on rare diseases come from scientific sources. If the resulting articles are taken as a set, 21% - 71% can be found in the PubMed database, depending on the disease in question. The search results for common diseases include only 8% up to 33% of contents from scientific journals. 37% up to 77% of the articles can also be found in the PubMed database. Thus, whoever wants to focus on scientific journals is better off with PubMed. However, even PubMed does not deliver a complete picture of the available scientific articles.

Overlaps Between Diagnosis and Therapy

To get more transparency in the market, it is essential to look for criteria that differentiate it. Therapeutics and diagnostics markets have been separated in the healthcare market for decades, and some large healthcare corporations focus on one of each. Market forecasts are often prepared exclusively for diagnostics (Miller et al., 2011). Even in hospitals, diagnosis and therapy are physically separated from each other and are often managed by different stakeholders. It is highly evident in large markets. Udelson and Stevenson, for example, explain differences between diagnosis and therapy within the heart failure market (Udelson & Stevenson, 2016).

Our results indicate that rare disease search results vary between therapy and diagnosis as well. Applying natural language processing, we find the following overlaps between hits (see Figure 5): Hits for rare diseases (RD_ALL) from the PubMed database reveal an overlap by an average of 22%. With Google, we observe an overlap of 27% and FindZebra returns results where diagnosis and therapy overlap on average by 46%. In the search results for common diseases (CD_ALL), PubMed hits overlap on average by 25%, Google by 17%, and FindZebra by an astounding 69%. Considering the first 100 hits only, the average values for PubMed and Google are almost identical; however, FindZebra reveals an overlap of about 70% for common diseases. Figure 5 depicts a summary of the results:

SUMMARY AND DISCUSSION

Studies by Krause et al. (2011) and Falagas et al. (2009) reveal that medical students and doctors can make better diagnoses using Google search results and studies by Tang and Ng (2006) and Lombardi et al. (2009) confirm it. Jhaveri et al. (2013) provide a more differentiated view as they discuss whether a Google search can replace the opinion of a medical expert. They confirm that medical specialists can achieve better results with their expert knowledge compared to less experienced doctors with Google. However, the authors suggest obtaining a first impression by using the search engine.

However, when it comes to scientific information from journals or conference papers, which is indispensable for the healthcare market and the healthcare professional, only a small fraction of the first 100 search engine hits are found in our study (for this study, Google is being used in Germany – results may differ from one country to another).

Additional information can be obtained by using FindZebra or PubMed. When it comes to diagnosis and therapy, PubMed appears the most comprehensive source of information. It is because MeSH codes for treatment and diagnosis may be used. PubMed delivers 25% of the same results on average for all search queries. The Google results overlap 27% for rare diseases and only 17% for frequent diseases. Only the FindZebra search engine seems to differ slightly, as the average overlap here is 59%. Since the limit of the interface of 10,000 documents is partially fully exhausted in the searches, overlaps are apparent, since the database FindZebra contains only about 36,000 articles in total.

Further investigations support this hypothesis since the intersections become more significant the more resulting hits are returned for a search. However, the analyses reveal that in rare disease searches, the overlaps increase to an average of 70% up to 95%. However, frequent disease searches show a slightly reduced average overlap of 50%. In summary, the search results for diagnosis and therapy indicate that PubMed and Google overlap by about a quarter. FindZebra, on the other hand, hardly differentiates between the results and often returns the same documents.

Since the search engines examined show hardly any overlaps between their search results, the question arises as to how far the contents of the resulting documents and websites differ. Word frequencies or word clouds help to get quick overviews of terms that are mentioned most frequently. Scientific articles on common diseases are less represented in search results of the search engine Google compared to those on rare diseases. It is striking that FindZebra returns on average about 1000 hits by searching for common diseases. It can be concluded that many irrelevant documents are returned as search results, mainly because the FindZebra database contains only about 36,000 documents in total.

FUTURE RESEARCH DIRECTIONS

Our research suggests that for rare diseases, the PubMed medical database (which comprises the MED-LINE database) is the tool of choice for a quick and up-to-date overview of the market. Nevertheless, the FindZebra database provides crucial additional information; unfortunately, it is not further developed. Nevertheless, also search engines like Google provide unique information. Thus, for rare diseases, a platform should be developed that integrates the three most essential portals with improved search and visualization possibilities. Our approach includes not only phenotype and genotype information but also multi-omics data because the PubMed database comprises valuable metadata. We are working on integrating this information with NLP and learning. Thus, this may provide additional valuable market information for patients, physicians, and other stakeholders.

CONCLUSION

Rare disease research requires expertise, but this paper shows that natural language processing and word clouds can be used to quickly gain an overview of rare diseases and achieve market transparency.

This work also responds to the trend that more and more people are using Internet search engines to diagnose diseases, most of them using search engines such as Google, Bing, or Yahoo. Since they often return several thousand search results, one person cannot read them all in detail. Therefore, using natural language processing appears to be an excellent alternative to get a quick overview of the most important parameters related to a rare disease.

This work, therefore, examines whether it makes sense to use Internet search engines such as Google to diagnose and search for therapeutic approaches to rare diseases. Natural language processing techniques are used to analyze search results from Google and medical databases. The study's subject is a list of 30 rare diseases from the National Organization for Rare Disorders (NORD, 2019) and the ten most common diseases of a study by the World Health Organization (Murray and Lopez, 2013).

The procedure is based on the STIRL model developed by Buchkremer et al. (2019), an approach to obtain a comprehensive overview of new scientific findings.

Related work highlights that using Google to diagnose rare diseases is useful and can lead to good results but does not replace seeking the opinion of an expert. Similarly, the use of Google as a diagnostic tool has an impact on the results. Google is optimized for keyword searches and performs worse when searching for large queries copied from medical case files.

For the comparison of search results from Google, the medical databases PubMed, and the search engine for rare diseases, FindZebra, in total, 512,585 search results with documents, abstracts, and websites on 60 different search terms in the scope of 180 search queries are analyzed. The study reveals that the search results for diagnosis and therapy in PubMed and Google overlap by about a quarter, but that FindZebra hardly differentiates between the results and often returns the same documents.

The differences between rare and common diseases are particularly evident in the low overlaps in diagnosis and therapy in the FindZebra search engine, the considerably larger intersections between the search engines, and a higher proportion of specialist articles in the Google results. Furthermore, as described above, rare diseases do not show a generalized distribution of search results in cluster analyses.

In order to quickly obtain comprehensive information on the rare diseases' healthcare market, we summarize the following:

Google is very well suitable for getting a quick overview of rare diseases and the healthcare market. However, it is far from complete and not very scientific.

FindZebra is also well qualified to get a quick overview of rare diseases, but the results are not very comprehensive and not up-to-date.

PubMed seems to be the source of choice, which is true not only for rare but also for common diseases. An analysis using natural language processing and text clouds delivers decisive information very quickly. PubMed has a clear advantage, especially when it comes to differentiating between diagnosis and therapy. The database is also updated daily.

Thus, to get an overview of a rare disease market, it is recommended to consult the scientific papers revealed by PubMed. For a more comprehensive view, all three portals should be consulted. It is strongly recommended to apply natural language processing algorithms offered by PubMed and MeSH in addition to fast text clouds and cluster analyses. For this purpose, training of healthcare market professionals is crucial.

REFERENCES

Abel, E. L. (2018). Syphilis: The History of an Eponym. *Names*, *66*(2), 96–102. doi:10.1080/0027773 8.2017.1415522

Almatarneh, S., & Gamallo, P. (2018). A lexicon based method to search for extreme opinions. *PLoS One*, *13*(5), 1–19. doi:10.1371/journal.pone.0197816 PMID:29799867

Brasil, S., Pascoal, C., Francisco, R., Ferreira, V. D. R., Videira, P. A., & Valadão, G. (2019). Artificial intelligence (AI) in rare diseases: Is the future brighter? *Genes*, *10*(12), 978. doi:10.3390/genes10120978 PMID:31783696

Buchkremer, R., Demund, A., Ebener, S., Gampfer, F., Jagering, D., Jurgens, A., Klenke, S., Krimpmann, D., Schmank, J., Spiekermann, M., Wahlers, M., & Wiepke, M. (2019). The Application of Artificial Intelligence Technologies as a Substitute for Reading and to Support and Enhance the Authoring of Scientific Review Articles. *IEEE Access: Practical Innovations, Open Solutions*, *7*(c), 65263–65276. doi:10.1109/ACCESS.2019.2917719

Christen, M., Boulding, W., & Staelin, R. (2009). Optimal market intelligence strategy when management attention is scarce. *Management Science*, *55*(4), 526–538. doi:10.1287/mnsc.1080.0988

Citron, D. T., & Ginsparg, P. (2015). Patterns of text reuse in a scientific corpus. *Proceedings of the National Academy of Sciences of the United States of America*, *112*(1), 25–30. doi:10.1073/pnas.1415135111 PMID:25489072

Cooper, M. C., Lambert, D. M., & Pagh, J. D. (1997). Supply Chain Management: More Than a New Name for Logistics. *International Journal of Logistics Management*, *8*(1), 1–14. doi:10.1108/09574099710805556

Dragusin, R., Petcu, P., Lioma, C., Larsen, B., Jørgensen, H., & Winther, O. (2011). Rare Disease Diagnosis as an Information Retrieval Task. In C. F. Amati G. (Ed.), Advances in Information Retrieval Theory. ICTIR 2011; Lecture Notes in Computer Science, vol 6931 (pp. 356–359). Springer Berlin Heidelberg. doi:10.1007/978-3-642-23318-0_38

Dragusin, R., Petcu, P., Lioma, C., Larsen, B., Jørgensen, H. L., Cox, I. J., Hansen, L. K., Ingwersen, P., & Winther, O. (2013). FindZebra: A search engine for rare diseases. *International Journal of Medical Informatics, 82*(6), 528–538. doi:10.1016/j.ijmedinf.2013.01.005 PMID:23462700

Faghfoury, H., Baruteau, J., Ogier de Baulny, H., Häberle, J., & Schulze, A. (2011). Transient fulminant liver failure as an initial presentation in citrullinemia type I. *Molecular Genetics and Metabolism, 102*(4), 413–417. doi:10.1016/j.ymgme.2010.12.007 PMID:21227727

Falagas, M. E., Ntziora, F., Makris, G. C., Malietzis, G. A., & Rafailidis, P. I. (2009). Do PubMed and Google searches help medical students and young doctors reach the correct diagnosis? A pilot study. *European Journal of Internal Medicine, 20*(8), 788–790. doi:10.1016/j.ejim.2009.07.014 PMID:19892310

Heimerl, F., Lohmann, S., Lange, S., & Ertl, T. (2014). Word cloud explorer: Text analytics based on word clouds. *Proceedings of the Annual Hawaii International Conference on System Sciences*, 1833–1842. 10.1109/HICSS.2014.231

Ian Fellows. (2018). *wordcloud: Word Clouds. R package version 2.6.* https://CRAN.R-project.org/package=wordcloud

Jhaveri, K. D., Schrier, P. B., & Mattana, J. (2013). Paging Doctor Google! Heuristics vs. technology. *F1000 Research, 2*, 1–15. doi:10.12688/f1000research.2-90.v1 PMID:24627777

Kang, Q., Hu, J., Yang, N., He, J., Yang, Y., Tang, M., & Jin, C. (2019). Marketing of drugs for rare diseases is speeding up in China: Looking at the example of drugs for mucopolysaccharidosis. *Intractable & Rare Diseases Research, 8*(3), 165–171. doi:10.5582/irdr.2019.01090 PMID:31523593

Kirca, A. H., Jayachandran, S., & Bearden, W. O. (2005). Market orientation: A meta-analytic review and assessment of its antecedents and impact on performance. *Journal of Marketing, 69*(2), 24–41. doi:10.1509/jmkg.69.2.24.60761

Krause, R., Moscati, R., Halpern, S., Schwartz, D., & Abbas, J. (2011). Can Emergency Medicine Residents Reliably Use the Internet to Answer Clinical Questions? *The Western Journal of Emergency Medicine, 12*(4), 442–447. doi:10.5811/westjem.2010.9.1895 PMID:22224135

Lombardi, C., Griffiths, E., McLeod, B., Caviglia, A., & Penagos, M. (2009). Search engine as a diagnostic tool in difficult immunological and allergologic cases: Is Google useful? *Internal Medicine Journal, 39*(7), 459–464. doi:10.1111/j.1445-5994.2008.01875.x PMID:19664156

Lorenzetti, D. L., Topfer, L. A., Dennett, L., & Clement, F. (2014). Value of databases other than medline for rapid health technology assessments. *International Journal of Technology Assessment in Health Care, 30*(2), 173–178. doi:10.1017/S0266462314000166 PMID:24774535

McKeown, K., Daume, H. III, Chaturvedi, S., Paparrizos, J., Thadani, K., Barrio, P., Biran, O., Bothe, S., Collins, M., Fleischmann, K. R., Gravano, L., Jha, R., King, B., McInerney, K., Moon, T., Neelakantan, A., O'Seaghdha, D., Radev, D., Templeton, C., & Teufel, S. (2016). Predicting the impact of scientific concepts using full-text features. *Journal of the Association for Information Science and Technology, 67*(11), 2684–2696. doi:10.1002/asi.23612

Miller, I., Ashton-Chess, J., Spolders, H., Fert, V., Ferrara, J., Kroll, W., Askaa, J., Larcier, P., Terry, P. F., Bruinvels, A., & Huriez, A. (2011). Market access challenges in the EU for high medical value diagnostic tests. *Personalized Medicine*, *8*(2), 137–148. doi:10.2217/pme.11.2 PMID:29783414

Minsky, M. (1961). Steps Toward Artificial Intelligence. *Proceedings of the IRE.*

Murray, C. J. L., & Lopez, A. D. (2013). Measuring the Global Burden of Disease. *The New England Journal of Medicine*, *369*(5), 448–457. doi:10.1056/NEJMra1201534 PMID:23902484

Narver, J. C., & Slater, S. F. (1990). The Effect of a Market Orientation on Business Profitability. *Journal of Marketing*, *54*(4), 20–35. doi:10.1177/002224299005400403

NORD. (2019). https://rarediseases.org/for-patients-and-families/information-resources/rare-disease-information/rare-disease-list/

R Core Team. (2018). *R: A language and environment for statistical computing*. R Foundation for Statistical Computing. https://www.R-project.org/

Sanderson, M., & Croft, W. B. (2012). The history of information retrieval research. *Proceedings of the IEEE, 100*, 1444–1451.

Schenkel, R., Broschart, A., Hwang, S., Theobald, M., & Weikum, G. (2007). Efficient Text Proximity Search. *Spire*, 287–299.

Sebastiani, F. (2002). Machine learning in automated text categorization. *ACM Computing Surveys*, *34*(1), 1–47. doi:10.1145/505282.505283

Spasic, I., Ananiadou, S., McNaught, J., & Kumar, A. (2005). Text mining and ontologies in biomedicine: Making sense of raw text. *Briefings in Bioinformatics*, *6*(3), 239–251. doi:10.1093/bib/6.3.239 PMID:16212772

Srinivasan, P. (2004). Text Mining: Generating Hypotheses from MEDLINE. *Journal of the American Society for Information Science and Technology*, *55*(5), 396–413. doi:10.1002/asi.10389

Svenstrup, D., Jørgensen, H. L., & Winther, O. (2015). Rare disease diagnosis: A review of web search, social media and large-scale data-mining approaches. *Rare Diseases*, *3*(1), e1083145. doi:10.1080/21675511.2015.1083145 PMID:26442199

Tang, H., & Ng, J. H. K. (2006). Googling for a diagnosis - Use of Google as a diagnostic aid: Internet based study. *British Medical Journal*, *333*(7579), 1143–1145. doi:10.1136/bmj.39003.640567.AE PMID:17098763

Udelson, J. E., & Stevenson, L. W. (2016). The future of heart failure diagnosis, therapy, and management. *Circulation*, *133*(25), 2671–2686. doi:10.1161/CIRCULATIONAHA.116.023518 PMID:27324362

Verzulli, R., Fiorentini, G., Lippi Bruni, M., & Ugolini, C. (2017). Price Changes in Regulated Healthcare Markets: Do Public Hospitals Respond and How? *Health Economics (United Kingdom)*, *26*(11), 1429–1446. doi:10.1002/hec.3435 PMID:27785849

Walewski, J. L., Donovan, D., & Nori, M. (2019). How many zebras are there, and where are they hiding in medical literature? A literature review of publications on rare diseases. *Expert Opinion on Orphan Drugs*, *7*(11), 513–519. doi:10.1080/21678707.2019.1684260

ADDITIONAL READING

Goeuriot, L., Jones, G. J. F., Kelly, L., Müller, H., & Zobel, J. (2016). Medical information retrieval: Introduction to the special issue. *Information Retrieval Journal*, *19*(1–2), 1–5. doi:10.100710791-015-9277-8

Jameel, S., Lam, W., & Bing, L. (2015). Supervised topic models with word order structure for document classification and retrieval learning. *Information Retrieval Journal*, *18*(4), 283–330. doi:10.100710791-015-9254-2

Kang, Q., Hu, J., Yang, N., He, J., Yang, Y., Tang, M., & Jin, C. (2019). Marketing of drugs for rare diseases is speeding up in China: Looking at the example of drugs for mucopolysaccharidosis. *Intractable & Rare Diseases Research*, *8*(3), 165–171. doi:10.5582/irdr.2019.01090 PMID:31523593

Köhler, S., Doelken, S. C., Mungall, C. J., Bauer, S., Firth, H. V., Bailleul-Forestier, I., Black, G. C. M., Brown, D. L., Brudno, M., Campbell, J., FitzPatrick, D. R., Eppig, J. T., Jackson, A. P., Freson, K., Girdea, M., Helbig, I., Hurst, J. A., Jähn, J., Jackson, L. G., ... Robinson, P. N. (2014). The Human Phenotype Ontology project: Linking molecular biology and disease through phenotype data. *Nucleic Acids Research*, *42*(D1), D966–D974. doi:10.1093/nar/gkt1026 PMID:24217912

Malerba, F., & Orsenigo, L. (2015). The evolution of the pharmaceutical industry. *Business History*, *57*(5), 664–687. doi:10.1080/00076791.2014.975119

Sardana, D., Zhu, C., Zhang, M., Gudivada, R. C., Yang, L., & Jegga, A. G. (2011). Drug repositioning for orphan diseases. *Briefings in Bioinformatics*, *12*(4), 346–356. doi:10.1093/bib/bbr021 PMID:21504985

Schatz, B. R. (1997). Information Retrieval in Digital Libraries: Bringing Search to the Net. *Science*, *275*(5298), 327–334. doi:10.1126cience.275.5298.327 PMID:8994022

Vanopstal, K., Buysschaert, J., Laureys, G., & Vander Stichele, R. (2013). Lost in PubMed. Factors influencing the success of medical information retrieval. *Expert Systems with Applications*, *40*(10), 4106–4114. doi:10.1016/j.eswa.2013.01.036

Wellman-Labadie, O., & Zhou, Y. (2010). The US Orphan Drug Act: Rare disease research stimulator or commercial opportunity? *Health Policy (Amsterdam)*, *95*(2–3), 216–228. doi:10.1016/j.healthpol.2009.12.001 PMID:20036435

Wise, A. L., Manolio, T. A., Mensah, G. A., Peterson, J. F., Roden, D. M., Tamburro, C., Williams, M. S., & Green, E. D. (2019). Genomic medicine for undiagnosed diseases. *Lancet*, *394*(10197), 533–540. doi:10.1016/S0140-6736(19)31274-7 PMID:31395441

KEY TERMS AND DEFINITIONS

Information Retrieval: A set of procedures, which mainly deals with the search in text files. The procedures are often described in the context of library work.

Market Orientation: To achieve market orientation, it is essential to know the elements of the market and their patterns of movement. The more is known about a market, the better is the resulting orientation.

Multi-Omics/Systems Medicine: An approach that considers diseases not only as a phenotypic (organic) phenomenon. It also takes into account, for example, bacteria and viruses (microbiome), chemical reactions (metabolomics), genes (genomics), and even the (social) environment.

Orphan Drug Act: The Act stands for a law legislated in the U.S.A. in 1983 to support R&D of medications for rare diseases. Reduced sales expectations for drugs due to low incidences can be partly compensated by government support.

Orphan/Rare Disease: An orphan or rare disease is affecting only very few people compared to the overall population.

PubMed/Medline: "Medline" denotes a medical database offered through the "PubMed" portal by the U.S. National Library of Medicine. To search for further medical information, it is recommended to use the databases "Embase" and "Chemical Abstracts."

Taxonomy/Ontology: A comprehensive semantic search in texts requires the classification of terms in a subject-specific context. This approach is sometimes also called lexicon-based. The purest form of a lexicon in this respect is the thesaurus. If these terms are arranged in a hierarchical structure, it is often called taxonomy, and if additional relations are given, ontology. MeSH (medical subject headings) stands for a well-known and comprehensive medical taxonomy.

Word Cloud: It represents a plotted distribution of the number of words in a given text. Words that occur more frequently appear more significant in the visualization.

ENDNOTES

[1]   https://www.webmd.com/
[2]   https://www.ncbi.nlm.nih.gov/pubmed/
[3]   https://www.who.int/healthinfo/global_burden_disease/estimates/en/index1.html
[4]   https://rapidminer.com/

Chapter 11
Quality Assurance in Computer–Assisted Translation in Business Environments

Sanja Seljan

https://orcid.org/0000-0001-9048-419X

Faculty of Humanities and Social Sciences, University of Zagreb, Croatia

Nikolina Škof Erdelja

Ciklopea, Croatia

Vlasta Kučiš

Faculty of Arts, University of Maribor, Slovenia

Ivan Dunđer

Faculty of Humanities and Social Sciences, University of Zagreb, Croatia

Mirjana Pejić Bach

Faculty of Economics and Business, University of Zagreb, Croatia

ABSTRACT

Increased use of computer-assisted translation (CAT) technology in business settings with augmented amounts of tasks, collaborative work, and short deadlines give rise to errors and the need for quality assurance (QA). The research has three operational aims: 1) methodological framework for QA analysis, 2) comparative evaluation of four QA tools, 3) to justify introduction of QA into CAT process. The research includes building of translation memory, terminology extraction, and creation of terminology base. Error categorization is conducted by multidimensional quality (MQM) framework. The level of mistake is calculated considering detected, false, and not detected errors. Weights are assigned to errors (minor, major, or critical), penalties are calculated, and quality estimation for translation memory is given. Results show that process is prone to errors due to differences in error detection, harmonization, and error counting. Data analysis of detected errors leads to further data-driven decisions related to the quality of output results and improved efficacy of translation business process.

DOI: 10.4018/978-1-7998-4240-8.ch011

INTRODUCTION

Use of computer-assisted translation (CAT) and machine translation technology is increasingly used in various business environments, such as in multilingual companies, societies, in industry, entertainment, and educational institutions or international events. Language service providers (LSPs) that offer translation services face competitive markets and digital transformation.

Digital transformation of the translation process has introduced various changes related to the whole business translation process, such as the use of CAT and machine translation technology, new jobs, task distribution, collaborative work, creating and sharing of digital resources and education of employees. In this competitive business environment, the use of CAT technology, used separately or integrated with machine translation, has gained considerable importance.

An increasing amount of work, short deadlines and collaboration in the same project give rise to an augmented number of errors in the translation process using CAT technology. Human verification of errors would be an extremely tedious, time-consuming and subjective task, inclined to errors. For this reason, the use of quality assurance (QA) tools helps to detect errors and possibly enable the categorization and counting of errors, can considerably contribute to the analysis of errors. Data analysis of error types could lead to further relevant decisions related to the translation business process, such as the building of language resources (e.g. lists of forbidden or preferred terms or list of abbreviations for translation), check of style formats depending on the language (e.g. number, currency and time formats), setup of QA tool profiles and creation of regular expressions detecting specific language errors, but also to the reorganization of business processes (e.g. introducing new jobs, such as language engineer and project manager, redistribution of tasks or segmentation of complex tasks).

In a business environment, data analysis has become an indispensable segment of any business process related to quality issues. This research can be used to improve the quality of the output product (here translation), identify weak points, and reorganize the business translation process. Data analysis of errors obtained by QA tools can serve to improve the efficiency of the CAT process and the quality of its output.

QA tools enable not only verification of target text, but also verification of the translation memories consisting of pairs of source and target segments, as well as compliance with client demands. Some QA tools can provide an additional asset, enabling language setup, control of content, control of layout, control of orthography and cultural formatting differences or check of terminology compliance with end-user demands. QA tools can provide significant help, but on the other hand, they differ regarding their setup characteristics, types of detected errors, ways of counting errors and integration possibilities. For this reason, the main goal of this research is to present the role of QA tools in error analysis, which can serve as a source for data analysis of errors performed in the CAT process and lead to future decisions. Existing researches of QA in CAT technology are mainly oriented to production level, concentrating on speed, analysis of error types, mistranslations, or post-editing, while researches related to QA of translation memory including source and target segments are scarce. As a translation memory represents the foundation for building high-quality resources used in CAT and machine translation technology, QA of translation memories directly affects the quality of the translated text.

The general aim of this research is to present the role of QA tools and data analysis of errors performed in the CAT process. The paper has three aims: i) to present a methodological framework for quality estimation of the translation memory which represents the basis for CAT technology ii) to perform a comparative evaluation of four QA tools with the aim of the harmonization of error types iii) to justify the introduction of QA tools into the digitally transformed process of translation, supported by CAT technology.

The research methodology consists of phases in a way that each activity gives output result, which serves as an input for the following phase. After the selection of four QA tools, the first phase includes the building of the translation memory, through the sentence alignment of the parallel English-Croatian text. In the second phase, the terminology base serves as a digital resource in the CAT process. This terminology base is created through the automatic terminology extraction process, followed by terminology selection. The final terminology base consisting of 100 terms serves as a control mechanism for the QA process. The third phase consists of the error categorization in order to perform the harmonization of different types of errors among the four selected QA tools. For the error categorization, the multidimensional quality (MQM) framework. The fourth phase consists of calculation of the level of mistake, taking into account detected, false and not detected errors - the smaller the level of mistake, the better the quality. In the next phase, error grouping is performed, for the criteria of fluency and adequacy. For each error type, weights are assigned (minor, major or critical), and penalties for criteria of adequacy and fluency calculated. The final step gives the quality estimation of the translation memory.

The paper organization is as follows: after the introduction part follows the section on related work. The research section presents the research methodology, tools and the process, including sentence alignment, creation of digital resources, the error categorization, assignment of error weights and the level of mistake analysis. Then results for each QA tool are given. The final section gives solutions and recommendations related to QA as an essential step of error analysis in the CAT process, affecting the quality of output results and the improved efficacy of the translation business process. At the end, suggestions for future research and a conclusion are given.

RELATED WORK

Quality Aspects

The aspect of quality in the translation had numerous definitions (Lommel et al., 2013; Czopik, 2014). In the narrow traditional sense, the quality was derived from literary translations, assuming perfect quality and style, being oriented to target text concerning the source text. With software development and localization, the quality was perceived more in the business environment, through identification and quantification of errors. With the development of machine translation tools and applications, the aspect of quality evolved and introduced the idea of "good enough" and "usable." For evaluation of machine translation, both human and automatic metrics are used, aiming to evaluate the quality of machine-translated texts. Today, data-driven decisions related to the quality are based on data analysis and make part of the whole Quality Management System (QMS).

Stejskal (2006) indicated that QA in the translation process traditionally included the three Ps: provider, process, and product. Chiocchetti et al. (2017) stated that QA was mainly used for the analysis of workflow, product or staff, processes, or people as the key elements. Seljan (2018a) identified several levels of the QA process, as part of the quality management system (QMS): workflow level (with different activities involved), production level (the use of QA tools), staff level (team experts) and users' aspects in a collaborative environment, software level and the output level.

The use of CAT technology can increase the number of errors due to large projects, collaborative work of translators, several language pairs, creating and sharing of new resources and short deadlines. Humans can perform QA, but this method is highly inconsistent, subjective, time-consuming, and prone to errors, differing considering evaluators, tools and methodology. For this reason, the use of QA tools that would perform consistently, would present great help. According to Dynamic Quality Framework Report by Meer and Görög (2015), the translation quality can be performed by different types of experts, experiencing various challenges (lack of knowledge, choosing an adequate metric, or lack of transparent evaluation criteria), which was one more reason for the standardization. According to Austermühl (2007) and Snell-Hornby (2006), various key drivers have an impact on the process of computer-assisted translation, including expectations in terms of quality, time and consistency, where quality has become a corporate issue. Muzii (2006) pointed out that the concept of quality was a relative concept that could take into account a set of expectations and users' requirements.

Quality Evaluation in CAT Technology

Existing researches on QA in the CAT process are mainly oriented to productivity and speed, to fuzzy matching techniques, to post-editing time or effort. Researches related to quality estimation through QA are mainly oriented to quality evaluation of the target text, while errors in the source text remain undetected.

Researches of CAT technology mainly examined productivity (Brkić et al., 2009; Federico et al., 2012) measured through speed and post-editing effort. Yamada (2011) researched the impact of translation memory in different styles (free and literal) to the translator's productivity. Zhang (2016) explored the influence of CAT software on the efficiency of technical translation through speed, quality, the possibility of mistranslation, term consistency and style. Kučiš and Seljan (2014) explored whether CAT technology and resources contributed to the quality and consistency of translation through analysis at several levels: lexical errors, spelling and punctuation, and syntactic errors. Results of t-tests showed statistically significant differences at p<0.002 confirming that the use of computer-assisted translation tools and resources, such as bilingual corpora, multilingual terminology bases, improved the quality of translation at the lexical, orthographic and also syntactic and stylistic levels. Gural and Chemezov (2014) investigated the efficiency of QA tools by counting the number of errors for five QA tools.

There were a few research types on QA analysis, such as in Makoushina (2007), who investigated eight translation QA tools from the practitioners' viewpoint and working environment or by Makoushina & Kockaert (2008) who classified QA tasks. Bogaert (2008) explored how terminology management affected translation and QA of translation. Kockaert et al. (2008) highlighted the need for effective translation where QA tools could guarantee consistency, transparency and impartiality at all levels, including punctuation, terminology, language register, and style. Seljan and Katalinić (2017) pointed out the importance of QA in a localization process, paying attention to tools and resources, processes, project management, and quality assessment, achieved through several methods and storage structures. Vázquez et al. (2013) investigated the post-editing effort from a statistical machine translation system and the translation memory, considering the amount of time, keystroke movements, and the resulting quality of translations.

Quality Evaluation in Machine Translation

Machine translation technology has become widely accessible, but the output quality was not always satisfactory, especially for less-resourced languages. Machine translation output can be used for a range of purposes, such as quick access to necessary information, for browsing or cross-lingual information retrieval, for individual use or in a business setting. Quality evaluation in machine translation generally falls into two main groups: human evaluation and automatic evaluation. Human evaluation is considered the "gold standard," but it is a long-term, subjective and laborious task. The most frequent criteria for the human evaluation of machine translation are adequacy and fluency, introduced by the Linguistic Data Consortium (2005). Adequacy denotes how well a target translation is translated in terms of meaning, while fluency denotes the quality in terms of style. Adequacy represents the degree to which the translation communicates information present in the original text and how much it preserves the meaning, whereas fluency refers to the degree to which the translation is well-formed, i.e. fluent according to the linguistic standards of the target language.

On the other hand, automatic metrics are low-cost, quick and consistent (always giving the same results for repeated usage), but also specific to machine translation system properties, as described in Koehn (2010). The main principle for the automatic metrics is the correlation with human evaluation. Various automatic metrics perform the quality evaluation in a fast and consistent manner, such as BiLingual Evaluation Understudy (BLEU) as in (Papineni et al., 2002; Coughlin, 2003), NIST by Doddington (2002), METEOR by Denkowski and Lavie (2011), GTM (F-measure), Word Error Rate (WER), Position-independent Error Rate (PER), Translation Edit Rate (TER), etc. The metrics differ in the way they measure similarity, while PER, TER and WER are distance error metrics. However, a hypothesis translation that is closer to a reference translation is considered better by all of the metrics.

Researches on the use of machine translation in business cases (Aiken & Ghosh, 2009) explored the use of machine translation in multilingual business meetings linked to the Google Translate service for instant messaging. Seljan and Dunđer (2014) researched the use of combined automatic speech recognition and machine translation in the domain of business correspondence. The research included results of the human evaluation and automatic metrics (WER and PER). In the research presented by Dunđer et al. (2020) the authors conducted an automatic evaluation of machine-translated Croatian-German and German-Croatian datasets, using BLEU, METEOR, RIBES and CharacTER metrics to evaluate machine translation at the corpus level for two online tools, showing deficiencies concerning dataset type and size and domain coverage.

Another aspect of measuring machine translation output is human post-editing time, productivity or human ranking of machine translation systems (e.g. by ordering of machine translation outputs by their quality). Machine translation system ranking seems to be an easier task to perform since it does not require specific skills (Zampieri & Vela, 2014; Guerberof, 2009). Brkić et al. (2011a) conducted machine translation system ranking for four tools, performed by automatic evaluation metrics (BLEU, NIST, F-measure) which were then correlated with human evaluation according to the criteria of fluency and adequacy, for two opposite language directions. Results showed that all metrics, as well as human evaluators, almost completely agreed on system ranking.

Maney et al. (2012) measured how various translation variables, such as a deleted verb, adjective, noun, pronoun, modified preposition or specific word order, affected the comprehension of machine-translated text. Some methods measured the effort needed to fix machine translation output and transformed it into the linguistically correct output. One of the metrics is WER, based on the Levenshtein distance (Levenshtein, 1966), counting a minimum number of insertions, deletions, and substitutions needed to convert the generated sentence (hypothesis) into the reference sentence. Another variant is the HTER (Human-targeted Translation Edit Rate) metric (Snover et al., 2006) which estimates translation post-editing rate at the sentence level (Specia & Farzindar, 2010), i.e. the fewest modifications (edits) required so that the machine translation system output becomes relatively fluent.

Digital Transformation and Datafication

Industry 4.0 has introduced changes in the business process of translation. LSPs (language service providers) perform more than just translation. They also perform desktop publishing (DTP), project management, the internationalization (I18n), the localization (L10n) of applications, globalization (G11n), transcreation in multilingual projects, marketing, the software globalization, website translation, and the localization or project management, using technologies of machine translation and CAT technology. The quality management system elaborates on the translation quality, as in EU institutions and bodies, in the Directorate-General for Translation (DGT) of the European Commission (Svoboda et al., 2017; Hansson, 2003). The European Commission – Directorate-General for Translation (2009) in the Programme for Quality Management in Translation points out the need for a quality assurance approach, which takes into account the various challenges and constraints.

Digital transformation in LSPs includes changes to task and distribution, process approach, education of employees and their engagement, data-based decision-making, customer focus, continuous improvement and innovations, and value-chain management. For this reason, the translation process is going through the reengineering process, introducing new tasks, types and distribution of jobs (language engineers, computational linguists, data analysts, project managers, and researchers), education and engagement of employees, data-driven decisions, and business process reorganization. Results in the study (Seljan, 2018b) showed that in micro and small translation companies, the lowest attention was given to data-based decision making, followed by leadership, systematic management and continuous improvement. Results showed the need for adaptation regarding the business organization, additional knowledge and types of jobs (language engineer, localization expert, data analyst, and PR manager).

Quality assurance is closely related to data-based decision making. Data is a valuable source of information for decisions related to translation business process reorganization (e.g. introduction of new types of jobs, separation of complex tasks, process changes, more time for specific tasks). Data obtained by QA can give insight into specific weak points of the translation process using CAT tools. Therefore, errors detected by QA can represent valuable data for further business decisions.

Quality assurance (QA) is often associated with the concept of quality control, as part of the quality management process.

Quality control represents the essential step of the quality management process (Seljan 2018a, 2018b), usually performed at the end of the process, in order to detect committed errors. Quality control is mainly product-oriented and conducted after the completed process.

On the other side, quality assurance (QA) is mainly performed before the beginning and during the process (Czopik, 2014; Seljan, 2018b), in order to prevent errors and to achieve the desired quality. QA might include various activities (e.g., planning, rules, procedures, templates for QA) useful for future similar types of projects.

Further steps, such as quality verification and validation, from developer and customer points of view, include various activities to check whether requirements are satisfied and to evaluate the needs of customers in order to provide constant feedback.

RESEARCH

The research on quality assurance in the CAT process included the English-Croatian language pair in the business correspondence domain. Figure 1 presented the methodology used in the research process through actions and results.

After the selection of QA tools and tool profiling, the following phase consisted of building the translation memory. Existing translations (English-Croatian texts) were used for the process of sentence alignment, enabling the building of translation memory (Seljan et al., 2007), revision, updating and use (Seljan & Pavuna, 2006). High-quality alignment represents the primary condition for further use of CAT tools (Brkić et al., 2011b), usually measured by precision, recall, and f-measure (Seljan et al., 2008; Seljan et al., 2010).

The created translation memory was a source for the further process of bilingual terminology extraction. After the automatic terminology extraction, 100 terms were selected and used to create the terminology base. This terminology base served as the control mechanism for checking compliant terminology.

The next phase included the error categorization since different tools considered different types of errors. The multidimensional quality metric (MQM) served as the framework for the error categorization. Each error type received a specific weight (minor, major or critical), and each error affected the criteria of fluency or the criteria of adequacy. Then penalties were calculated for both criteria of fluency and adequacy. In the next phase, the level of mistake took into account detected, false and not detected errors. The final result was the quality estimation of the translation memory quality. The second part of the research gave descriptive and non-parametric statistics (Kruskal-Wallis and Mann-Whitney tests).

METHODOLOGY

The research methodology consisted of several steps: the building of the translation memory and building the terminology base, the error categorization and assignment of error weights, calculation of the level of mistake, and quality estimation.

The first part of the research consisted of the sentence alignment process of English and Croatian parallel texts. The result of the alignment process was newly created translation memory, which contained 2250 translation units, i.e. parallel sentences from English and Croatian texts.

The following step consisted of the automatic extraction of the terminology. The resource for automatic terminology extraction was the translation memory. As a result of automatic terminology extraction, the list of 5500 term candidates was obtained, which was then filtered out.

Out of the suggested total number of 5500 automatically extracted terminology candidates, 100 terms were selected and used to create a terminology base for this research.

The newly created terminology base, consisting of 100 selected terms, was integrated into the CAT process and served as a resource in the QA process. This terminology base was a resource for verifying terminology consistency or checking the use of forbidden terms.

Figure 1. Research Methodology
Source: Authors' work, 2020

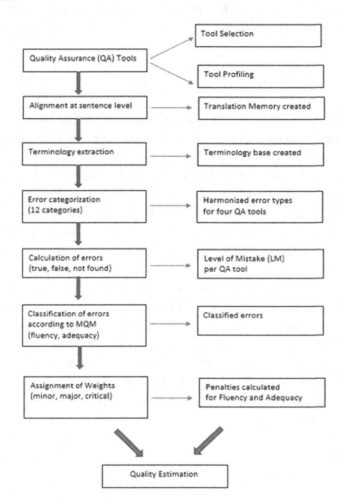

In QA analysis, four QA tools detected different types of errors and counted them in different ways. The multidimensional quality metric (MQM) served as a framework for the harmonization of error types and for the error categorization. The harmonization enabled the authors to set up the joint base of errors and to perform the comparable evaluation.

Errors were classified according to the multidimensional quality metrics (MQM) framework, using the criteria of accuracy and fluency. For each error type weights were assigned:

- minor,
- major,
- critical.

In the next step, the level of mistake was calculated, according to Gural and Chemezov (2014) for each of the selected QA tools – the smaller the level of mistake, the better the translation quality.

Penalties for the criteria of adequacy and fluency were calculated, as in Lommel et al. (2014), with the final aim to estimate the quality evaluation.

Error Categorization

For the error categorization, the multidimensional quality metric (MQM) framework served. MQM is a result of an EU-funded project "QTLaunchPad" (Multidimensional Quality Metrics (MQM) Issue Types (2015), created to offer a flexible framework helping to define categories for the assessment of the translation quality (Lommel, 2014).

The Multidimensional Quality Metrics (MQM) Issue Types (2015) defines more than 100 categories, which are classified hierarchically and which enable the use of categories at different levels. As in this study, errors can be examined at the top level by categories of fluency and adequacy or at a more fine-grained level, including subcategories. MQM metric can be used at different levels of granularity to identify more or less specific issues. Errors can be selected and implemented according to various needs.

At the top level, the MQM (2015) metric includes the following dimensions:

- Accuracy – referring to the information transferred in the target language. It is affected by the following types of errors: omission, non-translation, mistranslation, false friends, addiction, improper exact translation memory match, over translation, etc.
- Fluency – is related to the naturalness of expression in the target language. It is affected by errors such as agreement, word order, word forms, abbreviations, ambiguity, duplication, spelling, typography, etc.
- Design – is related to layout and formatting, including issues such as graphics and tables, fonts, formatting, markup, hyphenation, and overall layout, such as margins, formatting, color, page breaks, headers and footers, etc.
- Internationalization – includes the preparation of the source text for the localization, enabling the use of categories at different levels, including character support, embedded strings, language-specific tools, the localization support from locale convention.
- Locale convention – is associated with compliance with local conventions, such as formatting of time, currency, measures, telephone formats, etc.
- Verity – is related to issues of appropriate communication of the content in the target language, including end-user suitability, local-specific content, culture-specific reference, etc.
- Style – is closely related to fluency, but often treated separately, defined as "light style" or "engaging style," including the specific register, company style, or another specific style.
- Terminology – covers the use of domain-specific or client-specific terminology, which is one of the major concerns.

For Croatian as the target language, several types of research explored the use of MQM framework: for English/Russian-Croatian (Seljan & Dunđer, 2015a), for Croatian-German (Seljan et al., 2020), for different domains – e.g., sociological-philosophical-spiritual domain (Seljan & Dunđer, 2015b), legislation, technology, general – or combined with automatic speech recognition or with the summarization technology (Seljan et al., 2015) for five language pairs, showing problems with fluency, due to the characteristics of Croatian as a language with rich morphological system and relatively free word order.

Meer and Görög (2015) present the report on Dynamic Quality Framework (DQF), where the quality is dynamic, depending on the type of text, audience, and content. The focus of this research is not on the dynamic quality framework (DQF), but on static standalone or integrated tools used in the CAT process.

Tools

In this step, for four selected QA tools, language profiles were created. This research included standalone QA tools (Tool2, Tool3, Tool4), and one integrated tool (Tool1), where the QA made an integral part of the CAT tool. Among the other three standalone tools, Tool4 had a free version.

Tool Selection

In the QA process, four different tools considered different types of errors (e.g. punctuation, way of writing numbers, compliance of terminology and translation memory, URL addresses) and counted them in different ways (e.g. one error type was counted as one error, or each time when appearing). Different types of tools took into account different types of errors (Le Ny, 2014; Makoushina, 2007; Škof, 2017) that asked for the harmonization in order to be comparable. After the error detection and the harmonization of error types among tools, each tool's efficacy was calculated based on the number of errors:

- true errors detected by tools or confirmed errors,
- false errors detected by tools,
- not detected errors.

Tool Profiles

Different tools supported a different number of languages and mainly offered default profiles for supported languages. Such profiles included:

- terminology check for consistent use of terminology and non-translatable for source-to-target, target-to-source or both,
- warning for forbidden terms used,
- segmenting length based on words, characters or both,
- empty or identical segments,
- auto-translatable,
- formatting differences (bold, italic) and tags,
- number format (decimal point or decimal comma, negative sign, digit grouping symbol, warning if the number is >10 000), number grouping, digit to text conversion, exclusion list for numbers or numeronyms, range sign and spacing, etc.),
- punctuation differences (e.g. multiple spacing, end punctuation, brackets, quotations, special signs),
- measurements, tags, quotes, and apostrophes,
- letter case, orthography,
- omissions,
- URLs, etc.

Apart from the exact set of profile properties, some tools allowed regular expressions and export/ import options in a specific format, for example searching for the improper use of spaces around dashes in the target language.

Some tools offered an additional option for auto-correction – *suggested auto fix*, which could be useful in correcting formatting errors, spelling errors, deleting unnecessary blanks or adding non-existing blanks (e.g. deleting a blank before a comma, and adding a blank after a comma or full stop, question or exclamation mark). Some tools offered false suggestions, depending on resources used for the target language (e.g. suggesting a correction for misspelled words).

Untranslatables mainly related to brands (e.g. names of companies and brands), use of machines or devices (*Memory Stick™, SD*), or expressions that remained untranslated from the source text (e.g. *Copy to disk*). The client's specific list contained untranslatables, and all tools had the option to include a list of untranslatables. Similarly, the forbidden list, usually defined by a client, could also be included in QA tools for quality checking.

Alignment and Terminology Extraction

Translation memory was the output of the alignment process on the English-Croatian language pair in the business correspondence domain. After the automatic process of alignment, it was necessary to perform human verification to correct a few misaligned segments that occurred due to colon punctuation and hyphen, followed by lower letters. Verified exported translation memory contained 2250 aligned translation units.

In the next step, the translation memory served as a source for automatic terminology extraction. The list of automatically created terminology candidates was refined by the language engineer expert, who created the final list of 100 selected terms. This list served as a resource for the research purpose of QA in the CAT process.

From the previous researches performed by (Alhashmi, 2016; Chiocchetti et al., 2017; Seljan, 2018a), terminology evaluation and terminology management represented an imperative in the translation process, which was difficult to separate from the whole document production system. For the language-independent terminology extraction, the set up included defining of minimal and maximal lengths, delimiters, stop-words, and minimal frequency, resulting in a high number of term candidates (Seljan et al., 2017) which were then filtered out.

Out of a large number of automatically suggested term candidates, an expert selected 100 terms and used them to create the terminology base. This terminology base served as a control mechanism in the QA process to verify the terminological consistency and deviations.

Error Categorization

Different tools took into account different types of errors, which was handled through regular tool profiling and in the subsequent QA detection process. The harmonization among QA tools enabled the comparative analysis.

The following types of errors which appeared in the source and the target languages of the translation memory were considered:

- Orthography – in the source and target language;

- Terminology – wrong terminology use, compared with terminology base obtained by extraction process (Eng. *buying agent* – Cro. correct: *komisionar za kupnju*, instead of *komisionar za prodaju*; Eng. *sales* – Cro. *prodaja* instead of *kupovina*);
- Consistency of target text – conducted through consistency check in the target language, when the same segment had different translations (Eng. *commission* – Cro. *provizija, zastupnik*);
- Consistency of source text – conducted through consistency check of the source text, when having a different segment in the source text translated by the same segment in the target text (Eng. *agent, representative, deputy* – Cro. *zastupnik*);
- Capital letters – in segments of both languages (Eng. *Yours faithfully* – Cro. *srdačno*);
- Double spaces – which appeared between words or signs in source and target languages;
- Numbers – errors regarding inconsistent numbers between source and target language (Eng. *12,543.600* – Cro. *12.543,600* or *12 543,600*);
- Dates – e.g. Eng. *by March 1st 2010* – Cro. *do 1. ožujka 2010.*;
- Punctuation errors – inconsistencies in end punctuation (e.g. four dots in Croatian, instead of three, Eng. *to receive a monthly allowance of ...* – Cro. *mjesečni paušal od ...*);
- Quotation marks – e.g. Eng. *Company "ABC"* Cro. *kompanija „ABC"*);
- Repeated words around signs or phrases (Eng. *Firstly* – Cro. *Prvo naprije*);
- Spaces around signs – errors regarding incorrect use of spaces before or after signs (e.g. %, ©, °);
- URL errors – in cases when URLs were translated, not correctly written, or missing URL (e.g. www.servoce.sap.com/pam – www.service.sap.com/pam; www.goto... – www.ići...).

Level of Mistake

Each QA tool counted all types of errors, where t_{max} represented a maximal number of errors for each error type.

Level of mistake, as in Gural and Chemezov (2014), takes into account:

- t – number of true errors found by a tool,
- f – number of false errors,
- d – total number of all found errors (true and false), where (d = t + f),
- n – number of errors not found by the tool, (n = t_{max} - t), and was calculated as in (1) and (2).

$$LM = \frac{e*100}{d+n} \tag{1}$$

$$e = f + n \tag{2}$$

Based on the level of mistake for each tool, the translation quality was calculated.

In the research, four tools were analyzed in terms of error types. The second tool, closely followed by the third tool, achieved the best score and made the smallest mistake. The level of mistake was calculated for each tool:

level of mistake (Tool1) = 76.2%

level of mistake **(Tool2) = 55.85%**
level of mistake (Tool3) = 59.33%
level of mistake (Tool4) = 86.62%

Assigning Weights to Errors

In the next step, each error received an assigned weight, as in Yang et al. (2017):

- minor errors (weight 1) – including errors not affecting the content, such as blanks,
- major errors (weight 5) – including errors that affected the content, but did not understanding, such as orthography, spelling,
- critical errors (weight 10) – including errors that affected the meaning, such as omissions, untranslatables, specific grammatical errors, etc.

Each error with its assigned weight affected the criteria of Accuracy or Fluency:

- Accuracy:
  - Terminology – error weight: 10
  - Numbers – error weight: 10
  - Repeated words – error weight: 5
  - URL errors – error weight: 10
- Fluency:
  - Orthography – error weight: 5
  - Consistency of target text – error weight: 5
  - Consistency of source text – error weight: 5
  - Capital letter – error weight: 1
  - Double spacing – error weight: 1
  - Punctuation – error weight: 5
  - Quotation marks – error weight: 1
  - Spaces around signs – error weight: 1

The calculation of the translation quality estimation was as in Lommel et al. (2013):

$$TQ = 100 - AP - (FPT - FPS) - (VPT - VPS) \qquad (3)$$

where:

- TQ - translation quality (overall rating of quality),
- AP – accuracy penalty (sum of all penalties assigned to accuracy),
- FPT - fluency penalty for the target language (sum of all penalties assigned to fluency for the target language),
- FPS - fluency penalty for the source language (sum of all penalties assigned to fluency for the source language; if the source not assessed then FPS=0)

- VPT - verity penalty for the target language (sum of all penalties assigned to verity for the target language),
- VPS - verity penalty for the source language (sum of all penalties assigned to verity for the source language; if the source not assessed, then VPS=0).

The penalty was calculated for all error types, as in Lommel et al. (2013):

P =(Err_minor + Err_major • 5 + Err_critical • 10)/WordCount   (4)

where:

- P - penalty,
- Err_minor - minor errors,
- Err _major - major errors,
- Err _critical - critical errors,
- WordCount - total number of words (here target language words).

Calculations for adequacy penalty (AP) and fluency penalty (FP) gave the following results:

AP = 2.24
FP = 4.65

The final translation quality:

TQ = 100-AP-FP
TQ = 100-2.24-4.65
TQ = 93.11

Translated quality was affected by the total number of words of the target language (WordCount), a total number of true errors (t_{max}), and assigned weights. Errors which were not essential for understanding (weight 0) were also corrected, because of transmission into future projects.

RESULTS

Table 1 presented descriptive statistics on the total number of errors. The number of errors differed among tools as the tools counted errors in different ways. The total number of errors included errors in all categories: true errors with categories of orthography, terminology, capital letters, spaces, then false errors and errors not detected by the tool.

Several errors in the category of *Orthography* were directly related to spell-check, which was part of another tool (MS Word or Hunspell), or to additional options that were different among tools (such as writing in capital letters or combination, letters, and digits). Tool2 had the option to add the word into the dictionary, meaning that it would not appear as an error any more.

The error category *Terminology* was related to the created terminology base, which served as a control mechanism for checking compliant extracted terminology with the translation memory. Terminology consistency has considerable importance in the specific domain translations, here in business communication. In this paper, terminology evaluation considered terminology inconsistencies between the translation memory and the created terminology base. Although these texts did not contain the large terminology pool, all tools that had the option for terminology check detected terminology inconsistencies.

Tool1, Tool2 and Tool3 had options of additional formatting compatible with the target language. In Croatian, for decimal numbers, comma sign was used (0,25), and numbers higher than 10 000 separated by a blank character (full stop also permitted, but comma not allowed). Detected errors in this process included the wrong way of writing numbers. Tool2 and Tool3 had different punctuation options. Errors of punctuation represented the majority of the counting task (three dots in Croatian ritten next to the word followed by a blank).

Apart from the harmonization problems, QA tools counted errors in different ways. For the calculation of the level of mistake (LM), it was necessary to harmonize the number of detected true errors among tools (t), which were taken at the segment level, meaning that the error of the opening and closing quotation mark was one error and not two errors. The same segment could have more errors of different types, which counted additionally.

Errors were counted at the segment level, meaning that quotation errors at the beginning and the end of one segment was one error (and not as two errors), while errors in orthography were all counted several times. Tool1 and Tool4 did not offer an option for counting of ignored errors. In practice, it appeared that several false errors were higher than several true errors, which was the reason for the high level of mistake. False errors often include numbers (e.g. in source text written in letters and target text written in numbers, or false error in writing ordinal numbers 10th and 10.), punctuation (abbreviation Mr. and "*gospodin*" – in Croatian "*mister*" without full stop), different formats in abbreviations or terminology.

Figure 2 presented the total number of true errors and errors not found by the tool, and Figure 3 presented boxplot for true errors. The most of *true errors* were found by Tool2 (517), closely followed by two similar results, achieved by Tool1 (469) and Tool3 (456), whereas the Tool4 achieved the lowest score (162). Level of mistake results showed that the Tool2 obtained the best sore, with the lowest level of mistake (55.85%), followed by the Tool3 (59.33%).

Table 1. Descriptive Statistics - Total Errors

	Total_errors			
	Tool1	**Tool2**	**Tool3**	**Tool4**
Valid	12	12	12	12
Missing	0	0	0	0
Mean	157.417	97.667	86.750	70.167
Median	35.500	45.000	32.000	13.500
Range	888.000	252.000	478.000	434.000
Minimum	0.000	2.000	0.000	0.000
Maximum	888.000	254.000	478.000	434.000
Sum	1889.000	1172.000	1041.000	842.000

Source: Authors' work, 2020

Tool2 had the lowest number of not found errors (15), and it was the only tool that detected each type of error, although URLs were not properly detected. Regarding the number of *errors not found by the tool*, the Tool4 did not detect the most errors (370).

Figure 2. Errors per Tool
Source: Authors' work, 2020

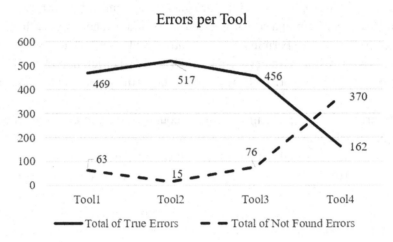

Figure 3. Boxplot for True Errors
Source: Authors' work, 2020

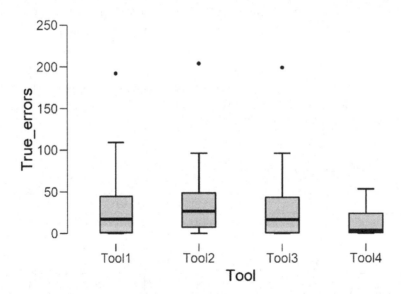

Although the tools gave different results of errors, a Kruskal-Wallis test showed that there was no statistically significant difference among the four QA tools at the level of significance α=0.05, regarding the total number of true errors.

According to the results of not found errors, each of two created categories contained two tools (category 1 – Tool1 and Tool2 and category 2 – Tool3 and Tool4). A Mann-Whitney test showed a statistically significant difference at the level of significance $\alpha = 0.05$ between the two groups of QA tools concerning the number of not found errors (p-value=0.043, p<0.05).

The final quality estimation for translation memory was 93.11%. Although some errors were not critical for understanding, it was necessary to fix them for future projects, as that translation memory could make an integral part of future projects. By correcting errors, the quality of the final product (translation) raised. Human correction of all errors ($t_{max}=532$) would be a long and tedious task and hard to accomplish. QA tools differed regarding setup characteristics, types of detected errors, ways of counting them and integration possibilities, but offered advantages of time, specific error detection and non-subjectivity, although pointed to the need for the harmonization of error types.

SOLUTIONS AND RECOMMENDATIONS

Besides indicated types of data used for the analysis, the suggestion is to keep track of other data, such as data related to time used for translation, time used for revision, number of revisions, post-editing effort, number of translators included in the task, consistency among translators, and their preferences related to the domain of translation. The use of QA tools that enabled the selection of specific error categories, chosen from the pool of standard error types, was a valuable source of information as they enabled data evaluation of error types during the CAT process.

The main limitation of this research is the use of only selected versions of QA tools. As new solutions develop, such as the Dynamic Quality Framework (DQF) integrating the MQM framework, further research would focus on investigating the use of QA tools integrating the DQF framework. The research would include analysis of time, post-editing effort and understanding of audience expectations (Czopik, 2014).

FUTURE RESEARCH DIRECTIONS

The use of CAT technology has become part of business processes in numerous agencies and institutions that provide various translation services. Due to the digital transformation of the translation process, including collaborative work, changes in the translation process (number of translators, task distribution), short deadlines and augmented amount of work, there is augmented risk of the high number of errors appearing during the CAT process.

For this reason, QA has become a necessary part of the CAT process. The use of QA tools enables data analysis of different types of errors, and thus can lead to relevant decisions related to the translation business process. Analysis of indicated QA errors enables future improvements related to QA task distribution (e.g. previous check of number formats, language style formats), the building of additional language resources (e.g. a list of forbidden terms, list of preferred terms) or check of untranslatables (URLs, brand names, specific expressions). Correction of various types of errors performed by humans would be a tedious and long-term task, prone to errors. Therefore, the use of QA tools is a necessary step to obtain data valuable for future decisions.

CONCLUSION

This paper presented a methodological framework for the quality estimation of translation memory in computer-assisted translation (CAT), using four selected QA tools. For the harmonization of error types, the MQM framework served, after which the error weight followed, calculation of penalties for accuracy and fluency, calculation of the level of mistake and the final quality estimation. Benchmarking of the quality estimation has moved from the traditional way to the data-based solutions in a business environment, as part of quality management systems (QMS).

The first aim of the research was to present a methodological framework for the quality estimation of the translation memory, which represented the basis for CAT technology. The research offered a framework for the quality estimation of the translation memory, which turned out to be complicated, prone to errors due to differences in performance, error detection, the error categorization, the error correction, and counting. The error counting and weight assignment affected penalty scores and the final score of quality estimation.

The second aim was to perform a comparative evaluation of four QA tools to harmonize error types. An analysis of four QA tools showed there was a need for harmonizing error types to conduct a thorough comparative evaluation. Existing QA tools enabled detection of errors but performed according to different principles. Interface and intuitiveness for some of the tools were not at the highest level, as well as additional options for defining profiles, auto-correction, and orthography check. Results showed that the tools detected various types of errors, however not in a harmonized approach.

Although all tools offered different options of error types, they allowed the option of ignoring detected errors. Different tools counted errors in different ways: some tools counted the same error twice, for example when finding wrong quotation marks, while others counted them once. The terminology base served as a control mechanism in the QA process and enabled the use of terminology compliant with end-user demands. Terminology QA looked at compliant, forbidden or inconsistent terminology in the translation memory. QA tools should detect these types of errors and prevent errors in the translation memory and in the final translation output. However, results showed differences in the detection of terminology errors and orthography among tools. The investigated standalone tools (Tool2, Tool3 and Tool4) were more oriented to quality assurance, and supported various options for setting up the language profiles, whereas Tool1 was an integrated commercial tool, but dating from previous versions.

The third aim of this paper was to justify the introduction of integrated QA tools into the digitally transformed translation process, supported by CAT technology. The high number of errors could affect the quality of the output result (here translation), especially important in specific domains, as when dealing with business contracts, legal documentation, public information or e-government documentation, medical guides and manuals or publicity materials in marketing campaigns. Besides the quality issue of the product (here translation), the error analysis can affect the translation business process concerning its processes, organization, job specialization and task distribution.

As presented, QA at the end of the translation process is a complicated, uneven, prone-to-errors, and time-consuming process that required additional time and engineering knowledge for specific tasks. QA represented an essential step in error analysis, leading do data-driven decisions. This research supported the assumption of QA integration into the digitally transformed process of translation, supported by CAT technology.

Errors detected by the QA process, point to specific weak points of the digitally transformed translation process. Corrections of detected errors are essential for future projects and the direct output - for the translation. Data analysis of detected errors can lead to further data-driven decisions affecting the CAT process, such as changes in the organization, process, time scheduling, job distribution, use of ICT tools or education requirements.

Translation quality assurance plays a crucial role in the translation business, connecting engineering knowledge, language and terminology, data analysis and statistics, management and marketing. Digital transformation of the translation process does not refer only to the platform including tools and resources. However, it encompasses changes in processes and people, values and innovations, leading to multilingual information management and a new type of Translation Industry, as part of the Industry 4.0.

REFERENCES

Aiken, M., & Ghosh, K. (2009). Automatic translation in multilingual business meetings. *Industrial Management & Data Systems, 109*(7), 916–925. doi:10.1108/02635570910982274

Alhashmi, A. (2016). *Embedding TQM in UAE translation organizations*. QScience Connect. Retrieved from https://www.qscience.com/doi/abs/10.5339/connect.2016.tii.3

Austermühl, F. (2007). Translators in the Language Industry – From Localization to Marginalization. In *Gebundener Sprachgebrauch in der Übersetzungswissenschaft* (pp. 39–51). Wissenschaftlicher Verlag.

Bogaert, van den J. (2008). Terminology and Translation Quality Assurance. *Revista Tradumatica, 6*, 1-10.

Brkić, M., Matetić, M., & Seljan, S. (2011a). Towards Obtaining High Quality Sentence-Aligned English-Croatian Parallel Corpus. Computer Science and Information Technology ICCSIT, 1068-1070.

Brkić, M., Seljan, S., & Bašić Mikulić, B. (2009). Using Translation Memory to Speed up Translation Process. *Proceedings of INFuture2009 - Digital Resources and Knowledge Sharing*, 353-363.

Brkić, M., Seljan, S., & Matetić, M. (2011b). Machine Translation Evaluation for Croatian-English and English-Croatian Language Pairs. *Proceedings of the 8th International NLPCS Workshop: Human-Machine Interaction in Translation*, 93-104.

Chiocchetti, E., Wissik, T., Lušicky, V., & Wetzel, M. (2017). Quality assurance in multilingual legal terminological databases. *The Journal of Specialised Translation, 27*, 164–188.

Coughlin, D. (2003). Correlating automated and human assessments of machine translation quality. *Proceedings of MT Summit, 9*, 23–27.

Czopik, J. (2014). Quality Assurance process in translation. *Translating and Computer, 36*, 77–85.

Denkowski, M., & Lavie, A. (2011). Meteor 1.3: Automatic metric for reliable optimization and evaluation of machine translation systems. *Proceedings of the Sixth Workshop on Statistical Machine Translation*, 85-91.

Doddington, G. (2002). Automatic evaluation of machine translation quality using n-gram co-occurrence statistics. *Proceedings of the Second international conference on Human Language Technology Research*, 138-145. 10.3115/1289189.1289273

Dunđer, I., Seljan, S., & Pavlovski, M. (2020). Automatic Machine Translation of Poetry and a Low-Resource Language Pair. *Proceedings of MIPRO 2020: Intelligent Systems.* (in press)

European Commission – Directorate-General for Translation. (2009). *Programme for Quality Management in Translation: 22 Quality Actions.* Retrieved from http://www.termcoord.eu/wp-content/uploads/2017/07/Programme-for-Quality-Management-in-Translation.pdf

Federico, M., Cattelan, A., & Trombetti, M. (2012). Measuring User Productivity in Machine Translation Enhanced Computer Assisted Translation. *Proceedings of AMTA 2012.*

Guerberof, A. (2009). Productivity and Quality in the Post-editing of Outputs from Translation Memories and Machine Translation. *International Journal of Localization, 7*(1).

Gural, S. K., & Chemezov, Y. R. (2014). Analysis of Efficiency of Translation Quality Assurance Tools. *Procedia: Social and Behavioral Sciences, 154,* 360–363. doi:10.1016/j.sbspro.2014.10.163

Hansson, J. (2003). *Total quality management – Aspects of implementation and performance: Investigations with a focus on small organizations* (Unpublished doctoral dissertation). Lulea University of Technology.

Kockaert, H., Makoushina, J., & Steurs, F. (2008). Translation quality assurance: what is missing? And what can be done? *Proceedings of XVIIIth FIT World Congress in Shanghai.*

Koehn, P. (2010). *Statistical Machine Translation.* Cambridge University Press.

Kučiš, V., & Seljan, S. (2014). The role of online translation tools in language education. *Babel, 60*(3), 303–324. doi:10.1075/babel.60.3.03kuc

Le Ny, B. (2014). *Quality Control in Human Translations: Use Cases and Specifications.* Retrieved from https://transread.limsi.fr/Deliverables/Deliverable_3.1.pdf

Levenshtein, V. I. (1966). Binary Codes Capable of Correcting Deletions, Insertions and Reversals. *Soviet Physics, Doklady, 10*(8), 707–710.

Linguistic Data Consortium. (2005). *Linguistic Data Annotation Specification: Assessment of Fluency and Adequacy in Translations.* Author.

Lommel, A. (Ed.). (2014). *Multidimensional Quality Metrics (MQM) Definition.* Retrieved from: http://www.qt21.eu/mqm-definition/definition-2014-08-19.html

Lommel, A., Uszkoreit, H., & Burchardt, A. (2014). Multidimensional Quality Metrics (MQM): A Framework for Declaring and Describing Translation Quality Metrics. *Revista Tradumatica: tecnologies de la traducció,* 455-463.

Lommel, A. R., Burchardt, A., & Uszkoreit, H. (2013). *Multidimensional Quality Metrics; A flexible System for Assessing Translation Quality.* Retrieved from http://www.mt-archive.info/10/Aslib-2013-Lommel.pdf

Makoushina, J. (2007). Translation quality assurance tools: Current state and future approaches. *Translating and the Computer, 29,* 1–39.

Makoushina, J., & Kockaert, H. (2008). Zen and the Art of Quality Assurance. Quality Assurance Automation in Translation: Needs, Reality and Expectation. *Proceedings of the International Conference on Translating and the Computer.*

Maney, T., Sibert, L., Perzanowski, D., Gupta, K., & Schmidt-Nielsen, A. (2012). Toward Determining the Comprehensibility of Machine Translations. *Proceedings of the 1st PITR*, 1-7.

Meer, van den J., & Görög, A. (2015). *Dynamic Quality Framework Report 2015: Results of the Evaluate Survey conducted in 2014.*

Multidimensional Quality Metrics (MQM) Issue Types. (2015). *German Research Center for Artificial Intelligence (DFKI) and QTLaunchPad.* Retrieved from http://www.qt21.eu/mqm-definition/issues-list-2015-12-30.html

Muzii, L. (2006). Quality Assessment and Economic Sustainability of Translation. *International Journal of Translation*, 9, 15–38.

Papineni, K., Roukos, S., Ward, T., & Zhu, W.-J. (2002). Bleu: A method for automatic evaluation of machine translation. *Proceedings of ACL*, 311-318.

Seljan, S. (2018a). Quality Assurance (QA) of Terminology in a Translation Quality Management System (QMS) in the Business Environment. *EU publications: Translation services in the digital world - A sneak peek into the (near) future*, 92-105.

Seljan, S. (2018b). Total Quality Management Practice in Croatian Language Service Provider Companies. *Proceedings of the ENTerprise REsearch InNOVAtion (ENTRENOVA)*, 461-469. 10.2139srn.3283755

Seljan, S., Agić, Ž., & Tadić, M. (2008). Evaluating sentence alignment on Croatian-English parallel corpora. *Proceedings of the 6th Int. Conf. on Formal Approaches to South Slavic and Balkan Languages - FASSBL 2008*, 101-108.

Seljan, S., & Dunđer, I. (2014). Combined Automatic Speech Recognition and Machine Translation in BSeusiness Correspondence Domain for English-Croatian. *International Journal of Computer, Information, Systems and Control Engineering*, 8(11), 1069-1075.

Seljan, S., & Dunđer, I. (2015a). Machine Translation and Automatic Evaluation of English/Russian-Croatian. *Proceedings of the "Corpus Linguistics 2015" Conference at the St. Petersburg State University*, 72-79.

Seljan, S., & Dunđer, I. (2015b). Automatic Quality Evaluation of Machine-Translated Output in Sociological-Philosophical-Spiritual Domain. *Proceedings of the CISTI 2015: 10th Iberian Conference on Information Systems and Technologies*, 2, 128-131. 10.1109/CISTI.2015.7170425

Seljan, S., Dunđer, I., & Pavlovski, M. (2020). Human Quality Evaluation of Machine-Translated Poetry. *Proceedings of MIPRO 2020: Intelligent Systems.* (in press)

Seljan, S., Dunđer, I., & Stančić, H. (2017). Extracting Terminology by Language Independent Methods. Forum Translationswissenschaft. *Translation Studies and Translation*, 141-147.

Seljan, S., Gašpar, A., & Pavuna, D. (2007). Sentence Alignment as the Basis For Translation Memory Database. *Proceedings of INFuture 2007 - Digital Information and Heritage*, 299-311.

Seljan, S., & Katalinić, J. (2017). Integrating Localization into a Video Game. *Proceedings of INFuture 2017: Integrating ICT in Society*, 43-55.

Seljan, S., Klasnić, K., Stojanac, M., Pešorda, B., & Mikelić Preradović, N. (2015). Information Transfer through Online Summarizing and Translation Technology. *Proceedings of INFuture2015: e-Institutions – Openness, Accessibility, and Preservation*, 197-210. 10.17234/INFUTURE.2015.24

Seljan, S., & Pavuna, D. (2006). Translation Memory Database in the Translation Process. *Proceedings of the 17th International Conference on Information and Intelligent Systems IIS 2006*, 327-332.

Seljan, S., Tadić, M., Šnajder, J., Dalbelo Bašić, B., & Osmann, V. (2010). Corpus Aligner (CorAl) Evaluation on English-Croatian Parallel Corpora. *Proceedings of the Conference Language Resources and Evaluation - LREC 2010*, 3481-3484.

Škof, N. (2017). *Utjecaj digitalnih resursa i alata na kvalitetu prijevoda u računalno potpomognutom prevođenju* (Diploma thesis). University of Zagreb.

Snell-Hornby, M. (2006). *The turns of Translation Studies. New Paradigms Or Shifting Viewpoints?* John Benjamins. doi:10.1075/btl.66

Snover, M., Dorr, B., Schwartz, R., Linnea, M., & Makhoul, J. (2006). A Study of Translation Edit Rate with Targeted Human Annotation. *Proceedings of the Association for Machine Translation in the Americas (AMTA)*, 223-231.

Specia, L., & Farzindar, A. (2010). Estimating Machine Translation Post-Editing Effort with HTER. *Proceedings of the AMTA 2010- workshop: Bringing MT to the User: MT Research and the Translation Industry*.

Stejskal, J. (2006) Quality assessment in translation. *MultiLingual*, 41-44.

Svoboda, T., Biel, Ł., & Łoboda, K. (2017). *Quality aspects in institutional translation. Multilingual Natural Language Processing, 8*. Language Science Press.

Vázquez, L. M., Rodríguez Vázquez, S., & Bouillon, P. (2013). Comparing Forum Data Post-Editing Performance Using Translation Memory and Machine Translation Output: A Pilot Study. Proceedings of Machine Translation Summit XIV.

Yamada, M. (2011). The effect of translation memory databases on productivity. In A. Pym (Ed.), *Translation research projects* (Vol. 3, pp. 63–73).

Yang, J., Ciobanu, D., Reiss, C., & Secară, A. (2017). *Using Computer Assisted Translation Tools' Translation Quality Assessment functionalities to assess students' translations*. The Language Scholar Journal.

Zampieri, M., & Vela, M. (2014). Quantifying the Influence of MT Output in the Translators Performance: A Case Study in Technical Translation. *Proceedings of the EACL Workshop on Humans and Computer-assisted Translation (HaCat)*, 93-98. 10.3115/v1/W14-0314

Zhang, L. (2016). A Study on the Efficiency Influence of Computer-Assisted Translation in Technical Translation. *Journal of Chemical and Pharmaceutical Research*, *8*(4), 801–808.

ADDITIONAL READING

Borges, J. L. (2018). A case study of a recommender system for Quality Estimation of Machine Translation based on linguistic features.

Brkić, M., Seljan, S., & Vičić, T. (2013). Automatic and Human Evaluation on English-Croatian Legislative Test Set. Lecture Notes in Computer Science - LNCS, 7816, 2013(1), 311-317.

Choudhury, R., & McConnell, B. (2013). *TAUS translation technology landscape report*. Published by TAUS BV, De Rijp, 12.

Huertas-Barros, E., Vandepitte, S., & Iglesias-Fernández, E. (2018). *Quality Assurance and Assessment Practices in Translation and Interpreting*. IGI-Global.

Karwacka, W. (2014). Quality assurance in medical translation. *The Journal of Specialised Translation*.

Seljan, S., Tucaković, M., & Dunđer, I. (2015). Human Evaluation of Online Machine Translation Services for English/Russian-Croatian. Advances in Intelligent Systems and Computing - New Contributions in Information Systems and Technologies, Springer, 353, 1089-1098.

Sun, D. (2017). The Role of Formalized Structured Translation Specifications in Translation Quality Assurance of Public Signs in China. *International Journal of English Linguistics*, *7*(5), 107. doi:10.5539/ijel.v7n5p107

Teixeira, C. S. C., Moorkens, J., Turner, D., Vreeke, J., & Way, A. (2019). Creating a Multimodal Translation Tool and Testing Machine Translation Integration Using Touch and Voice. *Informatics (MDPI)*, *6*(13), 13. doi:10.3390/informatics6010013

KEY TERMS AND DEFINITIONS

Alignment: The process of creating segment pairs in source and target languages used to create translation memory as a fundamental resource for computer-assisted translation and machine translation.

Computer-Assisted Translation (CAT): Implementation of interactive computer software in the translation process, which enables retrieving of already existing similar sentences from the translation memory when translating the new document. It includes the use of translation memory, terminology base and alignment modules, but can become integrated translation software.

Error Type: Refers to various types of errors (here in machine translation/computer-assisted translation process), basically according to the MQM framework.

Integrated Translation Software: Assumes computer software that integrates computer-assisted translation, terminology base and machine translation, possibly with other technologies, such as speech technology, optical character recognition (OCR), summarization, etc.

Machine Translation: Use of computer software/programs when translating from one natural language into another, performed by automatic machine translation or by integrated machine translation, which can include various technologies (e.g. automatic machine translation integrated with speech technologies, computer-assisted translation, optical character recognition (OCR), etc.)

Multidimensional Quality Metric (MQM) Framework: Provides a list of over 100 error types, classified into main categories (adequacy, fluency, verity, terminology, locale convention, design, internationalization) and subsequent subcategories, to harmonize error types.

Quality Assurance (QA): The process which identifies differences in translation between two languages, which can be differences in terminology, use of forbidden terms, layout differences, cultural differences (writing numbers, time, currency), signs, names, segments which are not translated (URL addresses), names, etc. in order to provide the high-quality translation.

Translation Memory: This is a textual database containing parallel segments (sentences, clauses, phrases, terminology, numbers) in source and target languages. Translation memory is the basis for building resources in computer-assisted translation tools and for building machine translation systems.

Section 3
Diversity Among Languages Over Natural Language Processing

Chapter 12

An Extensive Text Mining Study for the Turkish Language:
Author Recognition, Sentiment Analysis, and Text Classification

Durmuş Özkan Şahin
https://orcid.org/0000-0002-0831-7825
Ondokuz Mayıs University, Turkey

Erdal Kılıç
https://orcid.org/0000-0003-1585-0991
Ondokuz Mayıs University, Turkey

ABSTRACT

In this study, the authors give both theoretical and experimental information about text mining, which is one of the natural language processing topics. Three different text mining problems such as news classification, sentiment analysis, and author recognition are discussed for Turkish. They aim to reduce the running time and increase the performance of machine learning algorithms. Four different machine learning algorithms and two different feature selection metrics are used to solve these text classification problems. Classification algorithms are random forest (RF), logistic regression (LR), naive bayes (NB), and sequential minimal optimization (SMO). Chi-square and information gain metrics are used as the feature selection method. The highest classification performance achieved in this study is 0.895 according to the F-measure metric. This result is obtained by using the SMO classifier and information gain metric for news classification. This study is important in terms of comparing the performances of classification algorithms and feature selection methods.

DOI: 10.4018/978-1-7998-4240-8.ch012

INTRODUCTION

With the proliferation of the internet, the use of computers, mobile phones and tablets is increasing, and the amount of data is growing day by day. One of the sources of this increasing data type is non-structured textual documents. There is a significant increase in the number of data produced and stored in textual format. For this reason, automatically processing this data via computers and obtaining meaningful information from it will help researchers to develop new products. At the same time, the idea of text mining, a sub-branch of data mining, has appeared. Researchers aim to solve some problems with text mining techniques.

Text categorization can include supervised and unsupervised learning problems (Aggarwal and Zhai, 2012; Kadhim, 2019; Dasgupta and Ng, 2009 and Shafiabady et al., 2016). There is no training stage in unsupervised learning. Clustering algorithms are examples of these approaches. On the other hand, there is a training stage in supervised learning. Classification algorithms create a mathematical formula according to the training model. Classification is then carried out according to that mathematical formula. In a supervised text classification approach texts are divided into two parts, namely training and testing. Then, various rules are learned by classifiers according to the way the classification algorithms work on the training set. Classifiers apply these rules to the text in the test set and classify the text. There are many studies in published literature on text classification (Sebastiani, 2002). Examples include:

- Machine learning-based and text mining-based automatic electronic mail filtering (Clark et al., 2003)
- Classification of webpages (Sun et al., 2002)
- Author recognition (Stamatatos et al., 2000)
- Automatic extraction of text summary (Salton et al., 1997)
- Automatic question–answer system (Soricut and Brill, 2006)
- Sentiment analysis on texts (Dos Santos and Gatti, 2014)
- Document language identification (Artemenko et al., 2006)

In this study, three different Turkish text classification applications were performed. These are news classification, author recognition and sentiment analysis. In order to solve these text classification problems, all operations from the pre-processing step to obtaining the classification performance are explained in detail. In this way, the reader is shown how to make a Turkish text classification application in any programming language. It also explains what methods are used to improve the running time and performance of the classification algorithms. In order to increase classification performance, TF-IDF – a popular term weighting method – and classification algorithms with different working principles were used. Two different feature selection metrics were used to try and reduce the working time of the algorithms. Besides, the keywords extracted from the feature selection methods were compared and interpreted. This study uses many methods on different text classification problems and consequently contribute to existing published literature.

Use of Natural Language Processing and Text Mining in the Business World

Human language is one of the most basic features used by people to communicate and survive. A social person cannot avoid language in their daily life. Apart from speaking, we come across language via texts, signs, menus, emails, SMS, internet pages, advertisements and many other examples that can be found everywhere. In the same way, speech is a language feature in every area of our lives that we use to express ourselves even more easily than writing. Speaking in the mother tongue seems easy, but language acquisition is truly a challenging and time-consuming process. For example, learning a different foreign language is a very difficult process. Besides, language should be considered to be a living organism. Even in colloquial speech, there are many words and statements that change over time. The process of understanding natural language and thinking in natural language has a complex structure inside the brain. It is proposed to process this complex structure using computers by creating the idea of text mining and natural language processing.

Natural language processing and text mining are a broadly and rapidly evolving segment of today's digital technologies. The two concepts are closely interconnected. Text mining studies are data-mining studies that accept text as a data source. In other words, it aims to discover structured data within the text. Natural language processing uses various techniques to understand the complexities of human language. Both techniques benefit from each other. Natural language processing and text mining techniques are used in almost all sectors of the business world. Therefore, the techniques are performed quickly and regularly in the business world. Some areas, where natural language processing techniques and text mining techniques are frequently used in business are as follows:

Banking is one of the areas where natural language processing and text mining techniques are used most frequently (Hassani et al., 2018). The banking process has been very complicated for years. Customers often want to enquire about the bank's policies at the bank counter and since the policies are sometimes confusing, it takes time for customers to understand the policies. A banking assistant is recommended to work with a combination of natural language processing and machine learning techniques (Shah et al., 2017). In this way, chatbots are created where customers can ask about confusing situations.

General-purpose financial statements are shown as examples of increasing data. A business manager usually makes decisions for businesses by looking at these tables. It is not possible to obtain all the necessary information about the business from general purpose financial statements. This situation means the business value is not fully determined and the stakeholders may make the wrong decisions. For this reason, stakeholders turn to other sources. Annual reports, sustainability reports and integrated reports are examples of these resources. However, the analysis of the data contained in these reports becomes a problem for stakeholders, because statistical methods are insufficient in the analysis of these reports – which contain mostly unstructured data. Text mining is an analysis method that solves this problem and has been used frequently in the field of accounting in recent years (Yıldız and Ağdeniz, 2018).

One of the places featuring widespread use of computers is in hospitals. The doctors write reports about the patients they examine. These reports contain words and abbreviations that are difficult to understand. It is difficult for patients and their relatives to understand the report produced. Various machine learning algorithms and natural language processing techniques are used to overcome these difficulties (Leaman et al., 2015). In this way, it aims to let people without medical knowledge understand the reports.

Stock market index forecasting always attracts the attention of researchers due to its difficulty and economic importance. Many studies are using natural language processing and text mining techniques for stock market index prediction (Abdullah et al.; 2013, Khedr and Yaseen, 2017). Abdullah et al. (2013) worked on basic text mining steps by processing news, articles and comments about the stock market. Also, numerical data such as turnover and the volume of companies was used. This information was stored for estimation and analysis after processing. In the last step, the stock index was estimated by taking into account the risk factors based on standard deviation and correlation. In a similar study, data mining and emotion analysis techniques were applied to newspaper news to estimate the stock market index (Khedr and Yaseen, 2017). In addition to stock market index prediction, many financial predictions are made using natural language processing and text mining techniques (Xing et al., 2018).

Motivation

Text data is one of the main sources of increasing data stacks. Extracting meaningful information from these data is a significant problem. Researchers have been trying to make improvements in this field for many years. However, there are still many problems awaiting solutions in this area. One of these problems is the limited studies in the field of Turkish text mining. These problems are our main motivation. This study is primarily a Turkish text mining study. It also investigates three different problems through news classification, author recognition and sentiment analysis.

Contribution

The main contribution of this study is to present a systematic way to deal with Turkish text mining and apply solution methods to different problems. Readers interested in the field of text mining will satisfy most of their needs by acquiring the most basic information when reading this study. This work shows researchers who want to work in the field of text classification the steps they should follow from the very beginning to the end of any text classification application. In this way, readers will be able to develop a textual classification application. There are limited Turkish text mining studies in published literature. Together in this study, three different Turkish text mining applications were considered, and the results were examined thoroughly.

Organization

The study sections are organized as follows:

- Background
- Text Pre-processing and Feature Extraction
- Feature Selection Methods
- Solutions and Recommendations
- Results and Discussions
- Future Research Directions
- Conclusion.

Background: In the first part of the study, a summary of published literature related to author recognition for Turkish documents, sentiment analysis for Turkish sentences and categorization of Turkish texts are given. This part of the study is a brief survey.

Text Pre-processing and Feature Extraction: The second section outlines the basic steps that should be taken in text classification studies to the reader. This will enable readers to adopt basic text classification to any programming language.

Feature Selection Methods: In machine learning studies, feature selection can be considered as keyword selection in text classification. Keyword extraction is a method of information retrieval. How to do this and its mathematical representations will be explained in detail in a separate section.

Solutions and Recommendations: Three different studies will take place in this fourth section. These are author recognition using Turkish documents, sentiment analysis for Turkish sentences and categorization of Turkish texts. This is followed by a detailed explanation of the data sets and machine learning algorithms used in the study. For example, the distribution of the data sets used in the study during the training phase and test phase will be given. Also, the mathematical background of machine learning algorithms used in the study will be explained.

Results and Discussions: There are two different experimental results. The first of these is the Turkish keywords extracted from the three different studies. The second is the classification performance obtained from the machine learning algorithms.

Future Research Directions: In this section, the current unresolved problems in text classification studies are discussed, and the trend techniques frequently used by researchers in this field are highlighted.

Conclusion: The conclusions follow the basic text classification procedures and experimental results.

BACKGROUND

Although the history of computerized text classification applications goes back to the 1960s, it was in the late 1980s and early 1990s that they became more focused. In the early years, the majority of applications were based on the expert systems approach. In the text classification studies performed by expert systems, documents were divided into categories by the rules determined by the developer (Apté et al., 1994). With the increase in the amount of data and the number of categories, this system no longer worked because as the number of data increased, the number of rules increased. These are the disadvantages of rule-based systems.

With the development and reducing costs of electronic hardware parts such as memory and processors, the use of machine learning algorithms has become widespread and has been used on text classification problems. One of the most important of these algorithms is the support vector machine (SVM). The most important application of SVM for text classification is the Joachim (1998)'s study. Apart from this classifier, many machine learning algorithms, such as artificial neural networks (Ruiz and Srinivasan, 1998), Naive Bayes (Kibriya et al., 2004), K-Nearest Neighbor (Yang, 1999) and decision trees (Harrag et al., 2009) have been used extensively on text categorization.

In addition to supervised machine learning algorithms, unsupervised machine learning algorithms are also frequently used in the field of text mining. Unsupervised machine learning algorithms have extensively been studied with respect to textual information. With the use of these algorithms, solutions are created for document organization (Cutting et al., 2017), visualization (Cadez et al., 2003) and categorization (Bekkerman et al., 2001). Unsupervised algorithms used in text classification include hierarchical clustering (Willett, 1998), k-means clustering (Chen et al., 2010), probabilistic latent semantic analysis (Hofmann, 2013) and latent Dirichlet allocation (Blei et al., 2003).

In studies in recent years, data scientists have used graphics processing units (GPU) in machine learning to achieve groundbreaking improvements in a variety of applications, including image classification, video analysis, speech recognition, text classification and natural language learning processing (Deng, 2014). The GPU provides fast and efficient parallel computing. Due to its structure, deep learning is a system whose cost is proportional to its computational complexity. Thanks to the GPU, the usage of deep learning networks, which is more successful than classical machine learning algorithms, has become very popular in text classification in recent years.

In Turkey, there are reported to be 62.07 million internet users, according to January 2020 data (DataReportal, 2020). At the same time, the number of internet users has increased by 2.4 million between 2019 and 2020. More than 80 million people live in Turkey, where there are more than 50 million social media users according to January 2020 data. In addition to these data, 77.39 million mobile connections occurred in January 2020. This increase represents a serious amount of data that has to be processed because there are a limited number of studies on Turkish text mining – especially for author recognition and emotion analysis – this study aimed to contribute to the Turkish text classification area significantly.

There are studies on Turkish texts using different methods for different purposes. Naive Bayes, support vector machines and decision trees have been used in a study to find the author (Amasyalı and Diri, 2006). Also, classifying documents according to the text's genre and identifying the gender of an author are done automatically. The feature vector is generated by using the n-gram technique. The success in determining the author of the text, the genre of the text and gender of the author was found to be 83%, 93% and 96%, respectively. In another study, author recognition was performed on Turkish documents using ridge regression analysis (Kuyumcu et al., 2019). For the solution of the author recognition problem, the features obtained by applying the term frequency-inverse document frequency (TF-IDF) weighting method separately for word 1-3 n-grams and character 2-6 n-grams were combined and represented in vector space. An accuracy of 89.6% was obtained in that study.

The filtering of spam emails in Turkish has been performed by using artificial neural networks (Özgür et al., 2004). Seven hundred and fifty emails were used. Four hundred and ten of them were spam mail and the rest were normal mail. Terms were used as features. Both binary term weighting and probabilistic methods were applied. The mutual information method was implemented as a feature selection. The success in classifying kinds of mail was 90%. In another study on filtering spam emails in Turkish, the performance of Naive Bayes, support vector machines and artificial neural network methods were compared (Tantuğ and Eryiğit, 2006).

By scanning Turkish web pages, a data set of 22000 samples was created to determine the types of these pages (Hüsem and Gülcü, 2017). The n-gram technique was used to construct the feature vector. The information gain technique was used for feature selection. Naive Bayes and SVM were used as classification algorithms. When the number of categories was low, a 92.6% success rate was achieved, and a 79.45% success rate is achieved when the number of categories is high.

More than 20 methods have been tried to measure the similarity of Turkish documents (Keleş and Özel, 2017). The aim of the study was initially considered for the detection of plagiarism. Document similarity was processed in two different ways. In the first, document similarity was measured without a pre-processing step. In the second, document similarity was measured after a pre-processing step. According to the experimental results, it was observed that the pre-processing step increased the similarity detection performance. In all experiments, it was emphasized that the cosine similarity method was more successful than other distance criteria. A similar study was conducted to evaluate the similarities of Turkish words (Aydoğan and Karci, 2019).

A new data set called TTC-3600 was created by Kılınç et al., 2017. This data set consisted of news texts from various newspapers. The dataset consisted of 3600 documents, including 600 news items from six categories. These were the economy, culture–arts, health, politics, sport and technology. Five different classification algorithms were used. These were Naive Bayes, SVM, K-Nearest Neighbor (KNN), J48 and Random Forest. The experimental results showed that the best accuracy criterion value of 91.03% was obtained with the Random Forest classifier. In another study on this data set, the methods of document representation were compared (Yıldırım and Yıldız, 2018). These methods were the traditional bag of words and artificial neural network-based language models. The results indicated that the traditional method was still effective. In the same dataset, classification performance was improved by using a deep learning technique called Convolutional Neural Networks (Çiğdem and Çirak, 2019).

A sentiment analysis study was conducted on the data set containing the film interpretations in IMDB using various feature selection techniques (Kaynar et al., 2017). A data set with 1000 features, including 2000 film interpretations, were used. Seventy-five percent of the data set was reserved for the training phase and the remaining 25% was reserved for the test. Five different feature selection methods were tried and their performances were compared. These methods were chi-square, information gain, gain ratio, Gini coefficient, oneR and reliefF. SVM was used to compare classification performances. The best result was obtained by the Gini coefficient method.

Classification results for different machine learning algorithms were compared for the TREMO data set (Alpkoçak et al., 2019). This data set is constituted from the Turkish sentiment analysis field. Four different machine learning approaches were used. These were artificial neural networks, SVM, Random Forest and KNN algorithms. The first five characters of the words in the texts were used and the features were extracted. A mutual information algorithm was used in the feature selection stage. The most successful classification results were obtained by SVM and artificial neural networks. KNN gave the worst results.

Text data containing 444 opinions from the FATIH project were analyzed (Göker and Tekedere, 2017). TF-IDF weighting was performed on the terms to create the feature vector. Five different machine learning approaches were used. These were artificial neural networks, sequential minimal optimization, KNN, J48 and Naive Bayes algorithms. The highest achieving algorithm for the performance comparison was the sequential minimal optimization algorithm at 88.73%.

Apart from Turkish text classification and natural language processing studies, there are many studies in different languages such as Chinese (Shi et al., 2019), English (Liu et al., 2018), Arabic (Salloum et al., 2018) and Spanish (Cabezudo et al., 2019). Studies in these languages are summarized as follows:

English is the most preferred language worldwide as a foreign language. Therefore, many people use this language even if it is not their native language. Since the language of science is English and people who speak different languages communicate in English, a lot of textual data is produced in English. For these reasons, text classification and natural language processing studies are very often performed in English. Some of the English text mining studies are text summarization (Fattah and Ren, 2008), question answering (Ke and Hagiwara, 2017), sentiment analysis (Tripathi et al., 2015) and author profiling (Estival et al., 2007).

Chinese ranks first among the most spoken languages in the world. A total of 1,300,000,000 people speak Chinese around the world (Babbel Magazine, 2020). Since there are so many people speaking in this language, many researchers continue to study text mining in Chinese. Currently, there are some problems with Chinese text classification problems stemming from the structure of Chinese (Liu et al., 2019). For example, in a Chinese sentence, there is no space between words. For this reason, the tokenization structure becomes very difficult. Generally, the word segmentation approach is used for the solution of this problem. However, it is difficult to get accurate Chinese word segmentation results. To deal with these problems, a convolutional neural network (CNN) and long short-term memory (LSTM) networks based on deep learning are frequently used on Chinese texts (Zhang and Chen, 2016; Li et al.,

2018). With the use of these algorithms, good results are obtained for Chinese texts. In the sentiment analysis study on Chinese texts, the comments of Chinese tourists at hotels in Japan were examined (Carreónet et al., 2019) because there has been a remarkable increase in the number of tourists travelling from China to Japan in recent years. Due to this increase, hotel businesses in Japan needed reliable market research tools. These are considered to be a problem for the hotel industry in Japan. To solve this problem, researchers used text mining techniques (Carreónet et al., 2019). In this study, comments made by Chinese tourists for hotels in Japan were collected and processed. The Stanford Word Segmenter tool was used in the pre-processing of the texts, and the entropy technique based on the theory of information was used in the keyword extraction phase. With the support vector machines algorithm, there was an attempt to try and classify comments as positive or negative. The highest performance achieved was determined to be $F1 = 0.93 \pm 0.05$ and an accuracy $= 0.90 \pm 0.09$. According to the positive comments, the predictions of tourist density were provided to the hotels.

Arabic is among the popular languages of the world. Approximately 315 million people use this language as their first language (Babbel Magazine, 2020), and more than 250 million people use it as their second language. Therefore, Arabic is one of the languages that researchers are interested in for text classification studies. Although Arabic text classification studies are popular, the limited number of data sets is a problem for researchers working in this field. Both single-label and multi-label datasets are very limited to Arabic text classification (Elnagar et al., 2020). For this reason, it is difficult for researchers to try text classification techniques in Arabic. Researchers created both single-label (SANAD) and multi-label (NADIA) data sets (Elnagar et al., 2020). Both data sets were made freely available to the research community looking at Arabic computational linguistics. It was aimed at increasing the classification performance by applying deep learning techniques to the data sets created. While 96.94% success was achieved with the SANAD dataset, 88.68% success was achieved with the NADIA dataset. In another text classification study on Arabic, a linear discriminant analysis (LDA) technique was used (AbuZeina and Al-Anzi, 2018). Arabic is one of the richest languages in the world in terms of the number of words. For this reason, many features appear in Arabic text classification. The high number of features negatively affects classification performance and working time. To eliminate this situation, researchers used the LDA-based dimension reduction technique. When the results obtained in the study were compared to classical machine learning methods, it was emphasized that the LDA technique was promising in the classification of Arabic documents.

Another of the common languages in the world, like Arabic, is Spanish. Spanish is the official language of 20 countries. At the same time, more than 450 million people speak Spanish as their mother tongue (Babbel Magazine, 2020). Since many people speak Spanish, the number of resources produced in this language is quite high. Therefore many researchers want to work on text mining and natural language processing in the Spanish language. In the sentiment analysis study on Spanish texts, Spanish social media messages were examined (Plaza-del-Arco et al., 2019). Researchers proposed a study of different machine learning approaches to automatically recognize emotions in messages written in Spanish on social media. They focused on Spanish texts mainly because it is a major language used in social media. Also, researchers focused on this language because emotional analysis studies on Spanish documents are also limited in published literature. In addition to this study, Molina-González et al. (2015) suggested the integration of domain information for a Spanish polarity classification system, and Martínez-Cámara et al. (2015) carried out a study of different features and machine learning algorithms to classify the polarity of Spanish Twitter posts.

TEXT PRE-PROCESSING AND FEATURE EXTRACTION

Although texts are readable by computers using HTML, PDF, DOC and TXT, they are often not in a format that can be used directly by machine learning algorithms. Texts in these structures are known as non-structured data types. Therefore, before any text classification with any machine learning technique, the texts must be passed through various steps and converted into a type that the computer can understand. Figure 1 shows the pre-processing steps used to construct texts.

Figure 1. The Steps of Text Pre-processing

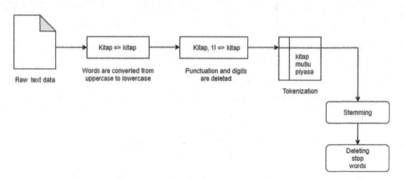

The same words in the text may be written in different forms. These words have the same importance. Therefore, all characters are converted from uppercase to lowercase so that all words in the text are in the same type. There are two important reasons for this transformation. The first is to reduce the total number of words by gathering words of the same structure and meaning into a single form. The second is to prevent the wrong classification result because the number of words will change. For example, the word "**hasta**" can exist in structures such as "**Hasta**" and "**HASTA**". Although they have the same importance, the computer considers these as three different terms. Thereby, they should be transformed into a single structure.

When the sentence "**Yazın en çok tüketilen meyveler karpuz, şeftali, kiraz ve üzümdür.**" is examined, if the comma (,) or dot (.) is not deleted from the sentence, terms such as "**karpuz,**" and "**üzümdür.**" are identified along with the punctuation. Since "**karpuz**" and "**karpuz,**" in another text or document will be different from each other, the frequency of these words will change. For this reason, punctuation, symbols and numbers are removed from the text.

Since words are processed in text classification, all words in the text should be obtained. For example, in the Java programming language, all the words in the text are taken into memory by using the **split()** method. Figure 2 shows how word separation is performed.

Figure 2. The Steps of Tokenization

In most instances, words that have the same meaning can be seen in morphologically different structures within the text. For instance, a plural suffix of the words and time suffix can be given as an example. Hence, in this case the words should be converted to the same structure by the stemming process. For this purpose, stemming libraries for different languages are available. Zemberek for Turkish and Porter Stemmer for English are examples (Zemberek, 2019; Porter Stemmer, 2019). Since this study is an example of Turkish text classification, the Zemberek library is used. This tool is recommended for Turkish. When working on a language other than Turkish, a natural language processing tool developed for that language should be used.

Apart from the Zemberek tool, there are also natural language processing tools developed for Turkish. These tools are (ITU NLP Toolkit, 2020) and (Turkish NLP Toolkit, 2020). ITU NLP Toolkit (2020) provides the Turkish NLP Tools and APIs developed by a Natural Language Processing group at Istanbul Technical University. The details of this work are given in Eryiğit, 2014. The Turkish NLP Toolkit (2020) contains implementations of several natural language processing and machine learning algorithms. Although initial implementations are based on the Turkish language, the system currently contains basic modelling in three languages, English, Turkish and Persian, respectively.

Some words can be seen frequently in each category. These words have no distinguishing features for a particular category. These words are known as stop words. The conjunctions and prepositions in the language can be given as examples. Table 1 gives some stop words for Turkish. Since these words appear in each category, they are eliminated by feature selection methods. However, to avoid the computational cost, a list of stop words should be created and these words should be eliminated directly in the pre-processing phase.

Table 1. Some Stop Words for Turkish

ama	biz	bir	en	bile
her	sey	gibi	değil	böyle
kadar	ancak	var	çok	hiç
ile	bu	ne	veya	göre

The Challenges of Natural Language and Text Processing in Turkish

Speaking and writing in Turkish is difficult. These situations also bring some difficulties in natural language processing and text mining studies of the Turkish language. These difficulties can be summarized as follows:

Turkish is a formal language based on a basic word order of Subject + Object + Verb. It is not possible to make any changes in the creation of words or when forming attachments, nor does it have any rules about the locations of sentence elements. Therefore, syntactic analysis is difficult. Even in official Turkish correspondence, the general structure of the Turkish language (Subject + Object + Verb) is only partially followed. In daily conversations, the subject is usually not used; this process is carried out by the verb. The use of transposed sentences is high and the highlighted parts are used close to the verb. For this reason, a large number of complex algorithms may need to be constructed. Unlike Turkish, attention is paid to the Subject + Verb + Object structure in English. Besides, using transpose sentences is rarely seen in English. As a result, it is relatively easier to process English than Turkish.

Turkish is a root-based language and a suffix one. Being a root-based language increases the intelligibility of the language. The fact that it is also a suffix language creates difficulties in language processing. The large number of suffixes that can be added makes it difficult to analyze the word. Also, the meaning can be completely changed with these additions. The number of synonyms and homophones is high in Turkish. This is why the number of words in Turkish is less than in other languages. A word can have many meanings and multiple words can be used instead of one word. To analyze the sentence properly, it is necessary to correctly determine the meaning of the word. This situation reveals some obstacles in natural language processing. There are also suffixes and prefixes to words in English. However, this is only true for some words. Consequently, again, it is relatively easier to process English than Turkish.

Document Representation

Texts must be converted to a numerical format to use machine learning algorithms on text data. In most text classification studies, a bag of words and the vector space model are preferred to convert text data into a format that computers can understand (Berry, 2004). In the bag of words approach, all the unique words in the training data sets form a vector. In other words, each document is represented by a vector.

$$doc_i = term_{1,i} - term_{2,i} - term_{3,i} - \ldots - term_{i,n} \tag{1}$$

In Equation 1, the document i is represented as a vector. Where n is the total number of words in the training data set. The vector is filled with the weight values of the terms using any term weighting method.

Term Weighting Approach

The most important reason for term weighting in text mining is to reveal the distinctive power of classification algorithms more clearly. For example, if any term appears too few times in some documents and too many times in other documents, this difference must have arisen through the term weighting approach. The most commonly used term weighting methods in text classification are binary term weighting and the TF-IDF methods (Salton and Buckley, 1988).

Binary Term Weighting

This is the most primitive and simple weighting method. If a term is used in the document, it is weighted as 1, otherwise, it is weighted as 0. The advantage of this method is that it is simple to use and has little computational cost. The disadvantage is that it does not make a distinction between terms. For example, a term seen ten times in the same document and a term seen once has the same significance. Another disadvantage is that the number of terms in the documents is ignored. For these reasons, binary term weighting is not as successful as other popular term weighting methods.

Term Frequency: Inverse Document Frequency (TF-IDF)

TF-IDF is one of the most important weighting methods. It was developed by (Jones, 1972; Jones, 2004). It is one of the first examples from information retrieval studies. The method is used for different purposes besides term weighting.

The TF-IDF consists of two factors: term frequency and inverse document frequency. The term frequency is calculated based on the document, while the inverse document frequency is calculated from the whole training set. There are many variations in the calculation of TF (Dogan and Uysal, 2019). The most commonly used TF is the number that specifies how many times a term appears in the document. In Equation 2, the TF-IDF value of any term t is calculated.

$$TF - IDF = TF \times \log \frac{total\ number\ of\ documents}{the\ number\ of\ documents\ containing\ the\ term\ t} \tag{2}$$

TF-IDF is used for different purposes in text classification studies. For example, in (Lan et al., 2008), TF-IDF is used for weighting, while in the (Taşcı and Güngör, 2013) study, it is used for feature selection. TF-IDF is used for weighting in this study.

FEATURE SELECTION METHODS

Machine learning algorithms usually take a long time to run due to their structure. At the same time, the operation of these algorithms is directly related to the size of the data. Document vectors are created by using all the words in the training sets. Therefore, documents are represented by tens of thousands of terms. Most of these terms do not contain important information as they do not positively affect the success of classification. The vector size will be very large, so memory and calculation problems will arise. In the previous subsection, techniques such as stemming words and removing stop words are used to reduce the vector size in the pre-processing stage. Although pre-processing methods and size reduction are used, a feature selection step is needed since it cannot solve the dimension problem completely. Feature selection is the process of finding a subset that best represents all words, rather than using all the terms in the bag of words. Thanks to feature selection:

- Memory wastage can be avoided by reducing the vector size.
- The running time of the text classification process can be reduced.
- Data considered as non-important or considered to be noise may be eliminated.
- Overfitting problems can be solved.

Feature selection methods are generally divided into three main groups (Rong et al., 2019). These are filters, wrappers and embedded methods. In addition to these methods, hybrid methods are also available (Hsu et al., 2019). Filtering is the most preferred method because the computation cost is low and easy to apply compared to the other two methods. Filtering methods are often statistical metrics that are derived from the number of occurrences of terms in their category or opposite categories (Şahin and Kılıç, 2019). Chi-Square (CHI), Information Gain (IG) and DF metrics are examples of filtering methods.

When selecting a feature with filtering methods, the selection is made in two different ways. These are local policies and global policies (Taşçı et al., 2013). In some studies, the local policy is called class-based, and the general policy is called corpus-based (Özgür et al., 2005). Local policies are a better approach to binary classification because the best keywords for each category are found separately (Özgür et al., 2005). As a result, a one-vs-all classification approach and local policy are applied in this study. In the general policy, a single feature vector is obtained by using some optimization techniques among the features obtained for each category. When the number of features is small, the local policy gives good classification achievements (Tasci and Gungor, 2008). When the number of features is too large, a general policy gives good classification achievements (Tasci and Gungor, 2008).

Chi-Square Metric

Chi-Square (CHI) metric is statistics-based and widely used for feature selection. In Equation 3, the CHI value is calculated for each feature value.

$$CHI = N \frac{(ad - bc)^2}{(a+c)(b+d)(a+b)(c+d)} \tag{3}$$

The CHI value of the term t_i in any class c_i is calculated in Equation 3. Where a represents the number of documents that contain the t_i term in c_i, b represents the number of documents that do not contain the t_i term in c_i, c represents the number of documents that contain the t_i term but do not belong to c_i and d represents the number of documents that do not contain the t_i term but do not belong to c_i. N indicates the total amount of documents (i.e. $N=a+b+c+d$). If the CHI value is 0, there is no relationship between the term and the category. As the CHI value increases, the relationship between the term and the category increases.

Information Gain

Information Gain (IG) generates a value. The produced value is the answer to the question of how important it is for the class. In Equation 4, the mathematical representation of information gain is given.

$$IG(t) = -\sum_{i=1}^{M} P(c_i) log P(c_i) + P(t) \sum_{i=1}^{M} P(c_i \mid t) log P(c_i \mid t) + P(t') \sum_{i=1}^{M} P(c_i \mid t') log P(c_i \mid t') \tag{4}$$

In Equation 4, M is the total number of categories, $P(c_i)$ means the probability that a document belongs to the class c_i in all categories, $P(t)$ means the probability that the term t is included in a document in the corpus, $P(t')$ means the probability that the term t is not included in a document in the corpus, $P(c_i|t)$ is the probability that the term t appears at least once in one of the documents in the class and $P(c_i \mid t')$ is the probability that the term t does not exist in any of the documents in the c_i class. The terms take values between 0 and 1 according to IG. The terms with the highest value are those that are most relevant to the category.

SOLUTIONS AND RECOMMENDATIONS

In this section, the methods used in the solution of the problems discussed in the study will be given. These are, respectively, the data sets used, the classification algorithms and the performance measures. The steps followed to solve the text classification problems are given in Figure 3.

Figure 3. The General Structure of Text Classification

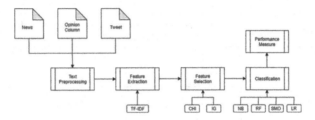

Data Sets Used

In this study, three different data sets were used. The first consisted of documents belonging to news texts received from Turkish newspapers (News Data Set, 2019). This data set normally consists of 13 categories. Six categories of the data set were used in this study. The distribution of the data set is given in Table 2.

Table 2. Distribution of Kemik Natural Language Processing Group News Data Set

Category	Number of Train Documents	Number of Tests Documents	Total Documents
economy	2285	980	3265
magazine	1954	838	2792
health	968	415	1383
politics	1294	555	1849
sport	6697	3300	9997
technology	539	232	771

The second data set was created for sentiment analysis (Çetin and Amasyalı, 2013). The data set was generated from twitter comments about GSM and telecommunication companies. Messages tagged "+" consisted of positive messages for companies and messages tagged "−" consisted of negative messages. Messages were short and often had typos. Therefore, it is a difficult data set to classify. The distribution of the data set is given in Table 3.

The third data set was the author detection data set (Mayda and Amasyalı, 2016). It was composed of the texts of the authors working in some newspapers. It was a balanced and difficult data set to categorize. The writing of six authors and their distributions are given in Table 4.

Table 3. Distribution of Kemik Natural Language Processing Group Tweets Data Set

Category	Number of Train Documents	Number of Tests Documents	Total Documents
+	529	227	756
-	900	387	1287

Table 4. Distribution of Kemik Natural Language Processing Group 500 Opinion Column Data Set

Author's Name	Number of Train Documents	Number of Tests Documents	Total Documents
Cüneyt Özdemir	35	15	50
Ece Temelkuran	35	15	50
İlber Ortaylı	35	15	50
İsmail Küçükkaya	35	15	50
Mustafa Balbay	35	15	50
Uğur Dündar	35	15	50

Classification Algorithms

In this study, four different classification algorithms were used according to the one-vs-all approach. The classification algorithms were Random Forest (RF), Naive Bayes (NB), sequential minimal optimization (SMO) and logistic regression (LR) techniques.

Random Forest

Random Forest is an easy to use, flexible machine learning algorithm. RF can be used for both classification and regression problems. The algorithm forms a random forest. The created forest is a collection of decision trees that are often trained with the bagging method. In other words, the Random Forest creates more than one decision tree. Then, it combines the forests to get an accurate and stable prediction.

Naive Bayes

Naive Bayes is a probability-based classification algorithm based on Bayes theorem. The NB classification aims to determine the class of data given to the system using calculations according to probability principles. Considering a problem with three classes, the algorithm will generate three different probability values to estimate the class of data. The data will be tagged according to the highest probability value. It is an algorithm that can give successful results with little training data. Compared to most classification algorithms, the computational cost is low.

Sequential Minimal Optimization Based Support Vector Machine

SMO is a supervised classification algorithm where a model is created based on training data. According to this model, the test data is included in a certain class. In the support vector machines model, the hyperplane is determined which separates the classes from each other. The determination of this hyperplane is based on maximizing the distance between the support vectors of the classes to process the classification.

Logistic Regression

Logistic Regression solves binary classification problems based on supervised machine learning and statistical models. In regression problems, a continuous variable is generally obtained as the output. In LR, the output is not always continuous. The algorithm can be used in many ways. In this study, results are obtained from the LR algorithm with the one-vs-all approach. Otherwise, the classification process cannot be performed. With this algorithm, the logistic function in mathematics is used to calculate the threshold value. Two classes are defined according to this logistic function. If the value of the logistic function is bigger than 0.5, the result is first class. Otherwise, the result is a second class.

Performance Measure

One of the biggest misconceptions in the studies using classification algorithms is to interpret the accuracy rate as classification success. Especially in imbalanced data sets, accuracy does not give much information about classification performance. In such cases, it would be useful to consider two metrics instead of the accuracy metric. These are recall and precision. Table 5 shows the confusion matrix.

Table 5. Confusion Matrix

ACTUAL			
+ CLASS	- CLASS		
True Positive	False Positive	+ CLASS	PREDICTION
False Negative	True Negative	- CLASS	

According to the confusion matrix, the True Positive (TP), False Positive (FP), True Negative (TN) and False Negative (FN) metrics are defined as follows:

TP: This is the case where + labelled instances are estimated as +.
FP: This is the case where − labelled instances are estimated as +.
TN: This is the case where − labelled instances are estimated as −.
FN: This is the case where + labelled instances are estimated as −.

The basic concepts used to evaluate the performance of the model are precision, recall and F-measure. Criteria for precision (π) and recall (ρ) are given in Equations 5 and 6, respectively.

$$\pi = \frac{TP}{TP + FP} \tag{5}$$

$$\rho = \frac{TP}{TP + FN} \tag{6}$$

Precision and recall criteria are not sufficient to give a meaningful comparison by themselves. The F-measure is defined for this purpose. The F-measure is calculated using Equation 5 and Equation 6, as given in Equation 7.

$$F = \frac{2\pi\rho}{\pi + \rho} \tag{7}$$

Since the application works in binary classification, the classification success of each category is calculated separately and an average F-measure is obtained.

RESULTS AND DISCUSSIONS

In this section, the results obtained from the data sets will be given. The results of the study will be presented in two different ways. Firstly, the keywords obtained from feature selection methods will be shown according to categories. Then, the performance of classification algorithms will be given. Classification achievements will be given separately according to feature selection methods.

Comparison of Keywords Extracted by Feature Selection Metrics

Since the working principle of each feature selection metric is different, the extracted keywords by these feature selection metrics are different. Which feature is selected is also an important parameter for the classification algorithms. Table 6 shows the top 10 features obtained from the news data set according to the CHI metric. The English meaning of Turkish words is given in parentheses in Table 6 to Table 11. English meanings for words with the same meaning are not given separately in other tables.

When Table 6 is analyzed, according to the CHI metric, 1 of the 60 words belonging to all categories is a common word. The word **takım** is seen in both the magazine and the sports category. This word, which is very important for the sports category, is misleading for the classification algorithm because it appears in another category. Apart from this word, the CHI metric did not find common words. This result indicated that the CHI metric generates distinguishing keywords.

Table 7 shows the top 10 features obtained from the news data set according to the IG metric. When Table 7 is examined, according to the IG metric, four of the 60 words belonging to all categories are common words. While there are 50 unique words, there are four common words. These words are **takım**, **oyun**, **başkan** and **futbol**. The word **takım** has appeared in the categories for the economy, magazines, sports and technology. The words **oyun**, **başkan** and **futbol** are selected as keywords in two different categories. The word **oyun** is used in the categories for the economy and sports. The word **başkan** is seen in the categories for magazines and politics. Finally, the word **futbol** is seen in the categories for magazines and sports.

When the keywords obtained from IG and CHI metrics are compared for the news data set, the CHI metric finds more unique words. When the extracted keywords in the economic category are compared,

Table 6. Kemik Natural Language Processing Group News Data Set - The best-distinguishing terms according to the CHI metric

Category	economy	magazine	health	politics	sport	technology
	milyar (billion)	dizi (series)	hastalık (disease)	parti (political party)	takım (team)	google
	yüzde (percentage)	şarkı (song)	hasta (patient)	başbakan (prime minister)	futbol (football)	bilgisayar (computer)
	şirket (company)	ünlü (famous)	tedavi (treatment)	milletvekil (deputy)	oyna (play)	apple
	sektör (sector)	sanat (art)	sağlık (health)	erdoğan (turkey president's surname)	kulüp (club)	android
	banka (bank)	film (film)	ilaç (drug)	terör (terror)	sezon (season)	iphone
Top 10 features	dolar (dollar)	posta (post)	uzman (expert)	tbmm (grand national assembly of turkey)	oyun (game)	cihaz (device)
	yatırım (investment)	takım (team)	vücut (body)	meclis (parliament)	saha (area)	windows
	piyasa (market)	sahne (scene)	prof (prof)	tayyip (turkey president's name)	transfer (transfer)	telefon (phone)
	lira (turkish lira)	sevgi (love)	besle (feed)	siyasi (political)	galatasaray (the name of football team)	teknoloji (technology)
	fiyat (price)	album (album)	cerrahi (surgical)	millet (nation)	fenerbahçe (the name of football team)	mobil (mobile)

Table 7. Kemik Natural Language Processing Group News Data Set - The best-distinguishing terms according to the IG metric

Category	economy	magazine	health	politics	sport	technology
	yüzde	dizi	hastalık	parti	takım	bilgisayar
	milyar	şarki	hasta	başbakan	futbol	google
	şirket	ünlü	sağlık	milletvekil	kulüp	kullan (use)
	takım	takim	tedavi	erdoğan	oyna	telefon
	sektör	başkan (president)	uzman	terör	sezon	teknoloji
Top 10 features	dolar	kaydet (save)	ilaç	meclis	saha	cihaz
	banka	film	prof	tbmm	fenerbahçe	apple
	yatırım	sanat	vücut	tayyip	galatasaray	takım
	piyasa	posta	hastane (hospital)	başkan (president)	oyun	mobil
	oyun	futbol	besle	siyasi	transfer	facebook

Table 8. Kemik Natural Language Processing Group Tweets Data Set - The best-distinguishing terms according to the CHI metric

Category	positive	negative
	hayat (life)	mesaj
	superonline (company name)	hayat
	teşekkür (thanks)	paylaş
	paylaş (share)	fatura (bill)
Top 10 features	tesekkurler (thanks)	selocan (ad film character)
	mesaj (message)	hala (still)
	manga (group)	para (money)
	turkcellmuzik (turkcell is a gsm operator)	gnctrkcll (youth package belonging to gsm company)
	ödül (prize)	allah (god)
	fiber (fiber)	edge (edge)

the CHI metric finds the word **fiyat**. This word is directly related to the economy. However, the IG metric cannot find it in the 10 most important words. When the keywords found using IG and CHI methods in the magazine category were compared, seven of the top 10 words were the same. The words **sahne** and **albüm** found by the CHI method can make a remarkable distinction in the magazine category. In the health category, both IG and CHI metrics found nine of the 10 keywords. The CHI metric selects **cerrahi**, and the IG metric selects **hastane**. Both selected words are distinctive in this category. In the politics category, both IG and CHI metrics found nine of the 10 keywords. The CHI metric selects **millet**, and the IG metric selects **başkan**. Both selected words are distinctive for this category. However, since the word **başkan** appeared in other categories, it adversely affected the success of the classification. Both IG and CHI metrics find the same words in the sports category. When the keywords found by IG and CHI metrics in the technology category were compared, seven of the top 10 words were the same. The words **android, iphone** and **windows** were found by CHI. However, the words **kullan, takım** and **facebook** were selected by IG.

Table 8 shows the top 10 features obtained from the Tweets data set according to the CHI metric. When Table 8 is analyzed, according to the CHI metric, three of the 20 words belonging to all categories were common words. These words were **hayat, paylaş** and **mesaj**. Having many keywords in common is a problem. This situation will undermine the performance of the classification algorithm. The prominent words in positive messages were **teşekkür, tesekkurler, ödül** and **fiber**. In negative messages, the words **fatura, para** and **edge** were selected.

Table 9 shows the top 10 features obtained from the Tweets data set according to the IG metric. When Table 9 is examined, according to the IG method, four of the 20 words belonging to all categories were common words. These words were **hayat, paylaş, ödül** and **mesaj**. Selecting a positive word such as **an** in the negative category as a keyword will mislead the classification algorithm. Examples of positive words discovered by the IG metric are the words **teşekkür, tesekkurler, fiber, mutlu** and **memnun**. The words **teşekkür, tesekkurler, mutlu** and **memnun** are very meaningful words for positive messages. These words may positively affect the classification performance. In particular, words **mutlu** and **memnun** are precise positive keywords.

Table 9. Kemik Natural Language Processing Group Tweets Data Set - The best-distinguishing terms according to the IG metric

Category	positive	negative
	hayat	mesaj
	superonline	hayat
	mesaj	paylaş
	paylaş	fatura
Top 10 features	teşekkür	selocan
	tesekkurler	hala
	ödül	para
	fiber	gnctrkcll
	mutlu (happy)	allah
	memnun (pleased)	ödül

Table 10 shows the top 10 features obtained from the 500 Opinion Column data set according to the CHI metric. When Table 10 is analyzed, according to the CHI metric, all keywords were selected differently from each other. The absence of common words for each author indicates that effective feature selection has been achieved.

Table 11 shows the top 10 features obtained from the 500 Opinion Column data set according to the IG metric. When Table 11 is analyzed, according to the IG metric, all keywords were used differently from each other. The IG metric did not find any common keywords like the CHI metric.

When the keywords obtained from IG and CHI metrics were compared in the Opinion Column data set, seven keywords related to Cüneyt Özdemir were common to both IG and CHI. Different words found with CHI were **bambaşka, twitter** and **dair**. IG selects **parti, fark** and **yine**. In both metrics, **birkaç** was selected as a keyword. This word was selected by metrics because it was not included in the stop word list. However, **birkaç** can be considered a stop word. All authors can use this word. There is no distinguishing feature of the word **birkaç**. Similarly, since the words **çünkü, kere** and **böylece** are not in the stop words list, they appeared in the keywords table. When the author Ece Temelkuran was examined, both metrics found seven common words. The CHI metric selected **neşe, ziyade** and **epey**, while the IG metric selected **başkan, türkiye** and **öldür**. Considering these three different words, CHI emphasized words related to the sentence structure used by the author. However, IG extracted keywords about the author's topics. When the features of author İlber Ortaylı were examined, 7 out of 10 words were found by both CHI and IG. İlber Ortaylı writes about Ottoman history. Selected keywords were directly related to history. For this author, the IG metric found the words **cihan, vilayet** and **tanzimat**, while the CHI metric found the words **bazı, ordu** and **paşa**. Five words – except the word **bazı** – are very meaningful and distinctive keywords for this author. IG and CHI feature selection methods found the same nine keywords for author İsmail Küçükkaya. The different words found were **bölgesel** and **ekonomik**. The word **bölgesel** was selected by CHI and the word **ekonomik** by IG. If the keywords of the author Mustafa Balbay are evaluated, 9 common words were found by CHI and IG. While the word **yelpaze** was selected by CHI, IG selected the word **parlamento**. The words found by IG are more discriminating compared to CHI. All keywords of the author Uğur Dündar were the same. Both CHI and IG cannot find a difference for this author.

Table 10. Kemik Natural Language Processing Group 500 Opinion Column Data Set - The best-distinguishing terms according to the CHI metric

Category	Cüneyt Özdemir	Ece Temelkuran	İlber Ortaylı	İsmail Küçükkaya	Mustafa Balbay	Uğur Dündar
	gözük (seem)	mühim (important)	imperator (imperial)	kritik (critical)	kasım (november)	okur (reader)
	yayımla (publish)	hala (still)	asır (century)	formül (formula)	vurgula (emphasise)	sevgi (love)
	çıkart (eject)	sebep (reason)	osmanlı (ottoman)	risk (risk)	sandık (chest)	dündar (author's surname)
	film	çünkü (because)	fransa (france)	washington (washington)	yelpaze (range)	yandaş (partisan)
Top 10 features	birkaç (some)	kere (times)	cihan (world)	olağanüstü (splendid)	tablo (table)	uğur (author's name)
	madem (as, since)	neşe (cheer)	vilayet (province)	küresel (global)	seçim (election)	operasyon (operation)
	bakın (look)	mesele (problem)	eski (old)	yönetim (management)	haziran (june)	vatan (motherland)
	bambaşka (disparate)	filan (and so on)	avusturya (austria)	stratejik (strategic)	ilişkin (related)	gözyaş (tear)
	twitter	ziyade (too much)	dahi (genius)	barış (peace)	sapta (determine)	iftira (slander)
	dair (about)	epey (quite)	tanzimat (reorganizations)	bölgesel (regional)	irade (will)	böylece (thus)

Table 11. Kemik Natural Language Processing Group 500 Opinion Column Data Set - The best-distinguishing terms according to the IG metric

Category	Cüneyt Özdemir	Ece Temelkuran	İlber Ortaylı	İsmail Küçükkaya	Mustafa Balbay	Uğur Dündar
	yayımla	mühim	imparator	risk	kasım	okur
	çıkart	çünkü	asır	kritik	vurgula	sevgi
	gözük	sebep	osmanlı	formül	seçim	dündar
	birkaç	hala	eski	washington	sandık	yandaş
	parti	mesele	fransa	yönetim	tablo	uğur
	film	kere	bazı	küresel	ilişkin	operasyon
Top 10 features	fark (difference)	başkan	avusturya	olağanüstü	haziran	böylece
	bakın	türkiye (turkey)	dahi	barış	parlemento (legislative assembly)	vatan
	madem	öldür (kill)	ordu (military)	stratejik	sapta	gözyaş
	yine (once again)	filan	paşa	ekonomik (economical)	irade	iftira

Comparison of the Performance of Classification Algorithms

The IG and CHI methods often select different features according to category. Due to these differences, feature vectors also differ. The performance of classification algorithms will change as a result of differences in the feature vector. In this subsection, the results were examined in two different ways. Firstly, classification performances are given according to the features obtained from the metrics. Secondly, the performance of classification algorithms were evaluated in their entirety. All figures given from Figure 4 to Figure 9 were drawn using the plot function of MATLAB (Matlab, 2020; Matlab Plot, 2020).

Figure 4 shows the results of the news data set. The CHI metric was used as a feature selection method in these results. SMO was the most successful classification algorithm when between 60 and 960 features are used. When the number of features was 60, the classification performance was 0.83 according to SMO.

Figure 4. Kemik Natural Language Processing Group News Data Set - Results from CHI metric

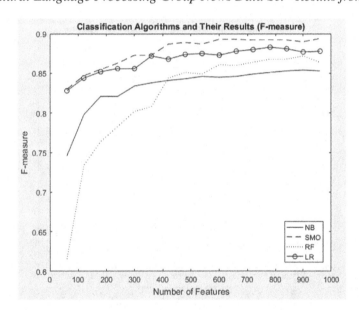

The classification performances obtained from NB, RF and LR algorithms for 60 features were 0.746, 0.616 and 0.828, respectively. The worst classification performance was achieved by the RF algorithm for up to 420 features. The RF algorithm outperformed the NB algorithm when the number of features exceeded 420. The best performance after the SMO algorithm was obtained by the LR algorithm. When the number of features was 780, the LR algorithm returned a value of 0.883. This result was the highest classification performance obtained by the LR algorithm. As the number of features increased, the performance of the algorithms generally increased. The best result obtained with the NB algorithm was 0.854. This result was obtained using 900 features. Similarly, the RF algorithm achieved the best results for 900 features, giving a result of 0.872.

Figure 5 shows the results of the news data set. The IG metric was used as a feature selection method for these results. SMO and LR were the most successful classification algorithms when 60 features were used. When the number of features was 60, the classification performance F-measure was 0.84 according to SMO and LR. The performance of the SMO algorithm outperformed the LR algorithm when using more than 60 features. The classification performances obtained from NB and RF for 60 features was 0.775 and 0.72, respectively. The worst classification performance was achieved by the RF algorithm. The RF algorithm outperformed the NB algorithm once the number of features exceeded 180. The best performance after the SMO algorithm was obtained by the LR algorithm. When the number of features was 840, the LR algorithm returned a value of 0.881. This result was the highest classification performance obtained by the LR algorithm. As the number of features increased, the performance of the algorithms generally increased. The best result obtained with the NB algorithm was 0.85. This result was obtained by using 900 features. The RF algorithm achieved the best results with 960 features with a value of 0.873.

Figure 5. Kemik Natural Language Processing Group News Data Set - Results from IG metric

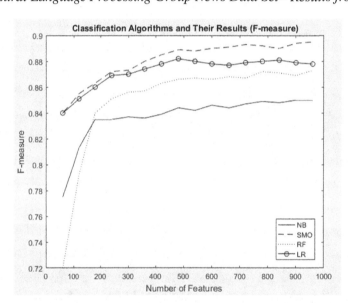

When Figure 4 and Figure 5 are taken into consideration, the IG metric gave better classification results than the CHI metric. This is the case when fewer features were used. Especially for the NB and RF algorithm, the result was more evident. For example, the NB algorithm gave a result of 0.746 in CHI with 60 features, while the NB algorithm using the same number of features returned a value of 0.775 with the IG method. When the RF algorithm was used instead of NB, the results were 0.616 and 0.72, respectively. These results showed that the keywords selected with the IG metric had a positive effect on classification performance. As the number of features increased, this difference in classification performance gradually decreased and the results converged. Considering the results from both metrics, the best results were obtained by the SMO algorithm with the IG metric for 960 features. This result was an F-measure of 0.895.

Figure 6 shows the results for the Tweets data set. The CHI metric was used as a feature selection method for these results. The highest performance was obtained by the RF algorithm. This result was 0.781 when 20 features were used. This result was also the best in Figure 6. The best result after the RF algorithm was obtained by the NB algorithm. Classification performance usually decreased when feature size increased with this dataset. This was because keywords were not distinctive for tweet messages. It also represented a different problem because the message size was short and there were many misspelled words. Since only word-based feature extraction was used, the classification algorithm could not distinguish the tweets messages well.

Figure 6. Kemik Natural Language Processing Group Tweets Data Set - Results from CHI metric

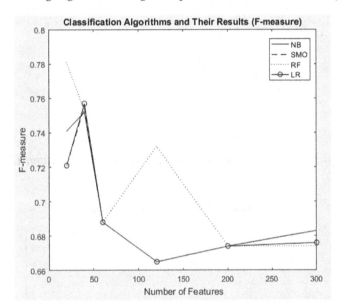

Figure 7 shows the results of the Tweets data set. The IG metric was used as the feature selection method in these results. The highest performance was obtained by the RF algorithm. This result was 0.767 when 20 features were used. This result was also the best in Figure 7. The best results after the RF algorithm were obtained by the NB and SMO algorithms. Classification performance decreased when feature size increased with this dataset.

When Figure 6 and Figure 7 were examined, the CHI gave better classification results than the IG metric. The differences between CHI and IG metrics were not important. For example, the NB algorithm gave a result of 0.741 in CHI with 20 features, while using the same number of features with the NB algorithm returned a value of 0.736 with the IG method. This also applied to the other algorithms.

Figure 8 shows the results of the 500 Opinion Column data set. The CHI metric was used as a feature selection method in these results. The highest performance was obtained by the LR algorithm using 60 features. The result obtained with the LR algorithm was 0.626. The best result in Figure 8 was 0.778 obtained by the NB algorithm with 960 features. When the number of features was increased, the performance of the classification usually improved.

Figure 7. Kemik Natural Language Processing Group Tweets Data Set - Results from IG metric

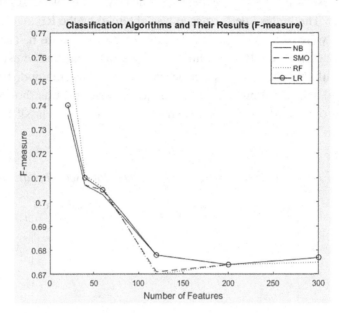

Figure 8. Kemik Natural Language Processing Group 500 Opinion Column Data Set - Results from CHI metric

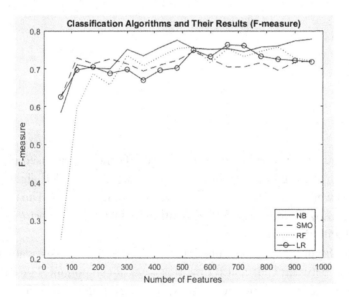

Figure 9 shows the results of the 500 Opinion Column data set. The IG metric was used as a feature selection method in these results. The highest performance was obtained by the SMO and LR algorithms using 60 features. The result obtained with the SMO and LR algorithms was 0.642. The best result in Figure 9 was 0.809 obtained by the NB algorithm using 660 and 720 features. When the number of features increased, the performance of the classification usually improved.

Figure 9. Kemik Natural Language Processing Group 500 Opinion Column Data Set - Results from IG metric

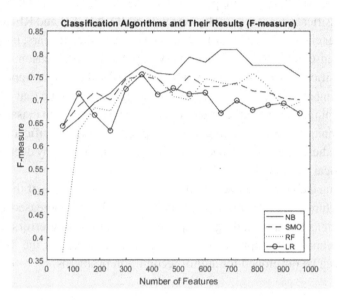

When Figure 8 and Figure 9 were examined, the IG metric gave better classification results than the CHI metric. This was the case when fewer features were used. Especially for the NB and RF algorithms, the result was more evident. For example, the NB algorithm gave a result of 0.584 in CHI with 60 features, while the NB algorithm using the same number of features returned a value of 0.63 with the IG method. When the RF algorithm was used instead of NB, the results were 0.25 and 0.367, respectively. These results showed that the keywords selected with the IG metric had a positive effect on the classification performance when fewer features were selected in comparison to the CHI metric. As the number of features increased, this difference in classification performance gradually decreased and the results converged. When the numbers of features were increased, the performance of the classification algorithms in the CHI metric usually improved. Considering the results from both metrics, the best results were obtained using the NB algorithm with the IG metric for 660 and 720 features. These results gave an F-measure of 0.809.

FUTURE RESEARCH DIRECTIONS

In text classification studies, researchers generally focus on two problems. The first is to increase the classification performance, while the second is to reduce the working time of the classification algorithms. In order to increase the classification performance, only TF-IDF term weighting technique was used in this study. However, there are many term weighting models in published literature. Therefore, classification performances can be improved by using different term weighting approaches. Many researchers also endeavour to develop new term weighting models. Therefore, a new term weighting model may appear in published literature. Feature selection is one of the important problems always waiting for effective solutions in the field of text classification to reduce the working time of classification algorithms. Therefore, effective feature selection methods are needed. In this study, only filter-based CHI and IG metrics were used. In addition, other filtering, wrapper or embedded techniques can be used.

In this study, the classification process took place with SMO, NB, LR and RF algorithms. In addition to these algorithms, other classification algorithms can be used. In recent years, increasing classification performance using the ensemble model has been very popular. For this reason, new ensemble models can be developed. Classification performance can be increased with similar approaches. In addition to classical machine learning algorithms, another machine learning technique that has become popular in recent years is deep learning. Considerable improvement can be achieved in classification achievements using deep learning techniques. Deep learning can be applied to news classification, author recognition and emotion analysis studies. Classification performance can be improved by deep learning, which gives better results than classical machine learning.

New feature extraction techniques for sentiment analysis studies are one of the open problems. With the addition of new features, classification performance can also be increased in sentiment analysis studies. Techniques such as n-gram, finding emoji, and removal spelling errors can be added to emotion analysis. These methods will improve classification performance. At the same time, new feature extraction approaches can be developed for author recognition problems.

CONCLUSION

In this study, a comprehensive Turkish text mining study has been presented. These are the classification of Turkish news, Turkish sentiment analysis and Turkish author recognition studies. It attempted to solve three different problems with classical machine learning techniques. Also, feature selection methods were tried to reduce the execution time of machine learning algorithms to obtain related keywords. In classifying news categories and opinion columns, more than 80% of classification performance was achieved. Nearly 90% success was achieved in separating news categories. In sentiment analysis, the classification performance did not exceed 78.1%. While it is enough to classify the news and authors, it is not enough to use words as a feature in sentiment analysis. The most successful result was generally obtained by the SMO algorithm when considering the keywords selected by both the IG metric and the CHI metric in the classification of news texts. When the feature selection methods were compared, the highest classification performance was found using the IG metric. After the SMO algorithm, the LR algorithm was the most successful algorithm. Compared to the NB algorithm and the RF algorithm, the NB algorithm gave better results when using fewer features. Nevertheless, as the number of features increased, the performance of the RF algorithm was better. Considering the keywords extracted from both the IG metric and the CHI metric in author recognition, the most successful result was usually obtained from the NB algorithm.

When the feature selection methods were compared, the highest classification performance was found using the IG metric. It would not be correct to make a general comparison for the performance of other algorithms other than the NB algorithm because the RF algorithm had the worst performance when the number of attributes was low. However, as the number of attributes increased, the performance of the RF algorithm often exceeded the LR and SMO algorithm.

Considering the keywords extracted from both the IG metric and the CHI metric in the sentiment analysis, the most successful result was generally obtained from the RF algorithm. When the feature selection methods were compared, the highest classification performance was found using the CHI metric. It would not be correct to make a general comparison for the performance of other algorithms other than the RF algorithm because the performance of the algorithms is almost the same. Considering the three different problems discussed in the study, it was seen that the classification performance obtained for sentiment analysis was lower than the others. Therefore, emotion analysis performance needs to be improved.

REFERENCES

Abdullah, S. S., Rahaman, M. S., & Rahman, M. S. (2013). Analysis of stock market using text mining and natural language processing. In *2013 International Conference on Informatics, Electronics and Vision (ICIEV)* (pp. 1-6). IEEE. 10.1109/ICIEV.2013.6572673

AbuZeina, D., & Al-Anzi, F. S. (2018). Employing fisher discriminant analysis for Arabic text classification. *Computers & Electrical Engineering*, *66*, 474–486. doi:10.1016/j.compeleceng.2017.11.002

Aggarwal, C. C., & Zhai, C. (2012). A survey of text classification algorithms. In *Mining text data* (pp. 163–222). Springer. doi:10.1007/978-1-4614-3223-4_6

Alpkoçak, A., Tocoglu, M. A., Çelikten, A., & Aygün, İ. (2019). Türkçe Metinlerde Duygu Analizi için Farklı Makine Öğrenmesi Yöntemlerinin Karşılaştırılması. *Dokuz Eylül Üniversitesi Mühendislik Fakültesi Fen ve Mühendislik Dergisi*, *21*(63), 719–725. doi:10.21205/deufmd.2019216303

Amasyalı, M. F., & Diri, B. (2006). Automatic Turkish text categorization in terms of author, genre and gender. In *International Conference on Application of Natural Language to Information Systems* (pp. 221-226). Springer. 10.1007/11765448_22

Apté, C., Damerau, F., & Weiss, S. M. (1994). Automated learning of decision rules for text categorization. *ACM Transactions on Information Systems*, *12*(3), 233–251. doi:10.1145/183422.183423

Artemenko, O., Mandl, T., Shramko, M., & Womser-Hacker, C. (2006). Evaluation of a language identification system for mono-and multilingual text documents. In *Proceedings of the 2006 ACM symposium on Applied computing* (pp. 859-860). ACM. 10.1145/1141277.1141473

Aydoğan, M., & Karci, A. (2019). Kelime Temsil Yöntemleri ile Kelime Benzerliklerinin İncelenmesi. *Çukurova Üniversitesi Mühendislik-Mimarlık Fakültesi Dergisi*, *34*(2), 181-196.

Babbel Magazine. (2020). *The 10 most spoken languages in the world*. Retrieved from https://www.babbel.com/en/magazine/the-10-most-spoken-languages-in-the-world

Bekkerman, R., El-Yaniv, R., Tishby, N., & Winter, Y. (2001). On feature distributional clustering for text categorization. *Proceedings of the 24th annual international ACM SIGIR conference on Research and development in information retrieval*, 146-153. 10.1145/383952.383976

Berry, M. W. (2004). Survey of text mining. *Computer Review*, *45*(9), 548.

Blei, D. M., Ng, A. Y., & Jordan, M. I. (2003). Latent dirichlet allocation. *Journal of Machine Learning Research*, *3*(Jan), 993–1022.

Cabezudo, M. A. S., Palomino, N. L. S., & Perez, R. M. (2015). Improving subjectivity detection for Spanish texts using subjectivity word sense disambiguation based on knowledge. In *2015 Latin American Computing Conference (CLEI)* (pp. 1-7). IEEE. 10.1109/CLEI.2015.7360018

Cadez, I., Heckerman, D., Meek, C., Smyth, P., & White, S. (2003). Model-based clustering and visualization of navigation patterns on a web site. *Data Mining and Knowledge Discovery*, *7*(4), 399–424. doi:10.1023/A:1024992613384

Carreón, E. C. A., Nonaka, H., & Hiraoka, T. (2019). *Analysis of Chinese Tourists in Japan by Text Mining of a Hotel Portal Site.* arXiv preprint arXiv:1904.13214.

Çetin, M., & Amasyalı, M. F. (2013). Supervised and traditional term weighting methods for sentiment analysis. In *2013 21st Signal Processing and Communications Applications Conference (SIU)* (pp. 1-4). IEEE. 10.1109/SIU.2013.6531173

Chen, Y., Qin, B., Liu, T., Liu, Y., & Li, S. (2010). The Comparison of SOM and K-means for Text Clustering. *Computer and Information Science*, *3*(2), 268–274. doi:10.5539/cis.v3n2p268

Çiğdem, A., & Çirak, A. (2019). Türkçe Haber Metinlerinin Konvolüsyonel Sinir Ağları ve Word2Vec Kullanılarak Sınıflandırılması. *Bilişim Teknolojileri Dergisi*, *12*(3), 219–228.

Clark, J., Koprinska, I., & Poon, J. (2003). A neural network-based approach to automated e-mail classification. In *Proceedings IEEE/WIC International Conference on Web Intelligence (WI 2003)* (pp. 702-705). IEEE. 10.1109/WI.2003.1241300

Cutting, D. R., Karger, D. R., Pedersen, J. O., & Tukey, J. W. (2017). Scatter/gather: A cluster-based approach to browsing large document collections. In *ACM SIGIR Forum* (Vol. 51, No. 2, pp. 148-159). New York, NY: ACM.

Dasgupta, S., & Ng, V. (2009). Topic-wise, sentiment-wise, or otherwise?: Identifying the hidden dimension for unsupervised text classification. In *Proceedings of the 2009 Conference on Empirical Methods in Natural Language Processing* (vol. 2, pp. 580-589). Association for Computational Linguistics.

DataReportal. (2020). *Digital 2020 report for Turkey.* Retrieved from https://datareportal.com/reports/digital-2020-turkey

Deng, L. (2014). A tutorial survey of architectures, algorithms, and applications for deep learning. *APSIPA Transactions on Signal and Information Processing*, *3*, 3. doi:10.1017/atsip.2013.9

Dogan, T., & Uysal, A. K. (2019). On Term Frequency Factor in Supervised Term Weighting Schemes for Text Classification. *Arabian Journal for Science and Engineering*, *44*(11), 1–16. doi:10.100713369-019-03920-9

Dos Santos, C., & Gatti, M. (2014). Deep convolutional neural networks for sentiment analysis of short texts. In *Proceedings of COLING 2014, the 25th International Conference on Computational Linguistics: Technical Papers* (pp. 69-78). Academic Press.

Elnagar, A., Al-Debsi, R., & Einea, O. (2020). Arabic text classification using deep learning models. *Information Processing & Management*, *57*(1), 102121. doi:10.1016/j.ipm.2019.102121

Eryiğit, G. (2014). ITU Turkish NLP web service. In *Proceedings of the Demonstrations at the 14th Conference of the European Chapter of the Association for Computational Linguistics* (pp. 1-4). Academic Press.

Estival, D., Gaustad, T., Pham, S. B., Radford, W., & Hutchinson, B. (2007). Author profiling for English emails. In *Proceedings of the 10th Conference of the Pacific Association for Computational Linguistics* (pp. 263-272). Academic Press.

Fattah, M. A., & Ren, F. (2008). Automatic text summarization. *World Academy of Science, Engineering and Technology*, *37*(2), 192.

Göker, H., & Tekedere, H. (2017). FATİH Projesine Yönelik Görüşlerin Metin Madenciliği Yöntemleri İle Otomatik Değerlendirilmesi. *Bilişim Teknolojileri Dergisi*, *10*(3), 291–299. doi:10.17671/gazibtd.331041

Harrag, F., El-Qawasmeh, E., & Pichappan, P. (2009). Improving Arabic text categorization using decision trees. In *2009 First International Conference on Networked Digital Technologies* (pp. 110-115). IEEE. 10.1109/NDT.2009.5272214

Hassani, H., Huang, X., & Silva, E. (2018). Digitalisation and big data mining in banking. *Big Data and Cognitive Computing*, *2*(3), 18. doi:10.3390/bdcc2030018

Hofmann, T. (2013). *Probabilistic latent semantic analysis*. arXiv preprint arXiv:1301.6705

Hsu, H. H., Hsieh, C. W., & Lu, M. D. (2011). Hybrid feature selection by combining filters and wrappers. *Expert Systems with Applications*, *38*(7), 8144–8150. doi:10.1016/j.eswa.2010.12.156

Hüsem, S. Ş., & Gülcü, A. (2017). Categorizing the Turkish web pages by data mining techniques. *In 2017 International Conference on Computer Science and Engineering (UBMK)* (pp. 255-260). IEEE. 10.1109/UBMK.2017.8093385

ITU NLP Toolkit. (2020). *ITU Turkish Natural Language Processing Pipeline*. Retrieved from http://tools.nlp.itu.edu.tr/index.jsp

Joachims, T. (1998). Text categorization with support vector machines: Learning with many relevant features. In *European conference on machine learning* (pp. 137-142). Springer.

Jones, K. S. (1972). A Statistical Interpretation of Term Specificity and its Retrieval. *The Journal of Documentation*, *28*(1), 11–21. doi:10.1108/eb026526

Jones, K. S. (2004). A Statistical Interpretation of Term Specificity and its Retrieval. *The Journal of Documentation*, *60*(5), 493–502. doi:10.1108/00220410410560573

Kadhim, A. I. (2019). Survey on supervised machine learning techniques for automatic text classification. *Artificial Intelligence Review*, *52*(1), 273–292. doi:10.100710462-018-09677-1

Kaynar, O., Arslan, H., Görmez, Y., & Demirkoparan, F. (2017). Feature selection methods in sentiment analysis. In *2017 International Artificial Intelligence and Data Processing Symposium (IDAP)* (pp. 1-5). IEEE.

Ke, Y., & Hagiwara, M. (2017). An English neural network that learns texts, finds hidden knowledge, and answers questions. *Journal of Artificial Intelligence and Soft Computing Research, 7*(4), 229–242. doi:10.1515/jaiscr-2017-0016

Keleş, M. K., & Özel, S. A. (2017). Similarity detection between Turkish text documents with distance metrics. In *2017 International Conference on Computer Science and Engineering (UBMK)* (pp. 316-321). IEEE. 10.1109/UBMK.2017.8093399

Khedr, A. E., & Yaseen, N. (2017). Predicting stock market behavior using data mining technique and news sentiment analysis. *International Journal of Intelligent Systems and Applications, 9*(7), 22–30. doi:10.5815/ijisa.2017.07.03

Kibriya, A. M., Frank, E., Pfahringer, B., & Holmes, G. (2004). Multinomial naive Bayes for text categorization revisited. In *Australasian Joint Conference on Artificial Intelligence* (pp. 488-499). Springer. 10.1007/978-3-540-30549-1_43

Kılınç, D., Özçift, A., Bozyigit, F., Yıldırım, P., Yücalar, F., & Borandag, E. (2017). TTC-3600: A new benchmark dataset for Turkish text categorization. *Journal of Information Science, 43*(2), 174–185. doi:10.1177/0165551515620551

Kuyumcu, B., Buluz, B., & Kömeçoğlu, Y. (2019). Author Identification in Turkish Documents with Ridge Regression Analysis. In *2019 27th Signal Processing and Communications Applications Conference (SIU)* (pp. 1-4). IEEE.

Lan, M., Tan, C. L., Su, J., & Lu, Y. (2008). Supervised and traditional term weighting methods for automatic text categorization. *IEEE Transactions on Pattern Analysis and Machine Intelligence, 31*(4), 721–735. doi:10.1109/TPAMI.2008.110 PMID:19229086

Leaman, R., Khare, R., & Lu, Z. (2015). Challenges in clinical natural language processing for automated disorder normalization. *Journal of Biomedical Informatics, 57*, 28–37. doi:10.1016/j.jbi.2015.07.010 PMID:26187250

Li, Y., Wang, X., & Xu, P. (2018). Chinese text classification model based on deep learning. *Future Internet, 10*(11), 113. doi:10.3390/fi10110113

Liu, J., Xia, C., Yan, H., Xie, Z., & Sun, J. (2019). Hierarchical Comprehensive Context Modeling for Chinese Text Classification. *IEEE Access: Practical Innovations, Open Solutions, 7*, 154546–154559. doi:10.1109/ACCESS.2019.2949175

Liu, Y., Yi, X., Chen, R., Zhai, Z., & Gu, J. (2018). Feature extraction based on information gain and sequential pattern for English question classification. *IET Software, 12*(6), 520–526. doi:10.1049/iet-sen.2018.0006

Martínez-Cámara, E., Martín-Valdivia, M. T., Ureña-López, L. A., & Mitkov, R. (2015). Polarity classification for Spanish tweets using the COST corpus. *Journal of Information Science, 41*(3), 263–272. doi:10.1177/0165551514566564

Matlab. (2020). *The official home of MATLAB software*. Retrieved from https://www.mathworks.com/products/matlab.html

Matlab Plot. (2020). *2-D line plot - MATLAB plot*. Retrieved from https://www.mathworks.com/help/matlab/ref/plot.html

Mayda, İ., & Amasyalı, M. F. (2016). Cross usage of articles and tweets on author identification. In 2016 Electric Electronics, Computer Science, Biomedical Engineerings' Meeting (EBBT) (pp. 1-4). IEEE. doi:10.1109/EBBT.2016.7483676

Molina-González, M. D., Martínez-Cámara, E., Martín-Valdivia, M. T., & Ureña-López, L. A. (2015). A Spanish semantic orientation approach to domain adaptation for polarity classification. *Information Processing & Management, 51*(4), 520–531. doi:10.1016/j.ipm.2014.10.002

News Data Set. (2019). *Kemik Natural Language Processing Group Tweets Data Set*. Retrieved from www.kemik.yildiz.edu.tr

Özgür, A., Özgür, L., & Güngör, T. (2005). Text categorization with class-based and corpus-based keyword selection. In *International Symposium on Computer and Information Sciences* (pp. 606-615). Springer.

Özgür, L., Güngör, T., & Gürgen, F. (2004). Adaptive anti-spam filtering for agglutinative languages: A special case for Turkish. *Pattern Recognition Letters, 25*(16), 1819–1831. doi:10.1016/j.patrec.2004.07.004

Plaza-del-Arco, F. M., Martín-Valdivia, M. T., Ureña-López, L. A., & Mitkov, R. (2019). Improved emotion recognition in spanish social media through incorporation of lexical knowledge. *Future Generation Computer Systems*.

Porter Stemmer. (2019). *The Porter Stemming Algorithm*. Retrieved from https://tartarus.org/martin/PorterStemmer/

Rong, M., Gong, D., & Gao, X. (2019). Feature Selection and Its Use in Big Data: Challenges, Methods, and Trends. *IEEE Access: Practical Innovations, Open Solutions, 7*, 19709–19725. doi:10.1109/ACCESS.2019.2894366

Ruiz, M. E., & Srinivasan, P. (1998). Automatic text categorization using neural networks. In *Proceedings of the 8th ASIS SIG/CR Workshop on Classification Research* (pp. 59-72). Academic Press.

Şahin, D. Ö., & Kılıç, E. (2019). Two new feature selection metrics for text classification. *Automatika (Zagreb), 60*(2), 162–171. doi:10.1080/00051144.2019.1602293

Salloum, S. A., AlHamad, A. Q., Al-Emran, M., & Shaalan, K. (2018). A survey of Arabic text mining. In *Intelligent Natural Language Processing: Trends and Applications* (pp. 417–431). Springer. doi:10.1007/978-3-319-67056-0_20

Salton, G., & Buckley, C. (1988). Term-weighting approaches in automatic text retrieval. *Information Processing & Management, 24*(5), 513–523. doi:10.1016/0306-4573(88)90021-0

Salton, G., Singhal, A., Mitra, M., & Buckley, C. (1997). Automatic text structuring and summarization. *Information Processing & Management, 33*(2), 193–207. doi:10.1016/S0306-4573(96)00062-3

Sebastiani, F. (2002). Machine learning in automated text categorization. *ACM Computing Surveys, 34*(1), 1–47. doi:10.1145/505282.505283

Shafiabady, N., Lee, L. H., Rajkumar, R., Kallimani, V. P., Akram, N. A., & Isa, D. (2016). Using unsupervised clustering approach to train the Support Vector Machine for text classification. *Neurocomputing*, *211*, 4–10. doi:10.1016/j.neucom.2015.10.137

Shah, K. B., Shetty, M. S., Shah, D. P., & Pamnani, R. (2017). Approaches towards building a banking assistant. *International Journal of Computers and Applications*, *166*(11), 1–6. doi:10.5120/ijca2017914140

Shi, L., Jianping, C., & Jie, X. (2018). Prospecting information extraction by text mining based on convolutional neural networks–a case study of the Lala copper deposit, China. *IEEE Access: Practical Innovations, Open Solutions*, *6*, 52286–52297. doi:10.1109/ACCESS.2018.2870203

Soricut, R., & Brill, E. (2006). Automatic question answering using the web: Beyond the factoid. *Information Retrieval*, *9*(2), 191–206. doi:10.100710791-006-7149-y

Stamatatos, E., Fakotakis, N., & Kokkinakis, G. (2000). Automatic text categorization in terms of genre and author. *Computational Linguistics*, *26*(4), 471–495. doi:10.1162/089120100750105920

Sun, A., Lim, E. P., & Ng, W. K. (2002). Web classification using support vector machine. In *Proceedings of the 4th international workshop on Web information and data management* (pp. 96-99). ACM.

Tantuğ, A. C., & Eryiğit, G. (2006). Performance Analysis of Naïve Bayes Classification, Support Vector Machines and Neural Networks for Spam Categorization. In *Applied Soft Computing Technologies: The Challenge of Complexity* (pp. 495–504). Springer. doi:10.1007/3-540-31662-0_38

Tasci, S., & Gungor, T. (2008). An evaluation of existing and new feature selection metrics in text categorization. In *2008 23rd International Symposium on Computer and Information Sciences* (pp. 1-6). IEEE.

Taşcı, Ş., & Güngör, T. (2013). Comparison of text feature selection policies and using an adaptive framework. *Expert Systems with Applications*, *40*(12), 4871–4886. doi:10.1016/j.eswa.2013.02.019

Tripathi, P., Vishwakarma, S. K., & Lala, A. (2015). Sentiment analysis of english tweets using rapid miner. In *2015 International Conference on Computational Intelligence and Communication Networks (CICN)* (pp. 668-672). IEEE.

Turkish N. L. P. Toolkit. (2020). *Turkish Natural Language Processing Toolkit*. Retrieved from http://haydut.isikun.edu.tr/nlptoolkit.html

Willett, P. (1988). Recent trends in hierarchic document clustering: A critical review. *Information Processing & Management*, *24*(5), 577–597. doi:10.1016/0306-4573(88)90027-1

Xing, F. Z., Cambria, E., & Welsch, R. E. (2018). Natural language based financial forecasting: A survey. *Artificial Intelligence Review*, *50*(1), 49–73. doi:10.100710462-017-9588-9

Yang, Y. (1999). An evaluation of statistical approaches to text categorization. *Information Retrieval*, *1*(1-2), 69–90. doi:10.1023/A:1009982220290

Yıldırım, S., & Yıldız, T. (2018). Türkçe için karşılaştırmalı metin sınıflandırma analizi. *Pamukkale Üniversitesi Mühendislik Bilimleri Dergisi*, *24*(5), 879–886.

Yıldız, B., & Ağdeniz, Ş. (2018). Muhasebede Analiz Yöntemi Olarak Metin Madenciliği. *World of Accounting Science*, *20*(2), 286–315.

Zemberek. (2019). *Zemberek Natural Language Processing Tool*. Retrieved from https://code.google.com/archive/p/zemberek/

Zhang, L., & Chen, C. (2016). Sentiment classification with convolutional neural networks: An experimental study on a large-scale chinese conversation corpus. In *2016 12th International Conference on Computational Intelligence and Security (CIS)* (pp. 165-169). IEEE.

ADDITIONAL READING

Aggarwal, C. C., & Zhai, C. (Eds.). (2012). *Mining text data*. Springer Science & Business Media. doi:10.1007/978-1-4614-3223-4

Cambria, E., & White, B. (2014). Jumping NLP curves: A review of natural language processing research. *IEEE Computational Intelligence Magazine*, *9*(2), 48–57. doi:10.1109/MCI.2014.2307227

Deng, X., Li, Y., Weng, J., & Zhang, J. (2019). Feature selection for text classification: A review. *Multimedia Tools and Applications*, *78*(3), 3797–3816. doi:10.100711042-018-6083-5

Forman, G. (2003). An extensive empirical study of feature selection metrics for text classification. *Journal of Machine Learning Research*, *3*(Mar), 1289–1305.

Jones, K. S. (2004). A Statistical Interpretation of Term Specificity and its Retrieval. *The Journal of Documentation*, *60*(5), 493–502. doi:10.1108/00220410410560573

Lan, M., Tan, C. L., Su, J., & Lu, Y. (2008). Supervised and traditional term weighting methods for automatic text categorization. *IEEE Transactions on Pattern Analysis and Machine Intelligence*, *31*(4), 721–735. doi:10.1109/TPAMI.2008.110 PMID:19229086

Otter, D. W., Medina, J. R., & Kalita, J. K. (2020). A Survey of the Usages of Deep Learning for Natural Language Processing. *IEEE Transactions on Neural Networks and Learning Systems*, 1–21. doi:10.1109/TNNLS.2020.2979670 PMID:32324570

Sebastiani, F. (2002). Machine learning in automated text categorization. [CSUR]. *ACM Computing Surveys*, *34*(1), 1–47. doi:10.1145/505282.505283

Zhai, C., & Massung, S. (2016). *Text data management and analysis: a practical introduction to information retrieval and text mining*. Association for Computing Machinery and Morgan & Claypool.

KEY TERMS AND DEFINITIONS

Feature: A structure that characterizes a system, an object, or a class and makes it distinct is called a feature.

Feature Extraction: It is a method frequently used in learning and image processing applications. In the field of text mining, it can be thought of as obtaining the words in the document.

Feature Selection: It is selecting and finding the most useful features in a data set. In other words, instead of using all the features in a data set, a subset of all features is obtained and used. It can also be considered as dimension reduction techniques.

N-Gram: They are words that consist of n-element subsets of a word. If N is equal to 1, 2, and 3, N-gram is called unigram, bigram, and trigram, respectively.

Stop Words: Stop words do not contribute to understanding because they are used very often.

Supervised Learning: It is a machine learning technique. It generates a function to match the inputs to the desired outputs.

Tokenization: Tokenization is defined as dividing a sentence into smaller meaningful units. Tokens are meaningful small units. Words, idioms can be given as examples of tokens.

Unsupervised Learning: It is a machine learning technique. It is used to estimate an unknown structure from unlabeled data.

Chapter 13
Sentiment Analysis of Arabic Documents:
Main Challenges and Recent Advances

Hichem Rahab
iD https://orcid.org/0000-0002-4411-0901
ICISI Laboratory, University of Khenchela, Algeria

Mahieddine Djoudi
iD https://orcid.org/0000-0002-2998-5574
TechNE Laboratory, University of Poitiers, France

Abdelhafid Zitouni
iD https://orcid.org/0000-0003-2498-4967
LIRE Laboratory, University of Constantine 2, Algeria

ABSTRACT

Today, it is usual that a consumer seeks for others' feelings about their purchasing experience on the web before a simple decision of buying a product or a service. Sentiment analysis intends to help people in taking profit from the available opinionated texts on the web for their decision making, and business is one of its challenging areas. Considerable work of sentiment analysis has been achieved in English and other Indo-European languages. Despite the important number of Arabic speakers and internet users, studies in Arabic sentiment analysis are still insufficient. The current chapter vocation is to give the main challenges of Arabic sentiment together with their recent proposed solutions in the literature. The chapter flowchart is presented in a novel manner that obtains the main challenges from presented literature works. Then it gives the proposed solutions for each challenge. The chapter reaches the finding that the future tendency will be toward rule-based techniques and deep learning, allowing for more dealings with Arabic language inherent characteristics.

DOI: 10.4018/978-1-7998-4240-8.ch013

INTRODUCTION

The evolution of Internet use in today's world is coupled with an important advancement in offering services for users. A tremendous amount of information and data is generated, and more needs emerge to take benefit from it (Liu, 2012). The importance of taking into accounts other opinions and advises in decision-making process (sales, voting, etc.) is a result of the neutrality of this information and its independence from any conflict of interest (Liu, 2015). When someone would sell a new product, ask for a service like a hotel booking or go to a new restaurant, or even take the decision in elections, he is no more limited to advice of family members and near friends. On Internet there are several web sites, discussion forums and social networks allowing their visitors to open debates and giving their comments on subjects, products and services of their interest (Guellil et al., 2019).

Sentiment analysis seeks to discover positive and negative sentiments about objects (ex. Cellular phones) and their attributes (image quality, weight, etc.) through natural language processing NLP, text mining and data-mining techniques (Aggarwal, 2018). Sentiment analysis aims to classify discovered people opinions into well-defined categories to facilitate hidden phenomenon understanding. Sentiment analysis can be seen as an automatic summarization of subjective documents, which allow positive or negative polarity extraction from textual documents (Pang & Lee, 2004). Opinion mining use is not limited to product reviews; it can reach user attitudes, political attitudes etc. (Aggarwal, 2018).

The application of sentiment analysis techniques covers a widespread of domains, such as business, politics, security and healthcare, to cite a few. Using sentiment analysis in healthcare domain can profit from available opinionated data in social media and web forums to help in the improvement of healthcare systems by controlling epidemics and guarantee a better care for patients (Ramírez-Tinoco et al., 2019). In the security domain, opinion mining can be used to control exchanged discussions in e-mails (Danowski, 2012), in social networks or even in phone conversations (Iskra et al., 2004). The available data at low cost in social media can be very beneficial to prevent possible perturbations in different events. This information can provide useful information for authorities and organizations, allowing them to take suitable decisions by understanding their people's mood (Subramaniyaswamy et al., 2017).

An important number of works in data mining and sentiment analysis is achieved in European languages, especially in English. Resources in these languages are available and enough in term of quantity and quality. However, in low resourced languages such as Arabic, the number of dedicated resources in very limited. Arabic is a Semitic language with more than 400 million speakers in 22 countries, and it is the fourth most used language in the Internet by 226 million users (*Internet World Stats*, n.d.). Arabic letters are used to write other languages, such as Person and Urdu. The Arabic language is also important as the language of the Holy Quran the book of 1.5 billion muslins around the world.

The aim of the present chapter is to provide sentiment analysis community, newcomers especially, with the important problematic questions and their last proposed solutions in the literature. The research questions that this chapter intends to answer are: what are the recent problems that sentiment analysis has to solve? What are the important methods used in sentiment analysis for the resolution of each problem? Are these methods sufficient to overcome the new challenges in the domain? And what will be the future tendency of the research in opinion mining and sentiment analysis? Unlike traditional surveys, listing sentiment analysis works according to adopted approaches and used methods and tools, the authors in this chapter extract, from literary works, the main challenges and their corresponding solutions. By the adopted methodology, the authors reach the new tendency in the domain, in order to respond to new challenges.

The chapter is organized as follows. The Second section presents related notions to Arabic language and sentiment analysis. In the third section, a literature review of recent works is included. The main challenges of Arabic sentiment analysis are described in section four. In the fifth section, the solutions and the recommendations, to the given challenges, are depicted. The next section gives future research directions in the domain. The chapter is concluded in the seventh section.

BACKGROUND

Characteristics of the Arabic Language

Arabic is a morphologically rich language characterized by coding, at the word level, a big amount of syntactic units of information (Tsarfaty et al., 2010). Arabic is the most important in the family of Semitic languages with; Amharic, Tigrinya, Hebrew, among others (Djoudi & Harous, 2008). Semitic languages family share a common characteristic of rich and complex morphology with similar syntactic generation rules (Marsi et al., 2005).

Arabic means, in this chapter, Modern Standard Arabic, which is, in our days, the most used form of the Arabic language in administration, education and media. Arabic is written from right to left, and Arabic alphabet is composed of 28 letters, three among them are considered long vowels Alif 'ا', Waw 'و', and Ya 'ي'. In addition, Arabic has a set of short vowels called diacritics. Diacritics are optional is most cases in Arabic texts; they are useful in a text to remove ambiguity and also to guide pronunciation (Boudad et al., 2017).

Arabic Lexicon

A word in Arabic can take one of the three forms; noun /Ăis.m/ (اسم), verb /fiɛ.l/(فعل) or particle/Har.f/ (فرح). A noun is a word which has a meaning and allows an entity or an object designation regardless any time, example /Alšajaraħ/ˈ (الشجرة) (tree), /AltaTaw~ur/(التطور) (development). Nouns can be grouped according to their origins into three categories; static nouns /Al ÂsmaA' AljaAmidaħ/ (الأسماء الجامدة) which are not derived from any others words, derived nouns /Al ÂsmaA' Almuš.taqaħ/ (الأسماء المشتقة) are obtained from other word called roots /jiðr/(جذر) and numbers nouns /ÂsmaA' Al ÂɛdaAd/ (أسماء الأعداد). In the difference of nouns, verbs allow designing event or meaning in relation to a well-determined time. In Arabic, there are three times; past, present and imperative. The past, or unaccomplished time / AlmaADiy/ (الماضي), designs an action accomplished before the pronunciation. In the present and the future /AlmuDaAriɛ/ (المضارع), the verb is not accomplished, and it is related to the present or future times (Saadane, 2015). Imperative designs an order, advice or suggestion to do an act.

Arabic Morphology

The morphological aspect is, perhaps, the most studied in Arabic language (Habash, 2010) as Arabic is a morphologically rich and complex language. Arabic is an agglutinated language in the sense that the same word can be formed by different terms. In this case, a set of clitics are attached to the word; each one represents a part of a sentence (Boudad et al., 2017).

Table 1. the verb /xaraja/ خرج (go out) in past, present and future

Time	انأ ÂnaA 'I'	نحن naH.n 'we'	تنأ Ânta You (m) [2]	تنأ Ânti You (f)	امتنأ ÂntumaA you (d)	متنأ Ântum You (pm)	نتنأ Ântun~a You (pf)
Past	خرجت	خرجنا	خرجتَ	خرجتِ	خرجتما	خرجتم	خرجتن
Present	أخرُجُ	نخرج	تخرج	تخرجين	تخرجان	تخرجون	تخرجن
Imperative	-	-	أخرج	أخرجي	أخرجا	أخرجوا	أخرجن

Table 2. the verb xaraja خرج (go out) in past, present and future (continued)

وه huwa He	Time	يه hiya She	امه humaA They (dm)	امه humaA They (df)	مه hum they (pm)	نه hun~a They (pf)
خرج	Past	خرجت	خرجا	خرجتا	خرجوا	خرجن
يخرج	Present	تخرج	يخرجان	تخرجان	يخرجون	تخرجن
-	Imperative	-	-	-	-	-

Derivation /Al ĂštiqAq/(الاشتقاق) is related to obtaining a word from another word, the root /Al maSdar/(المصدر). The root of a word may be different in pronunciation and part of speech category; even it has convenient meaning. Derivation variations in Arabic are seven: the active participle /Ăsm Al faAçil/(اسم الفاعل), the passive participle /Ăsm Al mafaçuwl/ (اسم المفعول), the resembling participle / AlSifa Almušabahah biAsm Al faAçil/ (الصفة المشبهة باسم الفاعل), the elative name /Ăsm Al tafDyl/ (اسم التفضيل), the time adverbial/Ăsm AlzamAn/(اسم الزمان), the place adverbial /Ăsm AlmakaAn/ (اسم المكان), and the noun of instrument /Ăsm AlÂlaħ/ (اسم الآلة).

Inflectional morphology design word variations among different grammatical categories by preserving the same meaning. Inflectional morphology is done according to (Boudad et al., 2017): time (past or present), mood (indicative, subjunctive, imperative, etc.), person (first, second, or third), number (single, dual or plural), genre (feminine or masculine), case (accusative, genitive or nominative), and voice (passive or active).

Sentiment Analysis

Sentiment analysis also known as opinion mining is a field that uses Natural Language Processing NLP, text mining and computational linguistics techniques in order to identify, extract and quantify sentiment and subjective information from text written in natural languages (Rahab et al., 2018). The expressions sentiment analysis and opinion mining are used interchangeably in most works in literature (Liu, 2010, 2012). However, some works may state the difference as in (Medhat et al., 2014) where the sentiment analysis is defined as the extraction and study of sentiments expressed in texts while opinion mining vocation is about analyzing people's opinion about an entity. One of the main applications of opinion mining is texts polarity classification when a document is studied to know whether it expresses a positive, negative, or neutral opinion.

Handling Levels

A sentiment analysis system may deal with opinionated documents, at several levels according to the nature of the study and the type of the document. Three levels are considered in sentiment analysis literature; the document level, the sentence level and the aspect level.

- **Document Level:** At the document level, the whole document is considered as a single unit; the opinion mining becomes a classification task and often a binary classification task (Aggarwal, 2018). This level is appropriate for sentiment analysis from reviews where a single entity is targeted in each document.
- **Sentence Level:** At this level, the document sentences are firstly classified into subjective and objective categories. Here, phrases may be parts of sentences, and a phrase can take the form of an idiom or a proverb (Ibrahim et al., 2015). In the second time subjective sentences will be classified into either positive or negative categories. The final step is the aggregation of individual sentences sentiment to obtain the whole document semantic orientation.
- **Aspect Level:** In the aspect or feature level, opinions toward entity aspects are studied individually. Aspect level is very useful in dealing with product reviews, where the reviewer may like some aspects of the product and dislike others. The task starts by extracting product aspects, for example from pros and cons of a product review (Liu, 2010), then opinions that target these aspects are obtained and calculated, the global review sentiment is calculated from sentiments about all aspects of the product (Ismail et al., 2016).

Classification Approaches

The first and the most used method is a machine learning-based, also called a corpus-based approach. In this approach a corpus of annotated documents is needed to train a classifier, the annotation can be manual (Mountassir et al., 2013; Rahab et al., 2019), automatic (Rushdi-Saleh et al., 2011) or by using a Crowdsourcing system (Abdul-Mageed & Diab, 2012a; Bougrine et al., 2017). In the next step, a set of features is selected to represent documents in the classification stage. In the classification, several methods are used in literature, and the most popular are Support Vector Machines, Naïve Bayes, and Decision trees, among others.

For the lexicon-based approach, a sentiment lexicon of words or phrases of known sentiment orientation is compiled, and sentiment orientation of documents is determined in function of the appearance of sentiment words and/or phrases. Sentiment lexicons creation can be manual, dictionary-based or lexicon-based. The manual technique is the most precise, but it is time-consuming and laborious; thus it is no more used alone, it is generally used in addition to other techniques as first cold start step and/or as final check step. The dictionary-based method starts with a manually created list of seed words with known sentimental orientation, then by propagation of this list using search engine corpora as WordNet or a thesaurus. An important characteristic of such technique is its domain independence.

The hybrid approach constitutes a combination of the aforementioned techniques, lexicon-based and machine learning approaches, at different levels of their implementation (Elshakankery & Ahmed, 2019).

Literature Survey

Sentiment analysis research had rapid growth in recent years; this advancement is due to its application in different domains. Works in Arabic sentiment analysis are still limited when compared with its importance in the world. A lot of effort is made in the last decade to reduce this gap, especially by developing dedicated resources (Abdul-mageed & Sandra, 2012; Al-hussaini & Al-dossari, 2017; Elnagar et al., 2018; Mahyoub et al., 2014; Rahab et al., 2019).

A lexicon of 2500 words from Sudanese dialect is manually collected from Twitter and other Arabic web sites in (Abdelhameed & Hernández, 2019). The collected data is then manually annotated as positive or negative by the authors. Before the classification step, the collected dataset is passed by a set of pre-processing subphases including; tokenization, removing stop words and stemming. The training dataset is formed by 608 positive words and 1246 negative ones. The authors use 646 tweets collected from Twitter as test dataset. The best classification result is obtained in term of F_mesure using support vector machines classifier.

HILATSA is a hybrid approach for dialectal Arabic sentiment analysis (Elshakankery & Ahmed, 2019). The approach is composed of a lexicon, a machine learning classifier, and a word learner. The lexicon is created by dialectal words collected from Twitter and manually annotated where, each word has three counts, the first is the number of times the word appears in positive tweets, the second for the number of times the word appears in negative tweets and the last for the number of times it has appeared in neutral tweets. Additional three lexicons were created for popular emotions, special intensification words, and popular dialectal idioms. Each tweet is preprocessed by a set of steps including detection of emotions from the emotion lexicon, removing numbers and non-Arabic words, removing the diacritical marks, converting letters with different formats in a unique one, using an algorithm to detect negation, stemming and detecting idioms from idioms lexicon. For Arabic people names, the authors use a list prepared by (Zayed & El-Beltagy, 2015) for the detection and elimination of person names in colloquial Arabic.

In order to study the sentiment analysis in Arabic reviews, two different datasets are used in (Rahab et al., 2019). The first dataset, SANA, is collected from Arabic newspaper web sites, while the second dataset is OCA (Opinion Corpus for Arabic) (Rushdi-Saleh et al., 2011) available online for research purposes. The reviews are manually annotated by MApTTER approach developed in the scope of the same work. For experimentation, three machine learning methods; Support Vector Machines, Naïve Bayes, and K-Nearest Neighbors were tested. Obtained performance differs with the used corpus and word vector model. The SANA corpus best results are obtained by application of the light stemming.

For Arabic named entity recognition ANER, a methodology of transfer learning using neural networks is built (Al-smadi et al., 2020). The authors developed a model Pooled-GRU with Multilingual Universal Sentence Encoder USE, in addition to the baseline Bi-LSTM-CRF developed earlier par the same authors. The experimental study is conducted using the WikiFANE$_{Gold}$ dataset, WikiFANE$_{Gold}$ consists of 8 main classes: (1) Person (PER), (2) Location (LOC), (3) Organization (ORG), (4) Vehicle (VEH), (5) Geopolitical (GPE), (6) Facility (FAC),(7) Weapon (WEA), and (8) Product (PRO). The eight main classes span over 50 more fine-grained classes. Both of the proposed models are trained and tested with the same dataset. The proposed model Pooled-GRU achieves 91% of accuracy and 90.25% of F1mesure outperforming the baseline model by around 17% in F1mesure.

ANETAC (Ameur, 2019) is a freely available dataset of English to Arabic named entity transliteration and classification (Hadj Ameur et al., 2019). ANETAC consists of 79,924 named entities divided into three classes: Person by 61.662, Location by 12.679 and Organization by 5.583 named entities. The authors divided their corpus into three subsets; training with 75.898 named entities, development with 1004 named entities and test with 3013 named entities. After a pre-processing step, the system identifies for each English sentence the set of names entities which it contains. Then, each English named entity is associated with a set of Arabic transliteration candidates. Finally, the best Arabic candidate will be selected in function of the obtained score. In the transliteration results, the performance of English-to-Arabic outperforms that of Arabic-to-English, and the authors report the need for more work to improve this later.

In the goal of comparing different methods of opinion spam detection in Arabic reviews, several investigations were carried out by saeed et al. (Saeed et al., 2019). The developed approach is based on three modules; pre-processing, extraction module and spam detection. In the pre-processing module, a set of operations are conducted including; tokenization, removal of non-Arabic content, normalization of words form, stop words removal and light stemming. In the extraction module, different n-gram models are constructed, and their polarity is determined by a sentiment lexicon of 17.000 words/phrases. To handle negation, the authors constructed a list of 50 negation words, and the extracted N-grams are checked to determine whether they are preceded by a negation. When an N-gram is preceded by a negation word, its polarity will be reversed. In the spam detection module, four methods are used: rule-based, machine learning, majority voting and stacking ensemble. In experimentation, two datasets were used. The first dataset is the Deceptive Opinion Spam Corpus (DOSC), it contains 1600 reviews translated from English to Arabic by Arabic expert translators. The second dataset is Hotel Arabic Reviews Dataset (HARD) (Elnagar et al., 2018); it consists of 94.052 reviews. The experimentation results show that spam detection is improved when using negation handling and the rule-based classifier outperforms machine learning classifier.

MAIN CHALLENGES OF ARABIC SENTIMENT ANALYSIS

Arabic Language Complexity

As explained in the background section and literature survey, Arabic has a set of inherent complex characteristics making Arabic sentiment analysis ASA and Arabic Natural Language Processing ANLP in general hard tasks. The Arabic script itself poses real challenges to the automatic process of the language. An Arabic letter may have several forms depending on its position in the word, in the beginning, in the middle, in the end, or alone. For example, the letter 'ب' /b/, in the beginning, takes the form 'بـ', in the middle 'ـبـ', in the end 'ـب', and when it is alone or after letters such 'ا' is written 'ب'as in the word 'باتك' /book/. Some letters may be used interchangeably by users of social media, for example, the letter Alif 'ا' /A/ has three forms 'أ', 'إ', 'آ', and 'ا', the letter yaA 'ي' /y/ can be written as "Alif maqsurah" 'ى' or as it 'ي'and the letter 'ة' can be replaced by haA 'ه' at the end of a word. This problem may produce different writing of the same word in different documents due to authors writing styles or even in the same documents by ignorance of the author.

A very challenging source of ambiguity in Arabic is the omission of diacritics, also known as short vowels. As Arabic is considered a consonantal language, the role of short vowels is handled as a secondary problem compared to consonants (Djoudi et al., 1989). In Arabic, there are eight short vowels, as shown in Table 3, also known as diacritic signs. In today's Arabic writing, diacritics are omitted in almost all Arabic documents, and native speakers can understand the meaning of a word from the context. These diacritic signs are conserved only in the writing of the Holy Quran and in children books and are usually absent in dialectal texts (Fadel et al., 2019). The absence of diacritics, in general, in Arabic texts constitutes a severe problem to face in Arabic Natural Language Processing tasks such as proper nouns extraction and text-to-speech conversion (Farghaly & Shaalan, 2009; Mubarak et al., 2019).

The fragmentation of a text into sentences is an important step in handling the sentiment in documents, and thus unlike Latin languages where a sentence starts with an upper case and is finished with a period, this situation is different in Arabic. Delimiting sentences is a real problem in Arabic documents due to: the absence of capital letters in Arabic, and also the lack in the use of punctuation marks by the Internet and social media users.

Tokenization in some languages such as English is limited to segmenting sequences of letters into words by means of space characters. In agglutinative languages such as Arabic, tokenization needs deep language knowledge, in fact an Arabic word may be segmented on so many tokens, that a set of clitics may be attached to it.

Table 3: Arabic short vowels (diacritics)

Diacritic	Description	Transliteration	Example		
			Arabic	**Transliteration**	**English**
َ	فتحة (fatHah)	a	دَهَنَ	dahana	He paints
ُ	ضمة (Dam~ah)	u	دُهِنَ	duhina	It is painted
ِ	كسرة (kas.rah)	i	دُهِنَ	duhina	It has been painted
ً	فتحتين (fatHatayn)	ā	كتاباً	kitaAbAā	Book (in the accusative)
ٌ	ضمتين (Dam~atayn)	ū	كتابٌ	kitaAbū	Book (in the nominative)
ٍ	كسرتين (kas.ratayn)	i	كتابٍ	kitaAbī	Book (in the genitive)
ّ	شدة (šad~ah)	~	كسّر	kas~ara	Break
ْ	سكون (sukuwn)	.	مسْجد	mas.jid or masjid	Mosque

Dialectal and Non-Arabic Content (Diglossia)

The Arab world is situated in the middle of the old world; this geographic region is the intersection between nations and civilizations for centuries. This situation influenced Arabic culture, population and language. The colonization movement in the nineteenth and twentieth centuries was the recent and the most influencing contact between the Arab world and the occident. One of the effects of such situation on the Arabic language is the introduction of borrowed words into Arabic daily conversations which contribute to form, in addition to other old languages such as Berber in North Africa, the Arabic Dialects. The coexistence of several forms of Arabic language in the Arab world and the simultaneous use of these varieties in an implicit manner is known as Diglossia (Ferguson, 1959). In the Arab world, there are three varieties of Arabic language which are used simultaneously: Classical Arabic, Modern Standard Arabic and Dialectal Arabic (also known as Colloquial Arabic). Dealing with these three forms is a considerable challenge facing the development of NLP systems; as a consequence, this will alter opinion mining development in Arabic.

Arabizi or Romanized Arabic

Arabizi (Duwairi et al., 2016; Guellil et al., 2020; Guellil, Adeel, et al., 2018; Masmoudi et al., 2019) or Romanized Arabic (Al-badrashiny et al., 2014; Masmoudi et al., 2015; Rushdi-Saleh et al., 2011) is an emergent writing style in the social media sites. Arabizi use is due essentially to the absence of Arabic keyboards in some phones and the speed nature of writing in SMS and Chat discussion. Transliteration is an important step in exploiting the Arabizi content, as most Arabic Natural Language Processing tools are developed for Arabic script (Masmoudi et al., 2019).

Arabizi is different from transliteration in the way that the later has a well-defined rule to transform each character from a source writing system to a destination one (e.g. see (Buckwalter, n.d.; Habash et al., 2007) for Arabic transliteration), while the former is without any standard to be fellowed by the writers. Another difference is that transliteration is a bidirectional function that allows for, in the case of the Arabic language, transforming a text from Latin characters to Arabic characters and the same system can be used to restitute the original Latin text from the transliterated output (Rahab et al., 2019). Another difference which concerns the purpose of each one, namely: Arabizi and transliteration, is that the main transliteration focus in Arabic is to allow non-Arabic speakers to read correctly Arabic texts, while Arabizi has emerged in the social media environment in the luck of Arabic keywords. Arabizi deals with dialectal Arabic in the almost all cases in the difference with transliteration, which is developed especially for MSA and can also deal with any kind of texts due to its well-defined rules.

The main problem in Arabizi transliteration is the absence of a standard of correspondence between Arabic and Latin letters. This problem leads to writing the same word in a very big number of forms, which creates an ambiguity situation to natural language processing systems. The use of abbreviations in Arabizi is another source of ambiguity as these abbreviations are very different from and Arab country to another, or even from one region to another in the same country. Example the use of 'hmd' which mean 'الحمد لله' /Al Hamdu lilah/ (thanks to god) or the use of the English word 'cool' to express the enthusiasm toward a person or an idea. The repetition of letters to express the intension in emotion is another source of difficulty in handling Arabizi content that the number of repetitions is different from a text to another, for example, the word 'jamiiiiiiiil' (nice) which is used to express intension of the Arabic word جميل /jamil/ (nice).

Proper Nouns Translation

Proper nouns translation from/to Arabic to/from foreign languages is a challenging problem in Arabic Natural Language Processing. This problem plays an important role in cross-language Information Retrieval and machine translation (Semmar & Saadane, 2013). In the USA after September 11, 2001, the authorities present a high level of interest to this problem especially in airports where the authorities would be able to well-checking people identity by security reasons (Farghaly & Shaalan, 2009). Sophisticated tools and methods for Arabic person names recognition are subject of interest.

The absence of standard leads to writing the same Arabic person name in a great number of transliteration forms. For example, the Arabic name 'محمد' /muham~ad/ may be transliterated as Mohamed, Muhammed, Muhamed, Mahomet, etc. Also, a Latin noun, English for example, can have a lot of corresponding Arabic nouns. The word 'Washington' can be written in Arabic; 'واشنطن', 'واشنغطن', 'وشنطن', etc.

One factor of difficulty in the person names extraction in the Arabic language is due to the absence of shorts vowels in Arabic texts. In Arabic, diacritics contribute to the determination of grammatical functions of words, for example, the short vowel /Dam~a/ (الضمة) serves to determine the nominative case which distinguishes the subject in Arabic sentences (Farghaly & Shaalan, 2009).

Opinion Spam

The increased amount of user-generated content in the web, especially in last years, leads to the absence of quality control of this content. Manual control of the huge available number of documents is a very difficult task and probably impossible. The importance of reviews opinion as an independent evaluation of products, events, politics etc. attracts spammers to promote their benefiting ideas as independent reviews. Spam content detection is a difficult and complex problem that spammers are usually working to invent new methods allowing them to infiltrate their data in the huge amount of user-generated content. In English language, methods to detect opinion spam are available, but in Arabic, this problem is still without well-established solutions (Abu Hammad & El-Halees, 2015).

Difficulties of spam detection in the Arabic language can be related to a set of factors. The first factor is the Arabic complex morphology compared to other languages such as English. The second factor is related to some Arabic writers whose use Arabic dialects rather than Modern Standard Arabic language in writing their reviews, this means that several Arabic Dialects can be encountered in the same document rather than a single language. The Spelling mistakes is an additional problem to the use of dialectal content, the users in social media products a lot of errors when writing their reviews, and this happens accidentally or by ignorance.

Opinion spam may be categorized in three classes; the untruthful opinion that wants to spread false positive reviews to promote products or viewpoints, or in the other side spreads false negative reviews to harm competitors' reputation of products or viewpoints. A second kind is opinions targeting a brand rather than a product. The non-reviews constitute an additional type of spam opinion content, which diffuses random reviews with irrelevant content (Jindal & Liu, 2008, 2007). A more severe problem is related to spammer groups; when several spammers construct a group in which they coordinate their efforts to control a given object. Spammer groups are damaging due to the fact that they generate more important content and are complicated de detect than spammers working each one alone (Wahsheh et al., 2013b).

Spam web pages are another type of undesirable content on the web. In the goal of increasing their ranking in search engines, such web pages owners use keywords irrelevant to their content to attract people to visit their websites (Wahsheh et al., 2013a).

SOLUTIONS AND RECOMMENDATIONS

Arabic Features Handling (Diacritics Problem Resolution)

Recent works adopt normalization of the input text to deal with problems related to Arabic language characteristics. For example, many works in Arabic sentiment analysis replace all variants of Alif such as 'أ', 'إ' and 'آ' with simple Alif 'ا', the letter 'ة' /ħ/ (TaA marbutah) with 'ه' /h/ (haA marbutah) and the letter 'ى' /ý/ is replaced by'ي'/y/ (Soliman et al., 2017). Even when the normalization resolves a problem, it removes the distinction between several words that may have different meanings and roles in a sentence such as 'أن' and 'إن'or 'على' and 'يلا' etc. (Farghaly & Shaalan, 2009). For tatwyl sign '—', it is simply eliminated because the only effect of this sign is the amelioration of the writing style. For diacritic signs, they are removed due to their absence from most documents, and their little impact in the sentiment orientation of texts.

Tokenization in Arabic must be handled while considering Agglutination property. A two-step approach for tokenization is followed in (Attia, 2007), the system distinguishes main tokens from sub-tokens. The first and intuitive step is to extract the main tokens using punctuation marks and white spaces. For sub-tokens, Attia's method consists of combining both morphological analysis and tokenization in different ways. The first method adopts a morphological analyzer and a tokenizer in the same function. The second method uses firstly a tokenizer, then introduces the morphological analyzer. The third method inverses the second; it starts with a morphological analysis which lists the words as possible tokens, then the tokenizer seeks for words in this list.

Automatic diacritization in Arabic is hot research problematic without definitive solutions. The implicit contextual features influence Arabic words meaning and affects diacritization output. A set of automatic diacritization tools such as Farasa (*Farasa*, n.d.) and MADAMIRA (Pasha et al., 2014), and approaches such as the deep learning-based approach Shakkala (Fadel et al., 2019) are developed. The most available methods and tools for automatic diacritization suffer from a high rate of diacritization errors, (Fadel et al., 2019) and this occurs especially at the end of words, this part is very important in Arabic words Part of Speech categorization and proper nouns identification.

Dialectal Content Handling

It is very important to develop suitable resources for each dialect to handle dialectal content in sentiment analysis tasks, thus the varieties in the arabic dialects make the use of resources developed for Modern Standard Arabic insufficient to conduct studies in those dialects (Farghaly & Shaalan, 2009).

Several tools and resources are created to take the Arabic dialectal content into consideration by sentiment analysis applications. Annotated corpora and opinion mining methods are developed for different Arabic dialects to cite a few; Algerian (Guellil, Azouaou, et al., 2018; Meftouh et al., 2012), Tunisian (Masmoudi et al., 2019, 2015; Mulki et al., 2018), Egyptian (El-Beltagy, 2016), Sudanese (Abdelhameed & Hernández, 2019), Palestinian (Jarrar et al., 2017).

Arabizi Transliteration

Arabizi transliteration refers to the process of converting an Arabic text written in Latin script to an equivalent Arabic text in Arabic script. For the fact that Arabizi texts are usually related to Dialectal

Arabic DA, the transliteration must take into consideration words of those dialects in any transliteration processes, unless it will confront serious problems with a big number of Arabizi words without Modern Standard Arabic MSA equivalent.

The transliteration of Arabizi texts into Arabic script is done by (Guellil et al., 2020) in a four steps approach.

1. An Arabic corpus for Arabizi is collected from Facebook social media network. The crawled corpus is used to generate a language model for Arabic Algerian Dialect. A pre-processing step is conducted in the goal to filter our non-Arabic words and sentences. The remaining words are used to generate the language model.

2. A set of transliteration rules are established in a way that every letter corresponds to one or several Arabic letters. When several Arabic letters are given, the authors sort them according to the probability of use in a way that the first generated word is the most probable to correspond to the right meaning and it is the word to be used in the case that anyone of the generated words corresponds to the language model. The established words are given in a well-organized table.

3. According to the above-elaborated table, for each word in the Arabizi document, a set of candidate words is generated. For example, the Arabizi word 'kraht' composed of five letters 'k', 'r', 'a'(in the middle), 'h' and 't' each of which has possible corresponding letters, so the result is $2*2*2*2*2=2^5$, i.e. the word has 32 possible candidates.

4. Selection of the best one between obtained candidates from the precedent step. From obtained candidates, the algorithm must select the one that corresponds to an entry in the language model constructed in the first step. In the case when no entry corresponds to the searched word, the first transliteration obtained according to the order of letters in the transliteration table is adopted.

Proper Nouns Recognition and Translation

Proper nouns recognition may be done on the basis of regularities of the Arabic language. For example, many Arabic person names use the word 'بن' /bn/ (son of) written in Latin as 'ben' or 'bin' in the composition of the name. This regularity may help to extract nouns that are not figuring in dictionaries (Farghaly & Shaalan, 2009).

Some recommendations are made to unify Arabic person names writing in Latin scripts. Such recommendations are; the exhaustive use of English letters to have a transliteration which is compatible with available systems, the use of capital and small letters indifferently, the name must be transliterated regardless of its parsing, handling composed names as one unit, for example, Abderrahmane, not Abed Errahmane and the transliteration of definite articles without considering sun versus moon letters. A post-processing phase is proposed, in which the first letter of a name will be capitalized, as in Latin languages (Alghamdi, 2009).

Arabic Sentiment Analysis Resources

Resources creation for morphologically rich languages such as Arabic face difficulties linked to the diversity in adopted labelling approaches (Abdul-Mageed & Diab, 2012a). Three approaches are followed for the creation of Arabic sentiment Analysis resources: manual approach, semi-automatic approach and automatic approach.

Sentiment Lexicon

The manual construction of lexicon is characterized by high precision and efficiency however this method is laborious and time-consuming, thus works adopting this approach are very limited (Abdul-Mageed & Diab, 2012b; Mataoui et al., 2016; Touahri & Mazroui, 2019). For semi-automatic creation, at first step automatic collection of lexicon entries is achieved, then manual checking is done on the obtained lexicon in the goal to limit semantic ambiguity and to ensure the high quality of each entry (El-Beltagy, 2016; Elshakankery & Ahmed, 2019; Guellil, Adeel, et al., 2018). Automatic creation of lexicon have three ways to do with; machine translation based construction, multi-languages based construction and construction merging both above methods (Guellil et al., 2019). Automatic construction is very used thanks to their construction speed and productivity (Altrabsheh et al., 2017; Badaro et al., 2014; ElSahar & El-Beltagy, 2015; Mohammad et al., 2016).

Sentiment Corpora

Collecting documents for corpus creation can be achieved in a manual or automatic manner. The manual collection refers to soliciting different sources such as web sites, discussion forums etc. Automatic creation refers to the use of a web crawler (dedicated script) that allows for the collection of documents from sources such as social networks. The automatic system may use specified queries including the country name, events, person names etc. in the goal of personalizing the desired output (Al-hussaini & Al-dossari, 2017).

An important step in developing sentimental corpora is annotation or labelling. Annotation affects collected documents into predefined categories. Different annotation methods can be found: automatic, manual and Crowdsourcing. Automatic annotation uses the websites rating system, the authors consider the middle point (for example 3 in a rating system of 5 points or 5 in a rating system of 10 points) as representative of the neutral class, above this point the document is considered positive and below this point, the document is labelled as negative (Aly & Atiya, 2013; Rushdi-Saleh et al., 2011). In the manual annotation, a set of human annotators, generally Arabic native speakers with specified skills, are asked to label the corpus with a set of given labels (Abdelhameed & Hernández, 2019; Abdul-Mageed & Diab, 2012a; Alotaibi & Anderson, 2016; Mountassir et al., 2013; Rahab et al., 2018, 2019). Crowdsourcing refers to a collaborative annotation where people are involved in a scientific task by an open call (Bou-grine et al., 2017). Different types of Crowdsourcing may occur according to the motivation of driving people to collaborate. The first intuitive manner to incite someone to do something is to pay him, and the share intent is related to the potential motivation to collaboration in a scientific project or the creation of a shared resource. Also, the enjoyment using games-with-a-purpose GWAP may be a motivation to such tasks (Poesio et al., 2017). In the goal to have a high level of homogeneity in the annotation and also a consistency with annotation purpose a set of guidelines are given to annotators in term of advice (Abdul-Mageed & Diab, 2012a; Rahab et al., 2019).

Opinion Spam Detection and Elimination

Opinion spam detection and elimination are crucial as such content may undermine the reputation and credibility of opinion sites. Opinion spam detection in Arabic is done through several approaches. The most used are rule-based approach and machine learning approach.

In their work to detect opinion spam in Arabic economic reviews, the authors in (Abu Hammad & El-Halees, 2015) use TBA dataset collected from three well-known booking websites; TripAdvisor, Booking and Agoda. To annotate their reviews as spam or non-spam the authors use a set of criterion; Reviews about brands only, Non-reviews, Irrelevant review, General review, Hotels that have 100% positive review, The contradiction in the review Body attributes, The contradiction between attributes, duplication and near-duplicate of features and duplicate or near-duplicate reviews. The authors use four machine learning techniques, namely: SVM, NB, ID3 and KNN.

Opinion can be categorized into spam and non-spam classes, and then the spam class may also be divided into low-level opinion spam and high-level opinion spam in (Wahsheh et al., 2013b). The level of opinion spam is determined according to the presence of URL links in the review. The low-level opinion spam is a review containing at least five consecutive numbers or the @ symbol, while the high-level opinion spam is a review with an URL blacklisted in a webspam list.

A web page analyzer is developed by the authors in (Wahsheh et al., 2013a), it allows analyzing web pages in accordance with a set of features. These features can be categorized into content-based and link-based features. Content-based features are features related to the content of the site, such as the duplication of some words or sequences of words in a meaningless manner. For link-based features, they correspond to the method by which the spammers choose the names of their links, like the use of expired domain names or the insertion of links into their pages as comments in many blogs and discussion forums.

FUTURE RESEARCH DIRECTIONS

Due to an urgent need in term of Arabic Natural languages processing tools in recent years, most of these tools and methods are developed following machine learning techniques. These aforementioned methods give rapid results which are not very expensive, and these results don't need deep research in the linguistic background of Arabic language (Farghaly & Shaalan, 2009). The problem of preparing well representative datasets is the main problem in the face of machine learning techniques; thus the future tendency in sentiment analysis in Arabic is the lexicon-based approaches and unsupervised methods (Medhat et al., 2014). These methods are characterized by the time and effort they need, in addition to a strong background in language skills. However, these methods have no need for training data. These methods are also domain-independent, so a system developed at a time may be used in several situations without basically changes.

In the machine learning approach, recent works have a tendency to use deep learning as sub-field in machine learning which is based on the human brain function. Deep learning is based on a set of hidden layer between and input and an output layers (Al-ayyoub et al., 2018). Several techniques are used in deep learning for the Arabic language, namely, Recurrent Neural Networks RNN (Al-smadi et al., 2017), Convolutional Neural networks (CNN)(Alayba et al., 2017), long short- term memory (LSTM) (El-Kilany et al., 2018) and deep neural networks (DNN)(Fadel et al., 2019) among others.

CONCLUSION

In this chapter recent challenges of sentiment analysis in Arabic documents are presented and discussed from a Natural Language Processing point of view. Arabic as a rich and complex morphology language

Figure 1. Main challenges and recent solutions to Arabic sentiment analysis

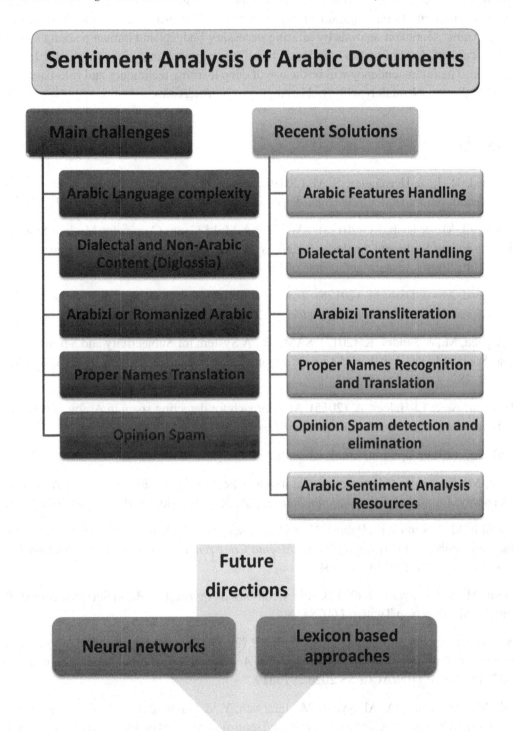

posed itself a set of difficulties making the task of opinion mining very difficult without real resolutions for these problems. In our days, scientific, economic and security needs allow the development of research in Arabic sentiment analysis by offering necessary budgets and human resources in the Arab world as in occident. A set of methods and tools handling sentiment analysis in the Arabic language are now available. The future tendency will be the use of deep learning techniques and rule-based approach in order to deal more adequately with Arabic language characteristics.

REFERENCES

Abdelhameed, H. J., & Hernández, S. M. (2019). Sentiment Analysis of Arabic Tweets in Sudanese Dialect. *International Journal of New Technology and Research, 5*(6), 17–22. doi:10.31871/IJNTR.5.6.20

Abdul-Mageed, M., & Diab, M. (2012a). AWATIF: A Multi-Genre Corpus for Modern Standard Arabic Subjectivity and Sentiment Analysis. *Language Resources and Evaluation Conference (LREC'12),* 3907–3914. http://www.seas.gwu.edu/~mtdiab/files/publications/refereed/13.pdf

Abdul-Mageed, M., & Diab, M. (2012b). Toward Building a Large-Scale Arabic Sentiment Lexicon. *6th International Global Wordnet Conference*, 18–22.

Abdul-mageed, M., & Sandra, K. (2012). SAMAR : A System for Subjectivity and Sentiment Analysis of Arabic Social Media. *3rd Workshop on Computational Approaches to Subjectivity and Sentiment Analysis,* 19–28.

Abu Hammad, A., & El-Halees, A. (2015). An approach for detecting spam in Arabic opinion reviews. *The International Arab Journal of Information Technology, 12*(1), 10–16.

Aggarwal, C. C. (2018). Opinion mining and sentiment analysis. *Machine Learning for Text,* (2), 413–434.

Al-ayyoub, M., Nuseir, A., Alsmearat, K., Jararweh, Y., & Gupta, B. (2018). Deep learning for Arabic NLP : A survey. *Journal of Computational Science, 26,* 522–531. doi:10.1016/j.jocs.2017.11.011

Al-badrashiny, M., Eskander, R., Habash, N., & Rambow, O. (2014). Automatic Transliteration of Romanized Dialectal Arabic. *Proceedings of the Eighteenth Conference on Computational Natural Language Learning,* 30–38. 10.3115/v1/W14-1604

Al-hussaini, H., & Al-dossari, H. (2017). A Lexicon-based Approach to Build Service Provider Reputation from Arabic Tweets in Twitter. *IJACSA, 8*(4).

Al-smadi, M., Al-zboon, S., Jararweh, Y., & Juola, P. (2020). Transfer Learning for Arabic Named Entity Recognition With Deep Neural Networks. *IEEE Access: Practical Innovations, Open Solutions, 8,* 37736–37745. doi:10.1109/ACCESS.2020.2973319

Al-smadi, M., Qawasmeh, O., Al-ayyoub, M., Jararweh, Y., & Gupta, B. (2017). Deep Recurrent neural network vs. support vector machine for aspect-based sentiment analysis of Arabic hotels' reviews. *Journal of Computational Science*. Advance online publication. doi:10.1016/j.jocs.2017.11.006

Alayba, A. M., Palade, V., England, M., & Iqbal, R. (2017). Arabic Language Sentiment Analysis on Health Services. *1st International Workshop on Arabic Script Analysis and Recognition (ASAR)*, 114–118. 10.1109/ASAR.2017.8067771

Alghamdi, M. (2009). Romanizing Arabic Proper Names : Saudi Arabia Experience. *International Symposium on Arabic Transliteration Standard: Challenges and Solutions.*

Alotaibi, S. S., & Anderson, C. W. (2016). Extending the Knowledge of the Arabic Sentiment Classification Using a Foreign External Lexical Source. *International Journal on Natural Language Computing*, *5*(3), 1–11. doi:10.5121/ijnlc.2016.5301

Altrabsheh, N., El-masri, M., & Mansour, H. (2017). Combining Sentiment Lexicons of Arabic Terms. *Twenty-Third Americas Conference on Information Systems*, 1–10.

Aly, M., & Atiya, A. (2013). LABR: A Large Scale Arabic Book Reviews Dataset. *Proceedings of the 51st Annual Meeting of the Association for Computational Linguistics (*Volume 2*: Short Papers)*, 494–498.

Ameur, M. H. (2019). *ANETAC*. https://github.com/MohamedHadjAmeur/ANETAC

Attia, M. A. (2007). Arabic Tokenization System. *Proceedings of the Association of Computational Linguistics (ACL'07)*, 65–72. 10.3115/1654576.1654588

Badaro, G., Baly, R., & Hajj, H. (2014). *A Large Scale Arabic Sentiment Lexicon for Arabic Opinion Mining*. Arabic Natural Language Processing Workshop Co-Located with EMNLP. doi:10.3115/v1/W14-3623

Boudad, N., Faizi, R., Oulad, R., Thami, H., & Chiheb, R. (2017). Sentiment analysis in Arabic: A review of the literature. *Ain Shams Engineering Journal*, *9*(July), 2479–2490. doi:10.1016/j.asej.2017.04.007

Bougrine, S., Cherroun, H., & Abdelali, A. (2017). Altruistic Crowdsourcing for Arabic Speech Corpus Annotation. *ACLing*, *117*(November), 133–144. doi:10.1016/j.procs.2017.10.102

Buckwalter, T. (n.d.). *Arabic Transliteration*. Retrieved December 18, 2019, from http://www.qamus.org/transliteration.htm

Danowski, J. A. (2012). Sentiment network analysis of taleban and RFE/RL open-source content about Afghanistan. *Open-Source Intelligence and Web Mining Conference [OSINT-WM], August*, 303–310. 10.1109/EISIC.2012.54

Djoudi, M., Fohr, D., & Haton, J.-P. (1989). Phonetic study for automatic recognition of Arabic. *First European Conference on Speech Communication and Technology, EUROSPEECH*, 268–271.

Djoudi, M., & Harous, S. (2008). Text Entry System for Semitic Languages on Mobile Devices. In *Handbook of Research on Mobile Multimedia* (pp. 772–782). IGI Global.

Duwairi, R. M., Alfaqeh, M., Wardat, M., & Alrabadi, A. (2016). Sentiment analysis for Arabizi text. 7th International Conference on Information and Communication Systems, ICICS, 127–132. 10.1109/IACS.2016.7476098

El-Beltagy, S. R. (2016). NileULex: A Phrase and Word Level Sentiment Lexicon for Egyptian and Modern Standard Arabic. *Proceedings of Tenth International Conference on Language Resources and Evaluation (LREC)*, 2900–2905.

El-Kilany, A., Azzam, A., & El-Beltagy, S. R. (2018). Using deep neural networks for extracting sentiment targets in arabic tweets. *Studies in Computational Intelligence*, *740*, 3–15. doi:10.1007/978-3-319-67056-0_1

Elnagar, A., Khalifa, Y. S., & Einea, A. (2018). Hotel Arabic-Reviews Dataset Construction for Sentiment Analysis Applications. *Intelligent Natural Language Processing: Trends and Applications*, 35–52.

ElSahar, H., & El-Beltagy, S. R. (2015). Building Large Arabic Multi-domain Resources for Sentiment Analysis. *International Conference on Intelligent Text Processing and Computational Linguistics*, 23–34. 10.1007/978-3-319-18117-2_2

Elshakankery, K., & Ahmed, M. F. (2019). HILATSA: A hybrid Incremental learning approach for Arabic tweets sentiment analysis. Egyptian Informatics Journal, 1–9. doi:10.1016/j.eij.2019.03.002

Fadel, A., Tuffaha, I., Al-jawarneh, B., & Al-Ayyoub, M. (2019). Arabic Text Diacritization Using Deep Neural Networks. *International Conference on Computer Applications & Information Security*, 2–9. 10.1109/CAIS.2019.8769512

Farasa. (n.d.). http://alt.qcri.org/farasa/

Farghaly, A., & Shaalan, K. (2009). Arabic natural language processing : Challenges and solutions. *ACM Transactions on Asian Language Information Processing*, *8*(4), 1–22. doi:10.1145/1644879.1644881

Ferguson, C. A. (1959). Diglossia. *Word*, *15*(2), 325–340. doi:10.1080/00437956.1959.11659702

Guellil, I., Adeel, A., Azouaou, F., Benali, F., & Hussain, A. (2018). Arabizi sentiment analysis based on transliteration and automatic corpus annotation. *9th Workshop on Computational Approaches to Subjectivity, Sentiment and Social Media Analysis*, 335–341. 10.18653/v1/W18-6249

Guellil, I., Azouaou, F., Benali, F., Hachani, A. E., & Mendoza, M. (2020). The Role of Transliteration in the Process of Arabizi Translation/Sentiment Analysis. In M. Abd Elaziz, M. A. A. Al-qaness, A. A. Ewees, & A. Dahou (Eds.), *Recent Advances in NLP: The Case of Arabic Language* (pp. 101–128). Springer International Publishing. doi:10.1007/978-3-030-34614-0_6

Guellil, I., Azouaou, F., & Hussain, A. (2018). SentiALG : Automated Corpus Annotation for Algerian Sentiment Analysis Introduction. *Proceedings of the International Conference on Brain Inspired Cognitive Systems*, 557–567. 10.1007/978-3-030-00563-4_54

Guellil, I., Azouaou, F., & Mendoza, M. (2019). Arabic sentiment analysis: Studies, resources, and tools. *Social Network Analysis and Mining*, *9*(56), 1–17. doi:10.100713278-019-0602-x

Habash, N. (2010). Introduction to Arabic natural language processing. In G. Hirst (Ed.), Synthesis Lectures on Human Language Technologies (Vol. 3, Issue 1). doi:10.2200/S00277ED1V01Y201008HLT010

Habash, N., Soudi, A., & Buckwalter, T. (2007). On Arabic Transliteration. In Arabic Computational Morphology (Vol. 49, Issue 4, pp. 15–22). doi:10.1007/978-1-4020-6046-5_2

Hadj Ameur, M. S., Meziane, F., & Guessoum, A. (2019). *ANETAC : Arabic named entity transliteration and classification dataset.* ArXiv Preprint ArXiv:1907.03110

Ibrahim, H. S., Abdou, S. M., & Gheith, M. (2015). Idioms-Proverbs Lexicon for Modern Standard Arabic and Colloquial Sentiment Analysis Idioms-Proverbs Lexicon for Modern Standard Arabic and Colloquial Sentiment Analysis. *International Journal of Computers and Applications*, *118*(11), 26–31. doi:10.5120/20790-3435

Internet World Stats. (n.d.). https://www.internetworldstats.com/stats7.htm

Iskra, D., Siemund, R., Borno, J., Moreno, A., Emam, O., Choukri, K., Gedge, O., Tropf, H., Nogueiras, A., Zitouni, I., Tsopanoglou, A., & Fakotakis, N. (2004). OrienTel -Telephony databases across Northern Africa and the Middle East Countries and technologies. *LREC*. http://citeseerx.ist.psu.edu/viewdoc/download?doi=10.1.1.360.7554&rep=rep1&type=pdf

Ismail, S., Alsammak, A., & Elshishtawy, T. (2016). A generic approach for extracting aspects and opinions of arabic reviews. *ACM International Conference Proceeding Series,* 173–179. 10.1145/2908446.2908467

Jarrar, M., Habash, N., Alrimawi, F., Akra, D., & Zalmout, N. (2017). Curras: An annotated corpus for the Palestinian Arabic dialect. *Language Resources and Evaluation*, *51*(3), 745–775. doi:10.100710579-016-9370-7

Jindal, N., & Liu, B. (2007). Review Spam Detection. *Proceedings of the 16th International Conference on World Wide Web*, 1189–1190. 10.1145/1242572.1242759

Jindal, N., & Liu, B. (2008). Opinion Spam and Analysis. In *Proceedings of the international conference on web search and data mining WSDM'08* (pp. 219–229). ACM. 10.1145/1341531.1341560

Liu, B. (2010). Sentiment Analysis and Subjectivity. In R. Herbrich & T. Graepel (Eds.), Handbook of Natural Language Processing (2nd ed., pp. 627–666). Microsoft Research Ltd.

Liu, B. (2012). Sentiment Analysis and Opinion Mining. *Synthesis Lectures on Human Language Technologies*, *5*(1), 1–167. doi:10.2200/S00416ED1V01Y201204HLT016

Liu, B. (2015). *Sentiment Analysis Mining Opinions, Sentiments, and Emotions.* Cambridge University Press. doi:10.1017/CBO9781139084789

Mahyoub, F. H. H., Siddiqui, M. A., & Dahab, M. Y. (2014). Building an Arabic Sentiment Lexicon Using Semi-supervised Learning. Journal of King Saud University - Computer and Information Sciences, 26(4), 417–424. doi:10.1016/j.jksuci.2014.06.003

Marsi, E., Bosch, A. van den, & Soudi, A. (2005). Memory-based morphological analysis generation and part-of-speech tagging of Arabic. *Computational Approaches to Semitic Languages*, 1–8.

Masmoudi, A., Habash, N., Khmekhem, M. E., Estève, Y., & Belguith, L. H. (2015). Arabic Transliteration of Romanized Tunisian Dialect Text: A Preliminary Investigation. *Lecture Notes in Computer Science*, *9041*, 608–619. doi:10.1007/978-3-319-18111-0_46

Masmoudi, A., Khmekhem, M. E., Khrouf, M., & Belguith, L. H. (2019). Transliteration of Arabizi into Arabic Script for Tunisian Dialect. *ACM Transactions on Asian and Low-Resource Language Information Processing (TALLIP), 19*(2), Article 32.

Mataoui, M., Zelmati, O., & Boumechache, M. (2016). A Proposed Lexicon-Based Sentiment Analysis Approach for the Vernacular Algerian Arabic. *Res Comput Sci, 110*(1), 55–70. doi:10.13053/rcs-110-1-5

Medhat, W., Hassan, A., & Korashy, H. (2014). Sentiment analysis algorithms and applications : A survey. *Ain Shams Engineering Journal, 5*(4), 1093–1113. doi:10.1016/j.asej.2014.04.011

Meftouh, K., Bouchemal, N., & Smaili, K. (2012). a Study of a Non-Resourced Language : an Algerian Dialect. *Proc. 3td International Workshop on Spoken Languages Technologies for Under-Resourced Languages (SLTU'12).*

Mohammad, S. M., Salameh, M., & Kiritchenko, S. (2016). Sentiment Lexicons for Arabic Social Media. *Tenth International Conference on Language Resources and Evaluation (LREC)*, 33–37.

Mountassir, A., Benbrahim, H., & Berraba, I. (2013). Sentiment classification on arabic corpora. A preliminary cross-study. *International Conference on Innovative Techniques and Applications of Artificial Intelligence, 16*(1), 259–272. 10.3166/dn.16.1.73-96

Mubarak, H., Abdelali, A., Darwish, K., Eldesouki, M., Samih, Y., & Sajjad, H. (2019). A System for Diacritizing Four Varieties of Arabic. *Proceedings of the 2019 Conference on Empirical Methods in Natural Language Processing and the 9th International Joint Conference on Natural Language Processing (EMNLP-IJCNLP)*, 217–222. 10.18653/v1/D19-3037

Mulki, H., Haddad, H., Ali, C. B., & Babao, I. (2018). Tunisian Dialect Sentiment Analysis : A Natural Language Processing-based Approach. *Computación y Sistemas, 22*(4). Advance online publication. doi:10.13053/cys-22-4-3009

Pang, B., & Lee, L. (2004). A Sentimental Education: Sentiment Analysis Using Subjectivity Summarization Based on Minimum Cuts. *42nd Annual Meeting on Association for Computational Linguistics*, 271–278. 10.3115/1218955.1218990

Pasha, A., Al-badrashiny, M., Diab, M., El Kholy, A., Eskander, R., Habash, N., Pooleery, M., Rambow, O., & Roth, M., R. (2014). MADAMIRA : A Fast, Comprehensive Tool for Morphological Analysis and Disambiguation of Arabic. *Proceedings of the Ninth International Conference on Language Resources and Evaluation (LREC'14)*, 1094–1101.

Poesio, M., Chamberlain, J., & Kruschwitz, U. (2017). Crowdsourcing. In Handbook of Linguistic Annotation (pp. 277–295). Academic Press.

Rahab, H., Zitouni, A., & Djoudi, M. (2018). SIAAC: Sentiment Polarity Identification on Arabic Algerian Newspaper Comments. In Applied Computational Intelligence and Mathematical Methods (Vol. 662, pp. 141–149). doi:10.1007/978-3-319-67621-0

Rahab, H., Zitouni, A., & Djoudi, M. (2019). SANA: Sentiment analysis on newspapers comments in Algeria. Journal of King Saud University - Computer and Information Sciences. doi:10.1016/j.jksuci.2019.04.012

Ramírez-Tinoco, F. J., Alor-Hernández, G., Sánchez-Cervantes, J. L., Salas-Zárate, M. del P., & Valencia-García, R. (2019). Use of Sentiment Analysis Techniques in Healthcare Domain. In Current Trends in Semantic Web Technologies: Theory and Practic (pp. 189–212). Springer International Publishing. doi:10.1007/978-3-030-06149-4_8

Rushdi-Saleh, M., Martín-Valdivia, M. T., Ureña-López, L. A., & Perea-Ortega, J. M. (2011). OCA: Opinion corpus for Arabic. *Journal of the American Society for Information Science and Technology*, *62*(10), 2045–2054. doi:10.1002/asi.21598

Saadane, H. (2015). *Le traitement automatique de l'arabe dialectalisé: aspects méthodologiques et algorithmiques* [These de doctorat].

Saeed, R. M. K., Rady, S., & Gharib, T. F. (2019). An ensemble approach for spam detection in Arabic opinion texts. Journal of King Saud University - Computer and Information Sciences. doi:10.1016/j.jksuci.2019.10.002

Semmar, N., & Saadane, H. (2013). Using Transliteration of Proper Names from Arabic to Latin Script to Improve English-Arabic Word Alignment. *International Joint Conference on Natural Language Processing, October*, 1022–1026.

Soliman, A. B., Eissa, K., & El-Beltagy, S. R. (2017). AraVec: A set of Arabic Word Embedding Models for use in Arabic NLP. *Procedia Computer Science*, *117*, 256–265. doi:10.1016/j.procs.2017.10.117

Subramaniyaswamy, V., Logesh, R., Abejith, M., Umasankar, S., & Umamakeswari, A. (2017). Sentiment analysis of tweets for estimating criticality and security of events. *Journal of Organizational and End User Computing*, *29*(4), 51–71. doi:10.4018/JOEUC.2017100103

Touahri, I., & Mazroui, A. (2019). Studying the effect of characteristic vector alteration on Arabic sentiment classification. Journal of King Saud University - Computer and Information Sciences. doi:10.1016/j.jksuci.2019.04.011

Tsarfaty, R., Sandra, K., Candito, M., Rehbein, I., & Foster, J. (2010). Statistical Parsing of Morphologically Rich Languages (SPMRL) What, How and Whither. In *NAACL HLT First Workshop on Statistical Parsing of Morphologically-Rich Languages* (pp. 1–12). ACL.

Wahsheh, H., Al-Kabi, M. N., & Alsmadi, I. (2013a). A link and Content Hybrid Approach for Arabic Web Spam Detection. *International Journal of Intelligent Systems and Applications*, *5*(1), 30–43. doi:10.5815/ijisa.2013.01.03

Wahsheh, H., Al-Kabi, M. N., & Alsmadi, I. (2013b). SPAR: A system to detect spam in Arabic opinions. *IEEE Jordan Conference on Applied Electrical Engineering and Computing Technologies, AEECT 2013*, 1–6. 10.1109/AEECT.2013.6716442

Zayed, O. H., & El-Beltagy, S. R. (2015). Named entity recognition of persons' names in Arabic tweets. *International Conference Recent Advances in Natural Language Processing, RANLP*, 731–738.

ADDITIONAL READING

Aggarwal, C. C. (2018b). Opinion mining and sentiment analysis. In Machine Learning for Text (pp. 413–434). doi:10.1007/978-3-319-73531-3_13

Farghaly, A., & Shaalan, K. (2009). Arabic natural language processing : Challenges and solutions. *ACM Transactions on Asian Language Information Processing*, *8*(4), 1–22. doi:10.1145/1644879.1644881

Guellil, I., Azouaou, F., Benali, F., Hachani, A. E., & Mendoza, M. (2020). The Role of Transliteration in the Process of Arabizi Translation/Sentiment Analysis. In M. Abd Elaziz, M. A. A. Al-qaness, A. A. Ewees, & A. Dahou (Eds.), *Recent Advances in NLP: The Case of Arabic Language* (pp. 101–128). Springer International Publishing., doi:10.1007/978-3-030-34614-0_6

Habash, N. (2010). *Introduction to Arabic natural language processing* (G. Hirst, Ed.). Vol. 3). Synthesis Lectures on Human Language Technologies.

Habash, N., Soudi, A., & Buckwalter, T. (2007). On Arabic Transliteration. In Arabic Computational Morphology (Vol. 49, pp. 15–22). doi:10.1007/978-1-4020-6046-5_2

Liu, B. (2012). Sentiment Analysis and Opinion Mining. *Synthesis Lectures on Human Language Technologies*, *5*(1), 1–167. doi:10.2200/S00416ED1V01Y201204HLT016

Liu, B. (2015). *Sentiment Analysis Mining Opinions, Sentiments, and Emotions*. Cambridge University Press. doi:10.1017/CBO9781139084789

Rahab, H., Zitouni, A., & Djoudi, M. (2019). SANA: Sentiment analysis on newspapers comments in Algeria. *Journal of King Saud University - Computer and Information Sciences*. . doi:10.1016/j.jksuci.2019.04.012

Wahsheh, H., Al-Kabi, M. N., & Alsmadi, I. (2013a). A link and Content Hybrid Approach for Arabic Web Spam Detection. *International Journal of Intelligent Systems and Applications*, *5*(1), 30–43. doi:10.5815/ijisa.2013.01.03

KEY TERMS AND DEFINITIONS

Agglutination: Is the representation of different part-of-speech POS elements in the same word.

Arabizi: Is a writing style that uses Latin script to write Arabic text without any kind of rules which leads to big differences in writing almost all Arabic words. The phenomenon emerged in the space of the Internet and especially by the spreading use of the smartphones without sophisticated Arabic keyboards.

Diacritic: Are signs playing the role of short vowels in the Arabic language, the diacritics signs, even omitted in most of the Arabic texts today, their role is primordial to guide the pronunciation and remove the ambiguity of an important number of Arabic letters.

Diglossia: Is a phenomenon appearing within some populations with a rich cultural heritage; in this situation people use more than one language at the same time.

Opinion: Is someone's viewpoint toward an entity based on their cultural, social and religious background. This point of view may be expressed in review, an article, a tv show or other media they have access to.

Opinion Holder: Is the person or organization claiming an opinion in a document, by an explicit or implicit manner.

Opinion Spam: Opinion that intends to influence the behaviour of Internet users by diffusing commercial, political, or social reviews in the goal to promote or discredit something. Spammers present themselves as independent reviewers without declaring their identity. The spammers may intend to promote their products or viewpoints or discredit the products or viewpoints of their competitors.

Sentiment: Is the positive or negative feeling of a person in response to an instantaneous event without a need to give any motivation. Thus, there is no neutral sentiment, but objectivity can be considered as a no-sentiment.

Transcription: Relays on writing a speech in a script as it is pronounced in the goal to guide the pronunciation of beginners in a language or to convert an audio speech to a text.

Transliteration: Is the process of moving a text from script to another in the goal to allow foreign readers of a language to read texts in this language. Word pronunciation is not considered here.

ENDNOTES

[1]   For transliteration adopted in this chapter See (Habash et al., 2007)

[2]   'm' for masculine, 'f' for feminine, 'd' for dual and 'p' for plural.

APPENDIX: ADOPTED TRANSLITERATION SYSTEM

The transliteration system followed in this chapter is the one proposed scheme in (Habash et al., 2007) and presented in the following table.

Table 4. Adopted transliteration system

Arabic Character	Description	Transliteration	Example		
			Arabic	**Transliteration**	**Signification**
ء	همزة	'	سماء	samaA'	Sky
آ	ألف مد	Ā	آمن	Āmana	Secured
أ	ألف بهمزة أعلى	Â	سأل	saÂala	Ask
ؤ	همزة على الواو	ŵ	مؤتمر	muŵtamar	Conference
إ	ألف بهمزة أسفل	Ă	إنترنت	Ăintarnit	Internet
ئ	همزة على الياء	ŷ	سائل	saAŷil	Liquid
ا	ألف	A	كان	kaAna	It was
ب	باء	b	بريد	bariyd	Post
ة	تاء مربوطة	ħ	مكتبة	maktabaħ or maktabaħŭ	Library
ت	تاء	t	تنافس	tanaAfus	Concurrence
ث	ثاء	θ	ثالثة	θalaAθaħ or θalaAθaħŭ	Three
ج	جيم	j	جميل	jamiyl	Beautiful
ح	حاء	H	حاد	HaAd	Prick
خ	خاء	x	خوذة	xawðaħ	Berets
د	دال	d	دليل	daliyl	Guide
ذ	ذال	ð	ذهب	ðahab	Gold
ر	راء	r	رفيع	rafiyς	Fine
ز	زاي	z	زينة	ziynaħ	Decoration
س	سين	s	سماء	samaA'	Sky
ش	شين	š	شريف	šariyf	Honest
ص	صاد	S	صوت	Sawt	Sound
ض	ضاد	D	ضرير	Dariyr	Blinded
ط	طاد	T	طويل	Tawiyl	Long
ظ	ظاء	Ď	ظلم	Ďulm	Injustice
ع	عين	ς	عمل	ςamal	Work
غ	غين	γ	غريب	γariyb	Strange
ف	فاء	f	فيلم	fiylm	Film
ق	قاف	q	قادر	qaAdir	Capable

continues on following page

Table 4. Continued

Arabic Character	Description	Transliteration	Example		
			Arabic	Transliteration	Signification
ك	فاك	k	كريم	kariym	Generous
ل	لام	l	لذيذ	laðiyð	Delicious
م	ميم	m	مدير	mudiyr	Director
ن	نون	n	رون	nuwr	Light
ه	هاء	h	هول	huwl	Devastation
و	واو	w	وصل	waSl	Receive
ى	ألف مقصورة	ý	على	çal ý	On
ي	ياء	y	تين	tiyn	Fig
َ	فتحة	a	دَهَنَ	dahana	He hangs
ُ	ضمة	u	دُهِنَ	duhina	It is hanged
ِ	كسرة	i	دُهِنَ	duhina	It is hanged
ً	فتحتين	ā	كتابأ	kitaAbAā	Book
ٌ	ضمتين	ū	كتابٌ	kitaAbū	Book
ٍ	كسرتين	i	كتابٍ	kitaAbī	Book
ّ	شدة (šad~ah)	~	كسّر	kas~ara	Break
ْ	سكون (sukuwn)	.	مسجد	mas.jidou masjid	Mosque
ـ	تطويل (taTwiyl) وأ كشيدة (kašiydah)	_	مسـجد	mas.___jid ou mas___jid	Mosque
ال	ال التعريف Definition Al	Al	المصلى	AlmuSal~a ý	Small mosque

Chapter 14
Building Lexical Resources for Dialectical Arabic

Sumaya Sulaiman Al Ameri
Khalifa University of Science and Technology, UAE

Abdulhadi Shoufan
iD https://orcid.org/0000-0002-3968-8637
Center for Cyber-Physical Systems, Khalifa University of Science and Technology, UAE

ABSTRACT

The natural language processing of Arabic dialects faces a major difficulty, which is the lack of lexical resources. This problem complicates the penetration and the business of related technologies such as machine translation, speech recognition, and sentiment analysis. Current solutions frequently use lexica, which are specific to the task at hand and limited to some language variety. Modern communication platforms including social media gather people from different nations and regions. This has increased the demand for general-purpose lexica towards effective natural language processing solutions. This chapter presents a collaborative web-based platform for building a cross-dialectical, general-purpose lexicon for Arabic dialects. This solution was tested by a team of two annotators, a reviewer, and a lexicographer. The lexicon expansion rate was measured and analyzed to estimate the overhead required to reach the desired size of the lexicon. The inter-annotator reliability was analyzed using Cohen's Kappa.

INTRODUCTION

Arabic is the official language of 22 countries, one of the six official languages of the United Nations and has more than 420 million speakers (Kamusella, 2017). Arabic has three varieties: classical Arabic (CA) used in Quran and old literature, modern standard Arabic (MSA) used in formal communication nowadays and dialectal Arabic (DA) which is the spoken variety (Habash, 2010). The last decade has experienced a growing interest in the natural language processing of dialectical Arabic. This growth is attributed to the wide usage of this language variety in social media (Guellil et al., 2019) and to the role of these media in the Arabic revolutions (Aouragh, 2016).

DOI: 10.4018/978-1-7998-4240-8.ch014

The topics treated by computational linguists for Arabic dialects can be assigned to one of four main categories (Shoufan & Alameri 2015):

1. Basic language analysis such as morphological and syntactical analysis (Maamouri et al. 2006; Habash et al., 2012; Masmoudi et al., 2015; Khalifa, 2017; Zalmout, 2018).
2. Building language resources such as lexica, corpora, treebanks, and wordnets (Graff et al., 2006; Cotterell and Callison-Burch, 2014; El-Beltagy, 2016; Qwaider et al., 2018).
3. Semantic-level analysis and synthesis, such as machine translation and sentiment analysis (Sawaf 2010; Duwairi et al., 2014; Medhaffar et al., 2017).
4. Identifying Arabic dialects, e.g., using speech recognition techniques (Kirchhoff and Vergyri 2005; El Haj et al., 2018; Ali, 2018).

Besides well-known challenges in NLP for Modern Standard Arabic (MSA) such as the lack of short vowel letters and the non-existence of capitalization, (Farghaly & Shaalan, 2009) processing Arabic varieties is challenged by the lack of language resources such as lexicons and annotated corpora. The few proposed solutions for building lexicons in the literature show two major restrictions. First, the lexicons are specific to one dialect only. This restriction is especially problematic when social media data should be processed because social networks cross the geographic borderlines and allow addressing topics that are of interest to most Arabic people regardless of their regions or countries. Thus, a relevant part of social media data can be described as multi-dialectical. Processing this data using a single-dialect language resource is not expected to provide desired performance. Second, the proposed lexicons are restricted in terms of annotation width, and some of them are even application-specific, e.g., for PoS tagging or sentiment analysis. The authors believe that the development of general-purpose lexicons is essential to serve different NLP applications. This does not only facilitate interfacing the lexicon to different tools. It also allows the community to concentrate its efforts towards building a sophisticated and comprehensive lexicon that can be used as a reference in many applications.

In this chapter, we propose a methodology for building lexical resources for Arabic dialects based on an in-depth requirement analysis that takes into consideration the restrictions described above. The technical solution denoted as the Lexicon Builder (LB) allows developing a cross-dialectical, general-purpose lexicon for Arabic dialects. The Lexicon Builder was conceived as a web application and deployed on a platform-as-a-service cloud. The LB was tested by a team of two annotators, a reviewer, and a Lexicographer. The system was evaluated and analyzed to estimate the overhead required to reach a desired size of the lexicon and to find the inter-annotator agreement.

The rest of the chapter is structured as follows. After reviewing some related literature as background, we present the design objectives and concepts of the Lexicon Builder. Then, the LB architecture and components are detailed. After this, some implementation and deployment aspects are given. Finally, the system evaluation is described.

LITERATURE REVIEW

In this section, we review previous work related to building lexical resources for Arabic dialects. This literature considers MSA too, but not exclusively. Related work that addressed lexical resources exclusively for MSA such as (Abuleil and Evens, 1998; Khemakhem et al., 2009; Attia et al., 2011; Khemakhem et al., 2012; Mohammad et al., 2016; Inoue et al., 2018) is not considered in this review.

Table 1 gives a comparative overview of important features of lexicons and lexicon building tools as covered in the literature and in this work. In this table, we use N/A when some feature is not applicable to the respective work. When the authors of some paper did not give information on some property, we used N/G to indicate this.

Graff et al. developed a manual approach for building an Iraqi lexicon for the purpose of morphological analysis (Graff et al., 2006). The main aspect of this approach is the differentiation between various pronunciation forms for the same skeletal form. This is important because different pronunciations can be found in the same dialect. The corpus consists of 20-hour recorded conversations, including 118,000 word tokens. A two-layer transcription is first performed, followed by extracting a structured word list that sorts the words by the frequency of their occurrences to improve the annotation effectiveness. The annotation starts with a morphological segmentation, followed by PoS tagging and adding an English gloss to each segment. The annotation can be iterated to make sure that all the diacritized forms, i.e., pronunciations of a skeleton are correctly annotated. The authors provide interesting information on the annotation process: The design of the database, the creation of the annotation tool, and the annotation of 13,000 distinct word forms took six calendar months. The work was carried out by the four authors in addition to an annotation crew of four people, who had part-time involvement in the project.

Diab et al. introduced a lemma-based Egyptian lexicon called THARWA with English and MSA translations (Diab et al., 2014). To build this lexicon, the authors used several existing monolingual and bilingual resources including the Hinds-Badawi Dictionary (Badawi and Hinds 1986), the Egyptian Colloquial Arabic Lexicon (Kilany et al., 2002), the Columbia Egyptian Colloquial Arabic Dictionary, and the SAMA Lexicon (Graff et al., 2009). Both manual and automatic techniques were used to edit, expand and verify the dictionary entries through a web interface. The publicly available lexicon contains more than 73,000 entries tagged with PoS, gender, number, rationality, morphological pattern, and morphological root.

Duh and Kirchhoff proposed a two-stage approach to generate a Levantine lexicon for the purpose of PoS tagging (Duh and Kirchhoff, 2006). In the first stage, a transcribed speech undergoes a morphological analysis using the MSA Buckwalter Morphological Analyzer (Buckwalter, 2004). This results in what the authors call Partially Annotated PoS Lexicon (PAL), which is essentially a list of tagged words and a list of untagged words. In the second stage a transductive learning algorithm is applied to the PAL to obtain the fully annotated PoS lexicon. The authors argue that this approach provides higher tagging accuracies when compared to a baseline lexicon that hypothesizes all PoS tags.

Al-Sabbagh and Girjiu proposed an approach for inducing an Egyptian Cairene lexicon using web mining (Al-Sabbagh and Girju, 2010). The approach relies on the scheme proposed by Rapp to find English German translations (Rapp, 1999), however, without using a seed dictionary. The acquisition of word co-occurrences of Egyptian Cairene Arabic (ECA) is conditioned by the word co-occurrences acquired for MSA. The lexicon assigns each ECA word an MSA equivalent, which facilitates using NLP solutions available for MSA. The approach includes PoS tagging of the ECA words by adopting the PoS of the MSA equivalents based on online MSA dictionaries. The approach was tested for 1000 ECA words.

Graff and Maamouri developed LMF-XML bilingual dictionaries for Moroccan, Syrian and Iraqi Arabic (Graff and Maamouri, 2012). This work was initiated by the Linguistic Data Consortium and Georgetown University Press to update and enhance three old dictionaries for English-speaking learners and to provide the dictionaries both in printed form and as an electronically accessible lexicon.

An approach for building a corpus and a bilingual dictionary for the Tunisian dialect is presented In Boujelbane et al. (2013) 's study. The lexicon was built based on explicit knowledge about the relation between the Tunisian dialect and MSA. This approach started with reviewing the Penn Arabic Treebank to specify the morphological, syntactical, and lexical differences between MSA and the Tunisian dialect. Then, dialectal rules and concepts were defined and used to create the bilingual lexicon.

Azouaou & Guellil constructed and enriched an Algerian Dialect French lexicon focused on sentiment analysis and opinion mining for social media (Azouaou & Guellil, 2017). They started with a lexicon that contains the most used words in French and their Algerian Dialect translations. Then, they added Algerian particle words and strong sentiment words. After this, they merged the two lexicons and replaced some letters with other letters which are used frequently in social media. Based on this, they automatically added words with different spelling variations and expanded the initially created lexicon from 1144 to 25086 words.

In Bouamor et al. (2018)'s study, the authors presented a corpus and a lexicon of 25 Arabic city dialects. The lexicon consisted of 1,045 entries in addition to their English, French and MSA transcriptions. The corpus included 12,000 sentences. 10,000 sentences thereof are translated into five Arabic dialects and the other 2000 into 25 Arabic dialects. To build the corpus, sentences from the Basic Traveling Expression Corpus (BTEC) were first selected and translated to the 25 or five Arabic dialects manually. For the lexicon, on the other hand, semi-automatic concept identification was used followed by manual lexicon population.

From this review and based on Table 1, we can classify the methodologies used to build dialectical lexicons in related work into two categories: Manual and Automated. Manual approaches start either from scratch as in (Graff et al. 2006) or from previously available resources such as in (Diab et al. 2014) and (Graff and Maamouri 2012). Also, the lexicon presented in (Boujelbane et al. 2013) was built manually, although the extracted rules were used for automated corpora generation. In contrast, automated approaches use computers to accelerate the process of finding word equivalents through web mining (Al-Sabbagh and Girju 2010) or to accelerate the tagging through machine learning (Duh and Kirchhoff 2006). In general, it can be expected that automated approaches cannot be used to perform comprehensive annotation of lexicon entries and are restricted to finding one or a few attributes of the words, e.g., MSA equivalent in (Al-Sabbagh and Girju 2010) or the PoS in (Duh and Kirchhoff 2006)). Additionally, automatic approaches cannot provide the accuracy level that is possible with human experts. On the other hand, manual annotation is very lengthy especially, when a comprehensive and reliable lexicon is sought. However, the overhead of the manual approach can be justified by the quality of the lexicon entries in terms of wide and deep annotation, as well as by the multi-purpose, multi-dialect features of the lexicon.

SOLUTIONS AND RECOMMENDATIONS

Lexicon Builder: Design Objectives and Concepts

The Lexicon Builder is a software solution for cooperative building of lexical data. To design it, we followed two groups of objectives: linguistic objectives and dependability objectives. The linguistic objectives represent the basic requirements of a lexicon and include accuracy, comprehensiveness, and flexibility. The dependability objectives relate to different requirements of the lexicon as well as the lexicon builder. These include accessibility, usability, efficiency, and security. In the following sections,

Table 1. Summary of literature on building lexical resources for Arabic dialects

Criteria		(Graff et al. 2006)	(Diab et al. 2014)	(Duh and Kirchhoff 2006)	(Al-Sabbagh and Girju 2010)	(Graff and Maamouri 2012)	(Boujelbane et al. 2013)	(Bouamor et al., 2018)	(Azouaou & Guellil, 2017)	Our Study
Lexicon Content	Supported dialects	Iraqi	Egyptian	Levantine	Egyptian	Iraqi, Syrian, Marroco	Tunisian	25 city dialects	Algerian	all dialects
	Number of entries	13,000	73,000	N/G	1000	18,000[1]	N/G	1045	25086	1300
	MSA equivalent	N/G	Yes	Yes	Yes	Some	Yes	Yes	No	Yes
	English meaning	N/G	Yes	N/G	N/G	Yes	Yes[2]	Yes	No	Yes
	Example	Yes	Yes[3]	No	Yes	Yes	Yes	Yes	Yes	Yes
	POS-tags	Yes	Yes	Yes	Yes	Yes	Yes	Yes	Yes	Yes
	Tagset size	N/G	34	20[4]	N/G	N/G	N/G	N/G	5	167
	Out of Vocabulary words tags (Foreign words, Abbreviations, Typos, etc.)	N/G	N/G	N/G	N/G	N/G	No	N/G	No	Yes
	Sentiment word tags	N/G	N/G	N/G	N/G	N/G	No	NG	Yes	Yes
Access to Lexicon	Access method for look-up users	Download	N/G[5]	N/A	N/G	Web	N/G	No	No	Yes
	API for other NLP tools	N/G	N/G	N/A	N/G	N/G	N/G	N/G	N/G	Web
	Multilevel PoS retrieval	No	N/G	N/A	N/G	N/G	N/G	N/G	N/G	Yes
Lexicon Building	Approach	Manual	Compilation	Machine learning	Statistical approach	Digitalization	Rule-based	Automatic lexicon population +Manual validation and annotation	Rule-based	Manual
	Distributed annotation	Yes	Yes	N/A	N/A[6]	Yes	No	Yes	N/G	Yes
	Reviewed annotation	Yes	Yes	N/A	Yes	Yes	N/G	Yes	No	Yes
	Data protection	N/G	N/G	N/A	N/G	N/G	N/G	N/G	N/G	Yes
Notes	(1)This number indicates the number of entries in the Iraqi dictionary; the rest is not mentioned. (2) Labelled as a gloss. (3) English gloss. (4) The tagset size in the approach is variable, but the one used in the experiment is 20. (5) The web application is used for annotation only as shown. (6) It uses the web to get the word meaning. (7) 300 entries were manually reviewed to test the approach.									

we describe these objectives and provide an overview of the design concepts followed and the technologies used to achieve these objectives as summarized in Table 2.

Linguistic Design Objectives and Concepts

1. Accurate Lexicon Content

The accuracy of lexical data is a primary requirement as it affects the acceptance of the lexicon by look-up users and computational linguists to a large extent. Depending on the lexicon type, the accuracy can relate to the word meaning, the words attributes or both as in our case. To assure data accuracy, the proposed Lexicon Builder supports Reviewed, Fine-Granular Annotation. Reviewed annotation means that a word cannot be made available by annotators. Rather, an expert must review the word annotation, make necessary revisions, and forward the task to a Lexicographer for final approval. For this purpose, a role-based user management system was developed as will be described in the section "Role-based User Management".

Fine-granular annotation describes the ability to annotate a word on a high level of details. This relates to several aspects, including the word part-of-speech and the origin dialect. The used tagset, for instance, does not only specify a word as a verb, but it describes its person, number, gender, tense, and mood. The word dialect can be specified not only on a regional level such as Levantine and Gulf but also on the country level.

Table 2. Requirements, design concepts, and supporting technologies for the dialectical lexicon

SR	Requirement	Design Concept	Techniques and Technologies
1	Accuracy	Reviewed Annotation	Role-based User Management
		Fine-Granular Annotation	Expanded Tagset
2	Comprehensiveness	Scalable Data Containers	Cloud and Relational DB
		Versatile Annotation	Relational DB
3	Flexibility	Layered Tagging	Relational DB
4	Accessibility	Remote Access	Client-Server Model
			Application Programmer Interface
5	Usability	Remote Annotation	Client-Server Model
		Friendly User Interface	Web Design
6	Efficiency	Fast Access	Cloud and JavaScript
		Distributed Annotation	Client-Server Model
			User Management
			Task Management
		Computer-Aided Annotation	Parser, Stemmer, Splitter, etc.
7	Security	Authentication and Authorization	Spring Security Framework

2. Comprehensive Lexicon Content

The size of a lexicon is essential for any useful application. To allow a continuous expansion of the lexicon with new entries, the Lexicon Builder relies on a relational database and a platform-as-a-service cloud as will be described later in the implementation section.

To serve different applications, the Lexicon Builder additionally allows versatile annotation. Annotators can translate the word into MSA as well as into English and add an example to explain the word in context. In addition to the mentioned dialectical origin and PoS tags, further attributes can be added to describe the word as foreign or transliterated. Stop words and abbreviations can also be specified. For different analyses of social media, misspelt words, grammatically wrong words, tweet-specific words, hashtags, and sentiment words are labelled. This will be outlined in section "System Architecture and Components".

3. Flexibility

NLP applications use tagsets with different sizes. This depends on the granularity level of annotation in the input dataset as well as on the capabilities of available NLP tools. Furthermore, computational linguists can trade off the PoS granularity against the computational overhead of the NLP solution at hand. In such cases, the lexicon should be able to return a word PoS on a specific granularity level. The Lexicon Builder allows this by maintaining a hierarchical structure of the tagset and by enforcing an annotation procedure that keeps this hierarchy. By this means, a later PoS retrieval on a specific level through the application user interface (API) is possible. Similarly, the dialectical origin of a word is stored on a regional level and on a country level so that a corresponding retrieval through the API is possible.

Dependability Design Objective and Concepts

1. Accessibility: To enhance accessibility, both the lexicon and the Lexicon Builder can be accessed remotely over the internet. The lexicon can be used through a web interface by look-up users and through an API by NLP application programmers. Also, the Lexicon Builder is accessed through a web interface to enable remote and distributed annotation.
2. Usability: Accessing the lexicon by look-up users and programmers is straight-forward. In contrast, the Lexicon Builder is a sophisticated system with diverse subsystems for the management of; the lexical database, the users, and the annotation tasks. We used advanced web technology to develop a friendly user interface that allows users with different roles to perform their tasks easily as will be described in the section "System Architecture and Components".
3. Efficiency: The retrieval of lexicon entries should be fast, especially when called by NLP tools through the application programmer interface. Fast retrieval can be assured using modern database technology as well as high-performance servers of cloud providers. On the other hand, building the lexicon itself is a lengthy process due to the wide and deep annotation and because of the required review and revision of new lexical entries. The collaborative distributed annotation is a solution to accelerate this process. Additionally, several techniques and tools are provided that help users during the annotation process. Colouring of previously annotated words, parsing, stemming, and word segmentation are examples for automatic functions that increase the annotation performance considerably.
4. Security: Lexicon entries should be kept authentic and secured against manipulation. Only authorized annotators, reviewers, and Lexicographers should have write access to the lexicon and Lexicon Builder functions. For that, a password-based authentication scheme is utilized.

System Architecture and Component

In this section, the models and techniques identified in the requirement analysis as summarized in Table 2, will be used to specify an architecture for the Lexicon Builder system.

Building lexical data is the core objective of the proposed system. The quality of the lexicon will strongly rely on the way this data is structured and related. Additionally, the lexicon entries need to be related to users (annotators and reviewers), tasks (the source of the data), and to other important data such as the tagset. Thus, the relational database forms a major architectural component in the Lexicon Builder system. The authors call this component Lexicon Builder Database (LBDB) as illustrated in Figure 1.

On the other end, the lexicon database should be accessed for expansion, update, and retrieval. For that, appropriate user and programmer interfaces should be provided. These interfaces form the second architectural component of the Lexicon Builder denoted as Lexicon Builder Interface (LBI).

To support and coordinate users' and programmers' access to the lexicon database, several linguistic functions, as well as control and management functions are required. The linguistic functions include a parser, a stemmer and a word splitter. The management functions relate to the user and task management. These and other auxiliary functions are embedded into one architectural component called the Lexicon Builder Controller (LBC), as depicted in Figure 1.

The LBC and the LBD run on the server system of a cloud platform, while the interface component resides on the client side. In the following sections, the three system components will be detailed starting with the LBDB followed by LBC and LBI.

Figure 1. Overview of the System Architecture

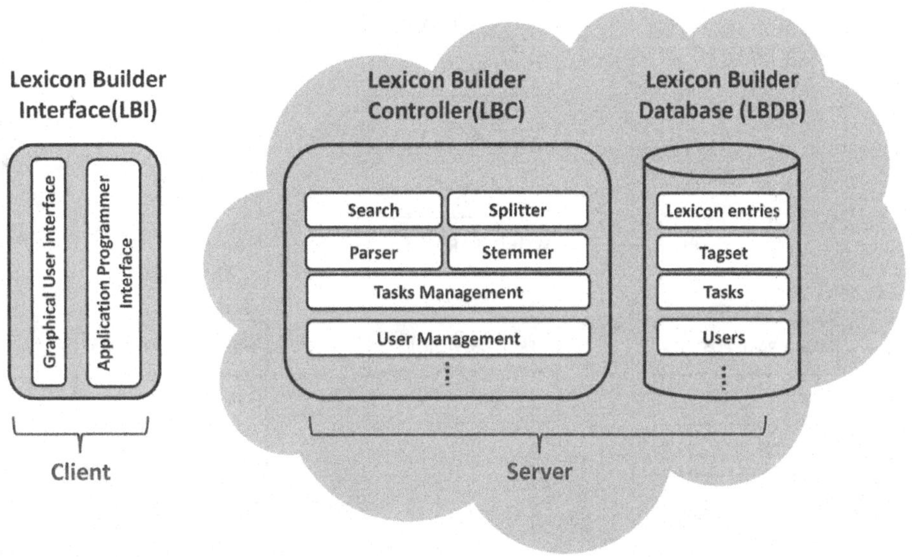

Lexicon Builder Database (LBDB)

The Lexicon Builder Database includes several tables that can be classified into two main categories. The first category includes the tables that are necessary for looking up the lexicon, such as the word table and the tagset table. This category is called the Lexicon Database (LDB). The second category comprises the tables that are required to build up the Lexicon Database, such as the user and the task tables. This category is referred to as the Builder Database (BDB) in the sequel.

Lexicon Database (LDB)

The LDB will be described following a top-down approach. The most important table in the LDB is the word table called LDB WORD. This table includes the following attributes:

1. LDB WORD ID
2. Lemma
3. ROOT ID: A link to the word root in the Root Table
4. BDB WORD ID: A link to the same word in the Builder Database
5. MSA equivalent
6. English Meaning
7. Gloss (the tweet or a part of it that includes the lemma)
8. Phonetic scheme (for future extension)
9. WordNet ID (for future extension)

Figure 2. Entity relationship diagram (ERD) of the lexicon database

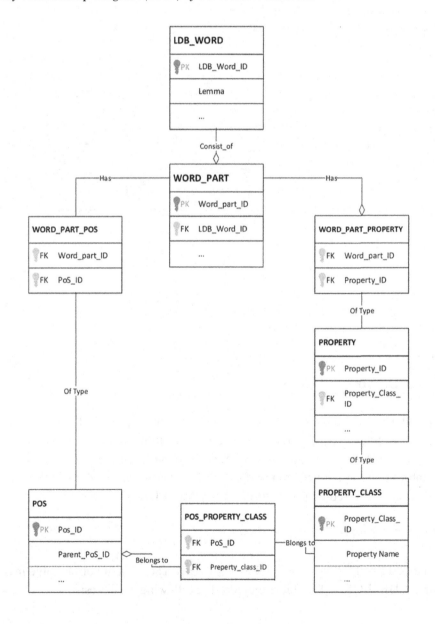

Arabic words can be composed of two or more parts with different parts-of-speech. The LDB_WORD table includes the word in its composite form. The relationship between this word and its parts is created using a second table called WORD_PART. This is a one-to-many relationship as one word can consist of many parts, as can be seen in Figure 2. Assume, for example, that the LDB_WORD table includes only two words that stem from the sentence "جامعتنا أحب" *ahb jam'etna* which means "I like our university". The part of the LDB_WORD table that includes the word identities and the lemmas are given in Table 3.

Table 3. LDB_WORD_ID table

LDB_WORD_ID	Lemma
1	أحب *ahb*
2	جامعتنا *jam'etna*

The WORD_PART table would have three entries as the word "جامعتنا" *jam'etna* is composed of the noun "جامعة" *jam'eh* (university) and the pronoun "نا" *na* (our), see Table 4.

Table 4. WORD_PART table

WORD_PART_ID	Part	Type	LDB_WORD_ID
1	"أحب" *ahb*	Main	1
2	"جامعة" *jam'eh*	Main	2
3	"نا" *na*	Main	2

Each word part has exactly one part-of-speech and can have up to four properties. The bridge tables WORD_PART_POS and WORD_PART_PROPERTY reflect these relationships by linking each word part to its PoS and its properties, respectively.

In our example, the content of these two tables is given in Table 5 and Table 6. Note that the entries in brackets are used for explanation only since they are not part of the table entries.

Table 5. WORD_PART_POS table

WORD_PART_ID	PoS_ID
1 (أحب) *ahb*	25 (imperfect verb)
2 (جامعة) *jam'eh*	4 (common noun)
3 (نا) *na*	4 (pronoun)

The table WORD_PART_POS is a bridge table that relates the WORD_PART to a part-of-speech table called PoS, see Table 19 in appendix 1. This table includes 47 parts-of-speech according to the hierarchy proposed by Khoja (Khoja et al. 2001). The table WORD_PART_PROPERTY is a bridge table that relates the WORD_PART to the property table, which is called PROPERTY. This table has 17 properties as shown in Table 7. Each property in the PROPERTY table belongs to one of six classes that are defined in an additional table called PROPERTY_CLASS as depicted in Table 8.

The PROPERTY_CLASS table relates to the PoS table for practical purposes related to the annotation process. In particular, when the annotator specifies the part-of-speech of a word, only the properties are displayed that are available for that part of speech. For example, when the annotator specifies a word as a verb, then no definiteness properties are displayed because this class of properties only applies to nouns. The relationship between PROPERTY_CLASS and PoS is realized using a bridge table named POS_PROPERRTY_CLASS that is depicted in Table 9.

Table 6. WORD_PART_PROPERTY table

WORD_PART_ID	PoS_ID
1 (أحب) *ahb*	1 (First person)
1 (أحب) *ahb*	6 (Neutral)
1 (أحب) *ahb*	7 (Singular)
1 (أحب) *ahb*	15 (Indicative)
2 (جامعة) *jam'eh*	5 (Feminine)
2 (جامعة) *jam'eh*	7 (Singular)
2 (جامعة) *jam'eh*	10 (Nominative)
2 (جامعة) *jam'eh*	13 (Definite)
3 (نا) *na*	1 (First person)
3 (نا) *na*	6 (Neutral)
3 (نا) *na*	9 (plural)
3 (نا) *na*	12 (Genitive)

The LDB_WORD table is also related to three other tables, which are the WORD_DIALECT, the ROOT, and the TAG tables, see Figure 3. The WORD_DIALECT table is a bridge table that links between the DIALEC_NATIONAL and LDB_WORD tables. The DIALECT NATIONAL table contains a list of 18 dialects each belonging to one dialectal region, see Table 10. There are five dialect regions stored in the DIALECT_REGIONAL table shown in Table 11.

A word can only have one root, whereas many words many share the same root. This is a one-to-many relationship. The table ROOT contains all the roots in the lexicon, and it is mapped to the LDB_WORD table by the ROOT_ID. For example, the words "كتب" *ktb*, "يكتبون" *yktbwn*, "كتبوا" *katabo* (equivalent to "he writes", "they write" and "they wrote", respectively) are all related to the root "كتب" *ktb* (equivalent to "he wrote"). This relation can be expressed in the ROOT and LDB_WORD tables as in Table 12 and Table 13, respectively. Note that Table 13 shows a part of the WORD table.

The last table that is mapped to LDB_WORD is the WORD_TAG table. This table relates the lexicon words to one or more tags listed in the TAG table shown in Table 14. The tags were chosen to capture

Table 7. PROPERTY table

PROPERTY ID	NAME	ABBREVIATION	PROPERTY CLASS ID
1	First	1st	2
2	Second	2nd	2
3	Third	3rd	2
4	Masculine	M	3
5	Feminine	F	3
6	Neutral	N	3
7	Singular	Sg	1
8	Dual	Du	1
9	Plural	Pl	1
10	Nominative	N	4
11	Accusative	A	4
12	Genitive	G	4
13	Definite	D	5
14	Indefinite	I	5
15	Indicative	In	6
16	Subjunctive	Sb	6
17	Jussive	Ju	6

Table 8. PROPERTY_CLASS table

PROPERTY CLASS ID	NAME
1	Number
2	Person
3	Gender
4	Nominal Case
5	Definiteness
6	Verbal Case

as many information as possible about the lexical entries. The Typo and Grammatically wrong tags can help find common typos and grammar mistakes. Transliterated and Foreign-word tags help to study the frequency of transliterated or foreign words in a specific dialect or medium (Twitter, Blogs, etc.). The MSA tag helps determine the percentage of common words between MSA and a certain dialect. Abbreviations, Tweet-specific, and Hashtag tags can help in characterizing texts related to social media. The Sentiment tag helps in collecting a list of words that represent emotions in a certain dialect which has many applications in information retrieval. The Stop-word tag identifies the stop words in a dialect.

Table 9. POS_PROPERTY_CLASS table

POS ID	PROPERTY CLASS ID
23	2
13	2
3	3
23	3
3	1
23	1
4	4
22	4
4	5
22	5

Figure 3. ERD of the lexicon database (continued)

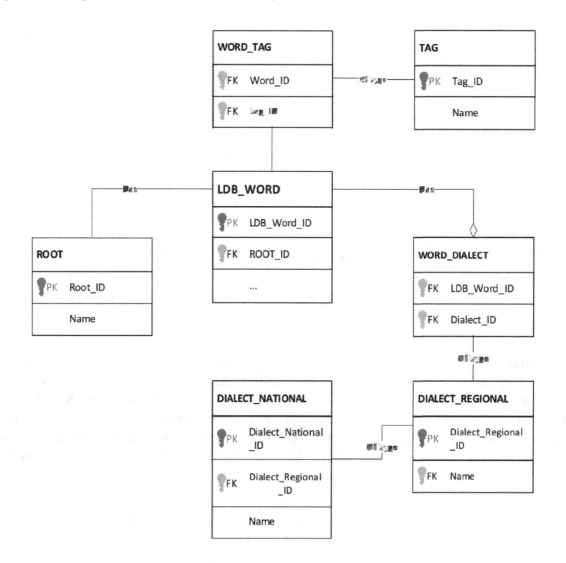

Table 10. DIALECT_NATIONAL table

DIALECT_NATIONAL_ID	NAME	DIALECT_REGIONAL_ID
1	Kuwaiti	1
2	Saudi	1
3	Emirati	1
4	Yemeni	1
5	Omani	1
6	Bahraini	1
7	Qatari	1
8	Moroccan	2
9	Tunisian	2
10	Libyan	2
11	Sudani	2
12	Algerian	2
13	Lebanese	3
14	Syrian	3
15	Palestinian	3
16	Jordanian	3
17	Iraqi	4
18	Egyptian	5

Table 11. DIALECT_REGIONAL table

DIALECT_REGIONAL_ID	NAME
1	Gulf
2	North Africa
3	Levantine
4	Iraqi
5	Egyptian

Table 12. ROOT table

ROOT_ID	NAME	..
1	*ktb* "كتب"	..

Table 13. LDB_WORD table

LDB_WORD_ID	LEMMA	ROOT_ID
1	يكتب *yktb*	1
2	يكتبون *yktbwn*	1
3	كتبوا *katabo*	1

Table 14. TAG table

TAG_ID	NAME
1	Typo
2	Grammatically Wrong
3	Transliterated
4	Foreign Word
5	MSA
6	Tweet Specific Word
7	Hashtag
8	Abbreviation
9	Sentiment
10	Stop Word
11	Unknown

Builder Database (BDB)

The Builder Database contains all the tables that facilitate the building and maintenance of the lexicon database, see Figure 4. Again, the BDB will be described using a top-down approach in the following. The most important table in this database is the BDB_WORD table that contains the following attributes:

1. BDB WORD ID
2. LDB WORD ID
3. WORD STATE ID
4. TASK ID
5. HISTORY ID
6. Single meaning tag
7. Position in task
8. Annotation duration

Each word in the lexicon can be in one of five different states listed in Table 15. The transition from one state to another can be described as a finite state machine, see Figure 5. When a word enters the system as a component of the task (e.g., a tweet) to be annotated, it goes into an initial state called *Pending*. From this state, the word can transit to one of two states: *Partially Annotated* or *Annotated*, depending on whether the word has received a partial or complete annotation, respectively. When a reviewer reviews and confirms the annotation, the word transits to the state *Reviewed*. Before a word is made available to users, it needs to be approved by a Lexicographer. Upon that, the word enters the state *Visible*. Only words in the visible state can be accessed by look-up users.

The HISTORY table keeps track of the lexicon words. For example, it records the creation time of each word, who annotated it and when. One advantage of these records is to track the progress of the lexicon building process and to evaluate the annotators' performance. The HISTORY table is connected to the table which contains all information related to the LBDB users. The MEMBERS table is related to the ROLE table. There are four roles in the Lexicon Builder: Admin, Lexicographer, Reviewer and Annotator. Table 16 and Table 17 show an example of the MEMBERS and ROLE tables respectively. The last table is the TASK table, which contains all information related to the annotation tasks. Some of the information saved in this table include the task source, the creation time of the task, its status, and the annotators to whom the task is assigned to.

Figure 4. Builder database ERD

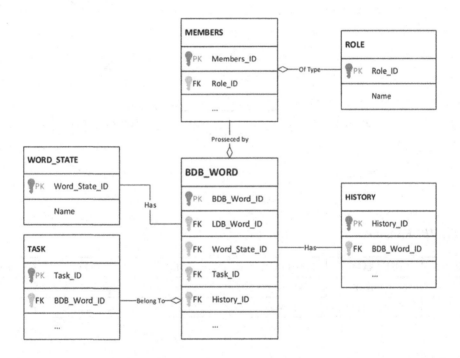

Table 15. WORD_STATE table

WORD STATE ID	NAME
1	Pending
2	Partially Annotated
3	Annotated
4	Reviewed
5	Visible

Figure 5. Word state transitions

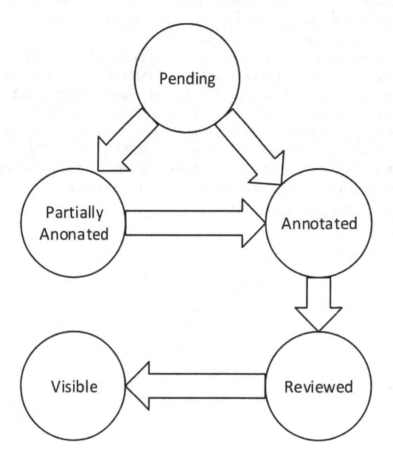

Table 16. MEMBERS table

MEMBER_ID	USERNAME	PASSWORD	ROLE	EMAIL	ENABLED
1	Abdulhadi	$2avKKoG..	1	example1@..	TRUE
2	Sumaya	DBWeZU..	2	example2@..	TRUE

Table 17. ROLE table

ROLE ID	NAME
1	Lexicographer
2	Admin

Lexicon Builder Controller (LBC)

The Lexicon Builder Controller forms the interface between the lexicon users and the lexicon database. It consists of several components that aid in building and managing the lexicon. These include tools for text analysis including a parser, a stemmer, and a word splitter, as well as functions for lexical search and statistics generation in addition to functions for user and task management.

Search

The search function enables a user to look-up a lexicon entry by entering a dialectical lemma, an MSA word, or an English word. When a dialectical lemma is entered, the search function returns the MSA equivalent, the English meaning, the PoS, the root, and an example (gloss). An advanced search option enables the user to enter a root and obtain all related lemmas. This option is especially useful to study the range of word inflexions used in a certain dialect. The search also supports partial entry when the user does not know the exact spelling.

Text and Word Analyzing Tools

The text analyzing tools help in preparing the tasks for annotation and support annotators in the annotation process. These tools include a parser, a stemmer, a text highlighter, and a word splitter. The parser reads an input text (annotation task) and converts it into a list of words that are ready for annotation. During that, the parser removes parts of the text that are irrelevant for the annotation such as special symbols including emotions. However, the original task is kept in the database unchanged for future analyses.

The Arabic stemmer determines the root of a given word. So, it helps in associating a lexicon lemma with its root as far as the latter is available. Using an automatic stemmer is highly important for efficient annotation. Our stemmer essentially relies on the solution proposed by Khoja in (Khoja et al. 2001). However, to allow portability and more flexible interfacing, the authors developed an object-oriented version.

The text highlighter uses different formatting methods to reflect the status of processed lemmas. When the annotator opens a task for annotation, the task is parsed and highlighted in different colours. Yellow-colour highlighting indicates that the lemma has not yet been added to the database. The green colour means that the lexicon has at least one annotated lemma with the same orthographic form. In this case, the annotator should view the list of available annotations of that lemma and decide whether one of these annotations covers the current occurrence of the lemma. Otherwise, the lemma will be added with new attributes. If the text is highlighted in green and underlined, then this means that the lemma was annotated in the current active session. Lemmas that are highlighted in blue belong to what we call single-annotation words. These are words that usually have only one annotation that is independent of the context. Prepositions belong to this class of words.

The Word Splitter is a tool that is initiated automatically when the user selects a word for annotation. First, the Splitter determines the word root by calling the Stemmer. Then, it determines the prefix and the suffix(es) of the word. After that, it displays the word parts is separate fields allowing the user to annotate each part independently as depicted in the example given in Figure 6. In this example, the word "كتابها" *ktabha* which means "her book" is split to two lemmas: "كتاب" *ktab*, i.e., "book" and "ها" *ha*, i.e., "her".

Figure 6. Word splitter

Lemma	كتب		≡ Merge	☐ **Single annotation word**
	ﻪ		كت	

The graphical user interface allows the user to reject the splitting proposed by the tools by pressing the Merge button. Also, the user can edit the suggested word parts if the splitter provided suboptimal results.

Task Management

As mentioned previously, the concept of a task in this work refers to a text segment that is ready for annotation. The task management component in the system architecture depicted in Figure 1 includes functions to create, edit, and delete tasks as well as functions to display the tasks in a way that reflects their status. Creating a task can be performed either by adding the task manually or by importing a list of tasks using import functions that include different API's such as a Twitter API[1].

In the context of annotation, a task can be in one of five states which are *New, Assigned, Partially Completed, Completed*, and *Reviewed*. A *New* task is a one that was added to the system but has not been claimed yet by any annotator. An *Assigned* a one that has been claimed by an annotator. A task is *Partially Completed* if some of its words are not annotated yet. A task is *Completed*, when all its words are annotated. A *Reviewed* task is a task that has been completed and reviewed. Only the elements of a *Reviewed* task can be activated by the Lexicographer to appear in the final lexicon table and to be made available for external access.

The annotated tasks are kept in the database and are linked to the annotations of their words. The motivation for this is to build an annotated corpus in the long term. Additional attributes are added to each task. In the case of tweets, these attributes include the author nickname, the author unique ID, the statuses count, the tweet location, the publication date, the number of the author's followers, the number of users the author is following, the author's location, and the author's real name as specified in her or his profile. This additional data is reserved for future purposes.

Role-Based User Management

The user management system is responsible for handling the processes of user creation, removal, and role assignment. It enables the *Admin* to create users through the lexicon interface. It also controls the views of the Lexicon Builder interface, depending on the privileges of each role. There are six different roles in our system, each of which has different permissions and views: *Admin, Lexicographer, Annotator, Reviewer, Guest* and *API*. Table 18 shows the different types of users and their respective privileges.

Lexicon Builder Interface (LBI)

In this section, we first explain how to use the lexicon and the Lexicon Builder by users and annotators through the user interface. Then, the programmer interface is described.

Table 18. Users privileges

Privilege		Admin	Annotator	Reviewer	Lexicographer	Guest	API
Create	User accounts	*					
	Annotation tasks				*		
View	User accounts	*					
	Annotation tasks		*	*	*		
	Task statuses		*	*	*		
	Lexicon entries statistics				*		
	Lexicon entries		*	*	*	*	*
Annotate			*	*	*		
Revise & approve	Annotator tasks			*			
	Reviewer tasks				*		
Search			*	*	*	*	*
Generate statistics report					*		

User Interface (UI)

The Lexicon Builder can be accessed from a computer or a mobile device. The search function is available for any user. Lexicographers, reviewers, and annotators have role-based interfaces.

The administrator manages user accounts through the web interface shown in Figure 7. She or he can create, delete, enable, or disable any of the users' accounts. To add new tasks to the system, the Lexicographer uses the Add New Task Interface shown in Figure 8 or uses an import function. Upon adding a task, the task appears in the annotators' view under the task list tab as shown in Figure 9.

An annotator can claim a task and start its annotation using the interface shown in Figure 10. As explained previously, once a task is claimed the text highlighter marks the task words depending on their states. After completing the annotation of a task, the reviewer can verify or revise the annotations. Following that, the task goes to the Lexicographer for final review and approval.

Application Programming Interface (API)

The API component gives our lexicon an interface to NLP applications. For users to connect to our application through the API, a request should be submitted to the Lexicon Builder admin. The admin creates a username and a password for the requester and generates an API key that is stored in the database for cross-matching. Then, the credentials are sent to the user via email. The client application needs to pass the provided credentials in the HTTP headers to be able to access the API. For example, if a tool needs to find the meaning of the word "عرب" *br'e* (equivalent to "out") through the API, an API search request should be generated with a certain format. Figure 11 shows a request and a response example.

The API also supports a level-specific PoS retrieval. That means that a valid API user can send a word or a paragraph to the Lexicon Builder and specify the level of tagging needed to get the word PoS or the paragraph PoS list (provided that the entries exist in the lexicon). There are four levels of tagging according to the hierarchy given in Figure 12. The first level includes the tags: noun, verb, particle,

Figure 7.

Figure 8. User interface of adding new task manually

Figure 9. Task list

residual and punctuation. The second level under verb contains: perfect, imperfect and imperative, and under the noun: adjective, numeral, pronoun, etc. Each level has certain properties. Each of these properties can be switched on or off. This technique allows a trade-off between accuracy and performance for NLP solutions.

Figure 10. User interface for word annotation

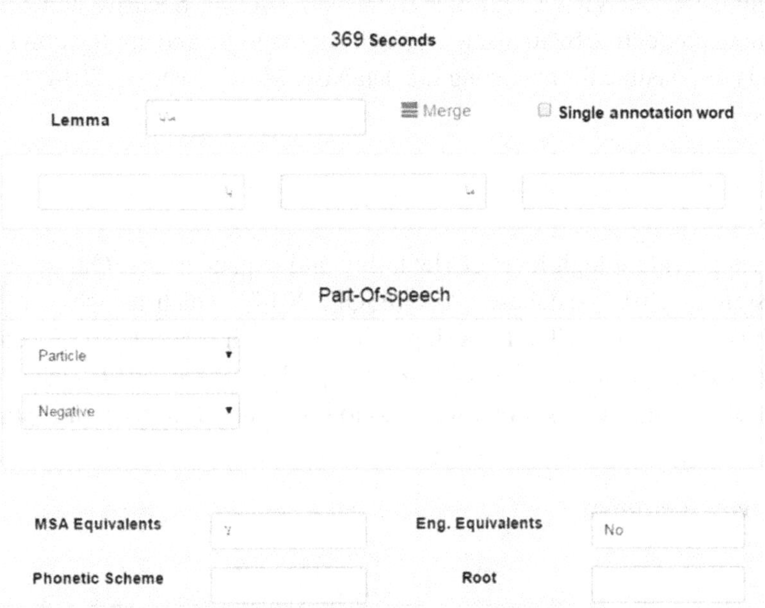

Figure 11. API request/response example

API request:
URL: http://arabic-lexicon.herokuapp.com/api/lemma/search?lemma=ذهب

Response sample:


```
{
    "lemmaResultList":[
        {
            "lemma":"ذهبت",
            "engEquivalent":null,
            "msaEquivalent":null,
            "gloss":"ذهبت الطالبة الصغيرة الى المدرسة",
            "root":"ذهب",
            "phoneticScheme":null,
            "tags":null,
            "foreignWord":"false",
            "dialects":[

            ]
        }
    ]
}
```


Implementation Aspects

Programming language and framework

The Lexicon Builder was built using Java[2] due to its cross-platform abilities and object orientation as well as the availability of a well-developed ecosystem around Java[2] such as the Spring framework (Spring Framework, 2013), Hibernate (Hibernate, 2013) and Maven (Maven, 2014). We adopted the

Spring framework (4.0) (Spring Framework, 2013) for implementing the Lexicon Builder because of the provided modules (Model-View-Controller framework, Spring Security and Spring core), which enabled us to be more productive by focusing on the business logic and application features. Hibernate (Hibernate, 2013) is responsible for managing the database. Maven (Maven, 2014) helps to resolve data dependency issues.

Database

Relational databases provide a high level of flexibility and expandability. Our application backend is powered by a PostgreSQL (9.4) database (PostgreSQL, 2014), which has shown good performance in similar applications and better Cloud offering compared with other database vendors. To improve system performance, we used Apache Lucene (4.8.0) (Apache Lucene, 2014), which is an open-source information-retrieval program that allows fast access to information saved in the database.

Figure 12. PoS tagging hierarchy

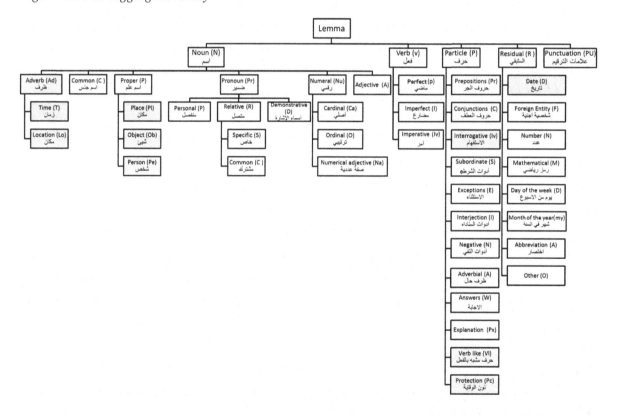

Cloud Deployment

We investigated three deployment options for our application: local server, infrastructure-as-a-service cloud, and platform-as-a-service cloud. The first option requires monitoring and has high cost and maintenance overhead. It is also difficult to scale. The second option is not as expensive; it is scalable, but it also requires monitoring and maintenance. The third option however is scalable, not expensive and has minimal maintenance and administration overhead. This is why we decided to deploy the Lexicon Builder on a platform-as-a-service cloud. Considering the nature of our system, it is an appropriate solution for us to transfer the server management to a cloud provider.

After surveying different cloud providers and comparing their services, the authors chose the Heroku cloud provider[3]. Heroku[3] is one of the leading platform-as-a-service clouds and is a subsidiary of salesforce[4]; a well-established company which assures reliability. It supports version control, which was very useful, particularly in the early development stage. Heroku[3] also supports a wide variety of add-ons and uses the Git method (Git, 2014) for committing the application code. The Git method is a way to deploy an application to the cloud, which pulls the code from the GitHub repository directly. Other cloud services require building the package on a machine before deploying it to the cloud, which might create errors depending on the operating system in use. For example, Windows sometimes changes text files while building the package. However, by using GIT, the deployment becomes machine-independent because it does not require building the package on the developer's machine before deployment.

Security

To secure the application, we used the Spring security framework (Spring Framework, 2013), which provides Java-based applications with access control techniques, including various authentication and authorization mechanisms (AlexLuke et al. 2014). The Spring security framework (Spring Framework, 2013) provides a security solution for the Lexicon Builder by facilitating the enforcement of many resistant access control methods and providing protection against various web application attacks. As an example, we protected the Lexicon Builder against Cross-Site Request Forgery (CSRF). This attack enables an attacker to use an authenticated user's credentials to perform actions that are only permitted for that user without his permission. It occurs when the attacker is able to generate exactly the same request expected by the target website. To protect against this attack, the Spring security framework (Spring Framework, 2013) provides a token (X-CSRF-TOKEN) that is unique for each session for all HTTP requests. This token cannot be predicted by the attacker; hence, it protects against CSRF.

System Evaluation

The Lexicon Builder was evaluated regarding two different aspects: the lexicon expansion rate and the inter-annotator agreement.

The lexicon expansion rate is a key aspect of the process of building lexical resources manually. Determining the number of words that can be annotated per hour and annotator helps to estimate the lexicon size after a given annotation period for a given number of annotators. From a project planning point of view, such an estimation is very helpful for determining the manpower or the time required to reach some lexicon size. To estimate the annotation performance of the presented Lexicon Builder, we tested it for the Emirati dialect with two annotators, one reviewer, and one Lexicographer who all had a good to very good knowledge in MSA grammar and morphology, which is necessary due to the detailed tagset used in the Lexicon Builder. The two annotators and the reviewer were native Emirati. The Lexicographer was a native Arabic but not a UAE citizen. We collected tweets in the UAE dialect using WISDOM (WISDOM, 2013) as a web analysis tool provided by Lockheed Martin Company[5] as well as using a Twitter API[1]. Collected tweets were preprocessed and added to the database as annotation tasks.

The annotators were first trained over a period of six hours to get familiar with the tools, the tagset and the annotation guidelines. Minimum guidelines were given to the annotators, such as: always making sure to annotate the word in its given context even if shown green (annotated lemma with the same orthographic form), maintaining the numbers written in words and numbers written in digits, If an English borrowed word such as computer is used in the dialect then the annotator should mark it as a word of that dialect, annotators should select all dialects they are certain that the given lemma is used in. After that, the annotators performed 121 hours of annotation over a period of three months. During this period, they annotated 1300 words, which corresponds to an annotation performance of 5.37 words per hour and annotator. The annotation time was measured word-wise using a timer embedded in the tools. The timer was started whenever the annotator clicked on a word for annotation and stopped upon saving the performed annotation for that word. The annotators were aware of this time measurement and that both the quality and the speed of the annotation are relevant for their work.

Similar time measurement was performed to estimate the review overhead. The authors found out that the reviewer took approximately one minute to review the annotation of one word on average. That means the reviewer has spent a total of 21.37 hours on the review, which makes 18% of the annotation time. The Lexicographer did not go through annotated words one-by-one, so far. Rather he verified the annotation work selectively and advised the reviewer during the annotation period continuously. We estimate that the Lexicographer has spent at least 10 hours on this work which makes almost 8% of the annotation time.

It is important to note that the measured annotation time does not consider the time taken to claim a task and to read and understand the task text before starting the actual word-by-word annotation. That means that the estimated annotation performance of 5.37 words per hour and annotator is an optimistic value. This metric should not be confused with general annotation performance because it only reflects the number of new words added to the lexicon.

We analyzed the impact of learning on the annotation performance. We found out that both annotators have improved their annotation performance between the first and the third months by more than 30%. This allows to say that the annotation performance improves with annotator's experience with the system. Based on this, we can assume that the estimated annotation performance of 5.37 words per hour and annotator is a pessimistic value. Whether this pessimistic factor can balance the optimistic factor above needs further investigation when more data is available in the future.

The second evaluation aspect is the inter-annotator agreement that reflects the reliability of the annotation system; thus, the quality of the lexicon entries. For this purpose, we used Cohen's Kappa (Artstein and Poesio 2008). We selected random tasks with a total of 104 words and calculated the agreement between the two annotators before the revisions of the reviewer and the Lexicographer. To investigate the impact of the level of details on the annotation reliability, the calculations were performed for the upper three levels of the tagset given in Figure 12. We found out that the inter-annotator agreement on Level 1, Level 2 and Level 3 is 0.95, 0.83, and 0.8 respectively. This shows that an increasing level of details causes more difficulty and more disagreement in the annotation. For example, it is easier to classify a word as a noun, verb or particle than classifying a pronoun as personal, relative or demonstrative. Nevertheless, the average inter-annotator agreement on all levels is 0.86, which shows a good understanding of the annotation guidelines and the Lexicon Builder system by the annotators.

FUTURE RESEARCH DIRECTIONS

The active research in Arabic NLP still did not give an answer to the question whether manual or automated methods should be used for building lexical resources for Arabic (Guellil et al. 2019). As has been shown in this chapter, the manual annotation is very lengthy, especially when a comprehensive and reliable lexicon is sought. However, the overhead of the manual approach can be justified by the quality of the lexicon entries in terms of wide and deep annotation, as well as by the multi-purpose and multi-dialect features of the lexicon. The proposed system offers the possibility for collaborative annotation and collective efforts toward expanding the lexicon in a reasonable time. For this, a community of annotators, reviewers, and Lexicographers should be built from different Arabic-speaking regions. Well-developed NLP tools for dialectal Arabic will be investigated, and collaborations with their developers will be sought towards developing Application Programming Interfaces (APIs) to allow these tools to access our lexicon. Scalability issues may arise if multiple tools have simultaneous access to our platform. These issues will be addressed considering hardware and software solutions. If the proposed model attracts community interest, it may be helpful to start adding some primitive linguistic functions which run on the lexicon data directly on the cloud so that the required bandwidth with requesting NLP tools is reduced. Such a networked solution will allow the collection of different data which can enhance our understanding of the requirements and the dimensions of Arabic NLP.

The proposed methodology for building lexicons can be useful for other languages and dialects which lack sufficient language resources. Automated and semi-automated methods were used to build lexical resources for specific NLP tasks such as sentiment analysis. In the future, we will investigate the possibility and performance of applying semi-supervised methods to expand the general-purpose lexicon starting from an initial seed built using the proposed annotation-based method.

CONCLUSION

This chapter presented the Lexicon Builder: a platform for collaborative, expert-reviewed building of lexical resources for Arabic dialects. The platform addresses the problem of lacking multi-purpose, multi-dialect lexicons for the spoken Arabic varieties. The Lexicon Builder was developed as a web application and deployed on a platform-as-a-service cloud. The test of the Lexicon Builder showed that the lexicon could be expanded at a speed of approximately 5 words per hour and annotator, in addition to an overhead of 18% for review 8% for final review and approval by a Lexicographer. Initial tests show that the platform supports reliable annotation: an inter-annotator agreement of 86% could be found. In the future, linguistic groups over the Arabic world will be called for collaborative expansion of the lexicon. When the lexicon reaches an appropriate size, interested NLP programmers will be granted access to the database.

REFERENCES

Abuleil, S., & Evens, M. (1998). Discovering lexical information by tagging Arabic newspaper text. *Proceedings of the Workshop on Computational Approaches to Semitic Languages - Semitic 98*, 1–7. 10.3115/1621753.1621755

Al-Sabbagh, R., & Girju, R. (2010). Mining the Web for the Induction of a Dialectical Arabic Lexicon. *Language Resources and Evaluation Conference (LREC)*.

AlexLuke, B., Taylor, L., & Winch, R. (2014b). *Spring Security Reference*. Retrieved December 20, 2019, from https://docs.spring.io/spring-security/site/docs/4.0.0.M1/reference/htmlsingle/#what-is-acegi-security

Ali, M. (2018, August). Character level convolutional neural network for Arabic dialect identification. *Proceedings of the Fifth Workshop on NLP for Similar Languages, Varieties and Dialects (VarDial 2018)*, 122-127.

Aouragh, M. (2016). Social media, mediation and the Arab revolutions. *Marx in the age of digital capitalism*, 482-515.

Apache Lucene. (4.8.0) [Software]. (2014). Retrieved from https://lucene.apache.org/

Artstein, R., & Poesio, M. (2008). Inter-Coder Agreement for Computational Linguistics. *Computational Linguistics*, *34*(4), 555–596. doi:10.1162/coli.07-034-R2

Attia, M., Pecina, P., Toral, A., Tounsi, L., & Genabith, J. V. (2011). A Lexical Database for Modern Standard Arabic Interoperable with a Finite State Morphological Transducer. *Systems and Frameworks for Computational Morphology Communications in Computer and Information Science*, 98–118.

Azouaou, F., & Guellil, I. (2017). A step by step construction of a lexicon between Algerian dialect and french. *The 31st Pacific Asia Conference on Language, Information and Computation PACLIC, 31*.

Badawi, E.-S., & Hinds, M. (1986). *A Dictionary of Egyptian Arabic: Arabic-English*. Librairie du Liban.

Bouamor, H., Habash, N., Salameh, M., Zaghouani, W., Rambow, O., Abdulrahim, D., ... Oflazer, K. (2018). The MADAR Arabic dialect corpus and lexicon. *Proceedings of the Eleventh International Conference on Language Resources and Evaluation (LREC 2018)*.

Boujelbane, R., BenAyed, S., & Hadrich Belguith, L. (2013). *Building bilingual lexicon to create Dialect Tunisian corpora and adapt language model*. ACL.

Buckwalter, T. (2004). *Buckwalter Arabic Morphological Analyzer Version 2.0* (LDC Catalog No: LDC2004L02). Retrieved from https://catalog.ldc.upenn.edu/LDC2004L02

Cotterell, R., & Callison-Burch, C. (2014). A multi-dialect, multi-genre corpus of informal written Arabic. *Proceedings of the Ninth International Conference on Language Resources and Evaluation (LREC'14)*, 241–245.

Diab, M., Al-Badrashiny, M., Aminian, M., Attia, M., Dasigi, P., & Elfardy, H. (2014). Tharwa: A Large Scale Dialectal Arabic-Standard Arabic-English Lexicon. *Proceedings of the Language Resources and Evaluation Conference (LREC)*.

Duh, K., & Kirchhoff, K. (2006). Lexicon acquisition for dialectal Arabic using transductive learning. In *Proceedings of the 2006 Conference on Empirical Methods in Natural Language Processing*. Association for Computational Linguistics. 10.3115/1610075.1610131

Duwairi, R., Marji, R., Sha'ban, N., & Rushaidat, S. (2014). Sentiment Analysis in Arabic tweets. *The 5th International Conference on. IEEE in Information and Communication Systems (ICICS).* 10.1109/IACS.2014.6841964

El-Beltagy, S. R. (2016, May). NileULex: a phrase and word level sentiment lexicon for Egyptian and modern standard Arabic. In *Proceedings of the Tenth International Conference on Language Resources and Evaluation (LREC'16)* (pp. 2900-2905). Academic Press.

El-Haj, M., Rayson, P., & Aboelezz, M. (2018, May). Arabic dialect identification in the context of bivalency and code-switching. In *Proceedings of the 11th International Conference on Language Resources and Evaluation*, (pp. 3622-3627). European Language Resources Association.

Git (2.0) [software]. (2014). Retrieved from https://git-scm.com/

Graff, D., Buckwalter, T., Jin, H., & Maamouri, M. (2006). Lexicon Development for Varieties of Spoken Colloquial Arabic. *Proceedings of the Fifth International Conference on Language Resources and Evaluation (LREC),* 999–1004.

Graff, D., & Maamouri, M. (2012). Developing LMF-XML Bilingual Dictionaries for Colloquial Arabic Dialects. *Proceedings of the Language Resources and Evaluation Conference (LREC),* 269–274.

Guellil, I., Azouaou, F., & Mendoza, M. (2019). Arabic sentiment analysis: Studies, resources, and tools. *Social Network Analysis and Mining, 9*(1), 56. doi:10.100713278-019-0602-x

Habash, N., Eskander, R., & Hawwari, A. (2012). A morphological analyzer for Egyptian arabic. In *Proceedings of the Twelfth Meeting of the Special Interest Group on Computational Morphology and Phonology.* Association for Computational Linguistics.

Hibernate framework (4.3.0) [Software]. (2013). Retrieved from https://hibernate.org/

Inoue, G., Habash, N., Matsumoto, Y., & Aoyama, H. (2018, May). A parallel corpus of Arabic-Japanese news articles. *Proceedings of the Eleventh International Conference on Language Resources and Evaluation (LREC 2018).*

Kamusella, T. (2017). The Arabic language: A Latin of modernity? *Journal of Nationalism. Memory & Language Politics, 11*(2), 117–145. doi:10.1515/jnmlp-2017-0006

Khalifa, S., Hassan, S., & Habash, N. (2017). A morphological analyzer for Gulf Arabic verbs. *Proceedings of the Third Arabic Natural Language Processing Workshop.* 10.18653/v1/W17-1305

Khemakhem, A., Elleuch, I., Gargouri, B., & Ben Hamadou, A. (2009). Towards an automatic conversion approach of editorial Arabic dictionaries into LMF-ISO 24613 standardized model. *Proceedings of the Second International Conference on Arabic Language Resources and Tools.*

Khemakhem, A., Gargouri, B., & Ben Hamadou, A. (2012). LMF standardized dictionary for Arabic Language. *International Conference on Computing and Information Technology - ICCIT.*

Khoja, S., Garside, R., & Knowles, G. (2011). *A tagset for the morphosyntactic tagging of Arabic.* Computing Department Lancaster University.

Kilany, H., Gadalla, H., Arram, H., Yacoub, A., El-Habashi, A., & McLemore, C. (2002). *Egyptian Colloquial Arabic Lexicon* (LDC catalog number LDC99L22).

Kirchhoff, K., & Vergyri, D. (2005). Cross-dialectal data sharing for acoustic modeling in Arabic speech recognition. *Speech Communication, 46*(1), 37–51. doi:10.1016/j.specom.2005.01.004

Maamouri, M., Bies, A., Buckwalter, T., Diab, M., Habash, N., Rambow, O., & Tabessi, D. (2006). Developing and using a pilot dialectal Arabic treebank. *Proceedings of the Fifth International Conference on Language Resources and Evaluation, LREC06.*

Maamouri, M., Graff, D., Bouziri, B., Krouna, S., Bies, A., Kulick, S., & Buckwalter, T. (2009). *LDC Standard Arabic Morphological Analyzer (SAMA) Version 3.1. Linguistic Data Consortium* (LDC2009E73).

Masmoudi, A., Habash, N., Ellouze, M., Est'eve, Y., & Belguith, L. H. (2015). Arabic Transliteration of Romanized Tunisian Dialect Text: A Preliminary Investigation. In *Computational Linguistics and Intelligent Text Processing* (pp. 608–619). Springer. doi:10.1007/978-3-319-18111-0_46

Maven (3.2.5) [Software]. (2014). Retrieved from https://maven.apache.org/

Medhaffar, S., Bougares, F., Estève, Y., & Hadrich-Belguith, L. (2017, April). Sentiment analysis of tunisian dialects: Linguistic ressources and experiments. In *Proceedings of the third Arabic natural language processing workshop* (pp. 55-61). 10.18653/v1/W17-1307

Mohammad, S., Salameh, M., & Kiritchenko, S. (2016, May). Sentiment lexicons for Arabic social media. In *Proceedings of the Tenth International Conference on Language Resources and Evaluation (LREC'16)* (pp. 33-37). Academic Press.

Postgre, S. Q. L. (9.4) [Software]. (2014). Retrieved from https://www.postgresql.org/

Qwaider, C., Saad, M., Chatzikyriakidis, S., & Dobnik, S. (2018, May). Shami: A Corpus of Levantine Arabic Dialects. *Proceedings of the Eleventh International Conference on Language Resources and Evaluation (LREC-2018).*

Sabry Farghaly, A. A. (2010). *Arabic computational linguistics.* Stanford University: CSLI Publications, Center for the Study of Language and Information.

Shoufan, A., & Alameri, S. (2015, July). Natural language processing for dialectical Arabic: A Survey. In *Proceedings of the second workshop on Arabic natural language processing* (pp. 36-48). 10.18653/v1/W15-3205

Spring framework (4.0) [Software]. (2013). Retrieved from https://spring.io/

WISDOM. (1.0) [software]. (2013). Retrieved from https://www.lockheedmartin.com/en-us/products/lm-wisdom.html

Zalmout, N., Erdmann, A., & Habash, N. (2018, June). Noise-robust morphological disambiguation for dialectal Arabic. In *Proceedings of the 2018 Conference of the North American Chapter of the Association for Computational Linguistics: Human Language Technologies*, Volume 1 *(Long Papers)* (pp. 953-964). Academic Press.

ADDITIONAL READING

Badaro, G., Baly, R., Hajj, H., Habash, N., & El-Hajj, W. (2014, October). A large-scale Arabic sentiment lexicon for Arabic opinion mining. In *Proceedings of the EMNLP 2014 workshop on arabic natural language processing (ANLP)* (pp. 165-173). 10.3115/v1/W14-3623

Beeston, A. F. L. (2016). *The Arabic language today.* Routledge. doi:10.4324/9781315512815

Farghaly, A., & Shaalan, K. (2009). Arabic natural language processing: Challenges and solutions. *ACM Transactions on Asian Language Information Processing*, *8*(4), 14. doi:10.1145/1644879.1644881

Guellil, I., Azouaou, F., & Mendoza, M. (2019). Arabic sentiment analysis: Studies, resources, and tools. *Social Network Analysis and Mining*, *9*(1), 56. doi:10.100713278-019-0602-x

Habash, N. Y. (2010). Introduction to Arabic natural language processing. *Synthesis Lectures on Human Language Technologies*, *3*(1), 1–187. doi:10.2200/S00277ED1V01Y201008HLT010

Maamouri, M., & Cieri, C. (2002, April). Resources for Arabic natural language processing. In *International Symposium on Processing Arabic* (Vol. 1).

Shaalan, K. (2010). Rule-based approach in Arabic natural language processing. *International Journal of Information and Communication Technology*, *3*(3), 11–19.

Shoufan, A., & Alameri, S. (2015, July). Natural language processing for dialectical Arabic: A Survey. In *Proceedings of the second workshop on Arabic natural language processing* (pp. 36-48). 10.18653/v1/W15-3205

KEY TERMS AND DEFINITIONS

Arabic Dialect: A variety of the Arabic language which is mostly spoken but has no standard written format.

Interrater Agreement: A statistical measure of the level of agreement between two or more raters.

Lexical Annotation: The process of assigning attributes to a word which should be added to a lexicon.

Lexicon Builder: A tool that helps in collaborative building of a lexicon.

Modern Standard Arabic: A formal variety of the Arabic language that is used in today's official communications.

Platform-as-a-Service (PaaS): A cloud service that provides users with a platform to create and manage applications without worrying about scalability or administration.

Relational Database: A structured set of data with relations between stored items of information.

ENDNOTES

[1]   https://developer.twitter.com/en/docs
[2]   https://www.java.com/en/download/
[3]   https://www.heroku.com/home
[4]   https://www.salesforce.com/
[5]   https://www.lockheedmartin.com/en-us/index.html

APPENDIX

Table 19. PoS table

POS ID	Name	Abbreviation	Level	Parent pos ID
1	Punctuation	PU	1	NULL
2	One Sentence Word	OSW	1	NULL
3	Noun	N	1	NULL
4	Common	C	2	3
5	Adverb	Ad	2	3
6	Time	T	3	5
7	Location	Lo	3	5
8	Proper	P	2	3
9	Place	Pl	3	8
10	Object	Ob	3	8
11	Person	Pe	3	8
12	Pronoun	Pr	2	3
13	Personal	P	3	12
14	Relative	R	3	12
15	Specific	S	4	14
16	Common	C	4	14
17	Demonstrative	D	3	12
18	Numeral	Nu	2	3
19	Cardinal	Ca	3	18
20	Ordinal	O	3	18
21	Numerical adjective	Na	3	18
22	Adjective	A	2	3
23	Verb	V	1	NULL
24	Perfect	P	2	23
25	Imperfect	I	2	23
26	Imperative	Iv	2	23
27	Particle	P	1	NULL
28	Prepositions	Pr	2	27
29	Conjunctions	C	2	27
30	Interrogative	In	2	27
31	Subordinate	S	2	27
32	Exceptions	E	2	27
33	Interjection	I	2	27
34	Negative	N	2	27

continues on following page

Table 19. Continued

POS ID	Name	Abbreviation	Level	Parent pos ID
35	Adverbial	A	2	27
36	Answers	W	2	27
37	Explanation	X	2	27
38	Verb like	Vl	2	27
39	Residual	R	1	NULL
40	Date	D	2	39
41	Foreign Entity	F	2	39
42	Number	N	2	39
43	Mathematical	M	2	39
44	Day of the week	D	2	39
45	Month of the year	my	2	39
46	Abbreviation	A	2	39
47	Other	O	2	39

Chapter 15
A Critical Review of the Current State of Natural Language Processing in Mexico and Chile

César Aguilar

(iD) https://orcid.org/0000-0003-1940-9933

Pontificia Universidad Católica de Chile, Chile

Olga Acosta

Singularyta SpA, Chile

ABSTRACT

This chapter presents a critical review of the current state of natural language processing in Chile and Mexico. Specifically, a general review is made regarding the technological evolution of these countries in this area of research and development, as well as the progress they have made so far. Subsequently, the remaining problems and challenges are addressed. Specifically, two are analyzed in detail here: (1) the lack of a strategic policy that helps to establish stronger links between academia and industry and (2) the lack of a technological inclusion of the indigenous languages, which causes a deep digital divide between Spanish (considered in Chile and Mexico as their official language) with them.

INTRODUCTION

This chapter presents a critical review about the evolution of natural language processing (NLP) in Mexico and Chile, in order to provide information that allows us to have an idea about the status of this line of research and development in both, as well as the challenges and future projections that can be currently identified. For the purposes of this work, these two countries are considered due to the strategic value they provide today to the relationship between academia and business, with a view to developing their own technological niche, which has a positive impact on the economy of both countries, and eventually become competitive internationally.

DOI: 10.4018/978-1-7998-4240-8.ch015

The justification of this text is justified by the shortage of academic papers that speak on the subject. In general, the issue has been approached from a business perspective, through reports that offer a summary view regarding the current state of language technologies in Latin America. However, as this chapter tries to show, the panorama is much more complex, especially if taken into account that the region is a multilingual area, where languages such as Spanish and Portuguese coexist with languages such as Nahuatl, Maya or the Mapuche, to mention just a few.

The methodology that has been used to obtain the information presented here consists of a review of several similar reports and documents generated by consultants and government entities, as well as some academics who have been interested in the subject. Therefore, without pretending to exhaust the problem, this chapter shows a description of the current state in NLP in both countries focusing on the following points:

i)   A general description of the projects carried out in both countries related to NLP.
ii) A briefly point out some collaborative initiatives between the two countries related to this topic.
iii) A summarized exposition about some advances made at the industrial level, emphasizing the potential that Chile and Mexico have to develop technologies that can innovate in the area.

Finally, some future challenges are identified, taking into account the strengths and weaknesses that exist today to invest in the development of language technologies in these two countries.

BACKGROUND

Nowadays, it is clear that technological development has transformed the science model that we inherited in the 20th century, especially when we focus on the relationship between theory and data. This has led to the creation of a **knowledge economy**, which is defined as the sector of the economy that uses information as a fundamental element to generate value and wealth through its transformation to knowledge. According to Powell and Snellman (2004), this kind of economy focuses on products and services based on knowledge-intensive activities, which contribute to accelerate the technical and scientific advance. Therefore, the key here is a greater reliance on intellectual capabilities than on physical inputs or natural resources.

The knowledge economy began in the second half of the 20th century, it is in the period from 1990 to the present that it has seen an exponential growth. As is known, this growth has led to financial restructuring, introducing a growing need to bet on technological innovation, particularly in the field of artificial intelligence.

For this reason, in recent years, economic clusters have been set up, specialized in the production of such technology on an industrial scale (e. g., the notorious cases of the United States and China), others in the development of investigations and specialized personnel for AI and similar areas (cases such as those of the European Union, Japan, India, Canada and so on), and finally groups of countries that have not yet made a full leap to the knowledge economy, and continue a role as producers of raw materials, just in the case of a region like Latin America.

THE SITUATION OF LATIN AMERICA

Latin America is currently in the transition from an economy that produces raw materials to other that conceives the knowledge as a generator of technological transformations. Nevertheless, such transition has not been easy. Since the last decade there is a fluctuation process, which has directly affected both the government and the industry in their ability to invest in science and technology. In the following graph, we can observe the variations of GDP around the world from 1963 to 2013:

Figure 1. Deceleration process in 50 years
Source: (Ovanesso & Plastino, 2017)

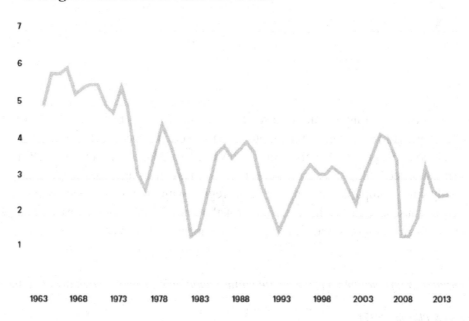

These variations have forced many regions or countries to make changes in their development models. For example, Asia has focused on the technology sector, and this has given it an economic growth compared with Latin America, according to the following graphic:

Figure 2 shows how East Asia and the Pacific zone have shown consistent growth in the technology sector since the 1960s. It should be noted here that, although in this first decade Latin America takes the lead (specifically, it includes here Argentina, Brazil, Chile, Colombia and Peru), for the 70s the situation is reversed: the investment that countries such as Japan, South Korea, China, Indonesia and others have focused on their technological development is practically the double compared to that of Latin America. Given the development achieved by the Asiatic region, a close relationship between economic development and productivity has been consolidated, where not only the use of technological resources is considered, but also their generation. In this sense, Latin America shows a decrease in productivity.

Figure 2. Average annual GDP growth (billions of dollars) between Asia and Latin America
Source: (Ovanesso & Plastino, 2017)

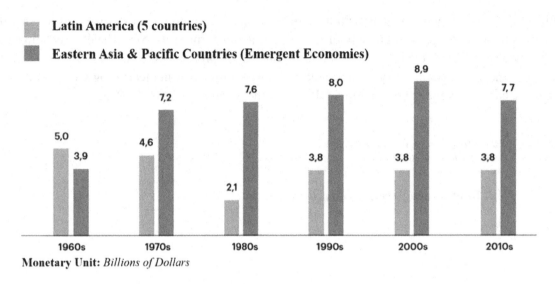

Monetary Unit: *Billions of Dollars*

One aspect to consider —thinking in the case of Latin America— is that knowledge economy does not pose a supremeness of the previous model, but rather is a complement that fosters a transformation oriented towards economic growth that gives an added value to productivity total factor (PTF). The benefits that investment in technology can generate, especially in artificial intelligence (AI), have a relevant impact, especially when comparing this impact in the region with other developed countries. Thus, AI has the capacity to cause an increase in economic growth rates in Latin America by up to a percentage point, in terms of its gross added value. In Figure 3 this impact by the AI can be observed:

Figure 3. Comparison around the increase in the annual economic growth rate between some countries in 2017
Source: (Ovanesso & Plastino, 2017)

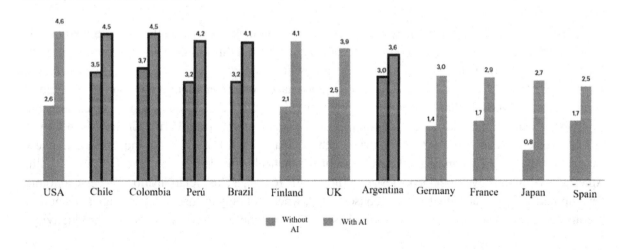

As seen here, countries like Chile, Colombia and Argentina stand out for achieving added value in their income by introducing AI-based technologies in their industries. However, this growth in Latin America is not constant, since it depends largely on the sale of natural resources, so it is not yet possible to reach a level of competitiveness that guarantees the consolidation of AI as an industrial activity.

LATIN AMERICA AND THE AI

Although the participation of Latin America became in the 80s, only in recent years has it shown substantial progress. Based on this behavior, several positive forecasts have been made, which recognize that there will be notable in this area. Moreover, there are countries in Latin America that have already managed to insert resources generated by AI into their industry.

Going into greater detail, it is necessary to notice differences regarding the advances that occur in the region between AI and industry: while countries like Argentina and Brasil support the consolidation of start-ups focused on the implementation of systems capable of solving tasks based on deep learning models and cognitive methods, others such as Colombia and Mexico are still in an exploratory phase, trying to encourage the use of methods based on neural networks or machine learning to solve problems.

Despite these differences, a trend observed is that there will be a greater investment towards this area. A projection that can be done is that North America, Europe and Asia will be the regions that will invest more money in that sector. Latin America and Africa will occupy a fourth and fifth place, respectively.

The Case of Mexico

In 2015, the **Government of Spain**, in collaboration with the **Spanish Society of Natural Language Processing (SEPLN)**[1], developed a national plan to promote the area of NLP, which aims to position this country as one of the main powers of these technologies for the Spanish language (Bel and Rigau, 2015). Taking this plan as a road map, in 2018 a study was carried out to know the situation of Spain and Mexico, two countries that are the ones with the greatest development capacity in the field of language technologies. This study was carried out by the consulting company **Track Global Solutions (TGS)**[2], in collaboration with the **Linguistic Engineering Group** (in Spanish, **GIL**)[3], affiliated with the **Institute of Engineering of UNAM**. Therefore, we identified the authors of this study with the abbreviation **TGS / GIL-UNAM** (2018).

According to this study, Mexico is seen as a strategic country both for its potential to be a large market interested in the acquisition of language technologies, as a collaborator in generating them. It should be noted that Mexico has carried out several initiatives to support this kind of technologies, the most relevant is the **Language Technology Thematic Network (RedTTL, 2007)**[4], supported by the **National Council of Science and Technology (CONACYT)**. This network brings together all the groups, researchers and professors working in the area of NLP.

The RedTLL aims to consolidate research in NLP, encouraging collaboration at national and international levels. Considering these collaborations, it will try to propose technological solutions to the problems of information processing that affect the country. This is important, especially considering some of the most relevant problems to solve, namely:

- Insufficient linguistic resources for Mexican Spanish

- Ignorance of the opportunities that NLP has in the business environment
- Little link between academia and industry
- Contradictions by the government regarding the research policies to follow

Thus, based on the data shown by the study by TGS and GIL, the agents participating in the language technology sector are:

On the other hand, the type of products sold are:

Figure 4. Agents identified in Mexico related to NLP
Source: (TGS/GIL-UNAM, 2018)

Public and private actors with policies and strategies of interest to the sector	Number of agents belonging to the NLP field	Other related agents
Public Organisms	0	16
Research groups dedicated to NLP	2	30
Companies focused on NLP	97	0
Total	126	46

According to Figure 5, the main focus of language technologies in Mexico is the semantic analysis of documents, which ranges from classic processes such as information retrieval and extraction, to opinion mining, configuring what is known as text analytics. Second, the development of technologies to process the written corpus takes precedence. Thirdly, systems for speech processing are relevant, especially for the business sector. The implementation of resources such as linguistic corpus, morphological analyzers, parsers, etc., is a purely academic task, with minimal industry participation.

Reviewing in more detail the data shown in Figure 5, it can see the performance of Mexican research research groups (affiliated to universities or research centers sponsored by the government) and private enterprises (either local or subsidiaries of international companies) in the field of speech technologies.

Figure 6, *grosso modo*, describes the state of art on speech technologies in the country. Following a general trend in the world, the private sector has focused on the development of chatbos for commercial purposes. In contrast, there is less work done around Speech-to-Text systems, or other similar applications.

On the other hand, in the case of written language technologies, the following are available:

Figure 7 shows a clear trend on the part of companies and research groups to solve problems related to information retrieval, design of search engines, automatic classification and clustering. Likewise, another relevant development line considered in the figure is information extraction, linked to other similar tasks as named entities recognition, term extraction, event extraction and text mining. A third

Figure 5. Types of NLP products marketed in Mexico
Source: (TGS/GIL-UNAM, 2018)

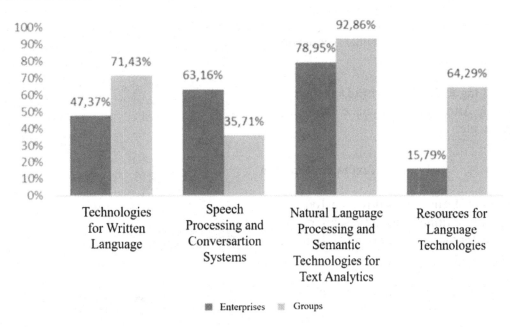

Figure 6. Landscape about Speech Technologies
Source: (TGS/GIL-UNAM, 2018)

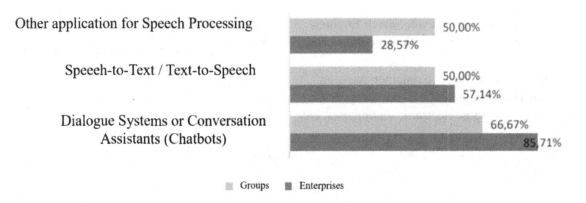

relevant research line is the opinion mining and the sentiment analysis, in order to respond to the interest that companies have in knowing the opinions that their clients have.

There are some lines of research that can have an immediate impact on the Government sector: this is the case of the NLP linked to Forensic Linguistics. Given the crisis caused by organized crime in Mexico, significant efforts have been made to develop systems that help to solve problems such as automatic fraud detection, or the recognition of acoustic patterns to identify criminals.

Figure 7. Landscape about Written Technologies
Source: (TGS/GIL-UNAM, 2018)

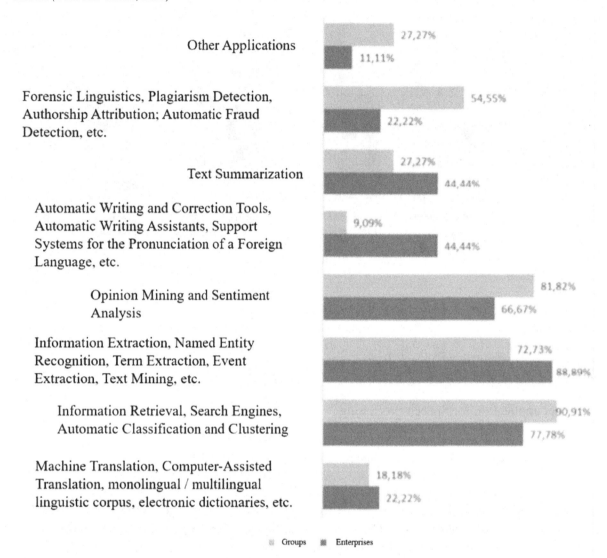

Finally, to complete this review regarding the state of the NLP in Mexico, its status in the academy must be considered. Specifically, this line of research is conceived primarily as part of Computer Science, given its relationship with AI. Likewise, this relationship also allows it to be linked to Engineering, especially in response to the formation of professional staff oriented to the development of applications.

However, there are no links of collaboration by the NLP with other branches of knowledge, including Linguistics. In Mexico, and in almost all of Latin America, it is considered that the NLP must be part of the so-called *Hard Sciences*, along with Mathematics or Physics, considering its location as part of the Computer Science.

In contrast, Linguistics (being a humanistic branch) is a *Soft Science*, so its approach to mathematical areas either stays on a theoretical level, or is nonexistent. The lack of collaboration between linguistics and NLP seriously affects Mexico's potential for the development of its own language technologies. Such contrast is better understood when analyzing the percentages of participation in the NLP area by university careers belonging to hard and soft sciences in Mexico:

Figure 8. Participation in the NLP area regarding both hard and soft scientific disciplines
Source: (TGS/GIL-UNAM, 2018)

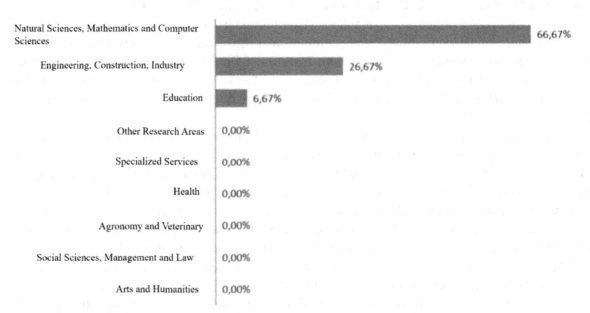

As can be seen in figure 8, in Mexico the university careers that have the greatest link with NLP are Natural Sciences (particularly Physics), Mathematics and Computer Sciences, with almost 66.67% enrollment. In a second position are the careers related to Engineering, Construction and Industry with almost 26.67%, and in a third position are the careers related to the Education area with 6.6%. In the case of the careers related to Language and Literature, they practically do not participate within the area, although it should be noted that there are some professors and researchers trained in these careers, who collaborate closely with research and development of NLP both in academia and in the industry.

Nowadays it is not feasible to develop resources for language processing without having a linguistic approach behind it. Having such an approach is extremely useful if addressing the automatic treatment of indigenous languages, an important challenge to solve, considering the variety of communities of speakers that communicate with a language other than Spanish. If Mexico is able to tackle this challenge, it has many possibilities to play a very important active role in the field of language technologies.

The Case of Chile

Since last 2019, the Government of Chile, together with the support of universities, research centers and business representatives, has directed its efforts to outline a national strategy to promote research and development in artificial intelligence. To achieve this, it has formed the **Commission for Future Challenges, Science, Technology and Innovation (CDFCTI)**[5], which has prepared a document entitled: *Inteligencia artificial en Chile. La urgencia de desarrollar una estrategia* (2019), which includes a detailed overview of the evolution and current state of the country in this area.

According to such a document, during the 1960s the first computers for data processing were introduced in Chile. Already in the 80s, with the arrival of personal computers, its use is widespread for both academic (research and teaching) and industrial purposes. In 2000, a significant advance was made in Chile in the field of AI thanks to the work of Ricardo Baeza-Yates and his colleagues, when they founded the **Center for Web Research (CWR)**[6] at the University of Chile (CDFCTI, 2019).

In 2006, the CWR had the support of Yahoo, which allowed it to be considered as a research laboratory at the international level, first under the coordination of Baeza-Yates, and later by Gonzalo Navarro. Currently, this center is part of the **Millennium Institute of Data Foundations (IMFD)**[7], sponsored since 2011 by the Ministry of Economy, Development and Tourism of the Government of Chile, within the program: *Millennium Scientific Initiative*. The IMFD is oriented to the development of projects on Data Science, AI and WEB Mining.

In line with the researches made by CWR and the IMFD, the work of César Hidalgo, an academic scholar and entrepreneur affiliated to the Artificial and Natural Intelligence Toulouse Institute (ANITI) of the University of Toulouse. Likewise, Hidalgo is the founder of Datawheel, a company specialized in the creation of data distribution and visualization systems. Datawheel is in charge of the administration of **Data Chile**, a digital platform that integrates, distributes and visualizes large volumes of public data about economy, technological development and social aspects of this country. The success achieved with Data Chile has allowed the implementation of similar platforms to collect data belonging to the USA and Africa. Thus, Hidalgo is nowadays one of the Chilean researchers with the greatest international projection in the field of AI, specifically in data visualization.

While the advances made by Baeza-Yates and Hidalgo provide Chile with an international impact, language technologies remain as an unknown field. In fact, the number of researchers in the country dedicated to the subject barely makes up a little more than a dozen, which is insufficient to meet needs both in the academy, in the industry or in the government itself. Considering such small number compared to the research groups and experts in Mexico, here is a list of the best known:

According to the study prepared by TGS / GIL-UNAM (2018), in Chile there are lack public programs in the field of language technologies that allow and promote business development. However, despite such lack of programs, Chile is one of the few countries in the region that tries, in the short term, to move towards a knowledge economy. In order to promote this movement, in 2018 the **Ministry of Science, Technology, Knowledge and Innovation** was created, precisely in charge of designing, implementing and coordinating policies that help to strengthen science and technology, particularly innovation processes both in the academy as in industry. It is precisely this Ministry that has launched in 2019 a national proposal for the development of AI in the country. It should be noted that this proposal recognizes that within the fields of research addressed by AI, the NLP plays a fundamental role. Thus, it is necessary that linguistic research, both theoretical and applied, be seen as one of the pillars of contemporary AI, especially if you want to boost its growth on an industrial scale.

Table 1. NLP Researchers in Chile

Researchers	University	Topics	Link
César Aguilar	Pontificia Universidad Católica de Chile	NLP, Corpus Linguistics, Digital Humanities	http://cesaraguilar.weebly.com
Rodrigo Alfaro	Pontificia Universidad Católica de Valparaíso	AI, NLP, Machine Learning, Text Mining, Data Science	www.rodrigoalfaro.cl
Héctor Allende	Pontificia Universidad Católica de Valparaíso	AI, Machine Learning, Predictive Analysis, Distributional Semantics	http://zeus.inf.ucv.cl/~hallende
John Atkinson	Universidad Adolfo Ibáñez	AI, NLP, Machine Learning, Text Mining, Text Analytics	https://ingenieria.uai.cl/profesor/john-atkinson
Felipe Bravo	Universidad de Chile	NLP, Data Mining, Data Science, Information Retrieval	https://felipebravom.com
Néstor Becerra	Universidad de Chile	AI, NLP, Speech Processing, Voice Recognition, Human-Computer Interfaces	www.lptv.cl/personas
Alejandro Figueroa	Universidad Andrés Bello	NLP, Information Retrieval, Data Mining, QA Systems	https://dci.unab.cl/alejandro-figueroa-amenabar
Rogelio Nazar	Pontificia Universidad Católica de Valparaíso	NLP, Corpus Linguistics, Term Extraction, Distributional Semantics	www.tecling.com/nazar/#Bio
Giovanni Parodi	Pontificia Universidad Católica de Valparaíso	Corpus Linguistics, Cognitive Linguistics, Language Technologies for Education, Discourse Analysis	www.giovanniparodi.cl
Jorge Pérez	Universidad de Chile	Databases, WEB Mining, Distributional Semantics, Computational Complexity	www.dcc.uchile.cl/jorge_perez
Bárbara Poblete	Universidad de Chile	Artificial Intelligence, Information Retrieval, WEB Mining, Opinion Mining	www.barbara.cl
Irene Renau	Pontificia Universidad Católica de Valparaíso	Corpus Linguistics, Term Extraction, Computational Lexicography,	www.elv.cl/elv/irene-renau
René Venegas	Pontificia Universidad Católica de Valparaíso	NLP, Corpus Linguistics, Computational Semantics, Discourse Analysis	http://renevenegas.cl/wp

Source: (TGS/GIL-UNAM, 2018)

Nevertheless, in spite of the foundational role of linguistics in the creation of AI, in Chile and Mexico there is a minimum participation of linguists in technological projects. One of the causes that the MCTCI considers influencing this preponderance of engineering faculties in AI is the lack of a critical mass of experts (both in academia and industry) who are capable of conducting research in this field (CDFCTI, 2019). Considering this lack of critical mass, one of the priorities that must be resolved in the coming years is the opening by the Humanities (not only of linguistics, but of other areas such as philosophy, sociology, librarianship or literature, among others) towards these new lines of research and development, with a view to achieving a real impact on the business sector.

LINGUISTIC DIVERSITY: THE CASE OF INDIGENOUS LANGUAGES

An important aspect that must be considered within the investigations in NLP in Latin America is its relationship with the indigenous languages of the region, whose speakers mostly suffer from a social, economic and legal marginalization since the time of the European Conquest and Colonization. However, the university income of young people belonging to these communities has been increasing in recent years, particularly in areas of technological training, which has provided opportunities to develop some electronic resources for their mother tongues.

In the case of Mexico, according to the Census conducted by the **National Institute of Statistics, Geography and Information** (INEGI, 2010), there are approximately 15 million people who recognize themselves as members of an indigenous group. On the other hand, in Chile there are about 2,185,792 people belonging to an ethnic group, according to the **National Socioeconomic Characterization Survey** (**CASEN**), applied in 2013 by the **Ministry of Social Development and Family** (MDSF) of the Government of Chile.

The Mexican indigenous communities with the highest number of population are outlined in Table 2.

Table 2. Larger Indigenous Populations in Mexico

Language	Population
Mayas	4,951,431
Nahuatls (or Aztecs)	2,870,784
Mixtecs	826,601
Zapotecs	700,000
Otomies	667.038
Rarámuris (or Tarahumaras)	121,835
Huicholes	43,929

Source: (INEGI, 2010)

Regarding the case of Chile, there are —at least— the native groups from Table 3.

Table 3. Larger Indigenous Populations in Chile

Language	Population
Mapuches	1,745,147
Aimaras	128,201
Mixtecs	826,601
Rapanuis	5,682

Source: (CASEN, 2013)

The relationship between these indigenous communities and their governments exposes many contrasts, ranging from serious attempts at conservation and insertion of such groups in today's society, to their ignorance, exclusion and marginalization, sustained by prejudices rooted since the times of European colonization. In order to illustrate these contrasts, from a very general perspective, at least two opposing lines of thought can be fixed:

a)   A conservative current, which considers that the indigenous groups in America, being minorities, need to be protected with respect to their relations with the rest of society (which, for the most part, is recognized as *mestiza* or *criolla*, that is, descendants of Indigenous and Europeans, whether Spanish, Portuguese, English, etc.). Such current has been interpreted and applied by many Latin American governments in different ways. However, a negative aspect that must be highlighted with respect to this trend is that it incorporates a policy of exclusion (whether explicit or implicit) that prevents these populations from integrating productively into the economic, cultural or political sectors of their respective countries. This current considers that indigenous groups are not interested in adopting computational knowledge and integrating it into their culture.

b)   An open current to a process of linking indigenous communities to contemporary societies in Latin America, seeing them as a sector capable of creating and maintaining their own integration models. This progressive vision has helped establish self-government options for these communities, and has also provided economic options that have a positive impact. Nevertheless, such a vision carries an implicit risk: the leave aside (either gradually or immediately) their cultural and linguistic roots, without considering its conservation for future generations.

Achieving a reconciliation between the two currents is extremely difficult. Thus, the Mexican Government has maintained a policy of integration towards its indigenous communities, which is established in its Political Constitution by recognizing the country as a Multicultural Nation. However, in practice, indigenous people suffers from racism and marginalization by Mexican society, despite the fact that the Mexican government fosters respect and admiration for pre-Columbian civilizations (particularly Nahuatl and Maya) as part of the Nationalist conception that Mexicans have about themselves. This conception has come to create constant tension among two opposing nation projects: (i) the conception of Mexico as a country with a unitary society, ethnically indivisible, represented mostly by the mestizo group, whose only language is Spanish, which admits variants, but in essence such a group is conceived as monolingual speakers of the Mexican dialect; (ii) the conception of Mexico as a multicultural country, inhabited by various ethnic groups, which have their own languages and dialect variants to communicate, and that would even redefine the conception of Mexico as a Pluri-National country, respecting the right of self-determination of these peoples, thus establishing cooperation agreements with a Federal Government (Benítez, 1989; Florescano, 1997).

The situation of indigenous communities in Chile is almost similar to that of Mexico, although there are significant differences. On the one hand, the Chilean state does not recognize itself as multicultural, but as a unitary, democratic and presidential nation. Based on this conception, the Chilean government does not make important ethnic distinctions, officially recognizing that its population is mostly mestiza.

On the other hand, Chile during the 19th century carried out a territorial expansion towards the south, specifically towards the regions of Araucanía. This resulted in military conflicts against the Mapuche tribes (mainly). Now, from the perspective of the Chilean Governments of that time, these military conflicts were considered as processes of occupation and pacification; while for the Mapuche people it was a genocide, which had entirely negative consequences: (i) significant reduction of population, (ii) submission to servile work (and even slavery), (iii) expropriation of collective lands and, (iv), an absolute denial of Mapuche culture and language (Mases, 1998; Cayuqueo, 2017).

As a result of these conflicts, today the Mapuche people are conceived as an independent nation, whose territory is occupied by the governments of Chile, mainly interested in exploiting their natural resources, but without recognizing that the Mapuches are their original inhabitants.

INDIGENOUS LANGUAGES AND NLP: THE ROAD TO A DIGITAL TRANSFORMATION

A fundamental problem for the indigenous peoples that live in Mexico and Chile is to achieve the conservation of their cultures and their languages in the face of the pressure exerted by their environment, specifically competing against Spanish, often considering it as the only official language of both countries, leaving aside the agreements and laws that have been set to promote bilingual education, as well as the dissemination of native languages through printed and electronic media (Kornai, 2013). The peoples who fail to solve this problem are absorbed by the mestizo majority, so that their culture and language are practically forced to die, according to Crystal's explanation of this phenomenon (2014).

The death of indigenous languages has been a problem of language policy in Chile and Mexico, especially confined to bilingual education projects that will enable speakers of indigenous languages integrate most mestizo population, which is Spanish monolingual (Riedemann, 2008; Barriga, 2018).

Given this consideration, for many years indigenous communities have been completely marginalized from any type of technological advance, which encompasses language technologies. Two concrete examples of this marginalization can be seen in a report prepared by the World Bank —entitled *Indigenous Latin America in the Twenty-First Century* (2015)— which provides percentages regarding access to mobile telephones, computers and the Internet among indigenous communities in Chile and Mexico (without considering here its native language):

(i)   In the case of Chile, in the year 2002, making a comparison between the mestizo (that is, non-indigenous) population, it has 55% access to cell phone services, along with 11% access to telephone services. Internet, while the possibility of having a computer at home was 11%. In the case of indigenous communities, access to these technological resources is less: 39% for cell phones, 4% for the Internet, and 10% for computers.

(ii) In the case of Mexico, contrasting the same items, in 2010 the mestizo population had 70% accessibility to cell phone services, 25% access to the Internet, while 34% had a computer at home. For their part, indigenous communities had 44% access to cell phone services, 8% access to the Internet, and only 13% could have a computer.

Having in mind these percentages, the World Bank indicates that in Latin America there is a deep digital and technological divide that affects a good part of its population, which has been observed and reported by other authors (Petrissans, 2002; Casas, 2004).

The critical point here is: although it is true that the scientific and technological divide that Chile and Mexico maintain with countries like the United States and Canada (or even with regions like Asia or Europe) is large, such a gap becomes deeper between the great mestizo population and indigenous communities. Thus, despite the fact that there is still an incipient development in language technologies, the mestizo population has much more possibilities of accessing this type of technology than indigenous groups. Likewise, this is one of the reasons why the vast majority of technology companies that emerge today in Chile and Mexico focus on the development of linguistic tools and resources for the processing of Spanish, and completely ignore indigenous languages.

In this sense, as Crystal (2015) explains, indigenous communities face a crucial dilemma in the current technological scenario: or they decide to conserve their native languages, knowing that this decision greatly reduces the possibility of accessing linguistic technologies that both governments and companies have for the majority of monolingual Spanish speakers; or they let their native languages die, since they do not have the knowledge or the capacity to establish collaboration agreements with companies and governments to develop these technological resources.

Looking at these two scenarios, it would seem that the technological future of indigenous languages in Chile and Mexico (and also for all of Latin America) is entirely negative. Nonetheless, it is possible to give it a positive turn, if we analyze options that allow us to understand how the technologies generated by the NLP can support not only the digital conservation of these languages, but also conceive them as a resource capable of generating economic and social benefits for both its potential users, as well as for people who are involved in the creation of such technology.

On the one hand, in the case of language conservation via the use of computational resources, since 2000 several proposals have been put forward to preserve and revitalize minority languages. Works such as those of Hinton and Hale (2001), Dyson, Hendriks and Grant (2007), as well as Dyson, Grant and Hendriks (2016) outline proposals that help use current technological resources to create linguistic corpus, annotated systems, electronic dictionaries and other similar tools, focused on these languages.

On the other hand, several initiatives have emerged to develop useful software and apps for the automatic treatment of this kind of languages. Whether for academic, social, or commercial purposes, there are currently several of these resources, available from WEB platforms. We mention below two examples of this type of initiative, which have been carried out in America, and which have had a positive impact on indigenous communities:

a) The apps developed by **Ogoki Learning Inc.**, a Canadian company coordinate by Darrick Baxter, which focuses on the creation of mobile services for native languages of Canada and the United States, specifically the Cree language (a language belonging to the Algonquian family). An important aspect of this company is that it has released the codes of its apps, so that other native communities can use them for free. Ogoki Learning can be characterized as a success story, it can be replicated in Mexico and Chile, considering not only its business model, but also taking advantage of free access to the codes of its apps, through reengineering process that allows adapting —*mutatis mutandis*— those apps to indigenous languages such as Náhualt, Maya, Mapuche and others, through the collaboration schemes between governmental or community entities.

b) Likewise, the **Summer Institute of Linguistics** (SIL), is the largest institution dedicated to the study of minority and aboriginal languages from all over the world, has developed in recent years several resources for the analysis of such languages, from linguistic corpus, systems of transcription, editors to create dictionaries and lexicons, etc. Given the constant activity of SIL in research and teaching, many computational linguists have taken great interest in collaborating with them, providing a large number of technological solutions for these languages, including those that are in danger of extinction.

Returning to the cases of Mexico and Chile, in both countries efforts are also being made to create both resources and electronic tools for processing indigenous languages.

An example is the work of Alfonso Medina, a researcher affiliated with El Colegio de México, who from the computational morphology has focused on developing automatic analysis models, independent of language, capable of differentiating lexical roots from suffixes (Medina and Buenrostro, 2003; Medina, 2007; 2008). The research and experiments carried out by Medina have focused mainly on two native languages: the Chuj, which is a language belonging to the Mayan family, which is spoken in the southern part of Mexico and Guatemala; and the Rarámuri (or Tarahumara), a language descended from the Yuto-Aztec family, spoken in northern Mexico, specifically in the province of Chihuahua.

Following a line similar to that of Medina and others, Gutierrez and Sierra —together with their colleagues— have developed the **Axolotl Project**, a parallel Nahuatl-Spanish corpus, which has been constructed from texts translated primarily by Christian missionaries during the 16th and 17th centuries in Mexico (Gutiérrez, 2015; Gutiérrez, Sierra and Hernández, 2016).

The work carried out around the **Axolotl Corpus** has allowed the evaluation of the performance of automatic tools for the morphological analysis of Nahuatl (Gutiérrez and Mijangos, 2018; Gutiérrez, Medina and Sierra, 2019). Such tools, in a short term, can be applied to other similar languages.

On the other hand, these works also have been useful to explore phenomena that help to graduate the *linguistic complexity*, considered as the ability of languages to generate combinations of elements, weighing the processing capacity required to perform such permutations (Juloa, 2008; Sampson, Gil and Trudgill, 2009; Baechler and Seiler, 2016). If such weighting is translated into a measurable parameter, it is feasible to make comparisons between human languages, as well as assess how difficult or not it is for a computer system to do some linguistic processing, particularly at the morphological and syntactic levels.

Keeping in mind the notion of linguistic complexity for typological studies of natural languages, it is possible to propose a new line of research in NLP, which focuses on developing mathematical models and computational resources to determine which languages may require greater processing capacity, given its morphological and / or syntactic complexity, and which others are more accessible. Similarities or differences regarding processing capacity can help to create effective algorithms to analyze human languages automatically. From this perspective, Mager *et al* (2018) delineate a promising overview to consider the indigenous languages of America as an object of study relevant for computational linguistics. Therefore, today there is a great interest in implementing computational resources for Nahuatl, it is special because it is one of the best preserved languages in Mexico thanks to its written production.

In the case of the Mayan, another indigenous language spoken in Mexico, there is the **Ko'ox Apps**[8], whose main objective is to support the learning of the Mayan language, similarly to what Ogoki Learning has done for the Algonquin, as mentioned above.

Another example of computational development is the implementation of the Mozilla Firefox WEB search engine in Mayan, under the initiative of **Mozilla Nativo**, a community that is in charge of adapting such search engine to native languages (Gómez, 2019). This implementation has been coordinated by Julio Ceballos, along with a team of programmers and linguists based in the province of Yucatán, one of the most important regions of the Mayan community.

Although there is still not so much literature that gives reference to these electronic resources for that language, in the short term there will be more computational resources, which will have a positive impact on the transition of the Mayan towards its conservation and dissemination in digital form (Acosta, 2019).

With regard to indigenous languages of Chile, which counts today with computational resources is the Mapudüngun (or Mapuche), thanks to the efforts of its speakers have been brewing since 2000 to establish a plan to revitalize their language (Catrileo, 2005). A significant advance in relation to such revitalization is the publication of the grammar elaborated by Smeets (2008). This grammar, in recent years, has served as a source of linguistic data, along with other Mapuche documents, for the compilation of the **Mapudüngun Lexicographic Corpus**, called **CORLEXIM** (2018), a project developed in collaboration between Belén Villena, who has focused on linguistic analysis, and Andrés Chandía, who has dedicated to the development of computational tools. Thus, on the one hand, the Villena's work has been oriented towards the generation of neologisms in Mapudüngun (2016). On the other hand, Chandía (2012) has implemented a morphological analyzer for Mapudüngun, based on finite-state transducers.

Finally, it is worth mentioning here the studies carried out by Scott Sadowsky, professor and researcher affiliated with the Pontifical Catholic University of Chile, as well as the Department of Linguistic and Cultural Evolution of the Max Planck Institute, in Jena, Germany. In collaboration with Paul Heggarty, affiliated with the Department of Linguistic and Cultural Evolution of the Max Planck Institute, both have carried out the **Sound Comparisons: Mapudungun Project**[9], which compiles sets of recordings, transcripts and graphics generated through Praat, made to Mapuche speakers who live in Chile and Argentina. The main objective of this project is to provide data that is useful for conducting typological interviews between languages. However, this data can be used for the design of acoustic analysis and dialogue systems, as well as others that require sound processing. Also, since 2000 Sadowsky has implemented two corpus with samples of Chilean and Mapuche Spanish: the **Sociolinguistic Corpus of Spoken Chilean Spanish (Coscach)**[10], and the **Dynamic Corpus of Chilean Spanish (Codicach)**[11]. One of the objectives for which Sadowsky compiled these corpus is to constantly monitor the relations and exchanges between Spanish and Mapuche, with a view to detecting how active this second language remains compared to the first, in order to support the conservation of Mapudüngun.

SOLUTIONS AND RECOMMENDATIONS

Historically, Latin America has been involved in AI and NLP with some 30 years of delay. Likewise, contrary to the integrating vision that has been taken in the United States regarding the existing relationship between Linguistics and Computer Sciences (Martin-Nielsen, 2012), in Latin America both AI and NLP have been assumed as purely computational areas, which have evolved apart from Linguistics. In fact, there are few linguists in the region that delve into a theoretical plane about some NLP problem: there is generally a rejection of establishing links with the Computer Sciences. Special mention deserves the only project —perhaps— carried out in Mexico, oriented towards the creation of the first electronic corpus for Mexican Spanish (Lara, Ham-Chande and García-Hidalgo, 1979): the **Dictionary of Mexican Spanish**, coordinated by Luis Fernando Lara. This corpus, started in the 70s, has become a pioneer reference for many subsequent research related to corpus linguistics and linguistic engineering since 2000 (Sierra, 2017). However, at the time, many Mexican linguists showed no interest in the computational processes for the creation of this corpus, and it is in recent years that the scope achieved by it has been revalued. This same disinterest is also shared by most Chilean linguists, whose research focuses more on linking language studies with teaching Spanish and foreign languages, than exploring other theoretical and/or applied topics.

However, despite such disinterest, there are several initiatives, both public and private, that attempt to encourage and consolidate the development of technological resources in the field of AI. In Mexico, a clear example is the network of **National Technological Institutes** that the Government has implemented since 1948. Today, this network has 254 sites, distributed throughout the country, which provide quality education to a population of Around 600 thousand students, at the undergraduate and graduate levels.

An important contribution provided by these technological institutes is that they provide specialization training with affordable costs, which allows many young people to pursue careers related to computer science. It has been under the initiative of the students of these institutes that electronic resources have been developed for indigenous languages, such as the mentioned **Ko'ox App**[12], designed for the Mayan language.

On the other hand, cities such as Mexico City, Monterrey and Guadalajara in Mexico, as well as Santiago in Chile, have established conditions for the generation of technological clusters, with a view to fostering an active transition to a knowledge economy by local industry. Examples of this are initiatives such as the **Jalisco Institute of Technology of Information** (IJALTI)[13], the **Cluster of Information and Communications Technologies** in Monterrey (CSOFTMTY)[14], both in Mexico, or the **Association of Chilean Technology Companies** (Chiletec)[15], in Chile.

While it is true that these initiatives do not yet take into account the NLP among their topics of interest, it is a matter of time before the strategic value of language technologies for the gestation of companies in AI is considered. In fact, in recent years, institutions with great weight in the linguistic community in Latin America such as the Language Academies, following the initiative proposed by the Royal Spanish Academy (RAE), have gradually become aware of the need to outline strategic projects in NLP for Spanish, although the digitization of indigenous languages has not yet been considered.

Therefore, we make here some recommendations in order to reflect on what paths can be followed in Chile and Mexico to promote and consolidate the NLP area:

- Encouraging university and technical training in this area, with the aim of developing professional profiles capable of solving problems related to lines of research related to NLP, computational linguistics and linguistic engineering. This is not trivial, because as Powell and Snellman (2004) explain, the knowledge economy necessarily goes through the creation of professional cadres that, over time, can be inserted in the academic, business and government sectors, generating a critical mass that has a positive impact to consolidate these lines of research in Latin America.
- Considering the adoption of strategic projects such as the initiative that the Government of Spain has implemented for the characterization and consolidation of language technologies, started from the in-depth study done by Bel and Rigau (2015). Although for Mexico there is currently an analysis on the state of the art of language technologies (TGS/GIL-UNAM, 2018), Chile still does not have a study of such magnitude (in fact, this chapter has already it is a first attempt to address this issue). However, it is necessary to have a clear census that documents: (i) how many professionals exist today in the academy, the government or the private company that have experience and interest in working in the NLP area: (ii) how many technological developments are now patented, or at least reported as prototypes; (iii) evaluate how short, medium and long-term terms can be established to generate a critical mass that allows the PLN area to be consolidated in both countries; (iv) locate strategic niches for the development of linguistic tools and resources that can solve the needs of the local market, and also have a relevant quality to be able to be exported to other countries that require them to process Chilean and Mexican Spanish for various purposes.
- Start without delay ta process of digitization and generation of tools for all the indigenous languages. Although it is true that today languages like Náhualt, Mayan or Mapuche already have some computational resources (as mentioned above), both in Chile and Mexico there are lan-

guages they do not have any technological resources such as electronic dictionaries, linguistic corpus or annotation and transcription systems, to name a few. It is essential to provide them with the opportunity to have their own linguistic technologies that help them coexist with Spanish on equal terms.

FUTURE RESEARCH DIRECTIONS

Keeping in mind the recommendations that we have raised in the previous section, we consider some lines of work to follow:

(i) Undertaking a census on the current situation of the linguistic technologies that are available today in Chile, whether they have been implemented by academic entities (research centers or universities), or by technology companies, similarly to the study carried out in Mexico under the initiative of the SEPLN, in collaboration with the UNAM Language Engineering Group (TGS/GIL-UNAM, 2018).

(ii) Collaborating in the implementation of strategic development plans for Chile and Mexico in the NLP area, which can define guidelines to be followed in the coming years, with the aim of channeling in the best way the efforts that people and institutions make today involved in that area.

(iii) Becoming aware of the critical situation that indigenous languages live in Chile and Mexico when they find themselves immersed in a digital divide, which prevents them from remaining as living languages even for their own speakers. The existence of this digital divide does not only affect the linguistic survival of these groups of speakers, but also limits their possibilities to integrate into society as users and potential developers of computer technologies.

CONCLUSION

This chapter has delineated a broad picture of the current state of research and development in NLP in Mexico and Chile. Thus, at the beginning there were some antecedents that would help place the NLP as a line of research and development inserted in the knowledge economy. Both countries are currently making significant efforts to move towards that economy. However, these efforts are still not enough to generate an industry focused on the creation of proprietary technology.

Once this background was given, the specific situations of the two countries to be evaluated were considered, considering: (i) their evolution within the field of the AI and the NLP; (ii) the impact that such a field has had on the local economy, as well as growth prospects, whether encouraged by the government, academia or private enterprise; (iii) the multilingual scenario of both Mexico and Chile, in order to observe whether there are initiatives (or not) to implement electronic resources for indigenous languages; and (iv) finally, offer a series of conclusions and observations on future perspectives.

The authors of this chapter consider that the data and reflections made focus attention on the challenges and scopes that are pending to be resolved for language technologies in Latin America, particularly the automatic treatment of indigenous languages such as Nahuatl, Mayan and Mapuche. The intention of this text, as has been pointed out, is to provide the international community in NLP with a clear overview of the existing reality of this field in the Latin American context, in order to recognize what are the chronic problems to be solved both on an industrial level, as in one of academic research.

REFERENCES

Acosta, F. (2019). *Ko'ox T'aano'on ich Máaya: Yucatec Maya Language Revitalization Efforts among Professional Educators in the State of Yucatán, México* (Master of Arts Dissertation). Raleigh, NC: North Carolina State University.

Barriga, R. (2018). *De Babel a Pentecostés. Políticas lingüísticas y lenguas indígenas, entre historias, paradojas y testimonios*. Secretaría de Educación Pública, Gobierno de México.

Bel, N., & Rigau, G. (2015). *Informe sobre el estado de las tecnologías del lenguaje en España dentro de la Agenda Digital para España*. Madrid: Secretaría de Estado de Telecomunicaciones y para la Sociedad de la Información, Gobierno de España. www.plantl.gob.es/tecnologias-lenguaje/PTL/Paginas/plan-impulso-tecnologias-lenguaje.aspx

Benítez, F. (1998). *Los indios de México. Antología*. Ediciones Era.

Casas, R. (2004). Conocimiento, tecnologia y desarrollo en America Latina. *Revista Mexicana de Sociologia, 66*, 255–277. doi:10.2307/3541453

Catrileo, M. (2005). Revitalización de la lengua mapuche en Chile. *Documentos Lingüísticos y Literarios, 28*, 10–17.

Cayuqueo, P. (2017). *Historia secreta mapuche*. Catalonia.

CDFCTI. (2019). *Inteligencia artificial en Chile. La urgencia de desarrollar una estrategia*. Santiago de Chile. Gobierno de Chile: https://eia.bcn.cl/images/c/c1/Inteligencia_Artificial_para_Chile.pdf

Chandía, A. (2012). *Dungupeyem1_alfa2_v0.1: un prototipo de analizador morfológico para el mapudüngun a través de transductores de estados finitos* (Master Thesis). Barcelona, Catalunya, Spain. Universitat Pompeu Fabra.

Crystal, D. (2014). *Language Death*. Cambridge University Press. doi:10.1017/CBO9781139923477

Dyson, L., Grant, S., & Hendriks, M. (2016). *Indigenous People and Mobile Technology*. Routledge.

Dyson, L., Hendriks, M., & Grant, S. (2007). *Information Technology and Indigenous People*. Information Science Publishing. doi:10.4018/978-1-59904-298-5

Florescano, E. (1997). *Etnia, estado y nación: Ensayo sobre las identidades colectivas en México*. Aguilar.

Gómez, D. (2019). Uso de las tecnologías de la información y la comunicación por universitarios mayas en un contexto de brecha digital en México. *Región y Sociedad, 31*. Advance online publication. doi:10.22198/rys2019/31/1130

Gutiérrez, X. (2015). Bilingual lexicon extraction for a distant language pair using a small parallel corpus. In *Proceedings of the 2015 Conference of the North American Chapter of the Association for Computational Linguistics: Student Research Workshop* (pp. 154-160). Denver, CO: ACL Publications.

Gutiérrez, X., Medina, A., & Sierra, G. (2019). Morphological segmentation for extracting Spanish-Nahuatl bilingual lexicon. *Procesamiento del Lenguaje Natural*, *63*, 41–48.

Gutiérrez, X., & Mijangos, V. (2018). Comparing morphological complexity of Spanish, Otomi and Nahuatl. In *Proceedings of the Workshop on Linguistic Complexity and Natural Language Processing (LC&NLP-2018)*. Santa Fe, NM: ACL Publications.

Gutiérrez, X., Sierra, G., & Hernández, I. (2016). Axolotl: a Web Accessible Parallel Corpus for Spanish-Nahuatl. In *Proceedings of the Tenth International Conference on Language Resources and Evaluation LREC 2016* (pp. 4210-4214). Portorož, Slovenia: European Language Resources Association (ELRA).

Hinton, L., & Hale, K. (2001). *The Green Book of Language Revitalization in Practice*. Academic Press. doi:10.1163/9789004261723

INEGI. (2010). *Population and Housing Census 2010*. México, Gobierno de México: www.inegi.org.mx/temas/lengua

Kornai, A. (2013). Digital Language Death. *PLoS One*, *8*(10), e77056. doi:10.1371/journal.pone.0077056 PMID:24167559

Lara, L.-F., Ham-Chande, R., & García Hidalgo, M. (1979). *Investigaciones lingüísticas en lexicografía*. El Colegio de México. doi:10.2307/j.ctv233mwx

Mager, M., Gutiérrez, X., Sierra, G., & Meza, I. (2018). Challenges of language technologies for the indigenous languages of the Americas. In *Proceedings of the 27th International Conference on Computational Linguistics COLING 2018* (pp. 55-69). Santa Fe, NM: ACL Publications.

Martin-Nielsen, J. (2012). It Was All Connected: Computers and Linguistics in Early Cold War America. In *Cold War Social Science* (pp. 63–78). New York: Palgrave Macmillan.

Mases, E. (1998). La cuestión social, la cuestión indígena. El destino final de los indios sometidos. Argentina y Chile, 1878-1885. *Estudios Sociales (Santo Domingo, Dominican Republic)*, *15*(1), 31–45. doi:10.14409/es.v15i1.2410

Medina, A. (2007). Affix discovery by means of corpora: experiments for Spanish, Czech, Ralámuli and Chuj. In *Aspects of Automatic Text Analysis* (pp. 277–299). Springer.

Medina, A. 2008. Affix discovery based on entropy and economy measurements. In *Proceedings of the Texas Linguistics Society X Conference: Computational Linguistics for Less-Studied Languages*. Austin, TX: University of Texas.

Medina, A. & Buenrostro, C. (2003). Características cuantitativas de la flexión verbal de Chuj. *Estudios de Lingüística Aplicada, 39*, 15-31.

Ministerio de Desarrollo Social y Familia. (2013). *National Socioeconomic Characterization Survey (CASEN)*. Santiago, Chile: Government of Chile. http://observatorio.ministeriodesarrollosocial.gob.cl/casen-multidimensional/casen/casen_2013.php

Ovanessoff, A., & Plastino, E. (2017). Cómo la inteligencia artificial puede generar crecimiento en Sudamérica. Reporte de investigación, Accenture, Buenos Aires, Argentina.

Petrissans, R. (2002). La brecha digital: Situación regional y perspectivas. *Estudios Internacionales (Santiago)*, *35*(138), 55–70.

Powell, W., & Snellman, K. (2004). The Knowledge Economy. *Annual Review of Sociology*. www.annualreviews.org/doi/full/10.1146/annurev.soc.29.010202.100037#_i2

RedTTL: Language Technology Thematic Network. (2007). National Council of Science and Technology (CONACYT), México: www.redttl.mx

Riedemann, A. (2008). La educación intercultural bilingüe en Chile: ¿ampliación de oportunidades para alumnos indígenas? *Indiana, 25*, 169-193. https://journals.iai.spk-berlin.de/index.php/indiana/article/view/1960

Sierra, G. (2017). *Introducción a los corpus lingüísticos*. IINGEN-UNAM.

Smeets, I. (2008). *A Grammar of Mapuche*. Mouton de Gruyter. doi:10.1515/9783110211795

TGS/GIL-UNAM. (2018). *Análisis del sector de tecnologías del lenguaje en México*. Ministerio de Asuntos Económicos y Transformación Digital, Gobierno de España. Madrid, Spain: www.plantl.gob.es/Paginas/Index.aspx

Villena, B. (2016). *Innovación léxica en mapudüngun: genuinidad, productividad y planificación* (Ph. D. Dissertation). Barcelona, Catalunya, Spain: Pompeu Fabra University.

World Bank Group. (2015). *Latinomérica Indígena en el Siglo XXI*. Washington, DC: World Bank Publications. http://documents.worldbank.org

ADDITIONAL READING

Beliz, G. (2018). *Algoritmolandia. Inteligencia artificial para una integración predictiva e inclusiva de América Latina*. Planeta.

Cambria, E., & White, B. (2014). Jumping NLP curves: A review of natural language processing research. *IEEE Computational Intelligence Magazine*, *9*(2), 48–57. doi:10.1109/MCI.2014.2307227

Gao, L., Chang, E., & Han, S. (2005). Powerful tool to expand Business Intelligence: Text Mining. Proceedings of Transactions on ENFORMATIKA, Systems Sciences and Engineering (pp. 110-115). Vol. 8. Budapest, Hungary. International Academy of Sciences.

Kuechler, W. (2016). Business Applications of Unstructured Text. *Communications of the ACM*, *50*(10), 86–93. doi:10.1145/1290958.1290967

Pejić-Bach, M., Bertoncel, T., Meško, M., & Krstić, Ž. (2020). Text mining of industry 4.0 job advertisements. *International Journal of Information Management*, *50*, 416–431. doi:10.1016/j.ijinfomgt.2019.07.014

Pejić-Bach, M., Krstić, Ž., Seljan, S., & Turulja, L. (2019). Text Mining for Big Aata Analysis in Financial Sector: A Literature Review. *Sustainability*, *11*(5), 1277. doi:10.3390u11051277

Pineda, L., Calvo, H., Villaseñor, L., Castro, N., Gelbukh, A., Hernández, Y., Jiménez, H., Montes, M., Pinto, D., Sánchez, F., & Sidorov, G. (2017). Lingüística computacional. In *La computación en México por especialidades académicas* (pp. 91–125). Academia Mexicana de Computación.

Reitman, W. (1984). *Artificial Intelligence Applications for Business*. Ablex Publishing.

Rodríguez, L., & Carnota, R. (2015). *Historias de las TIC en América Latina y el Caribe*. Ariel/Fundación Telefónica.

Solorio, Th., & Pedersen, E. (2010). *Proceedings of the NAACL HLT 2010 Young Investigators Workshop on Computational Approaches to Languages of the Americas*. Stroudsburg, PA, USA. Association for Computational Linguistics.

Tanev, S., Liotta, G., & Kleismantas, A. (2016). A business intelligence approach using web search tools and online data reduction techniques to examine the value of product-enabled services. *Expert Systems with Applications*, *42*(21), 7582–7600. doi:10.1016/j.eswa.2015.06.006

Villaseñor, L. (2018). *Panorama de las tecnologías del lenguaje en México*. Academia Mexicana de Computación.

KEY TERMS AND DEFINITIONS

Artificial Intelligence: It is an interdisciplinary line of research focused on the design and construction of intelligent machines, which are seen as agents capable of simulating human rationing that allow them to solve specific problems. An example is the development of machines capable of understanding and generating human language.

Computational Linguistics: It is a subfield of the NLP, oriented to develop useful mathematical models to understand and generate human language from computers and other similar electronic machines. Taking this orientation into account, computational linguistics maintains a close relationship with the cognitive sciences, in particular with cognitive psychology, as well as the philosophy of mind and language. Likewise, computational linguistics has established close ties with statistics, which has allowed it to interact with innovative lines of research such as machine learning, which has had a positive impact on its work projects.

Digital Divide: It refers to an unequal distribution regarding access and use of Information or Computational Technologies among communities. This inequality is due to political, economic, cultural, racial, gender, etc. Initially, the term focused on the lack of means to access the Internet, either by mobile phone or by computers. However, today it refers to any technological deficiency, so it can be used as a parameter to determine the distribution of wealth in a society, takes into account the technological divide as an indicator of the economic and social deficiencies that such communities suffer.

Knowledge Economy: It is an emerging economic area, oriented towards the creation of goods and services derived from the exploitation of specialized knowledge, provided by highly qualified workers. Such knowledge is acquired by these workers from their university studies, therefore universities acquire a strategic value as centers capable to generate innovation and disruptive knowledge. In this sense, the knowledge economy is located in a post-industrial stage, since it is oriented towards a services market, where what is exchanged, in addition to industrial and human resources, ideas, designs and useful concepts to improve the productivity.

Language Engineering: It is a line of research and development focused on creating electronic tools capable of processing natural language, either in oral or written format. Unlike NLP and computational linguistics, linguistic engineering has a more applied perspective, so its priority is the design and implementation of such tools.

Linguistic Death: It refers to a linguistic process that occurs when a language loses its last native speaker, thus leading to its extinction. In addition to this loss, the most serious problem occurs when there is no oral or written record of that language. Such a process is different from what has happened with Latin, since although this language lost its acoustic registers, in contrast it has extensive documentation, in addition to its evolution giving rise to new languages. The death of a language may be due to historical wear, or it may be caused by linguistic policies, e. g., in cases where a country decides to adopt one or more official languages, those that are not recognized with this status may tend to disappear over time.

Natural Language Processing: is an interdisciplinary research area that integrates theories and methods from linguistics and computer science, particularly artificial intelligence, in order to create models and tools for understanding and generate human language. Natural language processing can be divided into two major sub-domains: (i) computational linguistics, focused on solving theoretical questions involved in designing computational models of human language; and (ii) linguistic engineering, geared more towards the development of computational tools and resources capable of processing oral data (e.g.: sequences of dialogues) or written (e.g.: text corpora).

ENDNOTES

1.   For more details, see: www.sepln.org.

2.   For more details, see: www.trackglobalsolutions.com.

3.   For more details, see: http://grupos.iingen.unam.mx/iling/es-mx/Paginas/default.aspx.

4.   For more details, see: www.redttl.mx.

5.   For more details, see: www.anid.cl.

6.   For more details, see: http://www.cwr.cl.

7.   For more details, see: https://imfd.cl/en.

8.   For more details, see: https://lighthousecode.com.

9.   For more details, see: http://sadowsky.cl/mapu/index.html.

10. For more details, see: http://sadowsky.cl/coscach.html.

11. For more details, see: http://sadowsky.cl/codicach.html.

12. For more details, see: https://lighthousecode.com.

13. For more details, see: www.tci-network.org/organization/242/.

14. For more details, see: www.csoftmty.org.

15. For more details, see: https://chiletec.org.

Compilation of References

Abbes, M., Kechaou, Z., & Alimi, A. M. (2017). Enhanced deep learning models for sentiment analysis in Arab social media. *International Conference on Neural Information Processing*. 667-676. 10.1007/978-3-319-70139-4_68

Abdelhameed, H. J., & Hernández, S. M. (2019). Sentiment Analysis of Arabic Tweets in Sudanese Dialect. *International Journal of New Technology and Research*, 5(6), 17–22. doi:10.31871/IJNTR.5.6.20

Abdelhaq, H., Sengstock, C., & Gertz, M. (2013). EvenTweet: Online localized event detection from Twitter. *Proceedings of the VLDB Endowment International Conference on Very Large Data Bases*, 6(12), 1326–1329. doi:10.14778/2536274.2536307

Abdullah, S. S., Rahaman, M. S., & Rahman, M. S. (2013). Analysis of stock market using text mining and natural language processing. In *2013 International Conference on Informatics, Electronics and Vision (ICIEV)* (pp. 1-6). IEEE. 10.1109/ICIEV.2013.6572673

Abdul-Mageed, M., & Diab, M. (2012a). AWATIF: A Multi-Genre Corpus for Modern Standard Arabic Subjectivity and Sentiment Analysis. *Language Resources and Evaluation Conference (LREC'12)*, 3907–3914. http://www.seas.gwu.edu/~mtdiab/files/publications/refereed/13.pdf

Abdul-Mageed, M., & Diab, M. (2012b). Toward Building a Large-Scale Arabic Sentiment Lexicon. *6th International Global Wordnet Conference*, 18–22.

Abdul-mageed, M., & Sandra, K. (2012). SAMAR : A System for Subjectivity and Sentiment Analysis of Arabic Social Media. *3rd Workshop on Computational Approaches to Subjectivity and Sentiment Analysis*, 19–28.

Abel, E. L. (2018). Syphilis: The History of an Eponym. *Names*, 66(2), 96–102. doi:10.1080/00277738.2017.1415522

Abu Hammad, A., & El-Halees, A. (2015). An approach for detecting spam in Arabic opinion reviews. *The International Arab Journal of Information Technology*, 12(1), 10–16.

Abuleil, S., & Evens, M. (1998). Discovering lexical information by tagging Arabic newspaper text. *Proceedings of the Workshop on Computational Approaches to Semitic Languages - Semitic 98*, 1–7. 10.3115/1621753.1621755

AbuZeina, D., & Al-Anzi, F. S. (2018). Employing fisher discriminant analysis for Arabic text classification. *Computers & Electrical Engineering*, 66, 474–486. doi:10.1016/j.compeleceng.2017.11.002

Acosta, F. (2019). *Ko'ox T'aano'on ich Máaya: Yucatec Maya Language Revitalization Efforts among Professional Educators in the State of Yucatán, México* (Master of Arts Dissertation). Raleigh, NC: North Carolina State University.

Agarwal, B., & Mittal, N. (2013). Sentiment classification using rough set based hybrid feature selection. In *Proceedings of 4th Workshop on Computational Approaches to Subjectivity, Sentiment and Social Media Analysis* (pp.115-119). Academic Press.

Aggarwal, A., & Kumaraguru, P. (2014). *Followers or phantoms? An anatomy of purchased Twitter followers.* arXiv preprint arXiv:1408.1534

Aggarwal, C. C. (2018). Opinion mining and sentiment analysis. *Machine Learning for Text*, (2), 413–434.

Aggarwal, D. G. (2018). *Review Paper Sentiment Analysis: An Insight into Techniques, Application and Challenges.* Academic Press.

Aggarwal, C. C., & Zhai, C. (2012). A survey of text classification algorithms. In *Mining text data* (pp. 163–222). Springer. doi:10.1007/978-1-4614-3223-4_6

Aggarwal, D., Bali, V., & Mittal, S. (2019). An insight into machine learning techniques for Predictive Analysis and Feature Selection. *International Journal of Innovative Technology and Exploring Engineering*, 8(9S), 342–349. doi:10.35940/ijitee.I1055.0789S19

Agirre, E., & Soroa, A. (2009). Personalizing pagerank for word sense disambiguation. *Proceedings of the 12th Conference of the European Chapter of the Association for Computational Linguistics (EACL 2009)*, 33–41. 10.3115/1609067.1609070

Ahmad, M., Aftab, S., Muhammad, S. S., & Ahmad, S. (2017). Machine Learning Techniques for Sentiment Analysis: A Review. *International Journal of Multidisciplinary Sciences and Engineering.*, 8(3), 27–32.

Ahuja, R., Chug, A., Kohli, S., Gupta, S., & Ahuja, P. (2019). The impact of features extraction on the sentiment analysis. In *Proceedings of International Conference on Pervasive Computing Advances and Applications* (vol. 152, pp. 341-348). 10.1016/j.procs.2019.05.008

Aiken, M., & Ghosh, K. (2009). Automatic translation in multilingual business meetings. *Industrial Management & Data Systems*, 109(7), 916–925. doi:10.1108/02635570910982274

Ainur, Y., Yisong, Y., & Claire, C. (2010). Multi-level structured models for document-level sentiment classification. *Proceedings of the 2010 Conference on Empirical Methods in Natural Language Processing*, 1046–1056.

Al Omran, F. N. A., & Treude, C. (2017). Choosing an NLP library for analyzing software documentation: A systematic literature review and a series of experiments. In *Proceedings of the 14th International Conference on Mining Software Repositories*, (pp. 187-197). IEEE Press. 10.1109/MSR.2017.42

Alayba, A. M., Palade, V., England, M., & Iqbal, R. (2017). Arabic language sentiment analysis on health services. *2017 1st International Workshop on Arabic Script Analysis and Recognition (ASAR)*, 114-118.

Alayba, A. M., Palade, V., England, M., & Iqbal, R. (2017). Arabic Language Sentiment Analysis on Health Services. *1st International Workshop on Arabic Script Analysis and Recognition (ASAR)*, 114–118. 10.1109/ASAR.2017.8067771

Al-ayyoub, M., Nuseir, A., Alsmearat, K., Jararweh, Y., & Gupta, B. (2018). Deep learning for Arabic NLP : A survey. *Journal of Computational Science*, 26, 522–531. doi:10.1016/j.jocs.2017.11.011

Al-Azani, S., & El-Alfy, E. (2018). Emojis-Based Sentiment Classification of Arabic Microblogs Using Deep Recurrent Neural Networks. *2018 International Conference on Computing Sciences and Engineering (ICCSE)*, 1-6. 10.1109/ICCSE1.2018.8374211

Al-badrashiny, M., Eskander, R., Habash, N., & Rambow, O. (2014). Automatic Transliteration of Romanized Dialectal Arabic. *Proceedings of the Eighteenth Conference on Computational Natural Language Learning*, 30–38. 10.3115/v1/W14-1604

AlexLuke, B., Taylor, L., & Winch, R. (2014b). *Spring Security Reference.* Retrieved December 20, 2019, from https://docs.spring.io/spring-security/site/docs/4.0.0.M1/reference/htmlsingle/#what-is-acegi-security

Alfonseca, E., Pighin, D., & Garrido, G. (2013). HEADY: News headline abstraction through event pattern clustering. In *Proceedings of the 51st Annual Meeting of the Association for Computational Linguistics* (Vol. 1, pp. 1243-1253). Association for Computational Linguistics.

Alghamdi, M. (2009). Romanizing Arabic Proper Names : Saudi Arabia Experience. *International Symposium on Arabic Transliteration Standard: Challenges and Solutions.*

Alhashmi, A. (2016). *Embedding TQM in UAE translation organizations.* QScience Connect. Retrieved from https://www.qscience.com/doi/abs/10.5339/connect.2016.tii.3

Al-Hassan, A., & Al-Dossari, H. (2019). Detection of hate speech in social networks: a survey on multilingual corpus. *6th International Conference on Computer Science and Information Technology.* 10.5121/csit.2019.90208

Al-hussaini, H., & Al-dossari, H. (2017). A Lexicon-based Approach to Build Service Provider Reputation from Arabic Tweets in Twitter. *IJACSA, 8*(4).

Ali, F., Kwak, D., Khan, P., El-Sappagh, S., Ali, A., Ullah, S., Kim, K. H., & Kwak, K. S. (2019). Transportation sentiment analysis using word embedding and ontology-based topic modeling. *Knowledge-Based Systems, 174,* 27–42. doi:10.1016/j.knosys.2019.02.033

Ali, M. (2018, August). Character level convolutional neural network for Arabic dialect identification. *Proceedings of the Fifth Workshop on NLP for Similar Languages, Varieties and Dialects (VarDial 2018),* 122-127.

Al-kabi, Gigieh, Alsmadi, & Wahsheh. (2014). *Opinion Mining and Analysis for Arabic Language.* Academic Press.

Al-Makhadmeh, Z., & Tolba, A. (2020). Automatic hate speech detection using killer natural language processing optimizing ensemble deep learning approach. *Computing, 102*(2), 501–522. doi:10.100700607-019-00745-0

Almatarneh, S., & Gamallo, P. (2018). A lexicon based method to search for extreme opinions. *PLoS One, 13*(5), 1–19. doi:10.1371/journal.pone.0197816 PMID:29799867

Alorainy, W., Burnap, P., Liu, H., & Williams, M. L. (2019). "The Enemy Among Us" Detecting Cyber Hate Speech with Threats-based Othering Language Embeddings. *ACM Transactions on the Web, 13*(3), 1–26. doi:10.1145/3324997

Alotaibi, S. S., & Anderson, C. W. (2016). Extending the Knowledge of the Arabic Sentiment Classification Using a Foreign External Lexical Source. *International Journal on Natural Language Computing, 5*(3), 1–11. doi:10.5121/ijnlc.2016.5301

Alpkoçak, A., Tocoglu, M. A., Çelikten, A., & Aygün, İ. (2019). Türkçe Metinlerde Duygu Analizi için Farklı Makine Öğrenmesi Yöntemlerinin Karşılaştırılması. *Dokuz Eylül Üniversitesi Mühendislik Fakültesi Fen ve Mühendislik Dergisi, 21*(63), 719–725. doi:10.21205/deufmd.2019216303

Al-Sabbagh, R., & Girju, R. (2010). Mining the Web for the Induction of a Dialectical Arabic Lexicon. *Language Resources and Evaluation Conference (LREC).*

Al-smadi, M., Al-zboon, S., Jararweh, Y., & Juola, P. (2020). Transfer Learning for Arabic Named Entity Recognition With Deep Neural Networks. *IEEE Access: Practical Innovations, Open Solutions, 8,* 37736–37745. doi:10.1109/ACCESS.2020.2973319

Al-smadi, M., Qawasmeh, O., Al-ayyoub, M., Jararweh, Y., & Gupta, B. (2017). Deep Recurrent neural network vs. support vector machine for aspect-based sentiment analysis of Arabic hotels' reviews. *Journal of Computational Science.* Advance online publication. doi:10.1016/j.jocs.2017.11.006

Altrabsheh, N., El-masri, M., & Mansour, H. (2017). Combining Sentiment Lexicons of Arabic Terms. *Twenty-Third Americas Conference on Information Systems*, 1–10.

Aly, M., & Atiya, A. (2013). LABR: A Large Scale Arabic Book Reviews Dataset. *Proceedings of the 51st Annual Meeting of the Association for Computational Linguistics* (Volume 2: *Short Papers*), 494–498.

Amasyalı, M. F., & Diri, B. (2006). Automatic Turkish text categorization in terms of author, genre and gender. In *International Conference on Application of Natural Language to Information Systems* (pp. 221-226). Springer. 10.1007/11765448_22

Ameur, M. H. (2019). *ANETAC.* https://github.com/MohamedHadjAmeur/ANETAC

Andrea, A. D., Ferri, F., Grifoni, P., Guzzo, T. (2015). Approaches, Tools and Applications for Sentiment Analysis Implementation. *International Journal of Computer Applications, 125*(3), 26-33.

Ansari, G., Saxena, C., Ahmad, T., & Doja, M. N. (2020). *Aspect Term Extraction using Graph-based Semi-Supervised Learning.* arXiv preprint arXiv:2003.04968

Ansari, G., Ahmad, T., & Doja, M. N. (2018). Spam review classification using ensemble of global and local feature selectors. *Cybernetics and Information Technologies, 8*(4), 29–42. doi:10.2478/cait-2018-0046

Ansari, G., Ahmad, T., & Doja, M. N. (2019). Hybrid filter–wrapper feature selection method for sentiment classification. *Arabian Journal for Science and Engineering, 44*(11), 9191–9208. doi:10.100713369-019-04064-6

Anta, A. F., Chiroque, L. N., Morere, P., & Santo, A. (2013). Sentiment analysis and topic detection of Spanish Tweets: A comparative study of NLP techniques. *Procesamiento de Lenguaje Natural, 50*, 45–52.

Aouragh, M. (2016). Social media, mediation and the Arab revolutions. *Marx in the age of digital capitalism*, 482-515.

Apache Lucene. (4.8.0) [Software]. (2014). Retrieved from https://lucene.apache.org/

Apté, C., Damerau, F., & Weiss, S. M. (1994). Automated learning of decision rules for text categorization. *ACM Transactions on Information Systems, 12*(3), 233–251. doi:10.1145/183422.183423

Arendse, B. (2016). *A thorough comparison of NLP tools for requirements quality improvement* (Master's thesis). Utrecht University.

Arnold, D., Lorna, B., Siety, M., Humphreys, R. L., & Sadler, L. (1994). *Machine translation: An introductory guide.* Blackwells-NCC.

Aronson, A. R. (2001). Effective mapping of biomedical text to the UMLS Metathesaurus: the MetaMap program. *Proceedings. AMIA Symposium*, 17–21.

Artemenko, O., Mandl, T., Shramko, M., & Womser-Hacker, C. (2006). Evaluation of a language identification system for mono-and multilingual text documents. In *Proceedings of the 2006 ACM symposium on Applied computing* (pp. 859-860). ACM. 10.1145/1141277.1141473

Artstein, R., & Poesio, M. (2008). Inter-Coder Agreement for Computational Linguistics. *Computational Linguistics, 34*(4), 555–596. doi:10.1162/coli.07-034-R2

Asghar, M. Z., Khan, A., Ahmad, S., & Kundi, F. M. (2014). A review of feature extraction in sentiment analysis. *Journal of Basic and Applied Scientific Research, 4*(3), 181–186.

Asur, S., & Huberman, B. A. (2010). Predicting the future with social media. In *Proceedings of the 2010 IEEE/WIC/ACM International Conference on Web Intelligence and Intelligent Agent Technology-Volume 01*, (pp. 492–499). IEEE Computer Society. 10.1109/WI-IAT.2010.63

Atkinson, K. (2003). *GNU Aspell*. Retrieved from http://aspell.sourceforge.net/

Attia, M. A. (2007). Arabic Tokenization System. *Proceedings of the Association of Computational Linguistics (ACL'07)*, 65–72. 10.3115/1654576.1654588

Attia, M., Pecina, P., Toral, A., Tounsi, L., & Genabith, J. V. (2011). A Lexical Database for Modern Standard Arabic Interoperable with a Finite State Morphological Transducer. *Systems and Frameworks for Computational Morphology Communications in Computer and Information Science*, 98–118.

Austermühl, F. (2007). Translators in the Language Industry – From Localization to Marginalization. In *Gebundener Sprachgebrauch in der Übersetzungswissenschaft* (pp. 39–51). Wissenschaftlicher Verlag.

Avvenuti, M., Del Vigna, F., Cresci, S., Marchetti, A., & Tesconi, M. (2015). Pulling information from social media in the aftermath of unpredictable disasters. In *2015 2nd International Conference on Information and Communication Technologies for Disaster Management (ICT-DM)*, (pp. 258-264). IEEE. 10.1109/ICT-DM.2015.7402058

Aydoğan, M., & Karci, A. (2019). Kelime Temsil Yöntemleri ile Kelime Benzerliklerinin İncelenmesi. *Çukurova Üniversitesi Mühendislik-Mimarlık Fakültesi Dergisi*, *34*(2), 181-196.

Aziz, A. A., & Tao, L. (2016). Word embeddings for Arabic sentiment analysis. *IEEE International Conference on Big Data*, *7*, 3820-3825.

Azouaou, F., & Guellil, I. (2017). A step by step construction of a lexicon between Algerian dialect and french. *The 31st Pacific Asia Conference on Language, Information and Computation PACLIC*, *31*.

Babbel Magazine. (2020). *The 10 most spoken languages in the world*. Retrieved from https://www.babbel.com/en/magazine/the-10-most-spoken-languages-in-the-world

Baccianella, S., Esuli, A., & Sebastiani, F. (2010). SentiWordNet 3.0: An enhanced lexical resource for sentiment analysis and opinion mining. *LREC*, *10*, 2200–2204.

Badaro, G., Baly, R., & Hajj, H. (2014). *A Large Scale Arabic Sentiment Lexicon for Arabic Opinion Mining*. Arabic Natural Language Processing Workshop Co-Located with EMNLP. doi:10.3115/v1/W14-3623

Badawi, E.-S., & Hinds, M. (1986). *A Dictionary of Egyptian Arabic: Arabic-English*. Librairie du Liban.

Badjatiya, P., Gupta, S., Gupta, M., & Varma, V. (2017, April). Deep learning for hate speech detection in tweets. In *Proceedings of the 26th International Conference on World Wide Web Companion* (pp. 759-760). 10.1145/3041021.3054223

Bahdanau, D., Cho, K., & Bengio, Y. (2014, September 1). *Neural Machine Translation by Jointly Learning to Align and Translate*. Retrieved from https://arxiv.org/pdf/1409.0473v7

Baker, C. F., Fillmore, C. J., & Lowe, J. B. (1998, August). The berkeley framenet project. In *Proceedings of the 17th international conference on Computational linguistics-Volume 1* (pp. 86-90). Association for Computational Linguistics.

Balaji, P., Nagaraju, O., & Haritha, D. (2017). Levels of sentiment analysis and its challenges: A literature review. In *Proceedings of the 2017 International Conference on Big Data Analytics and Computational Intelligence (ICBDAC)* (pp. 436–439). IEEE. 10.1109/ICBDACI.2017.8070879

Barriga, R. (2018). *De Babel a Pentecostés. Políticas lingüísticas y lenguas indígenas, entre historias, paradojas y testimonios*. Secretaría de Educación Pública, Gobierno de México.

Bechara, A., Damasio, H., & Damasio, A. R. (2000). Emotion, decision making and the orbitofrontal cortex. *Cerebral Cortex (New York, N.Y.)*, *10*(3), 295–307. doi:10.1093/cercor/10.3.295 PMID:10731224

Beigi, G., Hu, X., Maciejewski, R., & Liu, H. (2016). An overview of sentiment analysis in social media and its applications in disaster relief. Sentiment analysis and ontology engineering, 313-340.

Béjoint, H. (2000). *Modern lexicography: An introduction*. Oxford: Oxford University Press.

Bekkerman, R., El-Yaniv, R., Tishby, N., & Winter, Y. (2001). On feature distributional clustering for text categorization. *Proceedings of the 24th annual international ACM SIGIR conference on Research and development in information retrieval*, 146-153. 10.1145/383952.383976

Bel, N., & Rigau, G. (2015). *Informe sobre el estado de las tecnologías del lenguaje en España dentro de la Agenda Digital para España*. Madrid: Secretaría de Estado de Telecomunicaciones y para la Sociedad de la Información, Gobierno de España. www.plantl.gob.es/tecnologias-lenguaje/PTL/Paginas/plan-impulso-tecnologias-lenguaje.aspx

Bengio, Y., Courville, A., & Vincent, P. (2013). Representation Learning: A Review and New Perspectives. *IEEE Transactions on Pattern Analysis and Machine Intelligence*, *35*(8), 1798–1828. doi:10.1109/TPAMI.2013.50 PMID:23787338

Benítez, F. (1998). *Los indios de México. Antología*. Ediciones Era.

Benson, E., Haghighi, A., & Barzilay, R. (2011). Event Discovery in Social Media Feeds. In *Proceedings of the 49th Annual Meeting of the Association for Computational Linguistics: Human Language Technologies*, (pp. 389-398). Association for Computational Linguistics.

Berry, M. W. (2004). Survey of text mining. *Computer Review*, *45*(9), 548.

Bhuta, S., Doshi, A., Doshi, U., & Narvekar, M. (2014). A Review of Techniques for Sentiment Analysis Of Twitter Data. *2014 International Conference on Issues and Challenges in Intelligent Computing Techniques (ICICT)*, 583-591. 10.1109/ICICICT.2014.6781346

Bird, S., Klein, E., & Loper, E. (2009). *Natural Language Processing with Python – Analyzing Text with the Natural Language Toolkit*. O'Reilly Media.

Birke, J., & Sarkar, A. (2006). A clustering approach for nearly unsupervised recognition of nonliteral language. 11th Conference of the European Chapter of the Association for Computational Linguistics, 329–336.

Bishop, C. M. (2006). *Pattern recognition and machine learning*. Springer-Verlag New York.

Blei, D. M., Ng, A. Y., & Jordan, M. I. (2003). Latent dirichlet allocation. *Journal of Machine Learning Research*, *3*(Jan), 993–1022.

Blitzer, J., McDonald, R., & Pereira, F. (2006). Domain Adaptation with Structural Correspondence Learning. In *EMNLP '06, Proceedings of the 2006 Conference on Empirical Methods in Natural Language Processing* (pp. 120–128). Association for Computational Linguistics. doi:10.3115/1610075.1610094

Bloem, C. (2017, July 31). *84 Percent of People Trust Online Reviews As Much As Friends. Here's How to Manage What They See*. Retrieved from https://www.inc.com/craig-bloem/84-percent-of-people-trust-online-reviews-as-much-.html

Bogaert, van den J. (2008). Terminology and Translation Quality Assurance. *Revista Tradumatica, 6*, 1-10.

Bojanowski, P., Grave, E., Joulin, A., & Mikolov, T. (2017). Enriching Word Vectors with Subword Information. *Transactions of the Association for Computational Linguistics*, *5*, 135–146. doi:10.1162/tacl_a_00051

Bollegala, D., & Shutova, E. (2013). Metaphor interpretation using paraphrases extracted from the web. *PLoS One*, *8*(9), e74304. doi:10.1371/journal.pone.0074304 PMID:24073207

Bolon-Canedo, V., Sanchez-Marono, N., Alonso-Betanzos, A., Benitez, J. M., & Herrera, F. (2014). A review of microarray datasets and applied feature selection methods. *Information Sciences*, *282*, 111–135. doi:10.1016/j.ins.2014.05.042

Bontcheva, K., Derczynski, L., Funk, A., Greenwood, M. A., Maynard, D., & Aswani, N. (2013). TwitIE: An open-source information extraction pipeline for microblog text. *International Conference Recent Advances in Natural Language Processing (RANLP)*, 83-90.

Bordagaray, M., dell'Olio, L., Fonzone, A., & Ibeas, Á. (2016). Capturing the conditions that introduce systematic variation in bike-sharing travel behavior using data mining techniques. *Transportation Research Part C, Emerging Technologies*, *71*, 231–248. doi:10.1016/j.trc.2016.07.009

Bouamor, H., Habash, N., Salameh, M., Zaghouani, W., Rambow, O., Abdulrahim, D., ... Oflazer, K. (2018). The MADAR Arabic dialect corpus and lexicon. *Proceedings of the Eleventh International Conference on Language Resources and Evaluation (LREC 2018)*.

Boudad, N., Faizi, R., Oulad, R., Thami, H., & Chiheb, R. (2017). Sentiment analysis in Arabic: A review of the literature. *Ain Shams Engineering Journal*, *9*(July), 2479–2490. doi:10.1016/j.asej.2017.04.007

Bougrine, S., Cherroun, H., & Abdelali, A. (2017). Altruistic Crowdsourcing for Arabic Speech Corpus Annotation. *ACLing*, *117*(November), 133–144. doi:10.1016/j.procs.2017.10.102

Boujelbane, R., BenAyed, S., & Hadrich Belguith, L. (2013). *Building bilingual lexicon to create Dialect Tunisian corpora and adapt language model*. ACL.

Braga, A. P., Ferreira, A. C. P. L., & Ludermir, T. B. (2007). *Redes neurais artificiais: teoria e aplicações*. LTC Editora.

Brandom, R. (2018, Sep 21). *PayPal bans Infowars for promoting hate*. Retrieved from https://www.theverge.com/2018/9/21/17887138/paypal-infowars-ban-alex-jones-hate-speech-deplatform

Brasil, S., Pascoal, C., Francisco, R., Ferreira, V. D. R., Videira, P. A., & Valadão, G. (2019). Artificial intelligence (AI) in rare diseases: Is the future brighter? *Genes*, *10*(12), 978. doi:10.3390/genes10120978 PMID:31783696

Bravo-Marquez, F., Frank, E., & Pfahringer, B. (2016). Building a Twitter opinion lexicon from automatically-annotated tweets. *Knowledge-Based Systems*, *108*, 65–78. doi:10.1016/j.knosys.2016.05.018

Brkić, M., Matetić, M., & Seljan, S. (2011a). Towards Obtaining High Quality Sentence-Aligned English-Croatian Parallel Corpus. Computer Science and Information Technology ICCSIT, 1068-1070.

Brkić, M., Seljan, S., & Bašić Mikulić, B. (2009). Using Translation Memory to Speed up Translation Process. *Proceedings of INFuture2009 - Digital Resources and Knowledge Sharing*, 353-363.

Brkić, M., Seljan, S., & Matetić, M. (2011b). Machine Translation Evaluation for Croatian-English and English-Croatian Language Pairs. *Proceedings of the 8th International NLPCS Workshop: Human-Machine Interaction in Translation*, 93-104.

Bruno, N. (2011). *Tweet first, verify later? How real-time information is changing the coverage of worldwide crisis events*. Retrieved June 1, 2020, from https://reutersinstitute.politics.ox.ac.uk/our-research/tweet-first-verify-later-how-real-time-information-changing-coverage-worldwide-crisis

Buchanan, M. (2008). This economy does not compute. *New York Times, 1.*

Buchkremer, R., Demund, A., Ebener, S., Gampfer, F., Jagering, D., Jurgens, A., Klenke, S., Krimpmann, D., Schmank, J., Spiekermann, M., Wahlers, M., & Wiepke, M. (2019). The Application of Artificial Intelligence Technologies as a Substitute for Reading and to Support and Enhance the Authoring of Scientific Review Articles. *IEEE Access: Practical Innovations, Open Solutions, 7*(c), 65263–65276. doi:10.1109/ACCESS.2019.2917719

Buck, D., & Buehler, R. (2012). Bike lanes and other determinants of capital bikeshare trips. *Proceedings of the 91st Transportation Research Board Annual Meeting.*

Buck, D., Buehler, R., Happ, P., Rawls, B., Chung, P., & Borecki, N. (2013). Are bikeshare users different from regular cyclists? A first look at short-term users, annual members, and area cyclists in the Washington, DC, region. *Transportation Research Record: Journal of the Transportation Research Board, 2387*(1), 112–119. doi:10.3141/2387-13

Buckwalter, T. (2004). *Buckwalter Arabic Morphological Analyzer Version 2.0* (LDC Catalog No: LDC2004L02). Retrieved from https://catalog.ldc.upenn.edu/LDC2004L02

Buckwalter, T. (n.d.). *Arabic Transliteration.* Retrieved December 18, 2019, from http://www.qamus.org/transliteration.htm

Bugmann, G. (1998). Normalized Gaussian radial basis function networks. *Neurocomputing, 20*(1-3), 97–110. doi:10.1016/S0925-2312(98)00027-7

Burnap, P., & Williams, M. L. (2014). *Hate speech, machine classification and statistical modelling of information flows on Twitter: Interpretation and communication for policy decision making.* Academic Press.

Burnap, P., & Williams, M. L. (2016). Us and them: Identifying cyber hate on Twitter across multiple protected characteristics. *EPJ Data Science, 5*(1), 11. doi:10.1140/epjds13688-016-0072-6 PMID:32355598

Buscapé. (2016). Retrieved September 28, 2016, from https://www.buscape.com.br/

Cabezudo, M. A. S., Palomino, N. L. S., & Perez, R. M. (2015). Improving subjectivity detection for Spanish texts using subjectivity word sense disambiguation based on knowledge. In *2015 Latin American Computing Conference (CLEI)* (pp. 1-7). IEEE. 10.1109/CLEI.2015.7360018

Cadez, I., Heckerman, D., Meek, C., Smyth, P., & White, S. (2003). Model-based clustering and visualization of navigation patterns on a web site. *Data Mining and Knowledge Discovery, 7*(4), 399–424. doi:10.1023/A:1024992613384

Cambria, E. (2016). Affective computing and sentiment analysis. *IEEE Intelligent Systems, 31*(2), 102–107. doi:10.1109/MIS.2016.31

Camilleri, S., Agius, M. R., & Azzopardi, J. (2020). Analysis of online news coverage on earthquakes through text mining. *Frontiers of Earth Science, 8*(141).

Camilleri, S., Azzopardi, J., & Agius, M. R. (2019). Investigating the relationship between earthquakes and online news. *2019 IEEE Second International Conference on Artificial Intelligence and Knowledge Engineering*, 203-210. 10.1109/AIKE.2019.00043

Carreón, E. C. A., Nonaka, H., & Hiraoka, T. (2019). *Analysis of Chinese Tourists in Japan by Text Mining of a Hotel Portal Site.* arXiv preprint arXiv:1904.13214.

Casas, R. (2004). Conocimiento, tecnologia y desarrollo en America Latina. *Revista Mexicana de Sociologia, 66*, 255–277. doi:10.2307/3541453

Catrileo, M. (2005). Revitalización de la lengua mapuche en Chile. *Documentos Lingüísticos y Literarios, 28*, 10–17.

Cayuqueo, P. (2017). *Historia secreta mapuche*. Catalonia.

CDFCTI. (2019). *Inteligencia artificial en Chile. La urgencia de desarrollar una estrategia*. Santiago de Chile. Gobierno de Chile: https://eia.bcn.cl/images/c/c1/Inteligencia_Artificial_para_Chile.pdf

Cellan-Jones, R. (2017, 20 March). *Google's crisis of confidence*. Retrieved from https://www.bbc.com/news/technology-39331204

Çetin, M., & Amasyalı, M. F. (2013). Supervised and traditional term weighting methods for sentiment analysis. In *2013 21st Signal Processing and Communications Applications Conference (SIU)* (pp. 1-4). IEEE. 10.1109/SIU.2013.6531173

Chalothom, T., & Ellman, J. (2015). Simple approaches of sentiment analysis via ensemble learning. Information Science and Applications, 631-639.

Chandía, A. (2012). *Dungupeyem1_alfa2_v0.1: un prototipo de analizador morfológico para el mapudüngun a través de transductores de estados finitos* (Master Thesis). Barcelona, Catalunya, Spain. Universitat Pompeu Fabra.

Chandni, Chandra, N., Gupta, S., & Pahade, R. (2015). Sentiment analysis and its challenges. *International Journal of Engineering Research & Technology (Ahmedabad)*, *4*(3), 968–970.

Chandrashekar, G., & Sahin, F. (2014). A survey on feature selection methods. *Computers & Electrical Engineering*, *40*(1), 16–28. doi:10.1016/j.compeleceng.2013.11.024

Chen, Y., Zhou, Y., Zhu, S., & Xu, H. (2012, September). Detecting offensive language in social media to protect adolescent online safety. In *2012 International Conference on Privacy, Security, Risk and Trust and 2012 International Conference on Social Computing* (pp. 71-80). IEEE. 10.1109/SocialCom-PASSAT.2012.55

Cheng, X., Xu, W., & Wang, T., Chu, W., Huang, W., Chen, K., & Hu, J. (2019). Variational Semi-Supervised Aspect-Term Sentiment Analysis via Transformer. In *Proceedings of the 23rd Conference on Computational Natural Language Learning (CoNLL)* (pp. 961–969). Hong Kong, China: Association for Computational Linguistics. 10.18653/v1/K19-1090

Chen, L., Chen, G., & Wang, F. (2015). Recommender systems based on user reviews: The state of the art. *User Modeling and User-Adapted Interaction*, *25*(2), 99–154. doi:10.100711257-015-9155-5

Chen, M., Li, W., Fortino, G., Hao, Y., Hu, L., & Humar, I. (2019). A dynamic service migration mechanism in edge cognitive computing. *ACM Transactions on Internet Technology*, *19*(2), 1–15. doi:10.1145/3239565

Chen, P., Sun, Z., Bing, L., & Yang, W. (2017). Recurrent Attention Network on Memory for Aspect Sentiment Analysis. In *Proceedings of the 2017 Conference on Empirical Methods in Natural Language Processing* (pp. 452–461). Copenhagen, Denmark: Association for Computational Linguistics. 10.18653/v1/D17-1047

Chen, X., Qiu, X., Zhu, C., & Huang, X. J. (2015). Gated recursive neural network for Chinese word segmentation. *Proceedings of the 53rd Annual Meeting of the Association for Computational Linguistics and the 7th International Joint Conference on Natural Language Processing*, *1*, 1744-1753. 10.3115/v1/P15-1168

Chen, Y., Argentinis, J. E., & Weber, G. (2016). IBM Watson: How cognitive computing can be applied to big data challenges in life sciences research. *Clinical Therapeutics*, *38*(4), 688–701. doi:10.1016/j.clinthera.2015.12.001 PMID:27130797

Chen, Y., Qin, B., Liu, T., Liu, Y., & Li, S. (2010). The Comparison of SOM and K-means for Text Clustering. *Computer and Information Science*, *3*(2), 268–274. doi:10.5539/cis.v3n2p268

Chetty, N., & Alathur, S. (2018). Hate speech review in the context of online social networks. *Aggression and Violent Behavior*, *40*, 108–118. doi:10.1016/j.avb.2018.05.003

Chiocchetti, E., Wissik, T., Lušicky, V., & Wetzel, M. (2017). Quality assurance in multilingual legal terminological databases. *The Journal of Specialised Translation*, *27*, 164–188.

Choi, W., Choi, S. J., Park, S., & Lee, S. (2019). Adversarial Style Transfer for Long Sentences. *2019 International Conference on Electronics, Information, and Communication (ICEIC)*. 10.23919/ELINFOCOM.2019.8706482

Cho, K., van Merriënboer, B., Bahdanau, D., & Bengio, Y. (2014). On the Properties of Neural Machine Translation: Encoder-Decoder Approaches. In *Proceedings of SSST-8, Eighth Workshop on Syntax, Semantics and Structure in Statistical Translation* (pp. 103–111). Doha, Qatar: Association for Computational Linguistics. 10.3115/v1/W14-4012

Christen, M., Boulding, W., & Staelin, R. (2009). Optimal market intelligence strategy when management attention is scarce. *Management Science*, *55*(4), 526–538. doi:10.1287/mnsc.1080.0988

Christy Daniel, D., & Shyamala, L. (2019). An insight on sentiment analysis research from text using deep learning methods. *International Journal of Innovative Technology and Exploring Engineering*, *8*(10), 2033–2048. doi:10.35940/ijitee.J9316.0881019

Çiğdem, A., & Çirak, A. (2019). Türkçe Haber Metinlerinin Konvolüsyonel Sinir Ağları ve Word2Vec Kullanılarak Sınıflandırılması. *Bilişim Teknolojileri Dergisi*, *12*(3), 219–228.

Citron, D. T., & Ginsparg, P. (2015). Patterns of text reuse in a scientific corpus. *Proceedings of the National Academy of Sciences of the United States of America*, *112*(1), 25–30. doi:10.1073/pnas.1415135111 PMID:25489072

Clark, J., Koprinska, I., & Poon, J. (2003). A neural network-based approach to automated e-mail classification. In *Proceedings IEEE/WIC International Conference on Web Intelligence (WI 2003)* (pp. 702-705). IEEE. 10.1109/WI.2003.1241300

Clement, J. (2019). *Share of adults in the United States who use the internet in 2019, by age group*. Retrieved from https://www.statista.com/statistics/266587/percentage-of-internet-users-by-age-groups-in-the-us/

Collomb, A., Costea, C., Joyeux, D., Hasan, O., & Brunie, L. (2014). A study and comparison of sentiment analysis methods for reputation evaluation. *Rapport de recherche RR-LIRIS-2014-002*.

Cooper, P. (2019). *28 Twitter Statistics All Marketers Need to Know in 2019*. Retrieved from https://blog.hootsuite.com/twitter-statistics/

Cooper, M. C., Lambert, D. M., & Pagh, J. D. (1997). Supply Chain Management: More Than a New Name for Logistics. *International Journal of Logistics Management*, *8*(1), 1–14. doi:10.1108/09574099710805556

Cortes, C., & Vapnik, V. (1995). Support Vector Machine. *Machine Learning*, *20*(3), 273–297. doi:10.1007/BF00994018

Cotterell, R., & Callison-Burch, C. (2014). A multi-dialect, multi-genre corpus of informal written Arabic. *Proceedings of the Ninth International Conference on Language Resources and Evaluation (LREC'14)*, 241–245.

Coughlin, D. (2003). Correlating automated and human assessments of machine translation quality. *Proceedings of MT Summit*, *9*, 23–27.

Crystal, D. (2014). *Language Death*. Cambridge University Press. doi:10.1017/CBO9781139923477

Cummins, N., Amiriparian, S., Ottl, S., Gerczuk, M., Schmitt, M., & Schuller, B. (2018). Multimodal Bag-of-Words for Cross Domains Sentiment Analysis. In *ICASSP-2018, Proceedings of the 2018 IEEE International Conference on Acoustics, Speech and Signal Processing (ICASSP)* (pp. 4954–4958). IEEE. 10.1109/ICASSP.2018.8462660

Cunha, T. M. D. (2013). *A criação de um sistema híbrido de tradução automática para a conversão de expressões nominais da língua inglesa*. Academic Press.

Cunha, T. M. D., & Silva, P. B. L. D. (2015a, November). A Criação de um Corpus de Sentenças Através de Gramáticas Livres de Contexto. In *Anais do X Simpósio Brasileiro de Tecnologia da Informação e da Linguagem Humana* (pp. 241–248). SBC.

Cunha, T. M. D., & Soares, D. D. F. B. (2015b, November). A Utilização de Atos de Diálogo em Sistemas de Diálogo para Dispositivos Móveis. In *Anais do X Simpósio Brasileiro de Tecnologia da Informação e da Linguagem Humana* (pp. 225–232). SBC.

Cutting, D. R., Karger, D. R., Pedersen, J. O., & Tukey, J. W. (2017). Scatter/gather: A cluster-based approach to browsing large document collections. In *ACM SIGIR Forum* (Vol. 51, No. 2, pp. 148-159). New York, NY: ACM.

Czopik, J. (2014). Quality Assurance process in translation. *Translating and Computer*, *36*, 77–85.

Dahou, A., Xiong, S., Zhou, J., Haddoud, M. H., & Duan, P. (2016). Word embeddings and convolutional neural network for Arabic sentiment classification. *The 26th International Conference on Computational Linguistics (COLING 2016)*, 2418-2427.

Dai, Z., & Yang, Z., Yang, Y., Carbonell, J., Le, Q., & Salakhutdinov, R. (2019). Transformer-XL: Attentive Language Models beyond a Fixed-Length Context. In *Proceedings of the 57th Annual Meeting of the Association for Computational Linguistics* (pp. 2978–2988). Florence, Italy: Association for Computational Linguistics. 10.18653/v1/P19-1285

Dalgleish, T., & Power, M. (2000). *Handbook of cognition and emotion*. John Wiley & Sons.

Danesi, M. (2002). *The puzzle instinct: The meaning of puzzles in human life*. Indiana University Press.

Danowski, J. A. (2012). Sentiment network analysis of taleban and RFE/RL open-source content about Afghanistan. *Open-Source Intelligence and Web Mining Conference [OSINT-WM], August*, 303–310. 10.1109/EISIC.2012.54

Dasgupta, S., & Ng, V. (2009). Topic-wise, sentiment-wise, or otherwise?: Identifying the hidden dimension for unsupervised text classification. In *Proceedings of the 2009 Conference on Empirical Methods in Natural Language Processing* (vol. 2, pp. 580-589). Association for Computational Linguistics.

Dash, M., & Liu, H. (1997). Feature selection for classification. *Intelligent Data Analysis*, *1*(1-4), 131–156. doi:10.1016/S1088-467X(97)00008-5

DataReportal. (2020). *Digital 2020 report for Turkey*. Retrieved from https://datareportal.com/reports/digital-2020-turkey

Davidson, T., Bhattacharya, D., & Weber, I. (2019). *Racial bias in hate speech and abusive language detection datasets*. arXiv preprint arXiv:1905.12516

Davitz, J. R. (2016). *The language of emotion*. Academic Press.

Della Pietra, S., Della Pietra, V., & Lafferty, J. (1997). Inducing features of random fields. *IEEE Transactions on Pattern Analysis and Machine Intelligence*, *19*(4), 380–393. doi:10.1109/34.588021

Deng, D., Jing, L., Yu, J., & Sun, S. (2019). Sparse Self-Attention LSTM for Sentiment Lexicon Construction. *IEEE/ACM Transactions on Audio, Speech, and Language Processing*, *27*(11), 1777–1790. doi:10.1109/TASLP.2019.2933326

Deng, L. (2014). A tutorial survey of architectures, algorithms, and applications for deep learning. *APSIPA Transactions on Signal and Information Processing*, *3*, 3. doi:10.1017/atsip.2013.9

Denkowski, M., & Lavie, A. (2011). Meteor 1.3: Automatic metric for reliable optimization and evaluation of machine translation systems. *Proceedings of the Sixth Workshop on Statistical Machine Translation*, 85-91.

Derczynski, L., Ritter, A., Clark, S., & Bontcheva, K. (2013). Twitter part-of-speech tagging for all: Overcoming sparse and noisy data. In *Proceedings of Recent Advances in Natural Language Processing* (pp. 198–206). Association for Computational Linguistics.

Desai, M., & Mehta, M. A. (2016). Techniques for Sentiment Analysis of Twitter Data: A Comprehensive Survey. *International Conference on Computing, Communication and Automation (ICCCA2016)*, 149-154. 10.1109/CCAA.2016.7813707

Desjardins, J. (2019). *What Happens in an Internet Minute in 2019?* Retrieved from https://www.visualcapitalist.com/what-happens-in-an-internet-minute-in-2019/

Devlin, J., Chang, M.-W., Lee, K., & Toutanova, K. (2018). *BERT: Pre-training of Deep Bidirectional Transformers for Language Understanding.* CoRR, abs/1810.04805

Diab, M., Al-Badrashiny, M., Aminian, M., Attia, M., Dasigi, P., & Elfardy, H. (2014). Tharwa: A Large Scale Dialectal Arabic-Standard Arabic-English Lexicon. *Proceedings of the Language Resources and Evaluation Conference (LREC).*

Dias-da-Silva, B. C. (2010). Brazilian Portuguese WordNet: A computational-linguistic exercise of encoding bilingual relational lexicons. *International Journal of Computational Linguistics and Applications, 1*(1-2), 137–150.

Digital Commerce 360. (2014). Retrieved August 18, 2016, from https://www.internetretailer.com/commentary/2014/12/04/how-many-online-stores-are-there-world?p=1

Dillinger, J. (2019, September 6). *List Of Countries By Internet Users.* Retrieved from https://www.worldatlas.com/articles/the-20-countries-with-the-most-internet-users.html

Djoudi, M., Fohr, D., & Haton, J.-P. (1989). Phonetic study for automatic recognition of Arabic. *First European Conference on Speech Communication and Technology, EUROSPEECH*, 268–271.

Djoudi, M., & Harous, S. (2008). Text Entry System for Semitic Languages on Mobile Devices. In *Handbook of Research on Mobile Multimedia* (pp. 772–782). IGI Global.

Doddington, G. (2002). Automatic evaluation of machine translation quality using n-gram co-occurrence statistics. *Proceedings of the Second international conference on Human Language Technology Research*, 138-145. 10.3115/1289189.1289273

Dogan, T., & Uysal, A. K. (2019). On Term Frequency Factor in Supervised Term Weighting Schemes for Text Classification. *Arabian Journal for Science and Engineering, 44*(11), 1–16. doi:10.100713369-019-03920-9

Dos Santos, C., & Gatti, M. (2014). Deep convolutional neural networks for sentiment analysis of short texts. In *Proceedings of COLING 2014, the 25th International Conference on Computational Linguistics: Technical Papers* (pp. 69-78). Academic Press.

Dragusin, R., Petcu, P., Lioma, C., Larsen, B., Jørgensen, H., & Winther, O. (2011). Rare Disease Diagnosis as an Information Retrieval Task. In C. F. Amati G. (Ed.), Advances in Information Retrieval Theory. ICTIR 2011; Lecture Notes in Computer Science, vol 6931 (pp. 356–359). Springer Berlin Heidelberg. doi:10.1007/978-3-642-23318-0_38

Dragusin, R., Petcu, P., Lioma, C., Larsen, B., Jørgensen, H. L., Cox, I. J., Hansen, L. K., Ingwersen, P., & Winther, O. (2013). FindZebra: A search engine for rare diseases. *International Journal of Medical Informatics, 82*(6), 528–538. doi:10.1016/j.ijmedinf.2013.01.005 PMID:23462700

Duan, X., Zhou, Y., Jing, C., Zhang, L., & Chen, R. (2018). Cross-domain Sentiment Classification Based on Transfer Learning and Adversarial Network. In *Proceedings of the 2018 IEEE 4th International Conference on Computer and Communications (ICCC)* (pp. 2302–2306). IEEE. 10.1109/CompComm.2018.8780771

Du, C., Tsai, M., & Wang, C. (2019). Beyond Word-level to Sentence-level Sentiment Analysis for Financial Reports. *Proceedings of the 2019 IEEE International Conference on Acoustics, Speech and Signal Processing (ICASSP)*. 10.1109/ICASSP.2019.8683085

Duch, W., & Jankowski, N. (1999). Survey of neural transfer functions. *Neural Computing Surveys, 2*(1), 163-212.

Duh, K., & Kirchhoff, K. (2006). Lexicon acquisition for dialectal Arabic using transductive learning. In *Proceedings of the 2006 Conference on Empirical Methods in Natural Language Processing*. Association for Computational Linguistics. 10.3115/1610075.1610131

Du, J., Gui, L., Xu, R., & He, Y. (2018). A Convolutional Attention Model for Text Classification. In X. Huang, J. Jiang, D. Zhao, Y. Feng, & Y. Hong (Eds.), Lecture Notes in Computer Science: Vol. 10619. *Natural Language Processing and Chinese Computing* (pp. 183–195). Springer International Publishing. doi:10.1007/978-3-319-73618-1_16

Dunđer, I., Seljan, S., & Pavlovski, M. (2020). Automatic Machine Translation of Poetry and a Low-Resource Language Pair. *Proceedings of MIPRO 2020: Intelligent Systems*. (in press)

Duwairi, R. M., Alfaqeh, M., Wardat, M., & Alrabadi, A. (2016). Sentiment analysis for Arabizi text. 7th International Conference on Information and Communication Systems, ICICS, 127–132. 10.1109/IACS.2016.7476098

Duwairi, R., Marji, R., Sha'ban, N., & Rushaidat, S. (2014). Sentiment Analysis in Arabic tweets. *The 5th International Conference on. IEEE in Information and Communication Systems (ICICS)*. 10.1109/IACS.2014.6841964

Dyson, L., Grant, S., & Hendriks, M. (2016). *Indigenous People and Mobile Technology*. Routledge.

Dyson, L., Hendriks, M., & Grant, S. (2007). *Information Technology and Indigenous People*. Information Science Publishing. doi:10.4018/978-1-59904-298-5

Ebrahimi, M., Yazdavar, A. H., & Sheth, A. (2017). Challenges of sentiment analysis for dynamic events. *IEEE Intelligent Systems, 32*(5), 70–75. doi:10.1109/MIS.2017.3711649

Egan, J. (2020). Marketing communications. SAGE Publications Ltd.

Ekman, P. (1984). Expression and the nature of emotion. *Approaches to Emotion, 3*(19), 344.

Ekman, P. (1999). Basic emotions. Handbook of Cognition and Emotion, 98(45-60), 16.

El-Assi, W., Mahmoud, M. S., & Habib, K. N. (2017). Effects of built environment and weather on bike sharing demand: A station level analysis of commercial bike sharing in Toronto. *Transportation, 44*(3), 589–613. doi:10.100711116-015-9669-z

El-Beltagy, S. R. (2016, May). NileULex: a phrase and word level sentiment lexicon for Egyptian and modern standard Arabic. In *Proceedings of the Tenth International Conference on Language Resources and Evaluation (LREC'16)* (pp. 2900-2905). Academic Press.

El-Beltagy, S. R., & Ali, A. (2013). Open issues in the sentiment analysis of Arabic social media: A case study. *2013 9th International Conference on Innovations in Information Technology (IIT)*, 215-220. 10.1109/Innovations.2013.6544421

El-Beltagy, S. R. (2016). NileULex: A Phrase and Word Level Sentiment Lexicon for Egyptian and Modern Standard Arabic. *Proceedings of Tenth International Conference on Language Resources and Evaluation (LREC)*, 2900–2905.

El-Haj, M., Rayson, P., & Aboelezz, M. (2018, May). Arabic dialect identification in the context of bivalency and code-switching. In *Proceedings of the 11th International Conference on Language Resources and Evaluation*, (pp. 3622-3627). European Language Resources Association.

El-Kilany, A., Azzam, A., & El-Beltagy, S. R. (2018). Using deep neural networks for extracting sentiment targets in arabic tweets. *Studies in Computational Intelligence, 740*, 3–15. doi:10.1007/978-3-319-67056-0_1

Elnagar, A., Khalifa, Y. S., & Einea, A. (2018). Hotel Arabic-Reviews Dataset Construction for Sentiment Analysis Applications. *Intelligent Natural Language Processing: Trends and Applications*, 35–52.

Elnagar, A., Al-Debsi, R., & Einea, O. (2020). Arabic text classification using deep learning models. *Information Processing & Management, 57*(1), 102121. doi:10.1016/j.ipm.2019.102121

ElSahar, H., & El-Beltagy, S. R. (2015). Building Large Arabic Multi-domain Resources for Sentiment Analysis. *International Conference on Intelligent Text Processing and Computational Linguistics*, 23–34. 10.1007/978-3-319-18117-2_2

Elshakankery, K., & Ahmed, M. F. (2019). HILATSA: A hybrid Incremental learning approach for Arabic tweets sentiment analysis. Egyptian Informatics Journal, 1–9. doi:10.1016/j.eij.2019.03.002

Eryiğit, G. (2014). ITU Turkish NLP web service. In *Proceedings of the Demonstrations at the 14th Conference of the European Chapter of the Association for Computational Linguistics* (pp. 1-4). Academic Press.

Estival, D., Gaustad, T., Pham, S. B., Radford, W., & Hutchinson, B. (2007). Author profiling for English emails. In *Proceedings of the 10th Conference of the Pacific Association for Computational Linguistics* (pp. 263-272). Academic Press.

Esuli, A., & Sebastiani, F. (2006). Sentiwordnet: A publicly available lexical resource for opinion mining. *LREC, 6*, 417–422.

European Commission – Directorate-General for Translation. (2009). *Programme for Quality Management in Translation: 22 Quality Actions*. Retrieved from http://www.termcoord.eu/wp-content/uploads/2017/ 07/Programme-for-Quality-Management-in-Translation.pdf

European Commission. (2018). *Mobility and Transport*. Retrieved from https://ec.europa.eu/transport/themes/sustainable_en

Evgeniou, T., & Pontil, M. (2001). *Support Vector Machines: Theory and Applications* (Vol. 2049). Springer. doi:10.1007/3-540-44673-7_12

Facebook. (2019). *Facebook Reports Second Quarter 2019 Results*. Retrieved from https://investor.fb.com/investor-news/press-release-details/2019/Facebook-Reports-Second-Quarter-2019-Results/default.aspx

Faculty. (2020). *Applying NLP to news articles to trace business sentiment*. Retrieved June 1, 2020 from https://faculty.ai/ourwork/applying-nlp-to-news-articles-to-trace-business-sentiment/

Fadel, A., Tuffaha, I., Al-jawarneh, B., & Al-Ayyoub, M. (2019). Arabic Text Diacritization Using Deep Neural Networks. *International Conference on Computer Applications & Information Security*, 2–9. 10.1109/CAIS.2019.8769512

Faghfoury, H., Baruteau, J., Ogier de Baulny, H., Häberle, J., & Schulze, A. (2011). Transient fulminant liver failure as an initial presentation in citrullinemia type I. *Molecular Genetics and Metabolism, 102*(4), 413–417. doi:10.1016/j.ymgme.2010.12.007 PMID:21227727

Fainsilber, L., & Ortony, A. (1987). Metaphorical uses of language in the expression of emotions. *Metaphor and Symbol, 2*(4), 239–250. doi:10.120715327868ms0204_2

Falagas, M. E., Ntziora, F., Makris, G. C., Malietzis, G. A., & Rafailidis, P. I. (2009). Do PubMed and Google searches help medical students and young doctors reach the correct diagnosis? A pilot study. *European Journal of Internal Medicine, 20*(8), 788–790. doi:10.1016/j.ejim.2009.07.014 PMID:19892310

Fang, H., Wu, F., Zhao, Z., Duan, X., Zhuang, Y., & Ester, M. (2016). Community-based question answering via heterogeneous social network learning. In *Proceedings of the Thirtieth AAAI Conference on Artificial Intelligence*, (pp. 122-128). AAAI Press.

Farasa. (n.d.). http://alt.qcri.org/farasa/

Farghaly, A., & Shaalan, K. (2009). Arabic natural language processing : Challenges and solutions. *ACM Transactions on Asian Language Information Processing*, 8(4), 1–22. doi:10.1145/1644879.1644881

Fattah, M. A., & Ren, F. (2008). Automatic text summarization. *World Academy of Science, Engineering and Technology*, 37(2), 192.

Federico, M., Cattelan, A., & Trombetti, M. (2012). Measuring User Productivity in Machine Translation Enhanced Computer Assisted Translation. *Proceedings of AMTA 2012*.

Fellbaum, C. (Ed.). (1998). WordNet: An Electronic Lexical Database. Cambridge, MA: MIT Press.

Feng, W., & Wang, J. (2012). Incorporating Heterogeneous Information for Personalized Tag Recommendation in Social Tagging Systems. In *Proceedings of the 18th ACM SIGKDD international conference on Knowledge discovery and data mining*, (pp. 1276-1284). Association for Computing Machinery. 10.1145/2339530.2339729

Ferguson, C. A. (1959). Diglossia. *Word*, 15(2), 325–340. doi:10.1080/00437956.1959.11659702

Florescano, E. (1997). *Etnia, estado y nación: Ensayo sobre las identidades colectivas en México*. Aguilar.

Forman, G. (2003). An extensive empirical study of feature selection metrics for text classification. *Journal of Machine Learning Research*, 3, 1289–1305.

Fortuna, P., & Nunes, S. (2018). A survey on automatic detection of hate speech in text. *ACM Computing Surveys*, 51(4), 1–30. doi:10.1145/3232676

Franco, W., Gomes, T. C. J. P. P., Castro, R., Andrade, R. M., & Castro, M. F. (2014). *Example-based dialog modeling for a mobile system*. Academic Press.

Frank, E., & Bouckaert, R. R. (2006). Naive bayes for text classification with unbalanced classes. In *Proceedings of 10th European Conference on Principles & Practice of Knowledge Discovery in Databases* (vol. 4213). 10.1007/11871637_49

Fu, X., Wei, Y., Xu, F., Wang, T., Lu, Y., Li, J., & Huang, J. Z. (2019). Semi-supervised Aspect-level Sentiment Classification Model based on Variational Autoencoder. *Knowledge-Based Systems*, 171, 81–92. doi:10.1016/j.knosys.2019.02.008

Galov, N., Krstic, B., & Chakarov, R. (2020). *67+ Staggering Online Review Statistics That Will Help You Improve Your Business in 2020*. Retrieved from https://hostingtribunal.com/blog/online-review-statistics/

Gal-Tzur, A., Grant-Muller, S. M., Kuflik, T., Minkov, E., Nocera, S., & Shoor, I. (2014). The potential of Social Media in delivering transport policy goals. *Transport Policy*, 32, 115–123. doi:10.1016/j.tranpol.2014.01.007

Gal-Tzur, A., Rechavi, A., Beimel, D., & Freund, S. (2018). An improved methodology for extracting information required for transport-related decisions from Q&A forums: A case study of TripAdvisor. *Travel Behaviour & Society*, 10, 1–9. doi:10.1016/j.tbs.2017.08.001

Galvao, A. M., Barros, F. A., Neves, A. M., & Ramalho, G. L. (2004, July). Persona-AIML: an architecture for developing chatterbots with personality. In *Proceedings of the Third International Joint Conference on Autonomous Agents and Multiagent Systems, 2004. AAMAS 2004.* (pp. 1266-1267). IEEE.

Gambäck, B., & Sikdar, U. K. (2017, August). Using convolutional neural networks to classify hate-speech. In *Proceedings of the first workshop on abusive language online* (pp. 85-90). 10.18653/v1/W17-3013

Ganin, Y., Ustinova, E., Ajakan, H., Germain, P., Larochelle, H., Laviolette, F., . . . Lempitsky, V. S. (2016). Domain-Adversarial Training of Neural Networks. *J. Mach. Learn. Res., 17*, 59:1-59:35. Retrieved from http://jmlr.org/papers/v17/15-239.html

Gao, G., Choi, E., Choi, Y., & Zettlemoyer, L. (2018). *Neural metaphor detection in context.* arXiv preprint arXiv:1808.09653

Gao, Z., Feng, A., Song, X., & Wu, X. (2019). Target-Dependent Sentiment Classification With BERT. *IEEE Access: Practical Innovations, Open Solutions, 7*, 154290–154299. doi:10.1109/ACCESS.2019.2946594

Garrão, M. D. U. (2001). Tradução automática: ainda um enigma multidisciplinar. In Congresso nacional de linguística e filologia (Vol. 5, pp. 8-12). Academic Press.

Gautam, G., & Yadav, D. (2014). Sentiment analysis of twitter data using machine learning approaches and semantic analysis. In M. Parashar (Ed.), *Proceedings of the 2014 Seventh International Conference on Contemporary Computing (IC3): 7 - 9 Aug. 2014, Noida, India* (pp. 437–442). Piscataway, NJ: IEEE. 10.1109/IC3.2014.6897213

Gaydhani, A., Doma, V., Kendre, S., & Bhagwat, L. (2018). *Detecting hate speech and offensive language on twitter using machine learning: An n-gram and tfidf based approach.* arXiv preprint arXiv:1809.08651

Gebhart, K., & Noland, R. B. (2014). The impact of weather conditions on capital bikeshare trips. *Transportation, 41*, 1205–1225. doi:10.100711116-014-9540-7

Gers, F. A., Schmidhuber, J., & Cummins, F. (2000). Learning to forget: Continual prediction with LSTM. *Neural Computation, 12*(10), 2451–2471. doi:10.1162/089976600300015015 PMID:11032042

Ghaleb, O. A. M., & Vijendran, A. S. (2017). The Challenges of Sentiment Analysis on Social Web Communities. *International Journal of Advance Research in Science and Engineering., 6*(12), 117–125.

Ghosh, A., & Veale, T. (2016). Fracking sarcasm using neural network. *Proceedings of the 7th workshop on computational approaches to subjectivity, sentiment and social media analysis*, 161-169. 10.18653/v1/W16-0425

Gibbs, R. W., Jr. (2010). The dynamic complexities of metaphor interpretation. *DELTA: Documentacão de Estudos em Linguística Teórica e Aplicada, 26*(SPE), 657–677.

Gieseke, F., Kramer, O. I., Airola, A., & Pahikkala, T. (2012). Efficient recurrent local search strategies for semi- and unsupervised regularized least-squares classification. *Evolutionary Intelligence, 2012*(5), 189–205. doi:10.100712065-012-0068-5

Gildea, D., & Jurafsky, D. (2002). Automatic labeling of semantic roles. *Computational Linguistics, 28*(3), 245–288. doi:10.1162/089120102760275983

Git (2.0) [software]. (2014). Retrieved from https://git-scm.com/

Gitari, N. D., Zuping, Z., Damien, H., & Long, J. (2015). A lexicon-based approach for hate speech detection. *International Journal of Multimedia and Ubiquitous Engineering, 10*(4), 215–230. doi:10.14257/ijmue.2015.10.4.21

Glorot, X., Bordes, A., & Bengio, Y. (2011). Domain Adaptation for Large-scale Sentiment Classification: A Deep Learning Approach. In *ICML'11, Proceedings of the 28th International Conference on International Conference on Machine Learning* (pp. 513–520). Omnipress. Retrieved from https://dl.acm.org/citation.cfm?id=3104482.3104547

Gojare, S., Joshi, R., & Gaigaware, D. (2015). Analysis and design of selenium webdriver automation testing framework. *Procedia Computer Science, 50*, 341–346. doi:10.1016/j.procs.2015.04.038

Göker, H., & Tekedere, H. (2017). FATİH Projesine Yönelik Görüşlerin Metin Madenciliği Yöntemleri İle Otomatik Değerlendirilmesi. *Bilişim Teknolojileri Dergisi, 10*(3), 291–299. doi:10.17671/gazibtd.331041

Gómez, D. (2019). Uso de las tecnologías de la información y la comunicación por universitarios mayas en un contexto de brecha digital en México. *Región y Sociedad, 31*. Advance online publication. doi:10.22198/rys2019/31/1130

Goodfellow, I. J., Pouget-Abadie, J., Mirza, M., Xu, B., Warde-Farley, D., Ozair, S., & Bengio, Y. (2014). Generative Adversarial Nets. In *NIPS'14, Proceedings of the 27th International Conference on Neural Information Processing Systems* (Vol. 2, pp. 2672–2680). MIT Press. Retrieved from https://dl.acm.org/citation.cfm?id=2969033.2969125

Goswami, S., Chakraborty, S., Ghosh, S., Chakrabarti, A., & Chakraborty, B. (2018). A review on application of data mining techniques to combat natural disasters. *Ain Shams Engineering Journal, 9*(3), 365–378. doi:10.1016/j.asej.2016.01.012

Graff, D., Buckwalter, T., Jin, H., & Maamouri, M. (2006). Lexicon Development for Varieties of Spoken Colloquial Arabic. *Proceedings of the Fifth International Conference on Language Resources and Evaluation (LREC)*, 999–1004.

Graff, D., & Maamouri, M. (2012). Developing LMF-XML Bilingual Dictionaries for Colloquial Arabic Dialects. *Proceedings of the Language Resources and Evaluation Conference (LREC)*, 269–274.

Grant-Muller, S. M., Gal-Tzur, A., Minkov, E., Nocera, S., Kuflik, T., & Shoor, I. (2014). Enhancing transport data collection through Social Media sources: Methods, challenges and opportunities for textual data. *IET Intelligent Transport Systems, 9*(4), 407–417. doi:10.1049/iet-its.2013.0214

Graves, A. (2012). Supervised Sequence Labelling with Recurrent Neural Networks (2nd ed.). In Studies in Computational Intelligence: Vol. 385. Berlin: Springer Berlin Heidelberg. doi:10.1007/978-3-642-24797-2

Greene, B. B., & Rubin, G. M. (1971). *Automatic grammatical tagging of English*. Department of Linguistics, Brown University.

Groves, D., & Way, A. (2005a). Hybrid data-driven models of machine translation. *Machine Translation, 19*(3-4), 301–323. doi:10.100710590-006-9015-5

Groves, D., & Way, A. (2005b). Hybrid example-based SMT: the best of both worlds? In *Proceedings of the ACL Workshop on Building and Using Parallel Texts* (pp. 183-190). Association for Computational Linguistics. 10.3115/1654449.1654490

Guellil, I., Adeel, A., Azouaou, F., Benali, F., & Hussain, A. (2018). Arabizi sentiment analysis based on transliteration and automatic corpus annotation. *9th Workshop on Computational Approaches to Subjectivity, Sentiment and Social Media Analysis*, 335–341. 10.18653/v1/W18-6249

Guellil, I., Azouaou, F., Benali, F., Hachani, A. E., & Mendoza, M. (2020). The Role of Transliteration in the Process of Arabizi Translation/Sentiment Analysis. In M. Abd Elaziz, M. A. A. Al-qaness, A. A. Ewees, & A. Dahou (Eds.), *Recent Advances in NLP: The Case of Arabic Language* (pp. 101–128). Springer International Publishing. doi:10.1007/978-3-030-34614-0_6

Guellil, I., Azouaou, F., & Hussain, A. (2018). SentiALG : Automated Corpus Annotation for Algerian Sentiment Analysis Introduction. *Proceedings of the International Conference on Brain Inspired Cognitive Systems*, 557–567. 10.1007/978-3-030-00563-4_54

Guellil, I., Azouaou, F., & Mendoza, M. (2019). Arabic sentiment analysis: Studies, resources, and tools. *Social Network Analysis and Mining, 9*(56), 1–17. doi:10.100713278-019-0602-x

Guerberof, A. (2009). Productivity and Quality in the Post-editing of Outputs from Translation Memories and Machine Translation. *International Journal of Localization, 7*(1).

Guo, W., Li, H., Ji, H., & Diab, M. (2013). *Linking Tweets to News: A Framework to Enrich Short Text Data in Social Media. Proceedings of the 51st Annual Meeting of the Association for Computational Linguistics*, 1, 239-249.

Gural, S. K., & Chemezov, Y. R. (2014). Analysis of Efficiency of Translation Quality Assurance Tools. *Procedia: Social and Behavioral Sciences*, *154*, 360–363. doi:10.1016/j.sbspro.2014.10.163

Gutiérrez, X. (2015). Bilingual lexicon extraction for a distant language pair using a small parallel corpus. In *Proceedings of the 2015 Conference of the North American Chapter of the Association for Computational Linguistics: Student Research Workshop* (pp. 154-160). Denver, CO: ACL Publications.

Gutiérrez, X., Medina, A., & Sierra, G. (2019). Morphological segmentation for extracting Spanish-Nahuatl bilingual lexicon. *Procesamiento del Lenguaje Natural*, *63*, 41–48.

Gutiérrez, X., & Mijangos, V. (2018). Comparing morphological complexity of Spanish, Otomi and Nahuatl. In *Proceedings of the Workshop on Linguistic Complexity and Natural Language Processing (LC&NLP-2018)*. Santa Fe, NM: ACL Publications.

Gutiérrez, X., Sierra, G., & Hernández, I. (2016). Axolotl: a Web Accessible Parallel Corpus for Spanish-Nahuatl. In *Proceedings of the Tenth International Conference on Language Resources and Evaluation LREC 2016* (pp. 4210-4214). Portorož, Slovenia: European Language Resources Association (ELRA).

Gu, Y., Qian, Z. S., & Chen, F. (2016). From Twitter to detector: Real-time traffic incident detection using Social Media data. *Transportation Research Part C, Emerging Technologies*, *67*, 321–342. doi:10.1016/j.trc.2016.02.011

Guyon, I., Weston, J., Barnhill, S., & Vapnik, V. (2002). Gene selection for cancer classification using support vector machines. *Machine Learning*, *46*(1–3), 389–422. doi:10.1023/A:1012487302797

Habash, N. (2010). Introduction to Arabic natural language processing. In G. Hirst (Ed.), Synthesis Lectures on Human Language Technologies (Vol. 3, Issue 1). doi:10.2200/S00277ED1V01Y201008HLT010

Habash, N., Eskander, R., & Hawwari, A. (2012). A morphological analyzer for Egyptian arabic. In *Proceedings of the Twelfth Meeting of the Special Interest Group on Computational Morphology and Phonology*. Association for Computational Linguistics.

Habash, N., Soudi, A., & Buckwalter, T. (2007). On Arabic Transliteration. In Arabic Computational Morphology (Vol. 49, Issue 4, pp. 15–22). doi:10.1007/978-1-4020-6046-5_2

Hadj Ameur, M. S., Meziane, F., & Guessoum, A. (2019). *ANETAC : Arabic named entity transliteration and classification dataset*. ArXiv Preprint ArXiv:1907.03110

Hamburg, M. (1974). *Basic statistics: A modern approach*. Houghton Mifflin Harcourt P.

Hampshire, R. C., & Marla, L. (2012). An analysis of bike sharing usage: Explaining trip generation and attraction from observed demand. *Proceedings of the 91st Annual Meeting of the Transportation Research Board*, 22–26.

Hanafiah, N., & Quix, C. (2014) Entity recognition in information extraction. In *6th Asian Conference on Intelligent Information and Database Systems*. (vol. 8397, pp. 113–122). 10.1007/978-3-319-05476-6_12

Han, J., & Kamber, M. (2006). *Data mining: Concepts and Techniques*. Morgan Kaufmann Publishers, Elsevier.

Han, J., Zhang, Z., Cummins, N., & Schuller, B. (2019). Adversarial Training in Affective Computing and Sentiment Analysis: Recent Advances and Perspectives [Review Article]. *IEEE Computational Intelligence Magazine*, *14*(2), 68–81. doi:10.1109/MCI.2019.2901088

Hansson, J. (2003). *Total quality management – Aspects of implementation and performance: Investigations with a focus on small organizations* (Unpublished doctoral dissertation). Lulea University of Technology.

Haochen, Z., & Fei, S. (2015). Aspect-level sentiment analysis based on a generalized probabilistic topic and syntax model. In *Proceedings of the Twenty-Eighth International Florida Artificial Intelligence Research Society Conference*. Association for the Advancement of Artificial Intelligence.

Hao, Y., Mu, T., Hong, R., Wang, M., Liu, X., & Goulermas, J. Y. (2019). Cross-domain Sentiment Encoding through Stochastic Word Embedding. *IEEE Transactions on Knowledge and Data Engineering*, *1*, 1. Advance online publication. doi:10.1109/TKDE.2019.2913379

Harrag, F., El-Qawasmeh, E., & Pichappan, P. (2009). Improving Arabic text categorization using decision trees. In *2009 First International Conference on Networked Digital Technologies* (pp. 110-115). IEEE. 10.1109/NDT.2009.5272214

Hassan, A., & Mahmood, A. (2018). Convolutional Recurrent Deep Learning Model for Sentence Classification. *IEEE Access: Practical Innovations, Open Solutions*, *6*, 13949–13957. doi:10.1109/ACCESS.2018.2814818

Hassani, H., Huang, X., & Silva, E. (2018). Digitalisation and big data mining in banking. *Big Data and Cognitive Computing*, *2*(3), 18. doi:10.3390/bdcc2030018

Hatzivassiloglou, V., & McKeown, K. (1997). Predicting the Semantic Orientation of Adjectives. In *Proceedings of the 35th Annual Meeting of the Association for Computational Linguistics and 8th Conference of the European Chapter of the Association for Computational Linguistics* (pp. 174–181). Madrid, Spain: Association for Computational Linguistics. 10.3115/976909.979640

Heimerl, F., Lohmann, S., Lange, S., & Ertl, T. (2014). Word cloud explorer: Text analytics based on word clouds. *Proceedings of the Annual Hawaii International Conference on System Sciences*, 1833–1842. 10.1109/HICSS.2014.231

Heimes, F., & van Heuveln, B. (1998). The normalized radial basis function neural network. In *SMC'98 Conference Proceedings. 1998 IEEE International Conference on Systems, Man, and Cybernetics (Cat. No. 98CH36218)* (Vol. 2, pp. 1609-1614). IEEE. 10.1109/ICSMC.1998.728118

Henry, N. (2017). Why app localization matters. *Localize Blog*. Available at https://localizeblog.com/app-localization-matters/

He, W., Zha, S., & Li, L. (2013). Social media competitive analysis and text mining: A case study in the pizza industry. *International Journal of Information Management*, *33*(3), 464–472. doi:10.1016/j.ijinfomgt.2013.01.001

He, X., & Lapedes, A. (1994). Nonlinear modelling and prediction by successive approximation using radial basis functions. *Physica D. Nonlinear Phenomena*, *70*(3), 289–301. doi:10.1016/0167-2789(94)90018-3

Hibernate framework (4.3.0) [Software]. (2013). Retrieved from https://hibernate.org/

Hinton, G., Deng, L., Yu, D., Dahl, G., Mohamed, A., Jaitly, N., Senior, A., Vanhoucke, V., Nguyen, P., Sainath, T., & Kingsbury, B. (2012). Deep Neural Networks for Acoustic Modeling in Speech Recognition: The Shared Views of Four Research Groups. *IEEE Signal Processing Magazine*, *29*(6), 82–97. doi:10.1109/MSP.2012.2205597

Hinton, L., & Hale, K. (2001). *The Green Book of Language Revitalization in Practice*. Academic Press. doi:10.1163/9789004261723

Hochreiter, S., & Schmidhuber, J. (1997). Long short-term memory. *Neural Computation*, *9*(8), 1735–1780. doi:10.1162/neco.1997.9.8.1735 PMID:9377276

Hodgkin, A. L., & Huxley, A. F. (1952). A quantitative description of membrane current and its application to conduction and excitation in nerve. *The Journal of Physiology, 117*(4), 500–544. doi:10.1113/jphysiol.1952.sp004764 PMID:12991237

Hofmann, T. (2013). *Probabilistic latent semantic analysis.* arXiv preprint arXiv:1301.6705

Howard, J., & Ruder, S. (2018). Universal language model fine-tuning for text classification. In *Proceedings of the 56th Annual Meeting of the Association for Computational Linguistics (*Volume 1*: Long Papers).* Melbourne, Australia: Association for Computational Linguistics. 10.18653/v1/P18-1031

Hsu, C.-C., & Ku, L.-W. (2018). SocialNLP 2018 EmotionX Challenge Overview: Recognizing Emotions in Dialogues. In *Proceedings of the Sixth International Workshop on Natural Language Processing for Social Media* (pp. 27–31). Melbourne, Australia: Association for Computational Linguistics. 10.18653/v1/W18-3505

Hsu, H. H., Hsieh, C. W., & Lu, M. D. (2011). Hybrid feature selection by combining filters and wrappers. *Expert Systems with Applications, 38*(7), 8144–8150. doi:10.1016/j.eswa.2010.12.156

Hu, M., & Liu, B. (2004). Mining and Summarizing Customer Reviews. In *KDD '04, Proceedings of the Tenth ACM SIGKDD International Conference on Knowledge Discovery and Data Mining* (pp. 168–177). New York, NY: ACM. 10.1145/1014052.1014073

Hu, M., & Liu, B. (2004). Mining and summarizing customer reviews. *Proceedings of the tenth ACM SIGKDD international conference on Knowledge discovery and data mining*, 168-177.

Hurley, L. (2019, December 9). *U.S. Supreme Court leaves in place Kentucky abortion restriction.* Retrieved June 1, 2020 from https://www.reuters.com/article/us-usa-court-abortion/u-s-supreme-court-leaves-in-place-kentucky-abortion-restriction-idUSKBN1YD1JX

Hüsem, S. Ş., & Gülcü, A. (2017). Categorizing the Turkish web pages by data mining techniques. *In 2017 International Conference on Computer Science and Engineering (UBMK)* (pp. 255-260). IEEE. 10.1109/UBMK.2017.8093385

Hussein, D. M. E. D. M. (2018). A survey on sentiment analysis challenges. *Journal of King Saud University-Engineering Sciences.*, *30*(4), 330–338. doi:10.1016/j.jksues.2016.04.002

Ian Fellows. (2018). *wordcloud: Word Clouds. R package version 2.6.* https://CRAN.R-project.org/package=wordcloud

Ibrahim, H. S., Abdou, S. M., & Gheith, M. (2015). Idioms-Proverbs Lexicon for Modern Standard Arabic and Colloquial Sentiment Analysis Idioms-Proverbs Lexicon for Modern Standard Arabic and Colloquial Sentiment Analysis. *International Journal of Computers and Applications, 118*(11), 26–31. doi:10.5120/20790-3435

Imran, M., Castillo, C., Diaz, F., & Vieweg, S. (2015). Processing social media messages in mass emergency: A survey. *ACM Computing Surveys, 47*(4), 67. doi:10.1145/2771588

INEGI. (2010). *Population and Housing Census 2010.* México, Gobierno de México: www.inegi.org.mx/temas/lengua

Inoue, G., Habash, N., Matsumoto, Y., & Aoyama, H. (2018, May). A parallel corpus of Arabic-Japanese news articles. *Proceedings of the Eleventh International Conference on Language Resources and Evaluation (LREC 2018).*

Internet World Stats. (n.d.). https://www.internetworldstats.com/stats7.htm

Iskra, D., Siemund, R., Borno, J., Moreno, A., Emam, O., Choukri, K., Gedge, O., Tropf, H., Nogueiras, A., Zitouni, I., Tsopanoglou, A., & Fakotakis, N. (2004). OrienTel -Telephony databases across Northern Africa and the Middle East Countries and technologies. *LREC.* http://citeseerx.ist.psu.edu/viewdoc/download?doi=10.1.1.360.7554&rep=rep1&type=pdf

Ismail, S., Alsammak, A., & Elshishtawy, T. (2016). A generic approach for extracting aspects and opinions of arabic reviews. *ACM International Conference Proceeding Series,* 173–179. 10.1145/2908446.2908467

ITU NLP Toolkit. (2020). *ITU Turkish Natural Language Processing Pipeline.* Retrieved from http://tools.nlp.itu.edu.tr/index.jsp

Jain, A., Tayal, D. K., & Rai, S. (2015). Shrinking digital gap through automatic generation of WordNet for Indian languages. *AI & Society, 30*(2), 215–222. doi:10.100700146-014-0548-5

Jang, B., Kim, I., & Kim, J. W. (2019). Word2vec convolutional neural networks for classification of news articles and tweets. *PLOS ONE, 14*(8), 1-20.

Jarrar, M., Habash, N., Alrimawi, F., Akra, D., & Zalmout, N. (2017). Curras: An annotated corpus for the Palestinian Arabic dialect. *Language Resources and Evaluation, 51*(3), 745–775. doi:10.100710579-016-9370-7

Jeong, H., Shin, D., & Choi, J. (2011). Ferom: Feature extraction and refinement for opinion mining. *ETRI Journal, 33*(5), 720–730. doi:10.4218/etrij.11.0110.0627

Jhaveri, K. D., Schrier, P. B., & Mattana, J. (2013). Paging Doctor Google! Heuristics vs. technology. *F1000 Research, 2*, 1–15. doi:10.12688/f1000research.2-90.v1 PMID:24627777

Jiang, M., Wu, J., Shi, X., & Zhang, M. (2019). Transformer Based Memory Network for Sentiment Analysis of Web Comments. *IEEE Access: Practical Innovations, Open Solutions, 1*, 179942–179953. Advance online publication. doi:10.1109/ACCESS.2019.2957192

Jindal, N., & Liu, B. (2007). Review Spam Detection. *Proceedings of the 16th International Conference on World Wide Web*, 1189–1190. 10.1145/1242572.1242759

Jindal, N., & Liu, B. (2008). Opinion Spam and Analysis. In *Proceedings of the international conference on web search and data mining WSDM'08* (pp. 219–229). ACM. 10.1145/1341531.1341560

Joachims, T. (1998). Text categorization with support vector machines: Learning with many relevant features. In *European conference on machine learning* (pp. 137-142). Springer.

Johnson, J. M., & Khoshgoftaar, T. M. (2019). Survey on deep learning with class imbalance. *Journal of Big Data, 6*(1), 27. doi:10.118640537-019-0192-5

John, V., Mou, L., Bahuleyan, H., & Vechtomova, O. (2019). Disentangled Representation Learning for Non-Parallel Text Style Transfer. In *Proceedings of the 57th Annual Meeting of the Association for Computational Linguistics* (pp. 424–434). Florence, Italy: Association for Computational Linguistics. 10.18653/v1/P19-1041

Jones, K. S. (1972). A Statistical Interpretation of Term Specificity and its Retrieval. *The Journal of Documentation, 28*(1), 11–21. doi:10.1108/eb026526

Jose, R., & Chooralil, V. S. (2016). Prediction of election result by enhanced sentiment analysis on twitter data using classifier ensemble Approach. In *Proceedings of the 2016 International Conference on Data Mining and Advanced Computing (SAPIENCE)* (pp. 64–67). IEEE. 10.1109/SAPIENCE.2016.7684133

Joshi, O. S., & Simon, G. (2018). Sentiment Analysis Tool on Cloud: Software as a Service Model. In *Proceedings of the 2018 International Conference On Advances in Communication and Computing Technology (ICACCT)* (pp. 459–462). Sangamner, India: Springer. 10.1109/ICACCT.2018.8529649

Joulin, A., Grave, E., Bojanowski, P., & Mikolov, T. (2017). Bag of Tricks for Efficient Text Classification. In *Proceedings of the 15th Conference of the European Chapter of the Association for Computational Linguistics: Volume 2, Short Papers* (pp. 427–431). Valencia, Spain: Association for Computational Linguistics. Retrieved from https://www.aclweb.org/anthology/E17-2068

Joyce, B., & Deng, J. (2017). Sentiment analysis of tweets for the 2016 US presidential election. In *Proceedings of the 2017 IEEE MIT Undergraduate Research Technology Conference (URTC)* (pp. 1–4). IEEE. 10.1109/URTC.2017.8284176

Jurafsky, D., Chahuneau, V., Routledge, B. R., & Smith, N. A. (2014). Narrative framing of consumer sentiment in online restaurant reviews. *First Monday, 19*(4). Advance online publication. doi:10.5210/fm.v19i4.4944

Jurafsky, D., & Martin, J. H. (2008). *Speech and Language Processing: An introduction to speech recognition, computational linguistics and natural language processing*. Prentice Hall.

Jurafsky, D., & Martin, J. H. (2014). *Speech and language processing*. Pearson London.

Jurka, T. P., Collingwood, L., Boydstun, A. E., Grossman, E., & van Atteveldt, W. (2013). RTextTools: A Supervised Learning Package for Text Classification. *The R Journal, 5*(1), 6. doi:10.32614/RJ-2013-001

Kaati, L., Omer, E., Prucha, N., & Shrestha, A. (2015, November). Detecting multipliers of jihadism on twitter. In *2015 IEEE International Conference on Data Mining Workshop (ICDMW)* (pp. 954-960). IEEE. 10.1109/ICDMW.2015.9

Kadhim, A. I. (2019). Survey on supervised machine learning techniques for automatic text classification. *Artificial Intelligence Review, 52*(1), 273–292. doi:10.100710462-018-09677-1

Kalchbrenner, N., Grefenstette, E., & Blunsom, P. (2014). A Convolutional Neural Network for Modelling Sentences. *Computation and Language.*, 655–665. doi:10.3115/v1/P14-1062

Kamble, S. S., & Itkikar, A. R. (2018). Study of supervised machine learning approaches for sentiment analysis. *International Research Journal of Engineering and Technology, 5*(4), 3045–3047.

Kamusella, T. (2017). The Arabic language: A Latin of modernity? *Journal of Nationalism. Memory & Language Politics, 11*(2), 117–145. doi:10.1515/jnmlp-2017-0006

Kang, Q., Hu, J., Yang, N., He, J., Yang, Y., Tang, M., & Jin, C. (2019). Marketing of drugs for rare diseases is speeding up in China: Looking at the example of drugs for mucopolysaccharidosis. *Intractable & Rare Diseases Research, 8*(3), 165–171. doi:10.5582/irdr.2019.01090 PMID:31523593

Kapil, G., Agrawal, A., & Khan, R. A. (2016, October). A study of big data characteristics. In *2016 International Conference on Communication and Electronics Systems (ICCES)* (pp. 1-4). IEEE.

Kar, A., & Mandal, D. P. (2011). Finding opinion strength using fuzzy logic on web reviews. *International Journal of Engineering and Industries, 2*(1), 37–43. doi:10.4156/ijei.vol2.issue1.5

Kaur, H., & Mangat, V., & Nidhi (2017). A survey of sentiment analysis techniques. *2017 International Conference on I-SMAC (IoT in Social, Mobile, Analytics and Cloud) (I-SMAC).* 10.1109/I-SMAC.2017.8058315

Kaushik, A., & Naithani, S. (2016). A comprehensive study of text mining approach. *International Journal of Computer Science and Network Security (IJC-SNS), 16*(2), 69-76.

Kayes, I., Kourtellis, N., Quercia, D., Iamnitchi, A., & Bonchi, F. (2015). The social world of content abusers in community question answers. *Proceedings of the 24th International Conference on World Wide Web*, 570-580. 10.1145/2736277.2741674

Kaynar, O., Arslan, H., Görmez, Y., & Demirkoparan, F. (2017). Feature selection methods in sentiment analysis. In *2017 International Artificial Intelligence and Data Processing Symposium (IDAP)* (pp. 1-5). IEEE.

Keleş, M. K., & Özel, S. A. (2017). Similarity detection between Turkish text documents with distance metrics. In *2017 International Conference on Computer Science and Engineering (UBMK)* (pp. 316-321). IEEE. 10.1109/UBMK.2017.8093399

Ke, Y., & Hagiwara, M. (2017). An English neural network that learns texts, finds hidden knowledge, and answers questions. *Journal of Artificial Intelligence and Soft Computing Research, 7*(4), 229–242. doi:10.1515/jaiscr-2017-0016

Khaled, A., Tazi, N. E., & Hossny, A. H. (2015). Sentiment Analysis over Social Networks: An Overview. *2015 IEEE International Conference on Systems, Man, and Cybernetics*, 2174-2179.

Khalifa, S., Hassan, S., & Habash, N. (2017). A morphological analyzer for Gulf Arabic verbs. *Proceedings of the Third Arabic Natural Language Processing Workshop*. 10.18653/v1/W17-1305

Kharde, V., & Sonawane, P. (2016). *Sentiment analysis of twitter data: A survey of techniques*. arXiv preprint arXiv:1601.06971

Khedr, A. E., & Yaseen, N. (2017). Predicting stock market behavior using data mining technique and news sentiment analysis. *International Journal of Intelligent Systems and Applications, 9*(7), 22–30. doi:10.5815/ijisa.2017.07.03

Khemakhem, A., Elleuch, I., Gargouri, B., & Ben Hamadou, A. (2009). Towards an automatic conversion approach of editorial Arabic dictionaries into LMF-ISO 24613 standardized model. *Proceedings of the Second International Conference on Arabic Language Resources and Tools*.

Khemakhem, A., Gargouri, B., & Ben Hamadou, A. (2012). LMF standardized dictionary for Arabic Language. *International Conference on Computing and Information Technology - ICCIT*.

Khoja, S., Garside, R., & Knowles, G. (2011). *A tagset for the morphosyntactic tagging of Arabic*. Computing Department Lancaster University.

Khumoyun, A., Cui, Y., & Lee, H. (2016). Real-time information classification in Twitter using Storm. *Bangkok 6th International Conference, 49*, 1-4.

Kibriya, A. M., Frank, E., Pfahringer, B., & Holmes, G. (2004). Multinomial naive Bayes for text categorization revisited. In *Australasian Joint Conference on Artificial Intelligence* (pp. 488-499). Springer. 10.1007/978-3-540-30549-1_43

Kilany, H., Gadalla, H., Arram, H., Yacoub, A., El-Habashi, A., & McLemore, C. (2002). *Egyptian Colloquial Arabic Lexicon* (LDC catalog number LDC99L22).

Kılınç, D., Özçift, A., Bozyigit, F., Yıldırım, P., Yücalar, F., & Borandag, E. (2017). TTC-3600: A new benchmark dataset for Turkish text categorization. *Journal of Information Science, 43*(2), 174–185. doi:10.1177/0165551515620551

Kim, Y. (2014). *Convolutional neural networks for sentence classification*. Academic Press.

Kim, S. B., Han, K. S., Rim, H. C. R., & Myaeng, S. H. (2006). Some effective techniques for naive bayes text classification. *IEEE Transactions on Knowledge and Data Engineering, 18*(11), 1457–1466. doi:10.1109/TKDE.2006.180

Kim, Y. (2014). Convolutional Neural Networks for Sentence Classification. In *Proceedings of the 2014 Conference on Empirical Methods in Natural Language Processing (EMNLP)* (pp. 1746–1751). Doha, Qatar: Association for Computational Linguistics. 10.3115/v1/D14-1181

Kingma, D. P., & Welling, M. (2013, December 20). *Auto-Encoding Variational Bayes*. Retrieved from https://arxiv.org/pdf/1312.6114v10

Kingsbury, P., & Palmer, M. (2002, May). From TreeBank to PropBank. In LREC (pp. 1989-1993). Academic Press.

Kintsch, W. (2000). Metaphor comprehension: A computational theory. *Psychonomic Bulletin & Review*, 7(2), 257–266. doi:10.3758/BF03212981 PMID:10909133

Kirca, A. H., Jayachandran, S., & Bearden, W. O. (2005). Market orientation: A meta-analytic review and assessment of its antecedents and impact on performance. *Journal of Marketing*, 69(2), 24–41. doi:10.1509/jmkg.69.2.24.60761

Kirchhoff, K., & Vergyri, D. (2005). Cross-dialectal data sharing for acoustic modeling in Arabic speech recognition. *Speech Communication*, 46(1), 37–51. doi:10.1016/j.specom.2005.01.004

Klebanov, B. B., Leong, B., Heilman, M., & Flor, M. (2014). Different texts, same metaphors: Unigrams and beyond. *Proceedings of the Second Workshop on Metaphor in NLP*, 11–17. 10.3115/v1/W14-2302

Kockaert, H., Makoushina, J., & Steurs, F. (2008). Translation quality assurance: what is missing? And what can be done? *Proceedings of XVIIIth FIT World Congress in Shanghai.*

Koehn, P. (2010). *Statistical Machine Translation*. Cambridge University Press.

Kohavi, R. (1995). A study of cross-validation and bootstrap for accuracy estimation and model selection. *IJCAI (United States)*, 14(2), 1137–1145.

Kohavi, R., & John, G. (1997). Wrappers for feature subset selection. *Artificial Intelligence*, 97(1-2), 273–324. doi:10.1016/S0004-3702(97)00043-X

Komesu, F., & Tenani, L. (2010). Considerações sobre o conceito de "internetês" nos estudos da linguagem. *Linguagem em (Dis) curso*, 9(3), 621-643.

Kornai, A. (2013). Digital Language Death. *PLoS One*, 8(10), e77056. doi:10.1371/journal.pone.0077056 PMID:24167559

Koswatte, S., McDougall, K., & Liu, X. (2015). SDI and crowdsourced spatial information management automation for disaster management. *Survey Review*, 47(344), 307–315. doi:10.1179/1752270615Y.0000000008

Kowsari, K., Meimandi, K. J., Heidarysafa, M., Mendu, S., Barnes, L. E., & Brown, D. E. (2019). Text classification algorithms: A survey. *Informations*, 10(4), 150. doi:10.3390/info10040150

Krause, T., & Grassegger, H. (2016). *Facebook's secret rules of deletion*. Retrieved from https://international.sueddeutsche.de/post/154543271930/facebooks-secret-rules-of-deletion

Krause, R., Moscati, R., Halpern, S., Schwartz, D., & Abbas, J. (2011). Can Emergency Medicine Residents Reliably Use the Internet to Answer Clinical Questions? *The Western Journal of Emergency Medicine*, 12(4), 442–447. doi:10.5811/westjem.2010.9.1895 PMID:22224135

Krijthe, J. (2015). Rtsne: T-distributed stochastic neighbor embedding using barnes-hut implementation. *R package version 0.10*. https://cran. r-project. org/package= Rtsne.

Krishnakumaran, S., & Zhu, X. (2007, April). Hunting Elusive Metaphors Using Lexical Resources. *Proceedings of the Workshop on Computational approaches to Figurative Language*, 13-20. 10.3115/1611528.1611531

Krizhevsky, A., Sutskever, I., & Hinton, G. E. (2012). ImageNet Classification with Deep Convolutional Neural Networks. In *NIPS'12, Proceedings of the 25th International Conference on Neural Information Processing Systems* - Volume 1 (pp. 1097–1105). Curran Associates Inc.

Kučiš, V., & Seljan, S. (2014). The role of online translation tools in language education. *Babel*, 60(3), 303–324. doi:10.1075/babel.60.3.03kuc

Kudo, T., Yamamoto, K., & Matsumoto, Y. (2004). Applying conditional random fields to Japanese morphological analysis. *Proceedings of the 2004 Conference on Empirical Methods in Natural Language Processing*, 230–237.

Kuflik, T., Minkov, E., Nocera, S., Grant-Muller, S., Gal-Tzur, A., & Shoor, I. (2017). Automating a framework to extract and analyse transport related Social Media content: The potential and the challenges. *Transportation Research Part C: Emerging Technologies, 77*, 275-291.

Kumar, A., & Sebastian, T. M. (2012). Sentiment Analysis: A Perspective on Its Past, Present and Future. *International Journal of Intelligent Systems and Applications*, 1–14.

Kumar, L., Somani, A., Bhattacharyya, P. (2017). *"Having 2 Hours to Write a Paper Is Fun!": Detecting Sarcasm in Numerical Portions of Text.* ArXiv, abs/1709.01950

Kumar, A., & Joshi, A. (2017). Ontology-Driven Sentiment Analysis on Social Web for Government Intelligence. *ICEGOV '17: Proceedings of the Special Collection on eGovernment Innovations in India*, 134–139. 10.1145/3055219.3055229

Kuyumcu, B., Buluz, B., & Kömeçoğlu, Y. (2019). Author Identification in Turkish Documents with Ridge Regression Analysis. In *2019 27th Signal Processing and Communications Applications Conference (SIU)* (pp. 1-4). IEEE.

Kwak, H., Lee, C., Park, H., & Moon, S. (2010). What is Twitter, a social network or a news media? In *Proceedings of the 19th international conference on World wide web* (pp. 591-600). ACM. 10.1145/1772690.1772751

Lafferty, J., McCallum, A., & Pereira, F. C. (2001). Conditional random fields: Probabilistic models for segmenting and labeling sequence data. *Proceedings of the 8th International Conference on Machine Learning*, 282–289.

Lakoff, G., & Johnson, M. (2020). The embodied mind. *Shaping Entrepreneurship Research: Made, as Well as Found*, 80.

Lakoff, G., & Johnson, M. (2008). *Metaphors we live by*. University of Chicago press.

Lambrecht, A., Tucker, C., & Wiertz, C. (2018). Advertising to Early Trend Propagators: Evidence from Twitter. *Marketing Science, 37*(2), 177–199. doi:10.1287/mksc.2017.1062

Lampert, C. H., Nickisch, H., & Harmeling, S. (2014). Attribute-Based Classification for Zero-Shot Visual Object Categorization. *IEEE Transactions on Pattern Analysis and Machine Intelligence, 36*(3), 453–465. doi:10.1109/TPAMI.2013.140 PMID:24457503

Lan, M., Tan, C. L., Su, J., & Lu, Y. (2008). Supervised and traditional term weighting methods for automatic text categorization. *IEEE Transactions on Pattern Analysis and Machine Intelligence, 31*(4), 721–735. doi:10.1109/TPAMI.2008.110 PMID:19229086

Lara, L.-F., Ham-Chande, R., & García Hidalgo, M. (1979). *Investigaciones lingüísticas en lexicografía*. El Colegio de México. doi:10.2307/j.ctv233mwx

Larochelle, H., Erhan, D., & Bengio, Y. (2008). Zero-data Learning of New Tasks. In *AAAI'08, Proceedings of the 23rd National Conference on Artificial Intelligence* (Vol. 2, pp. 646–651). AAAI Press. Retrieved from https://dl.acm.org/citation.cfm?id=1620163.1620172

Le Ny, B. (2014). *Quality Control in Human Translations: Use Cases and Specifications*. Retrieved from https://transread.limsi.fr/Deliverables/Deliverable_3.1.pdf

Leaman, R., Khare, R., & Lu, Z. (2015). Challenges in clinical natural language processing for automated disorder normalization. *Journal of Biomedical Informatics, 57*, 28–37. doi:10.1016/j.jbi.2015.07.010 PMID:26187250

LeCun, Y., & Bengio, Y. (1995). Convolutional networks for images, speech, and time series. The handbook of brain theory and neural networks, 3361(10), 1995.

LeCun, Y., Bengio, Y., & Hinton, G. (2015). Deep learning. *Nature, 521*(7553), 436–444. doi:10.1038/nature14539 PMID:26017442

Lee, D., Hosanagar, K., & Nair, H. (2018). Advertising Content and Consumer Engagement on Social Media: Evidence from Facebook. *Management Science, 64*(11), 4967–5460. doi:10.1287/mnsc.2017.2902

Lenzen, M., Sun, Y., Faturay, F., Ting, Y.-P., Geschke, A., & Malik, A. (2018). The carbon footprint of global tourism. *Nature Climate Change, 8*(6), 522–528. doi:10.103841558-018-0141-x

Letarte, G., Paradis, F., Giguère, P., & Laviolette, F. (2018). Importance of Self-Attention for Sentiment Analysis. In *Proceedings of the 2018 EMNLP Workshop BlackboxNLP: Analyzing and Interpreting Neural Networks for NLP* (pp. 267–275). Brussels, Belgium: Association for Computational Linguistics. 10.18653/v1/W18-5429

Levenshtein, V. I. (1966). Binary Codes Capable of Correcting Deletions, Insertions and Reversals. *Soviet Physics, Doklady, 10*(8), 707–710.

Levinson, B. (2019, June 10). *Don't Lie To Me: Integrating Client-Side Web Scraping And Review Behavioral Analysis To Detect Fake Reviews.* Undergraduate Research Scholars Program. Retrieved June 1, 2020 from http://hdl.handle.net/1969.1/175409

Li, N., Zhai, S., & Zhang, Z., & Liu, B. (2017). Structural Correspondence Learning for Cross-lingual Sentiment Classification with One-to-many Mappings. In *AAAI'17, Proceedings of the Thirty-First AAAI Conference on Artificial Intelligence* (pp. 3490–3496). AAAI Press. Retrieved from https://dl.acm.org/citation.cfm?id=3298023.3298075

Li, Z., & Wei, Y., Zhang, Y., & Yang, Q. (2018). Hierarchical Attention Transfer Network for Cross-Domain Sentiment Classification. *AAAI Conference on Artificial Intelligence; Thirty-Second AAAI Conference on Artificial Intelligence.* Retrieved from https://aaai.org/ocs/index.php/AAAI/AAAI18/paper/view/16873

Li, Z., & Zhang, Y., Wei, Y., Wu, Y., & Yang, Q. (2017). End-to-end Adversarial Memory Network for Cross-domain Sentiment Classification. In C. Sierra (Ed.), *IJCAI'17, Proceedings of the 26th International Joint Conference on Artificial Intelligence* (pp. 2237–2243). AAAI Press. Retrieved from https://dl.acm.org/citation.cfm?id=3172077.3172199

Liang, Y., Caverlee, J., & Mander, J. (2013). Text vs. images: On the viability of social media to assess earthquake damage. In *Proceedings of the 22nd International Conference on World Wide Web,* (pp. 1003-1006). ACM. 10.1145/2487788.2488102

Likert, R. (1932). A technique for the measurement of attitudes. *Archives de Psychologie.*

Li, M., Huang, L., Tan, C. H., & Wei, K. K. (2013). Helpfulness of online product reviews as seen by consumers: Source and content features. *International Journal of Electronic Commerce, 17*(4), 101–136. doi:10.2753/JEC1086-4415170404

Lincy, W., & Kumar, N. M. (2016). A survey on challenges in sentiment analysis. *International Journal of Emerging Technology in Computer Science & Electronics, 21*(3), 409–412.

Ling, P., Geng, C., Menghou, Z., & Chunya, L. (2014). *What Do Seller Manipulations of Online Product Reviews Mean to Consumers?* (HKIBS Working Paper Series 070-1314) Hong Kong Institute of Business Studies, Lingnan University, Hong Kong.

Linguistic Data Consortium. (2005). *Linguistic Data Annotation Specification: Assessment of Fluency and Adequacy in Translations.* Author.

Lin, H. C., Swarna, H., & Bruning, P. F. (2017). Taking a global view on brand post popularity: Six social media brand post practices for global markets. *Business Horizons, 60*(5), 621–633. doi:10.1016/j.bushor.2017.05.006

Li, P., Xu, W., Ma, C., Sun, J., & Yan, Y. (2015). IOA: Improving SVM based sentiment classification through post processing. *Proc. 9th Int. Workshop Semantic Evaluation, 545–550.* 10.18653/v1/S15-2091

Liu, B. (2010). Sentiment analysis and subjectivity. Handbook of Natural Language Processing, 2(2010), 627-666.

Liu, B. (2010). Sentiment Analysis and Subjectivity. In R. Herbrich & T. Graepel (Eds.), Handbook of Natural Language Processing (2nd ed., pp. 627–666). Microsoft Research Ltd.

Liu, B. (2012). Sentiment analysis and opinion mining. *Synthesis lectures on human language technologies, 5*(1), 1-167.

Liu, S., & Forss, T. (2015, November). New classification models for detecting Hate and Violence web content. In *2015 7th international joint conference on knowledge discovery, knowledge engineering and knowledge management (IC3K)* (Vol. 1, pp. 487-495). IEEE. 10.5220/0005636704870495

Liu, W., & Fu, X. (2018). Introduce More Characteristics of Samples into Cross-domain Sentiment Classification. In *ICPR 2018, Proceedings of the 2018 24th International Conference on Pattern Recognition (ICPR)* (pp. 25–30). IEEE. 10.1109/ICPR.2018.8545331

Liu, Y., Ott, M., Goyal, N., Du Jingfei, Joshi, M., Chen, D., . . . Stoyanov, V. (2019, July 26). *RoBERTa: A Robustly Optimized BERT Pretraining Approach.* Retrieved from https://arxiv.org/pdf/1907.11692v1

Liu, Z., Bai, X., Cai, T., Chen, C., Zhang, W., & Jiang, L. (2019). Improving Sentence Representations with Local and Global Attention for Classification. In *IJCNN 2019, Proceedings of the 2019 International Joint Conference on Neural Networks (IJCNN)* (pp. 1–7). Curran Associates, Inc. 10.1109/IJCNN.2019.8852436

Liu, B. (2010). Sentiment Analysis: A Multi-Faceted Problem. *IEEE Intelligent Systems.*

Liu, B. (2012). *Sentiment Analysis and Opinion Mining.* University of Illinois at Chicago, Morgan & Claypool Publishers. doi:10.2200/S00416ED1V01Y201204HLT016

Liu, B. (2015). *Sentiment Analysis Mining Opinions, Sentiments, and Emotions.* Cambridge University Press. doi:10.1017/CBO9781139084789

Liu, B., Blasch, E., Chen, Y. L., Shen, D., & Chen, G. (2013). Scalable sentiment classification for big data analysis using naïve bayes classifier. In *2013 IEEE International Conference on Big Data,* (pp. 99-104). Santa Clara, CA: IEEE. 10.1109/BigData.2013.6691740

Liu, G., & Guo, J. (2019). Bidirectional LSTM with attention mechanism and convolutional layer for text classification. *Neurocomputing, 337,* 325–338. doi:10.1016/j.neucom.2019.01.078

Liu, G., Xu, X., Deng, B., Chen, S., & Li, L. (n.d.). A hybrid method for bilingual text sentiment classification based on deep learning. *17th IEEE/ACIS International Conference on Software Engineering Artificial Intelligence Networking and Parallel/Distributed Computing (SNPD),* 93-98. 10.1109/SNPD.2016.7515884

Liu, H., Burnap, P., Alorainy, W., & Williams, M. L. (2019). A fuzzy approach to text classification with two-stage training for ambiguous instances. *IEEE Transactions on Computational Social Systems, 6*(2), 227–240. doi:10.1109/TCSS.2019.2892037

Liu, J., Wu, G., & Yao, J. (2006). Opinion searching in multi-product reviews. In *The Sixth IEEE International Conference on Computer and Information Technology* (pp. 25-25). IEEE. 10.1109/CIT.2006.132

Liu, J., Xia, C., Yan, H., Xie, Z., & Sun, J. (2019). Hierarchical Comprehensive Context Modeling for Chinese Text Classification. *IEEE Access: Practical Innovations, Open Solutions, 7,* 154546–154559. doi:10.1109/ACCESS.2019.2949175

Liu, Q., Zhang, H., Zeng, Y., Huang, Z., & Wu, Z. (2018). Content Attention Model for Aspect Based Sentiment Analysis. In *WWW '18, Proceedings of the 2018 World Wide Web Conference* (pp. 1023–1032). Geneva, Switzerland: International World Wide Web Conferences Steering Committee. 10.1145/3178876.3186001

Liu, R., Shi, Y., Ji, C., & Jia, M. (2019). A Survey of Sentiment Analysis Based on Transfer Learning. *IEEE Access: Practical Innovations, Open Solutions*, 7, 85401–85412. doi:10.1109/ACCESS.2019.2925059

Liu, Y., Yi, X., Chen, R., Zhai, Z., & Gu, J. (2018). Feature extraction based on information gain and sequential pattern for English question classification. *IET Software*, *12*(6), 520–526. doi:10.1049/iet-sen.2018.0006

Li, Y., Wang, X., & Xu, P. (2018). Chinese text classification model based on deep learning. *Future Internet*, *10*(11), 113. doi:10.3390/fi10110113

Loffler-Laurian, A. M. (1996). La traduction automatique. Presses Univ. Septentrion.

Lombardi, C., Griffiths, E., McLeod, B., Caviglia, A., & Penagos, M. (2009). Search engine as a diagnostic tool in difficult immunological and allergologic cases: Is Google useful? *Internal Medicine Journal*, *39*(7), 459–464. doi:10.1111/j.1445-5994.2008.01875.x PMID:19664156

Lommel, A. (Ed.). (2014). *Multidimensional Quality Metrics (MQM) Definition*. Retrieved from: http://www.qt21.eu/mqm-definition/definition-2014-08-19.html

Lommel, A. R., Burchardt, A., & Uszkoreit, H. (2013). *Multidimensional Quality Metrics; A flexible System for Assessing Translation Quality*. Retrieved from http://www.mt-archive.info/10/Aslib-2013-Lommel.pdf

Lommel, A., Uszkoreit, H., & Burchardt, A. (2014). Multidimensional Quality Metrics (MQM): A Framework for Declaring and Describing Translation Quality Metrics. *Revista Tradumatica: tecnologies de la traducció*, 455-463.

Long, M., Wang, J., Cao, Y., Sun, J., & Yu, P. S. (2016). Deep Learning of Transferable Representation for Scalable Domain Adaptation. *IEEE Transactions on Knowledge and Data Engineering*, *28*(8), 2027–2040. doi:10.1109/TKDE.2016.2554549

Loper, E., & Bird, S. (2002). Nltk: The natural language toolkit. In *Proceedings of the ACL-02 Workshop on Effective tools and methodologies for teaching natural language processing and computational linguistics-Volume 1*, (pp. 63–70). Philadelphia, PA: Association for Computational Linguistics.

Lorenzetti, D. L., Topfer, L. A., Dennett, L., & Clement, F. (2014). Value of databases other than medline for rapid health technology assessments. *International Journal of Technology Assessment in Health Care*, *30*(2), 173–178. doi:10.1017/S0266462314000166 PMID:24774535

Lu, G., Zhao, X., Yin, J., & Yang, W. , & Li, B. (2018). Multi-task learning using variational auto-encoder for sentiment classification. *Pattern Recognition Letters*. Advance online publication. doi:10.1016/j.patrec.2018.06.027

Luo, X., Zimet, G., & Shah, S. (2019). A natural language processing framework to analyse the opinions on HPV vaccination reflected in twitter over 10 years (2008 - 2017). *Human Vaccines & Immunotherapeutics*, *15*(7-8), 1496–1504. doi:10.1080/21645515.2019.1627821 PMID:31194609

Maamouri, M., Graff, D., Bouziri, B., Krouna, S., Bies, A., Kulick, S., & Buckwalter, T. (2009). *LDC Standard Arabic Morphological Analyzer (SAMA) Version 3.1. Linguistic Data Consortium* (LDC2009E73).

Maamouri, M., Bies, A., Buckwalter, T., Diab, M., Habash, N., Rambow, O., & Tabessi, D. (2006). Developing and using a pilot dialectal Arabic treebank. *Proceedings of the Fifth International Conference on Language Resources and Evaluation, LREC06.*

Maas, A. L., Daly, R. E., Pham, P. T., Huang, D., Ng, A. Y., & Potts, C. (2011). Learning Word Vectors for Sentiment Analysis. In *Proceedings of the 49th Annual Meeting of the Association for Computational Linguistics: Human Language Technologies* (pp. 142–150). Association for Computational Linguistics. Retrieved from https://www.aclweb.org/anthology/P11-1015

Maaten, L. d., & Hinton, G. (2008). Visualizing data using t-sne. *Journal of Machine Learning Research*, *9*(Nov), 2579–2605.

Madani, A., Boussaid, O., & Zegour, D. E. (2014). What's happening: A survey of tweets event detection. *Proceedings of the 3rd International Conference on Communications, Computation, Networks and Technologies*, 16-22.

Mager, M., Gutiérrez, X., Sierra, G., & Meza, I. (2018). Challenges of language technologies for the indigenous languages of the Americas. In *Proceedings of the 27th International Conference on Computational Linguistics COLING 2018* (pp. 55-69). Santa Fe, NM: ACL Publications.

Mahyoub, F. H. H., Siddiqui, M. A., & Dahab, M. Y. (2014). Building an Arabic Sentiment Lexicon Using Semi-supervised Learning. Journal of King Saud University - Computer and Information Sciences, 26(4), 417–424. doi:10.1016/j.jksuci.2014.06.003

Maitra, P., & Sarkhel, R. (2018). A K-Competitive Autoencoder for Aggression Detection in Social Media Text. In *Proceedings of the First Workshop on Trolling, Aggression and Cyberbullying (TRAC-2018)* (pp. 80–89). Association for Computational Linguistics. Retrieved from https://www.aclweb.org/anthology/W18-4410

Ma, J., & Hinrichs, E. (2015). Accurate linear-time Chinese word segmentation via embedding matching. *Proceedings of the 53rd Annual Meeting of the Association for Computational Linguistics and the 7th International Joint Conference on Natural Language Processing*, 1, 1733–1743. 10.3115/v1/P15-1167

Makhzani, A., & Frey, B. (2015). *Winner-take-all autoencoders*. MIT Press.

Makoushina, J., & Kockaert, H. (2008). Zen and the Art of Quality Assurance. Quality Assurance Automation in Translation: Needs, Reality and Expectation. *Proceedings of the International Conference on Translating and the Computer*.

Makoushina, J. (2007). Translation quality assurance tools: Current state and future approaches. *Translating and the Computer*, *29*, 1–39.

Maldonado, S., & Weber, R. (2009). A wrapper method for feature selection using support vector machines. *Information Sciences*, *179*(13), 2208–2217. doi:10.1016/j.ins.2009.02.014

Mamdani, E. H., & Assilian, S. (1975). An experiment in linguistic synthesis with a fuzzy logic controller. *International Journal of Man-Machine Studies*, *7*(1), 1–13. doi:10.1016/S0020-7373(75)80002-2

Maney, T., Sibert, L., Perzanowski, D., Gupta, K., & Schmidt-Nielsen, A. (2012). Toward Determining the Comprehensibility of Machine Translations. *Proceedings of the 1st PITR*, 1-7.

Manning, C. D., Surdeanu, M., Bauer, J., Finkel, J. R., Bethard, S., & McClosky, D. (2014). The stanford corenlp natural language processing toolkit. ACL (System Demonstrations), 55–60. doi:10.3115/v1/P14-5010

Manshu, T., & Bing, W. (2019). Adding Prior Knowledge in Hierarchical Attention Neural Network for Cross Domain Sentiment Classification. *IEEE Access: Practical Innovations, Open Solutions*, *7*, 32578–32588. doi:10.1109/ACCESS.2019.2901929

Manshu, T., & Xuemin, Z. (2019). CCHAN: An End to End Model for Cross Domain Sentiment Classification. *IEEE Access: Practical Innovations, Open Solutions*, *7*, 50232–50239. doi:10.1109/ACCESS.2019.2910300

Mark, H. (2019). *Nascar driver gaughan swims with the sharks at newport aquarium to teach kids about teamwork* [blog post]. retrieved from https://www.nkytribune.com/2016/09/nascar-driver-gaughan-swims-with-the-sharks-at-newport-aquarium-to-teach-kids-about-teamwork/. *Northern Kentucky Tribune.*

MarketsandMarkets. (2019). *Natural Language Processing Market by Component, Deployment Mode, Organization Size, Type, Application, Vertical And Region - Global Forecast to 2024.* Retrieved from https://www.reportlinker.com/p05834031/Natural-Language-Processing-Market-by-Component-Deployment-Mode-Organization-Size-Type-Application-Vertical-And-Region-Global-Forecast-to.html

Marsi, E., Bosch, A. van den, & Soudi, A. (2005). Memory-based morphological analysis generation and part-of-speech tagging of Arabic. *Computational Approaches to Semitic Languages*, 1–8.

Martínez-Cámara, E., Martín-Valdivia, M. T., Ureña-López, L. A., & Mitkov, R. (2015). Polarity classification for Spanish tweets using the COST corpus. *Journal of Information Science*, *41*(3), 263–272. doi:10.1177/0165551514566564

Martinez-Romo, J., & Araujo, L. (2013). Detecting malicious tweets in trending topics using a statistical analysis of language. *Expert Systems with Applications*, *40*(8), 2992–3000. doi:10.1016/j.eswa.2012.12.015

Martin, J. H. (2006). A corpus-based analysis of context effects on metaphor comprehension. *Trends in Linguistics Studies and Monographs*, *171*, 214.

Martin-Nielsen, J. (2012). It Was All Connected: Computers and Linguistics in Early Cold War America. In *Cold War Social Science* (pp. 63–78). New York: Palgrave Macmillan.

Mases, E. (1998). La cuestión social, la cuestión indígena. El destino final de los indios sometidos. Argentina y Chile, 1878-1885. *Estudios Sociales (Santo Domingo, Dominican Republic)*, *15*(1), 31–45. doi:10.14409/es.v15i1.2410

Masmoudi, A., Khmekhem, M. E., Khrouf, M., & Belguith, L. H. (2019). Transliteration of Arabizi into Arabic Script for Tunisian Dialect. *ACM Transactions on Asian and Low-Resource Language Information Processing (TALLIP)*, *19*(2), Article 32.

Masmoudi, A., Habash, N., Khmekhem, M. E., Estève, Y., & Belguith, L. H. (2015). Arabic Transliteration of Romanized Tunisian Dialect Text: A Preliminary Investigation. *Lecture Notes in Computer Science*, *9041*, 608–619. doi:10.1007/978-3-319-18111-0_46

Mass, H. D. (1972). Über den Zusammenhang zwischen wortschatzumfang und länge eines textes. *Lili. Zeitschrift für Literaturwissenschaft und Linguistik*, *2*(8), 73.

Masterman, M., & Kay, M. (1959). *Operational system (IBM-USAF Translator Mark I)*. Foreign Technology Division, USAF.

Mataoui, M., Zelmati, O., & Boumechache, M. (2016). A Proposed Lexicon-Based Sentiment Analysis Approach for the Vernacular Algerian Arabic. *Res Comput Sci*, *110*(1), 55–70. doi:10.13053/rcs-110-1-5

Mathews, S. M. (2019). Explainable Artificial Intelligence Applications in NLP, Biomedical, and Malware Classification: A Literature Review. *Advances in Intelligent Systems and Computing*, *998*, 1269–1292. doi:10.1007/978-3-030-22868-2_90

Matlab Plot. (2020). *2-D line plot - MATLAB plot*. Retrieved from https://www.mathworks.com/help/matlab/ref/plot.html

Matlab. (2020). *The official home of MATLAB software*. Retrieved from https://www.mathworks.com/products/matlab.html

Matthew, J. K., Spencer, G., & Andrea, Z. (2015). Potential applications of sentiment analysis in educational research and practice – Is SITE the friendliest conference? In *Proceedings of Society for Information Technology & Teacher Education International Conference 2015*. Association for the Advancement of Computing in Education (AACE).

Matthews, B. W. (1975). Comparison of the predicted and observed secondary structure of T4 phage lysozyme. *Biochimica et Biophysica Acta (BBA)-. Protein Structure, 405*(2), 442–451. doi:10.1016/0005-2795(75)90109-9 PMID:1180967

Maven (3.2.5) [Software]. (2014). Retrieved from https://maven.apache.org/

Mayda, İ., & Amasyalı, M. F. (2016). Cross usage of articles and tweets on author identification. In 2016 Electric Electronics, Computer Science, Biomedical Engineerings' Meeting (EBBT) (pp. 1-4). IEEE. doi:10.1109/EBBT.2016.7483676

McCarthy, P. M. (2005). *An assessment of the range and usefulness of lexical diversity measures and the potential of the measure of textual, lexical diversity (MTLD)* (Doctoral dissertation). The University of Memphis.

McCarthy, P. M., & Jarvis, S. (2010). MTLD, vocd-D, and HD-D: A validation study of sophisticated approaches to lexical diversity assessment. *Behavior Research Methods, 42*(2), 381–392. doi:10.3758/BRM.42.2.381 PMID:20479170

McClure, J., & Velluppillai, J. (2013). The effects of news media reports on earthquake attributions and preventability judgments: Mixed messages about the Canterbury earthquake. *Australasian Journal of Disaster and Trauma Studies, 2013*(1), 27–36.

McKeown, K., Daume, H. III, Chaturvedi, S., Paparrizos, J., Thadani, K., Barrio, P., Biran, O., Bothe, S., Collins, M., Fleischmann, K. R., Gravano, L., Jha, R., King, B., McInerney, K., Moon, T., Neelakantan, A., O'Seaghdha, D., Radev, D., Templeton, C., & Teufel, S. (2016). Predicting the impact of scientific concepts using full-text features. *Journal of the Association for Information Science and Technology, 67*(11), 2684–2696. doi:10.1002/asi.23612

Medhaffar, S., Bougares, F., Estève, Y., & Hadrich-Belguith, L. (2017, April). Sentiment analysis of tunisian dialects: Linguistic ressources and experiments. In *Proceedings of the third Arabic natural language processing workshop* (pp. 55-61). 10.18653/v1/W17-1307

Medhat, W., Hassan, A., & Korashy, H. (2014). Sentiment analysis algorithms and applications: A survey. *Ain Shams Engineering Journal. Elsevier., 5*(4), 1093–1113. doi:10.1016/j.asej.2014.04.011

Medina, A. & Buenrostro, C. (2003). Características cuantitativas de la flexión verbal de Chuj. *Estudios de Lingüística Aplicada, 39*, 15-31.

Medina, A. 2008. Affix discovery based on entropy and economy measurements. In *Proceedings of the Texas Linguistics Society X Conference: Computational Linguistics for Less-Studied Languages*. Austin, TX: University of Texas.

Medina, A. (2007). Affix discovery by means of corpora: experiments for Spanish, Czech, Ralámuli and Chuj. In *Aspects of Automatic Text Analysis* (pp. 277–299). Springer.

Meer, van den J., & Görög, A. (2015). *Dynamic Quality Framework Report 2015: Results of the Evaluate Survey conducted in 2014.*

Meftouh, K., Bouchemal, N., & Smaili, K. (2012). a Study of a Non-Resourced Language : an Algerian Dialect. *Proc. 3td International Workshop on Spoken Languages Technologies for Under-Resourced Languages (SLTU'12).*

Mikolov, T., Chen, K., Corrado, G. S., & Dean, J. (2013). *Efficient Estimation of Word Representations in Vector Space.* Retrieved from https://arxiv.org/pdf/1301.3781.pdf

Mikolov, T., Sutskever, I., & Chen, K., Corrado, G., & Dean, J. (2013). Distributed Representations of Words and Phrases and Their Compositionality. In *NIPS'13, Proceedings of the 26th International Conference on Neural Information Processing Systems - Volume 2* (pp. 3111–3119). Curran Associates Inc. Retrieved from https://dl.acm.org/citation.cfm?id=2999792.2999959

Mikolov, T., Sutskever, I., Chen, K., Corrado, G. S., & Dean, J. (2013). Distributed representations of words and phrases and their compositionality. Advances in neural information processing systems, 3111–3119.

Miller, G. A. (1995). WordNet: A Lexical Database for English. *Communications of the ACM, 38*(11), 39–41. doi:10.1145/219717.219748

Miller, G. A. (1998). *WordNet: An electronic lexical database.* MIT Press.

Miller, I., Ashton-Chess, J., Spolders, H., Fert, V., Ferrara, J., Kroll, W., Askaa, J., Larcier, P., Terry, P. F., Bruinvels, A., & Huriez, A. (2011). Market access challenges in the EU for high medical value diagnostic tests. *Personalized Medicine, 8*(2), 137–148. doi:10.2217/pme.11.2 PMID:29783414

Ministerio de Desarrollo Social y Familia. (2013). *National Socioeconomic Characterization Survey (CASEN).* Santiago, Chile: Government of Chile. http://observatorio.ministeriodesarrollosocial.gob.cl/casen-multidimensional/casen/casen_2013.php

Minsky, M. (1961). Steps Toward Artificial Intelligence. *Proceedings of the IRE.*

Mitchell, R. (2015). *Web Scraping with Python.* O'Reilly Publishers.

Mohammad, S. M. (2017). Challenges in sentiment analysis. In A practical guide to sentiment analysis. Springer.

Mohammad, S., Salameh, M., & Kiritchenko, S. (2016, May). Sentiment lexicons for Arabic social media. In *Proceedings of the Tenth International Conference on Language Resources and Evaluation (LREC'16)* (pp. 33-37). Academic Press.

Mohammad, S. M., Salameh, M., & Kiritchenko, S. (2016). Sentiment Lexicons for Arabic Social Media. *Tenth International Conference on Language Resources and Evaluation (LREC),* 33–37.

Mohammad, S. M., & Turney, P. D. (2010). Emotions evoked by common words and phrases: Using mechanical turk to create an emotion lexicon. In *Proceedings of the NAACL HLT 2010 workshop on computational approaches to analysis and generation of emotion in text,* (pp. 26–34). Los Angeles, CA: Association for Computational Linguistics.

Mohammad, S. M., & Turney, P. D. (2013). Crowdsourcing a word–emotion association lexicon. *Computational Intelligence, 29*(3), 436–465. doi:10.1111/j.1467-8640.2012.00460.x

Molina-González, M. D., Martínez-Cámara, E., Martín-Valdivia, M. T., & Ureña-López, L. A. (2015). A Spanish semantic orientation approach to domain adaptation for polarity classification. *Information Processing & Management, 51*(4), 520–531. doi:10.1016/j.ipm.2014.10.002

Moreno, R. E. V. (2004). Metaphor interpretation and emergence. *UCL Working Papers in Linguistics, 16,* 297-322.

Mountassir, A., Benbrahim, H., & Berraba, I. (2013). Sentiment classification on arabic corpora. A preliminary cross-study. *International Conference on Innovative Techniques and Applications of Artificial Intelligence, 16*(1), 259–272. 10.3166/dn.16.1.73-96

Mubarak, H., Abdelali, A., Darwish, K., Eldesouki, M., Samih, Y., & Sajjad, H. (2019). A System for Diacritizing Four Varieties of Arabic. *Proceedings of the 2019 Conference on Empirical Methods in Natural Language Processing and the 9th International Joint Conference on Natural Language Processing (EMNLP-IJCNLP),* 217–222. 10.18653/v1/D19-3037

Mulki, H., Haddad, H., Ali, C. B., & Babao, I. (2018). Tunisian Dialect Sentiment Analysis : A Natural Language Processing-based Approach. *Computación y Sistemas, 22*(4). Advance online publication. doi:10.13053/cys-22-4-3009

Müller, J., & Le Petit, Y. (2019). *Transport & Environment.* Retrieved from https://www.transportenvironment.org/sites/te/files/publications/2019_09_Briefing_LEZ-ZEZ_final.pdf

Müller, M. M., & Salathé, M. (2019). Crowdbreaks: Tracking health trends using public social media data and crowdsourcing. *Frontiers in Public Health*, *7*(APR), 81. Advance online publication. doi:10.3389/fpubh.2019.00081 PMID:31037238

Multidimensional Quality Metrics (MQM) Issue Types. (2015). *German Research Center for Artificial Intelligence (DFKI) and QTLaunchPad*. Retrieved from http://www.qt21.eu/mqm-definition/issues-list-2015-12-30.html

Murdoch, W. J., Singh, C., Kumbier, K., Abbasi-Asl, R., & Yu, B. (2019). Definitions, methods, and applications in interpretable machine learning. *Proceedings of the National Academy of Sciences of the United States of America*, *116*(44), 22071–22080. doi:10.1073/pnas.1900654116 PMID:31619572

Murray, C. J. L., & Lopez, A. D. (2013). Measuring the Global Burden of Disease. *The New England Journal of Medicine*, *369*(5), 448–457. doi:10.1056/NEJMra1201534 PMID:23902484

Muzii, L. (2006). Quality Assessment and Economic Sustainability of Translation. *International Journal of Translation*, *9*, 15–38.

Myagmar, B., Li, J., & Kimura, S. (2019). Cross-Domain Sentiment Classification With Bidirectional Contextualized Transformer Language Models. *IEEE Access: Practical Innovations, Open Solutions*, *7*, 163219–163230. doi:10.1109/ACCESS.2019.2952360

Nadali, S., Murad, M. A. A., & Kadir, R. A. (2010). Sentiment classification of customer reviews based on fuzzy logic. In *2010 International Symposium on Information Technology* (Vol. 2, pp. 1037-1044). IEEE. 10.1109/ITSIM.2010.5561583

Nadkarni, P. M., Ohno-Machado, L., & Chapman, W. W. (2011). Natural language processing: An introduction. *Journal of the American Medical Informatics Association*, *18*(5), 544–551. doi:10.1136/amiajnl-2011-000464 PMID:21846786

Nam, H., & Kannan, P. K. (2014). The Informational Value of Social Tagging Networks. *Journal of Marketing*, *78*(4), 21–40. doi:10.1509/jm.12.0151

Narver, J. C., & Slater, S. F. (1990). The Effect of a Market Orientation on Business Profitability. *Journal of Marketing*, *54*(4), 20–35. doi:10.1177/002224299005400403

Nasukawa, T., & Yi, J. (2003). Sentiment analysis: Capturing favorability using natural language processing. *Proceedings of the 2nd international conference on Knowledge capture*, 70-77. 10.1145/945645.945658

Neethu, M. S., & Rajasree, R. (2013). Sentiment analysis in twitter using machine learning techniques. In *2013 Fourth International Conference on Computing, Communications and Networking Technologies (ICCCNT)* (pp. 1–5). IEEE. 10.1109/ICCCNT.2013.6726818

News Data Set. (2019). *Kemik Natural Language Processing Group Tweets Data Set*. Retrieved from www.kemik.yildiz.edu.tr

Nickkar, A., Banerjee, S., Chavis, C., Bhuyan, I. A., & Barnes, P. (2019). A spatial-temporal gender and land use analysis of bikeshare ridership: The case study of Baltimore City. *City Cult. Soc*, *18*, 100291. doi:10.1016/j.ccs.2019.100291

Nigam, K., & Lafferty, J., & Mccallum, A. (1999). Using maximum entropy for text classification. In *IJCAI-99, Proceedings of the IJCAI-99 Workshop on Machine Learning for Information Filtering* (pp. 61–67). AAAI Press.

Nikos, E., Angeliki, L., Georgios, P., & Konstantinos, C. 2011. ELS: a word-level method for entity-level sentiment analysis. *WIMS '11 Proceedings of the International Conference on Web Intelligence, Mining and Semantics*.

Niu, X., & Hou, Y. (2017). Hierarchical Attention BLSTM for Modeling Sentences and Documents. Lecture Notes in Computer Science, 10635, 167–177. doi:10.1007/978-3-319-70096-0_18

Nobata, C., Tetreault, J., Thomas, A., Mehdad, Y., & Chang, Y. (2016, April). Abusive language detection in online user content. In *Proceedings of the 25th international conference on world wide web* (pp. 145-153). 10.1145/2872427.2883062

NORD. (2019). https://rarediseases.org/for-patients-and-families/information-resources/rare-disease-information/rare-disease-list/

Norouzi, M., Mikolov, T., Bengio, S., Singer, Y., Shlens, J., Frome, A., . . . Dean, J. (2014). Zero-Shot Learning by Convex Combination of Semantic Embeddings. In *2nd International Conference on Learning Representations, ICLR 2014*. Conference Track Proceedings.

Noura, F., Elie, C., Rawad, A. A., & Hazem, H. 2010. Sentence-level and document-level sentiment mining for Arabic texts. *Proceeding IEEE International Conference on Data Mining Workshops.*

Oliveira, L. P. (2009). Linguística de Corpus: teoria, interfaces e aplicações. *Matraga-Revista do Programa de Pós-Graduação em Letras da UERJ, 16*(24).

Oriola, O., & Kotzi, E. (2020). Evaluating Machine Learning Techniques for Detecting Offensive and Hate Speech in South African Tweets. *IEEE Access: Practical Innovations, Open Solutions, 8*, 21496–21509. doi:10.1109/AC-CESS.2020.2968173

Orkphol, K., Yang, W. (2019). Sentiment Analysis on Microblogging with K-Means Clustering and Artificial Bee Colony. *International Journal of Computational Intelligence and Applications, 18*(3).

Ortiz-Ospina, E. (2019, September 18). *The rise of social media*. Retrieved June 1, 2020 from https://ourworldindata.org/rise-of-social-media

Osimo & Mureddu. (2011). *Research Challenge on Opinion Mining and Sentiment Analysis.* Academic Press.

Ouyang, X., Zhou, P., Li, C. H., & Liu, L. (2015). Sentiment Analysis using Convolutional Neural Network. *2015 IEEE International Conference on Computer and Information Technology; Ubiquitous Computing and Communications; Dependable, Autonomic and Secure Computing; Pervasive Intelligence and Computing*, 2359-2364.

Ovanessoff, A., & Plastino, E. (2017). Cómo la inteligencia artificial puede generar crecimiento en Sudamérica. Reporte de investigación, Accenture, Buenos Aires, Argentina.

Owoputi, O., O'Connor, B., Dyer, C., Gimpel, K., Schneider, N. A., & Smith, N. A. (2013). Improved part-of-speech tagging for online conversational text with word clusters. *Proceedings of NAACL-HLT*, 380-390.

Özgür, A., Özgür, L., & Güngör, T. (2005). Text categorization with class-based and corpus-based keyword selection. In *International Symposium on Computer and Information Sciences* (pp. 606-615). Springer.

Özgür, L., Güngör, T., & Gürgen, F. (2004). Adaptive anti-spam filtering for agglutinative languages: A special case for Turkish. *Pattern Recognition Letters, 25*(16), 1819–1831. doi:10.1016/j.patrec.2004.07.004

Padró, L., & Stanilovsky, E. (2012). Freeling 3.0: Towards Wider Multilinguality. *Proceedings of the Eight International Conference on Language Resources and Evaluation (LREC'12).*

Panagiotou, N., Katakis, I., & Gunopulos, D. (2016). Detecting events in online social networks: Definitions, trends and challenges. In *Solving Large Scale Learning Tasks. Challenges and Algorithms* (pp. 42–84). Springer. doi:10.1007/978-3-319-41706-6_2

Pang, B., Lee, L., & Vaithyanathan, S. (2002). *Thumbs up? Sentiment classification using machine learning techniques.* Association for Computational Linguistics. Retrieved from https://dl.acm.org/ft_gateway.cfm?id=1118704&type=pdf

Pang, B., & Lee, L. (2004). A sentimental education: Sentiment Analysis using subjectivity summarization based on minimum cuts. In *Proceedings of the 42nd Annual Meeting on Association for Computational Linguistics*, (pp. 271-278). 10.3115/1218955.1218990

Pang, B., & Lee, L. (2008). Opinion Mining and Sentiment Analysis. *Foundations and Trends in Information Retrieval.*, 2(1), 1–135. doi:10.1561/1500000011

Pang, B., Lee, L., & Vaithyanathan, S. (2002). Thumbs up? Sentiment classification using machine learning techniques. In *Proceedings of the Conference on Empirical Methods in Natural Language Processing (EMNLP)*, (pp.79-86). 10.3115/1118693.1118704

Pan, S. J., Ni, X., Sun, J.-T., Yang, Q., & Chen, Z. (2010). Cross-domain Sentiment Classification via Spectral Feature Alignment. In *WWW '10, Proceedings of the 19th International Conference on World Wide Web* (pp. 751–760). New York, NY: ACM. 10.1145/1772690.1772767

Pan, S. J., & Yang, Q. (2010). A Survey on Transfer Learning. *IEEE Transactions on Knowledge and Data Engineering*, 22(10), 1345–1359. doi:10.1109/TKDE.2009.191

Pantel, P. (2005). Inducing ontological co-occurrence vectors. In *Proceedings of the 43rd Annual Meeting on Association for Computational Linguistics*, (pp. 125–132). Ann Arbor, MI: Association for Computational Linguistics.

Papineni, K., Roukos, S., Ward, T., & Zhu, W.-J. (2002). Bleu: A method for automatic evaluation of machine translation. *Proceedings of ACL*, 311-318.

Park, Y. J. (2018). Predicting the Helpfulness of Online Customer Reviews across Different Product Types. *Sustainability, MDPI*, 10(6), 1–20. doi:10.3390u10061735

Pasha, A., Al-badrashiny, M., Diab, M., El Kholy, A., Eskander, R., Habash, N., Pooleery, M., Rambow, O., & Roth, M., R. (2014). MADAMIRA : A Fast, Comprehensive Tool for Morphological Analysis and Disambiguation of Arabic. *Proceedings of the Ninth International Conference on Language Resources and Evaluation (LREC'14)*, 1094–1101.

Patel, V., Prabhu, G., & Bhowmick, K. (2015). A Survey of Opinion Mining and Sentiment Analysis. *International Journal of Computers and Applications*, 131(1), 24–27. doi:10.5120/ijca2015907218

Pease, A. (2011). *Ontology: A practical guide*. Articulate Software Press.

Pedregosa, F., Varoquaux, G., & Gramfort, A. (2011). Scikit-learn: Machine Learning in Python. *Journal of Machine Learning Research*, 12(85), 2825–2830.

Pelling, C., & Gardner, H. (2019, August). Two Human-Like Imitation-Learning Bots with Probabilistic Behaviors. In *2019 IEEE Conference on Games (CoG)* (pp. 1-7). IEEE. 10.1109/CIG.2019.8847995

Peng, F., Feng, F., & McCallum, A. (2004). Chinese segmentation and new word detection using conditional random fields. *Proceedings of the 20th International Conference on Computational Linguistics*, 562– 568. 10.3115/1220355.1220436

Pennington, J., Socher, R., & Manning, C. D. (2014). Glove: Global Vectors for Word Representation. *Proceedings of the 2014 Conference on Empirical Methods in Natural Language Processing (EMNLP)*. Retrieved from https://www.aclweb.org/anthology/D14-1162.pdf

Pereira, J. F. F. (2017). *Social Media Text Processing and Semantic Analysis for Smart Cities*. arXiv preprint arXiv:1709.03406

Perkins, J. (2014). *Python 3 text processing with NLTK 3 cookbook*. Packt Publishing Ltd.

Peters, B., Niculae, V., & Martins, A. F. T. (2018). Interpretable Structure Induction via Sparse Attention. In *Proceedings of the 2018 EMNLP Workshop BlackboxNLP: Analyzing and Interpreting Neural Networks for NLP* (pp. 365–367). Brussels, Belgium: Association for Computational Linguistics. 10.18653/v1/W18-5450

Petrissans, R. (2002). La brecha digital: Situación regional y perspectivas. *Estudios Internacionales (Santiago)*, *35*(138), 55–70.

Pinto, A., Oliveira, H. G., & Oliveira Alves, A. (2016). Comparing the performance of different NLP toolkits in formal and social media text. In *OpenAccess Series in Informatics, 51, 1-16*. Dagstuhl Publishing.

Piskorski, J., & Yangarber, R. (2013). Information extraction: Past, present and future. In *Multi-source, multilingual information extraction and summarization* (pp. 23–49). Springer. doi:10.1007/978-3-642-28569-1_2

Pitsilis, G. K., Ramampiaro, H., & Langseth, H. (2018). *Detecting offensive language in tweets using deep learning.* arXiv preprint arXiv:1801.04433

Plaza-del-Arco, F. M., Martín-Valdivia, M. T., Ureña-López, L. A., & Mitkov, R. (2019). Improved emotion recognition in spanish social media through incorporation of lexical knowledge. *Future Generation Computer Systems*.

Plutchik, R. (1980). A general psychoevolutionary theory of emotion. In R. Plutchik & H. Kellerman (Eds.), *Theories of Emotion* (pp. 3–33). Academic Press. doi:10.1016/B978-0-12-558701-3.50007-7

Poesio, M., Chamberlain, J., & Kruschwitz, U. (2017). Crowdsourcing. In Handbook of Linguistic Annotation (pp. 277–295). Academic Press.

Popoola, A., Krasnoshtan, D., Toth, A. P., Naroditskiy, V., Castillo, C., Meier, P., & Rahwan, I. (2013). Information verification during natural disasters. In *Proceedings of the 22nd International Conference on World Wide Web, WWW '13 Companion*, (pp. 1029-1032). New York. ACM. 10.1145/2487788.2488111

Porshnev, A., Redkin, I., & Shevchenko, A. (2013). Machine learning in prediction of stock market indicators based on historical data and data from twitter sentiment analysis. In *2013 IEEE 13th International Conference on Data Mining Workshops* (pp. 440-444). IEEE. 10.1109/ICDMW.2013.111

Porter Stemmer. (2019). *The Porter Stemming Algorithm.* Retrieved from https://tartarus.org/martin/PorterStemmer/

Postgre, S. Q. L. (9.4) [Software]. (2014). Retrieved from https://www.postgresql.org/

Powell, W., & Snellman, K. (2004). The Knowledge Economy. *Annual Review of Sociology.* www.annualreviews.org/doi/full/10.1146/annurev.soc.29.010202.100037#_i2

Powers, D. M. (2011). Evaluation: From precision, recall and F-measure to ROC, informedness, markedness and correlation. *Journal of Machine Learning Technologies*, *2*(1), 37–63.

Prasad, R., Dinesh, N., Lee, A., Miltsakaki, E., Robaldo, L., Joshi, A. K., & Webber, B. L. (2008, May). The Penn Discourse TreeBank 2.0. LREC.

Preoţiuc-Pietro, D., Volkova, S., Lampos, V., Bachrach, Y., & Aletras, N. (2015, September 22). Studying User Income through Language, Behaviour and Affect in Social Media. *PLoS One*, *10*(9), e0138717. Advance online publication. Retrieved June 1, 2020, from. doi:10.1371/journal.pone.0138717 PMID:26394145

Prescott, C. (2019, May 24). *Internet users, UK: 2019.* Retrieved from https://www.ons.gov.uk/businessindustryandtrade/itandinternetindustry/bulletins/internetusers/2019

Priyadarshini, R., Barik, R. K., Panigrahi, C., Dubey, H., & Mishra, B. K. (2020). An investigation into the efficacy of deep learning tools for big data analysis in health care. In Deep Learning and Neural Networks: Concepts, Methodologies, Tools, and Applications (pp. 654-666). IGI Global.

Provost, F. J., & Fawcett, T. (1997, August). Analysis and visualization of classifier performance: Comparison under imprecise class and cost distributions. *KDD: Proceedings / International Conference on Knowledge Discovery & Data Mining. International Conference on Knowledge Discovery & Data Mining*, 97, 43–48.

Qaiser, S., & Ali, R. (2018). Text Mining: Use of TF-IDF to examine the relevance of words to documents. *International Journal of Computers and Applications*, 181(1), 25–29. doi:10.5120/ijca2018917395

Qian, J., ElSherief, M., Belding, E. M., & Wang, W. Y. (2018). *Leveraging intra-user and inter-user representation learning for automated hate speech detection*. arXiv preprint arXiv:1804.03124

Quoc, L., & Tomas, M. (2014). Distributed representations of sentences and documents. *Proceedings of the 31 st International Conference on Machine Learning*, 32.

Qwaider, C., Saad, M., Chatzikyriakidis, S., & Dobnik, S. (2018, May). Shami: A Corpus of Levantine Arabic Dialects. *Proceedings of the Eleventh International Conference on Language Resources and Evaluation (LREC-2018)*.

R Core Team. (2018). *R: A language and environment for statistical computing*. R Foundation for Statistical Computing. https://www.R-project.org/

Rahab, H., Zitouni, A., & Djoudi, M. (2018). SIAAC: Sentiment Polarity Identification on Arabic Algerian Newspaper Comments. In Applied Computational Intelligence and Mathematical Methods (Vol. 662, pp. 141–149). doi:10.1007/978-3-319-67621-0

Rahab, H., Zitouni, A., & Djoudi, M. (2019). SANA: Sentiment analysis on newspapers comments in Algeria. Journal of King Saud University - Computer and Information Sciences. doi:10.1016/j.jksuci.2019.04.012

Rahman, J. (2012). *Implementation of ALICE chatbot as domain specific knowledge bot for BRAC U (FAQ bot)* (Doctoral dissertation). BRAC University.

Rai, S., & Chakraverty, S. (2017). Metaphor detection using fuzzy rough sets. In *International Joint Conference on Rough Sets*, (pp. 271–279). Olsztyn, Poland: Springer. 10.1007/978-3-319-60837-2_23

Rai, S., & Chakraverty, S. (2020). A Survey on Computational Metaphor Processing. *ACM Computing Surveys*, 53(2), 1–37. doi:10.1145/3373265

Rai, S., Chakraverty, S., & Garg, A. (2018b). Effect of Classifiers on Type-III Metaphor Detection. In *Towards Extensible and Adaptable Methods in Computing* (pp. 241–249). Springer. doi:10.1007/978-981-13-2348-5_18

Rai, S., Chakraverty, S., & Tayal, D. K. (2016). Supervised metaphor detection using conditional random fields. In *Proceedings of the Fourth Workshop on Metaphor in NLP*, (pp. 18–27). San Diego, CA: Association of Computational Linguistics. 10.18653/v1/W16-1103

Rai, S., Chakraverty, S., & Tayal, D. K. (2017a, May). Identifying metaphors using fuzzy conceptual features. In *International Conference on Information, Communication and Computing Technology* (pp. 379-386). Springer. 10.1007/978-981-10-6544-6_34

Rai, S., Chakraverty, S., Tayal, D. K., & Kukreti, Y. (2017b). Soft metaphor detection using fuzzy c- means. In *International Conference on Mining Intelligence and Knowledge Exploration*, (pp. 402–411). Springer. 10.1007/978-3-319-71928-3_38

Rai, S., Chakraverty, S., Tayal, D. K., & Kukreti, Y. (2018a). A study on impact of context on metaphor detection. *The Computer Journal*, *61*(11), 1667–1682. doi:10.1093/comjnl/bxy032

Rai, S., Chakraverty, S., Tayal, D. K., Sharma, D., & Garg, A. (2019). Understanding metaphors using emotions. *New Generation Computing*, *37*(1), 5–27. doi:10.100700354-018-0045-3

Raisi, E., & Huang, B. (2016). *Cyberbullying identification using participant-vocabulary consistency.* arXiv preprint arXiv:1606.08084

Rajput, K., Kapoor, R., Mathur, P., Kumaraguru, P., & Shah, R. R. (2020). Transfer Learning for Detecting Hateful Sentiments in Code Switched Language. In *Deep Learning-Based Approaches for Sentiment Analysis* (pp. 159–192). Springer. doi:10.1007/978-981-15-1216-2_7

Rameshbhai, C. J., & Paulose, J. (2019). Opinion mining on newspaper headlines using SVM and NLP. *Iranian Journal of Electrical and Computer Engineering*, *9*(3), 2152–2163. doi:10.11591/ijece.v9i3.pp2152-2163

Ramírez-Tinoco, F. J., Alor-Hernández, G., Sánchez-Cervantes, J. L., Salas-Zárate, M. del P., & Valencia-García, R. (2019). Use of Sentiment Analysis Techniques in Healthcare Domain. In Current Trends in Semantic Web Technologies: Theory and Practic (pp. 189–212). Springer International Publishing. doi:10.1007/978-3-030-06149-4_8

Ran, J. (2019). A Self-attention Based LSTM Network for Text Classification. *Journal of Physics: Conference Series*, *1207*, 12008. doi:10.1088/1742-6596/1207/1/012008

Ranjit, S., Shrestha, S., Subedi, S., & Shakya, S. (2018). Foreign Rate Exchange Prediction Using Neural Network and Sentiment Analysis. *2018 International Conference on Advances in Computing, Communication Control and Networking (ICACCCN)*. 10.1109/ICACCCN.2018.8748819

Rauchfleisch, A., Artho, X., Metag, J., Post, S., & Schäfer, M. S. (2017). How journalists verify user-generated content during terrorist crises. Analyzing Twitter communication during the Brussels attacks. *Social Media and Society*, *3*(3), 1–13. doi:10.1177/2056305117717888

RedTTL: Language Technology Thematic Network. (2007). National Council of Science and Technology (CONACYT), México: www.redttl.mx

Rehurek, R., & Sojka, P. (2010). Software framework for topic modelling with large corpora. *Proceedings of the LREC 2010 Workshop on New Challenges for NLP Frameworks*, 45-50.

Reinsel, D., Gantz, J., & Rydning, J. (2018, November). *The Digitization of the World From Edge to Core.* Retrieved June 1, 2020 from https://www.seagate.com/gb/en/our-story/data-age-2025/

Ribeiro, M. T., Singh, S., & Guestrin, C. (2016). Why Should I Trust You?": Explaining the Predictions of Any Classifier. In *KDD '16, Proceedings of the 22Nd ACM SIGKDD International Conference on Knowledge Discovery and Data Mining* (pp. 1135–1144). New York, NY: ACM. 10.1145/2939672.2939778

Ribeiro, M. T., Singh, S., & Guestrin, C. (Eds.). (2018). *Semantically equivalent adversarial rules for debugging NLP models.* Retrieved from https://www2.scopus.com/inward/record.uri?eid=2-s2.0-85061785761&partnerID=40&md5=be8d9d4a9111c0f0f6ba388f3dcc16bb

Riedemann, A. (2008). La educación intercultural bilingüe en Chile: ¿ampliación de oportunidades para alumnos indígenas? *Indiana*, *25*, 169-193. https://journals.iai.spk-berlin.de/index.php/indiana/article/view/1960

Rixey, R. A. (2013). Station-level forecasting of bikesharing ridership: Station network effects in three US systems. *Transportation Research Record: Journal of the Transportation Research Board*, *2387*(1), 46–55. doi:10.3141/2387-06

Rizos, G., Hemker, K., & Schuller, B. (2019). Augment to Prevent: Short-Text Data Augmentation in Deep Learning for Hate-Speech Classification. In *CIKM '19, Proceedings of the 28th ACM International Conference on Information and Knowledge Management* (pp. 991–1000). New York, NY: ACM. 10.1145/3357384.3358040

Rojas, R. (2013). *Neural networks: a systematic introduction.* Springer Science & Business Media.

Roncero, C., & de Almeida, R. G. (2015). Semantic properties, aptness, familiarity, conventionality, and interpretive diversity scores for 84 metaphors and similes. *Behavior Research Methods*, *47*(3), 800–812. doi:10.375813428-014-0502-y PMID:25007859

Rong, M., Gong, D., & Gao, X. (2019). Feature Selection and Its Use in Big Data: Challenges, Methods, and Trends. *IEEE Access: Practical Innovations, Open Solutions*, *7*, 19709–19725. doi:10.1109/ACCESS.2019.2894366

Rosenthal, S., Farra, N., & Nakov, P. (2017). SemEval-2017 Task 4: Sentiment Analysis in Twitter. In *Proceedings of the 11th International Workshop on Semantic Evaluation (SemEval-2017)* (pp. 502–518). Vancouver, Canada: Association for Computational Linguistics. 10.18653/v1/S17-2088

Rosen, Z. (2018). Computationally constructed concepts: A machine learning approach to metaphor interpretation using usage-based construction grammatical cues. *Proceedings of the Workshop on Figurative Language Processing*, 102–109. 10.18653/v1/W18-0912

Ross, B., Rist, M., Carbonell, G., Cabrera, B., Kurowsky, N., & Wojatzki, M. (2017). *Measuring the reliability of hate speech annotations: The case of the European refugee crisis.* arXiv preprint arXiv:1701.08118

Ruiz, M. E., & Srinivasan, P. (1998). Automatic text categorization using neural networks. In *Proceedings of the 8th ASIS SIG/CR Workshop on Classification Research* (pp. 59-72). Academic Press.

Ruiz, T., Mars, L., Arroyo, R., & Serna, A. (2016). Social Networks, Big Data and Transport Planning. *Transportation Research Procedia, 18*, 446-452.

Rushdi-Saleh, M., Martín-Valdivia, M. T., Ureña-López, L. A., & Perea-Ortega, J. M. (2011). OCA: Opinion corpus for Arabic. *Journal of the American Society for Information Science and Technology*, *62*(10), 2045–2054. doi:10.1002/asi.21598

Saadane, H. (2015). *Le traitement automatique de l'arabe dialectalisé: aspects méthodologiques et algorithmiques* [These de doctorat].

Sabry Farghaly, A. A. (2010). *Arabic computational linguistics.* Stanford University: CSLI Publications, Center for the Study of Language and Information.

Sa, C. A., Santos, R. L. D. S., & Moura, R. S. (2017). An approach for defining the author reputation of comments on products. In *International Conference on Applications of Natural Language to Information Systems* (pp. 326-331). Springer.

Saeed, R. M. K., Rady, S., & Gharib, T. F. (2019). An ensemble approach for spam detection in Arabic opinion texts. Journal of King Saud University - Computer and Information Sciences. doi:10.1016/j.jksuci.2019.10.002

Safrin, R. (2017). *Sentiment Analysis on Online Product Review.* Academic Press.

Sagha, H., Cummins, N., & Schuller, B. (2017). Stacked denoising autoencoders for sentiment analysis: A review. *Wiley Interdisciplinary Reviews. Data Mining and Knowledge Discovery*, *7*(5), e1212. doi:10.1002/widm.1212

Şahin, D. Ö., & Kılıç, E. (2019). Two new feature selection metrics for text classification. *Automatika (Zagreb)*, *60*(2), 162–171. doi:10.1080/00051144.2019.1602293

Sales, J. E., Barzegar, S., Franco, W., Bermeitinger, B., Cunha, T., Davis, B., . . . Handschuh, S. (2018, May). A Multilingual Test Collection for the Semantic Search of Entity Categories. In *Proceedings of the Eleventh International Conference on Language Resources and Evaluation (LREC 2018)*. Academic Press.

Salina, A., & Ilavarasan, E. (2014). Mining Usable Customer feedback from Social networking data for Business Intelligence. *GJMS Special Issue for Recent Advances in Mathematical Sciences and Applications, 13*(2), 1–9.

Sallab, A. A. A., Baly, R., Badaro, G., Hajj, H., Hajj, W. E., & Shaban, K. B. (2015). Deep learning models for sentiment analysis in Arabic. *Proceedings of the Second Workshop on Arabic Natural Language Processing*, 9–17. 10.18653/v1/W15-3202

Salloum, S. A., AlHamad, A. Q., Al-Emran, M., & Shaalan, K. (2018). A survey of Arabic text mining. In *Intelligent Natural Language Processing: Trends and Applications* (pp. 417–431). Springer. doi:10.1007/978-3-319-67056-0_20

Salminen, J., Hopf, M., Chowdhury, S. A., Jung, S. G., Almerekhi, H., & Jansen, B. J. (2020). Developing an online hate classifier for multiple social media platforms. *Human-centric Computing and Information Sciences, 10*(1), 1. doi:10.118613673-019-0205-6

Salton, G., & Buckley, C. (1988). Term-weighting approaches in automatic text retrieval. *Information Processing & Management, 24*(5), 513–523. doi:10.1016/0306-4573(88)90021-0

Salton, G., Singhal, A., Mitra, M., & Buckley, C. (1997). Automatic text structuring and summarization. *Information Processing & Management, 33*(2), 193–207. doi:10.1016/S0306-4573(96)00062-3

Samal, B. R., Behera, A. K., & Panda, M. (2017). Performance Analysis of Supervised Machine Learning Techniques for Sentiment Analysis. *2017 IEEE 3rd International Conference on Sensing, Signal Processing and Security (ICSSS)*, 128-133.

Samur, D., Lai, V. T., Hagoort, P., & Willems, R. M. (2015). Emotional context modulates embodied metaphor comprehension. *Neuropsychologia, 78*, 108–114. doi:10.1016/j.neuropsychologia.2015.10.003 PMID:26449989

Sánchez, J. (2018). *Cómo hacer turismo sostenible*. Retrieved from: https://www.ecologiaverde.com/como-hacer-turismo-sostenible-1216.html

Sanderson, M., & Croft, W. B. (2012). The history of information retrieval research. *Proceedings of the IEEE, 100*, 1444–1451.

Santorini, B. (1990). *Part-of-speech tagging guidelines for the Penn Treebank Project*. Technical report MS-CIS-90-47, Department of Computer and Information Science, University of Pennsylvania.

Santos, C. C. (2012). Os corpora eletrônicos nos estudos da tradução automática. *Revista Letras Raras, 1*(1), 48–64. doi:10.35572/rlr.v1i1.81

Santos, R. L. D. S., de Sousa, R. F., Rabelo, R. A., & Moura, R. S. (2016). An experimental study based on fuzzy systems and artificial neural networks to estimate the importance of reviews about product and services. In *2016 International Joint Conference on Neural Networks* (pp. 647-653). IEEE. 10.1109/IJCNN.2016.7727261

Sardinha, T. B. (2004). *Lingüística de corpus*. Editora Manole Ltda.

Save, A., & Shekokar, N. (2017). Analysis of cross domain sentiment techniques. *2017 International Conference on Electrical, Electronics, Communication, Computer, and Optimization Techniques (ICEECCOT)*. 10.1109/ICEECCOT.2017.8284637

Schenkel, R., Broschart, A., Hwang, S., Theobald, M., & Weikum, G. (2007). Efficient Text Proximity Search. *Spire*, 287–299.

Schmidt, A., & Wiegand, M. (2017, April). A survey on hate speech detection using natural language processing. In *Proceedings of the Fifth International Workshop on Natural Language Processing for Social Media* (pp. 1-10). 10.18653/v1/W17-1101

Schütze, H., Manning, C. D., & Raghavan, P. (2008). Introduction to information retrieval. In *Proceedings of the international communication of association for computing machinery conference* (p. 260). Academic Press.

Sebastiani, F. (2002). Machine learning in automated text categorization. *ACM Computing Surveys, 34*(1), 1–47. doi:10.1145/505282.505283

Seerat, B., & Azam, F. (2012). Opinion mining: Issues and challenges (A Survey). *International Journal of Computers and Applications, 49*(9), 42–51. doi:10.5120/7658-0762

Seljan, S. (2018a). Quality Assurance (QA) of Terminology in a Translation Quality Management System (QMS) in the Business Environment. *EU publications: Translation services in the digital world - A sneak peek into the (near) future*, 92-105.

Seljan, S. (2018b). Total Quality Management Practice in Croatian Language Service Provider Companies. *Proceedings of the ENTerprise REsearch InNOVAtion (ENTRENOVA)*, 461-469. 10.2139srn.3283755

Seljan, S., & Dunđer, I. (2014). Combined Automatic Speech Recognition and Machine Translation in BSeusiness Correspondence Domain for English-Croatian. *International Journal of Computer, Information, Systems and Control Engineering*, 8(11), 1069-1075.

Seljan, S., & Dunđer, I. (2015a). Machine Translation and Automatic Evaluation of English/Russian-Croatian. *Proceedings of the "Corpus Linguistics 2015" Conference at the St. Petersburg State University*, 72-79.

Seljan, S., Dunđer, I., & Stančić, H. (2017). Extracting Terminology by Language Independent Methods. Forum Translationswissenschaft. *Translation Studies and Translation*, 141-147.

Seljan, S., Agić, Ž., & Tadić, M. (2008). Evaluating sentence alignment on Croatian-English parallel corpora. *Proceedings of the 6th Int. Conf. on Formal Approaches to South Slavic and Balkan Languages - FASSBL 2008*, 101-108.

Seljan, S., & Dunđer, I. (2015b). Automatic Quality Evaluation of Machine-Translated Output in Sociological-Philosophical-Spiritual Domain. *Proceedings of the CISTI 2015: 10th Iberian Conference on Information Systems and Technologies*, 2, 128-131. 10.1109/CISTI.2015.7170425

Seljan, S., Dunđer, I., & Pavlovski, M. (2020). Human Quality Evaluation of Machine-Translated Poetry. *Proceedings of MIPRO 2020: Intelligent Systems*. (in press)

Seljan, S., Gašpar, A., & Pavuna, D. (2007). Sentence Alignment as the Basis For Translation Memory Database. *Proceedings of INFuture 2007 - Digital Information and Heritage*, 299-311.

Seljan, S., & Katalinić, J. (2017). Integrating Localization into a Video Game. *Proceedings of INFuture 2017: Integrating ICT in Society*, 43-55.

Seljan, S., Klasnić, K., Stojanac, M., Pešorda, B., & Mikelić Preradović, N. (2015). Information Transfer through Online Summarizing and Translation Technology. *Proceedings of INFuture2015: e-Institutions – Openness, Accessibility, and Preservation*, 197-210. 10.17234/INFUTURE.2015.24

Seljan, S., & Pavuna, D. (2006). Translation Memory Database in the Translation Process. *Proceedings of the 17th International Conference on Information and Intelligent Systems IIS 2006*, 327-332.

Seljan, S., Tadić, M., Šnajder, J., Dalbelo Bašić, B., & Osmann, V. (2010). Corpus Aligner (CorAl) Evaluation on English-Croatian Parallel Corpora. *Proceedings of the Conference Language Resources and Evaluation - LREC 2010*, 3481-3484.

Semmar, N., & Saadane, H. (2013). Using Transliteration of Proper Names from Arabic to Latin Script to Improve English-Arabic Word Alignment. *International Joint Conference on Natural Language Processing, October*, 1022–1026.

Serna, A., & Gasparovic, S. (2018). Transport analysis approach based on big data and text mining analysis from social media. *Transportation Research Procedia*, *33*, 291–298. doi:10.1016/j.trpro.2018.10.105

Serna, A., Gerrikagoitia, J. K., Bernabé, U., & Ruiz, T. (2017a). Sustainability analysis on Urban Mobility based on Social Media content. *Transportation Research Procedia*, *24*, 1–8. doi:10.1016/j.trpro.2017.05.059

Serna, A., Gerrikagoitia, J. K., Bernabe, U., & Ruiz, T. (2017b). A method to assess sustainable mobility for sustainable tourism: The case of the public bike systems. In *Information and Communication Technologies in Tourism 2017* (pp. 727–739). Springer. doi:10.1007/978-3-319-51168-9_52

Serna, A., Ruiz, T., Gerrikagoitia, J. K., & Arroyo, R. (2019). Identification of Enablers and Barriers for Public Bike Share System Adoption using Social Media and Statistical Models. *Sustainability*, *11*(22), 6259. doi:10.3390u11226259

Severance, C. (2013). *Python for informatics: Exploring information* (1st ed.). CreateSpace Independent Publishing Platform.

Shafiabady, N., Lee, L. H., Rajkumar, R., Kallimani, V. P., Akram, N. A., & Isa, D. (2016). Using unsupervised clustering approach to train the Support Vector Machine for text classification. *Neurocomputing*, *211*, 4–10. doi:10.1016/j.neucom.2015.10.137

Shah, D., Isah, H., & Zulkernine, F. (2018). Predicting the Effects of News Sentiments on the Stock Market. *2018 IEEE International Conference on Big Data (Big Data)*. 10.1109/BigData.2018.8621884

Shaheen, S. A., Guzman, S., & Zhang, H. (2010). Bikesharing in Europe, the Americas, and Asia: Past, present, and future. *Transportation Research Record: Journal of the Transportation Research Board*, *2143*(1), 159–167. doi:10.3141/2143-20

Shah, K. B., Shetty, M. S., Shah, D. P., & Pamnani, R. (2017). Approaches towards building a banking assistant. *International Journal of Computers and Applications*, *166*(11), 1–6. doi:10.5120/ijca2017914140

Shahnawaz, A. P. (2017). Sentiment Analysis: Approaches and Open Issues. *International Conference on Computing, Communication and Automation (ICCCA2017)*, 154-158.

Shang, W., Huang, H., Zhu, H., Lin, Y., Qu, Y., & Wang, Z. (2007). A novel feature selection algorithm for text categorization. *Expert Systems with Applications*, *33*(1), 1–5. doi:10.1016/j.eswa.2006.04.001

Sharef, N. M., Zin, H. M., & Nadali, S. (2016). Overview and Future Opportunities of Sentiment Analysis Approaches for Big Data. *Journal of Computational Science*, *12*(3), 153–168. doi:10.3844/jcssp.2016.153.168

Sharma, A., & Dey, S. (2012). A comparative study of feature selection and machine learning techniques for sentiment analysis. *Proceedings of the 2012 ACM Research in Applied Computation Symposium*, 1-7. 10.1145/2401603.2401605

Sharma, A., & Dey, S. (2012). An artificial neural network based approach for sentiment analysis of opinionated text. In *Proceedings of the 2012 ACM Research in Applied Computation Symposium* (pp. 37-42). ACM. 10.1145/2401603.2401611

Sharma, D., Sabharwal, M., Goyal, V., & Vij, M. (2019). Sentiment Analysis Techniques for Social Media Data: A Review. *First International Conference on Sustainable Technologies for Computational Intelligence. Proceedings of ICTSCI 2019,* 75-90.

Shi, L., Jianping, C., & Jie, X. (2018). Prospecting information extraction by text mining based on convolutional neural networks–a case study of the Lala copper deposit, China. *IEEE Access: Practical Innovations, Open Solutions, 6,* 52286–52297. doi:10.1109/ACCESS.2018.2870203

Shmueli, B., & Ku, L.-W. (2019). *SocialNLP EmotionX 2019 Challenge Overview: Predicting Emotions in Spoken Dialogues and Chats.* Retrieved from https://arxiv.org/abs/1909.07734

Shoufan, A., & Alameri, S. (2015, July). Natural language processing for dialectical Arabic: A Survey. In *Proceedings of the second workshop on Arabic natural language processing* (pp. 36-48). 10.18653/v1/W15-3205

Shutova, E. (2010). Automatic metaphor interpretation as a paraphrasing task. In *Human Language Technologies: The 2010 Annual Conference of the North American Chapter of the Association for Computational Linguistics,* (pp. 1029–1037). Association for Computational Linguistics.

Shutova, E., Sun, L., & Korhonen, A. (2010). Metaphor identification using verb and noun clustering. In *Proceedings of the 23rd International Conference on Computational Linguistics,* (pp. 1002–1010), Beijing, China. Association for Computational Linguistics.

Shuyo, N. (2010). *Language Detection Library for Java.* Retrieved from https://github.com/shuyo/language-detection/

Sierra, G. (2017). *Introducción a los corpus lingüísticos.* IINGEN-UNAM.

Silva, N. R., Lima, D., & Barros, F. (2012). Sapair: Um processo de análise de sentimento no nível de característica. *IV International Workshop on Web and Text Intelligence.*

Simões, A. (2004). *Parallel corpora word alignment and applications* (Doctoral dissertation).

Singh, J. P., Irani, S., Rana, N. P., Dwivedi, Y. K., Saumya, S., & Roy, P. K. (2017). Predicting the "helpfulness" of online consumer reviews. *Journal of Business Research, 70,* 346–355. doi:10.1016/j.jbusres.2016.08.008

Škof, N. (2017). *Utjecaj digitalnih resursa i alata na kvalitetu prijevoda u računalno potpomognutom prevođenju* (Diploma thesis). University of Zagreb.

Smeets, I. (2008). *A Grammar of Mapuche.* Mouton de Gruyter. doi:10.1515/9783110211795

Smiley, D., & Pugh, D. E. (2011). *Apache Solr 3 Enterprise Search Server.* Packt Publishing Ltd.

Snell-Hornby, M. (2006). *The turns of Translation Studies. New Paradigms Or Shifting Viewpoints?* John Benjamins. doi:10.1075/btl.66

Snover, M., Dorr, B., Schwartz, R., Linnea, M., & Makhoul, J. (2006). A Study of Translation Edit Rate with Targeted Human Annotation. *Proceedings of the Association for Machine Translation in the Americas (AMTA),* 223-231.

Snow, R., O'Connor, B., Jurafsky, D., & Ng, A. Y. (2008, October). Cheap and fast---but is it good?: evaluating non-expert annotations for natural language tasks. In *Proceedings of the conference on empirical methods in natural language processing* (pp. 254-263). Association for Computational Linguistics. 10.3115/1613715.1613751

Socher, R., Perelygin, A., Wu, J., Chuang, J., Manning, C. D., Ng, A. Y., & Potts, C. (2013, October). Recursive deep models for semantic compositionality over a sentiment treebank. In *Proceedings of the 2013 conference on empirical methods in natural language processing* (pp. 1631-1642). Academic Press.

Socher, R., Perelygin, A., Wu, J., Chuang, J., Manning, C. D., Ng, A., & Potts, C. (2013). Recursive Deep Models for Semantic Compositionality Over a Sentiment Treebank. In *Proceedings of the 2013 Conference on Empirical Methods in Natural Language Processing* (pp. 1631–1642). Seattle, WA: Association for Computational Linguistics. Retrieved from https://www.aclweb.org/anthology/D13-1170

Soliman, A. B., Eissa, K., & El-Beltagy, S. R. (2017). AraVec: A set of Arabic Word Embedding Models for use in Arabic NLP. *Procedia Computer Science, 117*, 256–265. doi:10.1016/j.procs.2017.10.117

Soman, S. J., Swaminathan, P., Anandan, R., Kalaivani, K. (2018). A comparative review of the challenges encountered in sentiment analysis of Indian regional language tweets vs English language tweets. *International Journal of Engineering & Technology, 7*(2), 319-322.

Sonagi, A., & Gore, D. (2013). Sentiment Analysis and Challenges Involved: A Survey. *International Journal of Scientific Research (Ahmedabad, India), 4*(1), 1928–1932.

Soricut, R., & Brill, E. (2006). Automatic question answering using the web: Beyond the factoid. *Information Retrieval, 9*(2), 191–206. doi:10.100710791-006-7149-y

Sousa, R. F., Rabêlo, R. A., & Moura, R. S. (2015). A fuzzy system-based approach to estimate the importance of online customer reviews. In *2015 IEEE International Conference on Fuzzy Systems* (pp. 1-8). IEEE. 10.1109/FUZZ-IEEE.2015.7337914

Spasic, I., Ananiadou, S., McNaught, J., & Kumar, A. (2005). Text mining and ontologies in biomedicine: Making sense of raw text. *Briefings in Bioinformatics, 6*(3), 239–251. doi:10.1093/bib/6.3.239 PMID:16212772

Specia, L., & Farzindar, A. (2010). Estimating Machine Translation Post-Editing Effort with HTER. *Proceedings of the AMTA 2010- workshop: Bringing MT to the User: MT Research and the Translation Industry.*

Spring framework (4.0) [Software]. (2013). Retrieved from https://spring.io/

Spss, I. I. B. M. (2011). IBM SPSS statistics for Windows, version 20.0. New York: IBM Corp.

Srinivasan, P. (2004). Text Mining: Generating Hypotheses from MEDLINE. *Journal of the American Society for Information Science and Technology, 55*(5), 396–413. doi:10.1002/asi.10389

Srivastava, R., & Bhatia, M. P. S. (2013). Quantifying modified opinion strength: A fuzzy inference system for sentiment analysis. In *2013 International Conference on Advances in Computing, Communications and Informatics* (pp. 1512-1519). IEEE. 10.1109/ICACCI.2013.6637404

Srivastava, R., & Bhatia, M. P. S. (2017). Challenges with sentiment analysis of on-line micro-texts. *International Journal of Intelligent Systems and Applications, 9*(7), 31–40. doi:10.5815/ijisa.2017.07.04

Štajner, T., Thomee, B., Popescu, A. M., Pennacchiotti, M., & Jaimes, A. (2013). Automatic Selection of Social Media Responses to News. In *Proceedings of the 19th ACM SIGKDD International Conference on Knowledge Discovery and Data Mining, KDD '13.* ACM. 10.1145/2487575.2487659

Stamatatos, E., Fakotakis, N., & Kokkinakis, G. (2000). Automatic text categorization in terms of genre and author. *Computational Linguistics, 26*(4), 471–495. doi:10.1162/089120100750105920

Stappen, L., Cummins, N., Meßner, E.-M., Baumeister, H., Dineley, J., & Schuller, B. W. (2019). Context Modelling Using Hierarchical Attention Networks for Sentiment and Self-assessed Emotion Detection in Spoken Narratives. In *Proceedings of the 2019 IEEE International Conference on Acoustics, Speech and Signal Processing (ICASSP)* (pp. 6680–6684). Brighton: IEEE. 10.1109/ICASSP.2019.8683801

Stejskal, J. (2006) Quality assessment in translation. *MultiLingual*, 41-44.

Strapparava, C., & Valitutti, A. (2004). Wordnet affect: an affective extension of wordnet. LREC, 4, 1083–1086.

Studer, R., Benjamins, R., & Fensel, D. (1998). Knowledge engineering: Principles and methods. *Data & Knowledge Engineering, 25*(1–2), 161–198. doi:10.1016/S0169-023X(97)00056-6

Subramaniyaswamy, V., Logesh, R., Abejith, M., Umasankar, S., & Umamakeswari, A. (2017). Sentiment analysis of tweets for estimating criticality and security of events. *Journal of Organizational and End User Computing, 29*(4), 51–71. doi:10.4018/JOEUC.2017100103

Su, C., Huang, S., & Chen, Y. (2017). Automatic detection and interpretation of nominal metaphor based on the theory of meaning. *Neurocomputing, 219*, 300–311. doi:10.1016/j.neucom.2016.09.030

Su, C., Tian, J., & Chen, Y. (2016). Latent semantic similarity based interpretation of chinese metaphors. *Engineering Applications of Artificial Intelligence, 48*, 188–203. doi:10.1016/j.engappai.2015.10.014

Sul, H., Dennis, A. R., & Yuan, L. I. (2014). Trading on Twitter: The Financial Information Content of Emotion in Social Media. *Proceedings of the Annual Hawaii International Conference on System Sciences*, 806-815.

Sun, C., Qiu, X., Xu, Y., & Huang, X. (2019). How to Fine-Tune BERT for Text Classification? In M. Sun, X. Huang, H. Ji, Z. Liu, & Y. Liu (Eds.), *LNCS sublibrary. SL 7, Artificial intelligence: v. 11856. Chinese Computational Linguistics: 18th China National Conference, CCL 2019, Kunming, China, October 18-20, 2019, Proceedings* (pp. 194–206). Cham: Springer. 10.1007/978-3-030-32381-3_16

Sun, A., Lim, E. P., & Ng, W. K. (2002). Web classification using support vector machine. In *Proceedings of the 4th international workshop on Web information and data management* (pp. 96-99). ACM.

Sun, S., Luo, C., & Chen, J. (2017). A Review of Natural Language Processing Techniques for Opinion Mining Systems. *Information Fusion, 36*, 10–25. doi:10.1016/j.inffus.2016.10.004

Svenstrup, D., Jørgensen, H. L., & Winther, O. (2015). Rare disease diagnosis: A review of web search, social media and large-scale data-mining approaches. *Rare Diseases, 3*(1), e1083145. doi:10.1080/21675511.2015.1083145 PMID:26442199

Svoboda, T., Biel, Ł., & Łoboda, K. (2017). *Quality aspects in institutional translation. Multilingual Natural Language Processing, 8*. Language Science Press.

Taboada, M., Anthony, C., & Voll, K. (2006). Methods for Creating Semantic Orientation Databases. *Proceeding of LREC-06, the 5th International Conference on Language Resources and Evaluation*. Retrieved from https://www.microsoft.com/en-us/research/publication/methods-for-creating-semantic-orientation-databases/

Taboada, M., Brooke, J., Tofiloski, M., Voll, K., & Stede, M. (2011). Lexicon-based methods for sentiment analysis. *Computational Linguistics, 37*(2), 267–307. doi:10.1162/COLI_a_00049

Tang, G., Müller, M., Rios, A., & Sennrich, R. (2018). Why Self-Attention? A Targeted Evaluation of Neural Machine Translation Architectures. In *Proceedings of the 2018 Conference on Empirical Methods in Natural Language Processing* (pp. 4263–4272). Brussels, Belgium: Association for Computational Linguistics. 10.18653/v1/D18-1458

Tang, D., Qin, B., & Liu, T. (2015). Document Modeling with Gated Recurrent Neural Network for Sentiment Classification. In *Proceedings of the 2015 Conference on Empirical Methods in Natural Language Processing* (pp. 1422–1432). Lisbon, Portugal: Association for Computational Linguistics. 10.18653/v1/D15-1167

Tang, D., Qin, B., & Liu, T. (2016). Aspect Level Sentiment Classification with Deep Memory Network. In *Proceedings of the 2016 Conference on Empirical Methods in Natural Language Processing* (pp. 214–224). Austin, TX: Association for Computational Linguistics. 10.18653/v1/D16-1021

Tang, H., & Ng, J. H. K. (2006). Googling for a diagnosis - Use of Google as a diagnostic aid: Internet based study. *British Medical Journal, 333*(7579), 1143–1145. doi:10.1136/bmj.39003.640567.AE PMID:17098763

Tang, H., Tan, S., & Cheng, X. (2009). A survey on sentiment detection of reviews. *Expert Systems with Applications, 36*(7), 10760–10773. doi:10.1016/j.eswa.2009.02.063

Tantuğ, A. C., & Eryiğit, G. (2006). Performance Analysis of Naïve Bayes Classification, Support Vector Machines and Neural Networks for Spam Categorization. In *Applied Soft Computing Technologies: The Challenge of Complexity* (pp. 495–504). Springer. doi:10.1007/3-540-31662-0_38

Tasci, S., & Gungor, T. (2008). An evaluation of existing and new feature selection metrics in text categorization. In *2008 23rd International Symposium on Computer and Information Sciences* (pp. 1-6). IEEE.

Taşcı, Ş., & Güngör, T. (2013). Comparison of text feature selection policies and using an adaptive framework. *Expert Systems with Applications, 40*(12), 4871–4886. doi:10.1016/j.eswa.2013.02.019

Tawunrat, C., Jeremy, E., 2015. Chapter Information Science and Applications, Simple Approaches of Sentiment Analysis via Ensemble Learning. *Lecture Notes in Electrical Engineering, 339*.

Taylor, A., Marcus, M., & Santorini, B. (2003). The Penn treebank: an overview. In *Treebanks* (pp. 5–22). Springer. doi:10.1007/978-94-010-0201-1_1

Techopedia. (2014, January 21). *Sentiment Analysis*. Retrieved from https://www.techopedia.com/definition/29695/sentiment-analysis

Templin, M. C. (1957). *Certain language skills in children; their development and interrelationships.* University of Minnesota Press. doi:10.5749/j.ctttv2st

TGS/GIL-UNAM. (2018). *Análisis del sector de tecnologías del lenguaje en México.* Ministerio de Asuntos Económicos y Transformación Digital, Gobierno de España. Madrid, Spain: www.plantl.gob.es/Paginas/Index.aspx

Thatha, V. N., Babu, A. S., & Haritha, D. (2019). An Enhanced Feature Selection for Text Documents. In *Smart Intelligent Computing and Applications* (pp. 21–29). Springer.

Thomas, B. (2013). *What Consumers Think About Brands on Social Media, and What Businesses Need to do About it Report.* Keep Social Honest.

Tian, Z., Rong, W., Shi, L., Liu, J., & Xiong, Z. (2018). Attention Aware Bidirectional Gated Recurrent Unit Based Framework for Sentiment Analysis. In W. Liu, F. Giunchiglia, & B. Yang (Eds.), *Knowledge Science, Engineering and Management* (pp. 67–78). Springer International Publishing. doi:10.1007/978-3-319-99365-2_6

Ting, I. H., Wang, S. L., Chi, H. M., & Wu, J. S. (2013, August). Content matters: A study of hate groups detection based on social networks analysis and web mining. In *Proceedings of the 2013 IEEE/ACM International Conference on Advances in Social Networks Analysis and Mining* (pp. 1196-1201). 10.1145/2492517.2500254

Tong, S., & Koller, D. (2001). Support vector machine active learning with applications to text classification. *Journal of Machine Learning Research, 2*(11), 45–66.

Torres, C. E. A. (2012). *Uso de informação linguística e análise de conceitos formais no aprendizado de ontologies* (Doctoral dissertation). Universidade de São Paulo.

Torruella, J., & Capsada, R. (2013). Lexical statistics and tipological structures: A measure of lexical richness. *Procedia: Social and Behavioral Sciences*, *95*, 447–454. doi:10.1016/j.sbspro.2013.10.668

Touahri, I., & Mazroui, A. (2019). Studying the effect of characteristic vector alteration on Arabic sentiment classification. Journal of King Saud University - Computer and Information Sciences. doi:10.1016/j.jksuci.2019.04.011

Tripathi, P., Vishwakarma, S. K., & Lala, A. (2015). Sentiment analysis of english tweets using rapid miner. In *2015 International Conference on Computational Intelligence and Communication Networks (CICN)* (pp. 668-672). IEEE.

Tsarfaty, R., Sandra, K., Candito, M., Rehbein, I., & Foster, J. (2010). Statistical Parsing of Morphologically Rich Languages (SPMRL) What, How and Whither. In *NAACL HLT First Workshop on Statistical Parsing of Morphologically-Rich Languages* (pp. 1–12). ACL.

Tseng, H., Chang, P. C., Andrew, G., Jurafsky, D., & Manning, C. D. (2005). A conditional random field word segmenter for sighan bakeoff 2005. *Proceedings of the fourth SIGHAN workshop on Chinese language Processing*, 168–171.

Tsvetkov, Y., Boytsov, L., Gershman, A., Nyberg, E., & Dyer, C. (2014, June). Metaphor detection with cross-lingual model transfer. In *Proceedings of the 52nd Annual Meeting of the Association for Computational Linguistics (Volume 1: Long Papers)* (pp. 248-258). 10.3115/v1/P14-1024

Tsytsarau, M., & Palpanas, T. (2012). Survey on mining subjective data on the web. *Data Mining and Knowledge Discovery*, *24*(3), 478–514. doi:10.100710618-011-0238-6

Turing, A. M. (1956). Can a machine think. *The World of Mathematics, 4*, 2099-2123.

Turkish N. L. P. Toolkit. (2020). *Turkish Natural Language Processing Toolkit*. Retrieved from http://haydut.isikun.edu.tr/nlptoolkit.html

Turney, P. D. (2002). *Thumbs up or thumbs down?: semantic orientation applied to unsupervised classification of reviews*: Association for Computational Linguistics. Retrieved from https://dl.acm.org/ft_gateway.cfm?id=1073153&type=pdf

Turney, P. D. (2002). Thumbs up or thumbs down?: semantic orientation applied to unsupervised classification of reviews. In *Proceedings of the 40th annual meeting on association for computational linguistics* (pp. 417-424). Association for Computational Linguistics.

Turney, P. D., & Littman, M. L. (2003). Measuring praise and criticism: Inference of semantic orientation from association. *ACM Transactions on Information Systems*, *21*(4), 315–346. doi:10.1145/944012.944013

Uchida, S., Yoshikawa, T., & Furuhashi, T. (2018). Application of output embedding on Word2Vec. *Proceedings of Joint Tenth International Conference on Soft Computing and Intelligent Systems and 19th International Symposium on Advanced Intelligent System*, 1433-1436.

Udelson, J. E., & Stevenson, L. W. (2016). The future of heart failure diagnosis, therapy, and management. *Circulation*, *133*(25), 2671–2686. doi:10.1161/CIRCULATIONAHA.116.023518 PMID:27324362

Uysal, A. K. (2016). An improved global feature selection scheme for text classification. *Expert Systems with Applications*, *43*(1), 82–92. doi:10.1016/j.eswa.2015.08.050

Uysal, A. K., & Gunal, S. (2012). A novel probabilistic feature selection method for text classification. *Knowledge-Based Systems*, *36*, 226–235. doi:10.1016/j.knosys.2012.06.005

Van Eck, N., & Waltman, L. (2010). Software survey: VOSviewer, a computer program for bibliometric mapping. *Scientometrics, 84*(2), 523-538.

van Rijsbergen, C. J. (1979). *Information Retrieval*. Butterworth-Heinemann.

Vapnik, V. N. (2000). *The Nature of Statistical Learning Theory*. Springer New York., doi:10.1007/978-1-4757-3264-1

Varghese, R., & Jayasree, M. (2013). A Survey on Sentiment Analysis and Opinion Mining. *IJRET: International Journal of Research in Engineering and Technology.*, 2(11), 312–317. doi:10.15623/ijret.2013.0211048

Vaswani, A., Shazeer, N., Parmar, N., Uszkoreit, J., Jones, L., Gomez, A. N., & Polosukhin, I. (2017). Attention is All you Need. In I. Guyon, U. V. Luxburg, S. Bengio, H. Wallach, R. Fergus, S. Vishwanathan, & R. Garnett (Eds.), Advances in Neural Information Processing Systems (Vol. 30, pp. 5998–6008). Curran Associates, Inc. Retrieved from http://papers.nips.cc/paper/7181-attention-is-all-you-need.pdf

Vázquez, L. M., Rodríguez Vázquez, S., & Bouillon, P. (2013). Comparing Forum Data Post-Editing Performance Using Translation Memory and Machine Translation Output: A Pilot Study. Proceedings of Machine Translation Summit XIV.

Veale, T., & Hao, Y. (2007). Comprehending and generating apt metaphors: a web-driven, case-based approach to figurative language. AAAI, 1471–1476.

Veale, T., & Hao, Y. (2008). A fluid knowledge representation for understanding and generating creative metaphors. In *Proceedings of the 22nd International Conference on Computational Linguistics-Volume 1*, (pp. 945–952). Manchester, UK: Association for Computational Linguistics. 10.3115/1599081.1599200

Verzulli, R., Fiorentini, G., Lippi Bruni, M., & Ugolini, C. (2017). Price Changes in Regulated Healthcare Markets: Do Public Hospitals Respond and How? *Health Economics (United Kingdom)*, 26(11), 1429–1446. doi:10.1002/hec.3435 PMID:27785849

Vidgen, B., Harris, A., Nguyen, D., Tromble, R., Hale, S., & Margetts, H. (2019, August). *Challenges and frontiers in abusive content detection.* Association for Computational Linguistics.

Vieira, J. P. A., & Moura, R. S. (2017). An analysis of convolutional neural networks for sentence classification. In *2017 XLIII Latin American Computer Conference (CLEI)* (pp. 1-5). IEEE. 10.1109/CLEI.2017.8226381

Vij, S., & Sharma, J. (2013). An Empirical Study on Social Media Behaviour of Consumers and Social Media Marketing Practices of Marketers. In *Proceedings of the 5th IIMA Conference on Marketing in Emerging Economies*. Indian Institute of Management, Ahmedabad.

Villena, B. (2016). *Innovación léxica en mapudüngun: genuinidad, productividad y planificación* (Ph. D. Dissertation). Barcelona, Catalunya, Spain: Pompeu Fabra University.

Vincent, P., Larochelle, H., Bengio, Y., & Manzagol, P.-A. (2008). Extracting and Composing Robust Features with Denoising Autoencoders. In *ICML '08, Proceedings of the 25th International Conference on Machine Learning* (pp. 1096–1103). New York, NY: ACM. 10.1145/1390156.1390294

Vohra, S., & Teraiya, J. (2013). Applications and Challenges for Sentiment Analysis: A Survey. *International Journal of Engineering Research & Technology (Ahmedabad)*, 2(2), 1–5.

Wadhwa, P., & Bhatia, M. P. S. (2013, February). Tracking on-line radicalization using investigative data mining. In *2013 National Conference on Communications (NCC)* (pp. 1-5). IEEE. 10.1109/NCC.2013.6488046

Wahsheh, H., Al-Kabi, M. N., & Alsmadi, I. (2013a). A link and Content Hybrid Approach for Arabic Web Spam Detection. *International Journal of Intelligent Systems and Applications*, 5(1), 30–43. doi:10.5815/ijisa.2013.01.03

Wahsheh, H., Al-Kabi, M. N., & Alsmadi, I. (2013b). SPAR: A system to detect spam in Arabic opinions. *IEEE Jordan Conference on Applied Electrical Engineering and Computing Technologies, AEECT 2013*, 1–6. 10.1109/AEECT.2013.6716442

Walewski, J. L., Donovan, D., & Nori, M. (2019). How many zebras are there, and where are they hiding in medical literature? A literature review of publications on rare diseases. *Expert Opinion on Orphan Drugs*, 7(11), 513–519. doi :10.1080/21678707.2019.1684260

Wallace, R. (1995). *Artificial linguistic internet computer entity (alice)*. Academic Press.

Wang, X., Jiang, W., & Luo, Z. (2016). Combination of Convolutional and Recurrent Neural Network for Sentiment Analysis of Short Texts. *Proceedings of COLING 2016, the 26th International Conference on Computational Linguistics: Technical Papers*. Retrieved from https://www.aclweb.org/anthology/C16-1229.pdf

Wang, A., Singh, A., Michael, J., Hill, F., Levy, O., & Bowman, S. (2018). GLUE: A Multi-Task Benchmark and Analysis Platform for Natural Language Understanding. In *Proceedings of the 2018 EMNLP Workshop BlackboxNLP: Analyzing and Interpreting Neural Networks for NLP* (pp. 353–355). Brussels, Belgium: Association for Computational Linguistics. 10.18653/v1/W18-5446

Wang, T., Wezel, F. C., & Forgues, B. (2015). Protecting Market Identity: When and How Do Organizations Respond to Consumers' Devaluations? *Academy of Management Journal*, 59(1), 135–162. doi:10.5465/amj.2014.0205

Warner, W., & Hirschberg, J. (2012, June). Detecting hate speech on the world wide web. In *Proceedings of the second workshop on language in social media* (pp. 19-26). Association for Computational Linguistics.

Waseem, Z., & Hovy, D. (2016, June). Hateful symbols or hateful people? predictive features for hate speech detection on twitter. In *Proceedings of the NAACL student research workshop* (pp. 88-93). 10.18653/v1/N16-2013

Weber, L., & Klein, P. A. T. (2003). *Aplicação da lógica fuzzy em software e hardware*. Editora da ULBRA.

Weiss, K., Khoshgoftaar, T. M., & Wang, D. (2016). A survey of transfer learning. *Journal of Big Data*, 3(1), 1817. doi:10.118640537-016-0043-6

Weizenbaum, J. (1966). ELIZA---a computer program for the study of natural language communication between man and machine. *Communications of the ACM*, 9(1), 36–45. doi:10.1145/365153.365168

Weng, J., Lim, E. P., Jiang, J., & He, Q. (2010). Twitterrank: finding topic-sensitive influential twitterers. In *Proceedings of the third ACM international conference on Web search and data mining* (pp. 261-270). ACM. 10.1145/1718487.1718520

Wiebe, J., Bruce, R., & O'Hara, T. P. (1999). Development and Use of a Gold-Standard Data Set for Subjectivity Classifications. *Proceedings of the 37th Annual Meeting of the Association for Computational Linguistics*. Retrieved from https://www.aclweb.org/anthology/P99-1032.pdf

Wiebe, J. (2000). Learning Subjective Adjectives from Corpora. In *Proceedings of the Seventeenth National Conference on Artificial Intelligence and Twelfth Conference on Innovative Applications of Artificial Intelligence* (pp. 735–740). AAAI Press. Retrieved from https://dl.acm.org/citation.cfm?id=647288.721121

Wiegand, M., Ruppenhofer, J., Schmidt, A., & Greenberg, C. (2018). *Inducing a lexicon of abusive words–a feature-based approach*. Academic Press.

Wikipedia. (2020, May 29). *Sarcasm*. Retrieved from https://en.wikipedia.org/wiki/Sarcasm#:~:text=From%20 Wikipedia%2C%20the%20free%20encyclopedia,sarcasm%20is%20not%20necessarily%20ironic

Wilks, Y. (1978). Making preferences more active. *Artificial Intelligence*, 11(3), 197–223. doi:10.1016/0004-3702(78)90001-2

Wilks, Y. (2008). *Machine translation: its scope and limits*. Springer Science & Business Media.

Willett, P. (1988). Recent trends in hierarchic document clustering: A critical review. *Information Processing & Management*, *24*(5), 577–597. doi:10.1016/0306-4573(88)90027-1

WilliamsD. (2020, March 5). *CNN Business*. Retrieved from https://edition.cnn.com/2020/03/04/business/target-commercial-race-reviews-trnd/index.html

Wilson, J. K. (2012). *Responding to natural disasters with social media: A case study of the 2011 earthquake and tsunami in Japan* (Master's thesis). Simon Fraser University.

WISDOM. (1.0) [software]. (2013). Retrieved from https://www.lockheedmartin.com/en-us/products/lm-wisdom.html

Wolfe, S. (2018, October 29). *Gab, the social network popular with the far right, has temporarily shut down after GoDaddy pulled its support.* Retrieved from https://finance.yahoo.com/news/gab-social-network-popular-far-162103840.html

World Bank Group. (2015). *Latinomérica Indígena en el Siglo XXI*. Washington, DC: World Bank Publications. http://documents.worldbank.org

Wu, X., Cai, Y., Li, Q., Xu, J., & Leung, H.-F. (2018). Combining Contextual Information by Self-attention Mechanism in Convolutional Neural Networks for Text Classification. Lecture Notes in Computer Science, 11233, 453–467. doi:10.1007/978-3-030-02922-7_31

Wu, C., Wu, F., Chen, Y., Wu, S., Yuan, Z., & Huang, Y. (2018). Neural metaphor detecting with cnn-lstm model. *Proceedings of the Workshop on Figurative Language Processing*, 110–114. 10.18653/v1/W18-0913

Wu, S., Liu, Y., Wang, J., & Li, Q. (2019). Sentiment Analysis Method Based on K-means and Online Transfer Learning. *CMC-Computers Materials & Continua*, *60*(3), 1207–1222. doi:10.32604/cmc.2019.05835

Xiang, G., Fan, B., Wang, L., Hong, J., & Rose, C. (2012, October). Detecting offensive tweets via topical feature discovery over a large scale twitter corpus. In *Proceedings of the 21st ACM international conference on Information and knowledge management* (pp. 1980-1984). 10.1145/2396761.2398556

Xian, Y., Lampert, C. H., Schiele, B., & Akata, Z. (2019). Zero-Shot Learning—A Comprehensive Evaluation of the Good, the Bad and the Ugly. *IEEE Transactions on Pattern Analysis and Machine Intelligence*, *41*(9), 2251–2265. doi:10.1109/TPAMI.2018.2857768 PMID:30028691

Xiao, P., Alnajjar, K., Granroth-Wilding, M., Agres, K., & Toivonen, H. (2016). Meta4meaning: Automatic metaphor interpretation using corpus-derived word associations. *Proceedings of the 7th International Conference on Computational Creativity (ICCC).*

Xing, F. Z., Cambria, E., & Welsch, R. E. (2018). Natural language based financial forecasting: A survey. *Artificial Intelligence Review*, *50*(1), 49–73. doi:10.100710462-017-9588-9

Xu, N. (2017). Analyzing multimodal public sentiment based on hierarchical semantic attentional network. In *Proceedings of the 2017 IEEE International Conference on Intelligence and Security Informatics (ISI)* (pp. 152–154). IEEE. 10.1109/ISI.2017.8004895

Xu, W., Sun, H., Deng, C., & Tan, Y. (2017). Variational Autoencoder for Semi-Supervised Text Classification. In *AAAI'17: Proceedings of the Thirty-First AAAI Conference on Artificial Intelligence* (Vol. 4, pp. 3358–3364). San Francisco, CA: AAAI Press.

Yadlapalli, S. S., Reddy, R. R., & Sasikala, T. (2019). Advanced Twitter sentiment analysis using supervised techniques and minimalistic features. Ambient Communications and Computer Systems, RACCCS 2019, 91-104.

Yamada, M. (2011). The effect of translation memory databases on productivity. In A. Pym (Ed.), *Translation research projects* (Vol. 3, pp. 63–73).

Yang, A. M., Lin, J. H., Zhou, Y. M., & Chen, J. (2013). Research on building a Chinese sentiment lexicon based on SO-PMI. Applied Mechanics and Materials, 263, 1688-1693.

Yang, Z., Dai, Z., Yang, Y., Carbonell, J., Salakhutdinov, R. R., & Le, Q. V. (2019). XLNet: Generalized Autoregressive Pretraining for Language Understanding. In *Advances in Neural Information Processing Systems 32* (pp. 5754–5764). Curran Associates, Inc. Retrieved from http://papers.nips.cc/paper/8812-xlnet-generalized-autoregressive-pretraining-for-language-understanding.pdf

Yang, Z., Yang, D., Dyer, C., He, X., Smola, A., & Hovy, E. (2016). Hierarchical Attention Networks for Document Classification. In *Proceedings of the 2016 Conference of the North American Chapter of the Association for Computational Linguistics: Human Language Technologies* (pp. 1480–1489). San Diego, CA: Association for Computational Linguistics. 10.18653/v1/N16-1174

Yang, J., Ciobanu, D., Reiss, C., & Secară, A. (2017). *Using Computer Assisted Translation Tools' Translation Quality Assessment functionalities to assess students' translations*. The Language Scholar Journal.

Yang, Y. (1999). An evaluation of statistical approaches to text categorization. *Information Retrieval, 1*(1-2), 69–90. doi:10.1023/A:1009982220290

Yang, Y., & Pederson, J. O. (1997). A comparative study of feature selection in text categorization. *Proceedings of the Fourteenth International Conference on Machine Learning*, 412-420.

Yanyan, Z., Bing, Q., & Qiuhui, S., & Ting, L. (2017). Large-scale sentiment lexicon collection and its application in sentiment classification. *Journal of Chinese Information Processing., 31*(2), 187–193.

Yıldırım, S., & Yıldız, T. (2018). Türkçe için karşılaştırmalı metin sınıflandırma analizi. *Pamukkale Üniversitesi Mühendislik Bilimleri Dergisi, 24*(5), 879–886.

Yıldız, B., & Ağdeniz, Ş. (2018). Muhasebede Analiz Yöntemi Olarak Metin Madenciliği. *World of Accounting Science, 20*(2), 286–315.

Yin, H., Liu, P., Zhu, Z., Li, W., & Wang, Q. (2019). Capsule Network With Identifying Transferable Knowledge for Cross-Domain Sentiment Classification. *IEEE Access: Practical Innovations, Open Solutions, 7*, 153171–153182. doi:10.1109/ACCESS.2019.2948628

Young, T., Hazarika, D., Poria, S., & Cambria, E. (2018). Recent trends in deep learning based natural language processing. *IEEE Computational Intelligence Magazine, 13*(3), 55–75. doi:10.1109/MCI.2018.2840738

Yousefpour, A., Ibrahim, R., Abdull Hamed, H. N., & Hajmohammadi, M. S. (2014). Feature reduction using standard deviation with different subsets selection in sentiment analysis. *Asian Conference on Intelligent Information and Database Systems*, 33-41. 10.1007/978-3-319-05458-2_4

Yousefpour, A., Ibrahim, R., & Hamed, H. N. A. (2017). Ordinal-based and frequency-based integration of feature selection methods for sentiment analysis. *Expert Systems with Applications, 75*, 80–93. doi:10.1016/j.eswa.2017.01.009

Yu, J., & Jiang, J. (2016). Learning Sentence Embeddings with Auxiliary Tasks for Cross-Domain Sentiment Classification. In *Proceedings of the 2016 Conference on Empirical Methods in Natural Language Processing* (pp. 236–246). Austin, TX: Association for Computational Linguistics. 10.18653/v1/D16-1023

Yu, Y., Duan, W., & Cao, Q. (2013). The impact of social and conventional media on firm equity value: A sentiment analysis approach. *Decision Support Systems, 55*(4), 919–926. doi:10.1016/j.dss.2012.12.028

Zadeh, A. H., & Sharda, R. (2014). Modeling brand post popularity dynamics in online social networks. *Decision Support Systems, 65*, 59–68. doi:10.1016/j.dss.2014.05.003

Zalmout, N., Erdmann, A., & Habash, N. (2018, June). Noise-robust morphological disambiguation for dialectal Arabic. In *Proceedings of the 2018 Conference of the North American Chapter of the Association for Computational Linguistics: Human Language Technologies,* Volume 1 *(Long Papers)* (pp. 953-964). Academic Press.

Zampieri, M., & Vela, M. (2014). Quantifying the Influence of MT Output in the Translators Performance: A Case Study in Technical Translation. *Proceedings of the EACL Workshop on Humans and Computer-assisted Translation (HaCat),* 93-98. 10.3115/v1/W14-0314

Zannettou, S., Caulfield, T., Blackburn, J., De Cristofaro, E., Sirivianos, M., Stringhini, G., & Suarez-Tangil, G. (2018, October). On the origins of memes by means of fringe web communities. In *Proceedings of the Internet Measurement Conference 2018* (pp. 188-202). 10.1145/3278532.3278550

Zayed, O. H., & El-Beltagy, S. R. (2015). Named entity recognition of persons' names in Arabic tweets. *International Conference Recent Advances in Natural Language Processing, RANLP,* 731–738.

Zemberek. (2019). *Zemberek Natural Language Processing Tool.* Retrieved from https://code.google.com/archive/p/zemberek/

Zeng, L., Starbird, K., & Spiro, E. S. (2016). #Unconfirmed: Classifying Rumor Stance in Crisis-Related Social Media Messages. In *Proceedings of the 10th International AAAI Conference on Web and Social Media (ICWSM 2016),* (pp. 747-750). AAAI Publications.

Zgusta, L. (2010). *Manual of lexicography* (Vol. 39). Walter de Gruyter.

Zhang, L., & Chen, C. (2016). Sentiment classification with convolutional neural networks: An experimental study on a large-scale chinese conversation corpus. In *2016 12th International Conference on Computational Intelligence and Security (CIS)* (pp. 165-169). IEEE.

Zhang, Z., & Saligrama, V. (2015). Zero-Shot Learning via Semantic Similarity Embedding. In *ICCV'15, Proceedings of the 2015 IEEE International Conference on Computer Vision (ICCV)* (pp. 4166–4174). ACM. 10.1109/ICCV.2015.474

Zhang, D., Xu, H., Su, Z., & Xu, Y. (2015). Chinese comments sentiment classification based on word2vec and svm perf. *Expert Systems with Applications, 42*(4), 1857–1863. doi:10.1016/j.eswa.2014.09.011

Zhang, L. (2016). A Study on the Efficiency Influence of Computer-Assisted Translation in Technical Translation. *Journal of Chemical and Pharmaceutical Research, 8*(4), 801–808.

Zhang, L., Wang, S., & Liu, B. (2018). Deep learning for sentiment analysis: A survey. *Wiley Interdisciplinary Reviews. Data Mining and Knowledge Discovery, 8*(4), e1253. doi:10.1002/widm.1253

Zhang, Q., Lu, R., Wang, Q., Zhu, Z., & Liu, P. (2019). Interactive Multi-Head Attention Networks for Aspect-Level Sentiment Classification. *IEEE Access: Practical Innovations, Open Solutions, 7,* 160017–160028. doi:10.1109/ACCESS.2019.2951283

Zhang, X., Zhao, J., & LeCun, Y. (2015). Character-Level Convolutional Networks for Text Classification. In *NIPS'15, Proceedings of the 28th International Conference on Neural Information Processing Systems* - Volume 1 (pp. 649–657). Cambridge, MA: MIT Press.

Zhang, Y., Barzilay, R., & Jaakkola, T. (2017). Aspect-augmented Adversarial Networks for Domain Adaptation. *Transactions of the Association for Computational Linguistics, 5*(1), 515–528. doi:10.1162/tacl_a_00077

Zhang, Z., Robinson, D., & Tepper, J. (2018, June). Detecting hate speech on twitter using a convolution-gru based deep neural network. In *European semantic web conference* (pp. 745-760). Springer. 10.1007/978-3-319-93417-4_48

Zhao, J., Wang, J., & Deng, W. (2015). Exploring bikesharing travel time and trip chain by gender and day of the week. *Transportation Research Part C, Emerging Technologies*, *58*, 251–264. doi:10.1016/j.trc.2015.01.030

Zhao, K., Stylianou, A. C., & Zheng, Y. (2018). Sources and impacts of social influence from online anonymous user reviews. *Information & Management*, *55*(1), 16–30. doi:10.1016/j.im.2017.03.006

Zheng, Z., Srihari, R., & Srihari, S. (2003). A feature selection framework for text filtering. *Proceedings of Third IEEE International Conference on Data Mining*, 705-708. 10.1109/ICDM.2003.1251013

Zhong, H., Li, H., Squicciarini, A. C., Rajtmajer, S. M., Griffin, C., Miller, D. J., & Caragea, C. (2016, July). Content-Driven Detection of Cyberbullying on the Instagram Social Network. IJCAI, 3952-3958.

Zhou, G., Zhu, Z., He, T., & Hu, X. T. (2016). Cross-lingual sentiment classification with stacked autoencoders. *Knowledge and Information Systems*, *47*(1), 27–44. doi:10.100710115-015-0849-0

Zhu, Y., Gao, X., Zhang, W., Liu, S., & Zhang, Y. (2018). A bi-directional LSTM-CNN model with attention for Aspect-level text classification. *Future Internet*. Advance online publication. doi:10.3390/fi10120116

Zhu, X. (2005). *Semi-supervised learning literature survey*. University of Wisconsin-Madison Department of Computer Sciences.

Zul, M. I., Yulia, F., & Nurmalasari, D. (2018). Social Media Sentiment Analysis Using K-Means and Naïve Bayes Algorithm. *2nd International Conference on Electrical Engineering and Informatics (ICon EEI)*, 24-29. 10.1109/IConEEI.2018.8784326

Zvarevashe, K., & Olugbara, O. O. (2018). A framework for sentiment analysis with opinion mining of hotel reviews. *Proceedings of the 2018 Conference on Information Communications Technology and Society (ICTAS)*. 10.1109/ICTAS.2018.8368746

About the Contributors

Fatih Pinarbasi is a research assistant at Istanbul Medipol University and a PhD student at Yildiz Technical University. His research areas are digital marketing and data mining.

M. Nurdan Taskiran was born in Istanbul, Turkey. She got her MA in English Literature and Language and a PhD in Communication Sciences. She has worked for Marmara University for 16 years and Kocaeli University for 14 years and three years for Samsun Ondokuz Mayıs University Communication Faculty. Now, she is an emeritus professor working for Istanbul Medipol University, School of Communication since 2017. She has articles in Turkish and English on visual semiotics including films, tv serials, and advertisements. She likes reading articles on media literacy, visual rhetorics and animal communication. She is married with two children.

* * *

Zitouni Abdelhafid received his PhD in computer science in 2008 from the University Mentouri of Constantine, Algeria. Currently working as Professor in University of Constantine 2 Abdelhamid Mehri. His research interests include Software Engineering, Cloud Computing, Multi Agent System, Szcurity, and Arabic text mining field. Pr. Abdelhafid Zitouni has published many articles in International Journals and Conferences. He supervises many Master and PhD students and peer-reviewed conference and journal papers in the above research topics

Olga Acosta is the CTO of Singularyta SpA, a company focused on the development of language technologies for text data analytics. Likewise, she is an assistant professor at the Pontifical Catholic University of Chile. She has a PhD in Computer Science from UNAM (Mexico). The research topics that interest her are: information retrieval, text mining, machine learning and deep learning.

Sumaya Sulaiman Al Ameri received her Master's degree in Engineering from Khalifa University, United Arab Emirates in 2014 with outstanding achievement. Awarded with the Young Emirati Researchers Prize (YERP) from the National Research Foundation. Also, she's one of the founders of the Emirates Digital Association for Women. She is currently managing data analytics projects in the Government sector. Sumaya lives in Abu Dhabi with her husband and family.

Gunjan Ansari has completed Ph.D.(Computer Engineering) in 2020 from Jamia Millia Islamia, Delhi. She received her B.E. (CSE) and M.Tech. (CSE) degree from Rajiv Gandhi Technical University, Bhopal. She published few research papers in reputed International Journals and Conferences. She also served as a reviewer of several International conferences and journals. She has experience of teaching postgraduate and undergraduate engineering students of over 17 years. Her areas of interest are Data Mining, Natural Language Processing and Machine Learning.

Rüdiger Buchkremer is currently Director at the Institute for IT Management and Digitization (ifid) and Professor of Computer Science at the FOM University of Applied Sciences Düsseldorf and the UCAM FOM Doctoral School of Business in Murcia, Spain. He focusses his research interests on artificial intelligence, in particular, natural language processing, applied to the search for therapies and diagnoses of diseases and systems medicine. He also worked in the pharmaceutical industry as Head of Research Information at the ALTANA Pharma Group. He also studied chemistry, physics, and mathematics at the Ruhr University in Bochum and received his Ph.D. in organic chemistry from Binghamton University, The State University of New York.

Stephen Camilleri is a Maltese graduate holding a Masters degree from the University of Malta, specializing in Artificial Intelligence. His research, which earned him the 2019 EGU Outstanding Student Poster and PICO (OSPP) Award, is focused on using text mining tools to automatically map in near real-time earthquake events with multilingual earthquake-related news articles, published by 23 leading news agencies across the world. The relationships derived from this research, in collaboration with Dr Joel Azzopardi and Dr Matthew R. Agius was published by Frontiers in 2020, in a technical paper entitled "The Analysis of online news coverage on earthquakes through text mining". The work complements the 2019 IEEE AIKE journal paper entitled "Investigating the relationship between earthquakes and online news", with the same collaborators, and the awarded poster presented in 2019 at the General Assembly of the European Geosciences Union (EGU) in Vienna. His recent success builds on the list of past achievements, including the University of London (Goldsmiths) Degree in Computing and Information Systems, where Stephen was awarded First Class Honours. His final dissertation entitled "Equity recommendation technique using fuzzy logic control" included an application, which made use of genetic programming, fuzzy logic control and sentiment analysis to establish the most promising stocks available on the market.

Shampa Chakraverty (B.E.-E.C.E Delhi University, M.Tech-IES, I.I.T. Delhi, P.hD- Comp Science, Delhi University) is professor in the Department of Computer Engineering at Netaji Subhas University of Technology, New Delhi. Her research interests are in NLP, E governance, Recommender Systems and Engineering Pedagogy.

Tiago da Cunha is an English Professor at the Languages Undergraduate course of the University of the International Integration of the Afro-Brazilian Lusophony. Phd in Linguistics focused in Computational Linguistics and Translation Studies.

Mahieddine Djoudi received a PhD in Computer Science from the University of Nancy, France, in 1991. His PhD thesis research was in Acoustic Phonetic Decoding for Standard Arabic Speech Recognition. He is currently working at Computer Science Department, Faculty of Fundamental and Applied

Sciences at the University of Poitiers, France and member of TechNE Technology Enhanced Learning Research Laboratory. His main scientific interests are: e-Learning, Mobile Learning, Cloud Computing, Information Literacy and Learning Analytics. He has published over 100 scientific papers. He is also a member of program committees, editor or reviewer for international journals or conferences proceedings. His teaching interests include Programming, Data Bases, Artificial Intelligence and Web Technology. He started and is involved in many research projects which include many researchers from different universities: Content Curation in Learning Analytics, Digital Practices Awareness, etc.

Ivan Dunđer, PhD, is a senior researcher at the Department of Information and Communication Sciences, Faculty of Humanities and Social Sciences, University of Zagreb. His research interests are algorithms and programming techniques in machine translation, natural language processing and information system modelling. He is a member of various professional associations.

Jon Kepa Gerrikagoitia is Computer Science Engineer by the University of Deusto 1993, Master of Science on Software Engineering by the University of Deusto 1995, and Computer Science Ph.D. by the Mondragon University in 2006. Currently, he is the Scientific and Technology Manager of BRTA (Basque Research and Technology Alliance), formed by 4 collaborative research centers and 12 technology centers with about 3.600 researchers, with the aim of developing advanced technological solutions for the Basque companies. His professional career of more than 20 years has been developed jointly in the academia and industry fields, tightly linked to Computer and Data Science, starting from IT, software architectures and web engineering to move towards Big Data Analytics and machine learning within the framework of Business Intelligence based in Internet, combining scientific and technology vision. He´s primary domain has been Advance Manufacturing, as has been in charge of the ICT and Automation research group in IK4-IDEKO, the technology center of DANOBATGROUP specialist in manufacturing and industrial production. The research area is incorporating the latest advances in ICT, Digital Automation and Data Science into the manufacturing and industrial production within the framework known as Industry 4.0. The digitization of the industry from the point of view of the machine tool builder is the main goal of the research group. He has participated actively in many research projects funded with public programs (EC, national, regional). Dr. Gerrikagoitia has contributed with numerous publications to scientific journals and has participated as keynote within diverse national and international events.

Sayani Ghosal is currently pursuing Ph.D. from Guru Gobind Singh Indraprastha University, New Delhi. She has done her M.Tech from Indira Gandhi Delhi Technical University for Women (Under Govt. of NCT of Delhi). She has done her B.Tech (CSE) from West Bengal University of Technology. She also has more than 4 Years of Industry Experience. Her area of interest includes Natural Language Processing, Machine Learning.

Divya Gupta is currently working as an Assistant Professor at Galgotias University, Greater Noida. She has received her M.Tech. (Master of Technology) in Software Engineering from Delhi Technological University and B.Tech. (Bachelor of Technology) in Information Technology from GGSIPU. Her research interests include Intelligent Systems, Web Mining and Web-based Software Engineering.

Shilpi Gupta is pursuing Ph.D. from Shobhit Institute of Engineering & Technology, Meerut. She is having teaching experience of more than 11 years. Her area of interest is data mining & machine learning.

Matthias Hölscher received a Bachelor's degree (BSc) in Software Engineering from Dortmund University of Applied Sciences and Arts (Germany) in 2016 and a Master's degree (MSc) in IT Management from the FOM-University (Germany) in 2019. His research interests include the use of artificial intelligence for natural language processing, especially in the field of healthcare. Currently, he holds a position as SAP consultant and project manager in various international engineering and software projects. He is also an agile coach and speaker for agile project management.

Amita Jain is working as an Asst. Prof. in Deptt of CSE at Ambedkar Institute of Advanced Communication Technology and Research, Delhi. She has done B.E. (CSE), M.Tech (IT). She did her Ph.D. in Computer Engg. from Jawaharlal Nehru University. She has a teaching experience of more than 18 years. She has published more than 50 research papers in topmost international journals including ACM transactions, Springer Verlag etc. She is also a reviewer on the panel of many IEEE, Elsevier, and Springer journals. She is currently supervising Ph.D. in the field of Artificial Intelligence and allied fields.

Vincent Karas received his B.Sc. in Engineering Science in 2014 and M.Sc. in Medical Technology and Engineering in 2018 at TU Munich, Germany. He is currently a PhD candidate with the Chair of Embedded Intelligence for Health Care and Wellbeing, University of Augsburg, Germany and BMW.

Erdal Kılıç received a Bachelor degree in Electrical Electronic Engineering from Karadeniz Technical University Trabzon in 1991. The Master degree in Electrical Electronic Engineering from Karadeniz Technical University in 1996. The PhD in Electrical and Electronic Engineering from Middle East Technical University Ankara in 2005. Currently, he is a Prof. Dr. in Ondokuz Mayıs University Department of Computer Engineering. His research interests include neural networks, machine learning and data mining.

Vlasta Kučiš, PhD, is associate professor at Faculty of Philosophy – University of Maribor. Her research interests are translations process, language analysis, intercultural communication and technology in translation. She is a member of various professional associations and participated in international and European projects.

Akshi Kumar is an Assistant Professor in the Department of Computer Science & Engineering at Delhi Technological University (formerly Delhi College of Engineering), New Delhi, India. She has been with the university for the past 11 years and was selected by the Union Service Public Commission, India for this post. She has received her Ph.D. in Computer Engineering from Faculty of Technology, University of Delhi in 2011. She completed her Master of Technology with honours in Computer Science & Engineering from Guru Gobind Singh Indraprastha University, Delhi in 2005. She received her Bachelor of Engineering degree with distinction in Computer Science & Engineering from Maharshi Dayanand University, India in 2003. Dr. Kumar has over 100 publications including published work in peer-reviewed and science cited journals. She has presented papers in international conferences and won best paper awards. She is a recipient of "commendable research award for excellence in research" at Delhi Technological University, 2018. She has also authored a monograph, 'Web Technology: Theory and Practice' published by CRC Press, Taylor and Francis Group and is an editor of the book 'A Roadmap to Industry 4.0: Smart Production, Sharp Business and Sustainable Development', Springer. Dr. Kumar has guided several doctoral and post-graduate scholars. She also has an Indian Patent published. She is an active reviewer and guest editor of many high impact journals of IEEE, MDPI, Springer and Elsevier.

Raimundo Moura is a graduate at Computer Science from Federal University of Piaui (1994), master's at Computer Science from Federal University of Pernambuco (1996) and PhD at Electric and Computer Engineering from Federal University of Rio Grande do Norte (2009). Currently, acting on the following subjects: formal languages and compilers, natural language processing and sentiment analysis and opinion mining in Web reviews (textual descriptions).

Mirjana Pejić Bach, PhD, is a full professor at the Faculty of Economics and Business University of Zagreb. Her research interests are data mining, system dynamics, web content analysis, and innovation. She has participated in a number of European projects. She is a member of various conference program committees and journal editorial boards. Mirjana has received several professional awards.

Ricardo Rabelo received the B.Sc. degree in computer science from the Federal University of Piauí, Brazil, in 2005, and the Ph.D. degree in power systems from the Sao Carlos Engineering School, University of Sao Paulo, Brazil, in 2010. His areas of research interest include smart grids, the Internet of Things, intelligent systems, and power quality.

Hichem Rahab is currently working as an Assistant Professor in department of Mathematics and computer science in the University of Khenchela, Algeria. He obtained his Master degree in Computer science from Batna University, Algeria, 2012. His research interest includes machine learning, opinion mining and sentiment analysis.

Sunny Rai is a faculty in the School of Engineering Science, Mahindra École Centrale, Hyderabad, India. She has completed her masters from GGS Indraprastha University and submitted her thesis for Ph.D. at University of Delhi, India. Her area of interest is Natural Language Processing, in particular Metaphor Processing/ Creative Text Processing, Social Computing, and Cognitive Linguistics.

Durmuş Özkan Şahin received a Bachelor degree in Computer Engineering from Süleyman Demirel University Isparta in 2013 and the Master degree in Computer Engineering from Ondokuz Mayıs University Samsun in 2016. Currently, he is a doctorate student in Computational Sciences. His research interests include machine learning, text mining, information retrieval and android malware analysis.

Björn W. Schuller received his diploma in 1999, his doctoral degree for his study on Automatic Speech and Emotion Recognition in 2006, and his habilitation (fakultas docendi) and was entitled Adjunct Teaching Professor (venia legendi) in the subject area of Signal Processing and Machine Intelligence for his work on Intelligent Audio Analysis in 2012 all in electrical engineering and information technology from TUM in Munich/Germany. Since 2017, he is Full Professor and Centre Digitisation.Bavaria (ZD.B) Chair of Embedded Intelligence for Health Care and Wellbeing at the University of Augsburg/Germany (ranked #801-900 as university in the ARWU Ranking 2019) in the Faculty of Applied Informatics and the Faculty of Medicine. At the same time, he is Professor of Artificial Intelligence in the Department of Computing at Imperial College London/UK (ranked #8 in THE World University Ranking 2018) since 2018 where he heads the Group on Language Audio & Music (GLAM), previously being a Reader in Machine Learning since 2015 and Senior Lecturer since 2013. Further, he is the co-founding CEO and current CSO of audEERING GmbH – a TUM start-up on intelligent audio engineering since its launch in 2012.

Sanja Seljan, PhD, is a full professor in Information and Communication Sciences, Faculty of Humanities and Social Sciences, University of Zagreb. Her research interests are data analysis and machine learning, language technologies in business, machine translation, natural language processing, text mining and information extraction. She is a member of various program and review boards of international conferences and journals, co-editor of seven publications. She is a project manager and collaborator in the domain of information and communication sciences.

Ainhoa Serna is lecturer and researcher at the University of the Basque Country UPV/EHU. During 20 years she has been lecturer and researcher at Mondragon Unibertsitatea (university) in Spain and has led the university's tourism and mobility research area since 2010. She earned her PhD in computer science from Mondragon Unibertsitatea (2006). She has led research teams from the university together with the Cooperative Research Center in Tourism (CICtourGUNE) on projects to develop tourism agenda in collaboration with the Basque Network of Science, Technology, and Innovation. Her research interests are related to Web Engineering, Natural Language Processing, Data Science and Semantic Web with a strong industry orientation. In 2010, she began her specialization in the field of tourism and human mobility. She has authored or co-authored over 50 publications on research themes related to urban mobility, transport, Big Data, Social Media and tourism. This work has been published in a wide-variety of languages, including English, Spanish and French. Since 2001, she has been responsible for Coordination in Postgraduate Studies (master's degrees, expert and advanced courses) and in competitive research projects financed by public administrations in Europe, Spain and Basque Country. Being principal investigator (PI) in more than 20 research projects and transferring knowledge to the productive sector through operating software, projects, technical reports and specialized seminars.

Abdulhadi Shoufan received his Dr.-Ing. degree from the Technische Universität Darmstadt, Germany in 2007. Currently, he is an Associate Professor of Electrical Engineering and Computer Science at Khalifa University, UAE. He is an expert in NLP for dialectical Arabic, information security, computer engineering, learning analytics, and engineering education.

Niraj Singhal is Ph.D. (Computer Engineering & Information Technology). He is Fellow and member of several International/National bodies. He is also serving as reviewer and member of advisory board for several International/National journals. He has guided more than hundred undergraduate engineering students for their project work and more than forty postgraduate engineering students for their thesis work. He is guiding many Ph.D. scholars too currently and some has already been submitted and awarded under his guidance. He has authored four handbooks with laboratory manuals for undergraduates. He has more than one hundred research publications to his credit in National/International journals/conferences of repute. He has twenty five years of rich experience of administration, coordinating and teaching at various levels. Presently working as Professor in the Department of Computer Science & Engineering at Shobhit Institute of Engineering & Technology, Meerut (Deemed to be University). His area of interest includes system software, web information retrieval and software agents.

Nikolina Škof Erdelja has M.A. degree in information sciences and linguistics, Faculty of Humanities and Social Sciences, University of Zagreb. She currently works in Ciklopea in IT department on projects using CAT technology.

Rogerio Sousa is a professor at the Federal Institute of Education, Science and Technology of Piauí. PhD student in Computer Science and Computational Mathematics at the University of São Paulo. Master in Computer Science at the Federal University of Piauí. Works in the area of Natural Language Processing.

Devendra K. Tayal is working as Professor in Department of Computer Science & Engg & Dean(Academic Affairs) in Indira Gandhi Delhi Technical University for Women, Kashmere Gate, Delhi, INDIA. Earlier he was Head in Department of Computer Science & Engg. He has done M.Tech(Computer Engg.), Ph.D(Computer Engg.) from Jawaharlal Nehru University. He has a teaching experience of more than 20 years. He did his research in the field of Intelligent Systems and has published more than 100 research papers in International Journals & Conferences. He is a member of International Advisory committee of International Journal of Computer Science, Hongkong and member of International Advisory Board of International Journal of Software Engg & Applications, Korea . Besides this, he is a referee on Editorial board of various International Journals including the famous "IEEE Transactions on Fuzzy Systems" having the SCI Impact Factor 4.26 . His area of interests include Intelligent Systems, Data-Mining, DBMS and Text Mining & Natural Language Processing.

Index

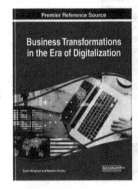
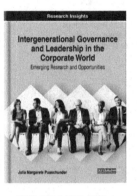

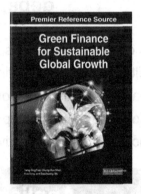

Ensure Quality Research is Introduced to the Academic Community

Become an IGI Global Reviewer for Authored Book Projects

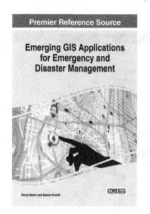

The overall success of an authored book project is dependent on quality and timely reviews.

In this competitive age of scholarly publishing, constructive and timely feedback significantly expedites the turnaround time of manuscripts from submission to acceptance, allowing the publication and discovery of forward-thinking research at a much more expeditious rate. Several IGI Global authored book projects are currently seeking highly-qualified experts in the field to fill vacancies on their respective editorial review boards:

Applications and Inquiries may be sent to:
development@igi-global.com

Applicants must have a doctorate (or an equivalent degree) as well as publishing and reviewing experience. Reviewers are asked to complete the open-ended evaluation questions with as much detail as possible in a timely, collegial, and constructive manner. All reviewers' tenures run for one-year terms on the editorial review boards and are expected to complete at least three reviews per term. Upon successful completion of this term, reviewers can be considered for an additional term.

If you have a colleague that may be interested in this opportunity,
we encourage you to share this information with them.

IGI Global Proudly Partners With eContent Pro International

Receive a 25% Discount on all Editorial Services

Editorial Services

IGI Global expects all final manuscripts submitted for publication to be in their final form. This means they must be reviewed, revised, and professionally copy edited prior to their final submission. Not only does this support with accelerating the publication process, but it also ensures that the highest quality scholarly work can be disseminated.

English Language Copy Editing

Let eContent Pro International's expert copy editors perform edits on your manuscript to resolve spelling, punctuaion, grammar, syntax, flow, formatting issues and more.

Scientific and Scholarly Editing

Allow colleagues in your research area to examine the content of your manuscript and provide you with valuable feedback and suggestions before submission.

Figure, Table, Chart & Equation Conversions

Do you have poor quality figures? Do you need visual elements in your manuscript created or converted? A design expert can help!

Translation

Need your documjent translated into English? eContent Pro International's expert translators are fluent in English and more than 40 different languages.

Hear What Your Colleagues are Saying About Editorial Services Supported by IGI Global

"The service was very fast, very thorough, and very helpful in ensuring our chapter meets the criteria and requirements of the book's editors. I was quite impressed and happy with your service."

– Prof. Tom Brinthaupt,
Middle Tennessee State University, USA

"I found the work actually spectacular. The editing, formatting, and other checks were very thorough. The turnaround time was great as well. I will definitely use eContent Pro in the future."

– Nickanor Amwata, Lecturer,
University of Kurdistan Hawler, Iraq

"I was impressed that it was done timely, and wherever the content was not clear for the reader, the paper was improved with better readability for the audience."

– Prof. James Chilembwe,
Mzuzu University, Malawi

Email: customerservice@econtentpro.com   **www.igi-global.com/editorial-service-partners**